C0-ARR-879

J 82 .D8 1959

United States. President
 (1953-1961: Eisenhower)

Public papers of the
 Presidents of the United

WITHDRAWN

PUBLIC PAPERS OF THE PRESIDENTS

OF THE UNITED STATES

PUBLIC PAPERS OF THE PRESIDENTS

OF THE UNITED STATES

Dwight D. Eisenhower

1959

Containing the Public Messages, Speeches, and

Statements of the President

JANUARY 1 TO DECEMBER 31, 1959

RAMAKER LIBRARY
NORTHWESTERN COLLEGE
ORANGE CITY, IOWA 51041

PUBLISHED BY THE
OFFICE OF THE FEDERAL REGISTER
NATIONAL ARCHIVES AND RECORDS SERVICE
GENERAL SERVICES ADMINISTRATION

U.S. GOVERNMENT PRINTING OFFICE: 1960

For sale by the Superintendent of Documents, U.S Government Printing Office
Washington 25, D.C. - Price $7.00

FOREWORD

THERE HAS BEEN a long-felt need for an orderly series of the Public Papers of the Presidents. A reference work of this type can be most helpful to scholars and officials of government, to reporters of current affairs and the events of history.

The general availability of the official text of Presidential documents and messages will serve a broader purpose. As part of the expression of democracy, this series can be a vital factor in the maintenance of our individual freedoms and our institutions of self-government.

I wish success to the editors of this project, and I am sure their work through the years will add strength to the ever-growing traditions of the Republic.

Dwight D. Eisenhower

PREFACE

IN THIS VOLUME are gathered most of the public messages and statements of the President of the United States that were released by the White House during the year 1959. A similar volume, covering the year 1957, was published early in 1958 as the first of a series. The President's foreword is reprinted from that volume.

Immediate plans for this series call for the publication of annual volumes soon after the close of each new calendar year, and at the same time undertaking the periodic compilation of volumes covering previous years. Volumes covering the years 1955 through 1959 are now available.

This series was begun in response to a recommendation of the National Historical Publications Commission (44 U.S.C. 393). The Commission's recommendation was incorporated in regulations of the Administrative Committee of the Federal Register issued under section 6 of the Federal Register Act (44 U.S.C. 306). The Committee's regulations, establishing the series, are reprinted at page 910 as "Appendix D."

The first extensive compilation of the messages and papers of the Presidents was assembled by James D. Richardson and published under Congressional authority between 1896 and 1899. It included Presidential materials from 1789 to 1897. Since then, there have been various private compilations, but no uniform, systematic publication comparable to the *Congressional Record* or the *United States Supreme Court Reports*.

For many years Presidential Proclamations have been published in the *United States Statutes at Large*. The Federal Register Act in 1935 required that Proclamations, Executive Orders, and some other official Executive documents be published in the daily *Federal Register;* but the greater part of Presidential writings and utterances still lacked an official medium for either current publication or periodic compilation. Some of them were interspersed through the issues of the *Congressional Record* while others were reported only in the press or were generally available only in mimeographed White House releases. Under these circumstances it was difficult to remember, after a lapse of time, where and in what form even a major pronouncement had been made.

CONTENT AND ARRANGEMENT

The text of this book is based on Presidential materials issued during the calendar year 1959 as White House releases and on transcripts of news conferences. Where available, original source materials have been used to protect against substantive errors in transcription. A list of the White House releases from which final selections were made is published at page 887 as "Appendix A."

Proclamations, Executive Orders, and similar documents required by law to be published in the *Federal Register* and *Code of Federal Regulations* are not repeated. Instead, they are listed by number and subject under the heading "Appendix B" at page 902.

The President is required by statute to transmit numerous reports to Congress. Those transmitted during 1959 are listed at page 908 as "Appendix C."

The items published in this volume are presented in chronological order, rather than being grouped in classes. Most needs for a classified arrangement are met by the subject index. For example, a reader interested in veto messages sent to Congress during 1959 will find them listed in the index under "veto messages."

The dates shown at the end of item headings are White House release dates. In instances where the date of the document differs from the release date that fact is shown in brackets immediately following the heading. Other editorial devices, such as text notes, footnotes, and cross references, have been held to a minimum.

Remarks or addresses were delivered in Washington, D.C., unless otherwise indicated. Similarly, statements, messages, and letters were issued from the White House in Washington unless otherwise indicated.

The planning and editorial work for this volume were under the direction of David C. Eberhart of the Office of the Federal Register, assisted by Warren R. Reid and Mildred B. Berry. The index was prepared by Dorothy M. Jacobson. Frank H. Mortimer of the Government Printing Office developed the typography and design.

Wayne C. Grover
Archivist of the United States

Franklin Floete
Administrator of General Services

March 15, 1960

CONTENTS

CONTENTS

LIST OF ITEMS

XIII

List of Items

XV

List of Items

List of Items

List of Items

List of Items

List of Items

List of Items

Page

List of Items

List of Items

List of Items

XXV

List of Items

XXVI

List of Items

XXVIII

List of Items

List of Items

List of Items

List of Items

List of Items

List of Items

Dwight D. Eisenhower

1959

1 ¶ Exchange of New Year Greetings Between the United States and the Soviet Union.

January 1, 1959

His Excellency
Kliment Efremovich Voroshilov
Chairman of the Presidium of the Supreme Soviet of the Union of the
  Soviet Socialist Republics
Moscow

I thank you for your message and, on behalf of the American people, I extend greetings to you, Prime Minister Khrushchev and the people of the Soviet Union as the New Year begins. I share the hope expressed in your message that the coming year will see a substantial improvement in the relations between our countries, and significant steps toward a lasting solution of the problems which endanger world peace.

Peaceful relations with other friendly countries are the hallmark of our American tradition and we seek always to develop and strengthen such relations. We profoundly hope that your wish for peaceful co-existence may bring about in 1959 genuine efforts to solve existing world problems. All of us know that mutual understanding and respect for the rights and legitimate aspirations of others could not fail to be beneficial to all peoples. It would enable the nations to strive more effectively for universal spiritural and material well-being.

As of this moment it seems to us critically important to apply the sentiments expressed in your message to the Berlin situation. In this connection, I cannot fail to recall your government's declaration of intentions toward the people of Berlin. In my view, they are not in accord with your expressed aspirations and hopes for peaceful coexistence. The United States Government repeats that, in an atmosphere devoid of any kind of coercion and threat, it would welcome discussion on the question of Berlin in the wider framework of the whole German problem and European security. Positive progress in this specific problem would, I deeply believe, give real substance to the hope that 1959 would witness great advances toward the goal of a just and lasting peace.

DWIGHT D. EISENHOWER

NOTE: The message from Mr. Voroshilov and Prime Minister Khrushchev follows:

To His Excellency Dwight D. Eisenhower President of the United States of America

On the occasion of the New Year we send to you, Mr. President, and also to the people of the United States of America congratulations and best wishes from the people of the Soviet Union and from us personally. We would like to express the hope that in the coming year our countries will unite their efforts in the search for a way towards the settlement of urgent international problems, for the cessation of the arms race and of the cold war which is hated by the people, with the aim of reducing dangerous tensions in international relations. The development of friendly cooperation on the basis of principles of peaceful coexistence between states would permit the deliverance of mankind from feelings of alarm for their future, from the fears of the dangers of a new war. We would like to express confidence that in this year there will be taken a decisive step in the direction of an improvement of Soviet-American relations, in the development of mutual understanding between our countries whose responsibility for the fate of the world is particularly great. This would be an important contribution of our countries to the healthy improvement of the whole international atmosphere and for the achievements of the great goal—the triumph of peace in the entire world.

K. VOROSHILOV
N. KHRUSHCHEV

The messages were released at Gettysburg, Pa.

2 ¶ Statement by the President on the Launching of a Space Probe by the U.S.S.R.   *January* 3, 1959

THE SUCCESSFUL launching, as announced by the Soviets, of a vehicle designed to pass near the moon, represents a great stride forward in man's advance into the infinite reaches of outer space. To the scientists and engineers assigned to this undertaking, a full measure of credit is due and we congratulate them on this achievement.

3 ¶ Remarks Upon Signing the Proclamation Admitting Alaska to the Union and the Executive Order Changing the Flag of the United States. *January* 3, 1959

GENTLEMEN, I think that all of us recognize this as an historic occasion. Certainly for myself I feel very highly privileged and honored to welcome the forty-ninth State into the Union.

Such a ceremony has not taken place in almost half a century, so at least I have the feeling of self-gratification that I am not just one of a group in this kind of ceremony.

To the State itself, to its people, I extend on behalf of all their sister States, best wishes and hope for prosperity and success. And to each of you gentlemen elected to high office to represent your new State, in both State and Federal offices, my congratulations, my felicitations, and my hope that we will all work together to the benefit of all forty-nine States.

Certainly, I pledge to you my cooperation in that effort.

And now, as far as these pens are concerned, I hope there's one for each of you people who has worked so hard to bring this about.

NOTE: The ceremony was held in the Cabinet Room at noon. Among those present were Senators-elect E. L. Bartlett and Ernest Gruening, Representative-elect Ralph J. Rivers, Acting Governor Waino Hendrickson, Michael A. Stepovich, former Governor of Alaska, and Robert Atwood, Publisher of the Anchorage Daily Times.

The new 49-star flag, to become official on July 4, was unfurled immediately after the President signed the documents.

Proclamation 3269 "Admission of the State of Alaska into the Union" and Executive Order 10798 "Flag of the United States" are published in the Federal Register (24 F.R. 79 and 81, respectively).

4 ¶ Statement by the President Honoring Charles A. Halleck and Joseph W. Martin. *January* 6, 1959

IT IS ALWAYS unfortunate that in a contest between one's friends the good fortune of one has to be at the expense of the other.

During the last six years I have met weekly, during Congressional Sessions, with Mr. Halleck and Mr. Martin and their associates. I have relied confidently on their advice and cooperation.

To Charlie Halleck, the new Republican Leader of the House, my warm congratulations. He will be a fine leader.

To Joe Martin my heartfelt thanks for his long years of loyal and effective service. I am sure that his rich experience and wise counsel will continue to be of great value to me, to our Party, and our country.

NOTE: Joseph W. Martin, Jr., of North Attleboro, Mass., was elected to the 69th Congress in 1924 and to each succeeding Congress. He served as Minority Leader in the 76th through the 85th Congresses, with the exception of the 80th and the 83d in which he served as Speaker of the House of Representatives.

Charles A. Halleck, of Rensselaer, Indiana, served continuously following his election to the 74th Congress in 1935. He was elected Minority Leader in the 86th Congress. During the 80th and 83d Congresses he served as Majority Leader.

5 ¶ Message to President de Gaulle of France Upon His Inauguration. *January* 9, 1959

[Released January 9, 1959. Dated January 8, 1959]

Dear General de Gaulle:

At this historic moment I deem it a privilege and honor to extend to you greetings and congratulations upon your inauguration as the first President of the Fifth French Republic.

France has a special place in the hearts of the American people. Moreover, you yourself have come to symbolize for us not only French valor and resolution in the face of adversity but also a dynamic and youthful France determined to go forward with renewed vigor and faith. For these reasons the American people join me in saluting the beginning of the Fifth Republic with great hope and confidence. We send to you and to the noble people you have the honor to lead a special message of friendship and of good wishes for your own future and that of the French nation.

The traditional friendship between our two peoples and our two Governments is firmly established in our foreign relations. I believe, however, that this is a most fitting occasion for us to rededicate ourselves to strengthening these ties and to build an ever more intimate and understanding partnership.

4

Please accept, Mr. President, my best wishes and the assurances of my highest esteem.

Sincerely,

Dwight D. Eisenhower

6 ¶ Annual Message to the Congress on the State of the Union. *January* 9, 1959

[Delivered in person before a joint session]

Mr. President, Mr. Speaker, Members of the 86th Congress, my fellow citizens:

This is the moment when Congress and the Executive annually begin their cooperative work to build a better America.

One basic purpose unites us: To promote strength and security, side by side with liberty and opportunity.

As we meet today, in the 170th year of the Republic, our Nation must continue to provide—as all other free governments have had to do throughout time—a satisfactory answer to a question as old as history. It is: Can Government based upon liberty and the God-given rights of man, permanently endure when ceaselessly challenged by a dictatorship, hostile to our mode of life, and controlling an economic and military power of great and growing strength?

For us the answer has always been found, and is still found in the devotion, the vision, the courage and the fortitude of our people.

Moreover, this challenge we face, not as a single powerful nation, but as one that has in recent decades reached a position of recognized leadership in the Free World.

We have arrived at this position of leadership in an era of remarkable productivity and growth. It is also a time when man's power of mass destruction has reached fearful proportions.

Possession of such capabilities helps create world suspicion and tension. We, on our part, know that we seek only a just peace for all, with aggressive designs against no one. Yet we realize that there is uneasiness in the world because of a belief on the part of peoples that through arrogance, miscalculation or fear of attack, catastrophic war could be launched.

Keeping the peace in today's world more than ever calls for the utmost in the nation's resolution, wisdom, steadiness and unremitting effort.

We cannot build peace through desire alone. Moreover, we have learned the bitter lesson that international agreements, historically considered by us as sacred, are regarded in Communist doctrine and in practice to be mere scraps of paper. The most recent proof of their disdain of international obligations, solemnly undertaken, is their announced intention to abandon their responsibilities respecting Berlin.

As a consequence, we can have no confidence in any treaty to which Communists are a party except where such a treaty provides within itself for self-enforcing mechanisms. Indeed, the demonstrated disregard of the Communists of their own pledges is one of the greatest obstacles to success in substituting the Rule of Law for rule by force.

Yet step by step we must strengthen the institutions of peace—a peace that rests upon justice—a peace that depends upon a deep knowledge and clear understanding by all peoples of the cause and consequences of possible failure in this great purpose.

I.

To achieve this peace we seek to prevent war at any place and in any dimension. If, despite our best efforts, a local dispute should flare into armed hostilities, the next problem would be to keep the conflict from spreading, and so compromising freedom. In support of these objectives we maintain forces of great power and flexibility.

Our formidable air striking forces are a powerful deterrent to general war. Large and growing portions of these units can depart from their bases in a matter of minutes.

Similar forces are included in our naval fleets.

Ground and other tactical formations can move with swiftness and precision, when requested by friendly and responsible governments, to help curb threatened aggression. The stabilizing influence of this capacity has been dramatically demonstrated more than once over the past year.

Our military and related scientific progress has been highly gratifying.

Great strides have been made in the development of ballistic missiles. Intermediate range missiles are now being deployed in operational units. The Atlas intercontinental ballistic missile program has been marked by rapid development as evidenced by recent successful tests. Missile training units have been established and launching sites are far along in construction.

New aircraft that fly at twice the speed of sound are entering our squadrons.

We have successfully placed five satellites in orbit, which have gathered information of scientific importance never before available. Our latest satellite illustrates our steady advance in rocketry and foreshadows new developments in world-wide communications.

Warning systems constantly improve.

Our atomic submarines have shattered endurance records and made historic voyages under the North Polar Sea.

A major segment of our national scientific and engineering community is working intensively to achieve new and greater developments. Advance in military technology requires adequate financing but, of course, even more, it requires talent and time.

All this is given only as a matter of history; as a record of our progress in space and ballistic missile fields in no more than four years of intensive effort. At the same time we clearly recognize that some of the recent Soviet accomplishments in this particular technology are indeed brilliant.

Under the law enacted last year the Department of Defense is being reorganized to give the Secretary of Defense full authority over the military establishment. Greater efficiency, more cohesive effort and speedier reaction to emergencies are among the many advantages we are already noting from these changes.

These few highlights point up our steady military gains. We are rightfully gratified by the achievements they represent. But we must remember that these imposing armaments are purchased at great cost.

National Security programs account for nearly sixty percent of the entire Federal budget for this coming fiscal year.

Modern weapons are exceedingly expensive.

The overall cost of introducing ATLAS into our armed forces will average $35 million per missile on the firing line.

This year we are investing an aggregate of close to $7 billion in missile programs alone.

Other billions go for research, development, test and evaluation of new weapons systems.

7

Our latest atomic submarines will cost $50 millions each, while some special types will cost three times as much.

We are now ordering fighter aircraft which are priced at fifty times as much as the fighters of World War II.

We are buying certain bombers that cost their weight in gold.

These sums are tremendous, even when compared with the marvelous resiliency and capacity of our economy.

Such expenditures demand both balance and perspective in our planning for defense. At every turn, we must weigh, judge and select. Needless duplication of weapons and forces must be avoided.

We must guard against feverish building of vast armaments to meet glibly predicted moments of so-called "maximum peril." The threat we face is not sporadic or dated: It is continuous. Hence we must not be swayed in our calculations either by groundless fear or by complacency. We must avoid extremes, for vacillation between extremes is inefficient, costly, and destructive of morale. In these days of unceasing technological advance, we must plan our defense expenditures systematically and with care, fully recognizing that obsolescence compels the never-ending replacement of older weapons with new ones.

The defense budget for the coming year has been planned on the basis of these principles and considerations. Over these many months I have personally participated in its development.

The aim is a sensible posture of defense. The secondary aim is increased efficiency and avoidance of waste. Both are achieved by this budgetary plan.

Working by these guide lines I believe with all my heart that America can be as sure of the strength and efficiency of her armed forces as she is of their loyalty. I am equally sure that the nation will thus avoid useless expenditures which, in the name of security, might tend to undermine the economy and, therefore, the nation's safety.

———————

Our own vast strength is only a part of that required for dependable security. Because of this we have joined with nearly 50 other nations in collective security arrangements. In these common undertakings each nation is expected to contribute what it can in sharing the heavy load. Each supplies part of a strategic deployment to protect the forward boundaries of freedom.

Constantly we seek new ways to make more effective our contribution to this system of collective security. Recently I have asked a Committee of eminent Americans of both parties to re-appraise our military assistance programs and the relative emphasis which should be placed on military and economic aid.

I am hopeful that preliminary recommendations of this Committee will be available in time to assist in shaping the Mutual Security program for the coming fiscal year.

Any survey of the free world's defense structure cannot fail to impart a feeling of regret that so much of our effort and resources must be devoted to armaments. At Geneva and elsewhere we continue to seek technical and other agreements that may help to open up, with some promise, the issues of international disarmament. America will never give up the hope that eventually all nations can, with mutual confidence, drastically reduce these non-productive expenditures.

II.

The material foundation of our national safety is a strong and expanding economy. This we have—and this we must maintain. Only with such an economy can we be secure and simultaneously provide for the well-being of our people.

A year ago the nation was experiencing a decline in employment and output. Today that recession is fading into history, and this without gigantic, hastily-improvised public works projects or untimely tax reductions. A healthy and vigorous recovery has been under way since last May. New homes are being built at the highest rate in several years. Retail sales are at peak levels. Personal income is at an all-time high.

The marked forward thrust of our economy reaffirms our confidence in competitive enterprise. But—clearly—wisdom and prudence in both the public and private sectors of the economy are always necessary.

Our outlook is this: 1960 commitments for our armed forces, the Atomic Energy Commission and Military Assistance exceed 47 billion dollars. In the foreseeable future they are not likely to be significantly lower. With an annual population increase of three million, other governmental costs are bound to mount.

After we have provided wisely for our military strength, we must judge how to allocate our remaining government resources most effectively to promote our well-being and economic growth.

Federal programs that will benefit all citizens are moving forward.

Next year we will be spending increased amounts on health programs;

on Federal assistance to science and education;

on the development of the nation's water resources;

on the renewal of urban areas;

and on our vast system of Federal-aid highways.

Each of these additional outlays is being made necessary by the surging growth of America.

Let me illustrate. Responsive to this growth, Federal grants and long term loans to assist 14 major types of capital improvements in our cities will total over 2 billion dollars in 1960—double the expenditure of two years ago. The major responsibility for development in these fields rests in the localities, even though the Federal Government will continue to do its proper part in meeting the genuine needs of a burgeoning population.

But the progress of our economy can more than match the growth of our needs. We need only to act wisely and confidently.

Here, I hope you will permit me to digress long enough to express something that is much on my mind.

The basic question facing us today is more than mere survival—the military defense of national life and territory. It is the preservation of a *way* of life.

We must meet the world challenge and at the same time permit no stagnation in America.

Unless we *progress,* we *regress.*

We can successfully sustain security and remain true to our heritage of freedom if we clearly visualize the tasks ahead and set out to perform them with resolution and fervor. We must first define these tasks and then understand what we must do to perform them.

If progress is to be steady we must have long term guides extending far ahead, certainly five, possibly even ten years. They must reflect the knowledge that before the end of five years we will have a population of over 190 million. They must be goals that stand high, and so inspire every citizen to climb always toward mounting levels of moral, intellectual and material strength. Every advance toward them must stir pride in individual and national achievements.

To define these goals, I intend to mobilize help from every available source.

We need more than politically ordained national objectives to challenge the best efforts of free men and women.   A group of selfless and devoted individuals, outside of government, could effectively participate in making the necessary appraisal of the potentials of our future.   The result would be establishment of national goals that would not only spur us on to our finest efforts, but would meet the stern test of practicality.

The Committee I plan will comprise educators and representatives of labor, management, finance, the professions and every other kind of useful activity.

Such a study would update and supplement, in the light of continuous changes in our society and its economy, the monumental work of the Committee on Recent Social Trends which was appointed in 1931 by President Hoover.   Its report has stood the test of time and has had a beneficial influence on national development.   The new Committee would be concerned, among other things, with the acceleration of our economy's growth and the living standards of our people, their health and education, their better assurance of life and liberty and their greater opportunities. It would also be concerned with methods to meet such goals and what levels of government—Local, State, or Federal—might or should be particularly concerned.

As one example, consider our schools, operated under the authority of local communities and states.   In their capacity and in their quality they conform to no recognizable standards.   In some places facilities are ample, in others meager.   Pay of teachers ranges between wide limits, from the adequate to the shameful.   As would be expected, quality of teaching varies just as widely.   But to our teachers we commit the most valuable possession of the nation and of the family—our children.

We must have teachers of competence.   To obtain and hold them we need standards.   We need a National Goal.   Once established I am certain that public opinion would compel steady progress toward its accomplishment.

Such studies would be helpful, I believe, to government at all levels and to all individuals.   The goals so established could help us see our current needs in perspective.   They will spur progress.

We do not forget, of course, that our nation's progress and fiscal integrity are interdependent and inseparable.   We can afford exerything we clearly need, but we cannot afford one cent of waste.   We must examine every item of governmental expense critically. To do otherwise would betray our nation's future. Thrift is one of the characteristics that has made this nation great. Why should we ignore it now?

We must avoid any contribution to inflationary processes, which could disrupt sound growth in our economy.

Prices have displayed a welcome stability in recent months and, if we are wise and resolute, we will not tolerate inflation in the years to come. But history makes clear the risks inherent in any failure to deal firmly with the basic causes of inflation. Two of the most important of these causes are the wage-price spiral and continued deficit financing.

Inflation would reduce job opportunities, price us out of world markets, shrink the value of savings and penalize the thrift so essential to finance a growing economy.

Inflation is not a Robin Hood, taking from the rich to give to the poor. Rather, it deals most cruelly with those who can least protect themselves. It strikes hardest those millions of our citizens whose incomes do not quickly rise with the cost of living. When prices soar, the pensioner and the widow see their security undermined, the man of thrift sees his savings melt away; the white collar worker, the minister, and the teacher see their standards of living dragged down.

Inflation can be prevented. But this demands statesmanship on the part of business and labor leaders and of government at all levels.

We must encourage the self-discipline, the restraint necessary to curb the wage-price spiral and we must meet current costs from current revenue.

To minimize the danger of future soaring prices and to keep our economy sound and expanding, I shall present to the Congress certain proposals.

First, I shall submit a balanced budget for the next year, a year expected to be the most prosperous in our history. It is a realistic budget with wholly attainable objectives.

If we cannot live within our means during such a time of rising prosperity, the hope for fiscal integrity will fade. If we persist in living beyond our means, we make it difficult for every family in our land to balance its own household budget. But to live within our means would be a tangible demonstration of the self-discipline needed to assure a stable dollar.

The Constitution entrusts the Executive with many functions, but the Congress—and the Congress alone—has the power of the purse. Ultimately upon Congress rests responsibility for determining the scope and amount of Federal spending.

By working together, the Congress and the Executive can keep a balance between income and outgo. If this is done there is real hope that we can look forward to a time in the foreseeable future when needed tax reforms can be accomplished.

In this hope, I am requesting the Secretary of the Treasury to prepare appropriate proposals for revising, at the proper time, our tax structure, to remove inequities and to enhance incentives for all Americans to work, to save, and to invest. Such recommendations will be made as soon as our fiscal condition permits. These prospects will be brightened if 1960 expenditures do not exceed the levels recommended.

Second, I shall recommend to the Congress that the Chief Executive be given the responsibility either to approve or to veto specific items in appropriations and authorization bills.[1] This would save tax dollars.

Third, to reduce Federal operations in an area where private enterprise can do the job, I shall recommend legislation for greater flexibility in extending Federal credit, and in improving the procedures under which private credits are insured or guaranteed. Present practices have needlessly added large sums to Federal expenditures.

Fourth, action is required to make more effective use of the large Federal expenditures for agriculture and to achieve greater fiscal control in this area.

Outlays of the Department of Agriculture for the current fiscal year for the support of farm prices on a very few farm products will exceed five billion dollars. That is a sum equal to approximately two-fifths of the net income of all farm operators in the entire United States.

By the end of this fiscal year it is estimated that there will be in Government hands surplus farm products worth about nine billion dollars. And by July 1, 1959, Government expenditures for storage, interest, and

---

[1] At this point the message, as recorded from the floor and printed in the Congressional Record, shows the following interpolation: I assure you gentlemen that I know this recommendation has been made time and again by every President that has appeared in this hall for many years, but I say this, it still is one of the most important corrections that could be made in our annual expenditure program, because this would save tax dollars. [*Applause*]

handling of its agricultural inventory will reach a rate of one billion dollars a year.

This level of expenditure for farm products could be made willingly for a temporary period if it were leading to a sound solution of the problem. But unfortunately this is not true. We need new legislation.

In the past I have sent messages to the Congress requesting greater freedom for our farmers to manage their own farms and greater freedom for markets to reflect the wishes of producers and consumers. Legislative changes that followed were appropriate in direction but did not go far enough.

The situation calls for prompt and forthright action. Recommendation for action will be contained in a message to be transmitted to the Congress shortly.

These fiscal and related actions will help create an environment of price stability for economic growth. However, certain additional measures are needed.

I shall ask Congress to amend the Employment Act of 1946 to make it clear that Government intends to use all appropriate means to protect the buying power of the dollar.

I am establishing a continuing Cabinet group on Price Stability for Economic Growth to study governmental and private policies affecting costs, prices, and economic growth. It will strive also to build a better public understanding of the conditions necessary for maintaining growth and price stability.

Studies are being undertaken to improve our information on prices, wages, and productivity.

I believe all citizens in all walks of life will support this program of action to accelerate economic growth and promote price stability.

III.

I take up next certain aspects of our international situation and our programs to strengthen it.

America's security can be assured only within a world community of strong, stable, independent nations, in which the concepts of freedom, justice and human dignity can flourish.

There can be no such thing as Fortress America. If ever we were reduced to the isolation implied by that term, we would occupy a prison, not a fortress. The question whether we can afford to help other nations that want to defend their freedom but cannot fully do so from their own means, has only one answer: we can and we must, we have been doing so since 1947.

Our foreign policy has long been dedicated to building a permanent and just peace.

During the past six years our free world security arrangements have been bolstered and the bonds of freedom have been more closely knit. Our friends in Western Europe are experiencing new internal vitality, and are increasingly more able to resist external threats.

Over the years the world has come to understand clearly that it is our firm policy not to countenance aggression. In Lebanon, Taiwan, and Berlin—our stand has been clear, right, and expressive of the determined will of a united people.

Acting with other free nations we have undertaken the solemn obligation to defend the people of free Berlin against any effort to destroy their freedom. In the meantime we shall constantly seek meaningful agreements to settle this and other problems, knowing full well that not only the integrity of a single city, but the hope of all free peoples is at stake.

We need, likewise, to continue helping to build the economic base so essential to the Free World's stability and strength.

The International Monetary Fund and the World Bank have both fully proven their worth as instruments of international financial cooperation. Their Executive Directors have recommended an increase in each member country's subscription. I am requesting the Congress for immediate approval of our share of these increases.

We are now negotiating with representatives of the twenty Latin American Republics for the creation of an inter-American financial institution. Its purpose would be to join all the American Republics in a common institution which would promote and finance development in Latin America, and make more effective the use of capital from the World Bank, the Export-Import Bank, and private sources.

Private enterprise continues to make major contributions to economic development in all parts of the world. But we have not yet marshalled the full potential of American business for this task, particularly in countries which have recently attained their independence. I shall present to this Congress a program designed to encourage greater participation by private enterprise in economic development abroad.

Further, all of us know that to advance the cause of freedom we must do much more than help build sound economies. The spiritual, intellectual, and physical strength of people throughout the world will in the last analysis determine their willingness and their ability to resist Communism.

To give a single illustration of our many efforts in these fields: We have been a participant in the effort that has been made over the past few years against one of the great scourges of mankind—disease. Through the Mutual Security program public health officials are being trained by American universities to serve in less developed countries. We are engaged in intensive malaria eradication projects in many parts of the world. America's major successes in our own country prove the feasibility of success everywhere.

By these and other means we shall continue and expand our campaign against the afflictions that now bring needless suffering and death to so many of the world's people. We wish to be part of a great shared effort toward the triumph of health.

IV.

America is best described by one word, freedom.

If we hope to strengthen freedom in the world we must be ever mindful of how our own conduct reacts elsewhere. No nation has ever been so floodlighted by world opinion as the United States is today. Everything we do is carefully scrutinized by other peoples throughout the world. The bad is seen along with the good.

Because we are human we err. But as free men we are also responsible for correcting the errors and imperfections of our ways.

Last January I made comprehensive recommendations to the Congress for legislation in the labor-management field. To my disappointment, Congress failed to act. The McClellan Committee disclosures of corruption, racketeering, and abuse of trust and power in labor-management affairs have aroused America and amazed other peoples. They emphasize the need for improved local law enforcement and the enactment of effective Federal legislation to protect the public interest and to insure the rights and economic freedoms of millions of American workers. Half-hearted measures will not do. I shall recommend prompt enactment of legislation designed:

To safeguard workers' funds in union treasuries against misuse of any kind whatsoever.

To protect the rights and freedoms of individual union members, including the basic right to free and secret elections of officers.

To advance true and responsible collective bargaining.

To protect the public and innocent third parties from unfair and coercive practices such as boycotting and blackmail picketing.

The workers and the public must have these vital protections.

In other areas of human rights—freedom from discrimination in voting, in public education, in access to jobs, and in other respects—the world is likewise watching our conduct.

The image of America abroad is not improved when school children, through closing of some of our schools and through no fault of their own, are deprived of their opportunity for an education.

The government of a free people has no purpose more noble than to work for the maximum realization of equality of opportunity under law. This is not the sole responsibility of any one branch of our government. The judicial arm, which has the ultimate authority for interpreting the Constitution, has held that certain state laws and practices discriminate upon racial grounds and are unconstitutional. Whenever the supremacy of the Constitution of the United States is challenged I shall continue to take every action necessary to uphold it.

One of the fundamental concepts of our constitutional system is that it guarantees to every individual, regardless of race, religion, or national origin, the equal protection of the laws. Those of us who are privileged to hold public office have a solemn obligation to make meaningful this inspiring objective. We can fulfill that obligation by our leadership in teaching, persuading, demonstrating, and in enforcing the law.

We are making noticeable progress in the field of civil rights—we are moving forward toward achievement of equality of opportunity for all people everywhere in the United States. In the interest of the nation and of each of its citizens, that progress must continue.

Legislative proposals of the Administration in this field will be submitted to the Congress early in the session. All of us should help to make clear that the government is united in the common purpose of giving support to the law and the decisions of the Courts.

By moving steadily toward the goal of greater freedom under law, for our own people, we shall be the better prepared to work for the cause of freedom under law throughout the world.

All peoples are solely tired of the fear, destruction, and the waste of war. As never before, the world knows the human and material costs of war and seeks to replace force with a genuine rule of law among nations.

It is my purpose to intensify efforts during the coming two years in seeking ways to supplement the procedures of the United Nations and other bodies with similar objectives, to the end that the rule of law may replace the rule of force in the affairs of nations. Measures toward this end will be proposed later, including a re-examination of our own relation to the International Court of Justice.

Finally—let us remind ourselves that Marxist scripture is not new; it is not the gospel of the future. Its basic objective is dictatorship, old as history. What *is* new is the shining prospect that man can build a world where all can live in dignity.

We seek victory—not over any nation or people—but over the ancient enemies of us all; victory over ignorance, poverty, disease, and human degradation wherever they may be found.

We march in the noblest of causes—human freedom.

If we make ourselves worthy of America's ideals, if we do not forget that our nation was founded on the premise that all men are creatures of God's making, the world will come to know that it is free men who carry forward the true promise of human progress and dignity.

DWIGHT D. EISENHOWER

NOTE: This is the text of the document which the President signed and transmitted to the Senate and the House of Representatives (H. Doc. 1, 86th Cong., 1st sess.).

The Address as reported from the floor appears in the Congressional Record of January 9, 1959 (vol. 105, p. 163).

7 ¶ Remarks and Discussion at the National Press Club. *January* 14, 1959

Mr. President, Mr. President-elect, and gentlemen:

It is a very distinct honor, not to say a valued privilege, to be able to participate in this way in your Golden Jubilee. I'm sorry that I couldn't have done it earlier, but at least I've gotten under the wire.

I understand that in the type of gathering that we have today, the speaker normally delivers a talk and is then questioned. Well, for those of you who have not been reading the newspapers, let me tell you that only last Friday I delivered a speech of 45 minutes and it would seem quite unnecessary to go through that, the topics I then suggested for consideration, because so far as I remember, I covered a great deal of the waterfront. And so, with no other word of apology except to disclaim the title that your president gave me of an authority, I assure you I am a worker in the vineyard and a student.

So with that word of apology, I suggest we go to the questions for the simple reason that those few who didn't read the papers may not be so aware of the wisdom of my words last Friday as they should be. [*Laughter*]

Mr. Horner: Thank you, Mr. President. As you know, sir, the question-and-answer period at our club differs somewhat from your news conference at the White House. In the standard news conference, correspondents rise for individual recognition. When recognized, they identify themselves and they put the questions. At the Press Club, the procedure is for the members of the audience to submit questions in writing which are sent up to the presiding officer and it is he who selects the questions asked and it is he who reads them. And I want to emphasize, Mr. President, that I do not write them. I do just read them. [*Laughter*]

And now, sir, for the first one: there were two themes in your State of the Union Message, one of expanding the cost of defense and of maintaining adequate sums for a growing population; the other on the need for fiscal responsibility. Can we do both of these things and, if so, how can they be done?

THE PRESIDENT. The real answer, in a word, is found in this truth, I think: that we can keep prices from rising unconscionably, and by doing so we can do exactly what the question propounds. Now I do want to say this: no one believes, of course, if he is a special advocate or a member of a particular lobby or pressure group that is seeking Federal funds, no one believes that the amounts that he has been allotted are quite sufficient. This truth has always been known to all of us.

It does take very earnest study, judgment, and decision to bring about this balance between outgo and income and still make adequate provision for security, make certain that we do not neglect those programs in which the Federal Government should participate for the welfare of our people, and still keep fiscal integrity and pay our way as we go. I say I believe if we can substantially keep under control the problem of risings costs, this not only can be done but will very soon account for substantial surpluses which will mean tax reform and eventually certainly some tax reduction.

Mr. Horner: Mr. President, what is your answer to critics who say the national economy cannot expand at a rate of 5 percent a year unless the Federal Government makes a bigger investment annually in public facilities of all kinds?

THE PRESIDENT. Well, I don't want to be a critic myself here, but I do not believe that that question is really the one we ought to be asking, because it is not the Federal Government that makes prosperity in this country. After all, we are talking within the reasonable future of a GNP of 500 billion, and now we are talking about spending for all purposes 77 billion, or a figure in that level. It is quite clear that the decisions of 175 million people and the way they make those decisions based upon their own needs is far more important than what the Federal Government does.

The Federal Government needs to lead, to point the way, to do the things, as Lincoln said, that people cannot do for themselves, such as providing for the national security. That kind of problem, they have to take initial and sole responsibility for.

But when it comes to the advancing and expanding our economy, that is by and large the business of America. The Federal Government can help, but our expenditures, our Federal money, will never be spent so intelligently and in so useful a fashion for the economy as will the expenditures that would be made by the private citizen, the taxpayer, if he hadn't had so much of it funneled off into the Federal Government.

Mr. Horner: Mr. President, is it correct to assume that if Congress maintains a balanced budget this year, that next year you will propose a reduction in individual income taxes?

THE PRESIDENT. Well, the first thing I believe we have to do is to reform our tax structure in a number of ways; I think some of you remember I mentioned this last Friday—the need for tax reform. The Secretary of the Treasury—by the way, a man who I think is in this field very brilliant and able—is already studying the kinds of reform we should have. I would not be prepared to say that we would be recommending next year, as the first move in this field, reduction of personal income tax. I do say we must reform our tax structure so that incentives are enhanced and not damaged.

And if the Congress does keep this budget balanced, I say that increases our prospect for that kind of reform, as I say, eventually a lowering of taxes all along the line.

Mr. Horner: Sir, in your State of the Union Message you said. "We must have teachers of competence. To obtain and hold them we need standards."

What do you have in mind, sir, by this—national minimum standards of pay, national standards for high school graduates, or what?

THE PRESIDENT. It is broader than just merely the pay of teachers. I am right now busily engaged in the business of getting together the kind of committee that I think will give us the widest representation from the whole spectrum of the American population, every walk of life, every party, every kind of philosophy that we can. If we can put together this kind of committee—and I preferably would like to see it financed privately so that there could be no dictatorial methods used—then we could begin to set up goals that would finally become standards.

Now let me give you just one or two examples. I happen to know of one district near Chicago where a very dedicated group of citizens went to work to make certain that their teachers were properly paid. The minimum salary of a qualified high school teacher in that school became $10,000. And pretty soon it was picked up by the whole district and the quality of teaching, the morale of the teacher and of the student and everybody else, went up high, very high.

Now, we have teachers for a purpose. They are one of the most and probably, in many ways, the most important group that we know in this whole country. But they are for a purpose, not an end in themselves. They are to take our children, to give them the proper kinds of standards, the moral, intellectual, and even physical standards we believe they should attain. So when we want to set a standard for this business of education, we have got to think of the problem, our needs, whether we should have completely classical or whether we should center on science alone. We must get a standard that brings us a well-rounded student at what you might call the end product, by the time he gets through high school.

This means facilities, buildings, adequate recreational and athletic types of material, fine teachers, and I could add dedicated parents that cooperate with the teachers. This is the kind of thing I am talking about. I believe it can be done, and I believe it will inspire us all to a better performance.

Mr. Horner: Mr. President, turning now to civil rights, the question is, in 1957 Congress passed, at your suggestion, a civil rights bill dealing largely with voting: do you think this Congress should pass civil rights legislation dealing specifically with problems arising from school segregation?

THE PRESIDENT. I think when we get into the field of law, here we must be very careful. I do believe in the law concerning voting, and I think we should have whatever correctives are necessary in the law in order to make certain that a qualified citizen's privilege of voting is not taken away from him for such inconsequential things as race, or creed, or origin. That to my mind is the first thing to do.

Now, when we get the Federal Government working by law in things that are known to be primarily State, we run into difficulties. One of them is the closing of schools. To my mind this is tragic. I tried to say the other day that I believe the image of America is not helped abroad when we have so many thousands of our children deprived of getting an education, by no fault of their own, and by the closing of the schools.

So I would say, first, I would like to see this problem of voting solved with whatever laws may be necessary. I would like to see extended the life of the Civil Rights Commission. I would like to see power more clearcut to make certain that they can examine into the difficulties about voting, the bars to it, and to get some kind of procedures that will make this privilege stand so that it will not be violated. And if this is done, it is my belief that now voters themselves—local voters, State voters, and national voters—will have a greater and finer opportunity to proceed with, you might say, the proper observance of their other rights.

But I do say that until all of us take again as a standard, a standard of living by the concepts of the Constitution, and try by our teaching, our example, our beliefs, expressed convictions—we are not going to get too far just by laws that operate specifically upon a State-supported activity because, as I say, if the State ceases that activity, then what do we do? That, to my mind, is a problem that takes time, dedication, but I do say this: it must be solved.

Mr. Horner: Mr. President, as you know, we have many questions here. I would like to shift, if you please, sir, to a topic, a favorite of all of us—politics. You said at a recent press conference that your political philosophy has not changed. Nevertheless, many people say you have drifted away from Modern Republicanism toward traditional Republican conservatism. Would you explain this, sir?

THE PRESIDENT. I am always amused, sometimes frustrated, in my attempt to define terms that I have heard, or have been coined. I happened once, I believe in '56, the fall of '56, to have used the term "Modern Republicanism." Because there was some question about that, I tried to define it, and I said as far as I am concerned, this is the application of Republican principles to modern problems and not to the problem of keeping the Union together, which was President Lincoln's great preoccupation.

We are talking about the problems that we encounter today. I do not see any difference so far as I am concerned between Modern Republicanism or another term that I liked, Theodore Roosevelt's, which was "Progressive Republicanism." I believe we should cling very, very firmly to the principles, to the vision, really, that our founders wrote into their great documents, and we should take those principles and apply them with problems of humans today.

At one time our population was 95 percent agricultural. Well, today I think it is something on the order of 10, or a little more or less. Of course problems are different, and therefore, let's meet the modern problems. I would appeal to all Republicans and such few Democrats that are here—[*laughter*]—to take very seriously this business of applying the real concepts of the Founding Fathers, applying them to problems today, and do it according to your own way and your thinking, because that is America. That is what keeps America strong. But I do not like terms that I don't understand myself. [*Laughter*]

Mr. Horner: Mr. President, if you will take just one more on politics, I will let you go at the press. You have indicated, sir, you will follow a strictly hands-off policy in selecting the Republican presidential nominee next year. Does that not run the risk of selection of a man with whose Republican political philosophy you do not agree?

THE PRESIDENT. I'm quite sure, Mr. President, that everybody would know that if a nominee were possibly made whose basic philosophy I could not go along with—whose general attitude toward the relationship of Government to the private citizen and to the State and to the community; who did not go along with my basic idea that only in a coalition of strong governments or at least an association through cooperation with strong governments can we make certain that freedom is not lost in the world; if any man could not go along with that kind of basic thinking, well, I would say this: I couldn't possibly support him, if my influence had anything to do with the matter. Therefore, I could—I won't, but I could—write out for you a list of half a dozen, or 10, or maybe a dozen fine, virile men in the Republican Party that I would gladly support. But I do say this: those are men, in my mind, who really want to see America go ahead, its economy sound, and to be very, very careful that our security is maintained, not only by our own building of armaments, with support, the cooperation of other governments that want to live in independence and in liberty. [*Applause*]

Mr. Horner: And now, sir, a question or so on the press. Which, sir, do you prefer, holding press conferences only when you have something specific to announce, or holding these conferences on a regularly scheduled basis, whether or not you have anything to volunteer?

THE PRESIDENT. I have had one sort of a predilection throughout my life. I never like to conform too much. And just to say that one particular day each week I am going to be in the same exact spot, the same exact time, sort of puts me down.

Now I have no objection, as long as we have got the time and something else isn't on the mind, I have no objection to doing it periodically. And I will say this: I cannot recall when there was any time that I felt that I had anything in my mind that I should tell the press at that particular moment, or in that particular way. After all, you can always issue statements or sometimes these newsreel cameras want to get hold of you and get a picture of you while you're saying these things. But I do like, and this contrary to some of the things I have seen in the paper, I do like the opportunity of meeting these people—not always, I say, periodically, and not on any stated time. I like to meet them and listen to their questions.

I also read that I sometimes get angry. Well, that is their idea. [*Laughter*] I don't believe I do.

I say they are a good institution. I would hate to see them relegated to a secondary place, but they are the President's press conferences, and so I think you ought to indulge him a little bit in the way he thinks they ought to be done, when they should be done.

Mr. Horner: Mr. President, a question on missiles. Sir, there seems to be a difference of opinion between Vice President Nixon and Senator Symington as to whether we are behind the Russians in missile development. Can you settle the argument?

THE PRESIDENT. First of all, as all of you here who go to my press conferences know, I never comment on the statements of any particular individual, either in a critical and only rarely in any other fashion. I will try to answer the question in my own way.

First, I would say this: it is absolutely fatuous and futile to try to balance, item by item, the progress of two great nations in their technology of defense. We do know that in certain types of missile development the Soviets have performed brilliantly indeed. But we have a defense, I must point out, that because it is defense must concentrate not only on one possible type of combat but every conceivable kind. We have to have balanced forces and not merely one that aims, let us say, at the destruction of cities or bases anywhere in the world.

Now in the missile field itself, I should think that if we did not believe that the other people were somewhat ahead in certain phases of the missile development, we would indeed be a little stupid, because they have been working at it for many years, and our urgent work in the long-range missile has started only something like 4 years ago.

Now in that time, I want to say with all the depth of understanding I believe I have, our scientists have made remarkable progress. There has been a speed of development that is exemplified here in these late months by many successful flights of the Atlas, by the fact that training units for those weapons are now being produced, their bases are being built, that certain of our intermediate, that is, the fairly long-range weapons, are some deployed. This kind of thing means that we are going very, very fast.

Also, to show that this is not just one item that we should consider, take airplanes. We have one plane now in the fighter squadrons flying at more than twice the speed of sound. There are a few of our bombers that are doing the same thing, and at great altitudes and at great efficiency.

So that to disturb ourselves too much that we have not yet caught up with another great power and people with great technical skill in a particular item, seems to me to show a lack of a sense of balance. And that is what we are concerned with, because we don't know anything about time, place, or character of any aggression that could occur. We have to be prepared, and we have got to be prepared to respond instantly. I think we are. We have made very remarkable progress. [*Applause*]

Mr. Horner: Mr. President, before we go overseas, we have a question here we would like for you to settle. As an old football star for Army, have you any inside information on why Earl Blaik is quitting as coach of West Point? [*Laughter*]

THE PRESIDENT. Again I must correct our President for the description he gives of me. I believe the brightest thing ever said about me in the papers was I had great promise. [*Laughter*] I was broken up so soon that whether that promise would have been fulfilled, I do not know.

But I would say this, and I would like to say it, as a matter of fact I am delighted at this chance to say it publicly: I have never known a man in the athletic world who has been a greater inspiration for the men he is teaching, for his athletes under his control, for a whole corps of cadets and, indeed, for everybody that has known him, than has been Earl Blaik. He has been indeed a very great man, and I think he has done a very remarkable job, a dedicated one, and I am quite sure that if he had been thinking only of Earl Blaik he would have been long since gone.

I don't mind telling you that I have written him a letter today trying to express my feeling of admiration and gratitude for a man who for these long—I think it is now 25—years has been at Dartmouth and at West Point doing a remarkable job for all of us. [*Applause*]

Mr. Horner: And now, sir, if you please, a few questions on foreign matters, foreign affairs.

Mr. President, both the Russians and we seem to favor negotiations on the future of Germany, but differ fundamentally on solutions to the problem. Do you have any new suggestions to make to Mr. Mikoyan which might break this dilemma?

THE PRESIDENT. Well, going backwards at that question, I should say that any effort to lay out something that was new that would be called a definite proposal would be quite a great mistake. I think that the most that would be expected of such an informal visit as Mr. Mikoyan is making would be that we would try to get behind each other's facial expressions and to see what we are really thinking. Is there an honest, peaceful motive behind these things? Are both of us really so sick of the burdens that we have to carry in the armament field that we want to find with some intelligence and some common approach a way out of this dilemma?

That is, I think, the most we could achieve from an informal visit such as this, if anything, because if you try to make a proposal, you get into what you might call a conference in which something is dotted and signed, and then it becomes really quite a job.

Now as to the different proposals of the Soviets and ourselves respecting Germany and Europe, we think it is just an exercise in futility to try to demilitarize, neutralize, and completely disarm a people as strong, as important, and virile as is the German people.

On the other hand, that being the general tenor of the Russian proposals, we oppose to that concept this one: that we would say we don't believe in the free arming of Germany in the sense that Hitler tried to rearm it. We would like to see Germany so intertwine itself with other European nations in its economy and its thinking and its defense exercises, that it doesn't have to do this. It is part of a community.

Now this has been started, insofar as the West is concerned, in Euratom, the Coal-Steel Community, and the Free Market, that kind of thing, and we think it is a very great development for the benefit and strength of Western Europe; the rest of Europe at this point, of course, cannot get in.

But it is also a development that almost proves they cannot be aggressive. They couldn't move except with the consent of a whole bevy of nations. How can you make a surprise aggressive move in such a way? It must be, as far as military is concerned, a defensive sort of organization.

But if we handled the thing separately—I mean separately from France, Belgium, Holland, Italy, and so on—we must remember this: this people cannot live in isolation, and the great movements toward integration in Europe that have now taken place, I think are proof that the West Germans at least, and I would personally believe all the German people, want to live in peace. We should be quite ready to make any assurances, make any material moves that would assure Russia that there is no danger from this people; and they should not, in our opinion, insist upon really making them as sort of a vacuum in both the security world, the economic, and every other, the political world. They shouldn't do it because it just won't work, in my opinion. [*Applause*]

Mr. Horner: Mr. President, why do you think Mr. Mikoyan is here?

THE PRESIDENT. Just before the luncheon there was a group of us sitting out here in the lobby and we were trying to work—as a matter of fact, I was trying to get it out from them what he wants. [*Laughter*]

I do recall this: sometime back—oh, I don't know, 10, 12, 18 months ago—I suggested that one of the things we ought to promote is more visits by our people. Now, some of this has been going on, and I even went so far as to suggest people that were deemed in Russia very important, and by that I meant even in the political world. It is hard for me to interpret the meaning of one meeting, but I would welcome more of them because I believe thoroughly that in the long run peaceful negotiation is going to grow out of one thing that I just mention with respect to a problem in our own country: better understanding of each other. That is going to be brought about, not by glaring across an iron curtain at each other, but getting together, our news, our ideas. I could make quite a speech on this one because it is something I have been entangled in for a long time. But at Geneva we had, as I recall, 17 programs we wanted to put over in October with the foreign ministers meeting, and one of the greatest was to increase our contacts, ideas, literature, books, movies, and above all, people.

So, I would say this: if this means that they are making an experiment in sending some of their higher people over here, I'm all for it. And I would again repeat a very prayerful hope that I expressed some time back: regardless of our own political and social views about a government, or about individuals, America should not forget the requirements of courtesy. [*Applause*]

Mr. Horner: Mr. President, do you consider Red China a potentially greater threat to the free world than Russia?

THE PRESIDENT. I don't believe in the measurable time, that on this you could make a really worthwhile conclusion or prediction. There is no question that the leaders of Red China are determined, by methods with which we are all familiar, to become an industrial power, which means that behind it, so far as we can see, they want to be a big military power, and they are going at that just as hard as they can.

Now, here is a people of 600 million, and I would think that if they continue in that line, with no change in objective, doctrine, or method, then we must indeed be watchful not only for ourselves but for other people that are friendly and who live closer to China.

But, of course, we would hope that as the instinctive urge of men for freedom, for the right to walk upright in the world, that that begins to create a ferment not only in the more western section of the Eurasian mass, but over in China as well; that, in my humble opinion, is something that must occur during these years, and I am sure we will have to use more mechanical methods, more material means of assuring our own security.

Until that happens, we have indeed got a bleak problem that must be solved.

Mr. Horner: Mr. President, I'm going to ask you if you will not reminisce a bit for us.

Some war historians would say one of your great contributions during World War II was your ability to bring men of divergent views together. Would you please, sir, recall for us some of your associations with Mr. Churchill and General Montgomery, General de Gaulle, and the other allied leaders?

THE PRESIDENT. First of all, it is a very dangerous question to ask of an old soldier, because you ask him to reminisce, and you really ask for something. [*Laughter*]

I think Mr. Churchill is one of those men that I have known that clearly deserves the title of great. I think this is the title that can be applied accurately to only a few men, because no matter how much we respect the capabilities of any individual, we never can use that title or that adjective, as I see it, until the man has been proven in a position of great responsibility.

He can be great in certain qualities; but great in the carrying of responsibility, like Mr. Churchill, is a very unusual qualification and one that entitles him, I think, overall to that designation. And this in spite of the fact that I probably had more differences of opinion, more quite warm arguments with Mr. Churchill than I suppose did any other person, certainly in the allied forces, because I happened to be of a nationality that he could not shut up if he wanted to.

Now, what I want to say is this: right down to the very moment of decision, this man could support his own conclusion, his own beliefs, more eloquently, more effectively than almost anyone I have ever known. You had to hang on tight to your basic conviction because the first thing you knew, he would shove you out of it, because either with pathos or humor or just sheer eloquence he was a very, very powerful debater. But when the decision was reached, he was absolutely loyal. Some of them he didn't like at all.

He was really not only to my mind a great man; he is certainly one of my greatest friends that is not of my nationality. There are, of course, other men. We couldn't go through the list.

I have often made public my admiration for General Bradley, and, of course, my almost veneration, in many ways, of General Marshall and others who served in the European and African theaters. Many of these people in the British services were indeed splendid people. One of them I think most of you never heard of, or not often. He was Air Chief Marshal Portal, now Lord Portal, one of the finest leaders that I have known, a very great mind.

Each of these men, like each of us, had his own strengths, and here and there I should think his weaknesses. I believe it is not profitable to try to show where you believe you were better than he was, or where you thought you could have done the job better if you had had someone else. We did win the war. [*Laughter and applause*]

And I am going to reminisce only in one little item showing the difference between foresight and hindsight. All of us who supported the concept of the Overlord operation had a very great case to prove, and often we had to prove it against our British friends. They had from their experience in World War I visions of Vimy Ridge, of Passchendaele, of Ypres, of those places where literally hundreds of thousands of British and Canadian men lost their lives, and often with not a single thing to show except maybe a few yards of territory. They had that kind of vision and they could not stand the idea of starting another operation like that by invading northern France.

The Americans believed somewhat different. We believed that didn't have to be true, particularly as we were building up a bomber force that was going for us to soften defenses and make very difficult the maneuvers of the opponent.

Now so far as the predictions were concerned, along these many months before even I went to Overlord and from there on down to late May, there were many predictions that we would probably have another Anzio or we would be penned in the beach, we would never get out, and I heard this expression: the tides would flow red with the blood of American and British youths and the beaches would be choked with their bodies.

Now you had to have a degree of confidence, maybe here and there, brashness. But I will say, all of the people in my staff, British and Americans, began to believe this: we began to believe we could win in a reasonable time.

The lowest prediction I ever heard from any political figure on either side of the water was 2 years after we landed. Indeed I heard one of the most prominent figures of the war say that if we were able to acquire, capture, Paris by Christmas 1944, the operation that we had then started would be known in history as the greatest of military operations of all time up to that moment.

We insisted we were going to be on the borders of Germany at Christmas, and if they had any sense they would surrender. Well, they didn't and I lost £5. But that is what we believed, all of us.

Now after that war was ended 11 months from the day we landed—as I say, the most optimistic prediction was 2 years—from that moment now there became many, many critics who showed how much more quickly it could have been won, and possibly it could have been. The only answer I can give you is we won. [*Applause*]

Mr. Horner: Again, Mr. President, we thank you. You have made a most significant contribution to the Golden Anniversary Celebration of the National Press Club, and in the doing have made considerable news, and we are grateful to you, sir.

Mr. President, I have just one short question remaining but before I ask that I would like to make an announcement. First, I would like to ask the members of the audience to remain in their places until the President and his party depart.

And now, sir, I would like to say the Board of Governors having agreed that you are well qualified as a source of news, has elected you to membership in the National Press Club. [*Applause*]

THE PRESIDENT. Thank you very much.

Mr. Horner: It is my honor and privilege, sir, to present this card to you, a card of membership in our club. And now for the final question—which you may answer in any way you like, sir, of course.

In 1948, as your retirement as Army Chief of Staff was nearing, you told the club your prescription for ideal retirement: "Put a chair on the porch, sit in it for 6 months, and then begin to rock slowly." [*Laughter*]

A few things have happened in the last 11 years. Is that still your idea of the best retirement? [*Laughter*]

THE PRESIDENT. I would like, gentlemen, to retire this long: until I really wanted to go to work some day. Not that I think I don't like to work now, but I have never had that opportunity in my life just to stay out of a job long enough even from the time I was a baby to say I really now want to get back. Because from the day I was almost a first-grader, I was helping earn my own living and I have always had something to do.

Now I don't know how long this type of retirement would last, but at least I want to sit in that chair until I really want to get out of it.

And now I want to say one thing about this card, for which I am very grateful. I understand, possibly erroneously but I hope it is true, that members of the press normally deal gently with their other members—[*laughter and applause*]—so I hope that possession of this card gives me a certain immunity that, up to this moment, has not been mine. Thank you. [*Laughter and applause*]

NOTE: The President spoke at 1:00 p.m. His opening words "Mr. President, Mr. President-elect" referred to John V. Horner of the Washington Evening Star, and William H. Lawrence of the New York Times.

8 ¶ Remarks at Annual Dinner of the Association of State Planning and Development Agencies. *January* 14, 1959

Mr. President, Mr. Chief Justice, Ladies and Gentlemen:

I'm delighted to have this moment to greet the members of the planning profession.

Planning has become an indispensable feature of living in this complex age.

Occasionally, people come to my office, or I meet them, and the word "planning" comes up. I am struck by the fact that so often the individual to whom I am talking seems to think there is something a little phony about the word planning. On the one end it's probably considered apparently academic or theoretical, with no practical application, and the other end of the spectrum it's rather an attempt to express an idea of being "bossy" in telling other people how they should live. And I normally try to get the matter in perspective by illustrating from military experience what planning is.

Now in World War II, I suppose there were—in the Pacific and in the Atlantic—let us say, 20 amphibious landings. And I say to these people, "How do you suppose these things happen?" Let's assume that we didn't have to plan to get the ships to sea or the people on them, we just thought we're out there. We had them. And now, suddenly, someone said "Well, let's land." Can you imagine the confusion and the defeat that would have been inflicted upon any such force? Actually, the days and weeks, and even months, and indeed in the case of Overlord, 2 years and 2 months of definite planning before it was accomplished, is usually my answer as to what planning means to success in positive operations.

Now, if you were in a wilderness, a home built without regard for planning might damage no one but the owner. But in crowded cities and under conditions where the boundaries of cities are colliding with each other, we must plan skillfully or the result is chaos.

Our past failures to look ahead resulted in wasteful use of land; overlapping, duplicating, and inefficient services; and critical congestion.

Growth in America has far outdistanced the forecasts of a generation ago. Right now—just a few blocks away—in the lobby of the Commerce building, a population clock registers an added American every 11 seconds—a net increase of approximately one million every 4 months. This means that just to keep our present level of living, we continuously need more houses, more schools, more hospitals, more streets and water supply systems, more waste treatment and air pollution works, more parks and recreational facilities.

Our population is only one reason that we must attract more first-rate people into the planning profession. We are a nation on the move; from country to city, from central city to suburbs, from metropolitan areas to urbanized regions in the corridors between metropolitan areas.

In the decade just past, 12 million people have moved into the suburbs—the largest population movement in the shortest time of our history. Today, the suburbs grow 7 times as fast as the cities. Someone has facetiously described one metropolitan area, of the West, as "100 suburbs in search of a city."

Clear it seems that in the not too distant future, the entire eastern seaboard, from Portland to Norfolk, will become one continuous urban area. A new term—megalopolis—has already slipped into our vocabulary to describe these giant groupings of central cities and suburbs.

We must see to it that this growth is not like that of Topsy. It must have method, commonsense, direction, and it must be orderly. This calls for new approaches to problems of expansion that have all but erased outmoded boundaries.

Urbanization does not recognize boundary lines, whether municipal, town, county, or State. Neither does a public facility, such as a water supply net, a transit system, or a program to reduce contamination of the air. And public services must follow the needs of the people and this means that more and more these services must cross, indeed ignore, traditional borders.

The Federal Government stands ever ready to help stimulate, and is making its facilities available to help, planning at the State and local level. But we are equally determined not to supersede local responsibility.

It is the States themselves, or States cooperating among themselves, with the power inherent in their sovereignties, which must provide authority for local, regional, and metropolitan area planning units.

But I must also add, as we plan for tomorrow, our efforts must embrace more than the initiative of government, no matter what its level.

To make our dollar go as far as possible our choice should be based on needs, objectively determined, and not on just the desirable.

I believe, as I stated recently, that such are the dimensions and problems of life in this great Nation, that we should set for ourselves a series of goals—goals that take into account our growth potential and define the methods needed for their attainment.

You as members of the planning profession are acutely aware of the need for imagination in setting some of these goals, including those applicable to rapid urbanization. To my mind this is the very core of intelligent planning.

So, to each of you, in your dedicated task of building a better America, I wish for you: opportunity, its fulfillment, and Godspeed. And thank you very much.

NOTE: The President spoke at the Statler Hilton Hotel, Washington, D.C. His opening words "Mr. President" referred to William D. Carlbach, President of the Association.

9 ¶ Statement by the President Following Announcement of Recipients of the President's Award for Distinguished Federal Civilian Service. *January* 16, 1959

THE DISTINGUISHED achievements of these Federal employees have contributed markedly to progress in law enforcement, foreign affairs, scientific research and missile development. Their accomplishments stand as a constant challenge and a lasting monument to the ingenuity and ability of Federal employees.

The strength of our Nation and its free institutions flows from the imagination, skill and special efforts of our people. All of us in positions of leadership in Government have an important responsibility to encourage the superior effort and constructive idea power that exists within the Federal service. These are the qualities that lead to progress. And progress is the necessary element in meeting the challenges of this age.

NOTE: The President made this statement in announcing his selection of the following persons to receive awards "for exceptional meritorious civilian service": James V. Bennett, Director, Bureau of Prisons, Department of Justice, for "outstanding leadership in directing the Bureau of Prisons and in establishing policies to improve correctional treatment of offenders"; Robert D. Murphy, Deputy Under Secretary of State for Political Affairs, for "resolving, with superlative diplomatic skill, many international crises that threatened the vital interests of the United States"; Doyle L. Northrup, Technical Director, Special Weapons Squadron, Department of the Air Force, for "his responsibility for the establishment of a network to detect atomic explosions anywhere in the world"; Hazel K. Stiebeling, Director, Institute of Home Economics, Department of Agriculture, for "her lasting contributions to the science of human nutrition and through this to the health of the American people"; and Wernher von Braun, Director, Development Operations Division, Army Ballistic Missile Agency, Department of the Army, for "his outstanding contributions in missile development and in the launching of the first United States satellite."

Gold medals were presented by the President to the award winners in a White House ceremony on January 20 at 10:30 a.m.

10 ¶ Annual Budget Message to the Congress: Fiscal Year 1960. *January* 19, 1959

To the Congress of the United States:

The situation we face today as a Nation differs significantly from that of a year ago. We are now entering a period of national prosperity and high employment. This is a time for the Government to conduct itself so as best to help the Nation move forward strongly and confidently in economic and social progress at home, while fulfilling our responsibilities abroad. The budget of the United States for the fiscal year 1960, transmitted herewith, will effectively and responsibly carry out the Government's role in dealing with the problems and the opportunities of the period ahead.

This budget proposes to increase our military effectiveness, to enhance domestic well-being, to help friendly nations to foster their development, to preserve fiscal soundness, and to encourage economic growth and stability, not only in the fiscal year 1960 but in the years beyond. And it clearly shows that these things can be done within our income.

We cannot, of course, undertake to satisfy all proposals for Government spending. But as we choose which ones the Government should accept, we must always remember that freedom and the long-run strength of our economy are prerequisite to attainment of our national goals. Otherwise, we cannot, for long, meet the imperatives of individual freedom, national security, and the many other necessary responsibilities of Government. In short, this budget fits the conditions of today because:

1. IT IS A BALANCED BUDGET.—My recommendations call for an approximate equality between revenues and expenditures, with a small surplus.

2. IT IS A RESPONSIBLE BUDGET.—By avoiding a deficit, it will help prevent further increases in the cost of living and the hidden and unfair tax that inflation imposes on personal savings and incomes.

3. IT IS A CONFIDENT BUDGET.—It anticipates, in a rapidly advancing economy, increases in revenues without new general taxes, and counts upon the unity and good judgment of the American people in supporting a level of government activity which such revenues will make possible.

4. IT IS A POSITIVE BUDGET.—It responds to national needs, with due

regard to urgencies and priorities, without being either extravagant or unduly limiting.

5. IT IS AN ATTAINABLE BUDGET.—Its proposals are realistic and can be achieved with the cooperation of the Congress.

Any budget is a financial plan. The budget for the Government is proposed by the President, but it is acted upon by the Congress which has the duty under the Constitution to authorize and appropriate for expenditures. Therefore, responsibility for the Government's finances is a shared one. Achievement of the plan set forth in this budget from here on depends upon congressional response, popular support, and developments in our economy and in the world.

Future Budget Outlook

The actions we take now on the 1960 budget will affect the fiscal outlook for many years to come. This budget was prepared in the light of the following general prospects for Government finances for the next few years.

Growth of revenues.—Our Nation's population and labor force will continue to increase. The output per hour of work on our farms and in our factories can also be expected to grow as it has in the past. With sustained economic expansion, with employment of our people and resources at high levels, and with continued technological advance, the value of total national production and income will be substantially larger in the future than it is today.

Economic growth generates higher personal incomes and business profits. Under our graduated income tax system, with present tax rates, budget receipts should grow even faster than national income, although the rise in receipts certainly will not be uniform from year to year. Also, some tax reforms and downward tax adjustments will be essential in future years to help maintain and strengthen the incentives for continued economic growth. With a balance in our finances in 1960, we can look forward to tax reduction in the reasonably foreseeable future. In the long run, taxes should be so arranged that in periods of prosperity some annual provision is made for debt reduction, even though at a modest rate.

Control of expenditures.—The estimated 1960 expenditures, while $3.9 billion less than in 1959, will still be $12.4 billion higher than in 1955, an average increase of almost $2.5 billion a year. These figures emphasize

37

that if we are to succeed in keeping total expenditures under control in the coming years we must recognize certain hard facts.

First, defense spending will remain extremely large as long as we must maintain military readiness in an era of world trouble and unrest. Until there is a significant and secure easing of world tensions, the actions by the Department of Defense to realign forces, close unneeded installations, and cut back outmoded weapons will achieve only relatively small expenditure reductions. Keeping our military structure capable and ready to meet any threat means that we must continue to strengthen our defenses. It is but a reflection of the world in which we live to stress again the fact that modern weapons are complex and costly to develop, costly to procure, and costly to operate and maintain.

Second, without one single new action by the Congress to authorize additional projects or programs, Government outlays for some of our major activities are certain to keep on rising for several years after 1960 because of commitments made in the past. For example, commitments for urban renewal capital grants have exceeded net expenditures by about $200 million or more for each of the last 3 years. Money to meet these commitments will be paid out in the years immediately ahead. Similarly, continued construction of the many water resources projects underway throughout the country will raise expenditures for these programs in the next 2 years beyond the current record amount.

Moreover, inescapable demands resulting from new technology and the growth of our Nation, and new requirements resulting from the changing nature of our society, will generate Federal expenditures in future years. As a matter of national policy we must, for example, make our airways measure up to the operational and safety needs of the jet age. We must not forget that a rapidly growing population creates virtually automatic increases in many Federal responsibilities.

Fiscal soundness and progress.—Both domestic and defense needs require that we keep our financial house in order. This means that we must adhere to two policies:

First, we must review all government activities as a part of the continuing budgetary process from year to year. Changing circumstances will inevitably offer opportunities for economies in a variety of existing Federal programs. If we do not make such reviews and act forthrightly on their findings, the combination of old commitments and new authorizations for new or enlarged Federal responsibilities could swell expenditures unnecessarily and inconsistently. Consonant with this policy of review, reductions have been recommended in this budget for 1960 appropriations which will affect expenditures not only in that year but also in later years. Furthermore, this budget contains proposals to modify certain activities and institute certain charges for special services. These recommendations are practicable and sound. They should be enacted.

Second, we must examine new programs and proposals with a critical eye. Desirability alone is not a sound criterion for adding to Federal responsibilities. The impact today and tomorrow on the entire Nation must be carefully assessed.

Our economy will continue to grow vigorously. This growth will produce additional Federal revenues, but it will not produce them without limit. We cannot take our resources for granted and we cannot spend them indiscriminately. We must deal with new conditions as they arise. We must choose what the Federal Government will do and how it will do it. If the choice is responsibly made, reductions obtained through economies and the rising revenues accompanying economic growth will produce surpluses which can be used to lessen the burden of taxes, meet the cost of essential new Government services, and reduce the public debt. The proposals in this budget have been formulated with these long-run objectives in mind.

BUDGET TOTALS

Budget expenditures are proposed to be held to $77 billion in fiscal 1960, which is $3.9 billion less than the estimated 1959 level of $80.9 billion.

With continued vigorous economic recovery, and with the relatively few new tax adjustments proposed herein, budget receipts in fiscal 1960 are expected to reach a total of $77.1 billion, an increase of $9.1 billion over fiscal 1959.

Thus a very modest surplus of about $0.1 billion is estimated for 1960, compared with a recession-induced deficit of $12.9 billion in the current fiscal year. This estimated balance assumes enactment of recommendations for extending present excises and corporation income taxes scheduled for reduction under existing law, for some new tax legislation to remove inequities and loopholes, for increased charges for special services,

39

and for reductions in some current programs. It also assumes that certain programs can be made self-financing by stepping up the sale of portfolio assets.

Financing of the $12.9 billion budget deficit for the current fiscal year will increase the public debt to $285 billion by June 30, 1959, $2 billion in excess of the present permanent debt limit. With a balanced budget in 1960, a $285 billion debt is indicated also for June 30, 1960. On the basis of these estimates, it will be necessary to renew the request made during the past session of Congress for a permanent debt ceiling of $285 billion and, further, to seek an increase in the temporary debt ceiling sufficient to cover heavy borrowing requirements during the first half of the fiscal year 1960, borrowings which would be repaid before June 30, 1960.

The new authority to incur obligations recommended for fiscal 1960 is $76.8 billion, which is slightly less than the estimates for expenditures and for receipts. Further reductions in new obligational authority can be attained in 1961 by the Congress enacting my recommendations for program modifications.

BUDGET TOTALS

[Fiscal years. In billions]

	1957 *actual*	1958 *actual*	1959 *estimate*	1960 *estimate*
Budget receipts.....................	$71.0	$69.1	$68.0	$77.1
Budget expenditures.................	69.4	71.9	80.9	77.0
Budget surplus (+) or deficit (−)...	+1.6	−2.8	−12.9	+0.1
New obligational authority...........	70.2	76.3	[1] 82.4	76.8

[1] Includes $8.7 billion of anticipated supplemental requests.

A consolidation of budget and trust fund transactions on a cash basis shows that the total Federal receipts from the public in fiscal 1960 are expected to exceed payments to the public by $0.6 billion. This figure exceeds the budget surplus in 1960 mainly because (1) cash payments of interest on redeemed savings bonds are less than the accrued interest included in budget expenditures and (2) trust fund receipts exceed trust fund expenditures.

40

FEDERAL GOVERNMENT RECEIPTS FROM AND PAYMENTS TO THE PUBLIC

[Fiscal years. In billions]

	1957 actual	1958 actual	1959 estimate	1960 estimate
Receipts from the public.............	$82. 1	$81. 9	$81. 7	$93. 5
Payments to the public..............	80. 0	83. 4	94. 9	92. 9
Excess of receipts over payments....	2. 1	....	....	0. 6
Excess of payments over receipts....	....	1. 5	13. 2	....

BUDGET RECEIPTS

Extension of present tax rates.—The budget outlook for 1960 makes it essential to extend present tax rates on corporation profits and certain excise taxes another year beyond their present expiration date of June 30, 1959.

Development of a more equitable tax system.—Considerable progress was made last year in removing unintended benefits and hardships from the tax laws. Continued attention is necessary in this area. As the budget permits, additional reforms should be undertaken to increase the fairness of the tax system, to reduce the tax restraints on incentives to work and invest, and wherever feasible to simplify the laws. I hope that the committees of the Congress will work with the Treasury Department in preparing further adjustments of our tax laws for the future.

I urge the Congress to take action now on certain specific changes to maintain or increase revenues and to make the laws more equitable. The Treasury Department has recently proposed an equitable plan for taxing the income of life insurance companies. Specific proposals for corrective amendments of the laws on taxation of cooperatives will be transmitted to the Congress shortly. The Treasury will also recommend an amendment specifying the treatment processes which shall be considered mining for the purpose of computing percentage depletion in the case of mineral products. This amendment, prompted by court decisions, is designed to prevent an unintended extension of percentage depletion allowances to the sales price of finished products; a similar recommendation with respect to cement and clay products was made to the Congress last year.

Other changes in tax rates.—In order to make highway-related taxes support our vast highway expenditures, excises on motor fuels need to be

41

increased 1½ cents a gallon to 4½ cents. These receipts will go into the highway trust fund and preserve the pay-as-we-go principle, so that contributions from general tax funds to build Federal-aid highways will not be necessary.

At the same time, to help defray the rising costs of operating the Federal airways, receipts from excises on aviation gasoline should be retained in general budget receipts rather than transferred to the highway trust fund. The estimates of budget and trust fund receipts from excise taxes reflect such proposed action. They also include a proposal to have users of the Federal airways pay a greater share of costs through increased rates on aviation gasoline and a new tax on jet fuels. These taxes, like the highway gasoline tax, should be 4½ cents per gallon. I believe it fair and sound that such taxes be reflected in the rates of transportation paid by the passengers and shippers.

BUDGET RECEIPTS

[Fiscal years. In billions]

	1958 actual	1959 estimate	1960 estimate
Individual income taxes	$34.7	$36.9	$40.7
Corporation income taxes	20.1	17.0	21.5
Excise taxes	8.6	8.5	8.9
All other receipts	5.7	5.6	6.0
Total	69.1	68.0	77.1

As part of my proposals referred to later in this message to return responsibility for certain Federal programs to the States—in this instance, responsibility for vocational education and for waste treatment facilities—Federal excise taxes on local telephone service should be revised effective July 1, 1960, to allow limited credits for telephone taxes paid to the States.

Revenues.—The resurgence of our economy has been stronger than was assumed in the budget estimates that were published last September. Consequently, budget receipts for the fiscal year 1959 are now expected to total $68 billion instead of the $67 billion estimated at that time.

The estimate of $77.1 billion in receipts for 1960 is contingent on enactment of the tax recommendations mentioned earlier. Of this estimate, approximately $76.5 billion reflects the increases in receipts under present tax rates and present tax sources while $0.6 billion is from new taxes and increased nontax sources.

The anticipated rate of recovery of revenues in fiscal 1960 may be compared with the experience of the fiscal years 1955 and 1956, which reflect the recovery from the recession of the calendar year 1954. After adjusting for comparability in corporate tax payment dates, the increase in revenues from 1955 to 1956 was more than the increase estimated in this budget. With similar forces of economic recovery at work today, I have confidence that our revenue estimate is sound and will be attained.

MAJOR PROGRAM RECOMMENDATIONS

Eleven key features of the budget recommendations are summarized below:

1. STRENGTHEN THE EFFECTIVENESS OF OUR ARMED FORCES BY FURTHER MODERNIZATION AND BY IMPROVED EFFICIENCY OF OPERATIONS; AND STRENGTHEN FREE WORLD SECURITY BY CONTINUED MILITARY ASSISTANCE TO OUR ALLIES.—This budget assures that essential defense needs are met. The budget recommendations will bolster the defense of our country against possible attack and enable our forces to respond more quickly and vigorously to any emergency. At the same time, and as part of our effort to keep America strong, this budget reflects policies to streamline operations, to remove duplication of weapons, to accentuate the principle and practice of unification, and to minimize maintenance costs—in short, to assure the maximum defense from each dollar expended. A realignment of the Armed Forces and a continuing reappraisal of existing defense activities are underway to accomplish these objectives. This can be illustrated by the changes in the composition of expenditures for the Department of Defense. While the estimated total expenditures for the Department will increase $145 million from 1959 to 1960, those for procurement of missiles and for research, development, test, and evaluation will rise more than $800 million.

In addition to strengthening our own Armed Forces, and recognizing the inseparability of free world defense, the budget continues to provide through military assistance the critical margin of weapons and equipment required by our allies who, with us, forge a strong shield against possible aggressors.

2. ASSIST FREE NATIONS IN THEIR ECONOMIC DEVELOPMENT THROUGH WELL-CONSIDERED PROGRAMS.—Today the less-developed nations—a score of which have attained independence since World War II—are struggling to improve their economic and social conditions. The success of these efforts is vital not only to the freedom and well-being of the millions of people within their boundaries but also to the population of the entire world. Fortunately, the free countries of the world are taking many actions together to promote trade with and to expand investment in such nations. As part of this joint effort, the following actions for the United States are recommended:

(*a*) Increase substantially our subscriptions to the International Bank for Reconstruction and Development and the International Monetary Fund. This should be done promptly.

(*b*) Bring the capitalization of our Development Loan Fund up to the amount originally recommended for the fiscal year 1959 by enacting a supplemental amount of $225 million.

(*c*) As a supplement to established institutions, create a joint development banking institution with our Latin American neighbors.

(*d*) Increase the emphasis on economic development in the mutual security programs through such measures as the appropriation of $700 million for the Development Loan Fund and $211 million for technical cooperation in fiscal 1960.

(*e*) Enact legislation to expand the mutual security investment guaranty program.

3. PROMOTE SCIENTIFIC RESEARCH AND SPACE EXPLORATION.—In the current fiscal year, total expenditures for basic and applied research and for scientific development have reached record amounts and a supplemental appropriation for 1959 to advance space technology is recommended.

For the fiscal year 1960, research and development expenditures will be increased still further, with emphasis on space exploration, peaceful uses of atomic energy, and basic science. Extensive space exploration investigations are being initiated, utilizing satellites and probes. Development work is going forward on high-energy fuel rockets, a million-pound thrust engine, and a nuclear rocket engine.

RESEARCH AND DEVELOPMENT EXPENDITURES

[Fiscal years. In millions]

	1958 actual	1959 estimate	1960 estimate
Department of Defense [1]	$2,314	$3,282	$3,692
Atomic Energy Commission	637	790	846
National Aeronautics and Space Administration	89	153	280
Department of Health, Education, and Welfare	179	236	250
Department of Agriculture	111	128	127
National Science Foundation	35	60	80
Other agencies	133	192	208
Total	3,498	4,841	5,484

[1] Figures for 1958, 1959, and 1960 are not fully comparable because of changes in appropriation structure; they also exclude about $2 billion of procurement funds in each year in support of research and development.

4. CARRY FORWARD CURRENT PUBLIC WORKS PROGRAMS—NOW LARGER THAN EVER BEFORE.—Increases were provided last year in construction programs for water resources, health facilities, public buildings, airways, and highways, partly to combat the recession. As a result, Federal expenditures for civil public works in fiscal 1960 will be the highest in history. It therefore seems both possible and prudent to take a breathing spell in the initiation of new projects. Accordingly, no additional funds are proposed in 1960 for starting new water resources projects, general office buildings, and veterans hospitals. Furthermore, reduced new spending authority is recommended for grants for local public and private hospitals, health research facilities, and for waste treatment works, although expenditures under earlier authorizations will continue to be high. Highway expenditures will increase in accordance with the program planned under the Federal Aid Highway Act, and modernization of airway facilities to meet operational and safety needs will go forward at a higher level of expenditure.

The combined outlay for reclamation, flood control, and navigation projects is estimated to be higher than ever before in 1960. Expenditures are expected to increase again in fiscal 1961 and to hold at that level in 1962 even without new starts beyond those for which initial appropriations have already been made. The new water resources projects authorized for starting in 1959 will be so spread out as to schedule initiation late in the year, wherever practicable, and, in a few cases, construction may be deferred until the fiscal year 1960.

CIVIL PUBLIC WORKS

Expenditures from budget and trust funds, including grants and loans to State and local governments

[Fiscal years. In millions]

	1958 actual	1959 estimate	1960 estimate
Highways and roads............................	$1,589	$2,559	$3,097
Water resources and related developments.........	971	1,031	1,089
Office buildings and post offices..................	78	200	310
Aviation and space flight facilities...............	110	195	233
Schools and hospitals...........................	183	215	201
Other structures...............................	175	343	312
Total...................................	3,106	4,543	5,242

5. CONTINUE AT A HIGH LEVEL PROGRAMS WHICH PROMOTE THE GEN-ERAL WELFARE OF OUR PEOPLE.—This budget makes provision for programs which are of utmost importance to our individual citizens. Expenditures for health research and for constructing various types of health facilities will be at a record level in 1960. Activities to improve education, especially in science and mathematics, will be increased significantly in 1960 as a result of programs started or expanded in fiscal 1959. Grants to States for vocational rehabilitation will be higher in 1960 than in 1959, with services provided to 314,000 disabled persons. Public assistance grants to the aged, the blind, the disabled, and to dependent children will continue to rise. Strengthened programs in the Food and Drug Administration are recommended.

Proposals will be made for widening the coverage of unemployment compensation, for extending and improving the minimum wage and 8-hour laws, and for providing added protection in labor-management relations. I am again proposing legislation to strengthen safeguards on the conduct of labor union affairs, including the strengthening of the law enacted last year requiring public reporting on union welfare and pension plans.

In the housing field, the budget recommends broadening the authority of the Federal Housing Administration and removing the ceiling on the total volume of mortgage insurance it can provide. Legislation is also recommended authorizing capital grants for urban renewal projects for a 6-year period. Annual contributions to local housing authorities for low-rent public housing projects will rise in 1960 as more projects are completed. Commitments by the Federal National Mortgage Association to purchase mortgages on housing for urban renewal areas for relocating displaced families and for the elderly will continue to rise in 1960.

6. FOSTER COMMUNITY DEVELOPMENT WITH INCREASED LOCAL PARTICIPATION.—The Federal Government is helping local communities meet many of the major problems of community development created by increasing population and growing urbanization. Federal expenditures for grants and long-term loans to assist 14 major types of capital improvements alone will reach an estimated $2.1 billion in 1960, or almost double the amount actually spent for these programs in 1958. By the close of fiscal 1960, commitments for future Federal expenditures for the same programs are estimated to be over $6 billion.

CAPITAL IMPROVEMENTS IN COMMUNITIES

Federal grants and long-term loans, excluding net operating expenses

[Fiscal years. In millions]

	Expenditures			Outstanding commitments, June 30, 1960 [1]
	1958 actual	1959 estimate	1960 estimate	
Airport grants....................	$43	$50	$55	$162
Area assistance loans (proposed).......	....	....	7	43
College housing loans................	165	234	186	329
Development corporation loans (Small Business Administration)............	....	4	15	6
District of Columbia construction grants and loans........................	11	15	16	73
Health research facilities construction grants........................	12	20	20	55
Hospital construction grants..........	105	123	128	288
Public facility loans.................	11	24	30	34
Public housing, annual contributions....	95	111	120	[2] 240
School construction grants to federally affected areas....................	80	78	51	98
Urban renewal capital grants.........	35	76	100	1,393
Urban renewal and relocation housing mortgage purchases................	20	122	181	450
Waste treatment works grants.........	17	30	30	82
Total, budget funds.............	594	887	939	3,253
Highway grants for urban areas (trust fund)...........................	534	911	1,136	2,929
Total, budget and trust funds.....	1,128	1,798	2,075	6,182

[1] Including allocations and program reservations.

[2] Estimated maximum annual payment to cover debt service on long-term bonds sold to finance projects. (Unamortized capital costs underwritten by Federal contributions are estimated at $5 billion.)

These totals show how rapidly direct Federal aid to communities is growing. They exclude many other Federal programs which indirectly assist development or redevelopment of communities, such as construction of river and harbor improvements and air navigation facilities, grants for intercity highways, purchases of general housing mortgages and guaranties of housing and business loans of many types. They also exclude Federal aid to communities for nonconstruction programs in such fields as health and welfare.

Federal programs should foster orderly development in a way that will encourage private participation and will share costs equitably among the beneficiaries and the various levels of government. Legislation will be proposed to meet these objectives in the programs for urban renewal, college housing, highways, airports, schools in federally affected areas, and construction of waste treatment facilities. The budget also provides for a new program to assist industrial redevelopment of areas which have severe and persistent unemployment. The Congress is urged to enact legislation for such assistance along the line I have recommended previously.

7. DISCONTINUE TEMPORARY EMERGENCY MEASURES AND STRENGHTHEN PERMANENT PROGRAMS FOR ECONOMIC STABILITY.— Among the governmental actions taken last year under the stress of the recession were two temporary measures involving substantial Federal expenditures.

Funds were advanced to the States and Territories to finance extended unemployment benefits for workers who had exhausted their regular benefits. Only 17 jurisdictions chose to receive these advances for all workers who could be made eligible. Five other States enacted their own legislation extending the period of benefits for those covered under the regular State program. Of the remaining States and Territories, some obtained Federal aid for extended unemployment benefits for veterans and Federal employees alone, while 17 had no extended benefit legislation of their own and did not take advantage of the Federal program at all. In view of the rapidity of the economic recovery and the lack of uniformity of State participation, it is now estimated that expenditures over the life of this program will be $206 million less than the $666 million appropriated for it.

Another temporary measure was the authorization for Government purchases of $1 billion of mortgages on low-cost housing. This full amount has been committed. By the end of fiscal 1959, it is estimated that the Government will have spent over $600 million for such mortgages and will have over $300 million of commitments still outstanding, for which expenditures will occur in 1960.

Direct emergency Federal expenditures for unemployment benefits and for emergency stimulation of home construction are unnecessary on a continuing basis. It is better to strengthen our essential continuing programs for economic growth and stability, and this budget so contemplates.

8. CONTINUE THE ADJUSTMENTS NEEDED FOR A FREER AGRICULTURAL ECONOMY WITH LESS RELIANCE ON THE FEDERAL TREASURY.—The agricultural sector of our economy is in the paradoxical situation of having more efficient farms than ever before and yet of being more dependent upon Federal financial aid. During the current fiscal year, budget expenditures for agriculture and agricultural resources are expected to reach a peak of $6.8 billion. For the coming year, they are estimated to decline to about $6 billion, mainly as a result of the termination of the acreage reserve of the soil bank.

About three-quarters of these expenditures are for price supports and other programs to stabilize farm prices and income. Other expenditures for agriculture consist primarily of payments for conservation; loans for rural electrification, telephones, and farm ownership and operation; and research and extension activities.

Last year, the Congress enacted some changes in price-support laws, but additional amendments are necessary to help our agricultural economy adjust to the continuing revolution in farming technology. Changes are also needed in other agricultural programs. Legislative proposals will be transmitted later which should help our agricultural economy gradually free itself from so much Government support and control.

9. REDUCE THE BURDEN ON THE GENERAL PUBLIC FOR SERVICES TO SPECIAL GROUPS.—Certain Government activities confer measurable special benefits on identifiable groups or individuals beyond the benefits to the general public. The cost of Federal services which convey special benefits should be recovered through charges paid by the beneficiaries rather than through taxes on the general public.

In furtherance of this principle, the recent Congress approved some adjustments in postal rates, and increased the fees for a few other relatively small services. On the other hand, it increased postal employees' pay and highway construction grants without providing the additional charges needed to finance such expenditures. As a result of these and other developments, further legislation is necessary to put the postal service on a self-supporting basis and to finance highway construction without drawing on the general revenues.

This budget recommends legislation to make the activities listed in the following table more nearly self-supporting.

ESTIMATED SAVINGS TO THE GENERAL TAXPAYERS FROM MORE ADEQUATE FEES AND CHARGES

[In millions]

	Fiscal year 1960	Full annual effect [1]
Support highway expenditures by highway-related taxes: [2]		
Finance deficiency estimated under present law............	$241.0	$818.0
Transfer financing of forest and public lands highways to trust fund..	41.0	41.0
Revise postal rates..	350.0	350.0
Charge specifically for use of Federal airways:		
Transfer aviation fuel taxes from highway trust fund to general fund...	34.0	34.0
Increase taxes on aviation fuels...........................	51.0	70.0
Revise fee schedule for noncompetitive oil and gas leases.......	....	14.0
Raise patent and trademark fees...........................	3.5	3.5
Miscellaneous increased fees and cost recoveries..............	11.5	20.8
Total...	732.0	1,351.3

[1] Net change on annual basis with present workload or first full fiscal year effect.
[2] Trust fund receipts, as distinct from budgetary savings, will be increased by an estimated net amount of $690 million in 1960 and nearly $900 million in subsequent years.

10. ENCOURAGE PRIVATE LENDING THROUGH FLEXIBLE INTEREST RATES FOR GOVERNMENT CREDIT PROGRAMS.—In a number of important cases, present legislation on programs for making loans, purchasing mortgages, and insuring or guaranteeing private loans sets inflexible and uneconomic restrictions on interest rates. This creates unneeded and hidden subsidies and requires excessive use of Federal funds by discouraging private lending.

To correct this situation, I recommend that for interest rates on new loans and commitments:

(*a*) The 4¾% ceiling on loans guaranteed by the Veterans Administration be replaced by a maximum rate not in excess of the rate for mortgages on sales housing insured by the Federal Housing Administration. This change will also have the effect of revising the interest rate ceiling on direct housing loans of the Veterans Administration.

(*b*) The ceilings of 4½% and 5% for rental (including armed services) and for cooperative housing mortgages insured by the Federal Housing Administration be increased to levels adequate to assure private financing.

(*c*) The present statutory interest rate of 2% for loans made by the Rural Electrification Administration be replaced by a rate which will cover the current cost to the Treasury of equivalent-term borrowing and other reasonable costs.

(*d*) The statutory standard for college housing loans made by the Housing and Home Finance Agency (the rate at present is 2⅞%) be amended to authorize a rate which will cover the current cost to the Treasury of equivalent-term borrowing and other reasonable costs.

(*e*) The 3½% ceiling on ship mortgage loans by the Maritime Administration be replaced by authority to charge the full costs of the loans.

Such actions by the Congress will encourage the participation of private capital, and, in the long run, will reduce Government expenditures significantly. At the same time, Government guaranties or insurance will continue to permit interest costs to borrowers more favorable than the rates charged in the open market for similar loans.

11. ACHIEVE LONG-RUN ECONOMIES BY ADAPTING PROGRAMS TO CHANGED CIRCUMSTANCES.—Changing conditions in recent decades have resulted in the enactment of hundreds of laws and the creation of vast new programs administered by new or enlarged agencies. In this same period, few Government programs or operations have been discontinued or reduced. Furthermore, in many cases, worthwhile objectives have been pursued with outmoded activities or methods and with accompanying excessive costs to taxpayers. This is a wasteful and inefficient way to conduct public business.

It is proposed in this budget that we start anew to amend the basic legislation for a number of Government programs and operations in order to adapt them to present circumstances and assure that they accomplish their objectives more effectively and with less cost.

IMPROVE CONTROL OVER THE BUDGET

Actions can and should be taken to achieve more effective control over the budget by improving present practices and procedures, especially those related to the consideration of budgetary requests.

Consider full fiscal situation.—The procedure used by the Congress for the review of fiscal matters is one which only the Congress itself can determine. Nevertheless, I believe that achievement of any overall fiscal objective is handicapped by the absence of arrangements under which the Congress can look at the fiscal situation as a whole. Such an arrangement was contemplated under a procedure established in the Legislative Reorganization Act of 1946, but apparently did not prove satisfactory to the Congress. Over the years since that arrangement fell into disuse, the executive branch has made considerable progress in achieving a more comprehensive consolidated executive budget which sets forth a financial plan, including the effect of proposed legislation. I sincerely hope that the Congress will again consider ways by which it can more effectively overcome the diffused consideration which results from separate appropriation bills, the provision of new obligational authority outside of the appropriations process, and the separate deliberations on revenue bills and the debt limit.

Item veto.—The item veto is another important and needed reform, regardless of whether appropriations are made in a number of bills or in a consolidated bill. In either case, the necessity of accepting or rejecting a bill in its entirety prevents the President from considering separable provisions on their own merits. Congress has recognized the value of an item veto by granting it to governors of our territories and insular possessions. Most States have adopted this device. Presidents of both parties, starting as far back as Ulysses S. Grant, have recommended an item veto. Legislation granting an item veto to the President should apply to legislative measures authorizing expenditures as well as to appropriation bills, and should include authority to reduce the amount of an appropriation as well as to strike out an item. The use of such a veto by a President would not remove the final authority of the Congress, which would still retain its constitutional power to override any specific veto.

Public enterprises.—The appropriation and fund structure of the Government needs a new review and some overhaul. For example, major lending programs and other business-type activities are now financed through revolving funds, which enable their expenditures and applicable receipts to be more easily related to each other and thus improve their operating flexibility. However, there are several notable exceptions— among them the Rural Electrification Administration, Farmers' Home Administration, and the power marketing agencies of the Department of the Interior. Legislation will be proposed to permit these enterprises to be budgeted through revolving funds. The possibility of converting still more business-type activities to a revolving fund basis will continue to be studied, with a view to making recommendations to the Congress.

More adequate control over the financial affairs of the Government could be achieved if all Government corporations which possess authority to draw money from the Treasury or to commit the Treasury for future expenditures were brought under the budget provisions of the Government Corporation Control Act. As in past years, legislation to accomplish this purpose will be again submitted to the Congress. I urge that it be enacted.

Legislation will also be proposed to incorporate the Alaska Railroad to facilitate its operations on a business-like basis.

Accrued expenditures and other controls.—In accordance with Hoover Commission recommendations, legislation was enacted last year to enable the Congress to exercise more direct control over the level of Government spending through limitations on accrued expenditures. As an initial step, this budget proposes such limitations for six appropriations. The beginning that can thus be made in improved congressional control should be extended as rapidly as experience warrants.

This budget extends the cost-based budgeting procedures which are necessary to get a proper measure of financial performance for many of the various agencies and programs. Further extensions will be made as agency accounting systems are made adequate to support them.

Continuing improvements.—Efforts to improve financial management practices need to be continued. Considerable progress has already been made by the executive agencies under the leadership of the joint accounting program which is sponsored by the Bureau of the Budget, the Treasury Department, and the General Accounting Office. But there remain a number of unsatisfactory situations, unimportant in earlier years of smaller budgets, that are now worthy of attention.

In the past, a number of appropriation items have been placed on a permanent basis and, in some of these cases, the major result achieved has been weaker control over the expenditures concerned. In addition, even though there are a few justifiable exceptions, the practice of providing authorizations to expend from debt receipts and contract authority outside the appropriation process is generally inconsistent with sound standards of budget practice.

Other inconsistencies occur in the system for making financial authority available to Government agencies. Some guaranty programs are fully funded by specific grants of obligational authority, some are partially funded, and others have an open-end call upon the Treasury. Some collections of funds now credited to miscellaneous receipts might be more properly credited against the related expenditures deliberately incurred to generate the receipts. Criteria for the use of revolving funds and trust funds have not been consistently applied.

Another problem in budgetary control has developed over the use of foreign currencies. In view of the volume of currencies generated by transactions under the Agricultural Trade Development and Assistance Act of 1954 and the numerous competing demands for their use for supplementary United States programs, more adequate procedures parallel to those governing dollar obligations are necessary. The action required by the Congress to authorize the use of certain of these currencies, for which a supplemental request will be transmitted for fiscal 1960, now relates to only a small portion of the currencies which will actually be used for Government programs.

The Director of the Bureau of the Budget is undertaking studies of the various weaknesses and inconsistencies mentioned herein to determine the most appropriate courses of action. Corrective recommendations will be made to the Congress as needed.

REVIEW OF MAJOR FUNCTIONS

The table below compares current estimates for each of the nine major functional categories in this budget with the actual figures for fiscal 1958 and the latest estimate for 1959. The recommendations and estimates

for 1960 are discussed in the sections of this message which follow the
table.

BUDGET EXPENDITURES

[Fiscal years. In millions]

Function	1958 actual	1959 estimate	1960 Estimate	1960 Percent of total
Major national security................	$44, 142	$46, 120	$45, 805	59. 5
International affairs and finance.......	2, 234	3, 708	2, 129	2. 8
Commerce and housing................	2, 109	3, 509	2, 243	2. 9
Agriculture and agricultural resources...	4, 389	6, 775	5, 996	7. 8
Natural resources....................	1, 543	1, 708	1, 710	2. 2
Labor and welfare...................	3, 447	4, 380	4, 129	5. 4
Veterans' services and benefits.........	5, 026	5, 198	5, 088	6. 6
Interest............................	7, 689	7, 601	8, 096	10. 5
General government..................	1, 356	1, 673	1, 735	2. 2
Allowance for contingencies...........	....	200	100	. 1
Total.........................	71, 936	80, 871	77, 030	100. 0

MAJOR NATIONAL SECURITY

The changes in emphasis in the four major national security programs
for the fiscal year 1960 reflect the growing armed strength of the United
States and its allies and the continuing modernization of defense methods.
The Department of Defense will significantly increase expenditures for
procurement of missiles and for development and evaluation of new
weapons, while reducing expenditures for other procurement and for
construction. The Atomic Energy Commission is advancing all phases
of its programs, particularly research in the peaceful uses of atomic
energy. Our allies' progress in equipping their armed forces and the
deliveries under military assistance in 1959 and prior years permit a
reduction in military assistance expenditures. Expenditures for stockpiling and expansion of defense production will be reduced because basic
stockpiling objectives for most materials are now fulfilled and because
many defense production expansion contracts have already been
completed.

Total expenditures for major national security programs in fiscal 1960
are estimated to be $45.8 billion.

55

MAJOR NATIONAL SECURITY

[Fiscal years. In millions]

Program or agency	Budget expenditures			Recommended new obligational authority for 1960
	1958 actual	1959 estimate	1960 estimate	
Department of Defense—Military Functions:				
Present program..................	$39,062	$40,800	$40,693	$39,287
Proposed legislation for construction...	....	....	252	1,563
Subtotal........................	39,062	40,800	40,945	40,850
Atomic energy:				
Present program..................	2,268	2,630	2,717	2,622
Proposed legislation..............	....	....	28	150
Subtotal........................	2,268	2,630	2,745	2,772
Stockpiling and expansion of defense production:				
Present program..................	625	378	140	....
Proposed legislation..............	....	....	125	....
Subtotal........................	625	378	265	....
Military assistance:				
Present program..................	2,187	2,312	1,600	....
Proposed legislation..............	....	....	250	1,600
Subtotal........................	2,187	2,312	1,850	1,600
Total........................	44,142	46,120	45,805	[1] 45,222

[1] Compares with $40,448 million of new obligational authority enacted for fiscal 1958 and $45,704 million (including $619 million of anticipated supplemental authorizations) estimated for fiscal 1959.

DEPARTMENT OF DEFENSE—MILITARY FUNCTIONS.—The defense program for 1960 calls for new appropriations of $40,850 million. This is $288 million less than the appropriations estimated for 1959. However, approximately $0.7 billion of the funds appropriated by the Congress for 1959 in excess of the amounts recommended will be added to the 1960 program.

Expenditures in 1960 are estimated at $40,945 million, which is $145 million more than in 1959 and about $1.9 billion more than the amount spent in 1958—continuing the upward trend which began in 1956. Over the 5-year period from 1955 to 1960, annual expenditures for defense will have increased by over $5.4 billion.

Recent developments.—In the 1959 budget message I recommended a substantial acceleration of our defense effort in selected areas to enable our military strategy, techniques, and organization to keep pace with the rapid strides in science and technology.

During the last year we have made substantial progress in accelerating or starting key programs. The Atlas intercontinental ballistic missile has successfully completed a full-range test and the first operational Atlas missiles will be at launching sites by the end of the current fiscal year. Additional missiles will be put in place in 1960. The first units of the intermediate range missile Thor have already been deployed to the United Kingdom and additional units of both Thor and Jupiter will be deployed during the next 18 months. Construction is already well along on the first five submarines which will be equipped to fire the Polaris solid fuel ballistic missile and the first such submarine will go into operation in the calendar year 1960. Construction of the sixth Polaris submarine has begun and three more are authorized and will be started in fiscal 1960. Coming along at a rapid rate is the Titan, an advanced liquid fuel intercontinental ballistic missile. Development work is progressing rapidly on a "second generation" solid fuel intercontinental ballistic missile, the Minuteman.

For air defense, the Nike-Hercules, which is capable of being armed with a nuclear warhead, is replacing the Nike-Ajax. The Bomarc ground-to-air missile, capable of destroying attacking aircraft at extended ranges, will, when operational, augment manned interceptor planes. To meet the threat of attack by ballistic missiles, the Nike-Zeus missile is being developed at an accelerated pace and construction is underway on a new ballistic missile early warning system.

A dispersal program for our strategic bomber force and its supporting tankers is nearing completion. To improve the effectiveness of the B–52 intercontinental bombers, the production of the Hound Dog air-to-ground missile has been accelerated.

Important scientific data have been obtained from the satellites and lunar probes launched to date. The recent successful use of the Atlas as a satellite clearly demonstrated the potential usefulness of satellites in the field of communications. The Department of Defense will continue to investigate satellite applications of specific military interest. Its space programs will be closely coordinated with those of the National Aeronautics and Space Administration.

The time has come to consolidate our position in key areas of defense affected by recent advances in missiles. Sufficient progress has been made on new weapons systems to permit us safely to eliminate marginal systems and to reduce the number of competitive projects. The solid fuel Pershing and Sergeant missiles will replace the liquid fuel Redstone and Corporal. Production of the Regulus II (a shipbased aerodynamic intermediate range missile) has been terminated, and the Rascal air-to-ground missile program has been canceled.

Because of a change in tactical concepts, the decoy missile Goose has been eliminated. The Seamaster jet powered seaplane project will be stopped. Other weapon systems of lesser importance have also been eliminated. No more appropriations are planned for the Jupiter and Thor intermediate range ballistic missiles after 1960, unless units in addition to those already being provided to our allies through the military assistance program should later be agreed upon.

Thus, by concentrating our efforts on the more advanced and more promising weapons systems, we can increase substantially the combat capabilities of our military forces with a relatively small increase in the overall cost of defense.

Reorganization of the Department of Defense.—The Department of Defense Reorganization Act of 1958, approved on August 6, 1958, is being put into effect.

A streamlined chain of command is being established running directly from the Secretary of Defense through the Joint Chiefs of Staff to unified and specified commands which have been given full operational control of the forces assigned to their commands. The organization of the Joint Chiefs of Staff has been strengthened to provide the Secretary of Defense with the military advice and assistance required for effective planning and direction. The committee system of the Joint Staff has been replaced by seven new directorates, including one for operations. Appropriate instructions have been issued to delineate the additional responsibilities of the Joint Chiefs of Staff and to outline their relationships with other agencies of the Department of Defense.

A director of defense research and engineering has been appointed to assure that all scientific and technological resources of the Department of Defense are put to the best possible use. I expect the new organization to provide more effective leadership, help to eliminate duplication, and develop an integrated research and development program.

In addition, improvements have been made in the administrative procedures of the Department of Defense. Operating methods in the Office of the Secretary of Defense have been improved. Nearly 200 committees have been abolished. The responsibilities and functions of the assistant secretaries are being clarified.

The job ahead is to develop within this organizational framework the management relationships that will improve the decision-making process, clearly fix responsibilities, and provide to all agencies of the Department a full understanding of the broad national requirements that determine our military policy. The attainment of this objective will provide the teamwork that is essential for the continued maintenance of an effective and, at the same time, economical defense effort.

Military personnel policy.—This budget provides for a military force of about the same overall size and composition in fiscal 1960 as that planned for the end of the current fiscal year. This force, however, will have significantly greater combat power as new weapons continue to be added to inventories.

The number of active duty military personnel during 1960 will continue at the level planned for the end of the current fiscal year except for a small reduction in the Air Force. Since the end of the Korean conflict, we have followed the policy of reducing numbers of military personnel as more powerful weapons become available to our forces. However, it has become increasingly apparent that the Communist bloc is following a policy of deliberately and constantly probing free world positions to test our determination to resist the further forcible expansion of Communist influence. Under these circumstances, it is prudent not to plan for any significant changes during fiscal 1960 in our deployments overseas or in our ready military forces at home.

A major effort has been made during the last few years to enhance the attractiveness of military service as a career. The most recent action along this line has been the enactment of military pay adjustments and adoption of recommendations of the Advisory Committee on Professional and Technical Compensation. Although these and earlier measures increase the average cost per man, they have had highly beneficial effects in all the services. The quality of inductees and enlistees has improved. The first term reenlistment rate has increased and the experience and skill levels have been raised. These improvements point to greater stability of personnel, smaller basic and technical training loads, and, over the longer run, may permit some further reductions in military personnel.

The objective of our defense effort today is the same as it has been in the past—to deter wars, large or small. To achieve this objective we must have a well rounded military force, under unified direction and control, properly equipped and trained, and ready to respond to any type of military operations that may be forced upon us. We have such a force now, and under this budget we will continue to have such a force.

Strategic forces.—A principal element of our deterrent power is the Strategic Air Command. The 43 wings of this Command are maintained at a high state of readiness and can react quickly and effectively to meet any major threat to our national security. This Command will be further strengthened during fiscal 1960 by additional deliveries of the improved B–52 intercontinental jet bomber and by the first deliveries of the new supersonic B–58 medium jet bomber together with additional KC–135 jet tankers. In addition, a new and important weapon will be provided by the introduction of Atlas missiles.

Our deterrent forces are complemented by the tactical units of the Army, Marine Corps, and Air Force and the mobile carrier task forces of the Navy, all with striking potential of great magnitude. The submarines designed to launch the Polaris missile will add significantly to our deterrent strength as they come into the fleet.

Air defense forces.—The North American air defense system is well established and is being improved constantly. Our forward warning line, which we operate jointly with Canada, stretches from the mid-Pacific around the northern edge of the continent and across the Atlantic approaches. Behind this line we have an extensive surveillance, tracking, and communications network. Elements of the structure are being tied together for operation by the semiautomatic ground environment (SAGE) system.

All the services contribute military elements to the unified command responsible for maintaining our air defense capability. The Air Force provides warning and control and the longer range weapons systems. The Army provides the shorter range weapons and over 70 Nike-Ajax and Nike-Hercules ground-to-air missile battalions will be in operation by the end of fiscal 1960. The Navy provides sea and air based radar which extend the early warning systems. National Guard units of many States participate in air defense. In addition, other regular and reserve forces of all the services stand ready in the event of need.

These forces, together with Canada's Air Defense Command, comprise the North American Defense Command and provide an air defense shield of growing effectiveness for the entire continent.

Sea control forces.—Historically, the Navy has been assigned the primary mission of controlling sealanes. In the conduct of amphibious warfare and antisubmarine campaigns, it is equipped to support the commands responsible for actions ranging from localized emergencies to large-scale military operations. It is ready to conduct prompt and sustained combat anywhere in the world at sea or adjacent to the sea, and is able to exploit the mobility, surprise, and concealment afforded by the world's free oceans.

The naval forces will operate 864 ships, including 389 warships, in 1960. The carrier task forces will be strengthened with new Forrestal-class carriers and higher performance aircraft possessing both conventional and atomic firepower. The cruiser, destroyer, and frigate forces are steadily acquiring a guided missile capability.

Special programs, including research and scientific studies, are underway to enhance our antisubmarine capabilities. Task forces of specially equipped ships and planes specifically designed for antisubmarine warfare are being employed.

Tactical forces.—The tactical elements of the ground, naval, and air forces combine to deal with situations short of general war or to carry out essential tasks in event of general war. These forces include 14 Army divisions organized along pentomic lines and able to deliver both nuclear and high explosive firepower. Many of these divisions are deployed overseas and are evidence of this Nation's determination to participate actively in the collective defense of the free world.

The Army divisions are supported by the tactical air wings of the Air Force, approximately half of which are deployed overseas. Other important elements of our tactical forces are the 3 divisions and 3 air wings of the Marine Corps. In areas adjacent to the seas these forces can also be supported by carrier-based aircraft.

Both the Army and Marine Corps divisions are backed up by a variety of support units organized to provide both nuclear and nonnuclear military power. Air and sea transportation for these forces are provided by the Air Force and the Navy.

The readiness of our tactical forces to respond to potential aggression was well demonstrated during the Lebanon and Quemoy crises.

Appropriation structure.—In my message to the Congress last year transmitting recommendations relative to our entire defense establishment, I pointed out the need for the Secretary of Defense to have adequate authority and flexibility to discharge his heavy responsibilities. One of the areas requiring attention is the pattern under which funds are appropriated.

This budget proposes a rearrangement of appropriations for the Department of Defense in terms of major purposes rather than of organization units. These broad categories are: (1) military personnel; (2) operation and maintenance; (3) procurement; (4) military construction; and (5) research, development, test, and evaluation. This rearrangement will permit consideration of the Department of Defense budget on a more uniform and more clearly understandable basis.

Operating costs.—The annual operating costs of the Department of Defense for active and reserve military personnel, for retired pay, and for operation and maintenance are approximately the same in 1960 as in 1959. They are estimated at about $22.3 billion in 1960, not taking into account credits of $0.4 billion in revolving funds. Savings from a somewhat lower average number of military personnel and somewhat smaller inventories of aircraft and ships to be supported in 1960 are offset by higher unit costs.

The average cost per man in uniform will be somewhat higher because of (1) required increases in the Government's social security contributions as employer, (2) additional longevity pay reflecting the larger proportion of career personnel, and (3) the proficiency pay provisions of the new military pay law.

The average cost of operating and maintaining each weapon and unit of equipment will be higher because they are more complex. Other elements of increased cost are the additional SAGE centers which will be operational in 1960, the increased cost of medical care for dependents of military personnel, and the larger number of family housing units which will have to be supported by the Department in 1960.

For the past 5 years, the Department of Defense has pursued a vigorous program to provide adequate housing for military personnel and their families, both within the continental United States and overseas. This program has met with significant success and sufficient numbers of units have been built or are under construction to satisfy a major part of the military requirements. With the recommended extension of the armed services mortgage insurance program for another year and with a more adequate interest ceiling, private enterprise and local community support should be able to meet most of the remaining requirements for military housing in the continental United States. Some new Government-operated housing will still be required, however, for new installations and certain existing installations in the United States and overseas.

Procurement, research, and construction.—Expenditures for procurement, research, development, test, and evaluation, and military construction are estimated at $19 billion for 1960. There is an increase over 1959 in the combined expenditures for procurement and for research, development, test, and evaluation and a decrease in expenditures for military construction. Missile systems in 1960 will take a larger share of total procurement expenditures and aircraft will take less. Ships and other weapons and equipment will take about the same amount as in 1959.

This budget will provide for the procurement of a total of 1,610 aircraft, including jet bombers and jet tankers, land based and ship based fighters, ship based attack aircraft, trainers, helicopters, and transports. Funds are also provided for the continuation of the development of the B–70, a new high altitude supersonic intercontinental bomber, and a new high speed interceptor.

Work will also continue, at about the same level as in 1959, on the development of a nuclear powerplant for military aircraft. Until such a powerplant is successfully developed, and the technical problems involved in operating a nuclear powered aircraft safely are solved, there is no practical military value in attempting to build the airplane itself. It is the judgment of my scientific advisers, which I approve, that the pace of this program should continue to be geared to valid technical considerations.

In addition to providing for the missiles discussed earlier, the budget also includes funds for a wide variety of tactical missiles, for both the ground and naval forces, and for additional quantities of air-to-air missiles.

The shipbuilding program proposed for 1960 includes another For-restal-class carrier, the eighth of its class. In line with the Navy's recommendation, this carrier will be conventionally powered. It is only good sense to wait until we have more experience with the construction of the first nuclear powered carrier authorized in the 1958 program before we start the construction of another.

The 1960 shipbuilding program also provides for 17 other new ships and for converting 13 ships to more modern types. In addition to the carrier, the ship construction program includes 6 guided missile destroyers and frigates, 3 nuclear powered attack-submarines, and 8 other vessels. Nine Polaris submarines have been authorized to date. This budget provides for the advance procurement of long lead time components for three additional Polaris submarines. Conversions include a cruiser, 8 destroyers, and 4 other vessels. This modernization will improve the antisubmarine warfare capabilities and extend the useful life of World War II destroyers.

Research will be conducted on, among other things, very early warning systems, ballistic missile defense, solid fuel chemistry, and the use of military satellites and other military vehicles for navigation and communication purposes. I am also requesting $150 million for the Department of Defense emergency fund—the same amount as provided for 1959—to provide for the exploitation of breakthroughs or unanticipated developments which may occur during the coming year.

Provision has been made for the essential needs of our ground forces. Included in this budget are funds for weapons, ammunition, engineering and training equipment for the Army and Marine Corps ground forces to enhance the combat power of the individual soldier.

Legislation for military operations.—There are a number of existing provisions of law concerning military personnel which will require legislative action during this session of Congress to extend the expiration dates. They include induction authorities under the Universal Military Training and Service Act, the special enlistment program authorized by the Armed Forces Reserve Act, the act suspending the permanent limitation on the authorized active duty strength of the Armed Forces, and the Dependents Assistance Act.

In the Department of Defense Appropriation Act for fiscal year 1959, the Congress enacted mandatory minimum strengths for the reserve components of the Army, an unprecedented departure from past policy. This action cuts deeply into the concept of flexibility overwhelmingly endorsed by the same Congress in the Department of Defense Reorganization Act of 1958. It is entirely inconsistent with a policy of promptly adjusting our military forces and concepts to rapidly changing world conditions and revolutionary advances in science and technology. Furthermore, I consider these mandatory provisions wasteful of resources that can be more appropriately applied elsewhere. I strongly urge, therefore, that the Congress repeal these mandatory provisions at an early date, and recommend that future defense appropriations contain no similar provisions.

The Departments of the Army, Air Force, and Commerce have for some years been operating long-line communications in Alaska. With Alaska now a State, a communications system should be developed which will be more responsive to the growing needs of the Alaskan economy and people, as well as to the needs of the Government agencies operating in that State. In my judgment, such a system can best be developed by private enterprise. I will therefore soon submit to the Congress proposed legislation to authorize the sale of these Government-owned communications facilities.

For the past several years the Department of Defense Appropriation Act has contained a rider which limits competitive bidding by firms in other countries on certain military supply items. This restriction is sharply at variance with the general law, popularly known as the Buy American Act. I strongly urge that the Congress not reenact this rider.

There are special problems involved in our present system of proficiency flying and its relationships to flight pay for personnel assigned to flying duty. The Secretary of Defense has been requested to make a study of these problems in the interest of improvements and economies.

Legislation on military property, construction, and procurement.— Changes in military concepts, weapons, and training requirements have markedly reduced or eliminated the need for some military installations and property while creating additional requirements for new types of facilities. Consideration should be given to legislation to streamline procedures and legal requirements for disposing of such obsolete facilities and real property. Such procedures would also reduce administrative costs of managing property and place property which is now exempt from State and local taxes on the tax rolls.

In this connection, section 601 of Public Law 155, 82d Congress, imposes restrictions on the executive branch of the Government with respect to certain real estate transactions of the Department of Defense. As stated in the budget message last year, the Attorney General has advised me that this provision of law reflects the exercise of legislative authority not warranted by the Constitution. I again recommend its immediate repeal.

The continued and rapid growth in the use of petroleum products has made questionable the need for maintenance of the relatively small naval petroleum reserves as a significant defense measure, since it would appear that the nationwide, even worldwide, petroleum industry must be relied upon to provide efficiently for our petroleum requirements in both peace and war. Accordingly, the administration will study (and I would hope the Congress would do likewise) the advisability of disposing of the anachronistic naval petroleum reserves, thereby relieving the Department of the Navy of an inappropriate responsibility and also providing additional revenue to the Federal Government.

This budget contains recommendations for $1.6 billion additional authorization for acquisition and construction of facilities for the Armed Forces. The details of this program are now under study in the Department of Defense and are subject to modifications in consonance with the program planning of the Armed Forces. The program will be held to the minimum requirements for facilities and installations essential to the modern weapons systems being made operational. I will submit at an early date both the additional authorizations and the related estimates of appropriations for the military construction programs.

Another matter which will require the attention of the Congress during this session is the expiration of the Renegotiation Act on June 30, 1959. This is the law under which excess profits gained on certain Government contracts and related subcontracts are recaptured by the Government through renegotiation. I recommend that this act be extended.

DEVELOPMENT AND CONTROL OF ATOMIC ENERGY.—Expenditures by the Atomic Energy Commission are expected to reach an all-time high of $2.7 billion in fiscal 1960. This large amount reflects our determination to maintain our position of world leadership in the field of nuclear military armaments until such armaments are brought under adequate international control and to promote the development of peaceful applications of atomic energy.

In the light of our offer to suspend tests of nuclear weapons for a 1-year period starting October 31, 1958, and in view of the negotiations for further suspension, the budget does not provide for any weapons tests in the fiscal year 1960. Under the circumstances, testing grounds in Nevada and the Pacific will be kept on a standby basis.

A satisfactory test suspension agreement, of course, is but a first step toward reducing the grave threat of nuclear warfare. This administration intends to explore all possible means of attaining armament control under adequate inspection guaranties despite the recent suspension of negotiations on means of avoiding surprise attack. I hope that we shall succeed. Until an acceptable agreement is reached, however, financial authorizations must be provided to continue development and production of nuclear weapons at current high levels to meet a variety of military needs.

Programs for the development of nuclear reactors for a variety of military propulsion and power applications will be continued at or above the high levels already attained.

Peaceful uses of atomic energy.—At the second Conference on the Peaceful Uses of Atomic Energy in Geneva during September 1958, the United States demonstrated the range and scope of its atomic research and development in the peaceful applications of this new energy source.

We plan to pursue energetically the promising technical approaches to civilian power reactors. We will emphasize efforts to reduce the cost of the reactor fuel cycle; such a reduction is basic to the attainment of economic atomic power. This budget provides for continuation of construction and for development, modification, and operation of a number of experimental and prototype power reactors owned by the Government, including operation of the atomic power station at Shippingport, Pa., the world's first nuclear powerplant devoted primarily to the production of electric energy. We will also continue substantial support of power reactor projects undertaken by groups outside of the Atomic Energy Commission.

The Commission in exercising its responsibility for direction of the civilian nuclear power development program will identify desirable projects to advance that program. In carrying out these projects the Commission will continue to work with the Nation's electric power producers, both privately and publicly owned, and will continue to seek cooperation from industry in order to utilize its experience and resources. In addition, exchange of technical information with foreign countries will be expanded through participation in international undertakings, especially the European Atomic Energy Community (Euratom) and the International Atomic Energy Agency.

Further investigations into the possible use of nuclear explosions for such peaceful purposes as mining and earth moving, known as Project Plowshare, will be conducted.

Legislation will be proposed in this session to carry out the recommendations of the Joint Federal-State Action Committee in the field of atomic energy, which would recognize certain State responsibilities for the protection of public health and safety.

The budget provides for a higher level of research in the physical and life sciences. Three large particle accelerators in the multibillion electron volt range will be put in operation in 1960. These new accelerators, together with two already completed, will produce valuable new information on the basic structure of the atomic nucleus. More advanced experimental devices will be fabricated and operated to explore the control of thermonuclear reactions. Also, as part of the life science program, the budget includes funds for the operation of the new Brookhaven Medical Center, where the first nuclear reactor designed primarily for medical research purposes is located.

STOCKPILING AND DEFENSE PRODUCTION EXPANSION.—Most of the objectives for the stockpile of strategic and critical materials have been substantially reduced as a result of new studies, and most of these reduced objectives have been met. Consequently, the need for new procurement has been sharply decreased. At the same time deliveries under contracts made during the Korean conflict to encourage expanded production of defense materials are declining. Substantial reduction in the Government's purchase commitments has also been achieved through negotiation with contractors.

For these reasons, expenditures for stockpiling and expansion of defense production are estimated to decline from $378 million in fiscal 1959 to $265 million in 1960. However, because the present authority is inadequate, legislation will be needed in 1959 to authorize an additional $325 million to finance probable deliveries in the next 2 years under existing contracts for expanding defense production.

MUTUAL SECURITY PROGRAM.—The mutual security program is designed to help strengthen the defense and bolster the political and economic stability of the free world. Through it the United States shares in worldwide efforts to meet the Communist threat and to help improve the standard of living of people in less developed nations. For the fiscal year 1960, I am recommending new obligational authority of $3,930 million for the mutual security program. Expenditures are estimated to be $3,498 million, which is $383 million less than in fiscal 1959.

The military assistance portion of the mutual security program, which is primarily related to our military defense effort, is discussed in this section of the message. The other portions of the mutual security program are directed primarily toward promoting stability and economic growth in less developed countries. They are discussed in the International Affairs and Finance section of this message.

The accomplishments, future needs, techniques, and interrelationships of military and economic assistance need to be reassessed in the light of continuing change in military technology and strategy and in economic and political conditions, and with consideration of new Communist techniques in waging the cold war. Therefore, I recently appointed a committee of outstanding citizens, with experience in government, the Armed Forces, and business, to appraise the military assistance program and the relative emphasis the United States should place on military and economic aid. Accordingly, in the present budget, provisions for the mutual security program are subject to whatever recommendations I may make in connection with my later transmission to the Congress of this program.

Military assistance.—In meeting the threats of Communist military aggression, the United States relies on two sources of strength, our own defense forces and the forces of more than 40 free-world nations, to many of whom we provide military assistance. Three of these, Korea, China, and Vietnam, are divided nations facing aggressive Communist-dominated forces across uneasy boundaries. Other recipients border on hostile Communist states, face potentially dangerous internal Communist movements, or are defenders of the great industrial communities of the free world.

Our primary concern is to insure the free world's ability to deter war and to retaliate against attack if deterrence fails. This we do through our own military capability and by providing intermediate and short-range missiles and other weapons to a number of our allies.

MUTUAL SECURITY PROGRAM

[Fiscal years. In millions]

Function and program	Budget expenditures			Recommended new obligational authority for 1960
	1958 actual	1959 estimate	1960 estimate	
Major national security:				
Military assistance..................	$2,187	$2,312	$1,850	$1,600
International affairs and finance:				
Development Loan Fund.............	2	125	200	700
Defense support.....................	874	815	780	835
Technical cooperation...............	140	159	170	211
Contingencies and other assistance.....	408	470	498	584
Subtotal........................	1,424	1,569	1,648	2,330
Total, mutual security............	3,611	3,881	3,498	[1]3,930

[1] Compares with new obligational authority of $2,764 million enacted for 1958 and $3,516 million (including $225 million of anticipated supplemental appropriations for the Development Loan Fund) estimated for 1959.

But the free world also faces the Communist threat of local aggression and military subversion. This danger is best met by conventional forces of the threatened countries. If necessary, the United States and other free-world nations would send reinforcements under the terms of regional pacts and bilateral agreements. Our allies, through their own efforts, are covering the bulk of the costs of operating and maintaining their forces. The United States supplies the critical military equipment that our partners cannot supply themselves and assists in the training of their officers and men.

The estimate of new obligational authority for military assistance in the fiscal year 1960 is $1,600 million. Expenditures in 1960, which will be made primarily from obligational authority enacted in previous years, are estimated to be $1,850 million, a reduction of $462 million from the amount estimated for 1959.

NONMILITARY DEFENSE.—Closely allied to our military preparedness are the nonmilitary civil defense and mobilization programs. These were reorganized last year under a new Office of Civil and Defense Mobilization, for which increased appropriations are recommended for 1960. These programs are discussed with other programs concerned with industry and community facilities in the Commerce and Housing section of this message, under which these expenditures are classified.

INTERNATIONAL AFFAIRS AND FINANCE

The United States is directing its diplomacy and devoting a substantial share of its economic resources to maintaining world peace and the security of free nations. In a world which still contains much want and suffering, it is a goal of our foreign policy to promote the economic stability and growth of less developed countries. This is as vital to us as it is to the countries concerned in the present world situation.

Although military danger persists, a strengthened free-world defense system enables less developed countries to concentrate much of their effort on needed economic progress. Increased international trade, private investment, public programs of lending, and technical assistance are essential to these efforts.

Expenditures for international affairs and finance are estimated to be $2.1 billion in the fiscal year 1960. This amount is $1.6 billion less than the expenditure estimate for 1959, mainly because of an additional and nonrecurring subscription of $1,375 million to the International Monetary Fund for which I am requesting authority for 1959.

Further expansion of trade was made possible when the Congress last year extended the reciprocal trade agreements legislation for 4 years. Under the authority of this act, we will seek additional agreements with friendly countries for mutually beneficial reductions of trade barriers.

The greater share of investment capital and technical ability in the United States and other highly developed countries is to be found in private hands. Less developed countries could benefit in greater measure from this large private reservoir by making investment more attractive to firms from other countries. The United States on its part invites negotiation of tax treaties designed to encourage its citizens to invest abroad. I will request legislation to expand the Mutual Security investment guaranty program, which offers guaranties to American private investors against losses on foreign investment that are caused by inconvertibility of currencies, expropriation, or war. The Export-Import Bank is actively seeking more private participation in its loans and is selling part of its portfolio to private investors, with the expectation of financing all of its operations in fiscal 1960 from receipts. The United States subscription to the capital of the International Bank for Reconstruction and Development helps that agency in channeling private capital into public loans to less developed countries.

INTERNATIONAL AFFAIRS AND FINANCE

[Fiscal years. In millions]

Program or agency	Budget expenditures			Recommended new obligational authority for 1960
	1958 actual	1959 estimate	1960 estimate	
Economic and technical development:				
International Monetary Fund subscription (proposed legislation).........	....	$1,375	....	....
Export-Import Bank...............	$340	243	−$6	....
Mutual security, economic:				
Development Loan Fund:				
Present program................	2	125	180	....
Proposed legislation..............	....	....	20	$700
Defense support:				
Present program................	874	815	515	....
Proposed legislation..............	....	....	265	835
Technical cooperation:				
Present program................	140	159	85	....
Proposed legislation..............	....	....	85	211
Contingencies and other assistance:				
Present program................	408	470	272	....
Proposed legislation..............	....	....	226	584
Other (primarily Department of Agriculture emergency famine relief abroad).........................	146	135	126	115
Conduct of foreign affairs:				
Department of State...............	175	242	212	204
Other...........................	2	4	4	2
Foreign information and exchange activities:				
United States Information Agency....	109	107	114	127
Department of State, exchange of persons...........................	24	25	24	24
President's special international program...........................	16	9	7	7
Total.........................	2,234	3,708	2,129	[1] 2,809

[1] Compares with new obligational authority of $3,983 million enacted for 1958 and $7,070 million (including $4,945 million of anticipated supplemental authorizations) estimated for 1959. The 1959 supplementals include proposed additional U.S. subscriptions to the International Bank for Reconstruction and Development of $3,175 million and to the International Monetary Fund of $1,375 million.

In addition, studies are being conducted by the Department of State
and the Business Advisory Council of the Department of Commerce on
ways to increase the role of private investment, management, and
technical training abroad.

International financial organizations.—To assist in economic development and in the sound expansion of trade, the United States participates
with other countries in international financial organizations and also
makes loans and grants directly to other nations. The multilateral and
bilateral approaches complement each other and both are essential to the
achievement of our objectives.

The International Bank for Reconstruction and Development extends
loans for capital investment, and the International Monetary Fund promotes sound foreign exchange policies and encourages trade by assisting
countries to overcome short-term foreign exchange problems. Both institutions have proved their worth as instruments of international financial cooperation. However, they cannot continue with the same effectiveness unless their present resources are supplemented. The executive
directors of each institution have recommended an increase in member
country subscriptions of 100% for the Bank and 50% for the Fund. I
request that the Congress promptly approve the United States share of
these recommended increases. Early approval will assure the other member countries that the increase in capitalization can be achieved quickly,
and thus encourage prompt action by them.

For the additional United States quota in the International Monetary
Fund, this budget includes $1,375 million as supplemental new obliga-
tional authority and as estimated expenditures in 1959. Of this amount,
$344 million is to be paid in gold and the balance of $1,031 million is
to be paid in the form of non-interest-bearing Treasury notes. The anticipated subscription to the International Bank of $3,175 million in the
fiscal year 1959 is included in the budget as new obligational authority
but not as an expenditure because it will be in the nature of a guaranty
fund. On the strength of guaranties from all its members, the Bank is
able to sell its bonds to private investors.

We are now negotiating with our Latin American neighbors concerning the establishment of an inter-American development banking institution which would facilitate the flow of public and private capital to
economic development projects in this hemisphere and would supplement

existing lending arrangements. This negotiation may result in a later request for legislation permitting United States participation in such an institution.

The administration is also currently studying the feasibility of establishing an international development association which would be affiliated with the International Bank for Reconstruction and Development and would make loans repayable wholly or partially in the borrower's currency.

Development Loan Fund.—In 1957, the United States established the Development Loan Fund to provide capital on terms more favorable than are normally available from other sources, including repayment in foreign currencies. The Development Loan Fund finances both public and private projects that clearly contribute to the basic development of a country but do not qualify for private loans or for financing by the International Bank for Reconstruction and Development or the Export-Import Bank.

The Development Loan Fund is now making loans in substantial numbers, and will have an increasing impact in assisting less developed economies. The Fund will have committed virtually its entire capital by the end of this month. Because of the vital importance to our foreign economic objectives of continuing this type of lending, a supplemental appropriation for fiscal 1959 of $225 million is recommended. This amount has already been authorized but not appropriated by the Congress. New obligational authority of $700 million is requested for fiscal 1960.

Defense support.—Many of our allies among the less developed countries maintain large military forces required for the common defense despite the added strain placed on their national economies by the continuing cost of these forces. To help prevent the living conditions and political stability of these countries from deteriorating because of the economic burden of their military forces, the United States provides economic aid through appropriations for defense support. This aid takes the form of food, textiles and other consumer goods, machinery, and raw materials. For fiscal 1960, new obligational authority of $835 million is requested for defense support.

Technical cooperation.—Through technical cooperation under the mutual security program the United States assists less developed countries to acquire technical, administrative, and managerial skills. This improvement of skills must go hand in hand with the financial and material resources made available for development. For 1960 an increase of approximately $40 million in new obligational authority is requested. This will enable the United States to train more foreign technicians and provide more American experts and demonstrational equipment, with emphasis on expanding programs in Africa. The increase will also permit the United States to pay its share of the expected greater contributions by member nations to the new United Nations special fund for technical assistance projects.

Contingencies and other assistance.—The mutual security program for 1960 includes a request for $200 million to be available for unforeseen contingencies and emergencies that may arise. In addition, appropriations will be requested for special assistance needed for the stability and progress of a number of countries not covered by other categories of aid and for such programs as our contributions to the worldwide malaria eradication program. Other special activities covered by the mutual security program are the United States contributions to the United Nations Children's Fund (UNICEF) and to refugee programs.

Legislation will be recommended to revise requirements on eligibility of countries for aid and thus provide the necessary additional flexibility to help nations that are resisting Soviet domination.

Conduct of foreign affairs.—The Department of State plans to open several new diplomatic and consular posts and to increase its staff dealing with problems of eastern Europe and international communism. Legislation will again be recommended to clarify the authority of the Secretary of State with regard to the issuance of passports. Legislation will also be recommended to reimburse Americans for certain property damage in Europe and the Far East during World War II for which compensation has not previously been authorized.

Foreign information and exchange activities.—The United States Information Agency will continue the major rebuilding of its radio facilities begun in fiscal 1959 to improve the reception overseas of the Voice of America. The cultural content of our information programs will be increased, more American books will be distributed abroad, and greater emphasis will be given to English-language teaching.

COMMERCE AND HOUSING

Over the past 6 years this administration has fostered major advances in the programs of the Federal Government for aviation, highways, urban renewal, the postal service, and aid to small business.

Expenditures for all commerce and housing programs in the fiscal year 1960 are estimated at $2.2 billion, which is $1.3 billion less than the estimated expenditures for 1959. The estimated reduction occurs primarily in the Federal National Mortgage Association and the Post Office Department. Reduced purchases of low-cost housing mortgages and administrative steps to increase receipts will enable the Association to finance its 1960 operations entirely from its current collections. The proposed legislation to provide more adequate postal rates and the absence of the large retroactive 1959 payments for pay and transportation will sharply reduce net budget expenditures for the postal service.

TRANSPORTATION AND COMMUNICATION.—In recent years, the Federal Government has had to take actions to meet emergency problems which have arisen in highways, railways, and aviation. These actions have sometimes been taken on a partial and piecemeal basis, without full consideration of the impact on other transportation programs. The Secretary of Commerce, at my request, is undertaking a comprehensive study of national transportation to identify emerging problems, redefine the appropriate Federal role, and recommend any legislation or administrative actions needed to assure the balanced development of our transportation system.

Space flight.—The National Aeronautics and Space Administration, organized in 1958, is initiating extensive scientific investigations with satellites and probes to increase our understanding of the earth's outer atmosphere; the moon and the planets; the earth's gravitational, magnetic, and electric fields; radiation from space; and other phenomena. Programs in the field of meteorology will look toward the ultimate establishment of a worldwide system of satellite weather observation, and in the field of communications will continue to experiment with the use of satellites to serve as relays for the intercontinental transmission of messages, voice, and television. Projects to increase our ability to place heavy objects in space include development of high energy fuel rockets, a million-pound thrust engine, and a nuclear rocket engine.

To promote rapid advancement of space technology, a supplemental

COMMERCE AND HOUSING
[Fiscal years. In millions]

Program or agency	Budget expenditures			Recommended new obligational authority for 1960
	1958 actual	1959 estimate	1960 estimate	
Promotion of aviation and space flight:				
National Aeronautics and Space Administration:				
Present program.................	$89	$146	$130	....
Proposed legislation..............	....	7	150	$485
Federal Aviation Agency:				
Present program.................	277	466	560	537
Proposed legislation..............	....	....	....	65
Civil Aeronautics Board............	38	58	63	63
Promotion of water transportation:				
Department of Commerce..........	174	212	232	279
Coast Guard.....................	219	238	250	260
Panama Canal....................	−1	13	5	....
Provision of highways................	31	36	1 3	(1)
Postal service:				
Present program.................	674	752	459	522
Proposed legislation..............	....	....	−350	−350
Community development and facilities:				
Urban Renewal Administration:				
Present program.................	58	80	104	1
Proposed legislation..............	....	....	....	252
Other.........................	21	39	40	7
Public housing programs.............	51	93	93	137
Other aids to housing:				
Federal Housing Administration......	−63	−62	−113	....
Federal National Mortgage Association.	−32	678	....	....
College housing loans..............	164	236	186	....
Veterans Administration:				
Present program.................	159	144	133	150
Proposed legislation..............	....	....	−33	....
Other.........................	−1	29	−24	10
Other aids to business:				
Small Business Administration........	71	157	164	201
Proposed legislation, area assistance...	....	....	10	55
Other.........................	44	48	40	52
Regulation of commerce and finance....	49	58	60	61
Disaster insurance, loans, and relief....	21	20	16	5
Civil and defense mobilization.........	66	60	65	87
Total........................	2, 109	3, 509	2, 243	2 2, 880

1 Reflects proposed financing of Federal-aid highways in national forests and public lands from highway trust fund.

2 Compares with new obligational authority of $5,863 million enacted for 1958 and $3,210 million (including $715 million of anticipated supplemental authorizations) estimated for 1959.

appropriation of $45 million is requested for 1959. Of this amount $21 million is for accelerating development of the technology of manned space flight and $24 million is for equipment and facilities for propulsion development and tracking. For 1960, I am requesting new obligational authority of $485 million, an increase of $135 million over the 1959 total; this includes the agency's aeronautical programs as well as its outer space activities.

Aviation.—Under the new Federal Aviation Agency, traffic control activities, both civil and military, are now being combined into a single system more capable of handling safely and efficiently the increasing number of planes of varying speeds. Expenditures for construction and operation of needed new facilities for the Federal airways system are accelerating as programs authorized in earlier years move from plans to performance. A newly established program to augment civilian facilities with existing air defense radar is now in effect and is being accelerated. At the same time, the extensive research underway will help us to resolve the even more difficult air traffic control problems of the future.

Legislation for Federal grants to aid local airport construction expires at the end of fiscal 1959. As I stated last year in disapproving legislation greatly expanding this program, the Federal Government should now begin an orderly withdrawal from the airport grant program. Legislation will therefore be recommended to authorize a transitional program of Federal grants to share the costs of basic facilities, such as runways and control towers. One-half—instead of three-fourths as in the expiring law—of the funds appropriated would continue to be available to the States on the basis of the existing apportionment formula. The other one-half would be available for expenditure on a discretionary basis. Revenue-producing facilities, such as terminals and hangars, should be financed locally. This program will require $65 million of new obligational authority in fiscal 1960, with somewhat smaller amounts in each of the following 3 years.

For the Federal Aviation Agency as a whole, including direct programs and airport grants, I recommend that the Congress provide new obligational authority of $602 million in 1960. Expenditures are estimated to be $560 million, which is $94 million more than in 1959 and almost four times the amount spent for these purposes in 1956.

Subsidy payments by the Civil Aeronautics Board to commercial air carriers are continuing to rise, primarily because of the increasing service to small communities. Practically all of the $63 million in payments estimated for 1960 will go to local service carriers including helicopter operators. The loan-guaranty program administered by the Board, by helping local service carriers to finance new equipment, should in the long run reduce the need for subsidy. Moreover, the Board has announced its intention to suspend service at any point where adequate traffic has not developed after a fair trial. This "use it or lose it" policy should help to prevent permanent certification of uneconomic service.

Airway user charges.—The magnitude of the burden on the general taxpayers for rising airway expenditures makes it essential that users of the facilities pay a greater share of the cost. To this end, legislation will be transmitted to raise the effective tax on aviation gasoline from 2 cents to 4½ cents in 1960 and to levy the same tax on jet fuels, which are now tax-free. These increased costs should be includible, along with other airline costs, in determining the rates charged the ultimate users of air transportation. Receipts from taxes on aviation gasoline should not be used for highways; they should be retained in the general fund instead of being transferred to the highway trust fund. These changes in revenue laws will increase general fund receipts by an estimated $85 million in fiscal 1960 and by somewhat larger amounts in subsequent years.

Promotion of water transportation.—The national maritime policies under which we now operate were laid down 23 years ago in the Merchant Marine Act of 1936. It is increasingly apparent that both the adequacy of and the need for those policies require reappraisal by the executive branch and the Congress. Accordingly, as a part of the general transportation study referred to earlier, the Secretary of Commerce will review the major problems of the shipping industry. As soon as his report is available, I hope the Congress will hold comprehensive hearings. We need new national policies and guidelines which can become effective at the earliest possible date.

At present, the bulk of our Merchant Marine consists of ships built during the years 1942 to 1946. Since existing law normally requires replacement of vessels at the age of 20 years, we must establish definitive policies on such questions as the realistic life span of merchant ships, the number of ships actually needed in our Merchant Marine, the extent to which their construction and operation should continue to be subsidized by the Government, and the pattern of trade routes that should be served by subsidized ships. There should also be an examination of present policies on such matters as foreign flag registration and the competition of foreign shipping.

In the meantime, the 1960 budget provides for a substantial ship construction program. New obligational authority of $129 million is recommended for construction subsidies and related programs in 1960. This appropriation will be used for replacing 14 needed cargo and combination passenger and cargo ships. It is not contemplated that any of it will be used for the passenger superliners authorized last year. I request that the Congress reconsider its action requiring that these superliners be built under direct Federal loans, which under present law would be made at an interest rate below that paid by the Government itself for comparable borrowed money.

The first nuclear powered merchant ship, the N.S. *Savannah,* is expected to be completed in January 1960. Research on improved nuclear propulsion of merchant ships is continuing. Legislation should be enacted to assure that nuclear materials may be distributed for use as fuel on United States merchant ships.

Some savings in maintenance costs will be realized by the Maritime Administration through disposal of surplus shipyards which it owns and through reducing preservation work on over 1,000 Liberty ships no longer suitable for mobilization.

Expenditures for operating subsidies to shipowners, estimated at $130 million, will be unchanged from 1959. A maximum of 330 ships are expected to be eligible for operating subsidies, including a limited number for new Great Lakes routes.

Urgently needed repair and modernization of Coast Guard equipment and facilities are provided for in the increase of $20 million in new obligational authority over the 1959 amount. This will not only improve the protection given life and property but will also save operating and maintenance costs in the future.

Highways.—The comprehensive highway program enacted in 1956 established the principle that highway users, rather than the general taxpayers, should pay the cost of Federal-aid highways. The larger contract authority enacted in 1958, however, will create a cumulative deficit in the highway trust fund under present law of $241 million by the end of the fiscal year 1960, and about $2.2 billion by the end of 1962.

To maintain the trust fund on a self-supporting basis, I am recommending a temporary increase of 1½ cents in highway fuel taxes, to

become effective July 1, 1959, and to remain in effect through the fiscal
year 1964. This increase is necessary to assure availability of the entire
1961 and 1962 Federal-aid highway authorizations without waiving provisions in the basic legislation which limit expenditures to the amounts
available in the trust fund.

HIGHWAY TRUST FUND

[In millions]

Fiscal year	Expenditures	Receipts	Year-end balance
Under existing legislation:			
1957	$966	$1,482	$516
1958	1,602	2,134	1,049
1959 estimate	2,553	2,143	639
1960 estimate	3,102	2,222	—241
1961 estimate	3,109	2,291	—1,059
1962 estimate	3,484	2,377	—2,166
After enactment of proposed legislation:			
1960 estimate	3,136	2,912	415
1961 estimate	3,180	3,175	410
1962 estimate	3,558	3,296	148

In addition, as I have previously recommended, the forest and public
land highways, which are an integral part of the Federal-aid system but
are now financed from general budget funds, should be transferred to
trust fund financing, and the revenues from aviation gasoline taxes which
are now allocated to highway construction should be retained in the
general fund. The net effect of these changes is that all Federal expenditures for Federal-aid highways will be paid from the highway trust fund
and the fund itself will be financed by highway users.

Postal service.—Since 1953 this administration has been using every
available method to improve the efficiency of the postal service, and to
place its operations on a self-supporting basis, except for a few subsidized
uses authorized by law.

In the last session the Congress took an important step by enacting the
first comprehensive increases in postal rates in a quarter century. The
increases, however, were considerably short of the minimum necessary
amounts which I had requested and were made more inadequate by pay
increases for postal employees for which no additional financing was
provided. As a result, new obligational authority of $522 million would
be required next year, under existing legislation, to finance the postal
deficit and the subsidized public services.

The Postal Policy Act of 1958 established, for the first time on a statutory basis, the principle that postal rates should be adequate to cover all costs of operating the postal establishment with certain exceptions. Consistent with this requirement, further revisions in rates should be enacted adequate to provide at least $350 million of additional revenues in 1960. Legislation for this purpose will be proposed in the near future.

An appropriation of $172 million is requested to reimburse the Post Office Department for public service costs not required to be covered by postal revenues. However, the concept of public services as defined in the act requires excessive costs to be charged against general Treasury revenues. Therefore, the Congress should correct this situation by amending the Postal Policy Act of 1958 to prevent these excessive charges and to assure a more equitable sharing of postal operating costs between mail users and the general public.

These increases in rates, together with the appropriations for public service items, should provide adequate funds, not only to meet the expanded requirements for postal service in 1960, but also to carry forward the research and capital programs already underway. As a result we can make needed progress in acquiring modern facilities and equipment adequate to take care of the steadily increasing mail volume in later years.

HOUSING AND COMMUNITY DEVELOPMENT.—A year ago I presented to the Congress a carefully considered program for revision and extension of the basic statutes governing several major housing and community development programs. Adjournment of the Congress without enactment of these recommendations has made it necessary to adopt temporary expedients to handle continuing applications for urban renewal capital grants and college housing loans until new authorizations can be made available. Emergency legislation has already been proposed to the Congress to provide the funds necessary for these programs and to increase the mortgage insurance authority available for the remainder of the fiscal year. In this message I shall emphasize comprehensive long-run changes needed in this important area.

Urban renewal.—The Federal Government is providing major assistance to communities in halting urban deterioration and replacing it with orderly redevelopment. Approximately 650 urban renewal projects are now underway or completed in more than 380 cities. These will involve an ultimate net cost estimated at about $2 billion, of which over $1.3 billion will be supplied by Federal capital grants. The Federal Government also has outstanding loans and loan guaranty commitments totaling about $700 million for temporary financing of these projects.

When urban renewal legislation was not enacted by the Congress last year, authority subject to the President's discretion had to be used to make available $100 million for capital grants. Since this authorization will soon be exhausted, the emergency legislation already proposed contains an additional $100 million for 1959 and also $100 million to restore the discretionary authority for future emergencies.

The Congress should act promptly upon four major revisions in the urban renewal laws:

(*a*) Assure the States and cities of continuing Federal support for urban renewal by authorizing capital grants of $1,350 million for the next 6 years. For each of the first 3 years, 1960–62, $250 million should be authorized, with $200 million annually for 1963–65. This forward authorization, together with administrative steps already taken to allocate the available funds equitably, should enable each community to develop a long-term community-wide plan which may then be financed in realistic annual installments.

(*b*) In accordance with the predominantly local benefits received, require States and cities to assume a gradually increasing share of the expense of buying and improving the land and of other net project costs. On projects initiated in fiscal 1960, the Federal Government should continue to pay two-thirds of the net cost and the State and local community one-third. In succeeding fiscal years the State and local share should increase by steps to 40, 45, and finally 50% in 1963–65. The increased non-Federal share should not prove onerous, since much of this contribution normally is provided through construction of improvements otherwise necessary and the increased property values in the completed projects will usually permit the local costs to be recovered in increased tax receipts, often within 10 years or less.

(*c*) Encourage more careful planning by requiring the States or communities to assume their share of the cost of planning from the start. At present the Federal Government advances the full amount for planning and the local share is paid only if the project actually goes forward.

(*d*) Aid nonresidential urban renewal projects by authorizing $150 million in loan commitments to assist local agencies to obtain financing from private sources. Projects of this type often can yield such substantial increases in property tax revenues that local communities should be able to finance them without requiring Federal grants.

Public housing programs.—By the end of the fiscal year 1960, over 475,000 federally aided public housing units will be occupied by about 2 million people, and the additional 110,000 units already authorized will be under contract for Federal contributions but will not yet be constructed. These 585,000 units should meet most of the demand for such housing by low-income families displaced by highway construction, urban renewal, or similar governmental action in the next few years. I shall not ask for authorization for any additional units.

Insurance of private mortgages.—Through the mortgage insurance programs of the Federal Housing Administration and the loan guaranty program of the Veterans Administration, the Federal Government is underwriting private credit for a substantial share of all houses built and purchased. Twice during the past calendar year, however, orderly planning and financing of home building have been jeopardized when increases in applications for mortgage insurance exhausted or threatened to exhaust the maximum amount of insurance authorized by law. The emergency housing legislation already recommended to the Congress would increase the existing limitation by $6 billion. I urge that the limitation be completely removed in general legislation so that this self-supporting program will be available at all times to insure adequate financing of housing.

Several other major legislative actions should be taken to permit insurance programs of the Federal Housing Administration to meet demonstrated needs:

(*a*) Enact permanent authority to insure property improvement loans;

(*b*) Authorize interest rates for insured armed services and other rental and cooperative housing mortgages adequate to assure private financing of such loans;

(*c*) Establish a new insurance program for mortgages on rental housing for elderly persons to replace the present limited program;

(*d*) Broaden the special mortgage insurance for families displaced by urban renewal and other Government programs to include more effective aids for rental housing;

(*e*) Extend for another year the authority to insure mortgages for military housing;

(*f*) Increase the maximum amounts of mortgages on sales housing eligible for insurance.

Veterans' housing loans.—The direct housing loan program of the Veterans Administration was extended and liberalized last spring as an antirecession measure. Requests for direct loans now exceed available funds in large part because the law does not permit interest rates that are adequate to attract private financing of guaranteed loans. I urge the Congress to act promptly to authorize the same flexibility in interest rates for the Veterans Administration as the Federal Housing Administration already has for comparable programs, and to extend the voluntary home mortgage credit program. These two actions should enable private lenders to meet a large share of the unsatisfied demand by veterans for Government loans, and will also reduce budget expenditures.

Mortgage purchases.—Under its special assistance programs, the Federal National Mortgage Association purchases certain types of insured or guaranteed mortgages. From 1956 through 1958 expenditures for these purchases have been exceeded by receipts from repayments and from sales of mortgages acquired under earlier purchase programs. In 1959, however, mortgage purchases will exceed repayments and sales, and net expenditures will jump to an estimated $678 million, as a result of the billion-dollar program authorized last spring by the Congress to purchase mortgages on low-cost housing at terms favorable to the borrowers.

For the fiscal year 1960, the Association will endeavor to cover its expenditures for mortgage purchases by receipts from mortgage sales and other sources. To make this possible without diverting the flow of new funds from the mortgage market, an estimated $335 million in Government-owned mortgages will be offered to investors in exchange for certain Government bonds which then will be retired.

To avoid unnecessary budget outlays in future years the Housing and Home Finance Agency is increasing its efforts to obtain private financing for programs now largely financed with special assistance funds. These efforts, aided by those of the Department of Defense, have already proved successful in obtaining adequate private credit for the armed services family housing program which, until last spring, had been financed mainly from Government funds. New commitments of over $400 million are anticipated for 1960, mainly for the purchase of mortgages on housing in urban renewal areas and housing for the relocation of families displaced by governmental actions. Since the agency is now permitted to control the prices at which it purchases such mortgages, the rapidly growing financing requirements can and should be met in substantial degree from private sources.

College housing.—No additional authorizations were provided for college housing loans by the Congress last year. Accordingly, while processing of loan applications has continued, only limited new commitments have been made. The emergency legislation already before the Congress would provide $200 million in new lending authority at once. This should be adequate to meet the needs for loans for at least the remainder of the fiscal year 1959.

For the fiscal year 1960, no additional new obligational authority is requested for college housing loans. However, an estimated $50 million in obligations owned by the Government will be offered to investors in exchange for certain Government bonds which then will be retired. This amount will be available for loans to take care of unusual cases during a transitional period from direct Government loans to other means of financing college housing needs.

About 60% of the demand for college housing loans in recent years has come from State universities and other public institutions. Such institutions normally can borrow privately on relatively favorable terms because of Federal tax exemptions on the income from their obligations. Nevertheless, they have been encouraged to borrow from the Federal Government by the low subsidized interest rates required by law since 1955. For the remainder of the present direct loan program, the law should be amended to remove this incentive to Federal borrowing by (a) denying eligibility for loans to any institution qualified to issue tax exempt securities and (b) placing in the law a requirement that interest rates cover costs on loans to all remaining eligible borrowers.

For the future, and in order that there may be no hiatus in providing Federal assistance where it is most needed, this budget suggests that the Congress include in general housing legislation provisions relating to college housing which would authorize a limited loan guaranty program. However, it seems to me that the continued needs of colleges and universities for housing should be considered within the framework of the general problems of education. The Department of Health, Education, and Welfare is now concluding its studies of these problems.

SMALL BUSINESS.—Recent enactment of the Small Business Investment Act and of legislation making the Small Business Administration a permanent agency is substantially strengthening Federal assistance to small businesses. New loan commitments to State and local development corporations and to newly authorized small business investment companies are estimated at $73 million in 1960, thereby putting to work a much larger amount of private capital. Efforts will be continued to assist small businesses in obtaining a fair share of Federal procurement, to advise them on Government property disposals, and to provide them with technical and management assistance. The new program of grants for research or small-business problems and counseling for small firms is getting underway. The expansion in loans can be financed largely by increased receipts anticipated from loans made in prior years, so that net expenditures of $164 million for the agency's business-aid programs will be only $7 million greater than in 1959.

AREA ASSISTANCE.—In disapproving the area redevelopment legislation enacted in the closing days of the last Congress, I expressed the hope that the next Congress would promptly pass a more soundly conceived program. The revised legislation which this administration is proposing would:

(*a*) Place the major responsibility on local citizens;

(*b*) Authorize loans to areas where unemployment has been well above the national average for 2 or more years;

(*c*) Authorize grants for technical assistance to these areas and to localities dependent upon a single industry or situated in rural low-income areas;

(*d*) Place leadership in the Department of Commerce, with the assistance of other Federal agencies.

To finance this program, I recommend initial appropriations in fiscal 1960 of $55 million. Based on the successful, comparable programs conducted by certain States, these appropriations should be adequate to meet the Federal share for redevelopment of all areas expected to qualify under the proposed legislation.

CIVIL AND DEFENSE MOBILIZATION.—Reorganization Plan No. 1 of 1958 merged the former Office of Defense Mobilization and the Federal Civil Defense Administration into the new Office of Civil and Defense Mobilization. This merger is now substantially completed and permits improved coordination of our nonmilitary defense. New obligational authority of $87 million is recommended for 1960.

Methods for formalizing the means by which the Office of Civil and Defense Mobilization utilizes appropriate resources of other departments and agencies are now being studied. The OCDM budget includes $12 million for financing the assigned responsibilities of such agencies in civil defense and mobilization programs.

It also includes $21 million to carry out legislation enacted last year for sharing with the States the cost of civil defense personnel and administration, and for providing radiological monitoring devices to States and cities for training and operational use.

During the past year the administration accelerated a program of public education on the effects of fallout with the aim of stimulating preparations for fallout protection. The new obligational authority for OCDM includes $11 million for the continuing support of this program and for research and demonstration on shelters.

AGRICULTURE AND AGRICULTURAL RESOURCES

Expenditures for agriculture and agricultural resources are surpassed in magnitude in the budget only by outlays for national security and for interest on the public debt. The continuing heavy impact of agricultural programs on the budget is mainly the result of the continued high volume of agricultural production and our long established and now largely outmoded system of farm price supports. This system of price supports is not suited to the technically more efficient agriculture that has been rapidly developing in this country. The system provides production incentives that impede needed adjustments and encourages the production of surpluses which, in turn, result in increased Government outlays for commodity loans and purchases, and for storage and interest costs.

Legislation is urgently needed, therefore, to make further revisions in the price support program. Recommendations will be sent to the Congress in a special message on agriculture. In this budget I am recommending extension of the Agricultural Trade Development and Assistance Act of 1954 (Public Law 480) and the Sugar Act, major changes in the rural credit programs, and a reduction in the advance authorization for the agricultural conservation program.

Estimated expenditures for agricultural programs in fiscal year 1960 are $6 billion, which is $779 million less than the estimate for the current year, but $1.6 billion more than was actually spent in 1958. The main part of the decrease expected in 1960 is in the soil bank program, because the acreage reserve portion terminated at the end of the 1958 crop year.

Total new authority to incur obligations requested for agriculture and agricultural resources in 1960 is $5.1 billion. This amount includes, among others, $2 billion to restore the capital impairment of the Commodity Credit Corporation resulting from price support losses, and $1.2 billion to reimburse the Corporation for estimated costs and losses under other programs financed through that agency. All of these Commodity Credit Corporation costs and losses are reflected in budget expenditures of 1959 and prior years.

Price supports and related programs.—Expenditures for price supports and other programs to stabilize farm prices and farm income will comprise about 75% of total expenditures for agriculture and agricultural resources in 1960.

Because of the many uncertainties with respect to future production, consumption, and exports of farm commodities, it is difficult to estimate the expenditures required for price supports. The budget assumes that crop yields in 1959 will be lower on the average than the record yields of 1958, but that a part of the land that was in the acreage reserve of the soil bank will be used to produce additional price-supported crops in the 1959 crop year. The shift of this idle land to crops will be a factor contributing to continued heavy Commodity Credit Corporation expenditures under existing laws.

Because of the technological revolution that is still increasing productivity in agriculture, farmers continue to produce more than can be marketed at home and abroad. Under our present open-end price support system, this excess production results in increased Federal loans and purchases and increased carryover inventories. Total loans and commodity inventories of the Commodity Credit Corporation on June 30, 1958, amounted to $7.1 billion. This accumulation is expected to rise to $9.1 billion by June 30, 1959, and still further to nearly $10.5 billion by June 30, 1960. To prevent continuation of huge Federal outlays, legislation will be proposed to make badly needed changes in the price support system.

Titles I and II of the Agricultural Trade Development and Assistance Act of 1954 expire on December 31, 1959. Sales of farm commodities

AGRICULTURE AND AGRICULTURAL RESOURCES

[Fiscal years. In millions]

Program or agency	Budget expenditures			Recommended new obligational authority for 1960
	1958 actual	1959 estimate	1960 estimate	
Stabilization of farm prices and farm income:				
Commodity Credit Corporation: [1]				
Price support, supply, and purchase programs....................	$987	$3,118	$2,880	$2,044
Public Law 480:				
Present program................	1,073	1,049	983	968
Proposed legislation.............	....	....	50	....
National Wool Act...............	57	21	81	48
Other...........................	177	233	224	193
Soil bank—acreage reserve..........	620	713	1	1
Removal of surplus agricultural commodities.....................	125	150	150	239
Sugar Act.......................	70	68	75	72
Other...........................	42	35	46	46
Subtotal......................	3,151	5,386	4,490	3,609
Financing rural electrification and rural telephones.........................	297	325	335	225
Financing farm ownership and operation:				
Farm Credit Administration.........	−3	4	2	2
Farmers' Home Administration.......	242	247	194	204
Conservation of agricultural land and water resources:				
Agricultural conservation program (including CCC loan)................	233	240	197	242
Soil bank—conservation reserve......	113	141	343	360
Soil Conservation Service, watershed protection, Great Plains program, and other........................	102	133	135	129
Research and other agricultural services.	255	299	301	294
Total, agriculture and agricultural resources.....................	4,389	6,775	5,996	[2] 5,065

[1] Certain expenditures for agriculture and agricultural resources which are shown elsewhere in this document under CCC are shown in this table under the soil bank programs for which the CCC serves as disbursing agent.

[2] Compares with new obligational authority of $6,257 million enacted for 1958 and $5,414 million (including $1,241 million for anticipated supplemental authorizations) estimated for 1959.

for foreign currencies under title I of this act and donations of commodities for relief purposes under title II have provided a temporary method of coping with some of the continuing excess production of farm commodities. This budget proposes extension of titles I and II of this act for 1 additional year, with an increase from $6,250 million to $7,750 million in the authorization for the Commodity Credit Corporation to incur costs and losses under title I.

The International Wheat Agreement between wheat importing and wheat exporting countries expires on July 31, 1959. The desirability of extending this agreement is currently being studied.

Although the Sugar Act, which serves to stabilize domestic sugar prices and assure adequate domestic supplies, does not expire until December 31, 1960, it is recommended that the act be extended at this time in order to give sugar producers needed time for production planning.

Agricultural credit programs.—The Rural Electrification Administration has made a major contribution to the development of rural America. Over 95% of our farms now have central station electric service compared with 11% in 1935. Expanding use of power in the areas served by electric cooperatives, however, requires substantial amounts of new capital every year to provide additional generating capacity and heavier transmission and distribution facilities. Rural industrial and nonfarm residential consumers, which already account for about one-half of total power sales by the REA system, are increasing their power consumption much faster than are farm consumers and comprise about 75% of the new customers being added. The prospective size of new capital requirements, together with the present state of development of the rural electric cooperatives, emphasizes the need to broaden the sources of capital from which the REA system may obtain the funds to finance needed expansion.

I am again proposing that legislation be enacted to assist both electric and telephone borrowers to obtain financing from private sources.

A reduction in the levels of the direct loan programs of the Farmers' Home Administration is recommended in this budget. Direct loans for farm ownership and for soil and water conservation are supplemented with private loans insured by the Federal Government. In order to attract additional private credit, the Secretary of Agriculture, under authority of present law, has raised the interest rate to be paid on insured farm ownership and soil and water loans from 4½ to 5%.

Legislation will also be proposed to place the Farmers' Home Administration on a revolving fund basis of operation. Under such legislation funds received in repayment of previous loans would be available for new loans and administrative expenses.

Conservation of agricultural resources.—Payments to farmers representing a sharing of the costs of conservation practices performed during the 1959 crop year will require $197 million in expenditures and $242 million in new obligational authority for fiscal 1960. These amounts are needed to pay for the advance authorization in the 1959 agricultural appropriation act, which exceeded my recommendation. For the 1960 crop year a reduced advance authorization of $100 million is recommended. This amount, along with other public programs in support of soil and water conservation, will provide substantial incentives for farmers to continue the soil and water conservation practices required to maintain our agricultural resource base.

With termination of the acreage reserve, many farm owners are expected to place larger acreage in the soil bank conservation reserve. This shift, together with an increase in rental payments, will result in an increase in expenditures from $141 million in fiscal 1959 to $343 million in 1960. The budget provides for an upper limit of $375 million on payments in the 1960 calendar year, which is the same as was provided for 1959.

No additional funds are recommended for 1960 to initiate construction on watershed projects under the Watershed Protection and Flood Prevention Act. However, funds available from the 1959 appropriation will permit starting construction on 60 projects in 1959 and 40 more in 1960.

Research and other agricultural services.—Expenditures for research, education, and other agricultural services financed from direct appropriations will be about the same in the fiscal year 1960 as in 1959, more than double the amount spent for these purposes in 1954. Research in foreign countries to increase industrial uses of agricultural commodities will be strengthened through the use of foreign currencies obtained from the sale of farm commodities abroad.

NATURAL RESOURCES

Expenditures for the development and conservation of natural resources are estimated at $1.7 billion in 1960, approximately the same as in 1959, which itself will be higher than any previous year. About two-thirds of the expenditures in 1960 will be for the development of water resources.

Work on many resource development projects underway was accelerated in the latter part of the fiscal year 1958 to aid in economic recovery, and the higher rate of construction has continued into 1959. To carry forward projects started in 1959 and earlier years will require some increases in appropriations for 1960. In view of this record program, no funds are provided in the 1960 budget for starting construction of new water resources projects. Further, the budget contemplates stretching out construction on some projects underway where this can be done without stopping work on the projects. Other programs will be continued at or below current levels. Even with these economies, total expenditures in 1960 for resources programs will remain at a record level.

NATURAL RESOURCES

[Fiscal years. In millions]

Program or agency	Budget expenditures			Recommended new obligational authority for 1960
	1958 actual	1959 estimate	1960 estimate	
Land and water resources:				
Corps of Engineers, civil functions....	$699	$725	$815	$865
Department of the Interior:				
Bureau of Reclamation............	226	270	250	256
Power marketing agencies.........	42	36	41	43
Indian lands resources............	46	64	61	56
Public domain and other.........	29	34	32	33
Saint Lawrence Seaway Development Corporation....................	48	17	4	....
Tennessee Valley Authority:				
Present programs................	38	46	8	15
Proposed legislation for revenue bond financing.....................	....	2	18	....
Federal Power Commission.........	6	7	7	7
Department of State and other.......	5	7	6	5
Forest resources.....................	174	194	186	192
Fish and wildlife resources............	60	69	70	70
Recreational resources...............	69	97	83	81
Mineral resources...................	59	78	78	68
General resource surveys and other.....	43	61	51	52
Total.........................	1,543	1,708	1,710	[1] 1,744

[1] Compares with new obligational authority of $1,456 million enacted for 1958 and $1,943 million (including $243 million of anticipated supplemental authorizations) estimated for 1959.

Water resources.—Flood control, navigation, irrigation, and related activities of the Corps of Engineers and the Bureau of Reclamation are expected to require expenditures of $1.1 billion in 1960—an all-time high. Of this amount, an estimated $869 million will be spent on construction.

In the years after 1960, an amount of $5 billion will be required to complete going projects, and annual expenditures in 1961 and 1962 will be even higher than in 1960. In view of this extremely high level of commitments and expenditures, the budget contemplates that in some cases work on new starts, for which appropriations were made for 1959, will be limited in that year largely to preconstruction activities, including land acquisition. No additional funds are requested to start new projects in 1960.

In the interest of sound water resources programs in future years, funds are recommended to continue investigations and advance planning and to assemble basic data for future projects. I continue to believe that, as part of sound advance planning, the Fryingpan-Arkansas project in Colorado should again be considered for authorization, but no appropriation to start construction should be enacted until the overall budgetary situation is more favorable.

Research will continue on processes for converting sea water and brackish water to fresh water. Design work and site selection for demonstration plants, initiated in fiscal 1959 under legislation enacted during the past session of the Congress, will be advanced in 1960.

One of the most pressing needs for achieving a sound water resources policy is the establishment of a consistent basis for cost sharing on flood control projects. Several distinguished commissions have emphasized the disruptive effects of requiring the Federal agencies responsible for flood protection works to operate under different and confusing cost-sharing standards. Legislation will be proposed to set a uniform basis of cost sharing for all projects not yet under construction that produce identifiable flood protection benefits to local areas. Under such legislation, non-Federal interests would bear at least 30% of the cost, with the value of lands, easements, and rights-of-way contributed locally counted as part of the non-Federal share. Operation and maintenance would be a State or local responsibility.

I again urge the Congress to take action early in this session to authorize the sale of revenue bonds by the Tennessee Valley Authority in order that the Authority may meet its needs for new generating facilities. Under such legislation the Congress would retain budgetary control of the program. This budget includes a supplemental authorization for fiscal 1959 of $200 million under the proposed revenue bond legislation.

To help improve financial management, legislation will be recommended for the establishment of revolving funds for the Bonneville, Southeastern, and Southwestern Power Administrations in the Department of the Interior. These Administrations market hydroelectric power generated at certain dams constructed by the Corps of Engineers and the Bureau of Reclamation. With this legislation, part of the receipts from these power sales would be used directly, subject to such limitations as may be included in appropriation acts, for financing the operation and maintenance expenses of the marketing agencies, thus reflecting the results of these business-type operations in the budget on a net basis.

Other resource programs.—In 1960, expenditures for conserving and developing the resources of the national forests, public domain lands, and Indian lands will be somewhat lower than in 1959. Receipts from management of these lands are estimated at $300 million in 1960, an increase of $22 million over the 1959 estimate. In accordance with this administration's policy to obtain a fair return for use of federally owned resources, legislation will be proposed to revise the fee schedule for noncompetitive oil and gas leases on lands in the public domain.

Scheduled construction on Indian reservations will permit progress in providing roads, irrigation and water systems, and buildings and utilities. The major share of building construction will go for schools for Indian children who reside on lands held in trust by the United States.

Expenditures in 1960 for fish and wildlife resources will be at about the present level. An increase is recommended to acquire lands for additional wildlife areas in 1960. Also, to aid the fishing industry, the fishery loan fund will be augmented by $3 million and mortgages for fishing vessels will be insured by the Bureau of Commercial Fisheries in the Department of the Interior.

This budget provides for the continued improvement of our national parks and the development of the national forests for recreational use. A supplemental 1959 appropriation is recommended to enable the recently established Outdoor Recreation Resources Review Commission to undertake the first comprehensive survey of outdoor recreational resources and needs. It is anticipated that the Commission's findings and recommendations will provide guides for Federal, State, local, and private interests in considering how to meet the increasing demands for outdoor recreation.

Under present methods of utilizing natural gas, helium is largely being dissipated into the atmosphere. This unique gas is needed for atomic energy and missile programs as well as industrial welding and certain types of aircraft. Legislation is recommended to conserve for future use the Nation's vital helium. Maximum private participation and financing in accomplishing this objective are contemplated.

LABOR AND WELFARE

The Federal Government's labor and welfare services have grown significantly in the last decade as new programs have been enacted and old ones broadened and expanded. Budget expenditures for labor and welfare will have doubled between 1950 and 1960. Including payments from trust funds as well as budget funds, there is an almost fourfold increase, from $5.3 billion in 1950 to an estimated $19.1 billion in 1960. Much of the increase in budget outlays has been for grants-in-aid to States and local governments, which in 1960 will comprise three-fourths of budget expenditures for labor and welfare programs.

Total expenditures for these programs are estimated at $4.1 billion. This is $682 million more than was spent for these programs in 1958 but $251 million less than the estimate for the current year. The decrease from 1959 to 1960 occurs chiefly because of the expiration on April 1, 1959, of the antirecession legislation for temporary Federal unemployment compensation payments. Excluding these temporary payments, estimated expenditures in fiscal 1960 are $161 million greater than in 1959. Significant increases are provided in 1960 for the defense education program initiated in fiscal 1959 and for higher public assistance grants as required by legislation enacted by the last Congress.

While continuing to support programs necessary to stimulate greater State and local effort in areas of critical national concern, this administration has consistently endeavored to strengthen our system of government by encouraging State and local governments to assume responsibility for many public needs which they can provide well without relying on

LABOR AND WELFARE

[Fiscal years. In millions]

Program or agency	Budget expenditures			Recommended new obligational authority for 1960
	1958 actual	1959 estimate	1960 estimate	
Promotion of science, research, libraries and museums:				
National Science Foundation: Basic research....................	$35	$60	$80	$94
Department of Commerce: Bureaus of Census and of Standards.......	16	41	105	120
Other........................	21	32	42	26
Promotion of education:				
National Science Foundation: Science education....................	15	51	60	67
Department of Health, Education, and Welfare:				
Defense education program........	....	65	110	150
Assistance for schools in federally affected areas.................	189	198	188	181
Vocational education and other....	57	62	63	63
Department of the Interior: Indian activities......................	54	60	57	59
Labor and manpower:				
Temporary extended unemployment compensation...................	48	412	....	....
Grants for administration of employment service and unemployment compensation...................	295	322	324	329
Other.........................	115	92	101	103
Promotion of public health:				
National Institutes of Health:				
Research grants and activities......	187	251	254	294
Grants for health research facilities and direct construction.........	14	24	27	20
Hospital construction grants........	106	124	129	101
Grants for construction of waste treatment facilities..................	17	30	30	20
Other.........................	222	240	238	229
Public assistance....................	1,797	1,987	2,022	2,038
Correctional and penal institutions......	34	41	45	59
Other welfare services...............	225	287	251	243
Total........................	3,447	4,380	4,129	[1] 4,196

[1] Compares with new obligational authority of $4,161 million enacted for 1958 and $4,158 million (including $273 million of anticipated supplemental authorizations) estimated for 1959.

Federal aid at all, or by financing a larger share from their own revenue sources. Therefore, toward this objective, legislation is again recommended to:

(*a*) Discontinue Federal grants for vocational education and for waste treatment works construction and adjust Federal revenue laws as recommended by the Joint Federal-State Action Committee so the States can assume full responsibility for these programs starting in the fiscal year 1961;

(*b*) Modify the provisions for aid to schools in areas affected by Federal activities;

(*c*) Increase State and local participation in the financing of public assistance programs.

Specific proposals will be transmitted to the Congress during this session on each of these matters and I urge the Congress to speed their enactment.

The rapid growth in our population, when added to the increasing complexity of our economy as a result of rapid technological advances, brings us face-to-face with increasingly difficult problems in the fields of health, education, and welfare. We cannot continue to deal with these problems on a year-to-year basis. We must, as a Nation, arrive at an understanding on long-term goals. At the same time we must endeavor to reach an understanding on the respective contributions that should be made by government at all levels and by private groups in order to achieve these goals. I have announced in my state of the Union message a series of studies designed to facilitate the reaching of such consensus.

Science, research, and education.—Expenditures for basic research, which provide the foundation for advancements in applied research and technology and assist in the support of our universities, will continue upward in 1960. Expenditures for the program of research grants by the National Science Foundation are expected to reach $80 million, an increase of $20 million above 1959 and more than double the 1958 amount. Basic research in other departments and agencies will continue to increase over past years. For all agencies combined, it is estimated that Federal expenditures for basic research will be about $500 million in the fiscal year 1960.

In the field of education, primarily in science and mathematics, this budget provides for increased expenditures by the National Science Foundation and the Department of Health, Education, and Welfare for programs initiated or enlarged in fiscal 1959.

The National Science Foundation programs are carried out through fellowships to individuals and grants to institutions of higher learning. They are chiefly directed toward providing encouragement and opportunity for capable students to undertake careers in science, improving courses of instruction in sciences, and providing advanced training for scientists and science teachers. For example, in 1960, 28,000 teachers—including one out of every six science and mathematics teachers in our high schools—will have the opportunity to attend institutes devoted to the improvement of teaching in these fields. Expenditures for the science education programs of the Foundation in the fiscal year 1960 are estimated at $60 million, an increase of $9 million above the 1959 level, and four times the expenditures in 1958.

The Department of Health, Education, and Welfare, under the National Defense Education Act of 1958, is initiating a program of repayable contributions to loan funds for college students and of grants-in-aid to States. The grants, which will run for 4 years, will help pay for the testing and counseling of high school students, the equipping of laboratories in the secondary schools, and related activities. The budget includes a supplemental appropriation for 1959 of $75 million to augment the $40 million already available in fiscal 1959 for the defense education program and provides $150 million in new obligational authority for fiscal 1960 pending further experience with the program.

Schools in federally affected areas.—Although education is primarily a responsibility of State and local governments, the Federal Government has an obligation to assist communities where large numbers of children of persons engaged in Federal activities impose an extraordinary burden on local school districts.

Programs to provide financial assistance to districts thus affected have been extended and liberalized several times since they were first started in 1950, despite the fact that they should be modified to assure greater and more equitable local responsibility. The Federal Government's responsibility is clear for those children whose parents both work and live on Federal property, and do not, therefore, pay local property taxes. On the other hand, it is only proper for the communities to bear the cost of educating children of those Federal personnel who, like all other residents, pay local taxes directly or indirectly for the support of public schools. In accordance with these principles, legislation will be recommended to place these aid programs on a more sound and equitable basis.

This budget includes appropriations of $181 million for these programs for the fiscal year 1960, the same amount as the appropriations provided by the Congress for fiscal 1959.

Government statistical and economic services.—The rapid growth of our economy and the effective operation of markets for goods and services requires prompt and accurate national statistical information, as well as improved organization in the Government for its analysis.

This budget recommends a major increase in funds for obtaining fundamental economic and demographic data through the 18th decennial census. It also provides for improvements in the compilation of regular price, construction, manpower, and related data to help produce more sensitive and useful information on which many private and Government policies are based. Additional price data will be collected for the Consumer Price Index by the Department of Labor, and a start will be made toward a revision of the index, which is to be completed in 5 years. Preparation of statistics on construction activities will be consolidated in the Department of Commerce. The responsibility for planning and publication of current comprehensive employment and unemployment statistics will be centralized in the Department of Labor, where the work on labor requirements will be strengthened.

Labor and manpower.—The growth of our economy depends in large measure upon the full use of our manpower resources and the effective operation of the free labor market. The Federal-State employment security system, with an estimated 54,000 State employees in 1,800 local offices, makes an important contribution to the functioning of that market. This budget provides $329 million of appropriations for grants to States for administration of employment service and unemployment insurance offices.

These grants are presently financed from an earmarked Federal tax which flows through the general budget even though it is not available for general Government purposes. Legislation is proposed to place an amount equal to the proceeds from this tax directly in a trust fund from which the necessary grants can be appropriated, and any balance used as a reserve for employment security and unemployment purposes. The administration of this program would then be financed in the same way as other social insurance programs.

Our unemployment compensation system has again demonstrated its importance in providing income for the unemployed and thereby supporting the economy while alleviating hardship. Temporary assistance of the kind provided by the Temporary Unemployment Compensation Act of 1958 is in no sense a substitute for widening the coverage of unemployment compensation and extending the duration of benefits and increasing benefit amounts under the Federal-State system. I have many times urged such action. I urge it again now with added conviction as a result of last year's experience.

I am again urging prompt enactment of effective statutory protection for workers and the public from the racketeering, corruption, and abuse of democratic processes which have been disclosed in the affairs of certain labor unions. Additional statutory protection in the field of labor-management relations will likewise be proposed to promote equity and stability in the relations among workers, unions, and employers. I shall make specific proposals in a special message on labor affairs.

Legislation is also recommended to provide equal pay for equal work, to revise the laws relating to hours of work on Federal construction projects, and to extend the coverage of the Fair Labor Standards Act so that several million more workers can receive its protection.

Last year Congress enacted legislation requiring regular reports and public disclosure of the provisions and finances of welfare and pension plans. Every effort is being made in administering the law to protect potential beneficiaries, and amendments to strengthen the basic authority will also be sought. In addition, the Administration recommended and the Congress authorized enforcement of safety codes for longshoremen and harbor workers to overcome certain hazardous conditions in the maritime industry. Supplemental appropriations for administering these new laws are recommended for 1959.

Public health.—Expenditures by the Department of Health, Education, and Welfare for health programs, including those for research and construction of health facilities in fiscal 1960 are estimated at $675 million—more than double the amount 5 years earlier.

Large and rapid increases in outlays for medical research and training by the National Institutes of Health have occurred simultaneously with expansion in related research by other agencies. In 1960, expenditures for such purposes are estimated to increase to $254 million, which is more than three times the amount 5 years ago. The impact of this expanded effort on medical schools and research institutions, as well as its implications for broader policy in education and health programs, requires careful appraisal. The Secretary of Health, Education, and Welfare is completing a review of our long-term objectives in the field of medical research and training. The results of this study in terms of program and costs, including indirect costs, will be made available to the Congress.

Another large component of the health programs consists of construction of hospitals and waste treatment works through grants, and of health research facilities through grants and direct financing. Expenditures in the fiscal year 1960 for these programs are estimated at $186 million, which is $8 million more than in the previous peak year 1959. Proposed new obligational authority has been reduced in a manner consistent with the policy outlined earlier in this message relative to public works. For hospital construction, the Congress provided a sharply increased 1959 appropriation for antirecession purposes, a sizable portion of which will be available for obligation in 1960.

The future of our health programs depends on an adequate supply of qualified personnel. Legislation is recommended to extend the programs, which expire on June 30, 1959, for training of professional nurses and for graduate training of public health personnel.

Social security and public assistance.—The Federal Government's responsibility for income maintenance should be mainly discharged through contributory, self-supporting social insurance. Today we have social insurance programs which help protect nearly all our people from loss of income due to old age, permanent disability, or death of the wage earner. The Federal old-age, survivors, and disability insurance system provides basic protection for nearly all workers; military personnel and railroad workers are covered in addition by special Federal systems; and Federal civilian employees are protected by special laws. The growth of the social security program since World War II is indicated below:

OLD-AGE, SURVIVORS, AND DISABILITY INSURANCE

[Fiscal years]

	1946 actual	1960 estimate
Percent of workers covered	60%	90%
Total annual benefits paid out (in millions)	$321	$10,510
Average monthly number of beneficiaries (in millions)	1.3	13.7

Despite this tremendous growth, and despite the primary responsibility of State and local governments for the economic security needs not met by social insurance, Federal expenditures for public assistance grants to States will continue to rise in 1960—chiefly because of the 1958 amendments to the Social Security Act. Legislation raising the Federal matching share or extending Federal participation to new groups has been enacted five times in the last six Congresses. The following table shows the growth in this program in the period since 1946:

PUBLIC ASSISTANCE GRANTS

[Fiscal years]

	1946 actual	1960 estimate
Federal expenditures (in millions)	$446	$2,018
Federal share in total expenditures	44%	57%
Average monthly number of recipients (in millions)	2.8	5.7

Under the authority of recent legislation, an advisory council is being appointed by the Secretary of Health, Education, and Welfare to study the whole structure and financing of our public assistance programs. I have asked the Secretary to present to this council, at the earliest possible time, the issue of what constitutes an appropriate Federal share in these programs. I have also requested him to develop recommendations, after consulting the council, which can be presented to the Congress to increase State and local participation in the cost of the public assistance programs beginning in 1961. In this connection, I believe we must keep in mind the fact that the Federal share of such expenditures has increased to more than 57% on an overall basis and runs as high as 80% in many cases. I believe that this trend is inconsistent with our American system of government. If it continues, the control of these programs will shift from our State and local governments to the Federal Government. We must keep the financing and control of these programs as close as we possibly can to the people who pay the necessary taxes and see them in daily operation.

A basic problem in the public assistance programs is achieving the goal of helping people to help themselves return to self-support. Solution of this problem requires studies into the causes of dependency and its prevention. It also requires better training of local case workers. This budget provides for cooperative work with the States in these two areas.

Other welfare services.—The rehabilitation of disabled people is rewarding in human as well as economic terms. This budget provides additional funds in 1960 for the Federal-State vocational rehabilitation program. It is estimated that services will be provided to 314,000 persons during 1960 and that the number rehabilitated will increase to 90,000.

Additional funds are included for the White House Conference on Children and Youth which I have called for 1960 so that the States, localities, private organizations, and Federal agencies can pool their knowledge of the best ways to meet the needs of our youth. Funds are also included in this budget for the 1961 White House Conference on Aging, which will provide an opportunity for all levels of Government and our many private organizations to find means through which they can contribute to a better life for our 15 million elderly citizens.

Railroad retirement insurance.—The railroad retirement system is a combination social insurance and industrial retirement program operated by the Government but self-financed from employment taxes on railroad workers and carriers. Several legislative steps should be taken to improve this system:

First, it should be placed on a sound actuarial basis. Although it is generally accepted that railroad retirement should be fully self-financed, studies made in recent years show that the system is incurring a substantial actuarial deficit. Therefore, taxes on railroad employment should be increased at the earliest possible time, without changing the status of such contributions for Federal income tax purposes.

Second, the wages covered for railroad retirement should be raised from $4,200 to $4,800 annually in line with the 1958 amendments for Federal old-age, survivors, and disability insurance. These two systems have been increasingly coordinated, particularly through the 1946 and 1951 amendments, but were not equally strengthened last year.

Finally, revisions should be made in the law governing Federal payments to the railroad retirement account for time spent by railroad workers in military service. According to the Comptroller General, the Government has already paid to the railroad retirement account an estimated $350 million more than will ever be required for the added cost of benefits resulting from military service previously rendered by railroad workers. Furthermore, the law requires Government contributions of several hundred million dollars on a 10-year installment basis to the old-age, survivors, and disability insurance trust funds for past military service, including the service of railroad workers for whom contributions have already been paid to the railroad retirement fund.

Legislation should be enacted to make the actual added cost of military service credits the basis of payment to the railroad account. This is the method already incorporated in law for military service by railroad workers before 1937 and is also the method specified for noncontributory service credits for old-age, survivors, and disability insurance purposes. Payment on this basis will save taxpayers an estimated $95 million in future appropriations for military service between 1948 and 1954. The past Government overpayments to the railroad system should be transferred to the old-age, survivors, and disability insurance trust funds as the annual installments of Government contributions to those funds become due. By providing the first such installment for 1960, this legislation will make unnecessary an $80 million appropriation from the general fund for that year.

VETERANS' SERVICES AND BENEFITS

The upward trend of expenditures in veterans' programs is expected to halt temporarily in the fiscal year 1960, mainly because declining workloads result in a decrease of $163 million for readjustment programs which have helped so many veterans of World War II and the Korean conflict to become reestablished in civilian life. Expenditures for disability and death compensation, which have increased in the last several years because higher rates were enacted, are expected to decrease somewhat in 1960 as the number of beneficiaries declines. However, expenditures for other permanent programs are continuing to increase, primarily because more veterans with disabilities not resulting from their military service are receiving hospital and medical care or pensions. The estimated total expenditures for veterans in 1960 of $5.1 billion are $110 million less than in 1959, and $62 million more than in 1958.

Most of the expenditures for veterans' benefits and services cannot be controlled by ordinary appropriation processes because the eligibility conditions and benefit rates are set by basic legislation, and payments must be made if eligible veterans apply.

This Nation has always shown deep gratitude and provided special benefits and privileges for its war veterans and their dependents, particularly for those veterans killed or disabled as a result of their service and for their widows and children. I am convinced that we will always continue compensation programs which reflect this policy. However, I believe that certain of our national policies and legislation governing

VETERANS' SERVICES AND BENEFITS

[Fiscal years. In millions]

Program or agency	Budget expenditures			Recommended new obligational authority for 1960
	1958 actual	1959 estimate	1960 estimate	
Readjustment benefits:				
Education and training..............	$699	$619	$490	$481
Loan guaranty and other benefits.....	92	105	107	107
Unemployment compensation (Department of Labor)...................	75	44	8	8
Compensation and pensions:				
Service-connected compensation......	2,024	2,065	2,043	2,043
Non-service-connected pensions.......	1,036	1,135	1,203	1,203
Burial expenses and other...........	44	57	61	61
Hospital and medical care, except construction........................	823	885	891	896
Hospital construction.................	33	45	55	20
Insurance and servicemen's indemnities..	43	44	49	54
Other services and administration (Veterans Administration and others):				
Present program...................	156	199	176	177
Proposed legislation................	....	....	5	5
Total..........................	5,026	5,198	5,088	¹ 5,054

¹ Compares with new obligational authority of $5,071 million enacted for 1958 and $5,125 million (including $122 million for anticipated supplemental authorizations) estimated for 1959.

other veterans programs should be modified. This is particularly true of the benefits provided to veterans and their families for disability or deaths not resulting from or related to military service. With veterans and their families constituting nearly half of our population, the cost of these veterans' benefits is high, and will continue to increase as our veterans advance in age.

Pensions.—We must continue veterans' pensions and increase pension rates for those who are without other resources, particularly if they have families. However, eligibility should be determined according to effective tests of need, both as to income and as to net worth, so that payments will no longer be made where the veteran or his family has adequate resources for basic necessities from other sources. Properly applied, I believe this approach can better serve those who are now in need and at the same time minimize the burden placed on taxpayers by present laws. I have, accordingly, asked the Administrator of Veterans Affairs to present to the Congress legislation both to provide more equitable treatment of needy veterans and to modernize the veterans' pension program in the light of social developments and changes.

Compensation.—Other veterans programs also merit close continuing attention. The Veterans Administrator will expedite and broaden the work underway in the Veterans Administration on revising standards for rating of disabilities. For some of the seriously disabled veterans, whose activities are greatly restricted, increases in compensation rates are warranted. Likewise, improved rehabilitation services should be provided for those few peacetime ex-servicemen with substantial service-connected disabilities.

Hospital and medical care.—This budget includes $891 million of expenditures for hospital and medical care for veterans in 1960. The increase of $6 million from 1959 is provided to improve the staffing and quality of service in the hospitals. Provision is made for hospital and domiciliary care for an average of 140,800 beneficiaries per day.

More than 2 million outpatient treatments or examinations for service-connected disabilities will be provided in 1960.

An appropriation of $20 million is recommended for modernization of hospital and domiciliary facilities; with balances from prior years, this appropriation will permit expenditures of $55 million for construction and modernization.

Administration.—Administrative expenditures associated with veterans programs will be lower in 1960 than in the current year because of declining workloads and increasing efficiency. Funds are provided for improving the top management and evaluation activities of the Veterans Administration. The application of modern high-speed automatic equipment to the large volume recordkeeping and clerical operations will be extended. This will produce significant administrative savings in future years.

INTEREST

Interest payments are estimated to rise $495 million to $8.1 billion in the fiscal year 1960. These payments, almost entirely for interest on the public debt, represent more than 10% of budget expenditures.

INTEREST

[Fiscal years. In millions]

Item	Budget expenditures			Recommended new obligational authority for 1960
	1958 actual	1959 estimate	1960 estimate	
Interest on public debt...............	$7,607	$7,500	$8,000	$8,000
Interest on refunds of receipts..........	74	92	87	87
Interest on uninvested funds...........	8	9	9	9
Total........................	7,689	7,601	8,096	8,096

Since the spring of 1958, market rates of interest have increased, reflecting the strong recovery of the economy. The rise in market rates requires the Treasury to pay higher interest on securities issued to refinance the heavy volume of maturing Government obligations, a large part of which were issued when interest rates were lower.

In addition to higher interest rates, the amount of interest payments depends on the size and composition of the public debt. It is anticipated that the public debt will reach $285 billion by the end of the fiscal year 1959. On the basis of the balanced budget I am presenting, the debt will be no higher at the end of 1960, although there will be a substantial temporary increase during the year.

GENERAL GOVERNMENT

Expenditures for general government activities are estimated at $1.7 billion in 1960, an increase of $62 million from 1959, primarily because of the volume of construction of Government office buildings started in earlier years, including the new office building for the House of Representatives.

General property and records management.—Initiation of new construction is being deferred in the fiscal year 1960 and no funds are recommended for starting new general office buildings. In 1959, a total of $208 million new obligational authority was enacted for this purpose. Hence, expenditures in 1960 for Government office buildings started in prior years will increase sharply.

Central personnel management.—The public interest requires a comprehensive analysis and modernization of Federal pay policies and systems. The salary and benefit systems for Federal civilian employees should

GENERAL GOVERNMENT

[Fiscal years. In millions]

Program or agency	Budget expenditures			Recommended new obligational authority for 1960
	1958 actual	1959 estimate	1960 estimate	
Legislative functions..................	$88	$104	$136	$92
Judicial functions....................	44	49	51	51
Executive direction...................	10	13	13	13
Federal financial management.........	502	566	563	566
General property and records management...........................	239	343	373	258
Central personnel management and employment costs.....................	140	215	211	215
Civilian weather services.............	39	49	51	52
Protective services and alien control.....	199	217	219	221
Territories and possessions and the District of Columbia..................	73	94	98	128
Other general government:				
Present programs...................	20	25	9	9
Proposed legislation for Alaska.......	....	....	10	10
Total........................	1,356	1,673	1,735	¹1,617

¹ Compares with new obligational authority of $1,417 million enacted for 1958 and $1,799 million (including $157 million for anticipated supplemental authorizations) estimated for 1959.

combine the best practices of progressive private employers with the special needs of the Government. Government policy should promote efficiency, maintain a clear relationship at all levels between pay and work performed, and assure compensation reasonably comparable with that in private employment. Although some progress has been made in recent years, the present system falls far short of meeting these objectives. Accordingly, I again urge the Congress to establish a Joint Commission on Civilian Employee Compensation in the Federal Government.

Statehood for Hawaii and home rule for District of Columbia.—I again recommend that the Congress enact legislation to admit Hawaii into the Union as a State, and to grant home rule to the District of Columbia. It would be unconscionable if either of these actions were delayed any longer.

Alaska.—I am highly gratified to be the first President in 47 years to have had the privilege of welcoming a new State into the Union. Alaska takes its place as the equal of the other 48 States with both the privileges and the responsibilities that go with statehood. Recommendations will be transmitted to the Congress concerning certain changes needed in Federal law as a result of Alaska's admission to the Union in order to apply to Alaska the same general laws, rules, and policies as are applicable to other States.

The size of the new State, its geographic location, present Federal ownership of 99% of the land area, and Federal administration of services provided elsewhere by private enterprise and State and local governments create problems not previously encountered when new States were admitted into the Union. Furthermore, some time will elapse before Alaska can benefit fully from the revenues to be derived from public lands and other resources to be made available to the State by the Statehood Act. The Federal Government is cooperating with Alaska in developing constructive solutions to these transitional problems.

In the long-run interest of both the State and the Nation, the Federal Government should not continue special programs in Alaska which, in other States, are the responsibility of State and local governments or of private enterprise. The Federal Government should provide such financial assistance as is necessary to facilitate transfer to the State of such programs as highway construction and maintenance, airport operations, and public health services. Therefore, legislation will be proposed to authorize the payment of transitional grants to the State of Alaska in an amount not to exceed $10.5 million for the fiscal year 1960 and in declining amounts for the subsequent four years. Under the proposed legislation Alaska could choose between receiving the entire transitional grant or requesting that a portion be used for financing continued Federal operations during an interim period.

Expenditures for the transitional grants to Alaska will be largely offset by the elimination of existing special Federal programs in Alaska. Alaska will, of course, be eligible to participate in regular Federal grant-in-aid programs on a comparable basis with the other States.

Other recommendations for legislation.—The last Congress enacted legislation to cover some of my most urgent proposals for amending the immigration laws. Legislation on the remaining proposals should be promptly enacted, and the expiring authority to issue visas to certain orphans and to aliens afflicted with tuberculosis should be extended.

I also recommend that the Congress direct special attention to the creation of additional Federal judgeships as proposed by the Judicial Conference, and the strengthening of Federal laws against organized crime.

To permit further timely improvements in the structure of the executive branch of the Government, I recommend that the Congress extend the Reorganization Act of 1949, as amended, which is effective only until June 1, 1959.

I again recommend that the President be authorized to make awards for distinguished civilian achievement.

CONCLUSION

This budget charts the course our Government should take as we embark on the decade of the 1960's. Since the end of World War II, the pace of achievement and universal change has quickened with each successive year, sharpening the need for adjustments in the relations of peoples and nations to each other. In the decade facing us, the challenges to representative government will be no less than in the past; indeed, the tasks which are certain to be laid upon the executive, legislative, and judicial branches will require from each increasing vision, understanding, and wisdom.

This budget is designed to serve the needs of the Nation as a whole as effectively as possible. It rejects the philosophy that the national welfare is best served by satisfying every demand for Federal expenditures.

Our objective, as a free Nation, must be to prepare for the momentous decade ahead by entering the fiscal year 1960 with a world at peace, and with a strong and free economy as the prerequisite for healthy growth in the years to follow. This can be achieved through Government actions which help foster private economic recovery and development, and which restrain the forces that would drive prices higher, and thereby cheapen our money and erode our personal savings. The first step is to avoid a budget deficit by having the Government live within its means, especially during prosperous, peacetime periods.

The 1960 budget reflects our determination to do this.

DWIGHT D. EISENHOWER

NOTE: As printed above, the following have been deleted: (1) illustrative diagrams and highlight summaries; (2) references to special analyses appearing in the budget document.

11   ¶ Statement by the President on the Annual
Budget Message.   *January* 19, 1959

[Recorded on film and tape]

Fellow Citizens:

Today I have sent to the Congress the Budget of the United States.

The Budget is the annual governmental plan for spending your Federal
tax money, which amounts to one dollar out of every five that all our
people earn. It comprises the proposals of the Government for assuring
the safety of our Nation, the well-being of our people and their continuing
prosperity. The program that I have sent to the Congress will enable us
to provide wisely for all these needs and will, at the same time, allow us
to live within our means.

The Budget is in balance.

This is important, because if the Government does not live within its
means, every American suffers. When the Government continues to run
deficits, inflation is the end result. And inflation means rising costs to
every housewife, a falling value to every pay envelope, and a threat to
the prosperous functioning of our economy. Every citizen, no matter
where he lives or what he does, has a vital stake in preventing inflation.

The President has the duty of representing all the interests of the entire
nation in his Budget recommendations.

But it is Congress—and Congress alone—that must enact the legislation
to carry out these recommendations.

The program in this Budget provides for:

—Accelerated modern weapons development, and a strong and adequate national defense program;

—Increases for dramatic exploration of outer space;

—The greatest investment for public works programs in the Nation's
history;

—Additional help to local communities to improve the health, education and welfare of citizens.

Many more programs are provided for in this balanced budget.

In the Government, as in your family, it is not possible to do all that
everyone would like to do—all at the same time. A budget is a way to
schedule priorities. And whatever choices are made, there will be objec-

tions from pressure groups that would put their own interests before the common welfare—that would like to see the Government spend more for their special projects. The Budget is not designed for special interests; the real purpose is to promote the good of all America.

I intend to do everything within my power to keep our country strong, our economy expanding, and Federal spending at a level that will make these objectives possible of attainment. I hope you will help.

Thank you.

12 ¶ Statement by the President on the Death of J. Ernest Wilkins. *January* 19, 1959

I HAVE just learned of the sudden and tragic passing of J. Ernest Wilkins. As former Assistant Secretary of Labor for International Labor Affairs and as a Member of the Civil Rights Commission, Mr. Wilkins was a gifted and dedicated public servant who contributed much to the public welfare of our country.

Mrs. Eisenhower and I extend our deepest sympathies to his family.

13 ¶ Exchange of Messages Between the President and President Frondizi of Argentina. *January* 19, 1959

His Excellency
Senor Dr. Arturo Frondizi
President of the Argentine Nation
Hotel Sumter
Charleston, South Carolina

On behalf of the American people I thank you for your message and extend to you their warm welcome to this nation—a welcome which I shall have the privilege of extending to you personally when I meet you in Washington tomorrow.

DWIGHT D. EISENHOWER

NOTE: President Frondizi's message follows:

The President
The White House

Flying over the coast of the United

States, I advance through you a fraternal greeting to the people of the United States of America and extend to Your Excellency the expressions of my sincere esteem.

ARTURO FRONDIZI

14 ¶ Remarks of Welcome to President Frondizi of Argentina at the Washington National Airport. *January* 20, 1959

Mr. President and Senora Frondizi:

It is a very great privilege and honor to welcome you here as the head of a great nation for whom our people feel the kindliest sentiments of deep friendship. It is particularly a privilege because this is the first time that the President of Argentina has come to our country while he is in office. So we take it that you are paying to our country a great compliment in the effort that you have made to visit and see something of our country.

I assure you that here you will find the warmest of welcomes because on the human side your country, as is ours, is hoping to promote those great values of freedom and life of all the people. And I am sure that because of that kinship in the appreciation of values, our people will look on this visit as the hope of both our countries that we will march forward in realization of those objectives more strongly and more tightly bound together.

I am sure that your visit can do nothing better than to strengthen the friendship between our two countries and to make certain of better cooperation between two nations who have so much in common.

It is a great privilege, I assure you, to have you and your lovely wife here in this Capital.

NOTE: President Frondizi responded (through an interpreter) as follows:

Mr. President:

With deep emotion as an American I arrive in this beautiful city which is your Capital to express personally the cordial feelings of friendship that unite our two Republics.

Although it is my privilege to be the first Argentine President to visit your great country, the links between the United States of America and the Argentine Republic have always been close and strong, ever since the first days of our existence as an independent nation. I thank you for the hospitality extended to me as one more expression of that friendship.

Mr. President, let me tell you of my sincere pleasure on making your acquaintance, a pleasure that is made even greater by the happy circumstance of today being the sixth anniversary of your Presidency.

As President of the Argentine Republic, I bring you the wishes of happiness of the Argentine people, who reaffirm, through me, their affection toward the great people of the United States of America.

Thank you, Mr. President.

15　¶ Annual Message Presenting the Economic Report to the Congress.　*January* 20, 1959

To the Congress of the United States:

I present herewith my Economic Report, as required by Section 3(a) of the Employment Act of 1946.

In preparing this Report, I have had the advice and assistance of the Council of Economic Advisers. I have also had the advice of the heads of executive departments and independent agencies of the Government. I set forth below, largely in the language of the Report itself, what I consider to be its salient conclusions and recommendations.

Economic Recovery in 1958

When the Economic Report was submitted to the Congress in January 1958, a contraction in production and employment that had started some six months earlier was still under way. The decline proved to be sharper than the 1953–54 recession, but it did not last as long. A recovery began in May 1958, and by the end of the year most of the ground lost had been regained. Gross national product, our broadest measure of the Nation's output of goods and services, was at an annual rate of $453 billion in the fourth quarter of the year. In dollars of constant purchasing power, this was almost equal to the highest output attained in the pre-recession period. Nearly a million more people were at work in December 1958 than in July, after allowance for seasonal changes. Although the number of persons unemployed was above 4 million in December, it was 1 million below the highest unemployment figure reached during the recession. Wage and salary income and consumer spending were at an all-time high, and the index of consumer prices had been virtually stable for six months, although about 2 percent higher than a year earlier.

Economic Policies in 1957–58

The events of the last 18 months show again the considerable capacity of our economy to resist contractive influences and to hold a downturn within fairly narrow limits.

Many factors contribute to this capacity. Chief among them are the industry and resourcefulness of our people, the strength and resiliency of our free competitive institutions, and the continuing operation in the American economy of powerful forces making for long-term growth.

Also of importance are features of our economic system that moderate the impact of contractive influences on personal income, and thus help to maintain demand. Increasingly, our people work in industries and occupations that are not readily affected by moderate economic declines. And such reductions in income as do result from lower production and employment are offset, to a considerable extent, by supplementary payments, notably by those made under the Federal-State system of unemployment insurance.

Governmental actions also played an important role in moderating the recession and helping to bring about a prompt and sound recovery. Monetary and credit policies were employed vigorously to assure ample supplies of credit. Legislation was enacted to lengthen temporarily the period of entitlement to unemployment benefits. Numerous actions were taken to spur building activity. Steps were taken to accelerate Federal construction projects already under way and to speed up projects supported by Federal financial assistance. Activities under a number of Federal credit programs, in addition to those in the housing field, helped counter the recession. And the acceleration of defense procurement, which was being undertaken in line with national security policy, exerted an expansive effect.

The 1957–58 recession shows that the major emphasis of Federal policies to counteract an economic downturn should be placed on measures that will act promptly to help shift the balance of economic forces from contraction to recovery and growth. Though an effective contribution can be made by the acceleration of public construction projects already under way, little reliance can be placed on large undertakings which, however useful they may be in the longer term, can be put into operation only after an extended interval.

The 1957–58 experience is also a reminder that there is no simple prescription for corrective action which can be applied with only minor variations in every business downturn. It emphasizes the importance, in a situation in which powerful corrective forces are at work, of avoiding hasty and disproportionate actions, such as tax reductions that needlessly endanger the prospects of future fiscal balance and prejudice the orderly revision of the tax structure.

As production, employment, and income moved upward in 1958, the economic policies of Government became increasingly concerned with keeping the recovery on a sound basis and promoting a sustainable long-term expansion. Monetary and credit policy was shifted with a view to limiting the expansion of bank credit to a sustainable pace. The large financing operations of the United States Treasury are being conducted with a view to enhancing the basic stability of our financial system and promoting sound economic growth. And the fiscal operations of Government are moving in the direction of restoring a balance between outlays and incomes and thereby countering potential inflationary tendencies.

The Economic Outlook

As 1959 opens, there is reason for confidence that the improvement in business activity which began in the second quarter of last year will be extended into the months ahead. Factors that influence decisions on business capital outlays have become more favorable, and an upturn in these expenditures may already be under way. Residential construction outlays should contribute further to economic expansion, especially if favorable action is taken by the Congress on recommendations made in the Report to provide a steadier and more assured flow of private funds into mortgages. Sales of United States products in foreign markets may increase as the pace of business activity abroad quickens and the trade position of primary producing countries is improved. The combined outlays of Federal, State, and local government units will continue to rise. Under the impact of these developments, the liquidation of inventories should soon come to an end; indeed, the gap between current sales and stepped-up production schedules may already have been closed. The effect of these favorable factors on employment and income can be expected to enlarge the markets for consumer goods and thereby to reinforce the conditions making for over-all economic expansion.

A Program for Economic Growth with Stable Prices

Our objective must be to establish a firm foundation for extending economic growth with stable prices into the months and years ahead. This will not come about automatically. To attain our goal, we must safeguard and improve the institutions of our free competitive economy. These are basic to America's unassailable economic strength. We must wage a relentless battle against impediments to the fullest and most effective use of our human and technological resources. We must provide incentives for the enlargement and improvement of the facilities that supplement human effort and make it increasingly productive. Finally, an indispensable condition for achieving vigorous and continuing economic growth is firm confidence that the value of the dollar will be reasonably stable in the years ahead.

Action to meet these challenges is required on many fronts, by all groups in our society and by all units of government.

The individual consumer can play an important part by shopping carefully for price and quality. In this way the American housekeeper can be a powerful force in holding down the cost of living and strengthening the principle that good values and good prices make good business.

Businessmen must redouble their efforts. They must wage a ceaseless war against costs. Production must be on the most economical basis possible. The importance of wide and growing markets must be borne in mind in setting prices. Expanding markets, in themselves, promise economies that help keep costs and prices in check.

Leaders of labor unions have a particularly critical role to play, in view of the great power lodged in their hands. Their economic actions must reflect awareness that the only road to greater material well-being for the Nation lies in the fullest realization of our productivity potential and that stability of prices is an essential condition of sustainable economic growth.

The terms of agreements reached between labor and management in wage and related matters will have a critical bearing on our success in attaining a high level of economic growth with stable prices. It is not the function of Government in our society to establish the terms of these contracts, but it must be recognized that the public has a vital interest in them. Increases in money wages and other compensation not justified by the productivity performance of the economy are inevitably inflationary. They impose severe hardships on those whose incomes are not enlarged. They jeopardize the capacity of the economy to create jobs for the expanding labor force. They endanger present jobs by limiting markets at home and impairing our capacity to compete in markets abroad. In short, they are, in the end, self-defeating.

Self-discipline and restraint are essential if reasonable stability of prices is to be reached within the framework of the free competitive institutions on which we rely heavily for the improvement of our material welfare. If the desired results cannot be achieved under our arrangements for determining wages and prices, the alternatives are either inflation, which would damage our economy and work hardships on millions of Americans, or controls, which are alien to our traditional way of life and which would be an obstacle to the Nation's economic growth and improvement.

The chief way for Government to discharge its responsibility in helping to achieve economic growth with price stability is through the prudent conduct of its own financial affairs. The budget submitted to the Congress for the fiscal year 1960, which balances expenditures with receipts at a level of $77 billion, seeks to fulfill this responsibility. If Government spending is held within the limits set in the proposed budget, the growth of our economy at the rate that may be expected would make it possible in the reasonably foreseeable future to provide, through a significant further step in tax reform and reduction, added incentives and means for vigorous economic growth and improvement.

Governmental actions in other areas can also help to maintain price stability as our economy expands. The Congress will be requested to amend the Employment Act of 1946 to make reasonable price stability an explicit goal of Federal economic policy, coordinate with the goals of maximum production, employment, and purchasing power now specified in that Act. Steps will be taken within the Executive Branch to assure that governmental programs and activities are administered in line with the objective of reasonable price stability, and programs for the enlargement and improvement of public information on prices, wages and related costs, and productivity will be accelerated.

The many continuing programs of Government that promote the expansion and improvement of our economy will be administered vigorously. Also, new legislation will be requested to strengthen competitive forces, to enhance personal welfare, to promote integrity in labor-management relationships and to foster better industrial relations, to assist local areas experiencing heavy and persistent unemployment, to make more effective use of the large Federal expenditures relating to agricultural price support, to promote conditions favorable to trade among nations, and to assist in the economic growth and development of the Free World.

Favorable consideration of these legislative proposals by the Congress will materially help to achieve the goals of vigorous, orderly, and sustainable economic progress within a framework of reasonable price stability.

All of our people, in view of their broad common interest in promoting the Nation's economic strength, can fully support this program.

DWIGHT D. EISENHOWER

NOTE: The message and the complete report (225 pages) are published in "Economic Report of the President, 1959" (Government Printing Office, 1959).

16 ¶ Toasts of the President and the President of Argentina. *January* 20, 1959

Mr. President, Senora Frondizi, Ladies and Gentlemen:

Something over ninety years ago, there was a very distinguished son of the Argentine who visited President Andrew Johnson. His name was Domingo Faustino Sarmiento. He was a scholar, a statesman, and a patriot. He came to this country as our friend, and we are proud to say that he went back as our greater friend. There was forged between him and between those whom he met a very strong friendship that lasted throughout his life. Subsequently he became President of Argentina, your distinguished predecessor.

Now you, Mr. President, come to meet us as the already freely elected President of the Argentine, and we devoutly hope that you, your lovely Senora, and your party, will go back with the same feeling that Sarmiento had—that you go back better friends of the United States than when you came here.

We feel that the historic friendship between your country and ours cannot fail to be strengthened by this visit, and we very much hope that you already have the feeling, here in this country, that feeling that is so graciously expressed in your language, "en su casa."

So, ladies and gentlemen, I hope that you will rise to drink with me a Toast to Dr. Arturo Frondizi, President of the Argentine, and Senora Frondizi.

NOTE: The President proposed this toast at a state dinner at the White House. President Frondizi responded (through an interpreter) as follows:

Mr. President, Mrs. Eisenhower, Ladies and Gentlemen:

It is with great emotion that I recall the memory which the President has just recalled of the visit to this country of the great Argentine, Domingo Faustino Sarmiento. He was a great educator. He was a great statesman. He left here to return to Argentina to preside over the destiny of our country at a time when the whole shape of our nation was in formation. He was a great son of Argentina. He was a great Democrat, and a great Argentine.

It is a particular source of emotion for me to hear President Eisenhower recall the memory of this very great man. I would like also to say at this moment that during my trip to the United States of America—and I believe I am speaking for my wife and all the members of my party—that we have felt here in the United States this warm spirit of friendship which exists between our two peoples.

We at the present time in Argentina are working to consolidate the democratic and free basis of our government, so that people may say of the American continent that it is a continent of brother nations, that it is a continent of freedom of justice and of respect for human dignity.

I would like to say, Mr. President, that the warmth of the welcome that we have received here in the United States—and this is a feeling that we will all carry away with us on our return to Argentina—has been of such a nature that during our visit to this great country, we have not felt that we are in a foreign country, but rather in a sister nation, to which we are joined by closest relations. And we will continue to work for these to be ever closer.

Ladies and gentlemen, I ask you to join me in Toasting the health, the prosperity, and the happiness of the great American people, and of President Eisenhower and his charming wife.

17 ¶ The President's News Conference of January 21, 1959.

THE PRESIDENT. Good morning, please sit down.

The United States has the opportunity and the privilege now for a few days of acting host to President Frondizi of the Argentine Republic and to his wife and party. The United States is very delighted to have the opportunity and hopes that out of this visit will grow even a better relation between the two countries. Incidentally, I am told that in the group here today are some 20 Argentinean press representatives, and it is a privilege to welcome them here at this press conference.

Any questions?

Q. Merriman Smith, United Press International: In Virginia, the State and Federal courts have ruled against laws that would have preserved school segregation. Yet the Governor of Virginia calls on his people to stand firm against integration. He says he has only begun to fight. Well, involved in this situation, sir, particularly in Norfolk, are the children of military personnel.

Now, if these schools remain closed, are you going to do anything to assure a public school education in Virginia and elsewhere for children of Federal personnel so situated?

THE PRESIDENT. Well, it's a very difficult question, and I have been going into it for a considerable time. There are something on the order of 15,000 students of this age in the city of Norfolk, and I think of this number about 5,500 are of military personnel, the sons and daughters of enlisted men and officers largely in the Navy.

Now, of this number of 5,500, something on the order of 500 are children of people that actually live on the post, that is, on the Federal reservation.

I have been informed that HEW and the Navy are now authorized by law to conduct educational operations that would be legal on the post. But I think the position with respect to the other 4,500 is not so clear. Of course, these folks all pay their taxes indirectly through the rents they pay, and also on the things they buy, sales taxes and all that sort of thing. So they are entitled to education, just like any other youngster of the city.

More than that, I should point this out—and many people do not know it—the Federal Government, over the past something like 8 or 9 years, has put in $900 million in building about 40,000 public schoolrooms and in this coming year has got something like 50 or 51 million in the budget for building schoolrooms, and something in the order of $135 million for conducting educational operations, all of this on the basis of these federally impacted areas, Norfolk being one.

Now, the only thing I can say with respect to that problem, which I think critical, is that both HEW and the Defense Department are working on it very hard to see whether at least that part of it, that responsibility, cannot be carried out.

Q. Ray L. Scherer, National Broadcasting Company: Mr. President, about the Mikoyan visit—first, what kind of a man did you find him to be; and second, what do you think that your talks with him might have accomplished?

THE PRESIDENT. Well, it would be pretty hard to give a real worthwhile opinion of an individual based on one fairly long conversation and one brief meeting with him, I think, back in 1945, probably on top of Lenin's Tomb in Moscow.

There is no question he is able, clever, and quick; and he is consistently, I might say, emphatic in his argument for and in favor of the Marxist doctrine as interpreted by Lenin and later other authorities of the Soviets. He is extremely intelligent.

Now, as to what might have been accomplished, as all of you know, there was no attempt at any negotiation. It was a statement of problems on both sides, trying to show some of the reasons why the positions in these issues were taken, as they are taken, by each side, and in an effort, therefore, to get a clearer understanding of the problems now existing. There were no new proposals of which I am aware at all.

With respect to his visit around the United States, I think that was somewhat more important; and for that reason, actually, I sent him a message, because I was very hopeful that he would carry back information that is accurate. No matter what or how much of it could be used for propaganda purposes, I would think for his own people he would be indeed accurate in his reporting. And I think there, one thing he must be sure of is that America wants peace, is ready to conciliate, is ready to match reasonableness with reasonableness, but it simply won't be pushed around. I believe he will understand that the American people believe that, just as much as does any official of the Government.

Q. William McGaffin, Chicago Daily News: Mr. President, you have always appealed for implementation of school desegregation on the grounds that Supreme Court orders must be obeyed. But many persons feel you could exert a strong moral backing for desegregation if you said that you personally favored it. If you favor it, sir, why have you not said so; if you are opposed to it, could you tell us why?

THE PRESIDENT. Because, I'll tell you why, I do not believe it is the function or indeed it is desirable for a President to express his approval or disapproval of any Supreme Court decision. His job, for which he takes an oath, is to execute the laws.

If he, in advance of such execution, says "I don't like it but I will do it," and in the other cases "I do like it, I will do it," he is constantly laying the whole law enforcement processes of the Federal Government open to the suspicion that he is doing his duty one time well and the other time not well.

I don't object to anyone else in the whole world disagreeing publicly with opinions or decisions of the Court, or agreeing with them. I say I have got a particular function and I think it would make it more difficult to carry out that function if I indulged in that kind of, let's say, personal action with respect to Court decisions.

Q. Lloyd M. Schwartz, Fairchild Publications: Mr. President, your Economic Report to Congress yesterday omits any proposal to raise the Federal minimum wage. I wonder whether this signifies that you feel any increase would not be justified and might be inflationary.

THE PRESIDENT. Well, I am not prepared to discuss all the details that are still under argument within my own administration in certain instances. I am soon to send down my recommendations with respect to the whole labor field.

But take the other part of your question. Anything, in my mind, now that is inflationary can almost be classed as bad. I think that the soundness of our economy, the stability of our dollar, in order that our economy can grow and expand, are some of the most important issues we have to meet now and solve them correctly.

Q. Edward P. Morgan, American Broadcasting Company: In that same economic message yesterday, Mr. President, you clearly underlined your feeling that unions had, as you put it, a particular critical role to play against inflation. Does this mean that you have become convinced that wages are more dangerous as an inflationary factor than prices, or does it mean that you think that labor and labor leaders have been less responsible than business in dealing with the problem?

THE PRESIDENT. Well, that's a rather long and involved question, and you make me go into motives of people. I can take the facts. Now, the facts are these, and I have said this long ago: any wage increase that is justified by increased productivity from any reasonable standard that wanted to be taken, that is not inflationary, it ought to be not only approved but we ought to make certain that it takes place.

When you do go, with wage rises, beyond increased productivity—and we always have to assume that you have gone from a reasonable base—now you do have something that is inflationary.

Now, in the same way, any manufacturer that says, "Because of this, I am just simply passing this on and adding a few more percentage points," I think he is guilty of something against the American people.

We have got a problem here that goes right across the board. You cannot excuse anybody in Government from responsibility, you cannot excuse the business leader, the labor leader, indeed, scarcely can you excuse any citizen. All of us have a problem to meet and to help solve.

Q. Mrs. May Craig, Portland (Maine) Press Herald: Mr. President, now that the Mikoyan visit has gone off without serious unpleasantness, may we expect visits perhaps from such persons as President Tito and President Nasser of Egypt?

THE PRESIDENT [*laughing*]. Well, maybe you better ask them, because I haven't had it suggested to me at the moment.

Q. Edward H. Sims, Columbia (S.C.) State and Record: Is Cape Canaveral in Florida going to continue to play an increasingly important part in the missiles program, or is emphasis going to be shifted gradually to the west coast?

THE PRESIDENT. I know of no plans for diminishing the importance of Canaveral whatsoever.

Q. Chalmers M. Roberts, Washington Post: Mr. President, in answering Mr. Smith's question, you mentioned the Federal aid to the so-called impacted areas. Was there an implication there, sir, that you are studying the possibility of asking Congress to deny that aid to areas under Court order to desegregate?

THE PRESIDENT. I didn't make any such implication whatsoever. I do believe this: that when you finally catch up with this problem, certain phases of it, I think the constructional part of it, might some day diminish. But I made no implication whatsoever.

Q. Robert C. Pierpoint, CBS News: Mr. President, some people have said that you seem to worry a little too much about inflation, sir, and perhaps not enough about the slow rate of growth of our economy. I would like to know how you feel about that.

THE PRESIDENT. Well, I can only say this: I've got a big Cabinet committee that has been appointed to study the subject, price stability for economic growth; and that takes the whole field, as far as I can see. The expanding economy is a thing that I believe I have talked more about than almost any individual that I know of, publicly. And the kind of concern that you speak of is really not two different problems—inflation or economic growth. I believe that economic growth in the long run cannot be soundly brought about except with stability in your price structure.

Q. John Scali, Associated Press: Mr. President, during the conferences which you had with Mr. Mikoyan, did he at any time give any hint or suggestion that the Soviet Union would be prepared to make the kind of concessions that would be necessary to settle such troublesome problems as Berlin and the future of Germany?

THE PRESIDENT. As I understood his conversations, this was their purport. He claims that every single proposition that the Kremlin has advanced has as its purpose peace, and it is truly a peace gesture, and therefore when we do not agree, we are negative, rigid, and are unready to meet these peaceful gestures.

I certainly, on my part, tried to make it clear that we are ready to explore anything, any time, any place, as long as there was reasonable chance, opportunity for advancing the peace. But merely to sit and to argue rigidly that any particular proposal that they make is certainly a step toward peace is a little bit hard to swallow.

Q. Garnett D. Horner, Washington Star: Mr. President, aside from the particular impact of the closed schools in Norfolk on the children of Federal workers, military personnel, could you comment on the situation posed by the Virginia Governor's call on his people to strengthen their defiance of the court decision?

THE PRESIDENT. Well, Mr. Horner, I don't know exactly what he means. Their own laws—allowing them to discriminate in giving aid to one particular district and not to another—have apparently been declared invalid by their Supreme Court. You know about the decisions of the United States Supreme Court.

It would appear that the laws in this matter, then, are clear as interpreted by the courts. If that is true—and let's remember again that I am not a lawyer, and I don't know that the court battle is finished—but if that is true, it would seem to me the question comes down: is the United States citizen, be he an official or be he a man that is working in civil life and outside of Government, ready to obey the laws of his State and of his Nation?   I think that is the real question that we have all got to meet.

Q. Carleton Kent, Chicago Sun-Times: Mr. President, what do you think of the proposal in the Senate to create a Federal conciliation service on civil rights matters?

THE PRESIDENT. Well, it's one I haven't studied particularly. Of course, in the Civil Rights Commission, in establishing it, recommending it—and certainly I am going to, as I have indicated before, recommend that it be continued—that was one of the things that we hoped would come about as a part of its duty of making certain that the voting rights of citizens were not interfered with by reason of race and color and so on.

Now, I don't believe that to put up an organizational part of Government with the function of conciliating these things would at the moment be fruitful, but I certainly could be convinced. My mind is not closed. I just haven't had the idea before.

Q. Rowland Evans, Jr., New York Herald Tribune: Mr. President, substantial figures in Congress have raised questions about the validity of your balanced budget. One yesterday said that it was a propaganda budget.

Against that backdrop, could you assess the state of your relations with the Democratic Congress——

THE PRESIDENT. Assess what?

Q. Mr. Evans: The state of your relations with the new and strongly Democratic Congress for the coming session, particularly with respect to welfare programs, such as housing and depressed areas.

THE PRESIDENT. Well, I thought I had made myself pretty clear in my State of the Union Message, my Budget Message, and the Economic Report. But with respect to the criticism of the budget, it is rather interesting to note that some say that the estimates of revenue are completely out of reason, although the range of estimates made by the greatest experts I know of hover somewhere between 75 billion and 78, and some a little bit higher than 78. Others complain bitterly because we are not spending enough money. One man even went to the extent of saying there ought to be $6 billion more at least, and $6 billion more of revenue to meet that particular increase. Others say costs ought to be brought down, we haven't done a good enough job in this. Others complain because we are putting some revenue legislation in the budget, although that is not only authorized but directed by the Budget Act of, I think, 1921—'20 or '21, something of that kind—which says that any time the expected revenues are not deemed by the President to be sufficient to cover the expenditures he thinks are necessary, he must propose measures for getting them.

But in any event, it seems like there is something that might be called budgetary schizophrenia that is affecting the critics of the budget, because they are on all sides of it.

I want to point out one thing: the budget has been called political, it has been called political propaganda. Now, I am not running for anything. I am just trying to do my best—what I believe, with all of the sound advice I can get, advice in Government and out of Government—to do my best for America.

If we get down to this business of who is using the budget as a political football, I assure you it is not I.

Q. Sarah McClendon, El Paso Times: Sir, in view of the rising demand for oil, and in view of the fact that we have greater danger than ever of submarines keeping our oil supply from overseas getting here, what made you all change your minds about selling the Navy petroleum reserves?

THE PRESIDENT [*laughing*]. I didn't change my mind. I will tell you who changed their mind. It started from a study from the end of the worthwhileness of these reserves, what to do with them; moreover, there have been so much exploration and production around them that many of these reserves were getting drained. And we had to begin to produce more oil than we wanted to merely because we couldn't now protect ourselves.

The whole problem of the naval reserves really belongs a long time back, about into the Teapot Dome thing. It is really not an important matter today, as I see it.

Q. Rod MacLeish, Westinghouse Broadcasting Company: Sir, on the Mikoyan visit, what do you think were Mr. Mikoyan's basic motives in coming here, and doing what he did?

THE PRESIDENT. Well, of course there has been so much speculation on that, that I doubt that it would do any good to expand it. But I think that he wanted to see two or three things done. One is that he probably could get a better opinion in the official circles, in Congress, and the executive department, as to whether or not we were talking the same language in the foreign field. And I was just assured last night, by one of the most important of our Democratic Senators, that he had got that understanding very clear, in his head. I think he possibly thought that he could create, possibly even in our own country, the theory that the business circles and professional and other circles—the whole civilian population—were completely unhappy with the policies the basis of which was founded in recent times, that those policies were wrong, and that they wanted them changed. I think he probably had a combination of motives. But I would certainly hesitate to give any emphasis to any one of them.

Q. Raymond P. Brandt, St. Louis Post-Dispatch: In your economic message, you said the alternative to inflation was Government controls. Can you tell us what controls you have in mind?

THE PRESIDENT. No, I don't have controls in mind, Mr. Brandt, because I despise them. I believe it is not truly a free economy if we are going to have federally imposed controls, and I want to try every single thing that is possible. But I do say if you get mounting inflation and we will not discipline ourselves, then something will have to be done, because otherwise our whole scheme of economy would just go out the window.

In an emergency, in a great emergency, our people will take these controls; and while we have a bit of black market, public opinion condemns it and the thing works fairly well for that period. But I really believe if you go that far in controls, you will find yourself having to control further. It is just like using morphine or something like that—you finally get to the point of too much, and then you certainly don't have any free economy, and that is what I am trying to preserve.

Q. Richard L. Wilson, Cowles Publications: Mr. President, in view of the attitude of the Democratic Congress, there has been considerable speculation that you might be required to use your power of veto to a greater extent than before. I would like to ask if you have considered that, and if you are prepared to use the power of veto on measures which you think are either borderline cases or not useful at all.

THE PRESIDENT. Well, now, to say when you will veto something and when you will not is a very difficult thing to decide in advance of the event, because you know this: we do not have the item veto where you could be quite specific about such things. Also, we have a habit of taking a bill that is a very necessary one, a good one, and by some maneuvering get into it various types of what I would call undesirable legislation. Now, the problem is very difficult for the Executive—what are you vetoing and what do you do when you do take this action?

After all, the Constitution puts the President right square into the legislative business by saying he must approve legislation after it is enacted; and then there is, of course, a method for the overriding. So he can't escape his responsibility.

I'd say this: if I thought that on balance a bill was bad for the Nation, I am going to veto it. If I do not believe that, then I will do my best to execute it as written.

Q. Pat Munroe, Chicago American: Mr. President, we know the anti-third term amendment can't be repealed in time to change your plans for retiring next year, but you have described it as being perhaps not wholly wise.

I wonder if you favor current efforts in Congress to repeal this amendment.

THE PRESIDENT. Well, I have made no effort in this line to find out the general thinking of the public or even of advisers, because it hasn't come up in that way as a specific question to be answered.

As I have said before, I do not believe it was a particularly wise decision. If the United States wants to take Mr. Smith—not specifying, but any other individual—and wants by its elective processes to make him the President in our system as it now is practiced, I see no objection to it, personally. And so, if I were asked to give an opinion officially on this now I would say I would rather see it repealed than be kept.

Q. Ruth S. Montgomery, Hearst Newspapers: Mr. President, do you think it would be a good idea this year for Mr. Nixon to make a trip to Russia?

THE PRESIDENT. Well, I don't know. But I think this: the visit of any individual that more or less publicizes a sort of, not routine, but sort of a normal exchange of visits, to my mind is all to the good. I am convinced from reports of people that have over the past year, year and a half, come back—these committees of the steel industry and professors and psychologists and numbers of people, committees like that—they come back and everyone reports this: the Russian people, as such, want peace just as earnestly, as seriously, as we do. And that, to my mind, is the great fact that has for all of us great hope. Because the more, therefore, we have people meeting people, I am certain the better is our situation.

Marvin L. Arrowsmith, Associated Press: Thank you, Mr. President.

NOTE: President Eisenhower's one hundred and forty-seventh news conference was held in the Executive Office Building from 10:30 to 11:00 o'clock on Wednesday morning, January 21, 1959. In attendance: 245.

18 ¶ Presidential Statement Upon Signing Executive Order Establishing the Committee on Government Activities Affecting Prices and Costs. *January* 23, 1959

ALTHOUGH the Government has many programs that affect prices and costs—including, of course, procurement—there is now no central mechanism for following their current operations to see whether they are being conducted, insofar as possible, in line with the need for reasonable stability of prices and costs. This newly established Committee will provide such a mechanism.

Each of the programs covered by this order operates under its own law and regulations, and each was set up for a specific purpose. What is needed today is a fresh look at how they are operating in the light of modern-day economic problems. We need to make sure that we are not contributing to the Nation's inflationary problems by the way in which we run our own Government business.

NOTE: Executive Order 10802, establishing the Committee, is published in the Federal Register (24 F.R. 557).

A list of the members of the Committee, as announced by Chairman Raymond J. Saulnier and released by the White House on February 18, follows: Elmer B. Staats, Assistant Director, Bureau of the Budget; Perkins McGuire, Assistant Secretary of Defense (Supply and Logistics); John M. McKibbin, Assistant Postmaster General; Royce Hardy, Assistant Secretary of the Interior; True D. Morse, Under Secretary of Agriculture; George T. Moore, Assistant Secretary of Commerce; John F. Floberg, member, Atomic Energy Commission; James T. Pyle, Deputy Administrator, Federal Aviation Agency; Franklin Floete, Administrator of General Services; John S. Patterson, Deputy Director, Office of Civil and Defense Mobilization; Henry O. Talle, Assistant Administrator for Program Policy, Housing and Home Finance Agency.

19 ¶ Message to the Baghdad Pact Ministerial Council in Karachi. *January* 26, 1959

I AM pleased that representatives of the nations associated in the Baghdad Pact are convening today in the Pact's Sixth Ministerial Council Session. I have followed the progress of this regional collective security organization with deep personal interest since its inception. The United States believes the instrumentalities which the member governments have created to carry out the Pact's purposes are making an important contribution to world peace. We are glad to participate in these activities.

I have asked Ambassador Henderson to represent the United States in your deliberations, and upon his return to report personally to the Secretary of State and me.

I send you my warm wishes for a fruitful meeting.

DWIGHT D. EISENHOWER

NOTE: This message was read at the opening meeting of the Council by Loy W. Henderson, Deputy Under Secretary of State and head of the U.S. Observer Delegation.

20 ¶ Memorandum on the 1959 Red Cross Campaign. *January 26, 1959*

Memorandum for the Heads of Executive Departments and Agencies:

The American Red Cross makes its annual appeal for funds in the month of March. This is one of the three campaigns authorized to be conducted within Executive Departments and Agencies.

The work of the Red Cross has wide benefits. During the year it responds to emergency calls for help from communities stricken by natural disaster—and it maintains many diverse programs of daily import to all citizens. Under charter by the Congress, it provides welfare services to the members of the Armed Forces and to their families at home and overseas.

Employees of the Federal Government, and members of the military establishment, have long given generous support to the Red Cross appeal for volunteers and funds. I hope you will encourage this fine tradition during the coming campaign in March.

DWIGHT D. EISENHOWER

21 ❡ The President's News Conference of *January* 28, 1959.

THE PRESIDENT. Good morning. Please sit down.

This noon, ladies and gentlemen, I am sending my message on labor to the Congress.

It has been prepared after exhaustive study of all the McClellan findings. The purpose is to cover all of the abuses and difficulties that were brought out by that committee, so as to improve the labor-management relationship, to protect every working man and woman in this country, so far as law can do it, and to protect the public.

So it will be a broadly based bill, because it is our conviction that this matter, if it is to be corrected, should be corrected at one time.

That is the proposal that I am making. I shall not talk this morning about the details of those recommendations because they are now going down at noon; but at a later time, why, of course, we can discuss them.

Any questions?

Q. Marvin L. Arrowsmith, Associated Press: Mr. President, how do you feel about the call at Des Moines and in substance last week by the Republican campaign chairman in Congress for you, yourself, to take a more decisive and a more active role in restoring that hibernating elephant you mentioned?

THE PRESIDENT. I believe that I have stayed right persistent in my support for what I believe to be moderate government in this country.

I believe that most Republicans understand this, know exactly what I mean, and support it.

It is, possibly, a difficult position to take as everybody who tries to take a middle-of-the-road position understands. You are subject to attack from both sides, and that is perfectly natural and proper, but you've got to take it from both sides. My own opinion is that anyone who doesn't understand what this administration has been standing for, after two platforms written by Republicans, and after six State of the Union Messages supported by budgetary and economic reports, must not have read as seriously as he should have.

Q. Merriman Smith, United Press International: Mr. President, wide circulation is being given today to a report that Chief Justice Warren has communicated to friends his feeling that your stand on school desegregation is too indecisive. The Chief Justice is represented this morning as being pained by what was described as your failure to take forceful action——

THE PRESIDENT. He is what?

Q. Mr. Smith: Your failure to take——

THE PRESIDENT. What is his reaction?

Q. Mr. Smith: He is described this morning as being pained——

THE PRESIDENT. Oh, oh!

Q. Mr. Smith: ——at what this story called your failure to take forceful action to implement the desegregation decision of the Court. If the Chief Justice has made known his feelings in this matter, would you like to do the same thing?

THE PRESIDENT. Well, so far as I am concerned, here is some irresponsible reporting.

I have told you people a dozen times or certainly frequently, exactly what I feel about a President commenting publicly upon decisions of the Supreme Court.

Now, I have regarded, and I am sure that everyone knows this also, I have regarded the Chief Justice as my personal friend for years. I know of no personal rift of any kind, and therefore I would believe that there is something that doesn't meet the eye here; and if the thing which you speak of is felt by the Chief Justice, I should think, and I am quite sure, that he is capable of telling me himself and doesn't have to take it to the public print.

Q. Peter Lisagor, Chicago Daily News: Mr. President, when Mr. Mikoyan was here, he made the point that he seemed to feel that there were divisions between the American people, or those he talked to, and Government policies in the cold war.

He also made this point when he got back to Moscow.

I wonder if you could tell us whether you have had any personal reflections from friends in private life who may have talked with Mr. Mikoyan, that the United States Government might make agreements with Russia if it had a less rigid position.

THE PRESIDENT. No, no, I didn't have any. What I did—I think I reported this to you once before, possibly not—I had reports from friends around the country that called me up, one of them in California, I recall, saying it was obvious there was an attempt on the part of Mr. Mikoyan to make this interpretation, that the people in the Government were particularly divided on certain points. It might be Berlin or some other question.

Now, because of these reports, in certain instances these friends made a special point of meeting with Mr. Mikoyan during the course of the evening and asserting their belief that the United States, in its firmness in refusing to retreat a single inch from its rights and from its obligations and responsibility, that all of us were one; it didn't make any difference whether it was in Government or civil life.

Now, I certainly tried to make that clear myself.

Q. William Knighton, Baltimore Sun: Mr. President, getting back to the Des Moines oratory again for a moment, have you given any serious consideration to the calling of another Mackinac conference in connection with the feelings of the leadership of the other people in the party?

THE PRESIDENT. For a long time—as a matter of fact, Mr. Knighton, starting back I think about November 6—I have been calling together people from the Republican Party and friends of the party to ask them to undertake very earnest studies of exactly what we should do to get on a better road in explaining what we are about, what we are doing.

Now, this is not confined to the professionals; this is trying to get educators, friends of mine from all walks of life cooperating with the groups that the Chairman, Mr. Alcorn, sets up, to see whether there is anything where we are just failing all along the line to put our story across. But thinking of a conference like Mackinac, I haven't anything like that at this moment. I do not rule it out if a group of responsible Republicans would want it done.

Q. Frank van der Linden, Nashville Banner: Sir, the Alaska statehood bill gives the new State of Alaska perpetual control over its local school system.

A constitutional amendment was introduced yesterday to give that same kind of local control over the schools to every State. Now, would you be in favor of Congress submitting such a constitutional amendment to the States?

THE PRESIDENT. Well, you are opening a matter that I have not even heard about. I didn't know that there was any difference in the responsibility and authority of the new State of Alaska as compared to other States.

I certainly would not make a comment on such a serious thing as approving, or let us say favoring because I wouldn't have any authority to approve, favoring a constitutional amendment until I had studied and looked at it.

Q. Robert G. Spivack, New York Post: Mr. President——

THE PRESIDENT. Oh yes. I believe that you wanted to be recognized. [*Laughter*]

Q. Mr. Spivack: Well, I made it.

I would like to ask you a question about your tactics in the fight against inflation.

Last—well, on February 7, 1957, the New York Times reported as follows: "President Eisenhower warned that the Government would have to impose price and wage controls unless business and labor used restraint to reinforce the Government's efforts to curb inflation."

Now, what I would like to know is why, or do you have any reason to feel that your repetition of this warning last week would be more effective now than it was then?

THE PRESIDENT. I say only this—of course, we don't have the whole context of the statement—certainly my meaning has been made clear time and time again. If we do not fight inflation effectively, eventually the people of this country are going to demand action that would be, in my opinion, antithetical to the whole concept of a true, free competitive enterprise. And when that happens, I think we have really gone quite a step backward; I hope that it never will happen.

If it becomes necessary, then it will be, as I say, a very sad day for America. But I keep warning to see whether I can have any influence whatsoever in keeping that condition from coming about.

Q. Edward T. Folliard, Washington Post and Times Herald: Mr. President, another question about the Des Moines Republican meeting.

A United States Senator, commenting on a message you had sent to the Republicans, said that the Republicans should stop copying the New Deal.

Do you feel that your administration has copied the New Deal?

THE PRESIDENT. So far as I know, I have copied nothing in this world except what I believe are the basic principles of Americanism, and then tried to apply those principles to the problems that now face us.

I still remind you that no one has ever stated, defined, the proper functions of government better than did Abraham Lincoln. You will recall he said: "The proper function of government is to do for people those things they cannot do at all, or not so well do individually." At the same time, he said: "And in everything else the government ought not to interfere."

I believe this is about as good a definition of the function of government as can possibly be made.

Different individuals in different times apply this kind of a truth, this generalization, to the problem today, and they come up with somewhat different answers. But I know this: this administration is dedicated to one thing, to take this kind of truth, this kind of principle, and apply it to the problems of today in the hope of seeing progress in America under a position of security in the world and with the best possible opportunity for developing a peaceful solution to international problems.

Q. Lloyd M. Schwartz, Fairchild Publications: Mr. President, what is your reaction to Premier Khrushchev's statement yesterday that Russia is now mass-producing these intercontinental ballistic missiles with pinpoint accuracy?

THE PRESIDENT. Well, I would say this: we seem very prone to give 100 percent credence to some statement of the Soviets if it happens to touch upon our own anxieties or beliefs or convictions, and then some other statement we dismiss completely and we say, "Why, that is just another repetition of the old baldfaced lie."

Now, I don't know exactly what Mr. Khrushchev has in mind. I do know this: our missile system is going forward as rapidly as possible under the guidance of the finest scientists that we can accumulate.

I believe that we are making, within the relatively short space of time we have had, remarkable progress. I think it is a matter for pride on the part of America, and not a constant—well, hangdog attitude of humiliation.

Now, I do admit we, in this particular field, when our faith was apparently given to the air-breathing missile rather than to the ballistic, we were slow in starting. But we have started; and from the earlier part of this administration, this progress has not only been on the basis of the most urgent priority, but it has been very remarkably successful.

Q. William H. Lawrence, New York Times: In 1952, sir, Senator Taft stated after a conference with you an agreement you had for a $60 billion budget within a 4-year period. This goal is no longer attainable. Is it because world conditions have worsened greatly?

THE PRESIDENT. Well I think, Mr. Lawrence, the best answer to that question is this:

First of all, of course, prices have gone up some—I would say about 8 percent since that period, in spite of all the Government's efforts to keep them down. And that means, in some ways, more than an 8 percent cost, because some of these costs when reflected in munitions seem to get in the order of, say, 20 percent increase. For example, I remember the last time that Secretary Wilson reported to me on outstanding contracts and bills; we had to appropriate $2½ billion more than had been calculated as the cost of those things.

The second thing was this: we were then in the midst of the Korean War, and no one knew what was going to be the cost of these great defense, military programs that have since become necessary.

Now, I don't think this is necessarily because of a worsening of the world situation; it is a realization of the need for a very large arsenal of complicated destructive weapons as long as we are to keep our deterrent power as strong and useful as we believe it must be.

Q. John Scali, Associated Press: Mr. President, Mr. Mikoyan in reporting on his trip to the United States on Saturday said that Russia might be willing to extend for a few days or a few months its Berlin deadline if talks with the West were under way by deadline time.

Do you think that such talks with the Russians before that deadline would be useful?

THE PRESIDENT. I think that any talks that deal fruitfully with the differences between our different peoples, our different governments, are useful.

I want to point out that the United States has constantly desired to get the political questions with which we are faced in a broader context, to try to solve these political questions as a matter of principle—get some basic agreement; and then within that context to get all different technical and, you might say, mechanical self-enforcing types of agreements like protection, better assurance against surprise attack, a banning of testing of all kinds of the nuclear weapons. This is the kind of agreement that we need if you are going to have a real effective result, but under which progress will be realized only, in my opinion, if we have a better general understanding about the peace of Europe, the readiness of both sides to renounce force and subversion in our efforts to maintain our positions in the world and to help our friends. And as to both sides, I would like to see some kind of a program that we could agree upon and which would have, within it, certain self-enforcing arrangements. By this I mean mutual inspection so that it would inspire mutual confidence.

With such things I believe we could count on real progress and finally a lightening of the load that all of us now have to carry.

Q. Mary Philomene Von Herberg, Pacific Shipper: In your Budget Message you asked Congress to reconsider its action last year in authorizing the superliners to be built under direct Federal loans. You pointed out that such Federal loans would enable the shipping companies to borrow money at a lower rate of interest than the Government itself pays.

I wondered, if Congress does as you requested of them, if you would be disposed to immediately request an appropriation to pay the Government's share for building these large passenger liners. One of them would be used on the Pacific and one would be on the Atlantic, and if you asked for it right away, they would start work on them right away; otherwise they are kind of stymied.

THE PRESIDENT. Well, there is no question that these two superliners were believed both by the shipping industry and by—I have forgotten all of the arguments now—certain sectors of the whole Defense Establishment to be necessary, or at least highly desirable in our shipping complement.

As of this moment, to answer your question, I cannot say now that if Congress did just so and so and so, that I would be prepared instantly. I would certainly, if Congress picked up my recommendation and enacted it, I would be right on the job to consider with people now what is the next move to make.

Q. Sarah McClendon, San Antonio Light: I want to know, sir, if you and Mrs. Eisenhower are going to Mexico within the next month, and if you will fly, and if you will go to Acapulco or Mexico City? [*Laughter*]

THE PRESIDENT. Well, I can tell you one thing: Mrs. Eisenhower is not going to be there, because that month is rather well mortgaged for her.

Now, I want to point out, there is nothing definite about any meeting right now with the new President. I am anxious to perpetuate the custom that I started with President Ruiz Cortines, of having informal talks, friendly chats, and really a friendly and useful correspondence—a correspondence that was made more valuable by the fact that we were personal acquaintances and, I have always thought more than that, friends.

Now, just when that can be done, I am not sure. Nothing is definite. But I do say this, I would like to see him.

Q. Raymond P. Brandt, St. Louis Post-Dispatch: Mr. President, at Des Moines one of the criticisms of your administration and of you personally is that you did not see enough of politicians and of legislators.

Have you any actions to take to answer that criticism?

THE PRESIDENT. You know, it's an odd thing—these criticisms and how they get publicized and widespread.

Starting way back in 1953 I had every single Congressman and every single Senator there was to my house. I had to do it in relays; it took a long time. I had them in just to make their acquaintanceship. And from that time onward, there has never been a time when I have not insisted time and again to the leaders, indeed, of both parties, that I am available and that when they want to see me about anything where they think I am making a mistake or about to make one or, indeed, that I just should start some new action, I would like to hear about it.

There have been, over the years, a great many of these individuals that I have invited, more often on my initiative than theirs, because possibly they don't want to bother me too much. At the same time, I don't feel I should nag them.

But if ever anyone has made clear his readiness to meet anyone of either side—Governor, Congressman, politician outside of office, or anything else—I have been always available.

And I particularly like to, used to get the educators in through stag dinners, things of that kind. I haven't done so much of that in later years because, as all of you know, I have tried to keep a schedule that is pretty logical and I think reasonable. But I still—as far as I know, there is no one ever denied a right to come to my office if there is any reasonable position on which he makes the request.

Q. Gordon White, Salt Lake City Deseret News: Senator Watkins was one of your better supporters——

THE PRESIDENT. Yes.

Q. Mr. White: ——and when he was defeated there were reports that there was some offering of a job for him, and I believe it has been 3 months now he has been back in Utah.

Is it correct to infer that you have been unable to find something for Senator Watkins?

THE PRESIDENT. Well now, there is no question about my respect for Senator Watkins. And, I think any discussion between him and me about a governmental job is rather a confidential matter.

There are certain posts that I would think he would be admirably fitted, but I have established certain criteria for appointments and it happens here that as a matter of age, in the only position that I knew of at the moment, he would be disqualified on that basis.

But let no one think that I have any loss of respect for his character, his ability, and his friendship.

Q. Garnett D. Horner, Washington Star: Mr. President, are you considering a meeting with former President Truman in the reasonably near future?

THE PRESIDENT. Well the only thing I know is that in this—I guess it's a bipartisan—national commission that is arranging for a celebration of President Lincoln's 150th anniversary, I suppose everybody is being invited to this affair here in Washington. That's the only thing I know where everybody might be present, because it is a bipartisan affair.

Q. Robert C. Pierpoint, CBS News: It has been about 3 weeks, sir, since Fidel Castro was successful in overthrowing the Cuban Government. I wonder if you could give us some of your impressions of Castro himself, and also tell us how you feel about some of the events that have developed since then?

THE PRESIDENT. No. I don't want to go into that kind of a thing.

But, I will tell you what I will do, I'll just say this: I am certain this Government and all the American people hope that his Government will be truly representative of the Cuban people, and that his Government will achieve the ability to reflect their views, their aspirations, and to encourage and help their progress.

Now, as far as to indulge in anything about his own personality—no.

Q. Charles E. Shutt, Telenews: I believe you stated, sir, that Mr. Mikoyan's visit in this country and your meeting with him was generally a good thing.

Do you believe there was sufficient value there, sir, to warrant a personal and formal meeting with Premier Khrushchev, a meeting similar to that; and do you have any plans to send Vice President Nixon to Russia?

THE PRESIDENT. It seems to me I am getting a lot of double- and triple-barreled questions this morning. [*Laughter*]

There have been no plans made to send anyone to Russia at this moment. Certainly I would not disagree with anyone's plan, if they want to do it, and if our Government thinks they should do it. But so far it has not been completely studied.

Now, so far as Mr. Khrushchev's visit is concerned, you couldn't do this in the informal way that Mr. Mikoyan did. Mr. Mikoyan came, I believe it was said, as a guest of the Embassy, and he got his visa on that basis.

Well, you couldn't do that with the head of the government, and it would be something entirely different, so I think the situations are not comparable.

Q. John Herling, Editors Syndicate: Recently, Ambassador Lodge took strong exception to a remark made by the Soviet Ambassador to the United Nations when the latter called the United States a capitalistic country.

Mr. Lodge replied that the United States is no longer capitalistic, but is a country of economic humanism.

Last night at Fordham University, Vice President Nixon, along the same lines, applauded the way U.S. labor leaders handled Mr. Mikoyan during his visit here, in contrast with that of some businessman.

Would you comment, sir, on what seems to be a new way of presenting the American image to the world?

THE PRESIDENT. Well, I think this: I don't believe that either of those people is necessarily wrong, because I believe there is no such thing as pure democracy, there is no such thing as pure competitive free enterprise; but there is, of course, the nearest thing we have to what you might call a pure government—a pure dictatorship.

Now, the pure dictatorship, at least in the case of Russia, has had to absorb into itself certain incentives of a material kind that they certainly at one time never did contemplate.

So, I would not say that our country is necessarily described as anything except a government, as Lincoln said, by, of, and for the people. I believe it's a true definition, even though we are a republic, not a democracy; but I believe the Government of the United States, and certainly we pray it always will be so, is responsive to the will of the people.   It doesn't make any attempt to make itself the power that rules and governs the lives, the ambitions, and aspirations of our people.

That is what I think America is.

Marvin L. Arrowsmith, Associated Press: Thank you, Mr. President.

NOTE: President Eisenhower's one hundred and forty-eighth news conference was held in the Executive Office Building from 10:30 to 11:02 o'clock on Wednesday morning, January 28, 1959. In attendance: 219.

22   ¶ Special Message to the Congress on Labor-Management Relations.   *January* 28, 1959

To the Congress of the United States:

In the State of the Union Message on January ninth, I reported again to the Congress on the need for enactment of effective Federal legislation designed:

To safeguard workers' funds in union treasuries against misuse of any kind whatsoever.

To protect the rights and freedoms of individual union members, including the basic right to free and secret election of officers.

To advance true and responsible collective bargaining.

To protect the public and innocent third parties from unfair and coercive practices such as boycotting and blackmail picketing.

There is submitted herewith for the consideration of the Congress a 20-point program which will eliminate abuses demonstrated by the hearings of the McClellan Committee, protect the public interest and insure the rights and economic freedoms of millions of American workers.

Complete and effective labor-management legislation, not a piecemeal program, is essential to assure the American public that true, responsible collective bargaining can be carried on with full protection to the rights and freedoms of workers and with adequate guarantees of the public interest.   These recommendations, when adopted, should do much to eliminate those abuses and improper practices which, I am firmly convinced, the American public expects and believes will be corrected through legislative action.   Equally important, they will do so without imposing arbitrary restrictions or punitive measures on the legitimate activities of honest labor and management officials.

143

I recommend legislation—

1. To require all unions to file detailed annual reports with the Department of Labor and furnish information to their members with respect to their financial operations.   These reports would be open to the public, including union members.

2. To require all unions to file with the Department of Labor, as public information, copies of their constitutions and bylaws and information as to their organization and procedures, which would be required to include provisions, which are observed, meeting minimum standards for periodic secret ballot elections of officers, for the removal of officers, and for the imposition of supervisory control over the affairs of subordinate bodies.

3. To require all unions to keep proper records on the matters required to be reported, open to examination by Government representatives and to permit union members, subject to reasonable conditions and upon request, to see and examine these records.

4. To require unions, union officers and agents, and employers to report and keep proper records with respect to any payments, transactions, or investments which create conflicts of interests or have as their objective the interference with the statutory rights of individual union members and employees.

5. To require that union officers hold and administer union funds and property solely for the benefit of the union members and for furthering the purpose of the union and to make this duty enforceable in any court in a suit for an accounting by the union or by members.

6. To require that unions observe minimum standards for the conduct of the elections of officers, including in addition to periodic elections, the right of members to vote in secret without restraint or coercion and upon due notice, uniform opportunity for all members to be candidates, procedures to ensure an accurate tabulation of votes, a ban upon the use of union or employer funds to promote candidacies for union office, and requiring constitutions and bylaws to contain detailed statements of election procedures and compliance with such procedures.

7. To require unions to observe minimum standards and to conform to the appropriate provisions of their constitution and bylaws in exercising supervisory control over the affairs of subordinate bodies; such control should be limited in purpose to correcting corruption, or the disregard of democratic procedures or other practices detrimental to the rights of

the members in the subordinate body, and assuring the performance of duties as a bargaining representative.

8. To place the administration of this legislation in the Secretary of Labor and to provide him with appropriate and adequate authority to issue regulations, investigate, subpoena witnesses and records, bring court action to compel compliance and to correct violations, and institute administrative procedures leading to decisions and orders, which would be subject to judicial review, necessary to effectuate the purposes of the legislation.

9. To prescribe criminal penalties for wilful violations of the Act, for concealment or destruction of records required to be kept, for bribery between employers and employee representatives, for improper payments by employers or their representatives to employees or employee representatives, for embezzlement of union funds, and for false entries or destruction of union books and records.

10. To preserve for union members any present remedies under State or Federal laws, in addition to those provided under this legislation.

11. To amend the secondary boycott provisions of the National Labor Relations Act so as to cover the direct coercion of employers to cease or agree to cease doing business with other persons; union pressures directed against secondary employers not otherwise subject to the Act; and inducements of individual employees to refuse to perform services with the object of forcing their employers to stop doing business with others; and to make clear that secondary activity is permitted against an employer performing "farmed-out struck work" and, under certain circumstances, against secondary employers engaged in work at a common construction site with the primary employer.

12. To make it illegal for a union, by picketing, to coerce an employer to recognize it as the bargaining representative of his employees or his employees to accept or designate it as their representative where the employer has recognized in accordance with law another labor organization, or where a representation election has been conducted within the last preceding 12 months, or where it cannot be demonstrated that there is a sufficient showing of interest on the part of the employees in being represented by the picketing union or where the picketing has continued for a reasonable period of time without the desires of the employees being determined by a representation election; and to provide speedy and effective enforcement measures.

13. To authorize the National Labor Relations Board to decline to take cases where the effect on commerce is relatively insubstantial and to permit the State courts and agencies to act with respect to these cases.

14. To eliminate the statutory prohibition which presently bars certain strikers from voting in representation elections, although their replacements are permitted to vote, and instead to leave the voting eligibility of strikers, as well as all others, to the administrative discretion of the National Labor Relations Board.

15. To authorize the Board, under carefully considered specific conditions, to certify building and construction trades unions as bargaining representatives without an election.

16. In order to speed up the orderly processes of election procedures, to permit the Board under proper safeguards to conduct representation elections without holding a prior hearing where no substantial objection to an election is made.

17. To equalize the onus of the non-Communist affidavit by extending it to employers, as well as unions, wishing to use the processes of the Act.

18. To make clear that parties to a valid collective bargaining agreement need not negotiate during the life of the agreement unless they have provided for, or agree to, the reopening of the agreement.

19. To authorize the designation by the President of an acting General Counsel of the Board when vacancies occur in that office.

20. To require that the Board be bipartisan in composition by providing that not more than three members of the Board may be of the same political party.

I urge that Congress give prompt and favorable consideration to this program. Its enactment, in my opinion, would contribute greatly to the protection of the public interest and the basic rights of individual working men and women.

DWIGHT D. EISENHOWER

23 ¶ Special Message to the Congress on Agriculture. *January* 29, 1959

To the Congress of the United States:

There are produced, in the United States, some 250 farm commodities. The law has required that prices of twelve of these be supported at prescribed minimum levels. It is this requirement, together with the level of required support, that has created our farm surplus problems. Farmers who produce cattle, hogs, poultry, fruits, vegetables, and various other products the prices of which are not supported—as well as those who produce crops the prices of which are supported at discretionary levels—have generally experienced growing markets rather than a build-up of stocks in warehouses.

Three of the twelve mandatory products (wheat, corn, and cotton) account for about eighty-five percent of the Federal inventory of price-supported commodities though they produce only twenty percent of the total cash farm income.

The price-support and production-control program has not worked.

1. *Most of the dollars are spent on the production of a relatively few large producers.*

Nearly a million and a half farms produce wheat. Ninety percent of the expenditures for price support on wheat result from production of about half of these farms—the largest ones.

Nearly a million farms produce cotton. Seventy-five percent of the expenditures for cotton price support result from production of about one-fourth of these farms—the largest ones.

For other supported crops, a similarly disproportionate share of the expenditure goes to the large producers.

For wheat, cotton, and rice producers who have allotments of one-hundred acres or more, the net budgetary expenditures per farm for the present fiscal year are approximately as follows:

	Per farm
Wheat	$7,000
Cotton	$10,000
Rice	$10,000

Though some presently unknown share of these expenditures will eventually be recovered through surplus disposal, the final cost of the operation will undoubtedly be impressively large.

Clearly, the existing price support program channels most of the dollars to those who store the surpluses and to relatively few producers of a few crops. It does little to help the farmers in greatest difficulty. For small operators the Rural Development Program approach, which helps develop additional sources of income, has clearly demonstrated that it is a far better alternative.

2. *The control program doesn't control.*

Mandatory supports are at a level which so stimulates new technology and the flow of capital into production as to offset, in large part, the control effort.

Despite acreage allotments and marketing quotas, despite a large soil bank program and despite massive surplus disposal, government investment in farm commodities will soon be at a new record high. On July 1, 1959, total government investment in farm commodities will total $9.1 billion. Investment in commodities for which price support is mandatory will total $7.6 billion, of which $7.5 billion will consist of those crops designated by law as basic commodities: wheat, corn, cotton, rice, peanuts, and tobacco. And these stocks are increasing rather than diminishing.

We already hold such huge stocks of wheat that if not one bushel of the oncoming crop were harvested we would still have more than enough for domestic use, export sales, foreign donation and needed carry-over for an entire year.

3. *The program is excessively expensive.*

When the 1958 crops have come into Government ownership, the cost, in terms of storage, interest and other charges, of managing our inventory of supported crops, for which commercial markets do not exist at the support levels, will be running at a staggering rate, in excess of a billion dollars a year. Unless fundamental changes are made, this annual cost will rise.

This sum is approximately equal to the record amount being spent in fiscal 1960 by the Federal Government on all water resource projects in the United States including power, flood control, reclamation and improvement of rivers and harbors.

During the present fiscal year, the net budgetary outlay for programs for the stabilization of farm prices and farm income will be $5.4 billion. $4.3 billion of this is for commodities for which price supports are mandatory. While some unpredictable part of this outlay will be recovered in later years through sales for dollars, sales for foreign currency and through barter, the cost will be great, especially when compared with the net income of all farm operators in the United States, which in 1958 was $13 billion. Budgetary expenditures primarily for the support of farm prices and farm income are now equal to about forty percent of net farm income.

Not a bushel of wheat nor a pound of cotton presently is exported without direct cost to the Federal Treasury.

Heavy costs might be justifiable if they were temporary, if they were solving the problems of our farmers, and if they were leading to a better balance of supplies and markets. But unfortunately this is not true.

These difficulties are not to be attributed to any failure on the part of our farm people, who have done an outstanding job of producing efficiently. They have in fact responded to the price incentive as farm people—and other people—traditionally have.

Our farm families deserve programs that build markets. Instead they have programs that lose markets. This is because the overall standards for the programs that they have are outdated relationships that existed nearly half a century ago. This was before sixty percent of our present population was born.

At that time it took 106 man hours to grow and harvest one-hundred bushels of wheat. In recent years it has taken not 106 but 22. Since then the yield of wheat has doubled. Similar dramatic changes have occurred for other crops.

It is small wonder that a program developed many years ago to meet the problems of depression and war is ill-adapted to a time of prosperity, peace, and revolutionary changes in production.

The need to reduce the incentives for excess production has been explicit in the three special messages on agriculture which I have previously sent to the Congress. The point has repeatedly been made by the Secretary of Agriculture in his testimony and in his statements to the Congress. The Congress has moved in the right direction but by an insufficient amount. There has been a general tendency to underestimate the pace at which farm technology has been moving forward. Hence there has been a tendency to underestimate the production-inducing effect of the prescribed minimum price support levels.

Recommendation

I recommend that prices for those commodities subject to mandatory supports be related to a percentage of the average market price during the immediately preceding years. The appropriate percentage of the average market price should be discretionary with the Secretary of Agriculture at a level not less than seventy-five and not more than ninety percent of such average in accordance with the general guidelines set forth in the law.   Growers of corn, our most valuable crop, have already chosen, by referendum vote, program changes which include supports based on such an average of market prices.

If, despite the onrush of science in agriculture, resulting in dramatic increases in yields per acre, the Congress still prefers to relate price supports to existing standards, the Secretary should be given discretion to establish the level in accordance with the guidelines now fixed by law for all commodities except those for which supports presently are mandatory.

Either of these changes would be constructive.   The effect of either would be to reconcile the farm program with the facts of modern agriculture, to reduce the incentive for unrealistic production, to move in the direction of easing production controls, to permit the growth of commercial markets and to cut the cost of federal programs.

As we move to realistic farm programs, we must continue our vigorous efforts further to expand markets and find additional outlets for our farm products, both at home and abroad.   In these efforts, there is an immediate and direct bearing on the cause of world peace.   Food can be a powerful instrument for all the free world in building a durable peace. We and other surplus-producing nations must do our very best to make the fullest constructive use of our abundance of agricultural products to this end.   These past four years our special export programs have provided friendly food-deficit nations with four billion dollars worth of farm products that we have in abundance.   I am setting steps in motion to explore anew with other surplus-producing nations all practical means of utilizing the various agricultural surpluses of each in the interest of reinforcing peace and the well-being of friendly peoples throughout the world—in short, using food for peace.

Certain details regarding the needed changes in law, particularly with reference to wheat, are appended to this message in the form of a memorandum to me from the Secretary of Agriculture.

Difficulties of the present program should not drive us to programs which would involve us in even greater trouble.   I refer to direct payment programs, which could soon make virtually all farm people dependent, for a large share of their income, upon annual appropriations from the Federal Treasury.   I refer also to various multiple price programs, which would tax the American consumer so as to permit sale for feed and export at lower prices.

To assist the Congress in discharging its responsibility, the Administration stands ready, as always, to provide the appropriate Committees with studies, factual data and judgments. Continuation of the price support and production control programs in their present form would be intolerable.

I urge the Congress to deal promptly with this problem.

DWIGHT D. EISENHOWER

NOTE: This message and Secretary Benson's memorandum dated January 19 are published in House Document 59 (86th Cong., 1st sess.).

24 ¶ Remarks to the Third National Conference on Exchange of Persons. *January* 30, 1959

Mr. Holland, Members of the Board of Trustees of the Institute of International Education, Ladies and Gentlemen:

It is a privilege to greet the members of this audience, all dedicated to the promotion of knowledge of all peoples by all other peoples.

The theme for this Conference, "World Peace through International Exchange of Persons," suggests one of the most promising gateways for reaching our most sought after goal—a just and lasting peace.

We realize that peace demands understanding. I know of no better single method of reaching mutual understanding than by multiplying our international contacts through people-to-people diplomacy. Fourteen years ago, delegates from the world over met in San Francisco to draft the United Nation's Charter. One experience that accompanied this meeting seems to have some relevance for us today.

To escape the tedious strain of weeks of conferences, a party of a geographer, a statesman, and a lawyer driven by an Army Sergeant took a trip to the Redwoods. Walking among the giant trees, the geographer remarked that while it would be a slight exaggeration to say that over every square mile of the earth's surface, dust particles from the entire earth's surface circulated, the statement was, to all intents, true.

To this, the statesman replied, "If only we might have the same interchange of peoples and ideas, our troubling problems of the San Francisco Conference would be resolved over night."

From the lawyer came the jesting comment, "This is the greatest violation of private property rights that I have ever heard."

But the final observation came from the Army Sergeant, "What this means to me," he said quietly, "is that we're all really living in each other's backyard."

Now each passing year since the drafting of the United Nation's Charter has brought new reminders of a closer relationship among the peoples of all nations. As the world has moved through tensions and intermittent crises, the importance of our interdependence has been strikingly driven home by far reaching developments in atomic fission, electronic communication, and swifter than sound flight. Today when the possibility of war carries with it a threat to the survival of civilization, the urgency of dealing effectively with all threats to peace is self-evident.

Mutual understanding is more than important—it is vital.

The exchange of persons is one approach by which we may work for understanding along many fronts. The need is for a continuous activity based upon the commonsense belief that understanding is an exportable item to all nations, including our own.

We are glad to welcome here to our shores students, educators, lawyers, scientists, artists, government officials, and others from distant lands, and it is equally important that Americans also enjoy the enriching experience of work and study in other nations. Such programs, I am happy to note, are receiving constant encouragement and support from the 139 public and private organizations that are represented here today.

Here I should say this group is growing very rapidly, because the statistics given to me yesterday, allowing me to write down 130—on the way over here, your President told me it was 139.

Now the education and training of our people for effective service in our Government's overseas activities is important. Because of this, the Secretary of State has recently appointed a Special Assistant for the Coordination of International Education and Cultural Relations. The exchange of persons is an essential feature of this training effort.

Now, peace is a goal that must never slip from focus. We have the resources and faith in ourselves to do our part for its attainment. But we must use these resources wisely. We must use some of our strength to bolster the free nations that, with us, stand as the defenders of freedom and which, with us, work for the achievement of a just peace.

For a moment may I digress to mention a related matter that deeply concerns all of us. I refer to the funds that are appropriated by the Congress every year to enable our friends around the world better to defend themselves and to maintain their independence through viable economies. Of all the money which this country lays out in one year, none of it contributes more to the security of our Nation and to freedom than that allocated to our mutual security programs.

Those in public and private life who would have us cut America's mutual aid and loan programs simply do not understand what these programs mean to peace and to America's safety.

Any cutback of present budgetary levels for our mutual security programs would require additional outlays for our own security forces, far greater than any amount that could possibly be so saved. Moreover such reductions would in the long run dilute the faith of our allies in America's determination and ability to exercise leadership for freedom. I shall do all in my power to insure that our friends around the world will not have their faith in these American purposes undermined.

Building friendships among nations through the exchange of individuals is not an idea of startling novelty. Nor is it work that can be undertaken only through a single program of grand design. The very term "People-to-people diplomacy" implies a healthy variety of programs— lots of them. To each of you here today, along with the organizations that you represent, and to the Institute of International Education which will have a 40th anniversary celebration tonight, I extend warmest congratulations on your exchange work.

I hope your joint efforts will ever grow and multiply. We need more individual diplomats from Main Street, from our farms, schools, laboratories—from every walk of life. People-to-people diplomacy means thousands of part-time ambassadors—all working for better relationships among all peoples. And the finest definition of an ambassador, you will recall, is this: "He is, above all else, a man of peace."

And I would like to add again my expression of appreciation to each member of the groups here assembled, because of the personal work used to make these ideals or purposes that I have so haltingly tried to express become a reality. I could think of no finer work that you are doing, for yourself, your family, your nation—indeed, for civilization.

Thank you very much. It has been a great privilege to be with you.

NOTE: The conference, held at the May-
flower Hotel, Washington, D.C., was sponsored by the Institute of International Education. The President's opening words
"Mr. Holland" referred to Kenneth Holland, President of the Institute.

25 ¶ Message to the Congress Transmitting the First Annual Report Under the National Aeronautics and Space Act. *February* 2, 1959

To the Congress of the United States:

Transmitted herewith, pursuant to Section 206(b) of the National Aeronautics and Space Act of 1958, is the first annual report on the Nation's activities and accomplishments in the aeronautics and space fields. This first report covers the year 1958.

The report provides an impressive accumulation of evidence as to the scope and impetus of our aeronautical and space efforts. Equally impressive is the report's description of the variety of fields being explored through the ingenuity of American scientists, engineers and technicians.

The report makes clear that the Nation has the knowledge, the skill and the will to move ahead swiftly and surely in these rapidly developing areas of technology. Our national capability in this regard has been considerably enhanced by the creation and organization of the National Aeronautics and Space Administration.

The report sets forth a record of solid achievement in a most intricate and exacting enterprise. In this record the Nation can take great pride.

DWIGHT D. EISENHOWER

NOTE: The message and the report are printed in House Document 71 (86th Cong.,
1st sess.).

26 ¶ The President's News Conference of *February* 4, 1959.

THE PRESIDENT. Please sit down.

Well, ladies and gentlemen, I got you out a little earlier this morning because, as you know, I am trying to go down to Georgia for the rest of the week.

I would like to talk for a few moments about two bills in the Congress, one the housing bill and one the airport bill.

The housing bill provides a much more expensive program than the budget does. For example, it has a very much expanded assistance to colleges—where we had about $200 million—of $575 million I believe it is, that kind of thing. There is additional money in some of the bills for direct loans for veterans. I recommended competitive rates of interest, which would make it unnecessary for the Federal Government to continue in the business of direct lending.

But, in any event, the effect of this bill in the Senate I think will be in the next several years about $1,300,000,000 more than I would recommend. Now, this means that in the very first bill the budget is to be unbalanced.

Many leaders of Congress in the past have talked to me—and I mean congressional leaders from both parties—about the need for keeping expenditures within our income, avoiding the cheapening of our money. I believe in that, and I am going to do every possible thing I can to keep expenditures within that level.

Now I wonder why, if we are going to ask for these new expenditures, and everybody admitting that deficit spending is certainly not a good thing, why doesn't each one of these bills include a measure for increasing taxes? That would be the straightforward, honest way to see whether the United States really wants this kind of thing.

I don't believe that we should have higher taxes, and I do not believe that the United States wants higher taxes. That means to me living within your income by avoiding unnecessary expenditures.

I stand on this, and you are going to hear me saying this often during the coming session. You will probably get weary of it, but it is honest and I think all of us should try to reason, with our own minds, what it means if we just go into this reckless spending.

Now, in the airport bill, the airport bill of the administration directs itself to one factor and one factor only: improving the safety of flying, whether it is in the air, takeoff, or when you are arriving. It does not interest itself in building a nice, lovely administration building and things that we would call, for the railroads, depots. The Federal Government did not build the terminals for either the railways or for the buses. I see no reason for doing it for the air terminals.

But this matter of safety is very, very important, emphasized again in the very sad accident this morning.[1]

Now, General Quesada informs me that there is no evidence that any failure of the airways safety system had anything to do with this particular accident, but this is sure: no money put into the building of the terminal, the administrative buildings, and other conveniences, could have avoided or helped to avoid that kind of accident.

I think we should put our money in that, and not into these things which are unnecessary, no matter how desirable they may seem to be to the locality. The locality ought to pay for those things, and the Government is certainly going to do its part to keep flying safe.

Remember, there are 35,000 individuals right now operating on this thing. I can give you all sorts of statistics. We have helped in the past. We have put money in 40 airports at which last year there was an average of less than 10 planes stationed.

There are all sorts of places where this money is not needed, but it is needed for improving flying safety, and that is what I believe we should do.

And, above all, let us remember—since we are doing necessary things— again we have the effect on budget. Why should we cheapen dollars, and in the airplane business having higher flying rates, and making everything more expensive, more expensive for the housewife and for you and for me and for everybody else? I am against it.

Now I have had my say.

Q. Dayton Moore, United Press International: Mr. President, do you consider Virginia's orderly start on integration of public schools to be a good model for other Southern States?

THE PRESIDENT. Well, I would put it in this way: I certainly feel that all of us should compliment the State officials who determined that there

---

[1] The President referred to an airplane crash near LaGuardia Airport, New York.

was going to be no evidence and no occurrence of violence in this kind of thing. I am certainly very proud of the parents, the way they performed their duties, and the children themselves.

There was one incident—I think it was reported in the papers yesterday or this morning—of this group of honor students in Norfolk themselves paying for advertisements in the local newspapers, to say that they wanted their schools opened and they wanted it done in an orderly fashion. This to my mind is the most important thing of all, because I believe we are beginning to understand that we must have some consideration for our fellow man if democracy is going to work. I think the evidence that a little education and a little effort to understand are growing is heartening indeed. But I repeat that I think all the officials and everybody else that was concerned should be complimented.

Q. John Scali, Associated Press: Mr. President, Soviet border guards have stopped an American Army truck convoy, and they have demanded the right to inspect it before they allow it to proceed. Could you tell us whether we have any intention of allowing the Soviet border guards to inspect such cargoes, and could you comment on this situation, generally?

THE PRESIDENT. The position we have always held is that the responsibility voluntarily undertaken by the four occupying powers of maintaining their forces in Berlin was one that did necessarily give the right of supporting those forces.

Now we felt that since we had to perform that responsibility, we had the right to bring in the kind of supplies and remove the same kind of supplies from that particular spot, Berlin. Therefore, we have never acknowledged any right of inspection on the part of another of the participating powers with respect to our cargoes and the kind of equipment and supplies we are carrying forward.

Now we feel, in other words, this is a violation of the agreements, implied if not always explicitly stated; because, naturally, the people that made these could not foresee every kind of little difficulty that could occur. So we believe it is a violation of the implied agreement, arrangement between the four. While up to this moment the protests have been only at the local level by the military, we have this morning lodged a vigorous protest with the Foreign Office in Moscow. Whether or not that message has yet been delivered, I do not know; but I do know we have sent it.

Q. Rowland Evans, Jr., New York Herald Tribune: Mr. President, in view of the transition in Virginia, I wondered whether you thought that strong civil rights legislation touching on education and integration in the schools could be more harmful than beneficial, whether you would discuss that for a moment.

THE PRESIDENT. Well, I do not know what is strong legislation and what is not strong. I do believe that legislation that is certain to exacerbate the whole situation, that is going to raise tempers and increase prejudices, could be far more harmful than good.

Now, I do believe there are certain aspects in which the laws show vacant spots; and certainly I, for one, will never propose anything of this kind where I do not believe that the American public would see it as moderate and decent and with the purpose of improving, not worsening, the situation. I believe if you try to do things that would give people the right, or at least even the possibility, of saying the Federal Government is trying to set up a great Federal police and give it the responsibility of seeing whether each citizen is doing his duty, is avoiding a violation of the law—that would be a wicked thing, and we are not trying to do anything like that.

Q. Sarah McClendon, Camden Courier-Post: Mr. President, Sarah McClendon of the Camden Courier-Post. [*Laughter*]

THE PRESIDENT. May I ask you, is that a new one?

Q. Mrs. McClendon: Well, somewhat.

Sir, in South Jersey there are hundreds of thousands of acres of land that could be had for a decent, adequate airport jet terminal to serve big cities, Washington and New York, by quick monorail facilities, and the officials in those counties have this plan well worked out.

Now, would you not say, on the contrary, that this New York airport terminal might have had something to do with that airplane crash, by reason of location, and maybe if there were more Federal funds for locating airports away from big cities, it might be safer.

THE PRESIDENT. Well, you are getting into a very involved question.

New York located that port, and I believe there was another one built out at Idlewild to take planes that were considered to be a little bit more difficult to handle.

Now, the particular kind of idea that you now describe, well, I have never heard it talked in governmental circles; I've never spoken to General Quesada, who I think is the authority in this field.

Still, I do believe it is, informally, something that people are talking quite a bit about—to get these long flights coming into areas where the maximum safety will be achieved, and then from there, either by helicopter or any other kind of a method, why, the distribution will be made.

But safety itself as we are studying it is devoted to the fields that do exist and are used, and this other is a much greater problem than what we have yet talked about.

Q. Rod MacLeish, Westinghouse Broadcasting Company: Sir, could you give us your assessment of Mr. Khrushchev's 6-hour oration before the Communist Party Congress in Moscow, especially his contention that competition should be on the economic level above everything else between our two countries?

THE PRESIDENT. Well, naturally we have had a number of briefings, but I think it would be really futile at such a meeting as this to try to go through the whole thing and try to get behind what you believe he is trying to do. After all, these speeches, these long speeches, are designed for domestic as well as foreign consumption.

I would merely say this: there is nothing that I can see in them that offers another avenue of hope for the free world. We have to design for ourselves such kinds of, you might say, plans or little programs that might possibly be acceptable and, therefore, would do something to crack this Iron Curtain complex that seems to plague us now.

Q. Raymond P. Brandt, St. Louis Post-Dispatch: Mr. President, another head of the ICA, International Cooperation Administration, has resigned. You have had about four in there. Is there any way that you could keep your dedicated people in that organization?

THE PRESIDENT. Well, I tell you, Mr. Brandt, that's one that after awhile everybody gets quite worn down, for this simple reason: every one of them believes in it as a matter of American policy and believes it is absolutely necessary to the safety of the free world. But they have a very hostile type of atmosphere in which to do their testifying and to get the appropriations that they believe—I say "very hostile"; there is a growing hostility. We have, as I recall, about halved the amounts that were put in this field, let's say 6 years ago. It is a very, very wearisome job that they have, and I can't blame them much; although I must say I hate to lose Mr. Smith, and I don't know who I am going to get yet to take his place.

Q. Garnett D. Horner, Washington Star: Mr. President, the Soviet Defense Minister bragged yesterday that they now have intercontinental missiles with hydrogen warheads that can hit any point in the world precisely and accurately, that make our nuclear weapons outdated. Could you comment on that, sir?

THE PRESIDENT. They also said that they invented the flying machine—[*laughter*]—and the automobile and the telephone and other things. Now I am not trying to be too facetious; I am trying to ask this one question of you people, though: why should you be so respectful of this statement this morning, if you are not so respectful of the other three?

I think there is always a design behind every Soviet pronouncement. Now I think you people probably know it already, but last night or this morning there was an Atlas firing that was absolutely successful; it was long range, and we think it was a very good performance.

I don't know what the words "pinpoint accuracy" mean. They sound to me like rather propaganda words.

Now I am not going to decry their accomplishments. But I am not going to get involved or worried about trying to take everything they could do in every field and placing an equation there and finding that it comes to equality.

We have got a very much more variegated, a more, we believe, balanced type of defensive organization than have they; and we believe that with the dispersion that we have and with the competence of our planes and supported as they are by the missiles that we have developed, that we have a very splendid posture today in the whole security field. And I would not be at all surprised that more statements of this kind will be made. Apparently, they are believed all around the world, and too implicitly.

Q. Richard L. Wilson, Cowles Publication: Mr. President, on the point that you were just speaking about, a great deal of controversy seems to center on the idea that the Russians have achieved some capability of knocking out our retaliatory capacity before we could actually use it.

THE PRESIDENT. Yes.

Q. Mr. Wilson: Could you throw any light on that general subject? Does it have any substance, does that idea have any substance at all?

THE PRESIDENT. Well, we don't believe it has. Quite naturally, if they are going to attack by surprise, there are going to be some losses suffered by American forces, and possibly by America itself in some other ways. That is just implicit in the opportunity that a dictator has to start a war himself.

Now, that is the reason that we have to be so alert. But as I have told you before, we are constantly improving our warning equipment.

We have dispersed through the building of new airfields, we have dispersed our strategic air force much more widely than it was a few years back. We have made alert arrangements until a very good portion of this whole force could be in the air in a matter of minutes; and on top of that, we have our own kinds of weapons that would be useful.

Now, if we were going to assume that our entire forces were going to be wiped out instantly so we would be helpless, then we must be figuring that these people—taking some factor of effectiveness and for near misses, let us say 70 percent or anything you want to, how many of these missiles are they going to send off in one volley all over this world to immobilize us? There finally comes such a thing as just a logical limit to capability, and we know that there is not that kind of capability existing in the world today.

And I will say this: our own capability is to make certain not only that our retaliatory power is strong, but gets more and more secure through our planning and development, more secure all the time; so that we do not believe that there is a relative increase in their capacity.

Q. Edward P. Morgan, American Broadcasting Company: Mr. President, may we explore another aspect of the housing problem. Your Civil Rights Commission has found evidences of discrimination and segregation in housing, not in the South this time, but in New York City.

Father Hesburgh of Notre Dame, who was at the hearings, calls it a national problem.

What do you feel is the Federal role in this national problem, and do you think perhaps that the proviso to withhold Government funds from housing projects that permit discrimination is of the same order of importance as holding down unnecessary spending in these problems?

THE PRESIDENT. Well, it seems to me always there is the effort to solve two problems at one time, in one major effort. Now, you want to solve the civil rights problem by housing, so therefore you have another facet of this problem attacked from a different way.

I think housing is important, and we continue to try to help with urban development. But we do believe that the Federal Government's share of urban development has been badly distorted in favor of the locality. It is the locality that is, after all, to be improved and made better, and we believe that something of the order of 35 percent should be the Federal portion, ratio, instead of 65.

Now, I do not know exactly—at this moment I certainly would not give a shotgun opinion—what I would say of giving such restrictions as you suggest in this urban development with respect to race. I personally believe these problems should not be put together and then try to solve them.

Q. Mrs. May Craig, Portland (Maine) Press Herald: Mr. President, Marshal Malinovsky also said that the United States should ponder the vulnerability of its shores.

THE PRESIDENT. Of what?

Q. Mrs. Craig: Should ponder the vulnerability of its shores, its coasts.

THE PRESIDENT. Oh, yes.

Q. Mrs. Craig: President Frondizi has told reporters that the Argentine Navy has depth-bombed submarines which refused to identify themselves off the Argentine shore. Will you tell us what you know of the activity of Russian submarines off our coasts and how vulnerable we are?

THE PRESIDENT. Well now, I will not tell you, for this simple reason: most of the information that I have in this field is of course through briefings, and I cannot tell you at this moment whether such as I have is in the restricted or confidential area or not.

You can go to the Secretary of Defense and ask him exactly the same question, and if he knows anything about it and knows whether he can give it, he will talk to you.

But I just feel that it is not wise for me, because my memory is simply not that good that I can tell you whether it is in the public domain or whether it is in the restricted field.

Q. William H. Lawrence, New York Times: Mr. President, do your introductory remarks about the housing and airport bills mean that in their present form they would be vetoed?

And, secondly, would you plan between now and final passage any effort by yourself to get together with the Democratic leaders to see if you could work out an agreed program?

THE PRESIDENT. I have consistently stuck to one policy: I never promise to veto or to approve. After all, that is something I cannot decide until the bill comes before me, until all of us, the administration and its officials, have had the chance to study the whole thing as it comes finally from the Congress.

Now in every possible way, everybody I meet from Congress, I talk to them about this problem; and I have seen no one yet that does not recognize the seriousness of the problem. It is a matter of judgment in two things, as I see it.

Some people say your aggregate is all right, but you distribute it badly and, therefore, "We will change it." Other people say, "Well, it would be very, very nice to have a balanced budget and therefore a sound dollar, but we would think it is more important to do some things we would like to do."

Now I am going to do everything I can to persuade people that I am talking sense in this matter and, if I am talking sense, this means that there has simply got to be some proximity, you might say, of target for all of us.

I am not going to say that I am going to veto this or that, based on a very minimum sum or a slight difference in policy. I am just simply saying this is so important I am never going to stop striving for it.

Q. Mr. Lawrence: May I ask one followup question, sir.

On the record, at least, sir, most of the people you see from Congress are Republicans, who numerically have very little influence.

THE PRESIDENT. Oh, yes, yes.

Q. Mr. Lawrence: I was wondering whether you plan a more aggressive effort to get together with the Democrats to have their leaders down on this sort of problem.

THE PRESIDENT. Well, I'll tell you. After all, there are, as you know, certain problems that we always get to them either through the Secretary of State, Secretary of Defense, or myself. [*Confers with Mr. Hagerty*]

As a matter of fact, I see them possibly more frequently than appears in the public press.

Q. Peter Lisagor, Chicago Daily News: Mr. President, you said that you did not think the American people wanted higher taxes. You also said that you thought localities ought to do some of the things, such as the airport. Governor Rockefeller of New York has found it necessary to move to get more taxes for what he regards as desirable programs.

Do you think the American people would be willing to accept tax increases from the State, rather than from the Federal Government? Do you think this is a better approach?

THE PRESIDENT. Well, I do not know, because I don't know the rate of that taxation for these several States. This is what I was talking about: the Federal rate of taxation and what I see as the American reluctance to accept higher rates, unless they can see that there is a clear emergency demanding now current action for which they can be persuaded to make the sacrifice. And I believe they will, if you have got an emergency thing. But now, let's remember we are planning for 20 years, 30 years, 40 years. We have got to live with this thing.

As we know, as the population grows we get more revenues; but we also get, in some of these things, very much higher costs. When we remember that our taxes run from—we have got a $600 exemption now, and we run up to 92 percent, I believe it is, in the very top ones—I think that income taxes, which are the things that the Federal Government mainly lives on, are getting about as high as you can keep them on the indefinite basis.

Now, I believe you can, for emergency, tough problems, I think you can do more than that.

Sterling F. Green, Associated Press: Thank you, Mr. President.

NOTE: President Eisenhower's one hundred and forty-ninth news conference was held in the Executive Office Building from 9:58 to 10:29 o'clock on Wednesday morning, February 4, 1959. In attendance: 214.

27 ¶ Special Message to the Congress on Civil Rights. *February 5, 1959*

To the Congress of the United States:

Two principles basic to our system of government are that the rule of law is supreme, and that every individual regardless of his race, religion, or national origin is entitled to the equal protection of the laws. We must continue to seek every practicable means for reinforcing these principles and making them a reality for all.

The United States has a vital stake in striving wisely to achieve the goal of full equality under law for all people. On several occasions I have stated that progress toward this goal depends not on laws alone but on building a better understanding. It is thus important to remember that any further legislation in this field must be clearly designed to continue the substantial progress that has taken place in the past few years. The recommendations for legislation which I am making have been weighed and formulated with this in mind.

First, I recommend legislation to strengthen the law dealing with obstructions of justice so as to provide expressly that the use of force or threats of force to obstruct Court orders in school desegregation cases shall be a Federal offense.

There have been instances where extremists have attempted by mob violence and other concerted threats of violence to obstruct the accomplishment of the objectives in school decrees. There is a serious question whether the present obstruction of justice statute reaches such acts of obstruction which occur after the completion of the court proceedings. Nor is the contempt power a satisfactory enforcement weapon to deal with persons who seek to obstruct court decrees by such means.

The legislation that I am recommending would correct a deficiency in the present law and would be a valuable enforcement power on which the government could rely to deter mob violence and such other acts of violence or threats which seek to obstruct court decrees in desegregation cases.

Second, I recommend legislation to confer additional investigative authority on the FBI in the case of crimes involving the destruction or attempted destruction of schools or churches, by making flight from one State to another to avoid detention or prosecution for such a crime a Federal offense.

All decent, self-respecting persons deplore the recent incidents of bombings of schools and places of worship. While State authorities have been diligent in their execution of local laws dealing with these crimes, a basis for supplementary action by the federal government is needed.

Such recommendation when enacted would make it clear that the FBI has full authority to assist in investigations of crimes involving bombings of schools and churches. At the same time, the legislation would preserve the primary responsibility for law enforcement in local law enforcement agencies for crimes committed against local property.

Third, I recommend legislation to give the Attorney General power to inspect Federal election records, and to require that such records be preserved for a reasonable period of time so as to permit such inspection.

The right to vote, the keystone of democratic self-government, must be available to all qualified citizens without discrimination. Until the enactment of the Civil Rights Act of 1957, the government could protect this right only through criminal prosecutions instituted after the right had been infringed. The 1957 Act attempted to remedy this deficiency by authorizing the Attorney General to institute civil proceedings to prevent such infringements before they occurred.

A serious obstacle has developed which minimizes the effectiveness of this legislation. Access to registration records is essential to determine whether the denial of the franchise was in furtherance of a pattern of racial discrimination. But during preliminary investigations of complaints the Department of Justice, unlike the Civil Rights Commission, has no authority to require the production of election records in a civil proceeding. State or local authorities, in some instances, have refused to permit the inspection of their election records in the course of investigations. Supplemental legislation, therefore, is needed.

Fourth, I recommend legislation to provide a temporary program of financial and technical aid to State and local agencies to assist them in making the necessary adjustments required by school desegregation decisions.

The Department of Health, Education, and Welfare should be authorized to assist and cooperate with those States which have previously required or permitted racially segregated public schools, and which must now develop programs of desegregation. Such assistance should consist of sharing the burdens of transition through grants-in-aid to help meet additional costs directly occasioned by desegregation programs, and also of making technical information and assistance available to State and local educational agencies in preparing and implementing desegregation programs.

I also recommend that the Commissioner of Education be specifically authorized, at the request of the States or local agencies, to provide technical assistance in the development of desegregation programs and to initiate or participate in conferences called to help resolve educational problems arising as a result of efforts to desegregate.

Fifth, I recommend legislation to authorize, on a temporary basis, provision for the education of children of members of the Armed Forces when State-administered public schools have been closed because of desegregation decisions or orders.

The Federal Government has a particular responsibility for the children of military personnel in Federally affected areas, since Armed Services personnel are located there under military orders rather than of their own free choice. Under the present law, the Commissioner of Education may provide for the education of children of military personnel only in the case of those who live on military reservations or other Federal property. The legislation I am recommending would remove this limitation.

Sixth, I recommend that Congress give consideration to the establishing of a statutory Commission on Equal Job Opportunity under Government Contracts.

Non-discrimination in employment under government contracts is required by Executive Orders. Through education, mediation, and persuasion, the existing Committee on Government Contracts has sought to give effect not only to this contractual obligation, but to the policy of equal job opportunities generally. While the program has been widely accepted by government agencies, employers and unions, and significant progress has been made, full implementation of the policy would be materially advanced by the creation of a statutory Commission.

Seventh, I recommend legislation to extend the life of the Civil Rights Commission for an additional two years. While the Commission should make an interim report this year within the time originally fixed by law for the making of its final report, because of the delay in getting the Commission appointed and staffed, an additional two years should be provided for the completion of its task and the making of its final report.

I urge the prompt consideration of these seven proposals.

DWIGHT D. EISENHOWER

28 ¶ Exchange of Messages Between the President and President Frondizi of Argentina.
February 5, 1959

His Excellency Dr. Arturo Frondizi
President of the Argentine Nation

Thank you for your gracious telegram of farewell and your good wishes which I wholeheartedly reciprocate. You have honored us by your presence in the United States. The warm response which your visit elicited here was a reflection of the strong friendship which we feel toward the Argentine Republic, as well as an impressive tribute to you personally. You may take pride in the impression which you created in the United States as the vigorous leader of a determined and forward-looking nation.

I welcomed this opportunity to get to know you and to learn at first hand your views on matters in which our Governments have a joint and continuing interest as partners in the community of free nations.

DWIGHT D. EISENHOWER

NOTE: President Frondizi's message follows:

I depart from the United States with a spirit overflowing with the emotions experienced during my stay in your great country. Permit me to express again my most sincere gratitude for the courtesies shown me during the course of the trip which I have just completed, the recollection of which will, for so many reasons, remain always with me. These have been days of true American brotherhood, the beneficial results of which for the promotion of friendship and constructive solidarity among the nations of the continent will be made increasingly evident with the passage of time.

I extend my most sincere wishes for the happiness of the American people and for the personal well-being of their illustrious leader.

ARTURO FRONDIZI

The messages were released at Thomasville, Ga.

29 ¶ The President's News Conference of *February* 10, 1959.

THE PRESIDENT. I should like to speak for a moment about Secretary Dulles.

As you know, he has applied for a leave of absence from his duties for some weeks to undergo a real physical check-up and for repair of a hernia.

I can't tell you how disappointed I am to know that he has had to go in the hospital, but how pleased I am that he has finally recognized that he just must do this. I have long urged him to do it.

But, because of the fact that I believe he is the most valuable man in foreign affairs that I have ever known, I believe that every clear-thinking man in the United States—I didn't mean to use "man" specifically; man and woman—any clear-thinking man or woman in the United States would pray for his early recovery and his complete restoration to vigor and health so he can get back on the job. America needs him and I think each one of us needs him.

I believe his performance over 6 years has been remarkable, a brilliant one, and I think it's almost a miracle that he hasn't had to go for a longer period of rest and healing than he is now undergoing.

The next thing I wanted to mention was this disaster in St. Louis. I believe the reports so far showed about 17 killed and about 300 people hurt as a result of this tornado. Mr. Hoegh has got his OCDM man on the job in St. Louis. He's got disaster experts on the way there. All the departments of Government have been alerted to giving every possible assistance to the mayor and to the local authorities. As of the moment, at least, the hospitals are capable of taking the injured in and caring for them, and there seems to be no danger that the matter cannot be handled locally and with such support as can be given, both moneywise and facilitywise, from the Federal Government, and handled as well as such sad things can be handled. At least they are on the job, every one of them.

That's all.

Q. Marvin L. Arrowsmith, Associated Press: Mr. President, could you size up the picture regarding Berlin from the standpoint of the Western allies, in the light of Mr. Dulles' latest report to you yesterday?

THE PRESIDENT. Well, I would think, Mr. Arrowsmith, there is very little to add to his statement. As he came back, he made the statement at the airport, and he told that he detected a greater unified purpose among the Western allies, their firmness in their purpose of enforcing their rights and not accepting the theory that the Soviets could abandon their agreed responsibilities and transfer them to officials or to the GDR.

Now I think that the points he made speak for themselves, and I don't think there is much to add to it.

Q. John Hightower, Associated Press: Mr. President, do you think that Mr. Dulles' illness would in any way delay the preparation for possible negotiations with the Soviet Union, or delay the negotiations themselves?

THE PRESIDENT. Well, not so far as I know. Of course the doctors don't make any exact predictions as to when a satisfactory return to his health will be achieved. But there has been suggested, for example, a foreign ministers meeting between the Soviets and some of the Western allies. That would take some preparation. There has been no agreement.

I believe the Russians themselves are more concerned, Mr. Khrushchev is concerned, in a head of government meeting, as he calls an informal and without an agenda type. Well, that would take still a great deal of preparation.

Actually, I think that Mr. Dulles is very hopeful that after he has the operation over, that he will get more time to do a little thinking at leisure about some of our European problems than he does normally here, badgered as he is by all kinds of requests for statements and speeches and going abroad and all the chores of the day. I think he is hopeful that he is going to get to think more about it, and I would really believe there would be no delay whatsoever in this kind of negotiation.

Q. J. F. Ter Horst, Detroit News: Mr. President, there has been a growing impression, or at least reports around the country, that in the course of the pursuit of normal military intelligence the U.S. planes sometimes play fox and hounds along the Turkish border in order to cause Soviet interceptors to scramble, and that therefore, or thereby, we can gain some knowledge of their preparedness and their procedures.

Was the plane that was shot down, our plane that was shot down last September, on such a mission?

THE PRESIDENT. Well, I will answer the first part of it very specifically: the orders are very strict on this matter. Now occasionally there are errors in navigation and sometimes there are storms and things of that kind; once in a while we believe there are false radio signals that will take a plane out of course. But any thought of playing fox and hounds, as you call it, to cause scrambling is contrary to orders.

Actually, I have forgotten now the limit, but I established it personally, sometime back a couple of years ago, and I am sure that this happening is accidental.

Q. Raymond P. Brandt, St. Louis Post-Dispatch: Can you tell us what progress is being made on that new committee you mentioned in your state of the Union address——

THE PRESIDENT. You mean——

Q. Mr. Brandt: ——on social trends. It's getting mixed up with Mr. Nixon's committee, I think.

THE PRESIDENT. No, it is not to be mixed up. It is sharply differentiated.

Actually, what I'm doing is to find the man who is capable of heading such a committee and who has the time to do it. I have had three or four in mind, and one is coming to see me in a day or so. I am pushing as hard as I can; but again, like it was in the assembly of the Civil Rights Commission, these things are not easy, to get exactly the right personnel you want.

Q. Harold R. Levy, Newsday: There are reports that the State Department's recommendation that Mr. Labouisse be appointed the Director of the ICA were, in effect, vetoed by Mr. Alcorn on political grounds.

Would you tell us, sir, what role the national committee plays in the selection of appointees?

THE PRESIDENT. Well, I'll tell you one thing: no one has got a right to veto or attempt to veto any selection I may make for appointment to any office.

Now, in every vacancy that occurs, we try to find a man that can fill it adequately, and with credit to himself, as well as to benefit the Government.

It is undoubtedly true, and everybody knows, that political considerations come in; but they are, so far as I'm concerned and have always been, secondary in the making of appointments to the good of the Government. The idea that someone can veto my selections, well, I would think they would be very bold, more bold than I'd think if they'd try it.

Q. Edward P. Morgan, American Broadcasting Company: Mr. President, from the school aid legislation that you sent up to the Hill yesterday, some people have concluded that you have decided that it's more dangerous to unbalance the budget now than to run the risk of more inadequately educated citizens later.

Could you discuss this dilemma with us in the context of determination between difficult fiscal values and human values?

THE PRESIDENT. Well, I am not so sure that you can differentiate. The human values in America are not going to be promoted unless we are sane and sensible in our fiscal policies. I know of nothing that could injure the great population—174 million people—we have got than to allow budgetary process to get out of control, fiscal measures going loosely, in such way that just inflation would absolutely be inevitable.

Of course we recognize the national need for better education, but also I am firmly committed to the idea that the primary and basic responsibility in these matters rests with the communities and with the States. The only thing that I think the Federal Government should do is to try to inspire or help them on the basis of need, and where need can be proved. Then I think the national benefit to be obtained out of having an educated citizenry overrides a mere matter of some dollars, particularly if you are trying to do it correctly, not by supporting education all over our country but to inspire and where necessary assist the localities to do their job.

Q. Frank Holeman, New York Daily News: Sir, a group of private doctors associated in humanitarian work is trying to get a Navy hospital ship out of the mothballs on the west coast for a mercy mission into Southeast Asia.

Sir, how would you feel about such a project?

THE PRESIDENT. Well, I think the project—I have read about it in all its details in a number of reports—I think it's a wonderful thing to do. I don't know of any better way in which you could bring to many thousands of people, many millions, the concern of the United States in humanitarian things.

Now, the only thing that I know is still in question is whether or not this matter has yet been financed by these private interests in the way that they think it should be and the way they believe they can. Once that assurance is there, the Navy will have the ship ready for them, I assure you.

Q. Robert C. Pierpoint, CBS News: From reports that we get, sir, Premier Khrushchev seems rather anxious to have you visit the Soviet Union. I was wondering, first of all if you think that might be a useful trip for you at this present time, or would you prefer to have him visit the United States, perhaps?

THE PRESIDENT. You say that it appears that he would like for me to come there.

Did you read the speech in which he suggested that I might come, and what he had to say, particularly about the United States as a whole, its leaders, and some of the language he used to describe us as a nation—and others, even more than myself? [1]

I would think that certainly I would have to wait for some more official type of, and more, let us say, persuasive kind of invitation than that.

Q. Charles E. Shutt, Telenews: The Congress, in passing legislation or proposing it, especially in the housing and airport fields, have put in for more funds than you have allocated in your budget. There is much speculation on the Hill, sir, that you may make up this deficit by cutting your foreign aid funds. Would you comment on that possibility, sir?

THE PRESIDENT. Well, I would say this: if there was any intention of increasing expenditures in this area at the expense of mutual security, then I'd say I could think of no policy that was more destructive of America's vast interests in the world than that one.

If there is any item that I know of that is calculated to give to each of us as a citizen of America the greatest possible return, it will be that mutual security appropriation. And the idea that this kind of proposition is to be advanced because of the known reluctance of America to indulge in a program that has been classified as giveaway, if that is the idea on which we are working, well, then I say that statesmanship is beginning to get of a very low order.

Q. Carleton Kent, Chicago Sun-Times: Mr. President, in 1956 an expression of interest by you swung the Republican convention to San Francisco.

The Republican National Committee is in the process of choosing the 1960 site now. Do you have any favorites this time?

THE PRESIDENT. As a matter of fact, I start off questioning your

---

[1] Earlier, on February 6, the Press Secretary to the President released the following statement at Thomasville, Ga.:

Premier Khrushchev's invitation to President Eisenhower to visit the Soviet Union occurred in a lengthy speech which contained very hostile references to United States' leaders. It seems strange that Premier Khrushchev, if he really welcomes a visit by the President, would extend it in such circumstances.

The President has no present plans to make such a visit—in fact he hasn't received any invitation, except through the reports of an off-hand invitation extended in a political speech.

Ever since he has been in office, President Eisenhower has always made it clear that he was willing to go anywhere in the world if, by so doing, such a visit would serve the cause of peace. Should future developments suggest that a visit to the Soviet Union—or anywhere else—would serve to advance this cause, then it certainly would be considered.

premise, Mr. Kent, because I may have expressed that preference, I don't recall; but I'd think my reaction would have been: "That's an awful long trip to make out to the convention."

Certainly, so far as the next convention is concerned, the matter is completely within the hands of the National Committee. So far as I am concerned, I would not think it either desirable or useful to express any preference myself.

Q. Mrs. May Craig, Portland (Maine) Press Herald: Mr. President, the new chairman of the Senate Foreign Relations Committee complains that some of our more recent top ambassadorial appointments have not been first rate. It is often complained by the State Department that Congress does not allow sufficient pay and allowances so that any but wealthy men can afford to take the top jobs.

What have you found in relation to that?

THE PRESIDENT. Well, Mrs. Craig, it is perfectly clear that—I don't know whether they are the top jobs, but the more expensive jobs cannot possibly be taken by anyone except individuals of considerable wealth.

I think most of us here have visited some of those embassies, and you see the staffs of assistants and servants, some hired locally but others carried over; they couldn't possibly be paid out of the allowances that the Government now permits.

However, I do say there are other posts in this world that I think are just as important, and they are filled by career people, merely because they are not so expensive. There are certain places that we have just made up our minds that no one but a career person can ever go there, and we hope that they won't get so expensive that they can't do it.

I really believe that we should increase our percentages of career people just so far as it can possibly be done.

Q. Lloyd M. Schwartz, Fairchild Publications: Mr. President, the Labor Department is reporting this morning that unemployment is up around five million. I wonder if you feel that this is a level that we have to live with for a while, or whether there is a chance for marked improvement in the spring months?

THE PRESIDENT. Well, first of all it's not above five million, it's 300,000 below five million.

Secondly, I don't for one minute accept that as a satisfactory level of unemployment.

Now, in the month of January, unemployment went up 616,000 which is really less than seasonal factors would normally compel. In addition, though, there were 200,000 more employed this month of January, and I am sure that the ratio of the unemployed to the labor force went down, even in January, about 1/10 of a point, from 6.1 to 6. So, I believe thoroughly that we are going to have a pickup as the year goes on. There are certainly areas in which it is much more slow than we should like, any of us would like, but this is sort of characteristic of recoveries. They come, they get spotty, and here and there things look fine; and in others, they are not so good. But I say this, never with any level of that kind could you say that you should be happy with it or content with it.

Q. Frank van der Linden, Nashville Banner: Sir, you had a meeting this morning with Senator Cooper from Kentucky, and that gives rise to two questions. The first is, have you managed to persuade Dr. Welch of the University of Kentucky to stay on the TVA Board; and the second one is, have you decided who will get the vacancy on the Sixth Circuit Court of Appeals?

THE PRESIDENT. Well—[*laughter*]—my answer to the second one is a very simple one: that when I have named that man it goes to the Senate before I make any public announcement. So that will come out just as quickly as it goes to the Senate.

Now the other one is this: I don't know whether we can persuade Dr. Welch to stay longer, but I would say this: I would very much hope that he would; and if I knew what considerations could influence him, I would use them.

But actually, however, I believe he has to go back soon to the university or he has lost a very favorable position in his retirement opportunities. I think it would be a very serious question for him.

Q. Edward T. Folliard, Washington Post: Mr. President, some people are worried because they say Russia's economy is growing much faster than ours.

Now you have taken your stand against what you regard as excessive Federal spending in order to ward off inflation.

What do you think, sir, of the argument that we ought to switch the emphasis and step up Federal spending and so—stimulate the growth of our economy?

THE PRESIDENT. Well, people apply this in many ways to all sorts of programs.

Right now, our GNP is about $453 billion, that's its rate. Procurement and services we get from the Government are about $54 billion; this is something on the order of 12 percent of that GNP; certainly it is not the decisive part. Therefore the expansion of your spending policies and the deleterious effects compared to the advantages that you get by $2 or $3 billion more expenditures in a 453 billion-dollar GNP seem to me to be completely overbalanced in favor of frugality and thrift and keeping your dollar sound.

I can't emphasize too often that millions and millions of people are living today in the security that their pensions offer them for their old age. If those pensions are going down in value each year by so much amount—as a matter of fact, from nineteen hundred and, I think, it was forty, I have forgotten the exact year, but at any rate in recent years our dollar has lost half its value—if that continues, that kind of thing, it is going to be disastrous for our kind of economy and for the welfare of our people. The expansion of your economy is not going to come out of that kind of spending. The expansion is going to come from the incentives that we give to our people for working hard, using their brains and keeping what they can earn as much as possible, so they spend their money themselves. That's the kind of economy we have, and not one where we can take off 2 or 3 billion and put it in and make it really a healthier affair. I just don't believe that the benefit, if any, to be gotten from such an expending program, compared to the bad effects of deficit spending today, would have any weight with us at all.

Q. Andrew F. Tully, Jr., Scripps-Howard: Sir, people are always speculating about your state of health. Could you tell us in any detail, sir, how you are feeling these days?

THE PRESIDENT. Well, I don't have much time to think about it. But I think I'm in good shape; the doctors say so, and I don't know who else should worry so much about it—[*laughter*]—as the doctors and myself.

Q. William Knighton, Baltimore Sun: Mr. President, you have spoken out against the third term amendment. Had there been no third term amendment, would you now be considering in your mind running for a third term? [*Laughter*]

THE PRESIDENT. First of all, I don't believe I ever spoke out against it. I said this—since I have never made a deep study of this thing, because what was the use—from my viewpoint, I said I thought on balance it was an unwise amendment.

However, there were so many people whose fears are very real that somebody who would get hold of the kind of military force we now have, get hold of it and use it as an instrument of establishment of centralized or dictatorship form of government, I would think that I could argue pretty well on either side of this one.

Let me point this out: our whole history, from the beginning, from 1787 until 1953, has been one of almost defenselessness in military forces. You remember—I realize I cover so many years now in a military career, but it was not too many years ago when the whole strength of the Army, including the Air Force, was 118,750. We would go down to the Congress, and I have sat in front, helping my bosses with the data, we'd ask for $50,000 more for something we thought was just terrific; and it would be cut off.

Now, even after World War II, we found this same trend had started in. And it started not as just a matter of congressional economy or of the Executive's economy, it's what America felt. We hoped that the United Nations were going to solve our problems. So this political policy that you ask about, I think has been sort of a concomitant with our military policy, because everybody knew there wasn't enough military, really, to go into control of the country.

Now, this is no longer true, and it might alter thinking.

The answer to your last question is "no."

Q. John R. Gibson, Wall Street Journal: In the past, in talking about inflation, you have said that you felt that if it got bad enough the people of the country will probably demand some sort of economic control. Have you or your advisers seen any hint yet that this sort of sentiment is building up in any fashion now?

THE PRESIDENT. Well, it's quite clear over some months now that prices have been remarkably stable. Actually we had this one period here, following '55, that we ran up about 6 percent. But over the past 6 years it's been stable, very stable compared to what much of our history is; and in the last 10 months, or something of that kind, prices have shown a very, very great stability.

Now this therefore tends, I think, to influence us to avoid looking ahead as far as we should. I believe as we look ahead there are many factors that demand that we use every bit of influence, of every kind of leadership there is available in the press, in different organizations, business and labor organizations, and in Government to keep this possibility off our immediate future. We must keep it back.

I am sure that the whole population would, if this thing got too bad, demand some kind of controls; this I would deplore with everything I have.

Q. Peter Lisagor, Chicago Daily News: In view of Mr. Dulles' leave, do you plan to devote more of your own time and energy to the conduct of foreign affairs?

THE PRESIDENT. Well, if I do, something else is going to suffer because I don't know of anything that I give as much time to, every week and every day, as I do to foreign affairs. Actually, I don't know of any Cabinet officer that I give half the time to that I do to Secretary Dulles; and if I go into any more personal conduct of the thing, then I am going to have to neglect a few other departments, that's sure.

Marvin L. Arrowsmith, Associated Press: Thank you, Mr. President.

NOTE: President Eisenhower's one hundred and fiftieth news conference was held in the Executive Office Building from 10:31 to 10:59 o'clock on Tuesday morning, February 10, 1959. In attendance: 217.

30 ¶ Remarks at the 17th Annual Meeting of the National Rural Electric Cooperative Association. *February 11, 1959*

Mr. President, Ladies and Gentlemen:

I am delighted to meet with the representatives of the rural electrification systems. I salute you and those you represent for a job well done.

I understand there has been a little advance billing here about my alleged views on matters of interest to you. Well, I am here to set forth my views accurately and frankly, in what I believe to be your own interest as in the interest of our country.

We all know that when the REA was born, less than 11 percent of our farms had central station electric service. And today, of course, you know that 95 percent of our farms have central electric service. Your record of meeting loan repayments on time or ahead of schedule is outstanding. Your achievements have encouraged the growth of both rural residences and rural industries.

Much of this growth has taken place these past 6 years. Since January 1, 1953, you have added some 800,000 new consumers; your net worth has more than doubled, every loan has been met.

All of us know that in these past 6 years, the REA has experienced the greatest financial growth in its history.

As we look ahead certainly we are anxious that the future growth of REA be based upon sound principles—principles that are sound for REA and for the entire nation.

America at this very moment is engaged in a great debate on the role of the Government in the lives of her citizens. A part of this debate revolves around the question: shall Government live within its means; shall our citizens, in prosperous times, meet the cost of the services they desire of their Government?

Or is it to be our established policy to follow the ruinous route of free republics of the past ages—the route of deficit financing, of inflation, of taxes ever rising, until all initiative and self-reliant enterprise are destroyed? This route, I remind you, is one that would surely torpedo all the great achievements of your organizations in the past quarter century.

My view on this issue is clear, and, I hope, well known.

I believe profoundly that we must, in these times, not fail to live within our income. I believe that this is the view of most Americans.

I believe all of us want a healthy, free economy—one that will produce growth in terms of real goods, real services, real wages. Surely none of us favors actions that tend to debase our currency.

I believe further that most of you and most of your organizations are equally dedicated to these principles. Moreover, now that your REA systems have arrived at a state of maturity, I am sure you want to make the kind of contribution all of us must make as citizens toward a goal of fiscal soundness throughout America. To this end, none of us should add to the burdens of the general citizenry by insisting upon a favored position.

Now I come to one point on which I realize full well there is disagreement. Parenthetically I feel obliged to say this: I believe we are not going to find decent solutions to any of these differences—or to any other serious problems facing our country—by resort to demagoguery that seeks support for a special position.

One difference of which I speak is the rate of interest paid by persons and agencies who borrow money from the Federal Treasury. Specifically I refer to programs—such as REA and college housing—in which borrowers do not pay interest rates equal to the cost of money to the Government and are capable of doing so.

I have recommended that the Congress authorize the Treasury to set these rates at a level that will recover the cost of the money loaned. This recommendation would not raise interest rates now in effect on outstanding REA loans, for these loans are firm contracts between your member cooperatives and the Federal Government.

Now such a development would unquestionably be in the public interest. I do not intend, nor does this administration believe, that these future interest rate changes would be harmful in any way, nor can they be, to your systems.

Here I hope you will indulge me in a little philosophizing about our Government and how it relates, to my thinking, to each one of us.

I believe that Government, at all levels, has certain clear obligations to you and to me. It owes us, for example:

security from external attack

protection of our person and property

protection in the exercise of all the individual rights guaranteed by our Constitution.

But beyond these things that the Government owes us, Government may, if it so chooses, do a number of things for all our people that benefit you and me as citizens. For example, it supports certain medical services, we need to establish schools to assist in the education of our children, and prevent pollution of the air and the water we use. But even beyond this, the Government may also undertake special activities in favor of particular groups, of which you and I may be members. This is sometimes done not only for humanitarian purposes, but also to equalize economic opportunity among different areas, or groupings, and to prevent disaster in some sector of our economy from hurting, too much, the entire economy and population of the country.

We have, for instance, farm programs, housing assistance, urban renewal, the REA, and so on and so on. The effort here is not to give to one group of citizens special privilege or undeserved advantage. Rather it is to see that equality of opportunity is not withheld from the citizen through no fault of his own.

These and many other things our Government does for you and me.

In return we have certain obligations to Government. Payment of taxes, obedience to the laws, readiness for military service in emergency are illustrations. In addition, it is our obligation, as I see it, if we belong to one of the groups for which the Government has made special provision, to use that help responsibly and constructively. It is up to us to do our level best to re-establish speedily our own equality of opportunity, and so share proportionately in the productivity of our economy.

I believe that when this has once been accomplished, and my special requirements satisfied, then certainly I do not need, do not deserve, and should not accept any special help from the Government. If I do so, I help deny equality of opportunity to all my fellow citizens. No longer am I a fully independent, sturdy, and useful member of society. Rather I am, to the extent I profit unfairly at the expense of others, dependent upon their bounty.

These beliefs lead to the conviction that the great success of REA justifies the adjustment in future interest rates that I have suggested.

I believe we have reached a point where REA is no longer an infant enterprise. You have grown wonderfully through your infancy and adolescence. My congratulations to you are not only enthusiastic, but deep and sincere. Now in your prideful maturity, it is my earnest desire to see the local enterprises you represent become even stronger and more self-sufficient.

I like to think that the program which lighted the farm homes of America will also help illuminate the path to sound finance, good government, and responsible citizenship.

It is my earnest desire that these broad gauge goals will unite us all as we plan confidently for your future and the future of our whole country.

Thank you and best wishes to you—all of you, and to your families— for the journey ahead. Goodbye. Thank you.

NOTE: The President spoke at the National Guard Armory. His opening words "Mr. President" referred to John M. George, President of the Association.

31   ¶ Remarks at the National Lincoln
Sesquicentennial Dinner.   *February* 11, 1959

Mr. Chairman, Mr. Vice President, and Distinguished Guests:

It is natural, I think, that speaking last in such a program as this, that
we should expect some duplication and repetition. But I should reassure you as I begin, by saying that my talk is only 5 or 6 minutes, so if
there are these inevitable duplications, I may hope and pray that you
do not find them lengthy or too boring.

Ninety-eight years ago today the President-elect of the United States
boarded a train in Springfield, Illinois, to start the long journey to his
Nation's capital. That same day a Washington newspaper reported the
election in Montgomery, Alabama, of another president, Jefferson Davis,
and from Fort Sumter came a report of "preparations for attack."

In bidding farewell to Springfield, Lincoln shared his innermost
thoughts with old friends. In part, he said: "I now leave, not knowing
when or whether ever, I may return, with a task before me greater than
that which rested upon Washington. Without the assistance of that
Divine Being Who ever attended him, I cannot succeed. With that assistance I cannot fail."

Four years and two months later Abraham Lincoln was dead—but the
union again united. Now, said Secretary of War Stanton, "he belongs to
the ages."

But Abraham Lincoln belongs not only to the ages, but to all humanity.
Immortality is his in the hearts of all who love freedom everywhere in
the world.

Each year two million people visit the Lincoln Memorial in
Washington.

In New Delhi, a Lincoln Society is establishing a museum in his honor.
High school students in Tokyo last summer ranked him as the most respected of all world figures.

"Of all the great national statesmen of history," Russia's Tolstoy
thought, "Lincoln is the only giant."

In the Caucasian Mountains, a wild chieftain asked of a visitor, "Tell
us about the greatest ruler in the world. We want to know something

about this man who was so great that he even forgave the crimes of his greatest enemies and shook brotherly hands with those who had plotted against his life."

The first President of modern China, Sun Yat-sen, found his three basic principles of government in Lincoln's Gettysburg Address.

For many years India's Prime Minister Nehru has kept, on the study table, a brass mold of Lincoln's right hand. "I look at it every day," Nehru tells us; "it is strong, firm and yet gentle . . . it gives me great strength."

The birth, 150 years ago, which we here honor, gave the Nation a son who a half-century later was summoned to lead our Republic through the tragedy of civil war. And as Lincoln fought for union and liberty he insisted always that "the struggle of today is not altogether for today— it is for a vast future also."

As we turn our eyes to that future, other words of his seem applicable. He said: "The tendency to undue expansion is unquestionably the chief difficulty. How to do something, and still not do too much, is the question. . . . I would not borrow money. I am against an overwhelming, crushing system. Suppose, that at each session, Congress shall first determine how much money can, for that year, be spared for improvements; then apportion that sum to the most important objects."

That the spirit of Lincoln be close at hand as we meet each successive challenge to freedom is the earnest hope of all Americans—indeed it is the hope of freedom's sentinels wherever they stand.

Pushing always ahead in our quest for a just peace and freedom for all men we can do no better than live by his prescription: "by the best cultivation of the physical world, beneath and around us; and the intellectual and moral world within us, we shall secure an individual, social, and political prosperity and happiness, whose course shall be onward and upward, and which, while the earth endures, shall not pass away."

Thank you very much.

NOTE: The President spoke at the Statler Hilton Hotel, Washington, D.C. The dinner, sponsored by the Lincoln Sesquicentennial Commission and the Lincoln Group of the District of Columbia, inaugurated ceremonies marking the 150th anniversary of Abraham Lincoln's birth.

Victor M. Birely, Vice Chairman of the Executive Committee of the Lincoln Sesquicentennial Commission, was chairman of the dinner meeting. Fred Schwengel, U.S. Representative from Iowa, served as President of the Lincoln Group of the District of Columbia.

32   ¶ Special Message to the Congress on Increasing the Resources of the International Bank for Reconstruction and Development and the International Monetary Fund.   *February* 12, 1959

To the Congress of the United States:

In the Bretton Woods Agreements Act of 1945 Congress authorized the participation of the United States in the International Monetary Fund and in the International Bank for Reconstruction and Development.

This act of leadership on the part of the Government of the United States made it possible to bring these two great international institutions into being and to launch a major effort among the nations of the free world designed to establish an effective and continuing system of international cooperation in the fields of monetary and exchange policy and economic development.

Since their foundation twelve years ago, the United States has given vigorous support to the Bank and the Fund.

The two institutions have been outstandingly successful.

The Bank has assisted on an increasing scale the economic growth of the less developed countries through well-conceived and intelligently executed development projects. The Fund, through the provision of wise counsel and timely financial assistance to member countries faced with balance-of-payments difficulties, has successfully promoted the adoption of sound fiscal, monetary and foreign exchange policies in member countries.

The international standing achieved by the Bank and Fund is such that the international economic system of today cannot successfully function without them. They are indeed vital to the continued economic growth and cohesion of the entire free world.

The National Advisory Council on International Monetary and Financial Problems, which is responsible for advising me with respect to United States relationships with the Bank and Fund, has now recommended that the resources of the Bank and Fund be increased.

I strongly concur in this recommendation. Accordingly, I ask that Congress, in accordance with the provisions of the Bretton Woods Agreements Act, authorize the United States Governor of the International

Monetary Fund to request and consent to an increase of 50 percent in the quota of the United States in the International Monetary Fund, and authorize the United States Governor of the International Bank to vote for an increase of 110 percent in the capital stock of the Bank, and, subject to said increase becoming effective, subscribe on behalf of the United States to 31,750 additional shares of stock of the Bank, amounting to a doubling of the United States subscription.

The recommended increase is necessary to enable the two institutions to continue to operate successfully over the years ahead. Our subscriptions are the only financial support we are required to give these institutions. Within the framework of their capital structure, they are self-supporting and do not require additional periodic contributions.

INTERNATIONAL MONETARY FUND

The International Monetary Fund has two primary tasks. It promotes international monetary cooperation and sound foreign exchange practices which are vital to the balanced growth of world trade and development. It also provides short-term financial assistance to member countries to help them stabilize their currencies, maintain or move toward convertibility, and overcome temporary balance-of-payments problems without resorting to restrictions or other practices which may be harmful to international cooperation. In its financial operations, the Fund utilizes the gold and currencies which have been provided to it by the member countries on the basis of their quotas. These operations consist of advances or drawings repayable in not more than three to five years.

Since the beginning of its operations, the Fund has made available about $4.1 billion to 36 countries. Of this sum $3.2 billion was actually drawn in cash; commitments of over $800 million under stand-by arrangements or lines of credit are still outstanding; and $100 million in such credits were allowed to expire unused. Approximately two-thirds of the total was provided during the past two years, and the total amount of drawings and unused stand-by commitments outstanding on December 31, 1958, was $2.6 billion. On that date, the Fund's holdings of gold and U.S. dollars available for new advances or commitments were $1.4 billion, compared with $3.5 billion at the end of 1956. In the light of past experience, this amount would not be adequate if calls on the Fund comparable to those of recent years were made. The Fund must maintain sufficient liquid resources to constitute a second line of reserves to which its members can turn with assurance at any time.

The proposed general increase of 50 percent in the resources of the Fund, together with larger increases requested by a few countries, will meet this need. These increases will raise the resources of the Fund by approximately $5 billion, of which gold and dollars will amount to some $2.3 billion. If these new resources are made available, the free world can have full confidence in the capacity of the Fund to perform its tasks in the coming years.

Under the Articles of Agreement of the Fund, when a quota is increased, the member must pay 25 percent of the increase in gold, and the balance in its currency. In our case, this means a payment of approximately $344 million in gold and $1,031 million in dollars. The latter will be held in non-interest bearing notes to be utilized only at such time as the Fund may need cash to meet drawings by its members.

I should like to stress the cooperative nature of this proposed increase in Fund resources. Three-fourths of the gold to be paid to the Fund will come from other countries. Moreover, the additional holdings of other leading currencies will be increasingly useful to the Fund, particularly in view of the recent extension of the convertibility of major European currencies. This increase in resources on a very broad base is assured by the provision that the increase will not become effective until members having 75 percent of present Fund quotas have consented to quota increases.

INTERNATIONAL BANK FOR RECONSTRUCTION AND DEVELOPMENT

The International Bank for Reconstruction and Development has, in its 12 years of operations, made loans of over $4 billion in 49 different countries and territories. The Bank's reconstruction loans were made in 1947, and since then the Bank has made loans of some $3.6 billion for productive development projects. Loans by the Bank are currently running at the rate of about $700 million per year. Most of these loans have been made to the underdeveloped areas of the world. The Bank's own financing and technical assistance activities have increased the pace of economic growth all over the free world. The Bank has also been able to act as a conduit and stimulant to the flow of private capital into less developed areas.

Under the charter of the International Bank, only a small part of its authorized capital is available for lending, and the Bank obtains its funds primarily through borrowings in the financial markets of the world. Most of its authorized capital is, in effect, a guarantee for these borrowings. The Bank has raised the equivalent of more than $2 billion through issuance of its bonds in several different currencies. Approximately $1.8 billion of such bonds are currently outstanding. These bonds are recognized throughout the world as high quality securities. Both because of the member countries' guarantees and because of the outstanding character of its record, the Bank has been able to borrow large sums of money at frequent intervals at rates of interest comparable to those on high-grade Government securities. This permits the Bank to fix interest rates on its own loans that do not impose undue burdens on the borrowing countries.

At present, and in the foreseeable future, the ability of the Bank to raise funds in the capital market of the United States will depend largely upon the guarantee inherent in this country's subscription. Under the current rate of Bank borrowing, the present amount of this guarantee will be exceeded in the next two years. If the Bank is to continue to play its full part in raising productivity and living standards, additional capital far beyond the amount covered by the existing United States subscription will be needed.

The proposed increase of 110 percent in the total capital of the Bank and of 100 percent in the United States subscription will permit the Bank to meet its needs for borrowed funds for a substantial period of time. No part of the increase in our subscription would be required to be paid in except to meet defaults on the Bank's obligations. There is no reason to believe that this contingent liability will become a real one.

As in the case of the Fund, the proposed increase in the capital of the Bank will not become effective until subscriptions have been received for approximately 75 percent of the existing capital. This will assure a wide participation by the member countries.

The Special Report of the National Advisory Council, which describes in detail the proposal to increase the resources of the Bank and Fund, is attached.

The entire free world needs sound currencies and orderly exchange systems to foster trade and economic growth and it needs capital which will support rising living standards and accelerate the pace of economic development in all of the member countries. The International Monetary Fund and the International Bank for Reconstruction and Development have achieved outstanding records as effective instruments toward these ends. For the well-being of the free world and in our own interest, it is essential that the proposed increases in the resources of these two institutions take place.

There is real urgency for prompt action. The United States has for many months been taking the lead in this important effort to equip the Bank and Fund to continue their work. The countries of the free world look to the United States, because of our economic strength, to set the pace by acting without delay to take up our subscription in the new stock of the Bank and to pay our quota increase in the Fund. I consider it to be most important for the United States Government to maintain the posture of leadership which it now occupies. To this end, I urge the Congress to enact the necessary legislation so that these increases may promptly be made effective, to ensure further progress toward realizing a better life for the peoples of the free world.

DWIGHT D. EISENHOWER

NOTE: The special report of the National Advisory Council on International Monetary and Financial Problems, referred to in this message, is published in House Document 77 (86th Cong., 1st sess.).

33 ¶ Remarks on the 25th Anniversary of the Export-Import Bank of Washington. *February* 12, 1959

Mr. President, Mr. Secretary, Ladies and Gentlemen:

I think it is a military crime to be surprised and mystified. I had a date with the Secretary of the Treasury and worked out with your President, Sam Waugh, that I was going to make a quiet, personal call, unknown to anyone except the three of us—I thought. I find here some of my writing friends with their photographers, and throughout the halls I find policemen all over the place. I think everything is entirely safe and in order. But I repeat, I am astonished, and surprised.

I came here—not to keep you people from the work that I know you want to be doing on your 25th birthday—but only to tell you how much we of the administration appreciate what you have done, how proud we are of the record that has been established by this Ex-Im Bank in the last 25 years. I am sure that you are just as proud of that record as any of the rest of us.

I am told, just this afternoon, that some of you are here that were at the first birthday of the Bank 25 years ago. Well, I am sure that it has been a career that has been most satisfying. Because all the way around the country—through Latin America, in other nations—the record of this Bank is for fair dealing, for human understanding, and for acting in a businesslike, canny way—not only for the welfare of the United States but for other nations. Your record of repaid loans and repayable loans, your infinitesimal portion of written-off loans is one that I can do nothing except to say congratulations to your Directors, the President, and to all of you. And of course, I hope that all of you are here for the next 25 years and that I can just be tottering around to hear about the Bank's record.

NOTE: The President spoke at the Export-Import Bank. His opening words "Mr. President, Mr. Secretary" referred to Samuel C. Waugh, President and Chairman of the Export-Import Bank, and Robert B. Anderson, Secretary of the Treasury.

34 ¶ Letter to Representative Halleck Concerning Citizens' Views on Excessive Government Spending. *February* 13, 1959

[Released February 13, 1959. Dated February 12, 1959]

Dear Charlie:

I am happy to have your February 9th letter, advising me that many citizens are making themselves heard on the subject of excessive governmental spending. This is most heartening news. I earnestly hope it foretells widespread public insistence that government, in these prosperous times, must live within its means.

I believe the public will soon realize, perhaps better than now, that we are engaged in a contest between the public interest and a wide array of special interests, each demanding increased public spending in its particular area. You have effectively called attention to the importance of this struggle. I assure you that I intend to continue doing my level best to persuade the Congress to act responsibly for the general good in the face of the incessant special pleas for increased public spending.

I am stimulated by the letters you enclosed and hope that you and your colleagues will receive many hundreds more in the same vein.

With warm regard,

Sincerely,

DWIGHT D. EISENHOWER

NOTE: In his letter, released with the President's reply, Minority Leader Halleck stated that he was enclosing letters typical of thousands received in response to his recent appeal to the American people. He further stated that a theme of fear of rising costs and higher taxes ran through the letters, and that they pledged all-out support for a responsible budget policy.

35 ¶ Statement by the President Following His Visit to Secretary Dulles in Walter Reed Hospital. *February* 14, 1959

I HAVE just visited Secretary Dulles. We had a good talk and he is resting well. His immediate response to the hernia operation, as the doctors indicated to me, has been very satisfactory. While I was with him, his doctors discussed with us their finding of the existence of malignancy not fully determined at this time as to extent but certain to require further treatment.

I express the thoughts and prayers of all of us that the results of his operation and the further course of treatment will be successful. In order to allow time for this purpose, the Secretary continues on leave of absence. I will, of course, be in close touch with him constantly.

36 ¶ The President's News Conference of *February* 18, 1959.

THE PRESIDENT. Please sit down.

I am quite sure I voice the sentiments of the United States in expressing satisfaction over the escape of Prime Minister Menderes from the terrible accident in the plane, and also expressing sympathy for the families of those who were lost.[1]

This afternoon I shall start on a short call to Mexico to meet President Lopez Mateos.

There is no agenda for the meeting. It would be quite natural to expect that we would be talking about a number of things of common interest, but the basic purpose is to pay my respects to the President of a great neighboring republic.

You all know that I have tried to make a special effort to keep in touch with our Canadian and Mexican friends, and I expect to continue to do that. So the trip will be very short; and from what I hear about the climate of Acapulco, I am quite sure it will be pleasant, and it will certainly be interesting to meet him.

I have no other announcements.

Q. Merriman Smith, United Press International: Mr. President, in recent days there have been at least two reports concerning Secretary Dulles; one, that he tried to resign and you refused to consider it, and then there have been other published reports, apparently emanating from Capitol Hill, that you have been sounding out certain Republicans on what you might do in event that it became necessary to select a successor to Mr. Dulles.

Now, in the light, against the background of these two reports, I wonder if you could discuss with us the Secretary's condition and how you view his future.

THE PRESIDENT. Well, I want to start off with a little reminiscing.

I once told General Marshall that there was a certain corps commander in the United States that I wanted to get over into Europe right away; I needed him and there was a corps needed such a man with such qualifications. I got a telegram saying, well, sure, he is a very fine man, but he is so crippled out in Walter Reed that the doctors won't assure you that he can move around. And I said, you send the man and I will send him to battle in a litter, because he can do better that way than most people I know. Now, I feel this way about Secretary Dulles. The doctors have assured me there is nothing in his disease that is going to touch his heart and his head, and that is what we want.

I am constitutionally responsible for conducting the foreign affairs of

---

[1] The President referred to an airplane crash near London, England.

the United States, and the man who has been my closest associate, certainly my principal assistant, and on whom all the responsibility for details has been resting, my closest friend and confidante in this whole business, is Secretary Dulles. I know of no man—in my knowledge—in the world that has equaled his wisdom and his knowledge in this whole complicated business.

Therefore, as long as Secretary Dulles believes that he is in shape to carry on, he is exactly the person I want.

So far as his offer to resign, I must tell you this is no new thing. His dedication and his selflessness is so great that from the very first day he came into this office, he has constantly said, "If ever, Mr. President, I become for you either a political or a national liability, remember you have my resignation always, to be accepted at your pleasure."

Well, now, of course, this has been his attitude. There has never been a specific statement ever that he wants to resign, because to be saying that would mean that he was ready to lay down his duties and responsibilities that he believes to be so important.

And so, I just say to you again, as long as he is ready to carry on, he is the man I want. And I have not discussed with anyone the possibility of his successor.

Q. William McGaffin, Chicago Daily News: Mr. President, the people who are concerned about freedom of information say that your administration has a bad record for bottling up information which they say the public is entitled to have. They would like to see you take the lead in correcting this situation.

THE PRESIDENT. Well, everybody seems to have ideas of many things, in particular when they have no responsibility.

A President has a very large organization to run. I have given my beliefs about the need for keeping certain information confidential until it can be published; and as quickly as it can be published in conformity with the security or other interests of the United States, then it should be given promptly because only with that kind of information can a public make up its mind as to what its own government should be.

Now, as an example of the kind of information not as security but which cannot be given out as quickly as it reaches the Government is this: take all of the reports on crops. If you publish this in advance or let it leak to get it before it could be evaluated and brought together, you could make it possible for a good many speculators to take advantage of this kind of thing.

So there is certain information, having nothing to do with the security, military security, of the United States, that cannot be promiscuously turned out, but it is given out as quickly as this is consistent with the best interests of the United States.

Now, on the part of security, there the people that are dealing with the problem—the State Department, the National Security Council, the Chiefs of Staff, the Secretary of Defense—those are the people who have to determine whether or not the item is really important from the security. Certainly we are not going to try to damage the security of the United States.

Q. Garnett D. Horner, Washington Star: Sir, there were introduced in the House yesterday 14 identical bills calling for a territorial form of home rule for the District of Columbia. There is also pending a proposal for a constitutional amendment to give the citizens of the District the right to vote for President and Vice President.

Could you express your opinions on both of those measures, sir?

THE PRESIDENT. Well, Mr. Horner, from the first day I was in this office, I have supported home rule.

Now, each year there seems to be some little change in detail, some new idea is brought up.

This year I have put in a bill that would make the District really on a territorial basis—you know, with an appointed governor and secretary, with a delegate in the Congress, and so on.

But I have not supported or have not suggested a constitutional amendment at this moment. I don't say my mind is closed to it; I just say I haven't done that.

Q. Chalmers M. Roberts, Washington Post: Mr. President, on the substance of the problem facing Secretary Dulles and the West in general, could you tell us whether you think the political and military changes in recent years affecting Europe are such that it might now be possible for the West to consider as part of the German reunification scheme some idea of thinning out our troops or troops on both sides, or of limiting weapons in central Europe?

THE PRESIDENT. Well, Mr. Roberts, I am not going here to start talking about the details or the possibilities that may come out of negotiations.

The West has shown time and again its readiness to negotiate, on the whole problem of Germany and the region, anything reasonable in which both sides can have confidence.

We don't want, and we realize it would be self-defeating, to build up anything that the Soviets could legitimately consider a menace on their border; we don't want to do that.

We want to do something that is decent; but to say now that one of the things that we want to throw in the pot, the thinning out of troops, and so on—there are a thousand factors each of which affects the others: the morale of the West, what their readiness is, what they believe about us, what our troops mean to them, even more than their actual strength.

I think that the best we can say is this: here we search for a just peace. That just peace is not going to come about until two sides can find some reasonable basis where these specific problems can be solved. Until that comes about, I think we have to do the best we can, stay strong, but always holding out a hand ready to be grasped if it will be grasped in good faith.

But I can't, I can't possibly at this moment, take the kind of detail of which you are speaking, and talk about it; because you are doing it out of context, and you couldn't do that one, really, without a long paper in front of you.

Q. William H. Lawrence, New York Times: Mr. President, may I ask a two-part question, sir?

Is there an allied agreement to use force, if necessary, to defend our rights in Berlin? And, two, if there is the risk of force, would you go to Congress for specific authority to act, as you did in the case of Formosa and the Middle East?

THE PRESIDENT. Again, Mr. Lawrence, you ask questions on matters each one of which has to be studied in its context—in other words, the situation at the time.

We have not said we are using force. We are saying we do not abandon our responsibilities. We will continue to carry them out, and it will be the responsibility of the other side if there is going to be any force; they have to use that to block our carrying out our responsibilities.

Q. Peter J. Kumpa, Baltimore Sun: Sir, in recent weeks we have heard reports that the Communists are gaining power in the government of Brigadier Kassem in Iraq.

I wonder if you could give us your evaluation of the situation, and tell us whether you are worried about it?

THE PRESIDENT. Well, I don't say I am worried about it, I don't like the word. Certainly I am concerned about it.

Frankly, the reports are not so clear, and the conclusions that we can reach are not so clean-cut that I could give you a yes or no answer to your question.

I would merely say this: here is one of those places where we hope that the forces within the country that want to live independently and in some measure of freedom will triumph over those where they want to have a dictatorial type of government or Communist type—by that I mean Communist; and certainly that is the kind of development we want to see come about.

Q. Charles W. Roberts, Newsweek: Sir, I would like to ask you two related questions. There have been reports recently that Secretary McElroy would like to leave the Cabinet this year; secondly, there have been a lot of reports that you have difficulty getting and keeping people in Government jobs, now that you are barred by the Constitution from running again, in the last 2 years of your administration.

Could you comment on both of those reports?

THE PRESIDENT. I will comment on them, yes.

First of all, Mr. McElroy did, when he accepted the job here, indicate there might be certain factors that might not allow him to go to the end of his term.

But I know this: he is dedicated to his job, and he has not brought up to me at this moment any expression of intention to quit at a particular time.

Now, next, about getting good men for this Government, I really believe it is a wrong premise that someone is starting, for this reason: I had a harder time when people thought they might be committed for 6 years of service than when they were for 2.

And I remember this: I believe the average person that takes a position in Government has a feeling, because of others' good opinion or under persuasion, that if he can do something for this country through a governmental job, that is a distinction that he rather likes. It is the kind of distinction that he can carry with him through his life, and maybe his children will think of it. Therefore, the very fact that he does not have to look forward to 8 years of this kind of, sometimes, tough work is a factor on the other side.

Now, there may be someone who is very politically motivated, who says, "Well, if I am going to have a job like that I want to be assured, I want to have it for a longer time." I think that is the minority, and it is not really the kind of person you are looking for.

So I would say the good man that believes you can persuade him that he has got something to deliver here, some service that he can give us, all of us, well, I don't think that he hesitates because of the fact that he may not have a longer job.

Q. David P. Sentner, Hearst Newspapers: Mr. Khrushchev said in Moscow yesterday that if we tried to shoot our way into West Berlin after Russia turns over the occupied area to East Germany, it would mean the beginning of war.

Mr. Khrushchev is also reported to have said that the recommendations of Senator Mansfield are more reasonable, apparently referring especially to the Senator's suggestion for direct negotiations between East Germany and West Germany.

Would you care to comment on both of those statements?

THE PRESIDENT. Well, I haven't read this speech except in a most abbreviated sort.

I would say this: he must be talking about shooting to stop us from doing our duty. After all, that is what is going to happen if it happens. We are not saying that we are going to shoot our way into Berlin.

We say we are just going to go and continue carrying out our responsibilities to those people, the ones that we agreed to undertake way back in 1945.

So that if we are stopped it will be somebody else using force.

Now, with respect to his comments on Senator Mansfield's speech, I wouldn't want to say anything at the moment.

Q. Thomas N. Schroth, Congressional Quarterly: Mr. President, among the Lincoln Day speeches last week was one by a Republican Senator who said we should not make a fetish out of balancing the budget. There are certain conditions that he named, the reversal of the economy or increased military threat, could make deficit spending more important than a balanced budget.

Would you say that conditions could change this year to make you change your mind on a balanced budget?

THE PRESIDENT. Well, I will say this: very manifestly, last year we didn't have a balanced budget, and we could foresee that it wasn't, and we didn't make any fetish about it. I don't know why suddenly a balanced budget is getting to be a bad word. I think it is rather a good thing to be a bit frugal and say that we can live within our income.

I do not know what is the future, and I can't even see beyond the next day; I am not a seventh son of a seventh son.

I say this: when the conditions allow it, and with the conditions of rising prosperity—remember, personal income in the month of January is the highest it has ever been in this country—this kind of thing opens up this great question: if we cannot live within our means as prosperity is growing and developing, when are we going to do it? And if we are going to always live under deficit spending, what is going to happen to our currency?

This question doesn't seem to me to demand any detailed answer. It is clear.

Now, on the other hand, it has sometimes seemed a little bit odd that we have to make our whole economic, in some strange way, economic cycle coincide with the time it takes the earth to get around the sun.

I sometimes wonder whether we shouldn't think of our budget balancing in terms of 5-year terms, or at least to include the length of time that we find the ordinary business cycle. Then you could have maybe a discussion on the balancing of the budget and living within your income on a little bit better basis. One year's budget is not the whole answer, and we didn't ask for it last year. I am asking for it this year because I think it is good for the country and I think we can do it in this kind of a period. I think we must do it.

Q. Edward P. Morgan, American Broadcasting Company: Sir, in a statement preliminary to an inquiry on inflation, the chairman of the Joint Congressional Committee on the Economic Report, Senator Douglas, says that we are in general agreement as to the desirability of three objectives of economic policy: substantially full employment, an adequate rate of economic growth, and substantial stability of the price level. How do those objectives strike you, sir, and could you tell us what Mr. Nixon's impending committee will do that this committee itself may not do? [1]

---

[1] A White House release of January 31 stated that the Vice President would serve as Chairman of the Cabinet Committee on Price Stability for Economic Growth, plans

THE PRESIDENT. Well, now, you are talking as the committee's objectives? Is that what you are talking about, or as the United States objectives?

Q. Mr. Morgan: I am reading from the New York Times, sir.

THE PRESIDENT. I know it, but——

Q. Mr. Morgan: It is indicated——

THE PRESIDENT. ——but whose objectives are these?

Q. Mr. Morgan: It is indicated that the Senator is speaking in terms of the country at large, implying that the committee's——

THE PRESIDENT. I think you will find exactly those things in the Economic Report. As a matter of fact, we even ask, I forget whether it was the Economic Report or the budget or my own speech, that the act be amended to make as one of our specific objectives keeping a stable dollar; and, of course, we want substantial full employment; we want an expanding economy, a healthy economy; and that means to us, means to anyone, I think, who studies this thing, a sound dollar.

So those objectives are perfectly fine. I have no quarrel with them whatsoever.

Now, what was the other, the second part?

Q. Mr. Morgan: The heart of my question, sir, was whether there was any confusion or duplication between the joint committee's inquiry and Mr. Nixon's impending inquiry.

THE PRESIDENT. None at all.

As a matter of fact, what he is doing is to find out what Government can do, what it can plan now and what it should be doing to promote these objectives; that is all.

Q. Alan S. Emory, Watertown Times: There has been some disappointment in New York State, sir, that while you are going to Canada for the St. Lawrence Seaway opening ceremony, the inference in the White House statement was that you might not be able to make the United States ceremony the following day. Is there any chance that you will be able to, sir?

THE PRESIDENT. Well, I have been to Massena, and certainly I have

for which were outlined in the State of the Union Message and the Economic Report. The release further stated that the Committee would serve as a continuing Cabinet group to study the problem of how to maintain reasonable price stability as an essential basis for achieving a high and sustainable rate of economic growth.

been to New York State; I have never been to Montreal, and this is a joint ceremony.

As it turned out, the day they fixed up—I thought I should take only a day, and it will probably be pretty bad. But I wouldn't see where there would be any hurt feelings, because I understand that the Queen and the Prince are going on all the way to Detroit——

Mr. Hagerty: Chicago.

THE PRESIDENT. Chicago—in their yacht to pay a visit to our Midwest through this channel. So I'd think there can be no hurt feelings anywhere, really.

Q. Robert C. Young, Chicago Tribune: Mr. President, you had breakfast this morning with Lawrence Kimpton, the chancellor of the University of Chicago in, I understand, connection with your National Goals Committee.

Could you tell us if you intend to appoint Mr. Kimpton chairman of that committee?

THE PRESIDENT. We didn't discuss appointments. We discussed the ideas and found a great deal of common ground in which we were interested.

I must say that it was, more than anything else, an opportunity to get to meet this man of whom I had heard so much. And I must say that what I had been told in the past was no better than my impression now; I think he is a very fine man.

Q. Raymond P. Brandt, St. Louis Post-Dispatch: Mr. President, the Treasury is paying very high rates on the short-term securities, and apparently finding great difficulty in selling bonds.

Does the administration have any plans to ask Congress to increase the 4¼ percent ceiling on bonds?

THE PRESIDENT. Well, of course, I think this: I think bonds should be marketed according to the demand, and I think if they are not, in the long run we run into difficulties. This applies to the mortgages on housing, Federal bonds, and everything else.

I think that if we are going to be a free enterprise country, we ought to take all of our debentures and our indebtedness and say, "All right, this money is going to earn this kind of return in this particular kind of an economy," whether it is on an upper leg or a lower leg, and I think if we don't try to do that, it would be bad.

Now, within the 4¼ we have always been able to do that. The reason your question is now pertinent is because the rate is getting close enough to make it look that you would have to sell bonds at a discount. Funny thing, they tell me under the law that you could offer a 4¼ bond and sell it at 95; but it is clear, as I understand the spirit of that law, that that would not be violated. I think we would have to go back to Congress if this situation, which I hope will not arise, really eventuates.

Q. Rod MacLeish, Westinghouse Broadcasting Company: Sir, can you give us your thoughts on Prime Minister Macmillan's proposed trip to Moscow?

THE PRESIDENT. There is nothing to say, particularly. He goes, of course, on the basis that he is returning a call that Bulganin and Khrushchev made to London a year ago or more. He does want to present to Mr. Khrushchev, of course, the views of his government, the problems that beset all Europe and really, indeed, all the world. Those have been, let's say, fairly concerted as to basis, and have been explained.

As a matter of fact, the last public statement that Mr. Dulles made, I think, brought that point out.

Q. Mr. MacLeish: Just one more aspect of that, sir. Have you discussed common objectives with Mr. Macmillan for this visit?

THE PRESIDENT. Oh, not this particular visit, no.

Q. Richard L. Wilson, Cowles Publications: Mr. President, in view of the circumstances, would you think it would be desirable to hold a foreign ministers conference on Berlin in Washington or New York or some other place in the United States?

THE PRESIDENT. Well, I think, Mr. Wilson, it is one of those questions that when the thing comes up, has to be determined then. I suppose you are—the circumstances of which you speak are Mr. Dulles' illness?

Q. Mr. Wilson: Yes, sir.

THE PRESIDENT. I would think that would have very little to do about it. Frankly, in talking to Mr. Dulles yesterday afternoon, why, we just decided that we were going right ahead because, after all, we have had here a man for 6 years with us, presenting his views constantly to the National Security Council; he is backed up by able men of his own choosing in his own department, and we want his brain and his heart, as I say, as long as we can have it. But I don't think we are going just to make details of operations, suggest that they revolve around the circumstance of his disability at the moment.

Q. J. F. Ter Horst, Detroit News: Despite the upswing in the economy, sir, heavy unemployment continues in places like Detroit and Pittsburgh and so on, as you well know.

A week ago Walter Reuther, to his own UAW, suggested that it might be a good idea for a march of the unemployed on Washington to dramatize their plight.

I have two questions, sir: what would you think of such a march and, second part, would you favor a move now in Congress to extend the 13-week unemployment compensation that was passed last year at your request?

THE PRESIDENT. Well, the first one, I believe that news item came out of Puerto Rico where people must be on the sunny beaches; I don't know whether they are going to march from there over to this foggy Washington or not. [*Laughter*]

Secondly, I don't see any good to be done, to come out of any such demonstration. Thirdly, I don't think this is the time to put the Federal Government back into this kind of a function when we are on a curve of rising prosperity.

Q. Spencer Davis, Associated Press: Would you give your estimate, sir, of relations between the United States and the Philippines? There have been indications in the past of some hurt feelings out there, that we have taken their friendship for granted.

Would you reply to that?

THE PRESIDENT. You have asked a question that could set me off on a very long dissertation.

I started working with the Philippines very intimately in 1935, and for some good bit over 4 years I was really employed or was one of the officers that was working under that government, that provisional government then under President Quezon. So I have lived with these problems of bases and jurisdiction and all the rest of it.

It is possible that sensitive peoples can decide that we are taking them too much for granted. But I would point out what the United States has tried to do. I think the record is very good, and I think that if people of good will get together and talk about these, there is really no difficulty.

The questions that really come in are psychological and a matter of pride rather than of great moment otherwise.

Q. Peter Lisagor, Chicago Daily News: Mr. President, have you given any thought to the appointment of a chief negotiator for these upcoming conferences in the event that Mr. Dulles physically could not negotiate them himself?

THE PRESIDENT. No.

Q. Lloyd M. Schwartz, Fairchild Publications: Mr. President, there seems to be considerable hostility in Congress to your proposed curbs on secondary boycotts and some types of picketing, and the tendency to separate that from the labor reform bill.

I wonder how you feel about that and what sort of priority you give to that type of thing.

THE PRESIDENT. Well, these are the two major differences between other bills put in and mine.

I personally believe that they are just a feature of decency and justice to the public and to the worker.

I think the blackmail picketing is unjustified, and I don't think that secondary boycotts should be tolerated.

Now, I have nothing whatsoever to say about Congress' opinion about this. I am giving my own. I think those two features should be right squarely in the bills.

Q. Mrs. May Craig, Portland (Maine) Press Herald: Mr. President, there are economy-minded members of both parties at the Capitol who think you can save money if every expenditure had to go through the Appropriations Committee rather than the backdoor payments direct from the Treasury to some agencies. Mr. Rayburn is for continuing the backdoor method.

My question is this: since you have refused to spend money actually appropriated when you didn't think it wise, could you also refuse the backdoor Treasury payments direct? [*Laughter*]

THE PRESIDENT. To go to the first question, the comment, I think that I should not comment on congressional methods for making money available. They have the power of the purse and they exercise it as they choose.

Now, when we get into this method of stopping some expenditures because they are deemed unwise, normally, or so far as I remember, I have done that only until I could go back to Congress and try to convince them that they have been mistaken, that this kind of floor under expenditures and strengths, for example, is not justified. If they are persistent, if they stick to this thing, I have no recourse except to execute the laws.

And I would say, with these other authorizations, if I did not follow the letter of the law instantly, I should certainly take it back to them, because I have no desire to be a dictator. And even though I sometimes think I know much better than some of these laws would seem to indicate, nevertheless when you come down to it, just like in any decision of the courts or anything else, I have to execute them. But I do have my right, I think, to go and put in a reclamor for a while and say I think they are not quite right.

Marvin L. Arrowsmith, Associated Press: Thank you, Mr. President.

NOTE: President Eisenhower's one hundred and fifty-first news conference was held in the Executive Office Building from 10:28 to 11:01 o'clock on Wednesday morning, February 18, 1959. In attendance: 261.

37 ¶ Remarks on Arrival at the Airport, Acapulco, Mexico. *February* 19, 1959

Mr. President, and Citizens of this great Republic:

Ever since the inauguration of your President, I have wanted to come to this country, that I may pay to him my respects as he takes over the great office of President and assumes the responsibilities and the authorities that devolve upon that office.

I do this because of the common knowledge in our own country—my country—that friendship with the Mexican people and with the Mexican government is, for us, a necessity.

We have with you a very long, common border. We do not want—ever—to see that border defended by guns and by the machines of war. We want it to be guarded by the friendship that lives within the hearts of your people and of ours. And that friendship must be borne and must be nurtured by a common respect for the human values that are the foundations for the forms of government we have.

Each of us, through different circumstances, has found independence and has developed liberty for each of its citizens. So that we can say with truth that the dignity of man, the rights of every individual are the motives that bind us together and makes certain that this friendship of which I speak shall never be destroyed.

I have been moved by your President's words in saying that on both sides he knows we are trying to solve our common problems in this spirit of understanding and of friendship. I can assure you, Mr. President, and I assure all your people, of our determination always to meet you halfway—we would hope more than halfway—that we may achieve this kind of result.

And now, sir, may I assure you that not only I but all the people of the United States would want me to say to you today: we hope, we trust, we pray, that the friendship between our two peoples will ever grow, so that we may be stronger in freedom, in justice, in prosperity—in the happiness of every single individual in each country down to the remotest village of our two countries.

Sir, this is a very great honor that you have permitted me to enjoy this morning, of coming to visit you on your home land. And for it, I assure you, I am grateful.

38 ¶ Joint Statement Following Discussions With President Lopez Mateos of Mexico. *February* 20, 1959

THE PRESIDENT of Mexico, Adolfo Lopez Mateos, and the President of the United States, Dwight D. Eisenhower, in a meeting on February 19 and 20, 1959, at Acapulco, Mexico, discussed informally and without an agenda, the general aspects of relations between the two countries.

The Presidents reconfirmed that relations between Mexico and the United States are excellent and are characterized by a spirit of good neighborliness, mutual understanding and respect. They agreed that these relations can and should attain even higher levels not only because both countries have an interest in expanding the areas in which they may jointly cooperate but also because in common endeavor they can make a contribution to the cause of a just and lasting peace through continued efforts to improve the welfare of mankind and through adherence to those principles of liberty under law which are fundamental to enduring good will among nations.

Recognizing that the great strides made in modern science have opened almost limitless opportunities for the future of mankind, the two Presidents are convinced that relations between countries must comprise not only harmonious living under the rule of international law and the promotion of mutual trade and intercourse but also encompass broad programs of mutual cooperation so that the benefits of civilization may be brought within the reach of all the peoples of the world.

In their conversations the two Presidents discussed impact on their two countries of the development of travel across their common frontier. In this Mexican port of surpassing beauty where thousands of Americans happily visit every year, the Presidents considered it particularly appropriate to express their pleasure with the growing number of their countrymen representing every walk of Mexican and American life who have made a two-way street of a common border.

The two Chiefs of State agreed completely that economic development is an objective of cooperation between nations. They noted with keen satisfaction the efforts made in this direction by the Organization of American States and concurred in the desirability of continuing and increasing those efforts to the greatest possible extent.

During discussions on the general nature of relationships between Mexico and the United States the two Presidents considered several specific matters of particular interest.

Since cotton is Mexico's major export commodity and one of great importance to the United States, the two Presidents agreed that their Governments should cooperate and consult together in their efforts better to protect the interests of both countries in this vital commodity.

Convinced that it would benefit both countries further to harness the waters of the river which is their common boundary the two Presidents were in agreement as to the desirability of constructing the Diablo Dam on the Rio Grande at a site which has been agreed upon by the International Boundary and Water Commission and they hope to conclude an agreement for the construction of the Dam as rapidly as possible.

The two Presidents reviewed the lead and zinc question and agreed that both countries should continue to study ways to reach a multilateral solution to this international problem without prejudice to further efforts by the two countries toward a solution consonant with the spirit of collaboration which exists in all their relationships. This same spirit of cooperation is shown in efforts to devise means for the strengthening of the international coffee market through the International Coffee Study Group, in which both Governments are participating.

They also agreed to instruct agricultural authorities of their two Governments to plan a coordinated attack on the screw worm problem which is causing grave damage to livestock in both countries. For this purpose it was agreed to explore the feasibility of a joint program of eradication utilizing radioactive isotopes. This agreement is illustrative of the benefits to be derived from peaceful uses of nuclear energy in both domestic and international affairs.

The Acapulco meeting was a meeting between friends. The two Presidents understood and appreciated each other from the beginning. They are determined to continue to collaborate on matters of mutual concern through their Governments and through international organizations. The meeting, moreover, confirmed anew that a personal relationship between the Presidents of Mexico and the United States is an essential element in fostering confidence and good will among the peoples of the two neighboring countries.

NOTE: This statement was released at Acapulco, Mexico.

39 ¶ Message to Prime Minister Macmillan of the United Kingdom on the Cyprus Agreement. *February* 20, 1959

[Released February 20, 1959. Dated February 19, 1959]

Dear Mr. Prime Minister:

Just at this moment I have received notice of the conclusion of an agreement between your Government and the Greek and Turkish Governments and the representatives of the Cypriot people concerning the future status of Cyprus. Though I am now visiting in Mexico, I feel impelled to send you instantly my sincere felicitations.

I know what your personal leadership has meant to the efforts to bring about a peaceful and equitable solution, and I share your satisfaction that the foundation has now been established for a settlement acceptable to the Cypriot people which at the same time contributes to the closer cooperation of Greece, Turkey, and the United Kingdom.

Please convey also to Mr. Lloyd, Mr. Lennox-Boyd, and Governor

Foot my admiration for the contribution which they have made in making this agreement possible.

With warm regard,

DWIGHT D. EISENHOWER

NOTE: This message was released at Acapulco, Mexico.

40 ¶ Message to Prime Minister Karamanlis of Greece on the Cyprus Agreement. *February* 20, 1959

[Released February 20, 1959. Dated February 19, 1959]

Dear Mr. Prime Minister:

I want you to know how very pleased I am by the recent developments concerning Cyprus and how deeply impressed I am by the spirit which you and Foreign Minister Averoff have demonstrated in making this possible.

The conclusion of an agreement on Cyprus is recognized throughout the world as a victory of common sense. I think that it is much more than that; it is also an imaginative and courageous act of statesmanship which cannot fail to strengthen and encourage the whole NATO alliance.

I believe it is particularly significant that a final solution now promises to be reached within the framework of close Greek-Turkish cooperation. This cooperation offers tremendous advantages, not only to the two countries but indeed the entire Free World and particularly the Cypriot people themselves.

I am very much aware of the difficulties which the problem has caused you and your Government. For this reason I am all the more appreciative of the perseverance and understanding which your Government has shown in reaching an agreement.

With warm personal regard,

DWIGHT D. EISENHOWER

NOTE: This message was released at Acapulco, Mexico.

41 ¶ Message to Prime Minister Menderes of Turkey on the Cyprus Agreement. *February* 20, 1959

[Released February 20, 1959. Dated February 19, 1959]

Dear Mr. Prime Minister:

The conclusion of an agreement on the substance of a Cyprus settlement by Turkey, Greece, and the United Kingdom, and the representatives of the Cypriot people is indeed a splendid achievement. A high order of statesmanship and resolution was needed to construct the basis for an equitable solution of this grave problem. I want you to know how much I admire your efforts, and those of your Foreign Minister, Mr. Zorlu, in the important negotiations which preceded the agreement.

The solution owes its impetus to Turkish-Greek understanding and cooperation. It will surely strengthen the NATO alliance and indeed the entire Free World.

I know that serious obstacles stood in the way. I can appreciate, all the more, the understanding and patience which were needed to achieve this significant step.

With warm personal regard,

DWIGHT D. EISENHOWER

NOTE: This message was released at Acapulco, Mexico.

42 ¶ The President's News Conference of *February* 25, 1959.

THE PRESIDENT. I have one short announcement this morning. When I was at Acapulco, with President Lopez Mateos, I invited him to come to the United States sometime at his convenience; he has accepted, to come sometime in the spring, although details of dates and so on are not yet determined. That's all.

Q. Marvin L. Arrowsmith, Associated Press: Mr. President, do you believe that it is worth while trying to negotiate with the Russians when Khrushchev informally rejects the idea of a foreign ministers conference on Germany, apparently without any advance notice to Macmillan at the very time he is in Moscow for talks on such matters?

And does this development raise doubts in your mind as to whether an eventual summit meeting would accomplish anything?

THE PRESIDENT. Well, Mr. Arrowsmith, we have at this minute exactly the same questions to answer that we have been trying to get good answers for for a long time—even prior to the time of my coming to this Office.

Now, the obviously, palpably, intransigent attitude of Mr. Khrushchev is, of course, not only—it has not only been well known, but it seems really to be emphasized. And at the moment when the logical purpose of Mr. Macmillan's visit was to try to create an atmosphere in which negotiations would be possible, this development is not one that, certainly, you could call hopeful.

This is the only logical attitude that the United States, and the West, as I see it, can take: first, that we are not going to give one single inch in the preservation of our rights, and of discharging our responsibility in this particular region, especially Berlin.

There can be no negotiation on this particular point of right, and of retention of responsibility.

Now, the United States has always made clear, we are always ready to negotiate when the other person will give us the slightest area or region in which to negotiate; but if there is to be a positive answer and a negative answer to give to any question before you do attempt to negotiate, then I can't see very much use for conferences. Indeed, if the same kind of attitude is shown insistently and always, why, I must say the future doesn't seem to hold much promise for negotiation.

Now this, in spite of the fact that there have been a number of things that have occurred. You will recall way back, there was a refusal to negotiate respecting the reunification of Austria. Well, that was accomplished. And down the road with respect to West Germany and so on, there have been other concessions; but they certainly come very rarely and from our viewpoint, at least, the refusals are so illogical that they do not promise a great deal for the establishment of a just peace. But, as I say, we have got to be ready, alert to opportunities to negotiate when there is any real promise of success, just as we are going to be strong and are strong and alert in making certain that others cannot take advantage of us or divide us by any kind of threat.

Q. Merriman Smith, United Press International: Mr. President, in this same vein there have been talks or reports from Moscow recently, talks of nonaggression pacts between Russia and certain other nations.

Do you have any reason to believe, sir, that a nonaggression pact with Soviet Russia today, without some element of control or inspection would have any more durability, validity, or value than agreements reached with Soviet Russia at Yalta, Potsdam, and Geneva?

THE PRESIDENT. Well, Mr. Smith, Mr. Dulles and I have always taken this position with respect to nonaggression pacts: everybody that is signatory to the United Nations agreement has already signed those pacts and therefore we see no need for them.

Now, on the other hand, I do not suppose we would have any great objection if there were in fact what you refer to as possibilities, practical possibilities for achieving confidence on each side that these treaties or this special treaty, rather than the general treaty, would be effectively carried out. And until you do have that kind of confidence coming out of some practical self-enforcing feature of the treaty, why then it would seem to me that they would have very little value.

Q. Rod MacLeish, Westinghouse Broadcasting Company: Sir, Khrushchev seems to be trying to get a summit conference instead of a foreign ministers conference.

Does this parliamentary or procedural difference change make any difference to us?

THE PRESIDENT. I would say this: all of you people are quite well acquainted with the constitutional difficulties that a President incurs when he goes abroad for one of these long conferences. But on top of that, there is this very great psychological reason: when the people of the world understand there is going to be a head of state or a head of government summit conference, they expect something to come out of it; and a feeling of pessimism and, in a way, hopelessness, I think, would be increased if you entered such a meeting and then nothing real came out of it as indeed, was the case at Geneva.

There was a great deal of talk about the spirit of Geneva, but frankly, before we went there, while we were there, and afterward, our Government said one thing: the proof of the sanity and the value of this Geneva meeting was going to be shown within the next few months when we went down to the concrete problems. And there we went over in October—the foreign ministers did—and we got exactly zero progress.

Now, I think it would be a very grave mistake to go to a summit conference unless there was some kind of preparation so that you could know the world could recognize the progress made.

Q. Peter Lisagor, Chicago Daily News: Mr. President, the Geneva talks on suspending nuclear tests have been dragging now for several months with the Russians seeming to insist upon a veto of the control system. Does the administration see any prospects of an agreement on that issue?

THE PRESIDENT. Well, frankly, I would say that hopes are not as strong as they were in the past.

We have, as you know, been quite ready to concede anything that did not seem to us absolutely needful in this regard. For example, at first we thought we should make any agreement about the cessation of tests a part of a major effort to reach general, or to begin general disarmament agreements.

Well, we said that isn't necessary, and so we receded from that. But we do say this: first, you cannot have a veto in any part of this process from the establishment of the control council right on down to the right of the groups to inspect the suspected areas at any moment. Any time you have a veto, the thing is defeated, and therefore what you might call the right, the inherent right of the parties to this agreement to make certain what has happened, if there is any physical evidence that something has happened, that right must be untrammeled.

That is what we have always insisted upon. In fact, it's a part of the basic feature we have always insisted upon. There must be some kind of substantive proof that we are each doing exactly what he promises to do. That's all there is to it.

And I'll tell you this: frankly, we very, very definitely want some kind of an agreement. We want to ease the tensions of the world, and I don't intend to make provocative speeches anywhere. I don't think it is good. But I do say this: we are going to be just as firm as anyone can be in maintaining the rights and the positions that we know are agreed upon, either in treaty or just in conformance with normal human decency.

Q. Robert G. Spivack, New York Post: This question is on a domestic problem, the matter of inflation.

Senator Kefauver has proposed that the steel industry forego a price increase if the steel union limits its wage demands to an amount equal to the average increase in productivity.

I'd like to know what you think about that proposal.

THE PRESIDENT. Well, I have not heard this particular one before.

Now, I have always urged that wage increases should be measured by increase of productivity, and I think that there would be no inflationary effect if they were measured by that criterion.

Now, exactly what the steel companies would have to have in this regard, it is possible they wouldn't have to have any increased price; I am talking a little bit out of my depth here because I am not an economist, but it looks to me like they wouldn't really have to have an increased cost if this wage drive was measured only by that single criterion.

I don't think the cost then should be any greater.

But, I will say this: we shouldn't be so prone, I think, to talk about and decry profits in our economy. You must remember that the people now expect all sorts of services from the Federal Government, starting with that of national defense and right on down to the last item that you want to find in HEW. We tax largely profits. We don't tax industrial activity as such, we tax profits. That is what the income tax is. So, if you are trying to get profits down to zero, you are going to have to find some other way of finding Federal revenue, ladies and gentlemen, if we are going to run this Government, I assure you.

Q. Felix Belair, New York Times: Mr. President, do you know from Mr. Dulles' doctors or otherwise whether there is a point at which you can determine, or the doctors, whether he will be able to resume full-time responsibility for the State Department?

THE PRESIDENT. Oh yes. There will come a point about this, and it will largely come between Mr. Dulles and myself. And I want to tell you this: don't think that Mr. Dulles wants a job—not by any manner of means. I have tried to make everybody see that here is a question of a man's dedication to duty and his loyalty to America.

Now, if he ever comes to the point that he cannot be restored to that degree of health where it will allow him to go and carry on his functions without hinder, as imposed by his physical condition, I know I couldn't possibly keep him.

There is no man that I admire and respect and like more than I do Mr. Dulles. But when it comes to that point, if it does, and I think all of us here of good heart would pray that it never comes, he is going to make that decision, make no mistake.

Q. Mr. Belair: Is there any indication when that time may come, I mean?

THE PRESIDENT. Well, when we found it the first time, we said it would be some weeks. Now, after all, I've forgotten the exact time that they said that this intensive period of treatment goes on. I think it will be shortly after that intensive treatment. Of course, after that, I think he would have to have some rest, because from what I understand, these things are not easy to take over the long period.

I must say this: he is reacting remarkably and the doctors are quite pleased with his progress today.

Q. William H. Lawrence, New York Times: Have you made any arrangements, sir, for direct consultations with Mr. Macmillan after he has concluded his talks in Moscow?

THE PRESIDENT. No, I haven't made any definite arrangements.

When he went there, there was some implication, understood implication, that he might find it necessary to report and discuss his findings and reactions in different capitals; he might even want to come here, but there has been nothing planned definitely.

Q. Mrs. May Craig, Portland (Maine) Press Herald: Mr. President, you have had several private talks that we know of with Senator Lyndon Johnson. Have you had similar talks with Speaker Rayburn, or is there a special area in which you need to talk to Senator Johnson?

THE PRESIDENT. The only time, I think, that you have to talk with the Leader of the Senate more than you do with the Speaker, is because you have the whole thing of confirmations and of treaties, and therefore a somewhat more intimate relationship to the whole business of foreign negotiation and activity. I think those would be the only places. And I must say, both these men, let's remember, are not only warm personal friends, but I think all of us have a common pride, understood by any other Texan, that we were all born in Texas. [*Laughter*] So I don't think there is any intimation whatsoever of differentiation, but it does happen in this one field you have more opportunities.

Q. Mrs. Craig: May I say the appropriations and taxes, of course, begin in the House.

THE PRESIDENT. Yes, but let me say this, too: it's very definitely a congressional thing to tax and to appropriate the money.

Q. Edward T. Folliard, Washington Post: Mr. President, this is a political question.

In your talk down at the National Press Club, you said that you could but would not give us a list of a half a dozen, ten, or a dozen men, fine, virile men, you described them, whom you would be glad to support for the Republican nomination for President.

THE PRESIDENT. No. I said support for election. Someone would have to nominate, because I said I would support them for election.

Q. Mr. Folliard: Well, that is weeks ago, and only two men are now talked about seriously for the Republican nomination. Do you think these, any of these 12 that you talked about will emerge, surface, so to speak? Would you encourage them to emerge? [*Laughter*]

THE PRESIDENT. I don't know of anyone that can do the job better than you people here.

This is what I believe—now, make no mistake, I am carefully avoiding saying that I am for or against anybody. But I do believe this: a political party has a certain facade, sort of, a certain face that becomes recognized. And I think that some of the features of this face have been distorted in popular conviction and imagination unfairly. I believe that we want a whole group of people that are dedicated to progress, to advancement both for our people, our economy, and our standing in the Nation, who are strong and can carry that kind of a policy and at the same time believe that we can destroy ourselves by unwise taxation, spending, and other economic features—we must not weaken ourselves that way.

Now that's the kind of a group that I'd like to see forming what I would call the facade of my particular political party.

Q. Laurence H. Burd, Chicago Tribune: Mr. President, the American Bar Association house of delegates in Chicago yesterday said that in view of the number of Supreme Court decisions on subversion that Congress should pass new laws tightening things up in this field.

Do you feel that gaps have been opened in this field by Supreme Court decisions and that new legislation is needed?

THE PRESIDENT. Well, Mr. Burd, I am not lawyer enough to say where, if any of these occur, they can be filled by legislation, and what other action would have to be taken, would be necessary.

I do want to establish my position that I have to take the law—and

I want to repeat this again—I have to take the law as it's interpreted by the Supreme Court, and that is the law of the land that I am called upon by oath to enforce.

Now, just what can be done, let's say, in spite of or because of Supreme Court decisions by the Congress itself to change that law, I am just not enough of a lawyer to know.

Q. Alan S. Emory, Watertown Times: Mr. President, the award by the Tennessee Valley Authority of a steam turbine contract to a British firm has aroused quite a bit of sentiment both in Congress and a number of localities around the country where heavy equipment is manufactured for restrictions on imports of this particular type of equipment.

Do you see any danger, sir, if this kind of outcry continues that Great Britain might decide to cut back on its recent liberalization of dollar trade?

THE PRESIDENT. Well, this calls, you might say, for a repetition of speeches that I have been trying to make for a long, long time.

I believe we have got to look at the welfare of all America. Now, ideally, we know that in each country in the world, the country ought to produce that thing for which itself is best suited and where its market is the most available. And then, it should buy those things it doesn't produce so well and sell these things in which it has great efficiency.

But all sorts of political bars have been produced through the years, and even the centuries, to impair the flow of trade that would come about because of a faithful adherence to this generalization. There are tariffs, there are cartels, there are quotas, there is every kind of thing in the world—monopolies. There is governmental purchase and selling, as opposed to a free enterprise system of buying and selling.

We are therefore not caught in an idealistic situation where you start, *de novo,* to solve a thing, you have to take the world as it now is. I believe that above everything else the United States should keep its cost down and try to liberalize trade. I believe that the reason we are having so much trouble competing with the other producing countries, not only within the neutral markets like Mexico, I think I gave you an example of that not long ago, but right here at home, we can't compete with them. Our costs are just too high. We cannot continue to increase these costs and have the kind of foreign trade that will make our own country prosperous.

Now, this means, of course, if you follow this thing in principle, you create different areas or particular points of difficulty. This is bad. We have got to take care of it, because these things have happened, again, by laws in the past. It's the whole purpose, though, of the Reciprocal Trade Act, not only started concretely in the time of Secretary Hull, but you go back to the time of McKinley and find that his finest speech was on reciprocal trade.

Everybody knows it must be done. The problem is, how do you get rid of the tremendous difficulties in order to make this reciprocal trade effective?

Now, here I think if we give way to the idea of just increasing tariffs along the line, and that is what you are implying by this question, I just believe we are making the gravest mistake we could make.

Q. Garnett D. Horner, Washington Star: Do you have any report, sir, on the condition of General Marshall, who is ill in North Carolina?

THE PRESIDENT. All I can say, Mr. Horner, is I keep in touch with General Marshall's condition daily, through the doctors at Walter Reed and my own doctor. And there is this, that with this second stroke he had, no question that it is a very, very serious illness; but so far as I can determine from the way they talk to me, he is progressing satisfactorily— satisfactorily is probably not the word; as good as could be expected. Now, I don't know that any of them have made any prognosis for me, but they are watching. That's all that I can say.

Q. John Scali, Associated Press: Another question on Secretary Dulles, sir.

THE PRESIDENT. Yes.

Q. Mr. Scali: During the past few days several Democratic Senators have suggested that you promptly replace Secretary Dulles with a successor. What do you think of such a suggestion?

THE PRESIDENT. Well, I'll try to be mild. [*Laughter*]

I would say this: those men, such as Senator Mansfield, Senator Sparkman, Senator Kennedy, Senator Capehart, who have publicly recognized the great value of Secretary Dulles to the United States and who have expressed very prayerfully their great hope that he will be spared to go on with this work, and that we can make arrangements until he can be so spared, if his health will permit, I think they are thinking of nothing but the welfare of the United States of America.

Q. James B. Reston, New York Times: Would you discuss with us, sir, the strategy in central Europe of how we do defend our rights in Berlin?

THE PRESIDENT. I can say this only: this is a matter that has been under discussion, under agreements by the several allies involved. It has been, of course, a part of the NATO discussions and decisions. I believe that the plans that they have made have never been published, so I couldn't talk about any details. But I can say this: that so far as I know, so far as any bit of information has ever come to me, all of these countries stand with us in the absolute necessity of being firm and defending those rights.

I can't say anything about any definite features of a plan.

Q. Mr. Reston: Is it proper to infer from that, sir, that you would believe if we were stopped from going into Berlin that the treaty, the NATO treaty would be invoked at that point?

THE PRESIDENT. I didn't say—no, I don't know that. I said this, I believe, here only last week or maybe it was two weeks ago: that so far as we were concerned, any act of actual war would have to be started, committed by someone else.

Now, that's the place where we stand.

Q. Sarah McClendon, Manchester (N.H.) Union Leader: Mr. President, since your budget came out many of the military experts have gone to the Capitol and they have testified; there have been great discrepancies in their testimony as to whether we have adequate defense.

Since that has come about, is there not some way to avoid public confidence being undermined and in view of the international situation, is there not some way that we can get these leaders and yourself to arrive at a reconciliation of views as to what we actually need for defense?

THE PRESIDENT. Well, I'm a little astonished at that question. I have been, certainly, all my life in this same problem. For the last 6 years I have had the final responsibility so far as the executive department and my position as Commander in Chief are concerned.

Now, very naturally there are conflicting views in any proposal that humans make. I would doubt that you could find any three people sitting in this room who, with respect to their idea of the way a newspaper ought to be operated, would give you identical views. [*Laughter*]

Now, you are certainly not going to get such identical views in people who, themselves, believe that in their service, in their own function, lies the safety of the United States. Someone has to make the decision. That happens to be the Commander in Chief.

I must say this, and I think possibly this is the first time that I have ever violated my own conception of humility and modesty: I think I am more able than any one of those individuals of whom you speak to make an overall decision on behalf of the United States in this vital matter, because I again assure you that just spending money does not make us stronger. Indeed, if you spend too much money, you will make us weaker. That is when the nicety of judgment comes in—what do we need; get that; get that by all means, and get no more.

Remember, our system is a balanced one. We should not concern ourselves so much with one single item. Somebody makes a demagogic talk about a missile, or somebody else about a different submarine or a piece of radar. You have got a whole level of balanced types of equipment, training, organization, and strategy that we believe fits our system.

As a matter of fact, just 2 or 3 nights ago Admiral Burke made a speech somewhere, I believe in Carolina, on this subject, and I thought it was indeed good.

Q. Charles W. Baily, Minneapolis Star and Tribune: A group of North Dakotans are down here today to talk to you about an irrigation project in their State. I wondered if you could tell us, does your "no new starts" policy—not starting any new construction of reclamation projects—does that extend to the withholding by the administration of reports from the Interior Department on the feasibility of future projects?

THE PRESIDENT. Oh, no. As a matter of fact, I have not only always urged studies, but a long time ago I got a Special Assistant, General Bragdon, and his whole purpose is to go over the whole field of public works in which the Federal Government participates. Indeed, he meets with the planning commissions and officers of each of the States in their conferences so as to coordinate these things so we can get the best value out of them.

But, to stop studying analyses or reports from the Interior, that would be the last thing I would ever think of.

Marvin L. Arrowsmith, Associated Press: Thank you, Mr. President.

NOTE: President Eisenhower's one hundred and fifty-second news conference was held in the Executive Office Building from 10:30 to 11:04 o'clock on Wednesday morning, February 25, 1959. In attendance: 229.

43 ¶ Remarks at the U.S. Savings Bond Conference. *February* 25, 1959

Mr. Secretary, Gentlemen:

I am delighted to be with you for a few moments this morning. I want to thank you for what you have done on behalf of the savings bond campaign and through that on behalf of the United States of America for its fiscal integrity and its economic soundness.

I have been told by the Secretary that through the efforts of this group, 40 percent of our savings bonds are accounted for by the enrollees in the various organizations that you people head or direct. That kind of record speaks for itself.

The readiness of our people to invest their savings into bonds is one of the features that we must count upon, if we are to have a successful America; if we are going to be able confidently and permanently to counter the Soviet threat to our form of life. It is the kind of thing that bespeaks morale and faith in America. Certainly without this kind of work, the debt management by the Federal Treasury would be much more difficult—I would say well-nigh impossible. And when we think that our debt is in the range where already we are spending for interest alone, without a single cent devoted to debt retirement, some eight billion dollars, we realize the kind of volume of work of which you are speaking.

Faith in our bonds certainly connotes a sound dollar. It means confidence in the American dollar, and confidence in the American dollar is certainly vital to our economic growth and expansion. If we are to keep this dollar sound, there are numbers of things that must be done—some by the individual citizen, some by business leaders, some by labor leaders, some by such organisms as the Federal Reserve Board, and some by the Federal Government directly.

One of the duties of the Federal Government is to be careful in expenditures—to make certain that it provides for the necessary operations of the Federal Government and does not waste a cent otherwise. We must do this in such a way as to live within our means. Certainly this is important. It is vital, when we are on a leg of a rising economic cycle. We simply cannot afford to be living now on deficit spending, no matter how much this might be justified in times of grave emergency or very unusual circumstances.

Now, we have many among us who are calling for heavier and heavier expenditures, saying that these heavier expenditures on the part of the Federal Government would mean and, in effect would cause, economic expansion. I cannot think of any doctrine or any statement that is so false as this one.

If the 174 million people of America don't know more about the spending of such money than does the Federal Government, then I for one submit we are getting in an awful fix. This is exactly what we do not want to do: appear under some kind of doctrine, making decisions of what the populace of our country want, what they desire and what they should have. These decisions to the major extent, to the most major extent you can possibly conceive of, should be in the hands of the people and in the localities where they live.

This cry for Federal expenditures claims as one of its features that we are tailoring all our expenditures to fit the possibility of a balanced budget.

Well now, let me say first: I don't know why a balanced budget should be a bad word, although some seem to think it is.

What we are talking about is this: finding out what is necessary. We know that we have to meet the Soviet threat. We know that for some years to come expenditures for this function are incalculable, they are almost astronomical—if I knew of a stronger adjective, I would use it. I would use everything except preposterous, because we have to do it.

But, if we are going to maintain our economic soundness, we do have to pay the interest on our debts, and we have to do those things that could be classed as necessary—of high priority in our whole Federal field. But each should be arranged in accordance to its importance and its priority. We must always remember that if the pressures of any particular group or a combination of groups keep us in an area of deficit spending—in order to get for the moment more dollars for itself—that will defeat not only the country but each group. This will be so because each such pressure group action will so depreciate our money that in the long run they won't be getting even so much as they thought they were. And certainly, what they will do to the United States will be terrible.

I have a little passage I want to read, so I do not make any mistakes in what I am trying to say. The fact of the matter is that there is nothing which is more positive and more important to be for than fiscal soundness—in spite of these people of whom I spoke, who said that if you believe in fiscal soundness then you are against everything that America needs. So I say, the most important factor to be for is fiscal soundness. This is an essential condition of our economic health. Without it we can have neither adequate military security nor the adequate provision of other needed services.

Let us not be misled. A balanced budget and all that it means today in the way of fiscal soundness is a highly positive objective. It is the advocates of unbalanced budgets and deficit spending in our present economic environment who are against rather than for the maintenance of healthy growth in America.

When the Government spends more money than it is getting in the form of taxes, the Treasury must do just exactly what a family or a business would have to do, under similar circumstances: it must go out and borrow whatever is needed to finish paying the bills. When part of the borrowing it must undertake comes from commercial banks, the money supply is increased and the conditions are created for an inflationary price rise. Inflation weakens the economy. It brings serious hardship to those of our citizens who are living on pensions or other fixed incomes, and works against those who are unable to bargain effectively for higher wages. Most dangerous of all, inflation weakens the incentive to save. It gives rise to a fear that the dollar will continue to decline in value and that speculation will be the only way to keep ahead of the game.

Secretary Anderson said just recently that if we ever do reach the point where people believe that speculation is safe and saving is a gamble then we are indeed in serious trouble.

Now my friends, I spoke about the Soviet menace. It is something that we have learned and are learning always to live with because it cannot be eliminated merely by wishful thinking. We can be strong in our understanding and in our intellects, in our spirit—meaning our morale— in our economy and in our military, to make sure that the United States will not have its rights violated or be unable to perform its responsibilities in the world.

But we can do all that and do it indefinitely and still have a sound and expanding economy, the kind of economy that will support and maintain that defense, if we will—each of us—only remember what are the stakes in this great struggle.

So I leave you by saying merely: savings, and the incentive to save, built this country.

We must not destroy this incentive. It is my conviction that the work you people here are doing is one of the vital steps in saving that incentive.

Thank you very much.

NOTE: The President spoke at the Sheraton-Park Hotel, Washington, D.C.

The Conference, attended by representatives of business and industrial concerns, was arranged by the Savings Bonds Division of the Treasury Department to solicit aid in promoting greater participation in payroll savings plans.

44 ¶ Remarks at the Dedication of a Statue of Simon Bolivar Presented by Venezuela. *February* 27, 1959

Dr. Uslar Pietri, Mr. Secretary, Your Excellencies, Distinguished Guests, Friends:

It is indeed a great honor to join with you in the dedication of this impressive statue to the memory of Simon Bolivar. He was the hero of more than two hundred battles for the emancipation of man from foreign bondage and for the democratic way of life.

In times of crises and hardship, every nation produces its heroes, its leaders. Many are good. Few are great. But on occasion a leader emerges whose goodness and whose greatness reach far beyond his own country and beyond his own time. Simon Bolivar was one of these. He belongs to your nation, surely. But the world claims him, too, as one of the true benefactors of mankind.

Liberator of half a continent, prophet and precursor of Pan American union, Simon Bolivar will long be remembered for his enduring contribution in the struggle for unity and independence in the New World.

He represents one of history's most brilliant personifications of adventure, tragedy, and glory.

The Venezuelan people have steadfastly maintained their faith in the ultimate realization of Bolivar's democratic ideals. It is therefore fitting that this ceremony should follow closely upon the inauguration of President Betancourt, chosen by his countrymen in an election so conducted as to typify the true meaning of democracy.

I cannot think of a more appropriate tribute to the Great Liberator and the principles for which he fought than this further evidence, as President

Betancourt has aptly described it, of the aptitude and capacity of the Venezuelan people to exercise their democratic prerogatives. The realization of Bolivar's dream in Venezuela through the determined efforts of his people is of the greatest importance in furthering the democratic aspirations of the American peoples throughout the hemisphere.

This dedication, then, will symbolize our mutual will to live and work together, in ever-increasing undertanding, for the common prosperity of our two nations.

Thank you very much.

NOTE: The statue was presented to the Government of the United States by the Government of Venezuela. The dedication ceremony was held at the Simon Bolivar Plaza, Virginia Avenue and 18th Street NW., Washington, D.C.

The President's opening words "Dr. Uslar Pietri, Mr. Secretary" referred to Dr. Arturo Uslar Pietri, Personal Representative of the President of Venezuela and head of the Venezuelan delegation to the dedication, and Christian A. Herter, Acting Secretary of State.

45 ¶ Statement by the President Recorded for the Opening of the Red Cross Campaign. *March 1, 1959*

My Fellow Americans:

At this time each year, it is my privilege to remind you that the month of March is "Red Cross Month." This is the time when we may pledge renewed support to those who serve us through the Red Cross.

Many years ago the founder of the Red Cross, Clara Barton, said that her organization stood for: "a peoples' help for the nation." That help has surely been given in full measure. It has been given to families crushed by disaster; it has been given to our men and women in uniform; it has been given to the victims of disease and accident. The pioneer work of Red Cross in Nursing, in First Aid, in Water Safety, and in many other community services has improved the lot of us all. This "peoples' help for the nation" continues unabated. Indeed, the work of the Red Cross has been accelerated by the growth of America's responsibilities and population.

The National Headquarters of the Red Cross is only a few blocks from the White House, and as Honorary Chairman I am kept informed of its work. For example, in mid-January I received a distressing report from the flooded areas of Ohio, Pennsylvania, and bordering States. I was glad to learn that emergency help was being given there to nearly twenty-two thousand families that had been driven from their homes. I know we must do our part now to see that the Red Cross has the money, the volunteers, and the enthusiastic support it needs to do the work which we expect it to do for us.

In some three thousand communities across the country, the Red Cross will ask for our support during the coming month—in its annual compaign for members and funds.

I urge you to give generously and offer to serve in the ranks of the Red Cross insofar as you are able. Such an organization needs both money and volunteers to do its neighborly work—in our land and around the world.

46 ¶ Letter to T. Keith Glennan, Administrator, National Aeronautics and Space Administration, Following the Launching of Space Probe Pioneer IV. *March 3, 1959*

Dear Dr. Glennan:

The successful launching early today of the space probe, Pioneer IV, marks yet another major step in scientific space exploration. The scientific information that is being sent back by its instruments should provide important additions to man's knowledge of the universe.

Please convey my warm congratulations for this splendid achievement to all who contributed to it in your own agency, in the Army, and among your scientific associates.

Sincerely,

DWIGHT D. EISENHOWER

47 ¶ Letter to the President of the Senate and to the Speaker of the House of Representatives Proposing Establishment of a Special Commission on Telecommunications. *March 3,* 1959

Dear —————:

The telecommunication systems of the United States are essential to the national security, to the safety of life and property, to international relations, to a better-informed public, and to the business, social, educational, religious and political life of the country. They are one of the Nation's most valuable assets.

Changing technology along with changing needs in Government and non-Government areas present problems in the telecommunication field which require searching examination. The situation is becoming no less complicated by prospective developments in satellites and space vehicles, as well as in defense weapons systems.

The Director of the Office of Civil and Defense Mobilization, on my behalf, convened a Special Advisory Committee on Telecommunication November 18, 1958, to review the role of the Federal Government in the management of telecommunications. The report of that Committee is now under study within the Administration.

It was not possible for the Special Advisory Committee during its brief existence to undertake a thorough and comprehensive study of the Government's role or to make detailed studies of such problems as radio frequency usage.

In order that such a study can be made, I recommend that the Congress establish a Special Commission on Telecommunications, to be composed of five members appointed by the President.

I have asked the Director of the Office of Civil and Defense Mobilization to transmit to you a draft of suggested legislation to carry out this recommendation, and to convey to you the details involved in the suggested studies, as recommended in the report of the Special Advisory Committee.

Sincerely,

DWIGHT D. EISENHOWER

NOTE: This is the text of identical letters addressed to the Honorable Richard M. Nixon, President of the Senate, and to ˋ the Honorable Sam Rayburn, Speaker of the House of Representatives.

The report of the Special Advisory Committee on Telecommunications, dated December 29, 1958 (31 pp., mimeographed), was released by the Office of Civil and Defense Mobilization.

The draft bill transmitted to the Congress by the Director of the Office of Civil and Defense Mobilization was incorporated in H.J. Res. 331 and S.J. Res. 76.

48 ¶ The President's News Conference of *March* 4, 1959.

THE PRESIDENT. I just had a message from Walter Reed, said that the Secretary was doing very well indeed and had reacted beautifully to this special treatment they gave him yesterday.

Q. Merriman Smith, United Press International: Mr. President, against the background of continuing tension between the East and West, could we ask, for a moment, about the debated need for increasing the defense strength of this country?

I ask specifically, sir, whether you feel that the present 15 minute ground alert for SAC is sufficient, or would you prefer, in times such as these, to have an airborne alert?

THE PRESIDENT. Well, no. I think the alert that is now observed is a good one, and certainly satisfactory for the present moment.

An air alert would be really worse than useless as defense against bombers. You would be much better to have your bombers on the ground.

Now the day will come when the principal threat, if this situation develops along the lines that it appears to be going—now at that time there will probably be a need for air alert; that is, some of your bombers in the air. They will have to be, of course, refueled more quickly because of the fact that they will have lost much of their fuel during their alert basis.

But at this moment, I would say the measures taken by the Defense Department are completely appropriate.

Q. John Scali, Associated Press: Mr. President, you have said there is no room for negotiation with the Soviets in our determination to uphold all our rights and responsibilities in Berlin.

Now, both the Republican and Democratic Parties appear united behind this stand. However, a number of persons, including former Secretary of State Acheson, have suggested that we take some concrete steps in advance to make it clear to the Soviets that we are absolutely determined to remove all obstacles which might be put in the way of access to and from Berlin, both on the land and in the air.

Among the suggestions that have been put forward have been an immediate mobilization of NATO defense forces, both on the land and in the air, with the return to the Continent of British and French divisions, possibly with Turkish and Italian reinforcements, as well as some steps at home to show that we are determined to see this thing through.

Could you comment on this thesis?

THE PRESIDENT. Well, you start off with this statement, that I said there was no room for negotiation.

Of course I always say there is room for negotiation. The only place that I said that we—they must be perfectly clear in their minds that we will not retreat from the exercise of the rights that are ours with respect to Berlin, and to carry the responsibilities that are laid upon us by these international agreements until eventually there is a new solution for the German problem.

But, our readiness to negotiate with respect to German peace and everything else has not only been emphasized time and again; if there were indeed no room for negotiation there, then there certainly would be no reason for any kind of a meeting.

Now, did you ever stop to think what a general mobilization would mean in a time of tension?

Ladies and gentlemen, we have been under periods of tension since '49, certainly—it was either '48 or '49 in the first Berlin situation.

Now, if you are going to keep a general mobilization for a long time in countries—democracies—such as ours, well, there is just one thing you have and that is a garrison state. General mobilization means all kinds of diversion of materials and other kinds of resources from the operation of a free economy; it means keeping your nation on a basis of readiness all the time.

This is, to my mind, not only futile; this would be the most disastrous thing we could do.

Q. James B. Reston, New York Times: Mr. President, when Mr. Dulles was in the hospital the first time, I recall that you suggested to

General Walter Bedell Smith that he come into the White House to assist you in the field of foreign affairs. Now, what happened to that idea at that time, and do you think it has any validity?

THE PRESIDENT. Do you think that I suggested that he come in?

Q. Mr. Reston: Yes, sir.

THE PRESIDENT. No. I have had General Smith, from time to time, talking to me, questions with which we'd both been familiar in the past. I don't think I ever asked him as a permanent adviser, at least I don't recall it if I did, Mr. Reston. And it has not been suggested at this moment.

Q. Garnett D. Horner, Washington Star: This question arises, sir, from a statement by Secretary of Defense McElroy in testimony before a House committee Monday—that, while it is still our policy not to strike the first blow in any possible future war, whether that is always true in the future is another matter.

Could you say if you can foresee any circumstances in which we might, so to speak, strike the first blow against a possible aggressor?

THE PRESIDENT. No, Mr. Horner. I will discuss that for a moment in this fashion: the right of self-preservation is just as instinctive and natural for a nation as it is for the individual. Therefore, if we know we are, at any moment, under a threat of attack, as would be evidenced by missiles or planes coming in our direction, then we have to act just as rapidly as is possible, humanly possible to defend ourselves.

But when you go beyond that point, I don't know exactly what this conversation meant, for the simple reason that I'm quite sure the Congress is not thinking of amending the Constitution and putting in the hands of the President the right to declare war. This is a congressional function and it must be observed. But I do point out that when you have got certain circumstances that put your life or could put your life or the Nation's life right at stake, then there is no time, and whatever would be necessary the President would then order.

Now, you know I'm certainly far from a complacent person. On the other hand, I don't think we ought to be thinking all the time, every minute, that while we are sitting here, we are very apt to get a bombing attack on Washington. The reason we have very great and expensive intelligence forces is to keep us informed as well as they possibly can. So, I don't believe we ought to be arguing some points too much, of this kind, because I believe we create more misapprehension than we do understanding.

Q. Carleton Kent, Chicago Sun-Times: Mr. President, last week a White House caller reported that you had sent a letter to Governor Rockefeller commiserating with him on his budget troubles. Could you tell us something of what you said to him and whether he replied, and what was in the reply?

THE PRESIDENT. Who told you this? [*Laughter*]

Q. Mr. Kent: Well, the Senator who called at the White House.

THE PRESIDENT. Well, I remember that I sent Nelson Rockefeller a note a couple of weeks ago. It certainly didn't require any answer, and I don't remember exactly what I said; but I do remember that I said we were at least two people that believe we ought to live within our means.

I didn't say anything about how you did it, but I did say that. [*Laughter*]

Q. Robert C. Pierpoint, CBS News: What is your reaction to the Russian note, or to the terms set forth by the Russians in that recent note proposing a foreign ministers conference?

THE PRESIDENT. As you know, this note, as usual, is very, very long, and of course it takes long and earnest study by our staffs before any detailed comment would be in order.

It starts off, of course, on the negative side, with the usual—oh, repetitions of their great efforts toward peace, charging us with all sorts of evil intentions. And it is filled with distortions.

There is one of them, by the way, I think I ought to correct. It is to the general effect that the United States, or the West, has rushed right in after the war to rearm West Germany. Now, there was no rearmament of West Germany that started at all until after West Germany had become a member of NATO in 1954.

East Germany had 50,000 troops under arms in 1950, and by 1953, had some 225–240,000 under arms in East Germany.

So this kind of distortion is the thing that we find constantly in the propaganda coming from the other side.

Now, on the more hopeful and positive side, you will find in the final paragraphs the admission that there could be something done by foreign ministers rather than heads of state, and indicating some—oh, lessening of the rigidity of the propositions they have heretofore advanced, certainly in the notes of, I think it was last November and of January.

So I would say: well now, you have at least that on the positive side; we are taking it for the moment just as optimistically as we can and, certainly, with our allies we will study how we can make any answer that could be constructive.

Q. Peter Lisagor, Chicago Daily News: Mr. President, in the past our position has been that we would not talk about Berlin as a free and demilitarized free city, or about separate peace treaties with West and East Germany.

From what you have just said, do you mean now that we might indeed go and talk to them about these problems at a foreign ministers conference?

THE PRESIDENT. No. I said that with respect to West Berlin and our rights and our responsibilities we could not abandon them, we never would abandon them. That is what I said.

Now, within the whole field of a peace treaty there could be very many different types of solutions, propositions, advanced; and I think all of them would have to be discussed in, as far as you could, a constructive manner.

Let's remember this: our policy and our agreement in 1955 at Geneva was that Germany would be reunited by means of free elections. For the moment, that has certainly been thrown overboard by the Soviets. They say the only possibility is by negotiation between these two separate Germanys.

Well, I don't see how that can possibly be a feature of any proposal made now. We stand, with our allies, as our policy is that the uniting of Germany would come about, should be by free elections.

Q. Mrs. May Craig, Portland (Maine) Press Herald: Mr. President, the Khrushchev-Macmillan communique praises an increase of trade between Britain and the Soviet Union, and said that a British trade mission would come soon to Moscow to increase it still further.

We had understood that the United States turned down Mr. Mikoyan's proposal for more trade on credit, particularly because of the slave labor there, and particularly also because they haven't paid us what they owe us.

Has there been or will there be a change in our trade policy toward the Soviet Union?

THE PRESIDENT. Well, Mrs. Craig, all I can say there, is this: there is a continuing committee, both in the State Department, and then it meets, you know, in Europe each year on the allied position on this business of trade with the Communists.

There have been changes made in not so much our policies but you might say in our specific items in which we are ready to see other countries trade. I do not believe that at this moment we are ready for any radical change in policy with respect to trade.

Q. Chalmers M. Roberts, Washington Post: Mr. President, Prime Minister Macmillan said in Moscow that he had advanced some new ideas, or tentative ideas on breaking the Geneva nuclear test suspension deadlock, and the British say that these were discussed with you before they were submitted.

Could you tell us something of the approach involved in this?

THE PRESIDENT. It is perfectly true that Mr. Macmillan had some different ideas than we have had expressed, and the study that we have given them so far does not reassure us that they are completely practical.

However, we have had no objection whatsoever to his bringing up these new ideas on his own, and to come back to us with such information as he could get. But I am not at liberty to discuss the details of what he suggested to me.

Q. Mr. Roberts: Could you say, sir, whether it involves the idea of establishing a threshold below which certain types of, say, underground explosions would be permitted?

THE PRESIDENT. I think I'd better not go any further into the details, Mr. Roberts.

Q. Kenneth M. Scheibel, Gannett Newspapers: Getting back to Governor Rockefeller, do you think that the stand that he has made on the budget issue in New York will advance or deter his chance of being the presidential nominee next year?

THE PRESIDENT. Well, now, there have been a number of things on my mind this week since I saw you, but that has not been one of them. [*Laughter*]

And I'll tell you this: at this distance, I am not one either to agree or disagree with the details of his budgetary plan, or to disagree and agree with his critics. I don't know enough about it.

I know what I read in the papers, and I know that he's got his troubles;

but he apparently is trying to attack it honestly, and if he attacks it honestly, why, there can be no great scar left on the solution that is attained.

Q. Roscoe Drummond, New York Herald Tribune: Mr. President, on the basis of what was said on both sides in Moscow, do you feel that Mr. Macmillan's visit has served a useful purpose, as far as practical or end results are concerned?

THE PRESIDENT. I think, Mr. Drummond, it's very difficult to speculate too much about that. But I will say this: I feel, frankly, it was a trip that had to be made, and since there were some moments that were a bit brighter than the others, because there were some places that it was quite dark, I think, all in all, certainly all Britain would feel better by the fact that he did go and see and talk.

Now, when you come down to the possibility that there may have been some lessening of this rigidity of which I speak in the Soviet attitude, that we can't tell until events unfold a little bit further.

Q. Charles W. Roberts, Newsweek: Sir, the Times of London and other British papers are saying today that because of Secretary Dulles' illness, the leadership of the Western World in the cold war has passed to Great Britain.

Do you feel that they must take a greater share of leadership in this situation?

THE PRESIDENT. Well, I never think of this business as resting exclusively upon individuals.

The United States has a present position that is unlike that of any other country, in the free world. Because of that position, American policy, American statement, American action is very significant, and that is what makes America a leader in the whole free world.

With respect to Secretary Dulles' illness, all of us, of course, deplore the absence of a man from his post who is so experienced, so wise, and so strong as this one.

Well, let's remember that he has been, over the years, himself selecting and training a team. There is a tremendous depth in the State Department of knowledge and understanding and capacity. And finally, whether I like it or not, I am constitutionally responsible for the conduct of the foreign affairs of the United States, and no two men have ever had a closer association and collaboration in such problems as these as have Secretary Dulles and I.

Now, I just can't tell what is going to be the length of time in which we'll have a relationship of this kind and a system of this kind, how long it's going to endure. We do have an Acting Secretary and he is responsible until I have designated someone else, or designated him in another capacity.

Q. Edward T. Folliard, Washington Post: Mr. President, the story is going around again that Mr. McElroy is going to resign as Secretary of Defense, and this has led to some criticism. The argument is that Mr. McElroy is thinking about leaving just about the time he has caught on to the job. The argument goes further that a successor, if he is another businessman, will just about have caught on to the job when your administration comes to an end.

Some people, including Walter Lippmann, think this job ought to go to a man versed in the art of government, in other words, a politician.

How do you feel about that, Mr. President?

THE PRESIDENT. I would just say this: I have been absolutely satisfied with Mr. McElroy's performance. I think he has learned his job quickly, and I think he has acted like a statesman and a very splendid public servant.

Now, I'm going to keep him just as long as I can, although I recall that when he accepted this post, he did say that he would have, sooner or later, to look to his own affairs, and he couldn't promise definitely that he could last out the whole tour. But, I'll say this: I know his sense of duty, and if things got tighter, well I think he'd forget all the rest of it at the time because he wouldn't want to break up the team then for anybody.

Q. David P. Sentner, Hearst Newspapers: Mr. President, what significance do you attach to the exploits of Pioneer IV?

THE PRESIDENT. I have been talking to the scientists about this, and of course I was highly pleased that the test came off as they planned. As you know, they did not plan to orbit the moon. Actually, my latest information as I came in here was that the thing was exactly 203,000 miles from us as we started this talk, but it's going past the moon I think on the order of about 37,000, plus or minus 2,000; it will be orbiting around the sun; and its signals, the signals it has transmitted, have been most interesting to our scientists, particularly in giving additional information on this belt of radioactivity that has been discovered around the earth and is of such tremendous interest to our scientists. That's about the answer.

Q. Gordon E. White, Chicago American: Mr. President, recalling that you won your first nomination in Chicago in '52, do you have any sentimental desire for the Republican Party to return to Chicago for its '60 convention? [*Laughter*]

THE PRESIDENT. I'll leave that to them. No, I have no feeling about it whatsoever.

Q. Sarah McClendon, Camden Courier-Post: Sir, this has to do with the nuclear ship *Savannah*——

THE PRESIDENT. Go right ahead, Mrs. McClendon.

Q. Mrs. McClendon: Thank you. This has to do with the nuclear ship *Savannah,* the first in history, and the cargo vessel you were so interested in.

THE PRESIDENT. Yes.

Q. Mrs. McClendon: About 2 weeks ago, New York Shipbuilding wrote a letter with the acceptance of the Maritime Administration, a letter to you, asking that you be the principal visitor and Mrs. Eisenhower sponsor this ship next July or August, depending upon your convenience; and they are very anxious to know if you would like to come——

THE PRESIDENT. Well, I'll tell you, just before Mrs. Eisenhower left she told me she had been invited to sponsor it, but she took a look and she said she'd have to come back and do a little bit more studying before she could give any answer to this thing.

Q. William McGaffin, Chicago Daily News: Mr. President, there is a report that the Democrats in Congress plan to hold back about $3 million [$3 billion] of the supplementals that you have requested for fiscal '59, and vote them in fiscal '60 instead. Their aim would be to make you unbalance your budget with your own requests. Have you any comment, sir?

THE PRESIDENT. Well, remember, balancing the budget is not of interest merely to ourselves. Our friends, the nations with whom we trade, the nations that are increasingly using the dollar as a medium of exchange, they are interested in the knowledge that we can pay our bills.

Now, we have had this very bad year from the standpoint of budgetary balance in 1957, when income was way down, and the expenditures, some of it due to one reason or other—one, to help increase employment, and the other brought about by sputnik complexes—caused a big gap.

Now, as quickly as we can get back to a pay-as-you-go basis, the freer the world will feel about this whole affair. Therefore, to unbalance a budget for political purposes, I couldn't imagine anything worse.

Now, I agree there are arguments to be brought about if you are going to take substantive matters of the needs of this country. I may think something is a luxury, someone else may think it's a need, but I have used my best judgment. I have used the judgment of all the advisers I can get in the whole administration to put down a balanced budget. That, to my mind, is one of the things that will keep our dollar stable, it will be one of the great influences in keeping the living costs from going up; and above all, it will be one of the things to inspire more confidence throughout the world in the American currency and American economy.

Q. Richard L. Wilson, Cowles Publications: In the communique issued by Macmillan and Khrushchev there was a reference to some kind of inspection and control within an agreed area of Europe.

I would like to ask if you have any renewed interest in the general idea of troop withdrawals or disengagement in central Europe?

THE PRESIDENT. I think the things of which you speak, if they ever come about, must be within a general agreement in which we have confidence.

I repeat, time and time and again, that any agreement in which we can have confidence and therefore take appropriate and accompanying actions such as some reduction in forces and reduction in alerts and reduction in expenditures, that must come about if there is some, you might say, self-enforcing element in these agreements so that we can have confidence.

I think, therefore, what we are talking about now are details of such a thing.

I believe you can start both from the general and from the detailed end. If you can take one problem, for example, inspection—there can be inspections which could be controlled; that's coming in it from the detailed angle. If you take from the general, then you have to have a stronger and better evidence of confidence on both sides.

Q. J. F. Ter Horst, Detroit News: Sir, a few moments ago you said that you thought the British people felt better because Mr. Macmillan had gotten together with Mr. Khrushchev.

Do you think the American people would feel better if you got together with this same gentleman?

THE PRESIDENT. No, it wouldn't necessarily—the cases wouldn't be the same.

For a long time there has been a great deal of pressure in his country for a meeting between himself and Mr. Khrushchev, and he did owe Mr. Khrushchev a return call from about a year or a year and a half ago; so there was no reason he shouldn't do this and nothing necessarily was expected out of it.

What I keep deploring is this idea of talking about summit meetings when you cannot see any possibility of a constructive step coming out of it. And if a constructive step does not come out of such a meeting, then in my mind the meeting should not be held.

Q. Edward P. Morgan, American Broadcasting Company: Along that same line, Mr. President, Mr. Khrushchev seems to have developed the unfortunate talent of being able to turn on and off international crises at will.

Under the curious circumstances that exist, including those of propaganda, do you feel that this is an international fact of life, so to speak, that we simply have to endure, or are there real ways in which we can put him diplomatically on the defensive?

THE PRESIDENT. Well, I think here and there you can; but the trouble of it is, here is a very strident and a very, you might say, pervasive propaganda machine, and it's being used to the very limit of capacity.

I don't mean to say that this can't be done once in a while, but we seem to understand it—I mean we as a people—more than it seems to get understood around the earth.

But, as to living with it, I would say this, Mr. Morgan: we are living in sort of a half world in so many things. We are not fighting a war, we are not killing each other, we are not going to the ultimate horror. On the other side of the picture, we are not living the kind of normal, what we'd like to call a normal life of thinking more of our own affairs, of thinking of the education and happiness of our children, and all that sort of thing that should occupy our minds.

Now, in many ways we are doing that, and one of the manifestations of that thing is this kind of propaganda and sometimes vituperation that is just poured at us all the time.

Therefore, we have two problems: one, not to allow ourselves to get thrown off balance, to get frightened, to get hysterical about the thing;

but on the other hand, don't be so indifferent that we are certain that it's just a cry of "Wolf."

We just must not ever be indifferent to what is happening in the world today.

Marvin L. Arrowsmith, Associated Press: Thank you, Mr. President.

NOTE: President Eisenhower's one hundred and fifty-third news conference was held in the Executive Office Building from 10:30 to 11:04 o'clock on Wednesday morning, March 4, 1959. In attendance: 236.

49 ¶ Letter to Secretary Flemming Reconstituting the Federal Council on Aging at Cabinet Level. *March 7,* 1959

Dear Mr. Secretary:

In recognition of the growing national importance of the needs and problems of our aging population, I have concluded that the present Federal Council on Aging, established by Presidential memorandum of April 2, 1956, should be strengthened.

The various resources and programs of the Federal Government must be utilized and coordinated in such a way as to provide maximum assistance in this field, consistent with Federal responsibility to State and local governments, to private groups, and to individuals themselves.

Accordingly, I am hereby reconstituting the Federal Council on Aging at Cabinet level.

It is my desire that this Council aid the various Federal agencies in improving the effectiveness of their programs in the field of aging.

The Council will be composed of the Secretary of Health, Education, and Welfare as Chairman, and of the following additional members:

The Secretary of Agriculture
The Secretary of Commerce
The Secretary of Labor
The Secretary of the Treasury
The Administrator of the Housing and Home Finance Agency
The Administrator of Veterans Affairs

I shall expect you as Chairman of the Council to invite those Federal departments and agencies that are not permanent members of the Council such as the Department of Defense, Civil Service Commission, Railroad Retirement Board, and National Science Foundation to participate when matters which are in their areas of responsibility come under consideration by the Council.   Provision also will be made for the Department of State and the Bureau of the Budget to have observers attend meetings of the Council.

Federal departments and agencies in their respective areas will continue to carry out their individual statutory responsibilities in the field of aging, cooperating with one another through the Council where appropriate and furnishing the Council such information and assistance, not inconsistent with law, as may be required for this cooperation.

Support of a small staff for the Council shall be by contribution of the permanent participating agencies subject to law.   I request you, as Chairman, to work out with such agencies a suitable scale of contribution which should bear a relation to the scope of the responsibility of each in the field of aging.   Agencies shall designate individuals within their own organizations as needed to carry out projects approved by the Council.

The Council is directed to initiate promptly and carry on continuing reviews of Federal programs for the aging and make recommendations to me and to the interested departments and agencies from time to time on how needs in this field can be better met.

At the onset, the Council shall prepare an analysis and evaluation of existing programs which I would like to have by September 30, 1959, at the latest.   This analysis should appraise the various Federal programs which affect the older people in our population and identify any areas in which further changes need to be considered in order to help extend the period of productive, healthy, and comfortable lives for people in this group.

The Council shall cooperate and assist the Secretary of Health, Education, and Welfare, as may be appropriate, in planning and coordinating the White House Conference on Aging.   It shall also carry out other interagency projects as may be appropriate and needed from time to time.

I shall look forward to receiving from you as Chairman periodic reports on the progress and recommendations of the Council.

Sincerely,

DWIGHT D. EISENHOWER

50   ¶ Remarks of Welcome to President Lemus of
El Salvador at the Washington National Airport.
March 10, 1959

MR. PRESIDENT, on behalf of the people of the United States, and of
the government and myself, I bid you a cordial welcome to the United
States.

This, of course, is not your first visit to our country. You are no
stranger here. But you have demonstrated in your position of great
responsibility such great awareness of the principles on which this country
was founded—you have been such a great supporter of those principles—
that it is a special privilege for me to have this opportunity to renew with
you an association and friendship that began back in Panama in 1956.

So, to you and Senora Lemus I say welcome, with the great hope that
you will find here an interesting and enjoyable experience, to say nothing
of meeting with people who will share with you such views about government and about the dignity of man.

So again—welcome, Mr. President.

NOTE: President Lemus responded
(through an interpreter) as follows:

Mr. President, it is a source of great
satisfaction and honor for me to be able
to express my thanks to you, to the
American government, and to the American people upon my arrival in this
country.

My government, myself, and the people
of El Salvador, have considered your invitation to visit this country to be a great
honor, and we are most happy that we
are able to do so.

As you have said, Mr. President, this
country is by no means unknown to me.
I come to this country where I have acquired part of my knowledge and part of
my culture, and for this reason I have a
particularly warm feeling toward this
country and its people.

I come from a country in Latin America, El Salvador—a country which is
mindful of its traditions and proud of its
history—and I am proud to be visiting

the great nation of the United States,
which has become the great leader of the
free nations, at a time when we must all
stand together. I feel that after my visit
here—after the opportunity of exchanging points of view and of expressing concerns—there will arise from this closer
and stronger relations between this great
country and the bloc of Latin American
nations of which we are a part.

This is all the more important at a
time when democracy is threatened in all
that makes it what it is. It is a time
when we must close ranks and stand
together.

Mr. President, I may affirm to you that
in this great struggle El Salvador will
stand shoulder to shoulder with the
United States, which has fought in the
past, and is fighting now, and will fight
in the future in defense of the rights of
man.

And our people have, for this reason,
the greatest feeling of warmth toward

your country, even in a struggle—if we must lay down our lives to defend freedom—that freedom may live.

For this reason, Mr. President, in the name of my wife, and in the name of the members of my party, and in the name of my government and my people, I would like to express my thanks to you for this magnificent reception that has been given to me this morning.

I would also like to express to you, Mr. President, my deep personal respects to Mrs. Eisenhower, as well as to express again my thanks.

51 ¶ Statement by the President Upon Signing Proclamation Governing Petroleum Imports. *March* 10, 1959

I HAVE today issued a Proclamation adjusting and regulating imports of crude oil and its principal products into the United States.

The Voluntary Oil Import Program has demonstrated to me the willingness of the great majority of the industry to cooperate with the Government in restricting imports to a level that does not threaten to impair security. I commend them, and to me it is indeed a cause for regret that the actions of some in refusing to comply with the request of the Government require me to make our present voluntary system mandatory.

The new program is designed to insure a stable, healthy industry in the United States capable of exploring for and developing new hemisphere reserves to replace those being depleted. The basis of the new program, like that for the voluntary program, is the certified requirements of our national security which make it necessary that we preserve to the greatest extent possible a vigorous, healthy petroleum industry in the United States.

In addition to serving our own direct security interests, the new program will also help prevent severe dislocations in our own country as well as in oil industries elsewhere which also have an important bearing on our own security. Petroleum, wherever it may be produced in the free world, is important to the security, not only of ourselves, but also of the free people of the world everywhere.

During the past few years, a surplus of world producing capacity has tended to disrupt free world markets, and, unquestionably, severe disruption would have occurred in the United States and elsewhere except for cutbacks in United States production under the conservation programs of the various state regulatory bodies.

The voluntary controls have been and the mandatory controls will be flexibly administered with the twin aims of sharing our large and growing market on an equitable basis with other producing areas and avoiding disruption of normal patterns of international trade.

The Director of the Office of Civil and Defense Mobilization will keep the entire program under constant surveillance, and will inform the President of any circumstances which in his opinion indicate the need for any further Presidential action. In the event price increases occur while the program is in effect, the Director is required to determine whether such increases are necessary to accomplish the national security objectives of the Proclamation.

The United States recognizes, of course, that within the larger sphere of free world security, we, in common with Canada and with the other American Republics, have a joint interest in hemisphere defense. Informal conversations with Canada and Venezuela looking toward a coordinated approach to the problem of oil as it relates to this matter of common concern have already begun. The United States is hopeful that in the course of future conversations agreement can be reached which will take fully into account the interests of all oil producing states.

NOTE: On February 28 the President, in a letter to the Secretary of the Interior, requested that the Voluntary Oil Import Program then in effect be continued through March 10 in order that he might have time to consider the findings and recommendations of the Director of the Office of Civil and Defense Mobilization resulting from a study of the effect of imports on crude oil and derivatives on the national security.

A report of the Special Committee to Investigate Crude Oil Imports dated March 6, 1959, and memorandums for the President from the Director of the Office of Civil and Defense Mobilization dated February 27 and March 4 respectively, were released with the President's statement and the proclamation.

Proclamation 3279, "Adjusting imports of petroleum and petroleum products into the United States," and amendments, Proclamations 3290 and 3328, are published in the Federal Register (24 F.R. 1781, 3527, 10133).

52 ¶ Toasts of the President and the President of El Salvador. *March* 10, 1959

Mr. President, Senora:

We are glad to welcome to this Capital and to this house the President of El Salvador and his charming wife.

In these days of tensions, no country can have any greater or more pride of possession than real friends. America—the United States of America—counts itself fortunate in its good friends. And friends and countries are not measured in value by the extent of territory or the size of their populations. They are, rather, measured by their constancy, their loyalty, and their dedication to their friends, to common values, priceless values that free men possess—above even life itself.

And it is because our country is bound to El Salvador by that kind of friendship, by that kind of mutual loyalty and common dedication to great principles and values, that I ask you all to stand to join with me in a Toast to the country of El Salvador and its President.

NOTE: The President proposed this toast at a state dinner at the White House. President Lemus responded (through an interpreter) as follows:

Mr. President, Mrs. Eisenhower, Ladies and Gentlemen:

It is for me a source of deep personal pride to have received an invitation of the President to visit the United States. But more than that, in the name of my government and in the name of the people of my country, El Salvador, I would like to express the feeling of gratitude and pride that we have on this occasion.

My country is small, perhaps, in the size of its territory, but it is great in the spirit which has always honored those human values and those spiritual values which have been the pride of great men of the earth.

My country which is small but which is proud of its traditions and of its history, has always maintained closest friendship with the United States. This is not a friendship which was born yesterday. This friendship has existed between our countries for more than a hundred years,

and my country, El Salvador, is proud of that friendship, which dates from the very beginnings of our independence, with your great nation—which has served as one of the leaders in the free world and in the respect of those same values to which we have such great devotion in our own country.

Because of this, Mr. President, it is a source of great pride for me to recall the great people of this country who have made such a contribution to the preservation of those values. And it is for the future of those people with whom we have always, as I have said, maintained such a close relationship from the very beginning of our history, that it is my joy, my pride tonight, to express to you our thanks for this invitation. In it our people see, through this expression to me, an expression of friendship from the people of the United States to the people of our country who together in union with the other peoples of the free world are building a freer world which we know cannot be destroyed.

And it is for that reason that I raise my glass to drink to your health and your happiness.

53 ¶ The President's News Conference of *March* 11, 1959.

THE PRESIDENT. The only announcement I have is that there are 24 editors visiting us this morning and if they are here, I certainly extend, on my behalf and I should think on yours, a cordial welcome to them.   They are from 24 different countries.

Q. Marvin L. Arrowsmith, Associated Press: Mr. President, you have been quoted as having told the congressional leaders with whom you met last week that you believe Soviet strategy in the Berlin crisis and over the long run is to get the United States to spend itself into bankruptcy.

Do you hold that view, and if you do, could you elaborate on it?

THE PRESIDENT. I don't know that it has any application, particularly, to the Berlin situation as of now; but I have said this time and time again. As a matter of fact you don't have to quote me, quote the Communists. If you have read their books and their writings, why, you know that one of the things by which they hope to weaken the free world is to show that free enterprise can't work, can't afford to do the things it needs to do.

Q. Thomas N. Schroth, Congressional Quarterly: Mr. President, both Houses of Congress plan to take up the Hawaiian statehood bill today. Do you have any words of encouragement for them?

THE PRESIDENT. For a long number of years I have been talking on this same subject.   I didn't realize they were both coming up, coming up today.   But I think in my very latest State of the Union Message, I said again that I hoped that this would be acted on promptly.   And I still do.

Q. Merriman Smith, United Press International: Sir, do you foresee anything on the international scene to cause an increase in your defense budget beyond the present 40.9 billion, or anything that might delay the decrease in the Army and Marine Corps—manpower?

THE PRESIDENT. Well, this is a subject, of course, that is under discussion all the time.   What you do and what must be done is a production of a defensive plan, the nearest you can get of a consensus on this vital subject by those people who are best informed and who believe that we must negotiate always in this business of seeking a just peace from a position of strength.

Now, you make out a plan and you follow that plan.   You do not want, and, as a matter of fact, it would be ruinous to be pushed off this plan time and again by something suddenly described as a crisis.

I have argued and urged for years that we are living and we are going to live in a tense period because of the actions and the attitude of the Communist imperialism.

Communist imperialism is never going to decrease the pressure of its efforts to promote world revolution, resulting in the communization of the world and with Moscow at the head.

Now, they focus these tensions, or they find some way where they can make it very difficult for the free world to carry on its planned program of strengthening the associations among the several nations that are free and trying to remain free and to keep our defenses strong and adequate, as we seek this just peace.

Now, every time one of these incidents, or one of these, you might say, these foci of tension occur, we have something that's called a crisis, and everybody has a new answer.

Whether it is sputnik or it's Quemoy or it's Korea or whatever it is, what we have to do is to stand steady, as I see it, to be alert, to watch what we are doing, and to make certain that we know how and where we would have to produce action, if action became necessary.

What I am trying to point out is this: that adequacy of our defenses is not going to be especially increased or strengthened by any particular sudden action in response to one of these moments of increased tension.

We are certainly not going to fight a ground war in Europe. What good would it do to send a few more thousands or indeed even a few divisions of troops to Europe?

I do not see why we would think that we—with something of a half a million troops, Soviet and some German in East Germany, with 175 Soviet divisions in that neighborhood—why in the world would we dream of fighting a ground war? When our allied forces were capable of winning wars in that region, it was in World War II. No matter who they had been fighting, they could have done so. But after all, our divisions which were from two to three times the strength of the average of that time against us, totaling, I suppose, 120 divisions in the West, were supported by the most powerful air forces and navies of that time that could be put together.

Now, we don't want to get into that kind of a miscalculation, and certainly that kind of an error. We want to keep adequate forces and we want to keep as strong in our hearts and our heads as we do in our military, and then carry forward our policies, our firmness in supporting our rights, carrying out our responsibilities in the world, keeping our friends together, and remembering that we just simply cannot be always following someone else's lead. We have to take our own positive plan and follow it.

Q. Garnett D. Horner, Washington Star: Mr. President, what you have just said implies a part of the answer to this question, but the news reports today from Berlin say that some top allied officials there are convinced in the light of Mr. Khrushchev's visits that only the clearest warning of nuclear war would deter the Soviets from trying to carry out its plan for Berlin.

So, the question is: is the United States prepared to use nuclear war if necessary to defend free Berlin?

THE PRESIDENT. Well, I don't know how you could free anything with nuclear weapons.

I can say this: the United States and its allies have announced their firm intention of preserving their rights and responsibilities with respect to Berlin. If any threat, or any push in the direction of real hostilities is going to occur, it's going to occur from the side of the Soviets.

Now, if that would become reality, and I don't believe that anyone would be senseless enough to push that to the point of reality, then there will be the time to decide exactly what the allies would, in turn, expect to do.

Q. William McGaffin, Chicago Daily News: Mr. President, some economists contend that the auto and steel industries have helped bring on inflation by raising prices despite drops in demand. Do you agree, sir?

THE PRESIDENT. I haven't seen that particular point discussed. I suppose you are talking about some recent report, and I have not seen it discussed.

Q. Mr. McGaffin: Well, Mr. President, the argument is that instead of a classical type of inflation, this is one brought on by administered prices, that certain industries are so powerful that they can control prices, and during the recent recession, for instance, it was remarked that prices kept on going up although we were in a recession, and this was said to be because of these industries who were able to administer prices.

THE PRESIDENT. Well, you raised a particular facet of this argument which has been going on a long time but I don't think I am particularly qualified to discuss it this morning. I would want to talk to Dr. Saulnier and some of my other associates on that subject, so I could find the statistics on the thing to see whether the premises from which we start such a discussion are correct.

Q. Raymond P. Brandt, St. Louis Post-Dispatch: Can you give the administration's position on extending the unemployment pay benefits?

THE PRESIDENT. Yes. The administration's position is that this was undertaken as an emergency program of last year, and particularly, one compelling reason being because it was the year in which State legislatures were not in session.

I think for some 20 years this has been completely a State program, and the Federal participation has been a very, very slight charge for overhead, so as to help the administrative expenses of the States; otherwise, it is not Federal, it is State.

Now, we are waiting for the legislatures to come into session, which they are this year. The problem is to see exactly what they will do.

With respect to this plan that we produced last year, there were only 17 States that took full advantage of it; 19 others continued payments or made the payments to veterans and, I believe, Federal workers who were out of work, but those were the only ones. So the position of the administration is now that this becomes a State responsibility.

Q. Mr. Brandt: Would you agree to let it go until the end of this fiscal year? I understand it expires on March 31, or something like that.

THE PRESIDENT. One of the things at this moment, Mr. Brandt, is this: the principle is that I believe the Federal Government should not be in the State business here, but I haven't got such a rigid position about this that I wouldn't listen to something that might be considered an adjustment at this moment.

Q. Spencer Davis, Associated Press: Last November, sir, you created a commission headed by Mr. William Draper to look into the relative emphasis of economic and military aid in the mutual security program.

Could you give us a report, or a preliminary report, on their findings to date?

THE PRESIDENT. They are going to give me an interim report, interim recommendations, very soon, I understand. I have not seen them all but I do know from correspondence that they are very, very concerned about the whole program.

Q. Sarah McClendon, El Paso Times: Sir, to some people in recent years it has seemed that the office of Secretary of Defense has lessened somewhat in prestige and planning for the military.

I wonder if you would tell us if you see the Secretary of Defense as a man who sort of takes orders from the White House and State Department, or as an adviser to you on modern strategy?

THE PRESIDENT. Well, I think it would be difficult for me right now to review all of my relationships with all of the several subordinates I have in this Government, and they are many.

But I will say this: Mr. McElroy is where he is because I respect him. I believe in his powers of judgment, and I believe that he is just as spendid a man as could be found in this country for the job. If I thought for one moment that he was just a "yes man" taking my suggestions and carrying them out, he wouldn't be there.

I have never had that kind of a subordinate and I never expect to have one. His own judgment and his own dedication to his job is what I depend on, his own brain and intellectual capacity.

Q. John Scali, Associated Press: Mr. President, Premier Khrushchev has added a new wrinkle to his Berlin proposal, namely, he would now allow minimum numbers of American, British, and French troops, as well as Russian troops, to remain in the western sectors if we accepted his proposal to make West Berlin a free city. What do you think of this suggestion?

THE PRESIDENT. I'd say first of all that I would not expect ever to be in the business of reacting instantly to one of Mr. Khrushchev's wisecracks or whatever he calls it, that we take as a serious suggestion. We have allies. We try to apply in the free world the same kind of procedure in the reaching of decisions that you do in a democracy. We have discussion and lively debate, and then we try to figure out what is best for all America.

Well now, this is our system when dealing with our allies. You don't expect to have a doctor hit you on the knee with a rubber hammer and your foot jump quickly up and have that kind of a system in responding to suggestions of Mr. Khrushchev's about anything.

And I say right now, we have four nations conferring among themselves as to an answer on the latest Russian note; that having been concerted, NATO will be consulted and we go ahead on that basis. And that is exactly what we will do to reply to anything else.

Now, violating everything I have said, I'd say I don't think much of it. [*Laughter*]

Q. Chalmers M. Roberts, Washington Post: Mr. President, how serious do you consider the Berlin situation, and do you consider that the American public is sufficiently aware of the possibility of war in this situation?

THE PRESIDENT. I personally think that the American public is more soberly aware of the true situation than a lot of people around this town. We are so close to ourselves around here that we have a great possibility of stirring ourselves up. It's like one staff officer making work for another, so you get still another one to do it.

Now, this country knows it's a serious situation. They wouldn't be voting this kind of money for defense forces and for mutual security—which, to my mind, is the most vital part of our whole defense forces—they wouldn't be voting this kind of money unless they knew it was serious. And certainly I think there has been enough in the papers, enough in public statements for the whole free world, to say nothing just of the American population, to know that it is serious.

But what I decry is: let's not make everything such an hysterical sort of a proposition that we go a little bit off halfcocked. We ought to keep our steadiness, is what I plead for, steadiness in meeting this whole business, whether it be in Quemoy or Berlin or anywhere else.

Q. Edward P. Morgan, American Broadcasting Company: I wonder if part of your answer to Mr. Smith's question implied a sharp reduction in the importance of the ground forces?

And I wondered if you would answer that question against this background, sir: some of your critics in defense policy are attempting to challenge your military judgment by pointing out, for example, that you are willing to spend several millions, I think the number they mentioned was 90 millions, for jet transport planes for the administrative use of the White House and the Pentagon, whereas the expenditure of some 60 million more would bring an additional 55,000 men to the Army and the Marine Corps.

THE PRESIDENT. Well, I think your arithmetic and some of your premises that you quote are wrong.

First of all, I believe 55,000 men would be somewhere in the rate of 250 million for a year.

Secondly, I have never asked for a jet plane and I'm not sure that I'll ever be riding in one. One reason I haven't asked for a jet plane is because of the paucity of fields in the United States. When I ride in a plane, I want to be able to go into any State that occurs to me to go, whereas you have to pick and choose when you are going into these places with these big jet planes.

So, I have authorized, I forget whether it is either two or three, jet planes for the military, and I know of no other way they can decide— of transport types—whether or not they are efficient and effective means for supporting the logistics of the forces.

Now, when you come down to, you say, "marked decrease," I don't think that an army of 870,000 is a small army. And I don't see why we should get so hysterical or so excited about it. Actually there has been an effort, apparently, to relate the Berlin situation to the fact that we should have a lot more ground forces.

What would you do with more ground forces in Europe? Does anyone here have an idea?

Would you start a ground war? You wouldn't start the kind of ground war that would win in that region if that were going to make the way you had to enforce your will. You have got to go to other means. You couldn't possibly, between now and summer, any time, put the kind of divisions from all the countries in the world that could meet that kind of a threat. Did you ever stop to think the number of American divisions that were ready for action in the first 2 years of war, World War II?

These things aren't done in a minute. So, I say to you, we just don't want to be fighting battles where we are always at a disadvantage, and I mean battles, whether they are political, economic, or military. I don't want to be at a disadvantage. That's all.

Q. Mr. Morgan: May I just clarify one point, sir?

THE PRESIDENT. Yes.

Q. Mr. Morgan: Does this mean that you are confident that the ground forces as they now exist are capable of handling our side of any so-called brush fire situation that might break out?

THE PRESIDENT. I'd say this: if we can't, then the war's gotten beyond a brush war, and you have got to think in much, much bigger terms.

Q. Mrs. May Craig, Portland (Maine) Press Herald: Sir, the Constitution gives to Congress the power to provide for the common defense and raise and support armies, maintain and provide a navy.

Now, aside from the wisdom of what Congress says, where technically do you get the right to thwart the will of Congress, for instance in cutting the Army and the Marine Corps, quite aside from Berlin, or for not spending the money which they give you for missiles, submarine missiles or whatever they be?

Where do you get the right not to do what Congress says in providing for the common defense?

THE PRESIDENT. Well, I'll say this: first of all, I am Commander in Chief, and I use the forces that are given me.

Now, I have pointed out a number of times that I am not going to try deliberately and continuously to, as you say, thwart the will of Congress. I think Congress is sometimes mistaken, and I think in the past they have made some very bad mistakes in dealing with defense.

All right; I try to get them to correct. If they persist in such a thing as this, I'll have to put these people, I suppose, in the forces. Where will I put them? Well, just some place where it's nice to keep them out of the way, because I don't know what else to do with them.

Q. Edward T. Folliard, Washington Post: Mr. President, as you know, it has been said that the administration puts a balanced budget ahead of national security.

Suppose that our Federal Treasury were in better shape; suppose you could look forward to a surplus? Would you then be willing to spend more money on the armed forces, or would you still say that they are adequate?

THE PRESIDENT. I would say that I would not spend money on the armed forces of the United States as such.

Now, I would very much like to get some of our allies in better position to do their part in this job, and there are a number of other things that you might call ancillary or strengthening the United States in other ways—from its educational system to some other place where I would probably spend some more money.

I'm just tired even of talking about the idea of a balanced budget against national security; I don't see where this thing ever comes into it.

I say that a balanced budget in the long run is a vital part of national security.

Let us just assume this: we know that every time you get new formations in the defense forces, that increases expenses, and they keep growing with their maintenance, and you get into mass procurement and maintenance should go up. So let's go up 5 billion this year and then 10 billion more and then 7 and 8 and 9—where is our economy going? Everybody with any sense knows that we are finally going to a garrison state. If we want to do this, let's meet this problem, or if we say we want to avoid that, let's say for every increase that people believe ought to be in these formations, let's ask for the taxes.

Why doesn't anyone have the courage to get right up and say "I want 55,000 men"—maybe they want them sometimes because they'll be stationed at nice convenient places—why don't they say "But we want the taxes for it"?

I think that this problem is a little bit more comprehensive than just getting hold of another 10,000 or 15,000 young men, take them out of civil life and put them in uniform.

We have got the job of keeping the United States just as strong at home in everything we are trying to do as we have abroad. And the way we are going to keep it abroad is to keep the United States a big partner in a whole bevy of free nations that are activated by the same kind of things we want to do, which is to preserve the dignity of man and his opportunities to fulfill himself in this world.

Q. Felix Belair, New York Times: Under the heading of preparedness, sir, would you address yourself to alleged inequities arising from the draft, namely that as we are calling on fewer numbers now, I think 7,000 this summer as compared with 11 last year, these inequities increase, particularly in the more populous areas; some were called but many more were not called. I was wondering if you had any general ideas about it.

THE PRESIDENT. No, I don't think I could contribute anything at this moment.

It's been a problem that has always been with the United States from the moment that we started the draft in the First World War.

I have, as a young officer, made studies on these and analyses and reports and everything else, and I would say this: today more than ever, you need good men in the services. You cannot just take a man who can just be a hewer of wood and a carrier of water. He has got to be a fellow that can do more than that and capable of absorbing more instruction.

Now, there is one other thing that deals with this whole problem we are talking about, men. Two years ago I think it started, three years, there was a hue and cry to increase the salaries for all of the military services, salaries and pay, and one of the big reasons was to get good men and keep good men in the services so that a big percentage of them would make careers. The argument was presented to me time and time again that if we would only do this, we could soon get away from a draft; people would stay in, our armies would be so efficient that we would actually save money and cut down costs by the reduction in the numbers of people we had to have in. That was the argument at that time.

Now, we want to get all these good men but we still shout for numbers. Although the Chiefs of Staff, as a corporate body, said the budget is adequate, each one of them has got his own reservations when he wants what *he* wants.

Q. Peter Lisagor, Chicago Daily News: Mr. President, in answer to earlier questions, you seemed to have ruled out the possibility of a ground war in central Europe.

You also said, I believe, that nuclear war doesn't free anyone.

Is there, therefore, an in-between response that we could make in the event that the Russians really started trouble over Berlin?

THE PRESIDENT. I think we might as well understand this—might as well all of us understand this: I didn't say that nuclear war is a complete impossibility. I said it couldn't as I see it free anything. Destruction is not a good police force. You don't throw hand grenades around streets to police the streets so that people won't be molested by thugs.

This is exactly the way that you have to look at nuclear war, or any other. Indeed, even in the bombing of the, you might say, relatively moderate type that we had in World War II, we destroyed cities, but not to compel anything except the enemy to allow our ground forces to move forward.

And, I must say, to use that kind of a nuclear war as a general thing looks to me a self-defeating thing for all of us. After all, with that kind of release of nuclear explosions around this world, of the numbers of hundreds, I don't know what it would do to the world and particularly the Northern Hemisphere; and I don't think anybody else does.

But I know it would be quite serious.

Therefore, we have got to stand right ready and say, "We will do what is necessary to protect ourselves, but we are never going to back up on our rights and our responsibilities."

Marvin L. Arrowsmith, Associated Press: Thank you, Mr. President.

NOTE: President Eisenhower's one hundred and fifty-fourth news conference was held in the Executive Office Building from 10:29 to 11:00 o'clock on Wednesday morning, March 11, 1959. In attendance: 255.

54 ¶ Joint Statement Following Discussions With the President of El Salvador.
March 13, 1959

PRESIDENT Jose Maria Lemus, of the Republic of El Salvador, today concluded a three-day State Visit to Washington, departing for New York at 9:15 a.m.

During the course of the State Visit President Lemus and the President of the United States held useful discussions on matters of interest to both countries. These talks dealt primarily with United States-El Salvador relations but also included an exchange of views on significant developments in inter-American affairs.

While in Washington President Lemus addressed a Joint Meeting of both houses of Congress, and he and members of his Party conferred with the Acting Secretary of State and other United States Government officials. After leaving Washington President Lemus will visit New York, Springfield, Illinois, Houston, Texas, and New Orleans and will meet governmental, cultural, and business leaders.

I.

The two Presidents reaffirmed the traditional close ties of friendship and cooperation between their countries and are confident that the people of El Salvador and the United States will continue to enjoy the benefits of this close association in the future. The Chief Executives of the two countries recognized that these relationships are based upon mutual respect and upon loyalty to the same principles of democracy and individual rights. The two Presidents noted the fact that the United States and El Salvador continue to stand shoulder to shoulder with those nations of the world acting in defense of these worthy objectives and would continue to strive for peace and justice.

II.

The two Heads of State discussed the problems created for the coffee-producing nations, including the Republic of El Salvador, by the decline of coffee prices in the world market. It was recognized that the health of the economy of El Salvador is heavily dependent upon export earnings for this commodity and that the United States is deeply interested in the situation of the coffee-producing countries. It was agreed that the two countries would continue to work through the Coffee Study Group to seek, in cooperation with principal coffee-producing and consuming nations, reasonable ways of ameliorating the general situation in the world coffee trade.

III.

The President of El Salvador and the President of the United States discussed recent developments in the field of the economic integration of Central America and creation of a common market in that area. It was agreed that the establishment of an economically sound system for the integration of the economies of the Central American Republics and for a common market comprising those nations would be beneficial and would receive the support of the Governments of El Salvador and the United States. The two Presidents agreed that these steps could make a significant contribution to the industrial development of Central America, to the stimulation of capital investment in those nations, and to the steady improvement of the welfare of the people. This subject will receive continued study by the two Governments with a view to taking appropriate action to carry on those sound plans already contemplated.

IV.

The two Presidents discussed the proposals to establish an Inter-American Development Banking Institution and agreed upon the need to act in support of sound plans to establish such an institution. They recognized the need for stimulation of Latin American economic development through increased availability of capital from both public and private sources on a sound basis. It was agreed that such an inter-American institution, when properly established, would be a valuable supplementary source of capital for the nations of Latin America. In accordance with this position the United States would also continue its present loan programs in Latin America.

V.

President Lemus and President Eisenhower were deeply aware of the need for the greatest possible mutual understanding among the American Republics and believe that the understandings reached and the personal relationships developed will contribute to the steady strengthening of the traditionally close inter-American ties.

JOSE MARIA LEMUS
DWIGHT D. EISENHOWER

55 ¶ Special Message to the Congress on the Mutual Security Program. *March* 13, 1959

To the Congress of the United States:

A year ago in concluding my message to the Congress on the Mutual Security Program I described it as of transcendent importance to the security of the United States. I said that our expenditures for mutual security are fully as important to our national defense as expenditures for our own forces. I stated my conviction that for the safety of our families, the future of our children, and our continued existence as a nation, we cannot afford to slacken our support of the Mutual Security Program.

The events of the intervening year have vividly demonstrated the truth of these statements. In this one year there have been crises of serious proportions in the Middle East, in the Far East, and in Europe. In each of these the strength built by our Mutual Security Program has been of immeasurable value.

At the time of the difficulty in Lebanon the uneasy balance of the Middle East would have been far more seriously endangered if it had not been for the stability of other Middle Eastern countries which our Mutual Security Program had helped build. Without our Mutual Security aid, Jordan, under severe pressures, would have faced collapse, with the danger of flaring conflict over her territory.

In the Far East, the firm stand of the Republic of China against the Communist attack on Quemoy would not have been possible without the arms and training furnished by our Mutual Security Program and by the high morale promoted by the economic progress we have helped forward on Taiwan. This successful local defense blunted an aggression which otherwise could have precipitated a major conflict.

In Europe today the Soviet Union has made demands regarding the future of Berlin which, if unmodified, could have perilous consequences.

The resoluteness with which we and our allies will meet this issue has come about in large measure because our past programs of economic and military assistance to our NATO allies have aided them in strengthening the economies and the military power needed to stand firm in the face of threats.

While our Mutual Security Program has demonstrated a high value in these tense moments, its military and economic assistance to other areas has undoubtedly had an equal value in maintaining order and progress so that crises have not arisen.

REALITIES OF 1959 AND AHEAD

I believe that these events of the past year and the stern, indeed harsh, realities of the world of today and the years ahead demonstrate the importance of the Mutual Security Program to the security of the United States. I think four such realities stand out.

First, the United States and the entire free world are confronted by the military might of the Soviet Union, Communist China, and their satellites. These nations of the Communist Bloc now maintain well-equipped standing armies totaling more than 6,500,000 men formed in some 400 divisions. They are deployed along the borders of our allies and friends from the northern shores of Europe to the Mediterranean Sea, around through the Middle East and Far East to Korea. These forces are backed by an air fleet of 25,000 planes in operational units, and many more not in such units. They, in turn, are supported by nuclear weapons and missiles. On the seas around this land mass is a large navy with several hundred submarines.

Second, the world is in a great epoch of seething change. Within little more than a decade a world-wide political revolution has swept whole nations—21 of them—with three-quarters of a billion people, a fourth of the world's population, from colonial status to independence— and others are pressing just behind. The industrial revolution, with its sharp rise in living standards, was accompanied by much turmoil in the Western world. A similar movement is now beginning to sweep Africa, Asia, and South America. A newer and even more striking revolution in medicine, nutrition, and sanitation is increasing the energies and lengthening the lives of people in the most remote areas. As a result of lowered infant mortality, longer lives, and the accelerating conquest of famine, there is underway a population explosion so incredibly great that in little more than another generation the population of the world is expected to double. Asia alone is expected to have one billion more people than the entire world has today. Throughout vast areas there is a surging social upheaval in which, overnight, the responsibilities of self-government are being undertaken by hundreds of millions, women are assuming new places in public life, old family patterns are being destroyed and new ones uneasily established. In the early years of independence, the people of the new nations are fired with a zealous nationalism which, unless channelled toward productive purposes, could lead to harmful developments. Transcending all this there is the accompanying universal determination to achieve a better life.

Third, there is loose in the world a fanatic conspiracy, International Communism, whose leaders have in two score years seized control of all or parts of 17 countries, with nearly one billion people, over a third of the total population of the earth. The center of this conspiracy, Soviet Russia, has by the grimmest determination and harshest of means raised itself to be the second military and economic power in the world today. Its leaders never lose the opportunity to declare their determination to become the first with all possible speed.

The other great Communist power, Red China, is now in the early stages of its social and economic revolution. Its leaders are showing the same ruthless drive for power and to this end are striving for ever increasing economic output. They seem not to care that the results—which thus far have been considerable in materialistic terms—are built upon the crushed spirits and the broken bodies of their people.

The fact that the Soviet Union has just come through a great revolutionary process to a position of enormous power and that the world's most populous nation, China, is in the course of tremendous change at the very time when so large a part of the free world is in the flux of revolutionary movements, provides Communism with what it sees as its golden opportunity. By the same token freedom is faced with difficulties of unprecedented scope and severity—and opportunity as well.

Communism exploits the opportunity to intensify world unrest by every possible means. At the same time Communism masquerades as the pattern of progress, as the path to economic equality, as the way to freedom from what it calls "Western imperialism", as the wave of the future.

For the free world there is the challenge to convince a billion people in the less developed areas that there is a way of life by which they can have bread *and* the ballot, a better livelihood *and* the right to choose the means of their livelihood, social change *and* social justice—in short, progress *and* liberty. The dignity of man is at stake.

Communism is determined to win this contest—freedom must be just as dedicated or the struggle could finally go against us. Though no shot would have been fired, freedom and democracy would have lost.

This battle is now joined. The next decade will forecast its outcome.

The fourth reality is that the military position and economic prosperity of the United States are interdependent with those of the rest of the free world.

As I shall outline more fully below, our military strategy is part of a common defense effort involving many nations. The defense of the free world is strengthened and progress toward a more stable peace is advanced by the fact that powerful free world forces are established on territory adjoining the areas of Communist power. The deterrent power of our air and naval forces and our intermediate range missile is materially increased by the availability of bases in friendly countries abroad.

Moreover, the military strength of our country and the needs of our industry cannot be supplied from our own resources. Such basic necessities as iron ore, bauxite for aluminum, manganese, natural rubber, tin, and many other materials acutely important to our military and industrial strength are either not produced in our own country or are not produced in sufficient quantities to meet our needs. This is an additional reason why we must help to remain free the nations which supply these resources.

The challenge that confronts us is broad and deep—and will remain so for some time. Yet our gravest danger is not in these external facts but within ourselves—the possibility that in complacent satisfaction with our present wealth and preoccupation with increasing our own military power we may fail to recognize the realities around us and to deal with them with the vigor and tenacity their gravity requires.

We have the national capacity and the national program to surmount these dangers and many more. We have the strength of our free institutions, the productivity of our free economy, the power of our military forces, a foreign policy dedicated to freedom and respect for the rights of others, and the collective strength of our world-wide system of alliances.

The effectiveness of all these in meeting the challenge confronting us is multiplied by our Mutual Security Program—a powerful and indispensable tool in dealing with the realities of the second half of the twentieth century.

I should like to outline how the principal elements of this program will serve the vital interests of our country in Fiscal Year 1960.

THE MUTUAL SECURITY PROGRAM FOR FISCAL YEAR 1960

The Mutual Security Program which I propose for Fiscal Year 1960 is in the same pattern and has the same component parts as the program which the Congress enacted at the last session. To carry forward this program I ask $3,929,995,000.

I ask these funds to attain the two basic objectives of the Mutual Security Program: military security and economic and political stability and progress.

THE MILITARY SHIELD

In view of the maintenance by the Communists of armed force far beyond necessary levels and the repeated evidences of willingness to use a portion of that force where the Communist leaders believe it would be a successful means to a Communist end, it is rudimentary good sense for the peoples of the free nations to create and maintain deterrent military strength. We do this not through choice but necessity. It is not in our nature to wish to spend our substance on weapons. We would like to see these outlays shifted to the economic benefit of our own nation and our friends abroad striving for economic progress.

Because the need for military strength continues, we seek to build this strength where it can most effectively be developed, deploy it where it can most effectively be used and share the burden of its cost on as fair a basis as possible. To this end, we and over forty other nations have joined together in a series of security pacts. Some of our allies and close friends have joined in other supporting agreements. We have also made certain individual undertakings such as the Middle East Resolution.

Each of the free nations joined in this world-wide system of collective security contributes to the common defense in two ways: through the creation and maintenance of its individual forces; through the support of the collective effort.

For our own military forces, which form a major element in the total security pattern, I have asked the Congress to make available $40.85 billion, to which must be added approximately $2.8 billion for atomic programs, largely for defense purposes. For our contribution of military materiel and training assistance to the collective security effort, I now ask the Congress to make available $1.6 billion. This amount is far below that needed for our share of the cost of improving, or even providing essential maintenance for the forces of our allies. It is a minimum figure necessary to prevent serious deterioration of our collective defense system.

These two requests, one for our own defense forces, the other for our share in supporting the collective system, are but two elements in a *single* defense effort. Each is essential in the plans of the Joint Chiefs of Staff for our national security. Each is recommended to you by the same Joint Chiefs, the same Secretary of Defense, and the same Commander-in-Chief.

Dollar for dollar, our expenditures for the Mutual Security Program, after we have once achieved a reasonable military posture for ourselves, will buy more security than far greater additional expenditures for our own forces.

Two fundamental purposes of our collective defense effort are to prevent general war and to deter Communist local aggression.

We know the enormous and growing Communist potential to launch a war of nuclear destruction and their willingness to use this power as a threat to the free world. We know also that even local aggressions, unless checked, could absorb nation after nation into the Communist orbit—or could flame into world war.

The protection of the free world against the threat or the reality of Soviet nuclear aggression or local attack rests on the common defense effort established under our collective security agreements. The protective power of our Strategic Air Command and our naval air units is assured even greater strength not only by the availability of bases abroad but also by the early warning facilities, the defensive installations, and the logistic support installations maintained on the soil of these and other allies and friends for our common protection.

The strategy of general defense is made stronger and of local defense is made possible by the powerful defensive forces which our allies in Europe, in the Middle East, and the Far East have raised and maintain on the soil of their homelands, on the borders of the Communist world.

These military forces, these essential bases and facilities constitute invaluable contributions of our partners to our common defense. On our part we contribute through our military assistance program certain basic military equipment and advanced weapons they need to make their own military effort fully effective but which they cannot produce or afford to purchase.

As we move into the age of missile weapons, this plan of collective security will grow in importance. Already intermediate range ballistic missiles are being deployed abroad. Our friends on whose territory these weapons are located must have the continued assurance of our help to their own forces and defense in order that they may continue to have the confidence and high morale essential to vigorous participation in the common defense effort.

The funds I now ask for military assistance are to supply to these partners in defense essential conventional weapons and ammunition for their forces and the highly complex electronic equipment, missiles and other advanced weapons needed to make their role in the common defense effective.

As already pointed out these funds are asked on a minimal basis. Continuation of a sufficient flow of materials and of sufficient training for the year can be attained only by some additional cannibalizing of the pipeline, already reduced to a point where flexibility is difficult.

To summarize, through the Mutual Security Program our friends among the free world nations make available to us for the use of our forces some 250 bases in the most strategic locations, many of them of vital importance. They support ground forces totaling more than 5 million men stationed at points where danger of local aggression is most acute, based on their own soil and prepared to defend their own homes. They man air forces of about 30,000 aircraft of which nearly 14,000 are jets, 23 times the jet strength of 1950 when the program started. They also have naval forces totaling 2500 combat vessels with some 1700 in active fleets or their supporting activities.

Over the years of our combined effort, these allies and friends have spent on these forces some $141 billion, more than 6 times the $22 billion we have contributed in military assistance. During calendar year 1958 they contributed $19 billion of their own funds to the support of these forces. On our part we have created and maintain powerful mobile forces which can be concentrated in support of allied forces in the most distant parts of the world. We know it would be impossible for us to raise and maintain forces of equal strength and with the immeasurable value of strategic location. Without the strength of our allies our nation would be turned into an armed camp and our people subjected to a heavy draft and an annual cost of many billions of dollars above our present military budget.

Because the military assistance program is a vital part of our total defense, and to be certain that it serves its intended purpose fully and effectively, I have appointed a bipartisan Committee of prominent Americans of the highest competence to examine this program and its operation thoroughly. I have asked them to make a report of their findings on the program, including its proper balance with economic assistance. Since its formation in late November of last year, the Committee has been vigorously pursuing its study, including personal visits to all major areas where military assistance is being rendered. The Committee has already indicated to me that it will recommend an increase in the level of commitments for vital elements of the military assistance program, primarily for the provision of weapons to the NATO area. I expect to receive its written interim report shortly. I will, of course, give this report my most careful attention and will then make such further recommendations as are appropriate.

MAINTAINING ECONOMIC STABILITY

While our own and our allies' military efforts provide a shield for freedom, the economic phases of our Mutual Security Program provide the means for strengthening the stability and cohesion of free nations, limiting opportunities for Communist subversion and penetration, supporting economic growth and free political institutions in the newly independent countries, stimulating trade and assuring our own nation and our allies of continuing access to essential resources.

Two of these programs, Defense Support and Special Assistance, are specifically directed towards helping maintain order, stability and, in certain countries, economic progress, where these are of material importance to the welfare of the United States itself.

Defense Support. For most of our allies and friends the cost of the share which they bear of the common defense effort constitutes a heavy burden on their economies. Our NATO allies in Western Europe bear this entire economic burden themselves, receiving from us only advanced weapons and other essential items of military equipment and certain training. But for others, the burden of defense vastly exceeds their limited resources. They therefore are forced to turn to us for economic help in maintaining political and economic stability.

We supply this assistance through our defense support program to twelve nations in which we are helping to arm large military forces. Eleven of these nations—Greece, Turkey, Iran, Pakistan, Thailand, Laos, Cambodia, Viet-Nam, the Philippines, the Republics of China and Korea—lie along or are narrowly separated from the very boundaries of the Sino-Soviet Bloc, subjected daily to the pressures of its enormous power.   Several of them are also the sites of major U.S. military installations.   The twelfth, Spain, is the strategically located site of other bases used by the United States.   Together these twelve nations are supporting three million armed forces—nearly one-half of the total forces of the free world.

Despite their proximity to Communist forces, most of these nations have pledged themselves to the world-wide collective defense plan.   Greece and Turkey are among our NATO allies.   Pakistan, Thailand, and the Philippines are among our SEATO allies and Cambodia, Laos, and Viet-Nam are protected through SEATO.   Turkey, Iran, and Pakistan are active members of the Baghdad Pact which forms a connecting link of free world defenses between NATO and SEATO.   Korea, the Republic of China, and the Philippines are joined with us in special mutual defense agreements.

For defense support, to make possible the needed contributions of these twelve nations to the common defense, I ask $835 million.   I ask the Congress to recognize these economic needs of our partners and to provide the full amount I request.

Over two-thirds of this sum will be used for Turkey, Viet-Nam, Taiwan and Korea.   These courageous and strategically located nations—three of them the free areas of divided nations—are directly faced by heavy concentrations of Communist military power.   Together they contribute nearly two million armed forces in the very front lines of the free world's defenses.   These nations depend for survival on our defense support program.   The remaining third of the funds will be for the eight other nations which rely on this help to enable them to make their valuable contributions to the common defense without serious harm to their economies.

These nations are contributing heavily to the defense effort in keeping with their abilities.   Reducing the defense support we provide them will compel a reduction in the forces we wish them to maintain in our common defense or place a heavy additional burden on the already low standards of living of their people.

Special Assistance. There are a number of other nations and areas of the world whose need is so great and whose freedom and stability are so important to us that special assistance to them is essential. In North Africa, for example, the newly independent Arab nation, Tunisia, is struggling to improve the economic and social conditions of its people while under strong external pressures. Its neighbors, Morocco and Libya, are also striving to build economic progress upon their newly acquired political independence. Another new nation, the Sudan, is an important link between the Arab world and rapidly growing Central Africa and is intently working to maintain its independent course of progress in the face of strong Communist and other outside pressures. These nations are all new outposts of freedom in whose success we are deeply interested.

During the last year, as I have mentioned, Jordan has been subjected to severe pressures. Should Jordan be overwhelmed, the peace and stability of the Middle East would be endangered. But with its very limited internal resources, Jordan desperately needs continued substantial outside help.

West Berlin is a solitary outpost of freedom back of the Iron Curtain. In addition to the firm support which we and our NATO allies have assured West Berlin in the face of current Soviet threats, it is important that we show our support of its people by continuing our economic assistance to the beleaguered city.

Programs for Health. I have on several occasions during the recent past sought to focus public attention on the great opportunity open to the United States in the field of health. The United States will continue to support and promote the accelerating international fight against disease in the coming fiscal year. The great campaign to eradicate the world's foremost scourge, malaria, is moving into its peak period of activity and need for special assistance funds. Of more than a billion people formerly exposed to the disease, half have now been protected and the movement is gaining strength and momentum as a true international effort. The substantial progress of this campaign as well as modern medical potential generally have opened new vistas of the conquest of mass disease through pooling of efforts.

I ask the Congress to make available funds to continue the program for development of medical research programs begun last year by the World Health Organization with the help of a grant from the United States. I also propose that the United States explore whether practical and feasible means can be found whereby progress can be made toward equipping those nations whose needs are greatest to provide in a reasonable time pure drinking water for their people as a method of attack on widespread water-borne diseases.

Added to the health programs now being carried on by our bilateral programs and through our voluntary contributions to the United Nations, these new programs will raise the health activities proposed for Fiscal Year 1960 under the Mutual Security Program to a total value of some $84 million, exclusive of loans by the Development Loan Fund in this field. The total effort of the United States in the field of international health, including among other activities those conducted by the Department of Health, Education, and Welfare, will approximate 100 million dollars.

For the nations I have mentioned and several others, for West Berlin, for such programs as those for health, for support to certain of our American sponsored schools abroad and for our contribution to the United Nations Emergency Force I ask $272 million in Special Assistance funds. I believe that the close examination which I expect the Congress to give each of these special needs will show that this request is conservative.

AIDING ECONOMIC PROGRESS

The requests for funds for defense support and special assistance which I have outlined thus far are directed primarily at maintaining political and economic stability. But in our dynamic world of multiple revolutions this is far from enough.

In many nations of Asia and Africa per capita incomes average less than $100 a year. Life expectancies are half those of the more advanced nations. Literacy averages twenty-five percent. Affected by the revolutionary drives which are sweeping their regions, the peoples of the areas will tolerate these conditions no longer—and they should not. They are intently determined to progress—and they deserve to do so. If they cannot move forward, there will be retrogression and chaos, the injurious effects of which will reach our own shores. These newly independent peoples look to their present generally moderate governments for leadership to progress. If they do not find it, they will seek other leadership, possibly extremists whose advent to power would not only endanger the liberties of their own people but could adversely affect others, including ourselves.

Above all, these people must have hope that they can achieve their economic goals in freedom, with free institutions and through a working partnership with other citizens of the free world.

The leaders of the Soviet Union and Communist China are intently aware of the great revolutionary surges in these less developed areas, many of which are on the borders of the Communist Bloc. Seeing in these new trends an historic opportunity, they have reversed their attitude of hostility to all nations not under their direct control. Five years ago they entered on a great diplomatic and economic campaign of wooing the new nations of Asia and Africa, even attempting to push their drive into Latin America. I reported on this campaign of trade and aid in my message to the Congress last year. It has increased in intensity in the intervening time. Communist Bloc military and economic credits to 17 selected nations exceeded a billion dollars in 1958 alone, bringing the present total to $2.4 billion. The number of technicians supplied to 17 countries of Asia and Africa rose from 1,600 in 1957 to 2,800 in 1958.

Our own programs of technical cooperation and capital assistance are not mere responses to Communist initiatives. The reverse is true. This year will mark the tenth anniversary of our Point Four program. Capital assistance for development has been flowing to nations needing our help for many years. Even if the Communist Bloc should revert tomorrow to its previous icy treatment of all free peoples, we would continue the warmth of our interest in and help to their determined efforts to progress.

Nevertheless, it is imperative that we understand the real menace of the Communist economic offensive. The great contest in half the globe, the struggle of a third of the world's people, is to prove that man can raise his standard of living and still remain free—master of his individual destiny and free to choose those who lead his government. The Communist economic offensive presents the grave danger that a free nation might develop a dependence on the Communist Bloc from which it could not extricate itself. This must not happen. We and other nations of the free world must provide assurance that no nation will be compelled to choose between bread and freedom.

The United States is determined to do its part in providing this assurance.   For this purpose, in addition to channels of private investment and existing financing institutions, we have created two carefully designed instruments of national policy: the technical cooperation program and the Development Loan Fund.

Technical Cooperation.   To carry on our technical cooperation program some 6,000 skilled American men and women are now working in 49 countries and 9 dependent territories which have asked our help. They are advising high officials on problems of administering new governments.   They are helping farmers raise their incomes by teaching them better methods of cultivation, irrigation and fertilization and by introducing more productive seeds, poultry and livestock.   They are planning with local scientists for uses of atomic power and isotopes.   They are attacking disfiguring and debilitating diseases and helping to increase the health and vigor of untold millions.   They are helping to organize the educational systems which will bring literacy and the knowledge which is the power for progress.

In order to transfer our modern technical knowledge even more effectively, we will bring next year over 10,000 of the rising leaders of the less developed areas to study in the United States or in specially developed training programs in other countries.

To provide for the work of our technicians abroad and for these training programs I ask $179.5 million for Fiscal Year 1960.   The increase in this sum over the current year is to expand programs recently begun in the newly independent and emerging countries of Africa, to intensify activity in Asian nations and to augment substantially cooperative programs with countries of Latin America.

I also ask $30 million to be available for our contribution to the companion technical cooperation and special projects programs of the United Nations, initiated by our own government.   I anticipate that increasing contributions by other members in the year 1960 will call for this increased contribution on our part.

As in recent years, I believe we should continue our annual contribution of $1.5 million to the technical cooperation program of the Organization of American States.

The Development Loan Fund.   Administrative and technical skills, though essential to economic growth, cannot of themselves make possible the rate of progress demanded of their governments by the peoples of the newly independent nations. For this progress they must have capital—capital for the roads, telecommunications, harbors, irrigation and electric power which are the substructure of economic progress and for the steel mills, fertilizer plants, and other industries which are fundamental to general economic growth.

Just as in the early decades of our own national development we depended upon the more highly developed nations of that period—England, France, and others—for capital essential to our growth, so do the new nations of this era depend on us and others whose economies are well established.

Two years ago the Congress, the Executive Branch, and several distinguished private organizations re-examined the needs of the newly independent nations for outside development capital and of the then existing sources. The independent but unanimous conclusion of these studies was that existing sources were and for the foreseeable future would be inadequate to meet even the most pressing needs. They recommended that there be established a new institution to provide long-term credits on flexible terms.

In the light of these findings, I recommended to the Congress and it established the Development Loan Fund, an agency of the United States Government especially designed to advance loans on a businesslike basis for sound projects which cannot find financing from private or established governmental sources.

The Development Loan Fund in its little more than a year of active operation has established the sound and useful position that was foreseen for it. In this short time it has taken under consideration $2.8 billion in screened requests for loans. It has later determined that some $600 million were unacceptable or more appropriate for private or other public financing. Of its total capital of $700 million thus far made available by the Congress, it had by mid-February, 1959, committed $684 million for loans to projects in 35 countries. For all practical purposes it is now out of funds for further loan commitments and has before it applications totaling over $1.5 billion with more being received almost daily.

In order that the Fund may continue to meet the most urgent needs of the nations depending on us, I have asked the Congress for a supplemental appropriation of $225 million to be available in the Fiscal Year

1959. This appropriation is under authorizations previously made but not used.

When I made my original recommendation to the Congress in 1957 for the establishment of the Development Loan Fund I urged that it be provided with capital for three years of operation and stated that based on observation of its progress within that period I would ask for longer-term capitalization commencing in Fiscal Year 1961. The Congress chose to authorize capital initially for two years of operation. I now ask that the Congress authorize and appropriate $700 million to become available in Fiscal Year 1960, the third year of the Fund. This sum will allow the Fund a level of activity no higher than it established in its first year of operation.

Consideration should continue to be given to capitalization procedures that will allow better long-range planning.

Private Investment. These governmental programs of technical cooperation and capital financing of course only augment the investment in progress which comes from private sources. But they are indispensable and probably will be for a number of years because private investment, though very significant in the Western Hemisphere, does not and cannot in the near future be expected to supply more than a fraction of the capital needed by the new nations of Asia and Africa.

In order to encourage increased private investment in these areas, our Government has already undertaken a system of guaranties against loss from non-convertibility of foreign currency receipts and from expropriation, confiscation, and war. To further stimulate such investment, I now request that legislation be enacted to allow similar guaranties against risks of revolution, insurrection, and related civil strife. I propose also that the Congress double the availability of such guaranties.

CONTINGENCY FUND AND OTHER PROGRAMS

The experience of this year has shown, as in the past, that there will arise each year contingencies for which funds will be urgently needed—but which cannot be foreseen at all or with sufficient clarity to program in advance. For the current year I asked $200 million for such eventualities. Heavy demands, arising from the crises in the Middle East and from needs elsewhere, have already been made on the $155 million appropriated—with several months of the fiscal year remaining. I still believe that $200 million is the smallest sum which safety and prudence recommend and I ask that this sum be provided for Fiscal Year 1960.

I recommend that we continue our support of the United Nations Children's Fund, our help in the resettlement of refugees from Communism, our program of atoms-for-peace, and certain other small programs we are now engaged in. The International Cooperation Administration will need an increase in its administrative funds, particularly to help obtain more persons of high qualifications for service abroad and to strengthen our representation at key posts in Africa and Latin America. For all these purposes I ask $112 million.

SOME FISCAL CONSIDERATIONS

The total sum I request for the Mutual Security Program for Fiscal Year 1960, $3,929,995,000 is slightly less than I asked last year. Each category and item in it has been weighed in terms of the contribution it will make to the achievement of the important objectives the program is designed to serve. The total amount is well under one percent of the gross national product our country will enjoy in the coming year. It is approximately five percent of our national budget. The greater part will go for military equipment to our allies and for economic support directly related to defense. The remainder, for aid to the economic growth we are most anxious to promote amounts to less than two percent of our national budget, under one-third of one percent of our national production. At the end of the present fiscal year the military assistance pipeline will be at the lowest level in its history and will be further reduced by next year's expenditure which will substantially exceed the new appropriation I am now asking. The economic assistance pipeline will, as in recent years, be barely enough to keep the program flowing without serious interruption.

The true measure of this national security program is what we have gotten and will get for our expenditures and what the cost would be without it. Over the years we have received returns many times the value of our investment.

Our first great work, the Marshall Plan, cost less than projected, ended on time, and revived Western Europe from the destruction of the war to a group of thriving nations, now among our best customers and strongest allies, many of whom are now joining with us in assistance to the newly independent nations.

Our military and economic aid has been indispensable to the survival and gradual progress of nation after nation around the perimeter of Asia from Greece to Korea and others in Africa and our own hemisphere. When I hear this program described as a "give-away" or "aid to foreigners at the expense of domestic programs", I wonder what sort of America we would have today—whether any funds would be available for any domestic programs—whether all of our substance would not today be devoted to building a fortress America—if we had not had such a program: if the key nations of Europe had been allowed to succumb to Communism after the war, if the insurrectionists had been allowed to take over Greece, if Turkey had been left to stand alone before Soviet threats, if Iran had been allowed to collapse, if Viet-Nam, Laos and Cambodia were now in Communist hands, if the Huks had taken control in the Philippines, if the Republic of Korea were now occupied by Communist China.

That none of these tragedies occurred, that all of these nations are still among the free, that we are not a beleaguered people is due in substantial measure to the Mutual Security Program.

CONCLUSION

The realities of this era indicate all too clearly that the course of our country will be deeply affected by forces at work outside our borders. These forces if left to exploitation by extremists will inevitably lead to changes destructive to us. Yet with wisdom and tenacity it lies within our power to frustrate or to shape these forces so that the peoples directly concerned and our own nation may be benefited.

We cannot safely confine government programs to our own domestic progress and our own military power. We could be the wealthiest and the most mighty nation and still lose the battle of the world if we do not help our world neighbors protect their freedom and advance their social and economic progress. It is not the goal of the American people that the United States should be the richest nation in the graveyard of history.

In the world as it is today—and as it will be for the foreseeable future—our Mutual Security Program is and will be both essential to our survival and important to our prosperity. It not only rests upon our deepest self-interest but springs from the idealism of the American people which is the true foundation of their greatness. If we are wise we will consider it not as a cost but as an investment—an investment in our present safety, in our future strength and growth, and in the growth of freedom throughout the world.

DWIGHT D. EISENHOWER

56 ¶ Presidential Statement Upon Signing Order Establishing Federal Council for Science and Technology. *March* 13, 1959

LESS THAN twenty years ago, Federal support of science was about 100 million dollars annually. Today, this annual investment in research and development has grown to over five billion dollars, and a large fraction of these Federal funds is spent in laboratories owned and operated by private groups. It is the responsibility of the Federal Government to encourage in every appropriate way the scientific activities of non-Government institutions; but it is apparent from the size of these Federal expenditures that the policies and practices of the Federal Government can exert an immediate and substantial effect on the Nation's private scientific institutions as well as on Government laboratories.

I believe that the new Federal Council for Science and Technology can effectively aid the objective of improving the ways in which the Federal Government uses and supports science. Moreover, the report of my Science Advisory Committee on "Strengthening American Science" also pointed to a number of opportunities for advancing our total national program. I expect the new Council to consider and evaluate these opportunities and to encourage all Government agencies further to increase the quality of their efforts in these fields. By fostering greater cooperation among Federal agencies in planning their research and development programs, by facilitating the resolution of common problems, and by reviewing the impact of Government policies on the programs of non-Governmental institutions, the Council should be able to contribute greatly to the development and advancement of our national programs in these important and critical areas.

NOTE: Executive Order 10807, establishing the Federal Council for Science and Technology, is published in the Federal Register (24 F.R. 1897).

The Science Advisory Committee report "Strengthening American Science" (Government Printing Office, 1958) was made public by the President on December 28, 1958, and is summarized in a note in the 1958 volume, this series, p. 869.

57 ¶ Radio and Television Report to the American People: Security in the Free World. *March* 16, 1959

[Delivered from the President's Office at 9:30 p.m.]

My Fellow Americans:

Tonight I want to talk with you about two subjects:

One is about a city that lies four thousand miles away.

It is West Berlin. In a turbulent world it has been, for a decade, a symbol of freedom. But recently its name has come to symbolize, also, the efforts of Imperialistic Communism to divide the free world, to throw us off balance, and to weaken our will for making certain of our collective security.

Next, I shall talk to you about the state of our Nation's posture of defense and the free world's capacity to meet the challenges that the Soviets incessantly pose to peace and to our own security.

First, West Berlin.

You have heard much about this city recently, and possibly wondered why American troops are in it at all.

How did we get there in the first place? What responsibilities do we have in connection with it and how did we acquire them?

Why has there developed a situation surrounding this city that poses another of the recurring threats to peace that bear the stamp of Soviet manufacture?

Let's begin with a brief review of recent history.

We first acquired rights and responsibilities in West Berlin as a result of World War II. Even before the war ended, when the defeat and capitulation of Nazi Germany were in sight, the Allied Powers, including the Soviet Union, signed agreements defining the areas of occupation in Germany and Berlin which they would assume.

273

As a result, Germany and the City of Berlin, were each divided into four zones, occupied by American, British, French, and Soviet troops, respectively.

Under the wartime agreements I have mentioned, the Western Allies entered into occupation of West Berlin and withdrew our Armies from the Soviet Zone. Accordingly, the boundary of the Soviet Zone, like our presence in Berlin, was established upon the basis of these same agreements.

Also by agreement among the occupying powers, the Western Allies— the United States, the United Kingdom, and France—were guaranteed free access to Berlin.

Here in my office is a map of Germany. The light portion of the map is West Germany—the darker portion is East Germany. The lighter gray lanes are the air corridors to Berlin—and the dotted lines show both the main roads and railroads that give us access to the city. Notice that the City of Berlin is one hundred and ten miles inside East Germany; that is, it is one hundred and ten miles from the nearest boundary of West Germany.

Here is the territory, now in East Germany that was taken by our Army in World War II and was turned over to the Russians by political agreement made before the end of the War.

Now at the end of World War II our announced purpose and that of our wartime associates was the pacification and eventual unification of Germany under freedom.

We jointly agreed to undertake this task. Ever since that time, the United States has continuously recognized the obligation of the Allied Governments under international law to reach a just peace settlement with Germany and not to prolong the occupation of Germany unnecessarily.

The public record demonstrates clearly that such a settlement has been frustrated only by the Soviets. It quickly became evident that Soviet leaders were not interested in a free unified Germany, and were determined to induce or force the Western Powers to leave Berlin.

Ten years ago Senator John Foster Dulles, now our great Secretary of State, described the basic purpose of the Soviet government. He said that purpose was, and now I am quoting: "no less than world domination, to be achieved by gaining political power successively in each of the many areas which had been afflicted by war, so that in the end the

United States, which was openly called the main enemy, would be isolated and closely encircled." That is the completion of the quotation.

The current Berlin effort of the Soviets falls within this pattern of basic purpose.

The first instance of unusual pressure, clearly evidencing these purposes, came in 1948 when the Communists imposed a blockade to force the protecting Western troops out of Berlin and to starve the people of that City into submission.

That plan failed. A free people and a dramatic airlift broke the back of the scheme.

In the end the Communists abandoned the blockade and concluded an agreement in 1949 with the Western Powers, reconfirming our right of unrestricted access to the city.

Then, last November, the Soviets announced that they intended to repudiate these solemn obligations. They once more appear to be living by the Communist formula that "Promises are like pie crusts, made to be broken."

The Soviet Government has also announced its intention to enter into a peace treaty with the East German puppet regime. The making of this treaty, the Soviets assert, will deny our occupation rights and our rights of access. It is, of course, clear that no so-called "peace treaty" between the Soviets and the East German regime can have any moral or legal effect upon our rights.

The Soviet threat has since been repeated several times, accompanied by various and changing suggestions for dealing with the status of the city. Their proposals have included a vague offer to make the Western part of Berlin—though not the Eastern part, which the Soviets control— a so-called "free city."

It is by no means clear what West Berlin would be free from, except perhaps from freedom itself. It would not be free from the ever present danger of Communist domination. No one, certainly not the two million West Berliners, can ignore the cold fact that Berlin is surrounded by many divisions of Soviet and Eastern German troops and by territory governed by authorities dedicated to eliminating freedom from the area.

Now a matter of principle, the United States cannot accept the asserted right of any government to break, by itself, solemn agreements to which we, with others, are parties. But in the Berlin situation, both free people and principle are at stake.

What, then, are the fundamental choices we have in this situation?

First, of course, there is the choice which the Soviet rulers themselves would like us to make. They hope that we can be frightened into abdicating our rights—which are indeed responsibilities—to help establish a just and peaceful solution to the German problem—rights which American and Allied soldiers purchased with their lives.

We have no intention of forgetting our rights or of deserting a free people. Soviet rulers should remember that free men have, before this, died for so-called "scraps of paper" which represented duty and honor and freedom.

The shirking of our responsibilities would solve no problems for us. First, it would mean the end of all hopes for a Germany under government of German choosing. It would raise, among our friends, the most serious doubts about the validity of all the international agreements and commitments we have made with them in every quarter of the globe. One result would be to undermine the mutual confidence upon which our entire system of collective security is founded.

This, the Soviets would greet as a great victory over the West.

Obviously, this choice is unacceptable to us.

The second choice which the Soviets have compelled us to face, is the possibility of war.

Certainly, the American and Western peoples do not want war. The whole world knows this. Global conflict under modern conditions could mean the destruction of civilization. The Soviet rulers, themselves, are well aware of this fact.

But all history has taught us the grim lesson that no nation has ever been successful in avoiding the terrors of war by refusing to defend its rights—by attempting to placate aggression.

Whatever risk of armed conflict may be inherent in the present Berlin situation, it was deliberately created by the Soviet rulers.

Moreover, the justice of our position is attested by the fact that it is ardently supported with virtual unanimity by the people of West Berlin.

The risk of war is minimized if we stand firm. War would become more likely if we gave way and encouraged a rule of terrorism rather than a rule of law and order. Indeed, this is the core of the peace policy which we are striving to carry out around the world. In that policy is found the world's best hope for peace.

Now our final choice is negotiation, even while we continue to provide for our security against every threat. We are seeking meaningful negotiation at this moment. The United States and its allies stand ready to talk with Soviet representatives at any time and under any circumstances which offer prospects of worth-while results.

We have no selfish material aims in view. We seek no domination over others—only a just peace for the world and particularly, in this instance, for the people most involved.

We are ready to consider all proposals which may help to reassure and will take into account the European peoples most concerned.

We are willing to listen to new ideas and are prepared to present others. We will do everything within our power to bring about serious negotiations and to make these negotiations meaningful.

Let us remind ourselves once again of what we cannot do.

We cannot try to purchase peace by forsaking two million free people of Berlin.

We cannot agree to any permanent and compulsory division of the German nation, which would leave central Europe a perpetual powder mill, even though we are ready to discuss with all affected nations any reasonable methods for its eventual unification.

We cannot recognize the asserted right of any nation to dishonor its international agreements whenever it chooses. If we should accept such a contention the whole process of negotiation would become a barren mockery.

We must not, by weakness or irresolution, increase the risk of war.

Finally, we cannot, merely for the sake of demonstrating so-called "flexibility" accept any agreement or arrangement which would undermine the security of the United States and its Allies.

The Soviet note of March 2nd appears to be a move toward negotiation on an improved basis. We would never negotiate under a dictated time limit or agenda, or on other unreasonable terms. We are, with our Allies, however, in view of the changed tone of the Soviet note, concerting a reply to that note.

It is my hope that thereby all of us can reach agreement with the Soviets on an early meeting at the level of foreign ministers.

Assuming developments that justify a summer meeting at the Summit, the United States would be ready to participate in that further effort.

Our position, then, is this: we will not retreat one inch from our duty. We shall continue to exercise our right of peaceful passage to and from

West Berlin. We will not be the first to breach the peace; it is the Soviets who threaten the use of force to interfere with such free passage. We are ready to participate fully in every sincere effort at negotiation that will respect the existing rights of all and their opportunity to live in peace.

Today's Berlin difficulty is not the first stumbling block that International Communism has placed along the road to peace. The world has enjoyed little relief from tension in the past dozen years. As long as the Communist empire continues to seek world domination we shall have to face threats to the peace, of varying character and location. We have lived and will continue to live in a period where emergencies manufactured by the Soviets, follow one another like beads on a string.

Whatever the length of that period, we shall have to remain continuously ready to repel aggression, whether it be political, economic, or military. Every day our policies of peace will be subjected to test. We must have steadiness and resolution, and firm adherence to our own carefully thought-out policies.

We must avoid letting fear or lack of confidence turn us from the course that self-respect, decency, and love of liberty point out. To do so would be to dissipate the creative energies of our people upon whom our real security rests. This we will never do.

Now to build toward peace and maintain free world security will require action in every field of human enterprise. It can only be done by the nations of the Free World working together in close cooperation, adjusting their differences, sharing their common burdens, pursuing their common goals. We are carrying out just such an effort. We call it mutual security.

We recognize that freedom is indivisible. Wherever in the world freedom is destroyed, by that much is every free nation hurt.

If the United States, alone, had to carry the full burden of defending its interests from the Communist threat, we would have to draft a much larger portion of our manhood into the armed services, spend many more billions of treasure, and put a more intense strain on all our resources and capacities. We would become more and more like a garrison state.

Fortunately, we do not have to adopt such a desperate course. Nearly 50 nations have joined with us in a cooperative effort to protect freedom.

This system of mutual security allows each nation to provide the forces which it is best able to supply.

Now what is the strength of these forces? What are we contributing to the joint effort? What can we count on from our Allies?

Let's look first at our own contribution. Let us look at it from the viewpoint of our own security.

Of late I—and I am sure the American people—have heard or read conflicting claims about our defenses.

We have heard that our military posture has been subordinated to a balanced budget, jeopardizing our national defense.

We have heard that our defenses are presently—or they will be some-time in the future—inadequate to meet recurrent Communist threats.

We have heard that more manpower in our forces than I have recommended is essential in the present circumstances, for psychological reasons if for no other.

My friends, such assertions as these are simply not true. They are without foundation. It is not likely, however—and this is indeed fortunate—that such assertions will lead the Soviet Union to miscalculate our true strength.

The design of our defense is the product of the best composite judgment available for the fulfillment of our security needs.

First, we are devoting great sums for the maintenance of forces capable of nuclear retaliatory strikes. This capability is our indispensable deterrent to aggression against us.

The central core of our deterrent striking force is our Strategic Air Command with its long range bombers. They are reinforced by naval aircraft, missiles of varying types, and tactical fighter bombers. This array will soon include weapons of even greater power and effectiveness.

The capacity of our combined striking forces represents an almost unimaginable destructive power. It is protected by a vast early warning system and by powerful air defense forces.

More and more this great retaliatory force will feature intermediate as well as long-range missiles capable of reaching any target on the earth. As we steadily go through the transition period from bomber to missile as the backbone of this striking force, we nevertheless continue replacing bombers, powerful as we know them now to be, with others of greater power, greater range, and greater speed. In this way we take care of the needs of this year and those immediately ahead, even as we plan, develop, and build for the future.

We are engaged in an endless process of research, development, and production to equip our forces with new weapons.

This process is tremendously costly, even should we consider it only in terms of money. If we are to master the problem of security over a prolonged period, we cannot forever borrow from the future to meet the needs of the present.

Therefore, we must concentrate our resources on those things we need most, minimizing those programs that make less decisive contributions to our Nation. Effective defense comes first.

Today there is no defense field to which we are devoting more talent, skill, and money than that of missile development.

I'd like to have you look at this chart showing three lists of missiles.

The first list shows seventeen different types of missiles now in use by our Armed Forces.

The second list shows missiles that will be available for use in 1959. There are eleven different types.

The third list shows thirteen more types of missiles now in the research and development stages. In all there are forty-one types of missiles.

Now there is, of course, a constant parade of improvement, with newer and better weapons constantly crowding out the older and less efficient ones.

The first model of any new piece of equipment is always relatively primitive. The first sewing machine, the first typewriter, the first automobile—all left much to be desired. And even the rockets that dazzle us today will soon become the Model T's—the Tin Lizzies—of the Missile Age.

We must never become frozen in obsolescence.

In addition to the forces comprising our retaliatory striking power, we have potent and flexible naval, ground, and amphibious elements. We have a growing array of nuclear-powered ships, both submarines and surface vessels.

World-wide deployment of Army divisions, including missile units, increases the ability of the U.S. Army and the Marines to rapidly apply necessary force to any area of trouble. At home, the Strategic Army Corps is ready and able to move promptly as needed to any area of the world.

I believe that the American people want, are entitled to, can indefinitely pay for, and now have and will continue to have a modern, effective, and adequate military establishment. In this overall conviction, I am supported by the mass of the best military opinion I can mobilize, and by scientific and every other kind of talent that is giving its attention to a problem to which I personally have devoted a lifetime.

As all thoughtful citizens know, our own security requires the supplemental and reinforcing strength provided by the free world's total.

In the Far East, nations with which we are associated in a common defense system have over a million trained soldiers standing watch over the free world frontiers.

In Europe, the efforts of fifteen nations are united in support of freedom.

In global totals, our friends are contributing over 200 ground divisions, 30,000 aircraft, and 2500 combatant naval vessels to the task of defending the free world.

For every soldier we have under arms, our free world Allies have five.

Through each of these stout efforts we strengthen the bonds of freedom.

Our mutual security program supports this joint undertaking by helping to equip our partners with the weapons they cannot by themselves provide, and by helping them keep their economies strong.

This mutual effort provides a constructive, long-term answer to the recurrent crises engineered by the Communists. It strengthens the stability of free nations, and lessens opportunities for Communist subversion and penetration. It supports economic growth and gives hope and confidence to the cause of freedom. It is America's strongest instrument for positive action in the world today.

Last Friday I sent to the Congress a special message presenting my recommendations for this important part of our defense and security program for the coming year. Let me repeat that definition of that program: it is an important part of our defense and security program for the coming year. In my judgment, there is no better means of showing our resolution, our firmness, and our understanding of the Communist challenge than to support this program in full measure.

These funds are vital to our national and free world security.

Any misguided effort to reduce them below what I have recommended weakens the sentries of freedom wherever they stand.

In this conviction, also, I am supported by the military experts of our Government.

————————

Fellow Americans, of one thing I am sure: that we have the courage and capacity to meet the stern realities of the present and the future. We need only to understand the issues and to practice the self-discipline that freedom demands.

Our security shield is the productivity of our free economy, the power of our military forces, and the enduring might of a great community of nations determined to defend their freedom.

We Americans have been, from the beginning, a free people—people who by their spiritual and moral strength and their love of country provide the mainspring for all we have done, are doing, and will do. In those truths we place our faith.

So, together with our Allies we stand firm wherever the probing finger of any aggressor may point. Thus we lessen the risk of aggression: thus we shall with resolution and courage, struggle ever forward to the dream of a just and permanent peace.

God helping us, we shall stand always equal to the challenge.

Thank you, and goodnight.

NOTE: The missile chart to which the President referred is published in the Congressional Record of March 18, 1959 (vol. 105, p. A2312).

58 ¶ Remarks of Welcome to President O'Kelly of Ireland at the Washington National Airport. *March* 17, 1959

Mr. President, Mrs. O'Kelly, members of your party, ladies and gentlemen:

It is indeed a signal honor to welcome here to America the first President of Ireland who has ever visited our shores. And it is particularly felicitous that we can welcome him on the birthday, the anniversary, of the great Irish saint—some fifteen hundred years since his death.

Now as I welcome you, Mr. President, I find myself in a rather difficult situation, and I am sure that the protocol officers of our two governments wouldn't know exactly how to solve the problem.

It is this: today everybody in the United States is Irish.

Now, those who look Irish and sound Irish and have Irish names, they don't have to prove this in any way. But anyone with the name Eisenhower must wear something green—which I have.

In any event, all of us are Irish.

So, I would say that for this day at least, though you come as the official President of Ireland, in our hearts you are President for all of us. So this particular welcome that I extend to you is not only as from the President of the United States but one of your subjects, because of your particular position in relationship to the patron saint of Ireland, St. Patrick.

Welcome again to all of you.

NOTE: President O'Kelly responded as follows:

Mr. President, I salute my most distinguished subject.

I thank you, sir, for your most kind words of welcome, which have touched me deeply. They are an expression of the great American tradition of hospitality. They also reflect that close friendship and mutual understanding which have always so happily existed between Ireland and the United States of America.

I am very sensible, Mr. President, of the great honor you did me and my country in inviting me to come to the United States as your guest. But I am most profoundly grateful that you should have asked me to come at this particular time. It is, as you have so graciously said, a happy augury that the first official visit of the President of Ireland should begin on St. Patrick's Day. On this day the Irish honor the Apostle of the Gael but we are not alone in doing so. Nowhere, I venture to say, is this feast celebrated with greater enthusiasm than here in the United States. We in Ireland remember with gratitude the unfailing sympathy and generous help which Ireland has always received from the American people. We recall with pride the part played in the history of your Republic by Irish men and Irish women, and we admire with an unqualified admiration the remarkable achievements of this great nation, and the pre-eminent position it has achieved.

But above all, we rejoice that the United States has always remained true to the high purpose and the noble ideals of the Founding Fathers which in the words of Abraham Lincoln—whom we especially honor this year—contain as he said, the germ which has vegetated and still is to grow and expand into the universal liberty of mankind.

Permit me once more, Mr. President, to thank you for your cordial welcome, and to assure you how honored and privileged I feel personally to renew acquaintance with this great country and its noble President and people.

59 ¶ Toasts of the President and the President of Ireland.   *March* 17, 1959

Mr. President, Mrs. O'Kelly, and My Friends:

It is a delightful privilege that I have this evening to welcome the President of Ireland to this country, to this capital city, to this house.   I think only an Irishman could possibly have the language, the terminology, to describe the close feeling, the feeling of affection that America has for Ireland.

Now, my name, wouldn't it sound funny if I tried to say O'Eisenhower? Nevertheless, I think I sum up the feeling of an Irishman in America when he tries to say to you: Welcome—welcome—to a people that are so very dear and close to us.

It is not, I think, just because there are so many Irish in America. And I don't think it's because they have had such a big part in helping to win the wars in which we have been so unfortunate to indulge.   And I don't think it's particularly just because they like a fight!   But there is something almost romantic even in their names.   Whether it's O'Shaughnessey or whether it's O'Kelly, there's something, a sort of a feeling that is quite individual.   I think the American senses this, and whether the Irishman is what we used to call a "gandy dancer" on the railroad or whether he is occupying the highest places in Government or in business or in the professions, there is still a rather fine feeling when you go up to him and say, "How do you do, I am glad to see you."

I have learned during the course of this day with you, sir, that all of these qualities that the Irish have, to inspire affection, admiration, and liking, you have in full measure.

And I am quite certain that in saying that, I mean only that you are representative of this lovely island from which you come, and the people that have sent you here as our guest.

So as I pay again a tribute to this wonderful feeling of warm friendship that has never been broken between Ireland and ourselves—and incidentally, Mr. President, I have always wondered how you people can call yourselves neutral, you are in every fight there is—and maybe that's another reason we like you—but in any event, as I try to express that feeling of warm friendship that we know exists between your people and ours, and which we know shall never be broken, I can do it in no better terms than merely to request you to stand up and drink with me to Ireland, its President and his charming lady.   Mr. President!

NOTE: The President proposed this toast at a state dinner at the White House. President O'Kelly responded as follows:

Mr. President, Madam, Ladies and Gentlemen:

Maybe you can all hear me, but you might not all be able to see me—I stand up as tall as I can. But I am profoundly grateful to your President for the most gracious and kindly and friendly words spoken about me. Deep down in my heart I have always had good reason to have affection for the United States and its people. But after today and their wonderful demonstration in this great city, the capital of this great nation, and your most kind and all too generous remarks about me personally, I am overflowing with affection, not alone for the United States and its people, but for the two Eisenhowers. God bless you both.

I am profoundly grateful for this opportunity of being here as President of Ireland. But first of all, Mr. President, I would like to express my very deep appreciation of your great kindness in inviting me to come to this country as your official guest.

This visit marks for me one of the highlights of a long public career which began in the early days of this century, and which comes to a close in a few months' time. On the 24th of June I walk out of the President's House in Dublin, and I become a "has been."

I count myself fortunate that my official activity lay within those particular years. They have seen the suppression of freedom in countries dear to you, sir, and to me. But they have also seen the emergence of freedom in many nations old and new. The Irish nation, which as you have so kindly said more than once, Mr. President, is among the oldest on the earth—is one of these that has won its freedom in recent times. I thank God that it should have been given to me to witness, though still unfortunately for less than the entirety of our ancient land, the realization of the dreams and the endeavors of many generations of Irishmen, and to have the privilege of playing some part myself—and my wife—in that realization.

Our generation has seen, too, the rise of this great Republic of the United States of America to new pinnacles of glory and of power, and also of responsibility. No more than in Ireland has the outstanding material progress of this country been so warmly welcomed, nowhere have the efforts of the American government and people, to give in their international conduct an example of justice and the rule of law, been more generally applauded than in Ireland.

For seeking ourselves no advantages at the expense of others, we profoundly appreciate that the leading world power in the world today should dedicate itself so unselfishly to the cause of peace and should be so lavish of its own resources in that great cause.

I know, Mr. President, that your invitation to me was above all intended to mark the close friendship between our two nations. That friendship dates from the very beginning of American independence, and reflects the equal attachment of our two peoples to freedom, justice, and tolerance.

And there are very few of us in Ireland but have some ties of blood within this great community. I think it is true to say—maybe a slight exaggeration, but not much—that there is hardly a family in Ireland that hasn't relatives in the United States. I think that is true.

The debt of my country to yours in this regard was well expressed by Walt Whitman in the poem to old Ireland, when he wrote, "What you wept for was translated, passed from the grave, the winds favored and the sea sail'd it, and now with rosy and new blood, moves today in a new country."

I can think of no higher tribute to

Ireland than that the President of the United States of America should mark in such a signal manner the feast day of our nation, the apostle of St. Patrick, under whose special protection we stand and through whose labors was implanted in us those many centuries ago the gift of the Christian heritage.

This heritage our people have always cherished, and through it they have been privileged to contribute to the spiritual store of other nations, and not least of the American nation, to which we are now attached by so many ties and such a wealth of grateful memories.

Your most cordial welcome adds a precious new chapter to the noble record of our relations and one of which my country shall always be proud and sensible. And no humble or great citizen in that nation be more proud and more sensible of the honor done than your humble friend, the President of Ireland! Your health, sir!

60   ¶ Statement by the President Upon Signing the Hawaii Statehood Bill. *March* 18, 1959

IT HAS given me great satisfaction to sign the Act providing for the admission of Hawaii into the Union.

Since my inauguration in 1953 I have consistently urged that this legislation be enacted, so the action of the Congress so early in this session is most gratifying.

Under this legislation, the citizens of Hawaii will soon decide whether their Islands shall become our fiftieth State. In so doing, they will demonstrate anew to the world the vitality of the principles of freedom and self-determination—the principles upon which this Nation was founded 172 years ago.

NOTE: As enacted, the Hawaii Statehood Bill (S. 50) is Public Law 86-3 (73 Stat. 4).

61   ¶ Letter to Governor Quinn Certifying to the Enactment of the Hawaii Statehood Bill. *March* 18, 1959

Dear Governor Quinn:

In accordance with the provisions of Section 6 of Public Law 86-3, I am very happy to certify to you the fact that I approved the law today, March 18, 1959.

As you start the procedure that will, I hope, result in the admission of Hawaii into the Union as a State on equal footing with the other States, you and the people of Hawaii have my very best wishes.

Sincerely,

Dwight D. Eisenhower

62 ¶ Letter to the Director, Bureau of the Budget, Concerning the Admission of Hawaii.
March 18, 1959

Dear Mr. Stans:

In view of the imminent admission of the State of Hawaii into the Union, it is essential that the Federal Government promptly initiate a careful study of the effects of statehood and develop a systematic and coordinated program for effecting an orderly transition from territorial status to statehood.

I believe that the Bureau of the Budget should assume leadership for Executive Branch action in this area, beyond the regular responsibilities of the Department of the Interior, as it has done, at my request, in the case of Alaska statehood. Therefore, I am asking you, with the cooperation of the interested departments and agencies, to undertake the task of reviewing the implications of Hawaii statehood, developing a comprehensive plan for accomplishing the transition, and presenting to me recommendations for dealing with any matters requiring my attention.

Sincerely,

Dwight D. Eisenhower

63 ¶ Letter to Mr. Steve Stahl, Chairman, National Taxpayers Conference, on Preserving Our National Economic Strength.   *March* 18, 1959

Dear Mr. Stahl:

I appreciate very much your letter expressing the support of the National Taxpayers Conference for a balanced budget and sound management of our Government's fiscal affairs.

In response to your request for suggestions as to how your Association can best aid in preserving our Nation's economic strength, I'm sure you realize I would not want to be in the position of an expert devising a detailed prescription. However, assuming that I had a post such as yours in the National Taxpayers Conference, first I would want to help citizens gain a better understanding as to the facts of the Government's fiscal position. They need to know that our failure to keep the budget in balance next year can result in growing difficulties in public debt financing, and certainly will mean further postponement of overdue tax revision. Future years are already threatened with more deficits because of built-in growth factors in existing legislation.

I should want to assist members to understand the increased danger of inflation if the Government is forced to continue deficit spending in a period of rising incomes and prosperity. I assume that they would need no help to see the implications of inflation to their savings, their pensions, their personal budgets, and the value of their take-home pay. This would certainly destroy any indifference to inflation.

Next, I'd try to help citizens to form a balanced opinion on the major issues which have arisen in the current discussion of the Federal budget. Point out to them, for example, that the budget which I have recommended contains 45.8 billion dollars for the basic features of our national security, and that to support this kind of expenditure we must examine all non-defense items with a careful eye.

We must remind ourselves that the danger we face is only in part a military one; that the threat of Soviet communism is likewise an economic threat.

Finally, of course, your members should realize that they and other citizens have the greatest control over the outcome of the budget for the next fiscal year. Public opinion is still the determining force in our public affairs. If the Government is to follow the course of fiscal responsibility in the conduct of its business, the informed citizens of our Nation must speak up to the Congress without delay.

Whether or not the above is helpful, I assure you that I am grateful for the effort you are personally making.

With best wishes to you and to the National Taxpayers Conference, I am

Sincerely,

DWIGHT D. EISENHOWER

NOTE: Mr. Stahl's letter was released with the President's reply. The executive officers of State taxpayers associations, associated as the National Taxpayers Conference, met in Washington at the Sheraton-Park Hotel, March 16–18.

64 ¶ Toasts of the President and President O'Kelly of Ireland at a Luncheon for President Eisenhower. *March* 19, 1959

Mr. President, Mrs. O'Kelly, Your Excellency the Archbishop, Distinguished Guests and Friends:

I think each of us can sense something of the spirit of warm friendship that has been brought to our people during these two or three days by the President of Ireland and his lovely lady.

We thank Ireland for sending him over here. We thank them for coming.

This spirit—this changed spirit in Washington that I sense so keenly—is reflected even among ourselves. It seems to me I am getting more smiles from the Democrats than I have had in a long time. And certainly I feel more kindly to everybody in the city because of having met you, President O'Kelly.

I think it is well that it is so. In the years that stretch out ahead of us, we must be friendly among ourselves. We must be close to our good friends—and Ireland is among the front rank of our good friends. We must have faith in ourselves. We must have faith in each other—and faith in our God.

These are the sentiments that I have been listening to from our friend, the President, for these past two or three days. I have had an uplift of spirit because of the things I have heard during this visit.

So it is with extraordinary pleasure and satisfaction that I ask you all to stand to drink with me the health of the Irish people—and, above all, to their President and his lady.

NOTE: This toast was proposed in response to a toast by President O'Kelly at a luncheon which he gave in honor of President Eisenhower at the Mayflower Hotel, Washington, D.C. In his opening words the President referred to the Most Reverend Patrick A. O'Boyle, Archbishop of Washington.

The toast proposed by President O'Kelly follows:

Mr. President, Mrs. Eisenhower, Mr. Speaker, Your Excellency the Archbishop, Your Excellencies, Ladies and Gentlemen:

I know how busy your President is, and though I would like to spend some time repeating again for you the things you have heard many times of the excellencies associated with and incorporated in your President, I must refrain.

I do want, though, just before I leave Washington, to express again my most profound gratitude to you, Mr. President, and to you, Madam, and to all the people of Washington, D.C., for the warmth, the overwhelming warmth of the welcome the President of Ireland has received since his coming here.

It has been something that I could never have dreamed could have happened—that's the truth.

The warmth of feeling exhibited here for Ireland—I couldn't take it all for myself, though I would like to, as if it were

meant for me—but it was meant for Ireland, and that's the same thing.

And then, that gracious, noble gesture of the President at the airport the other day, describing himself as—for Patrick's Day—my subject, that will never be forgotten in Ireland's history.

So, I am profoundly grateful, in Ireland's name.

I pray God to give you strength and power and health and happiness and prosperity. To you, your good lady, and your great people—on whom so much depends today, God be with you always.

I would ask you, ladies and gentlemen, to join with me in drinking the health of the President of the United States.

65 ¶ Statement by the President on the House Appropriations Committee's Rejection of the Development Loan Fund. *March* 20, 1959

I HAVE just learned of the action of the Appropriations Committee of the House of Representatives rejecting all funds for the continuation of the Development Loan Fund.

This irresponsible action, if not rectified, will do the gravest injury to the whole position of the United States in the world today. As I told the Congress when I requested these funds, the Development Loan Fund has committed virtually all of its appropriated funds and must have additional funds now. The only alternative is to turn a deaf ear to all loan requests from our friends until fiscal year 1960 funds become available through authorization and appropriation several months from now.

The commitment of virtually all of the capital of the Fund was made by formal letters of commitment and other pledges signed and delivered under my authority and publicly announced both here and abroad. It is now contended by those seeking to cut off this vital arm of our foreign policy that the Fund still really is well supplied with money because these actions did not constitute commitments.

These commitments are firm. They have been made at my direction under provisions of law and in accord with my Constitutional authority.

They must be honored. They, therefore, leave us without funds for further commitments.

I recommended, and the Congress established, the Development Loan Fund as a major instrument of United States leadership in the world. The action today, if not reversed, will represent a long step backward toward isolating our country and weakening our national security.

NOTE: This statement was released at Gettysburg, Pa.

66 ¶ Toasts of the President and King Hussein I of the Hashemite Kingdom of Jordan. *March 24, 1959*

Your Majesty, Distinguished and Honored Guests from your country, and Friends:

It is truly an honor and a privilege to welcome to this country, on behalf of the American people, King Hussein of the Hashemite Kingdom of Jordan.

He has been admired as the head of his nation, but he has also been so courageous that his name has become symbolic of courage in the world.

Since the American people, Your Majesty, honor and admire courage as much as any other quality, they have for you a real feeling of friendliness and admiration. They recognize what the leaders of your country, headed by yourself, have been able to do in the face of very great trials and pressures. You have withstood the temptations that have been placed before you to weaken in defense of your principles and your rights.

So I am sure this company would like to give a salute to you in a toast to your health and happiness and prosperity.

Gentlemen, His Majesty the King!

NOTE: The President proposed this toast at a luncheon at the White House. King Hussein responded as follows:

Mr. President, gentlemen:

I should like to thank you very much indeed for your kind words. I should like to thank you for giving me the opportunity today, despite your engagements, to have the pleasure to spend this time with you and the gentlemen present here.

It has always been one of my dearest wishes to be able to visit this great country, and to personally thank you, Mr. President, for all the help and encouragement you have given me during a time of great difficulty in which I, and the country I am privileged to serve, have had to pass. I always remember our friends and remember the difficulties we faced. I am very happy that we have managed to pass through that difficult stage, and that I now have this opportunity to come here to thank you, and to spend a period of time with you, which has been most pleasant.

We have been meeting with kindness and hospitality everywhere. I am sure that not only myself, but all of the group that has come with me and are present here, join me in giving our sincere thanks for all the warmth and kindness we have met here.

I hope, as well, that the good relations between our two countries will always remain very strong. We believe in the same things, and we have the same path. I assure you that as far as we are concerned in Jordan, we will continue to fight the best way we can—no matter what the difficulties may be—to preserve our independence, the integrity of our country and our beliefs, and to defend the whole nation, the Hashemite Kingdom of Jordan.

It is a great privilege and honor. I should like to ask you gentlemen to join me now in a toast to your good health and happiness.

67 ¶ The President's News Conference of *March* 25, 1959.

THE PRESIDENT. Good morning. Please sit down.

We'll go to questions.

Q. Merriman Smith, United Press International: Mr. President, do you feel that the results of your meeting with Prime Minister Macmillan will lead to a reduction of tensions with Russia; and in this connection, sir, what, if any, conditions do you attach to your attending a summer summit conference?

THE PRESIDENT. Well, first of all, the first part of your question—all of this exercise of negotiating and dealing with the Soviets has as its basic purpose the reduction of tension. We have been, the free world has been, trying to bring that about for a good many years.

Now, with respect to conditions laid down in the notes, as you people well know, all of these notes have to be coordinated with our friends, including NATO. This has now been done. Our note will be sent very shortly; and very quickly after that, as quickly as it can be done, it will be released.

So I would suggest for the actual letter of our intentions there is a place to find it, and very quickly.[1]

---

[1] On the following day the Department of State released the note, dated March 26, from the U.S. Government to the Soviet Government concerning the United States proposal that a meeting of the foreign ministers of France, U.S.S.R., the United Kingdom, and the United States be convened in Geneva on May 11 to consider questions relating to Germany, including a peace treaty with Germany and the question of Berlin. The note is published in the Department of State Bulletin (vol. 40, p. 507).

Now, I just will say this one thing: I have been talking for some years now about the convictions that I hold with respect to this whole business. I have never changed them; I don't expect to change them, unless there is something cataclysmic or, let us say, unexpected, rather, that comes along and that would bring some change.

Q. Robert C. Pierpoint, CBS News: Mr. President, do we have any new proposals to discuss with Premier Khrushchev at the summit, and if so, could you tell us something about them?

THE PRESIDENT. No, I can't go into any detail of that, because this is exactly, of course, what the exercise of coordinating with our friends has to do with. We have to be with them as a unit when we make any kind of proposals. There will be many proposals made, but I couldn't discuss them now.

Q. John Scali, Associated Press: Sir, what do you think of the idea of a series of summit conferences where the world leaders could get off in some secluded spot and discuss informally the problems of the world?

THE PRESIDENT. Well, it is rather difficult to visualize such a thing. If you meet with a group of world leaders, it is rather hard to keep the spotlight off of it. And if you are going to talk, doing this informally, it would be with the batteries of interpreters and recorders and all that sort of thing. It would almost inevitably change, I think, into something rather formal.

I will say merely this: if, assuming that we have an atmosphere that permits periodic negotiation, gives some hope of its beneficial effects for our country and for the free world, well, certainly I would never decline to go along in that kind of an effort.

Q. Chalmers M. Roberts, Washington Post: Sir, on a related question, could you tell us the value of Project Argus as you understand it now, and especially whether the results are likely to lead you to alter the nuclear test ban proposal by limiting the ban to tests only in the atmosphere, for example.

THE PRESIDENT. The Argus tests were conducted under conditions that required new methods of evaluation of the results. And they were conducted outside of the atmospheric tests, so that there would be no additional fallout.

Those results, by the way, were picked up from Explorer IV. That is why we put up the Explorer IV, and it was the instrument from which we have gotten all the information that we have gotten.

Now, the purpose had to do both with the IGY, that is the International Geophysical Year, and it had also certain security aspects. Those results have been under study for a good long time—months, really. And only now have my scientific people separated out the IGY information, which we are obligated to make public to the world, and those things which have a potential military value. This has been done. And today, or maybe it is tomorrow—today, I guess—today there is quite a report that will be available to you; I would say later in the day.[2]

Now, as to whether or not this will lead to some agreement that we would have a ban that would be only in the atmosphere—in other words, where additional radioactive material would come into the atmosphere—I cannot tell. With us, the basic question has been that of veto: can we establish a system where each can have confidence in the reports of the other. And if that has been done, why I imagine there are a hundred tangents that could be explored and discussed in such a meeting.

Q. Mrs. May Craig, Portland (Maine) Press Herald: Mr. President, you have spoken of the difficulty of you as President leaving the country for any length of time. Would you like to have a summit conference in the United States with Mr. Khrushchev attending?

THE PRESIDENT. Well, of course, if I tried to make that conference here, I would know of no place you could do it except in the United Nations Building. You see, the job of having all these simultaneous translation instruments, and of the building, the accommodation, so set up that it can be done, that would be the only place. And New York is a very crowded place.

There is another thing: if I am here, I am on the flank of this whole group of nations to be talking, and it is a little bit unfair, I think, to ask them all to come over here, because they all have to go a long distance. The purpose would be to get into a central point.

Now, I don't mean to say that I bar this idea from consideration. I just say we have not taken it seriously as one of the prospects at the moment.

Q. Charles W. Roberts, Newsweek: Mr. President, without anticipating the message that will go out to the Soviets, I would like to ask about your use of the word "justify" in your broadcast a week ago Monday.

---

[2] The report on the Argus experiment, prepared under the direction of the President's Science Advisory Committee and the IGY Committee of the National Academy of Sciences, was released by the White House on March 26.

You said that we wouldn't go to the summit unless it were justified by a foreign ministers conference. Would the breakdown of a foreign ministers conference justify it as well as real progress toward an agreement?

THE PRESIDENT. I have been questioned in many quarters about the use of that word. I thought that it was clear, and I meant when I used it only this, that there was progress that justified it.

Now, if somebody else has taken a different meaning, or a different possibility, contingency, it is different from what I had at the moment I made the talk.

Q. Edward T. Folliard, Washington Post: Mr. President, there has been some comment in print over the fact that you did not have Vice President Nixon at Camp David for the talks. It was suggested that he was absent because you want to appear neutral in the prospective battle between Mr. Nixon and Governor Rockefeller. Would you care to comment?

THE PRESIDENT. You are making a rather unusual premise there—this is all between Mr. Nixon and Mr. Rockefeller. [*Laughter*]

No, I'll tell you: we thought about asking Mr. Nixon. He is busy. He has got here some other things he was talking about and thinking about when we were up at Camp David. And then I myself undertook to get him in. We did have quite a long meeting to keep him fully acquainted with every single idea that we discussed.

And I have no idea of tempering my actions or my own thinking according to the possibilities of a political contest that may come about at some future time.

Q. Laurence H. Burd, Chicago Tribune: Mr. President, what is your feeling about a plan which we were told was discussed at Camp David for some kind of weapons freeze or ceiling in an area of central Europe?

THE PRESIDENT. I don't know who could have told you that. If anyone did, they would do it without my consent and without the consent of any others at the conference. And if I should attempt to say whether or not this question was discussed, or with any ideas put forward, then I would be compelled, I think, to talk and tell you everything we talked about. I don't think that would be justified.

Q. Lloyd M. Schwartz, Fairchild Publications: Mr. President, did you have occasion to reassure the British on objections they have raised to several recent restrictive U.S. trade actions, including the possibility of smaller quotas on wool fabrics?

THE PRESIDENT. Well, yes, we talked. As a matter of fact—and this of course was outside any secret realm—everybody knows that we are concerned about this thing. I believe it is not only the wool fabrics, but it is electrical machinery and I believe some activities in the airplane realm.

Now, both of us agreed this: to study it as seriously, as exhaustively as we can, because both of us believe in what we call the principle of interdependence. We believe that you cannot keep a coalition of free countries, each with its own problems, its own aspirations, its own special conditions—you cannot bring them together, keep them close together, unless we adopt cooperative measures that do promote the interests of all. And to be too selfish, or, let us say, too shortsighted in looking at our own possible advantage for the moment—I think the greatest need is to look at the long-term benefits of the whole group, because with that group our own fortunes are tied up.

Q. John R. Gibson, Wall Street Journal: Mr. President, on the trade matter, your recent action on controls for oil imports has raised some question in the country about whether or not you are going back in your longtime opposition to price control. There was an action in there relating to price regulation, perhaps. Would you comment?

THE PRESIDENT. Well, the only comment in that statement was that the committee would have to continue its study on this oil agreement to see whether or not the security of the Nation did demand any increased prices. And I meant it just exactly that way, because—look here: suppose you make a decision, OCDM makes a decision, that the national security is involved in certain quotas or certain actions to protect a particular industry in our country. Now, if you would run the prices too high, you could be very definitely weakening the national security of our country because you could hurt our economy to the point that it would be indeed difficult to keep our security on the level we want.

So what I am trying to say is, here, you have got problems that act and interact and react on each other in such a way that you just can't make a complete, perfect decision today, or one that you hope will be a practicable one, and know that it is going to be exactly the right one a year later.

Q. J. F. Ter Horst, Detroit News: Sir, yesterday the House approved your Development Loan Fund by reversing the action of a powerful committee, the Appropriations Committee. Since this would not have been possible without strong Democratic support, do you think you were a little hasty last fall, or perhaps ill-advised, in the campaign to label Democrats as wild or reckless spenders?

THE PRESIDENT. If you will just go back to all my speeches, you will find that I carefully defined the people, not a whole party, and I carefully made that clear. I said there were some that were reckless spenders, and I talked about it, and I think it was perfectly legitimate as a political argument in a political fight.

Q. Raymond P. Brandt, St. Louis Post-Dispatch: Senator Byrd says he has urged you to veto the appropriation bills which were substantially larger than your recommendations.

Do you have an understanding with Senator Byrd?

THE PRESIDENT. I don't even have an understanding with my own budget officer or my Secretary of the Treasury. There is no one who knows, until a bill is before me—not even I—whether or not that bill is going to be vetoed.

Now, I do respect Senator Byrd's position in this whole business, because he agrees, as I do, in the theory that we simply must get Federal expenditures into a better status than they have been and are threatening to become today.

Q. Sarah McClendon, San Antonio Light: Sir, the farmers of the Rio Grande Valley have hundreds of acres of cabbages which they want to give to the hungry coal miners and their families in Kentucky and Pennsylvania and other States. They have offered to give this and to pack it for shipment. There is no legal way to get it up there under the present setup, unless you have some emergency funds that perhaps you could use for this. The railroads say they cannot take it for free, although that is permissible by law.

THE PRESIDENT. Well, I hadn't heard about this cabbage, but I am all for it—*[laughter]*—because I happen to be one of those people who like cabbage in all its forms.

So, if we can get it to them, why, I will look into it, I promise you.[3]

───────────

[3] The President later referred to the Department of Agriculture for study, the question dealing with food shipments into Kentucky. A memorandum from Acting Secretary of Agriculture, True D. Morse, dated and released April 6, stated that while no cabbage had been offered to the Government by Texas growers, it was his understanding that private transportation had been arranged for the donated cabbage. Mr. Morse further noted that substantial amounts of other surplus farm products were being distributed by the Government to needy persons in Kentucky.

Q. Rutherford M. Poats, United Press International: Can you give us your comments, sir, on the Tibetan revolt and your views as to the prospects or possibilities of any outside assistance to the rebels?

THE PRESIDENT. Frankly, I looked at the thing again this morning. Our reports are so fragmentary, so—as a matter of fact—sketchy, that there is very little to deduce from the occurrence, except that the people of Tibet were very much disturbed and have become very restive under the control exercised over them, and apparently the Chinese have had to bring in some reinforcements. There has been a very considerable amount of guerrilla type of fighting, and I believe some burning in some parts of the city.

But we don't know enough about it to make a conclusion at this moment.

Q. Roland Evans, Jr., New York Herald Tribune: Mr. President, Congress is leaving town this week for the Easter recess, halfway through the first session. Would you assess the record so far, and tell us whether you are satisfied with the actions of Congress to date.

THE PRESIDENT. I think, Mr. Evans, I have been asked that question in every session of every Congress we have had, along about the Eastertime.

I don't believe there is any way—no one can predict Congress, as far as I know. Its actions come in spurts. Usually in the first part of the session there is a lot of studying and talking and speechmaking, and then suddenly there are a lot of bills up for real action. I know that they come in very rapidly at the last minute, because I have such stacks on my desk at the end that it is a wonder you can get them all signed in time. So I think it is just futile to try to evaluate their accomplishments today or what we expect in the future.

Q. Marvin L. Arrowsmith, Associated Press: Mr. President, what would be your attitude regarding a summit conference if before such a meeting could be arranged the Russians were to sign a separate peace treaty with East Germany?

THE PRESIDENT. Well, I don't know that—first of all—let's start with this. I believe they did sign a treaty and filed it with the United Nations some time back, several months. I believe that any signature by itself would not necessarily have any effect particularly because of this. We are talking about actions, and we are quite sure and clear in our own minds that the mere signing of a new peace treaty, or a so-called peace treaty, or a codicil to that treaty, an addendum, would not in itself vitiate our rights which we are determined to protect.

Q. Peter Lisagor, Chicago Daily News: On the summit, again, Mr. President, in the past you have indicated many times that you thought the summit conferences were not very good means of diplomacy unless they met to ratify previous agreements. How do you feel now about the argument that the only man in Russia you can do business with is Soviet Premier Khrushchev?

THE PRESIDENT. Well, I think it is perfectly clear that he is the only man who has the opportunity, let us say, the authority really to negotiate. If you had anyone else with whom you were negotiating—except in detail, or method or procedure or agenda, things like that—I really believe that the only way that man could do anything would be to be on the telephone all the time with Moscow. So in effect you would be negotiating directly with Moscow. And I think that there is probably some validity to the argument that if you are going to talk really substantive measures, and hope to get some agreement that can be valid on both sides, considered valid on both sides, that he has got to get into the picture pretty well.

I want to make this very clear. This doesn't mean that anyone can command anybody else to come to a summit meeting. You can't bluff them or blackmail them or anything else. This is to be a meeting, if there is one, of heads of government who are acting voluntarily and because of their beliefs in the possibilities, with some kind of grounds for such a belief, that real measures can be discussed profitably by all of us.

Q. Don Oberdorfer, Knight Newspapers: Mr. President, the workers in the steel mills are already tightening their belts for what seems to them to be an inevitable steel strike this summer.

Isn't there anything that the public or the Government or you, yourself, can do to head off this new injection of price-wage inflation, and do you have any plans along this line?

THE PRESIDENT. Well, I think you know that some time ago I appointed a very high-ranking Cabinet committee to study all of these matters of inflation and of the expansion of our economy without inflation, a sound dollar, and so on, and they have been studying very earnestly.

Now, I have to make it clear that it has been the policy of this Government to keep outside the business of collective bargaining, and not to inject itself into that process, so far as any specific recommendation is made.

But over and over again I have said, with all the emphasis I can, that here is a place, if the United States is to go ahead economically, continue to go ahead, here is a place where labor and management must show statesmanship on both sides. Frankly, I would expect, as a measure of their statesmanship, to see whether it can be brought about, in their argument, that whatever it is, that there need be no advancement in the price of the commodity the public has to pay.

The reason that I say this so emphatically is this: while this is a matter between the steelworkers and the steel companies, the whole public is affected by everything they do, and it would be completely out of character for me to pretend to ignore it and wash my hands, like Pontius Pilate; I don't mean to do that. But I do mean to say, if we are going to retain the methods and the procedures that belong properly in a free economy, they must do it, and they must do it in such a way that the price is not compelled to go up.

Q. Kenneth M. Scheibel, Gannett Newspapers: Mr. President, another question on Congress: what do you think of the practice of some Congressmen of putting their relatives on the payroll, or renting the front porch to the Government?

THE PRESIDENT. I believe I will let the editors answer that one. [*Laughter*]

Q. Henry N. Taylor, Scripps-Howard: Sir, in reference to this Soviet peace treaty with East Germany which you referred to, you mentioned it being signed several months ago. I think we are aware of a draft peace treaty which they have said they might sign with East Germany, or at least propose.

THE PRESIDENT. I could be mistaken, but I am sure that they filed a document with the United Nations some months back. If they didn't, I will correct it and make an apology for my error. But that is what I remember.

Now, they do, of course, talk about a new one, but that has a different kind of meaning, because some of the things that were in that one, as I understand it, they now want to put in another one, so they call it a new one, I guess.

Q. Frank Bourgholtzer, NBC News: Mr. President, can you tell us anything now about the role you think Secretary Dulles may play in these forthcoming negotiations?

THE PRESIDENT. Well, I don't know right now, of course. I talked to Secretary Dulles 30 minutes ago, and he is planning to leave for Florida on Monday, I think it is. Everything going well, he will go down there for a period of recreation and convalescence. The doctors will be watching him closely, of course, and hope he can be back in harness in a reasonable time. But as long as he is capable of working, that is, as long as he can feel physically that he can work, in some capacity, I will never let him go—that I can assure you.

Q. David P. Sentner, Hearst Newspapers: Mr. President, in connection with your talks with British Prime Minister Macmillan, there have been confusing and contradicting reports concerning whether you actually agreed on an unconditional summit meeting. Would you care to clear that up for us?

THE PRESIDENT. Well, now, isn't that odd? So far as I know, no one that engaged in that conference made any statement about this whatsoever. So there is some reporting around here I don't understand; although someone read me excerpts where one said in effect that Mr. Macmillan had put one on my jaw, and the other paper said I sort of hit him over the head with a ball bat or something. Now, I think we just better wait to see what comes out in these documents.

Q. John Herling, Editors Syndicate: Mr. President, in view of the continuing high level of unemployment, despite our strong industrial comeback, what obligations, sir, executive and legislative, do you believe fall upon the Federal Government to cope with such unemployment, which is of course very acute in some areas at the present time.

THE PRESIDENT. You are talking, I suppose, about the effects of increased mechanization and automation. I had a Governor come in to see me the other day. He stated this—he told a number of coal miners that were now laid off from the peak level of employment, and he was told that with methods now used, you could get back to peak production with the employment in his State only of an additional 2,000 people. This is a problem that is going to take all the best brains that there are. But I am quite sure that just arbitrary political action from the Federal Government is not going to do it.

Q. Frank van der Linden, Nashville Banner: Sir, there is increasing speculation in the newspapers that Senate Majority Leader Lyndon Johnson may be the Democratic presidential nominee next year. I wonder, sir, if you think he is well qualified and if he would be hard for the Republicans to beat. [*Laughter*]

THE PRESIDENT. The only thing I will say about this is that the Senator has been one of my warm personal friends for many years, and like myself he belongs to the "Cardiac Club." [*Laughter*]

Q. Charles H. Mohr, Time Magazine: Regarding your remarks about Secretary Dulles, Mr. President, have you had any preliminary reports from the doctors that indicate that the radiation treatments have perhaps retarded the disease, already in such a hopeful way that you are pretty sure he is going to come back after that Florida vacation, or have the doctors reported to you yet?

THE PRESIDENT. The doctors just say "We will give you our final answer when we can be sure of it"—that this is not the time yet to make a prognosis in which they could have any real confidence.

Marvin L. Arrowsmith, Associated Press: Thank you, Mr. President.

NOTE: President Eisenhower's one hundred and fifty-fifth news conference was held in the Executive Office Building from 10:29 to 11:00 o'clock on Wednesday morning, March 25, 1959. In attendance: 260.

68 ¶ Statement by the President Concerning Disclosure of Information on Fallout.
March 25, 1959

TO MY knowledge, there has been no suppression of information on fallout. One particular Department of Defense report, dealing with this subject, a summary of which was furnished to the Joint Committee on Atomic Energy on February 19, was originally classified because it dealt with certain operational techniques affecting the national security. At the Committee's request, those portions of the summary report containing the tentative conclusions derived from this operation to date, were declassified.

It was pointed out to the Committee that the data were subject to different interpretations by different technical experts. Therefore the Department of Defense had indicated that in view of the preliminary nature of the information, in its judgment it should not be publicly released until it has been more thoroughly evaluated. The recent release of the differing interpretation of these data by the Department of Defense and the Atomic Energy Commission does not represent fundamental disagreements but rather emphasizes the preliminary nature of these findings.

Every effort is being made by this Government to develop the facts about fallout and to disclose these facts fully to the public. The Atomic Energy Commission is spending about $18,000,000 a year on research on problems associated with radiation standards and protection. In addition, there are other substantial expenditures for sampling and analysis for national and worldwide fallout studies. As Chairman McCone pointed out in his testimony yesterday, in Fiscal Year '60 the figures for radiation standards and protection will be increased to $20,000,000.

The National Academy of Sciences has asked its committees on the biological effects of radiation hazards to consider and appraise the present state of scientific knowledge in this field, the degree of potential hazard from such radiation, and to recommend further research that should be undertaken. This means that the excellent comprehensive study made under the auspices of the Academy nearly three years ago will now be brought up to date by competent scientists.

Everyone in Government who has a responsibility with respect to this matter feels it of the greatest importance that we be diligent in our study of this problem.

NOTE: On March 22 the Chairman of the Joint Committee on Atomic Energy made public declassified portions of letters from the Department of Defense and the Atomic Energy Commission, dated February 19 and March 21 respectively, relating to fallout. This is the recent release referred to by the President.

On April 3 a White House release stated that in view of the attention focused on radiological health matters the President had directed that a report should be made on the status of plans of the executive branch. Referring to comments by the Secretary of Health, Education, and Welfare at his March 16 press conference, and to the Atomic Energy Commission Chairman's March 24 testimony before the Joint Committee, as to the need for a review of the organizational problems involved, the April 3 release stated that, at the President's request, a

joint study of Federal organization of radiological health activities was well under way.

This study resulted in recommendations leading to a Presidential order establishing the Federal Radiation Council (Executive Order 10831, August 14, 1959, 24 F.R. 6669).

The White House release of August 14, announcing the establishment of the Council, noted that the President had approved a series of recommendations to be carried out upon enactment of proposed legislation under which certain regulatory responsibilities of the Atomic Energy Commission would be transferred to the States by agreement with the Commission. Public Law 86–373 (71 Stat. 688), approved September 23, 1959, amended the Atomic Energy Act of 1954 with respect to cooperation with the States and provided for the reestablishment of the Federal

Radiation Council with increased membership and broadened functions.

On August 22, the White House announced at Gettysburg, Pa., that the President had appointed the Secretary of the Department of Health, Education, and Welfare as Chairman of the Council.

69   ¶ Letter to Meade Alcorn, Chairman of the Republican National Committee, Concerning His Resignation.   *April* 1, 1959

Dear Meade:

Your decision to resign as Chairman of the Republican National Committee causes me great regret, as I know it will the vast number of Republicans with whom you have worked closely during the twenty-six months of your stewardship. The zeal with which you have devoted yourself to the work of the Party has been an inspiration to all those who are fostering Republican ideals at every level of government.

You have been an outstanding spokesman for our Party, and have represented it forthrightly and with honor throughout the length and breadth of the land. The program which you have recently initiated to build for the future will, I confidently expect, be a major milestone in Republican history.

Particularly heartening to me has been your constant emphasis upon the role of youth. On the vision and the vigor that they bring to the councils of our Party depends significantly the ability of Republicans, as a political entity, to contribute through future decades to the shaping of sound and effective governmental policies. I am confident that in their achievements to come, you will see frequent and satisfying reflections of your own dedicated efforts.

Although you will soon be relinquishing your official responsibilities as Chairman, I know there will be many calls on you for further assistance, and I hope to see you often as you visit here.

With gratitude for your fine services, and warm personal regard,

Sincerely,

DWIGHT D. EISENHOWER

P.S. Not long ago I saw a copy of the Resolution of thanks for your services adopted by the National Committee at its meeting in Des Moines. I agree with every word the Committee had to say; the Resolution expresses the affection, admiration and respect in which the rank and file of the Republican Party hold you.

NOTE: Mr. Alcorn served as chairman of the Republican National Committee from February 1, 1957, to April 11, 1959. His letter was released with the President's reply.

70   ¶   Remarks at the Opening Session of the Ministerial Meeting of the North Atlantic Council. *April* 2, 1959

Mr. President, Mr. Secretary General, Your Excellencies, and Distinguished Guests:

It is for me a great privilege and a great pleasure to welcome to Washington the Secretary General of the North Atlantic Treaty Organization, and the Foreign Ministers of the NATO nations.

As I review the list of the distinguished persons of this audience, I find the names of many old friends and colleagues from times past, including the early days when I myself was associated directly with NATO. It is indeed heartwarming to greet you here this morning.

And I think it would be somewhat miraculous if an old soldier should find it possible to restrain the impulse to reminisce just a bit about those early days when we were trying to organize and to bring together the military portions of the NATO alliance.

In doing so, I visited each of the countries. I went to see their heads of state, heads of government, the chiefs of the armed services, and as many members of the governments and of the citizens of the country as I could possibly see.

There was only one message that I had to carry. I knew that the basic purpose of the alliance was already achieved. Here in this room 2 years earlier there had been brought about that union of hearts and of purpose that was affirmed in the treaty under which we still operate.

But the achieving of the strength that could realize a particular passage of the Bible that comes to mind, was still to be realized. That passage in St. Luke says, "When a strong man armed keepeth his palace, his goods are in peace." That was what we had to do.

To the members of the armed services and to the governments, then,

I had one simple message. It was this: look at the hand. Each finger is not of itself a very good instrument for either defense or offense, but close it in a fist and it can become a very formidable weapon of defense.

So, our job was to make each finger stronger, sturdier, so as to get a fist that could defy anyone that would think of aggression against the free world, and the values that it is still defending as it was then defending.

I would like to ask each delegation, each individual from another country, to carry back to those countries my affectionate greetings and my warm remembrance of the kindness and the cooperation they then gave to me some 8 or 9 years ago. It was a very great privilege—I think one of the most interesting experiences of my entire military life.

Today we celebrate the tenth anniversary of this Organization. Founded as an alliance to assure our defense against the threat of aggression, NATO has grown into a powerful security-community by means of which the free people of 15 nations pursue the goal of a durable peace with justice.

Now for generations each nation, including my own, pursued this aim through its own individual efforts. But the galloping pace of technology and the upheavals of modern war brought the world suddenly to a new stage of its existence. By 1945 Americans together with all other peoples recognized the urgent need for a new relationship among nations.

That year the establishment of the United Nations organization lifted hopes the world over that all peoples would at last join together in a universal quest for peace and justice. Momentarily it seemed that mankind at long last had begun to put aside the weapons of war in favor of the tools of peace. But quickly it became evident that the aftermath of World War II had brought, along with this opportunity, new dangers of fearful and unusual significance.

War for all nations has always meant privation, suffering, and death. But with the advent of nuclear science the possibility of war suddenly threatened entire civilizations. Almost simultaneously a new dictatorship reached such great power that it openly challenged the concepts of justice and freedom which our respective nations adhere to and support. So challenged, no free nation dedicated to peace and the preservation of priceless human values could adopt aggression as a countermeasure. But all quickly realized that to stand firmly in defense of their people and those peoples' rights, they had to act in unison.

The stake was not merely the security of our nations from military onslaught; the true issue was our ability to protect the spiritual foundations of Western civilization against every kind of ruthless aggression, whether the attack should be military, economic, or political.

Out of this realization was born the North Atlantic Treaty Organization. Its immediate purpose was the prevention of war by deterring military aggression in Europe. The task presented many difficulties, one of which was that there was no guiding precedent. But out of necessity and through the good will of member nations, we succeeded within a few short years in building a substantial defensive establishment.

Since NATO was formed there has been no further Communist advance in Europe—either by political or by military means. And while our military efforts have obviously required economic sacrifice, they have by no means stunted the economic growth of member countries. Instead, there has been a notable increase in production, trade, and living standards among the NATO peoples during the 10 years of NATO's existence.

NATO is unique in many respects. Of these, the most important by far is our common support of spiritual and moral values. Each nation has of course its heritage of religion, language, literature, music, education, and other elements of culture which give real meaning to life. But among all, there is a close kinship because of a common belief in the freedom and the dignity of man. All of us are devoted to the twin ideals of peace and justice—neither of which can live long without the other.

Sustained by a conviction in the rightness of our cause, by faith in ourselves and in each other, NATO has grown steadily in its capacity to assure our common security.

And our alliance is developing an ever-growing political cohesion. The Permanent Council, under the chairmanship of the able and dedicated Mr. Spaak, is becoming an effective mechanism for harmonizing the policies of the Atlantic peoples. By our association we have created possibilities for new and unprecedented forms of economic cooperation among the free peoples of Europe. Together we have laid the foundation for intimate Atlantic partnership in other fields, such as science and technology. All these achievements of the past decade merely point the way for an accelerated progress ahead.

Thus united in purpose and sustained by our moral, economic, and military power, the member nations begin the second decade of their association in NATO.

We shall always keep open the door of honest discussion—even to those whose creed is world domination. Our governments conduct continuous—almost daily—discussions and negotiations with the Soviet Union. We use regular diplomatic establishments, special committees, organs of the United Nations, and occasional meetings of responsible political leaders. No means are overlooked that give rise to promise of constructive results.

We shall continue these negotiations and discussions. We shall continue to make concrete and realistic proposals for disarmament, for a just solution of the problems of Germany, for European security, and for cooperation in the newly-opening realm of outer space.

Although we shall always avoid substituting illusion for reality, we shall continue to strive for a more general and far-reaching, but always practical, settlement of differences with the Soviets.

The need, as we reach for a lasting peace with justice, is the abandonment of the Communist purpose of world domination.

We shall never cease to encourage such a change. Meanwhile, we must be prepared during the years ahead to live in a world in which tension and bickering between free nations and the Soviets will be daily experiences. So, to live confidently, freedom's greatest requirement is unity—the unity which is the very life-blood of NATO.

On this base we propose to build the road leading toward lasting peace and universal justice.

Building this road will require courage—courage to stand fast in the face of menace and of threats.

It will require sacrifice—sacrifice needed to maintain and improve our collective strength over a long period of time.

It will require perseverance—perseverance to explore every avenue which offers reasonable hope for just solutions to the issues between ourselves and the Soviet Union.

All these qualities the free nations possess in full measure—we must never tire or weaken in our practice of them.

Those who respect the dignity of man will not flinch before the magnitude of the task. Rather they will prove once again that greatness of spirit and love of liberty will overcome the forces of atheistic materialism and coercion and give to all the nations, under God, the blessings of security, along with a just and durable peace.

Thank you very much.

NOTE: The President spoke at the Departmental Auditorium. His opening words "Mr. President, Mr. Secretary General" referred to Joseph M. A. H. Luns, President of the North Atlantic Council and Minister of Foreign Affairs of the Netherlands, and Paul-Henri Spaak, Secretary General of NATO.

71 ¶ Address at the Gettysburg College Convocation: The Importance of Understanding. *April 4,* 1959

Mr. Chairman, President Paul, Members of the Board of Trustees, Members of the Faculty, the Alumni, Student Body, and the Friends of Gettysburg College:

As one who in 1914 first visited Gettysburg College when I was still a West Point cadet, who years later had the great distinction of receiving from this institution its honorary doctorate, and who, in recent years, became an official resident of Adams County and your neighbor, I congratulate Gettysburg College on having recorded 127 years of faithful service to its community and to the nation.

And I am reminded also that I owe a debt to this institution of personal gratitude. During the 86th year of its existence—41 years ago—Gettysburg College, through some of its fraternities, made available a home for my family and me during the months that we served here in World War I. I am happy to have the opportunity, again, to thank the entire Gettysburg College family for its thoughtfulness in arranging for us, in the crowded community of that war year, a much needed place to live.

———

Now like any other individual invited to speak on a subject of his own choosing before a collegiate group, I have been confronted with the need for making one or two decisions.

One of these has been the selection of a subject that you here might consider to be both current and interesting.

Another has been the length of the time I might need for its exposition.

Napoleon, reflecting upon the desirable qualities of a political constitution, once remarked that such a document should preferably be short, and always vague in meaning. Unfortunately he did not comment upon the appropriate length and character of a talk commemorating Founder's Day at a liberal arts college. But if I do not wander too far from my text, I can, at least, attain respectable brevity—and I do assure you that there will be nothing vague about the convictions I express.

I shall not attempt to talk to you about education, but I shall speak of one vital purpose of education—the development of understanding—understanding, so that we may use with some measure of wisdom the knowledge we may have acquired, whether in school or out.

For no matter how much intellectual luggage we carry around in our heads, it becomes valuable only if we know how to use the information—only if we are able to relate one fact of a problem to the others do we truly understand them.

This is my subject today—the need for greater individual and collective understanding of some of the international facts of today's life. We need to understand our country's purpose and role in strengthening the world's free nations which, with us, see our concepts of freedom and human dignity threatened by atheistic dictatorship.

If through education—no matter how acquired—people develop understanding of basic issues, and so can distinguish between the common, long-term good of all, on the one hand, and convenient but shortsighted expediency on the other, they will support policies under which the nation will prosper. And if people should ever lack the discernment to understand, or the character to rise above their own selfish short-term interests, free government would become well nigh impossible to sustain. Such a government would be reduced to nothing more than a device which seeks merely to accommodate itself and the country's good to the bitter tugs-of-war of conflicting pressure groups. Disaster could eventually result.

Though the subject I have assigned myself is neither abstruse nor particularly difficult to comprehend, its importance to our national and individual lives is such that failure to marshal, to organize, and to analyze the facts pertaining to it could have for all of us consequences of the most serious character. We must study, think, and decide on the governmental program that we term "Mutual Security."

The true need and value of this program will be recognized by our people only if they can answer this question: "Why should America, at heavy and immediate sacrifice to herself, assist many other nations, particularly the less developed ones, in achieving greater moral, economic, and military strength?"

What are the facts?

The first and most important fact is the implacable and frequently expressed purpose of imperialistic communism to promote world revolution, destroy freedom, and communize the world.

Its methods are all-inclusive, ranging through the use of propaganda, political subversion, economic penetration, and the use or the threat of force.

The second fact is that our country is today spending an aggregate of about 47 billion dollars annually for the single purpose of preserving the nation's position and security in the world. This includes the costs of the Defense Department, the production of nuclear weapons, and mutual security. All three are mutually supporting and are blended into one program for our safety. The size of this cost conveys something of the entire program's importance—to the world and, indeed, to each of us.

And when I think of this importance to us, think of it in this one material figure, this cost annually for every single man, woman, and child of the entire nation is about 275 dollars a year.

The next fact we note is that since the Communist target is the world, every nation is comprehended in their campaign for domination. The weak and the most exposed stand in the most immediate danger.

Another fact, that we ignore to our peril, is that if aggression or subversion against the weaker of the free nations should achieve successsive victories, communism would step-by-step overcome once free areas. The danger, even to the strongest, would become increasingly menacing.

Clearly, the self-interest of each free nation impels it to resist the loss to imperialistic communism of the freedom and independence of any other nation.

Freedom is truly indivisible.

To apply some of these truths to a particular case, let us consider, briefly, the country of Viet-Nam, and the importance to us of the security and progress of that country.

It is located, as you know, in the southeastern corner of Asia, exactly halfway round the world from Gettysburg College.

Viet-Nam is a country divided into two parts—like Korea and Germany. The southern half, with its twelve million people, is free, but poor. It is an under-developed country—its economy is weak—average individual income being less than $200 a year. The northern half has been turned over to communism. A line of demarcation running along the 17th parallel separates the two. To the north of this line stand several Communist divisions. These facts pose to South Viet-Nam two great tasks: self-defense and economic growth.

Understandably, the people of Viet-Nam want to make their country a thriving, self-sufficient member of the family of nations. This means economic expansion.

For Viet-Nam's economic growth, the acquisition of capital is vitally necessary. Now, the nation could create the capital needed for growth by stealing from the already meager rice bowls of its people and regimenting them into work battalions. This enslavement is the commune system—adopted by the new overlords of Red China. It would mean, of course, the loss of freedom within the country without any hostile outside action whatsoever.

Another way for Viet-Nam to get the necessary capital is through private investments from the outside, and through governmental loans and, where necessary, grants from other and more fortunately situated nations.

In either of these ways the economic problem of Viet-Nam could be solved. But only the second way can preserve freedom.

And there is still the other of Viet-Nam's great problems—how to support the military forces it needs without crushing its economy.

Because of the proximity of large Communist military formations in the North, Free Viet-Nam must maintain substantial numbers of men under arms. Moreover, while the government has shown real progress in cleaning out Communist guerillas, those remaining continue to be a disruptive influence in the nation's life.

Unassisted, Viet-Nam cannot at this time produce and support the military formations essential to it, or, equally important, the morale—the hope, the confidence, the pride—necessary to meet the dual threat of aggression from without and subversion within its borders.

Still another fact! Strategically, South Viet-Nam's capture by the Communists would bring their power several hundred miles into a hitherto free region. The remaining countries in Southeast Asia would be menaced by a great flanking movement. The freedom of twelve million people would be lost immediately, and that of 150 million others in adjacent lands would be seriously endangered. The loss of South Viet-Nam would set in motion a crumbling process that could, as it progressed, have grave consequences for us and for freedom.

Viet-Nam must have a reasonable degree of safety now—both for her people and for her property. Because of these facts, military as well as economic help is currently needed in Viet-Nam.

We reach the inescapable conclusion that our own national interests demand some help from us in sustaining in Viet-Nam the morale, the economic progress, and the military strength necessary to its continued existence in freedom.

Viet-Nam is just one example. One-third of the world's people face a similar challenge. All through Africa and Southern Asia people struggle to preserve liberty and improve their standards of living, to maintain their dignity as humans. It is imperative that they succeed.

But some uninformed Americans believe that we should turn our backs on these people, our friends. Our costs and taxes are very real, while the difficulties of other peoples often seem remote from us.

But the costs of continuous neglect of these problems would be far more than we must now bear—indeed more than we could afford. The added costs would be paid not only in vastly increased outlays of money, but in larger drafts of our youth into the Military Establishment, and in terms of increased danger to our own security and prosperity.

No matter what areas of Federal spending must be curtailed—and some should—our safety comes first. Since that safety is necessarily based upon a sound and thriving economy, its protection must equally engage our earnest attention.

As a different kind of example of free nation interdependence, there is Japan, where very different problems exist—but problems equally vital to the security of the free world. Japan is an essential counterweight to Communist strength in Asia. Her industrial power is the heart of any collective effort to defend the Far East against aggression.

Her more than 90 million people occupy a country where the arable land is no more than that of California. More than perhaps any other industrial nation, Japan must export to live. Last year she had a trade deficit. At one time she had a thriving trade with Asia, particularly with her nearest neighbors. Much of it is gone. Her problems grow more grave.

For Japan there must be more free world outlets for her products. She does not want to be compelled to become dependent as a last resort upon the Communist empire. Should she ever be forced to that extremity, the blow to free world security would be incalculable; at the least it would mean for all other free nations greater sacrifice, greater danger, and lessened economic strength.

What happens depends largely on what the free world nations can, and will, do.

Upon us—upon you here—in this audience—rests a heavy responsibility. We must weigh the facts, fit them into place, and decide on our course of action.

For a country as large, as industrious, and as progressive as Japan to exist with the help of grant aid by others, presents no satisfactory solution. Furthermore, for us, the cost would be, over the long term, increasingly heavy. Trade is the key to a durable Japanese economy.

One of Japan's greatest opportunities for increased trade lies in a free and developing Southeast Asia. So we see that the two problems I have been discussing are two parts of a single one—the great need in Japan is for raw materials; in Southern Asia it is for manufactured goods. The two regions complement each other markedly. So, by strengthening Viet-Nam and helping insure the safety of the South Pacific and Southeast Asia, we gradually develop the great trade potential between this region, rich in natural resources, and highly industrialized Japan to the benefit of both. In this way freedom in the Western Pacific will be greatly strengthened and the interests of the whole free world advanced. But such a basic improvement can come about only gradually. Japan must have additional trade outlets now. These can be provided if each of the industrialized nations in the West does its part in liberalizing trade relations with Japan.

One thing we in America can do is to study our existing trade regulations between America and Japan. Quite naturally we must guard against a flooding of our own markets by goods, made in other countries, to the point where our own industries would dry up. But the mere imposition of higher and higher tariffs cannot solve trade problems even for us, prosperous though we be. We too must export in order to buy, and we must buy if we are to sell our surpluses abroad.

Moreover, unless Japan's exports to us are at least maintained at approximately their present levels, we would risk the free world stake in the whole Pacific.

There is another fact that bears importantly upon this situation. In international trade our competitors are also our customers. Normally, the bigger the competitor, the bigger the customer. Japan buys far more from us, from the United States, than she sells to us. She is our second largest customer—second only to Canada. Last year she bought $800 million in machinery, chemicals, coal, cotton, and other items—and thus made jobs for many thousands of Americans. She paid for these with American dollars earned largely from the goods she sold to us. If she had earned more dollars she would have bought more goods, to our mutual advantage and the strengthening of freedom.

Now I turn to one other case, where the hard realities of living confront us with still a further challenge. I refer to West Berlin, a city of over two million people whose freedom we are pledged to defend.

Here we have another problem but not a unique one. It is part of a continuing effort of the Communist conspiracy to attain one overriding goal: world domination.

Against this background we understand that the mere handing over of a single city could not possibly satisfy the Communists, even though they would particularly like to eliminate what has been called the "Free World's Show Case behind the Iron Curtain." Indeed, if we should acquiesce in the unthinkable sacrifice of two million free Germans, such a confession of weakness would dismay our friends and embolden the Communists to step up their campaign of domination.

The course of appeasement is not only dishonorable, it is the most dangerous one we could pursue. The world paid a high price for the lesson of Munich—but it has learned the lesson well.

We have learned, too, that the costs of defending freedom—of defending America—must be paid in many forms and in many places. They are assessed in all parts of the world—in Berlin, in Viet-Nam, in the Middle East—here at home. But wherever they occur, in whatever form they appear, they are first and last a proper charge against the national security of the United States.

Because mutual security and American security are synonymous.

These costs are high—but they are as nothing to those that would be imposed upon us by our own indifference and neglect, or by weakness of spirit.

And though weakness is dangerous, this does not mean that firmness is mere rigidity, nothing but arrogant stubbornness. Another fact, basic to the entire problem of peace and security, is that America and her friends do not want war. They seek to substitute the rule of law for the rule of force, the conference table for the battlefield.

These desires and their expressions are not propaganda. They are aspirations felt deeply within us; they are the longings of entire civilizations based upon a belief in God and in the dignity of man. Indeed, they are the instinctive hopes that people feel—in all nations—regardless of curtains. People everywhere recoil from the thought of war as much as do any of us present here in this peaceful gathering.

Tensions are created, primarily, by governments and individuals that are ruthless in seeking greater and more extensive power. Berlin is a tension point because the Kremlin hopes to eliminate it as part of the free world. And the Communist leaders have chosen to exert pressure there at this moment. Naturally they always pick the most awkward situation, the hard-to-defend position, as the place to test our strength and to try our resolution. There will never be an easy place for us to make a stand, but there is a best one.

That best one is where principle points. Deep in that principle is the truth that we cannot afford the loss of any free nation—for whenever freedom is destroyed anywhere we are ourselves, by that much weakened. Every gain of communism makes further defense against it harder and our security more uncertain.

A free America can exist as part of a free world, and a free world can continue to exist only as it meets the rightful demands of people for security, progress, and prosperity. That is why the development of South Viet-Nam and Southeast Asia is important; why Japanese export trade is important; why firmness in Berlin is important.

It is why Communist challenges must always be answered by the free world standing on principle, united in strength and in purpose.

This is the true meaning of mutual security.

It is the idea that by helping one another build a strong, prosperous world community, free people will not only win through to a just peace but can apply their wonderful, God-given talents toward creating an ever-growing measure of man's humanity to man.

But this is something that will come only out of the hard intellectual effort of disciplined minds. For the future of our country depends upon enlightened leadership, upon the truly understanding citizen.

We look to the citizen who has the ability and determination to seek out and to face facts; who can place them in logical relationship one to another; who can attain an understanding of their meaning, and then act courageously in promoting the cause of an America that can live, under God, in a world of peace and justice. These are the individuals needed in uncounted numbers in your college, your country, and your world.

Over the one hundred and twenty-seven years of Gettysburg College's existence, its graduates have, in many ways, served the cause of freedom and of justice. May the years ahead be as fruitful as those which you now look back upon with such pride and with such satisfaction.

Thank you very much indeed.

NOTE: The President's opening words "Mr. Chairman, President Paul" referred to John S. Rice, President of the Board of Trustees, and Dr. Willard S. Paul, President of Gettysburg College.

72 ¶ Statement by the President on the Observance of World Health Day. *April* 7, 1959

ON THIS day, the 11th anniversary of the adoption of the constitution of the World Health Organization, it is a privilege to join with my fellow citizens and with citizens of other nations in observing World Health Day.

The theme of this year's observance, "Mental Illness and Mental Health in the World Today," calls attention to the necessity of learning more about the nature of mental illness and applying more fully the knowledge we now have of ways to maintain sound mental health. This is one of the great areas of human need which requires our active concern working in concert with our neighbors in the United Nations.

73 ¶ Message to President Garcia of the Philippines on Bataan Day. *April* 8, 1959

[Released April 8, 1959. Dated April 7, 1959]

ON THE seventeenth Anniversary of Bataan, a campaign of heroic memory, I extend best wishes to you and to the people of the Philippines on behalf of the people of the United States.

The bonds of brotherhood forged in the gallant defense of Bataan and Corregidor are part of the tradition which unites our two countries. Our continuing effort to defend and encourage the growth of democratic institutions throughout the world is a corollary of this tradition. In this campaign, we will together press on to win the victory: Peace with honor and progress for mankind.

It is a privilege to join you in commemorating the indomitable spirit of Bataan.

DWIGHT D. EISENHOWER

NOTE: This message was released at Augusta, Ga.

74 ¶ Letter to the Director, Bureau of the Budget, on Interagency Cooperation in Aviation Matters. *April* 10, 1959

[Released April 10, 1959. Dated April 9, 1959]

Dear Mr. Stans:

I am enclosing a copy of a report by Mr. E. R. Quesada on the implementation of the Curtis Report on "Aviation Facilities Planning." Mr. Quesada's report indicates a high percentage of implementation of the recommendations made by Mr. Curtis. However, the recommendation pertaining to the replacement of the Air Coordinating Committee by arrangements for interagency cooperation in keeping with the intent of the Federal Aviation Act of 1958 is still not implemented.

I should like the Bureau of the Budget to undertake an analysis of this recommendation and to present to me, as soon as possible, recommendations for such action as may be found desirable and appropriate. Your analysis should identify areas of aviation activity in which interagency cooperation will be required and should suggest efficient and workable arrangements for bringing about such cooperation.

Sincerely,

DWIGHT D. EISENHOWER

NOTE: This letter and the Quesada report (4 mimeographed pages) were released at Augusta, Ga. Mr. Quesada submitted this report in his capacity as Special Assistant to the President, in which he continued to serve until May 8, 1959. Mr.

Quesada was serving also, at this time, as Administrator, Federal Aviation Agency. The report "Aviation Facilities Planning" (Government Printing Office, 1957) was submitted to the President by Mr. Quesada's predecessor in this post, Edward P. Curtis, on May 10, 1957.

75 ¶ Remarks at the Seventh Annual Republican Women's Conference. *April* 13, 1959

Mrs. Williams, Chairman Morton, my friend Meade Alcorn, Fellow Republicans All:

Meeting this dynamic group of Republican workers—full of enthusiasm and full of pride in the achievements of our party, is an uplifting experience. I was more than pleased, I was delighted to see the response of each group of delegates to the salute played by the orchestra to each of our States.

For myself, I had a little difficulty. Born in Texas, raised in Kansas, having served in the United States in many stations throughout the country, finally getting a voting residence in New York, and transferring later to Pennsylvania, with a mother from Virginia, a father from Pennsylvania, my wife born in Iowa and raised in Colorado, I didn't know exactly where my first loyalty fell except in the point of time.

Nevertheless, it was really a thrill for me to see the enthusiasm with which each person, each individual in those delegations, greeted the sound of their State song. Because, as loyalty goes to each State, and as our hearts beat faster when we see or hear something that reminds us of that beloved area, we think always, at bottom, of the United States of America. And frankly, in a word, I believe that the whole program of the Republican Party, its reason for being is to serve better than any other group can the United States of America. On that, there is no question.

Now I must say—and this is for the record—that if the women of our party now mobilize for the 1960 drive the kind of national campaign that they have twice participated in so successfully in the past 7 years, the result, once again, will be victory.

I have never been accused of being a smart politician. But I am this smart: I found out, as long ago as 1952, that there are more women in the United States than there are men. And I have always tried to let them know that I knew that.

We all know that our party is outnumbered in registrations—badly so in some of the States.

To win, all of us have to work hard.

There is a little story that suggests something of the tactical problem faced by the Grand Old Party.

During a visit to Switzerland, before World War I, the German Kaiser conducted an exhaustive examination of the Swiss Army. One evening he turned to the Commanding Colonel to say: "Your soldiers are brave, carefully disciplined, and they shoot well. But you are only a half million. Suppose we march a million men against you. What would you do then?" "We'd each shoot twice, Your Excellency," answered the Colonel quickly without the slightest flicker of emotion.

So—we Republicans need simply to work twice as hard. We are not working at shooting anybody. We are working to send in twice as many recruits as we ever had before, so we work twice as hard for that purpose.

Now you women have come to Washington for this Conference, and those you represent back home, and you have time and again demonstrated your readiness to work without ceasing and at top speed—and that is what we need. You have proved that mere numbers as measured by party registration is not the answer, but that belief in a cause and down-to-earth work—hard work—wins elections.

Your own confidence and optimism—what I have seen here tonight—are the ingredients of success that you must always seek to transmit to others. In getting across the facts to others, it is well to remember that knowledge is not taught, it is caught. This is why your enthusiasm becomes so vitally important as we seek to persuade others to march under our Republican standard. The leader who is obviously dedicated to a cause and shows his pride in its service will certainly draw to himself an increasing army of friends, followers, and associates.

We Republicans are justly proud of the steady accomplishments made since January 1953. Our prosperity, the increased standard of living for Americans, and security for ourselves and our friends through strength and understanding, are facts beyond dispute. They are worthy of your pride. But they have resulted from faithful adherence to the Republican creed.

That creed has been lived and expounded by a long line of distinguished Republicans, from Lincoln onward. They have invariably insisted upon the security of our Nation;

upon the liberty and rights of the individual, and his free opportunity to better himself in every legitimate way;

upon respect for the rights and the responsibilities of the several States;

upon honesty in Government;

upon fiscal integrity; and

upon an expanding economy, based upon a dollar that, earned today, will buy tomorrow and day after an equal amount of groceries.

Republicans hold that the level of Federal spending should be measured by necessity, not by political opportunism. No one has ever spent himself into prosperity; many have spent themselves into insolvency. As Republicans we are proud of such words as thrift and frugality and efficiency. Whenever you apply these words to Federal activities and spending, Americans will listen to you attentively, because today everybody knows that everybody pays additional taxes for political extravagance. Your many written and verbal messages to me on this subject are evidence of the emphasis you place upon economy in Government.

Such convictions as these, conveyed to others with the vigor and enthusiasm I have seen here this evening, will present to all America an energetic and tireless and confident Republican Party.

I might say that I know that every one of us is a busy individual. Whether you are principally occupied in your home, or in an office, whether you may be in the public service, whatever you do, the loyalty and work for the Republican Party is a bit of an extracurricular service. It is a service of dedication, indeed loyalty and love, and therefore it can be the most powerful and effective thing that we can produce.

I want to say, on my own behalf, I think at times—at least in spite of other critics—that I am quite busy myself. But so far as I am able, so far as time and endurance and strength will permit, I am with you to the bitter end, not only this election of 1960 but in every possible way to make the Republican Party that effective political instrument that will lead America into the path that we know to be correct.

The Republican Party is and will continue to be dedicated to one basic purpose—the security, freedom, and the prosperity of our people.

Working ceaselessly in this cause, Republicans, Independents, discerning Democrats, and new voters can and will achieve political victory. In doing so, they will win the opportunity to serve effectively and with devotion our Nation, her citizens, and the cause of peace with justice.

Thank you—and goodnight, ladies.

NOTE: The President spoke at a dinner meeting at the Statler Hilton Hotel, Washington, D.C. His opening remarks "Mrs. Williams, Chairman Morton" referred to Mrs. Clare Williams and Senator Thruston B. Morton, Assistant Chairman and Chairman of the Republican National Committee, respectively.

76 ¶ Remarks to the 15th Annual Washington Conference of the Advertising Council. *April* 13, 1959

Mr. Gray, Members and Friends of the Advertising Council:

This is the seventh time that I have had the honor of meeting with this group. Always before I have spoken extemporaneously, but I thought as a change of pace that it might be a good idea to take the results of some of my Augusta contemplation and put it on paper and therefore address you from notes.

First of all, of course, it is a great privilege to welcome you back to Washington, and once again you have my sincere thanks for the significant contributions you have made in developing a better public understanding of the important issues that confront our Nation.

I am especially grateful for your response to the serious economic challenge we experienced during the past year.

Each of you will recall that when you were meeting here last May we were still at a very low point in the recent recession. Production was off, unemployment was up and pessimistic voices were loud in the land.

Although the basic soundness of our economy was not in jeopardy, there was a danger that the prophets of doom might undermine confidence to the point where normal recovery would be unnecessarily and seriously retarded. It was perfectly possible for us to talk ourselves into far worse circumstances than we actually were.

Obviously many of you recognized this possibility. Even before I met with you last year you had launched your now-famous Confidence Campaign, designed to put all the talk about recession back into a proper perspective.

This Confidence Campaign was a material factor influencing the recovery movement that started last summer. Many other specific factors of course played a part in bringing about the upturn. But this matter of confidence—of morale—is fundamental to any human activity.

Without confidence, constructive action is difficult—often impossible. With it, miracles can be performed.

So I know you are all pleased to see the gains that recovery continues to chalk up. Total employment in March this year stood at nearly 64 million—a million above February, and a million and a half above a year ago. Unemployment at the end of March stood at 4 million 362 thousand—a drop of about 4 hundred thousand from the February total. We have every reason to believe that this trend will continue. Personal incomes are setting records each month, and the Gross National Product is now running at an all time high of 464 billion dollars a year. And, what is vitally important—we have been making this recovery while maintaining the soundness and honesty of our dollar! The Consumer Price Index has held steady for nearly a year—which means that the recovery figures are genuine gains in actual buying power and goods produced.

We have made a fine start, and all the hard work we've done so far has paid off in stability. But we can't afford to relax for a single minute.

Some have told me that I am too concerned about this problem of inflation because for several months the indices have been reasonably steady.

They forget that it is too late to repair a leaky roof when the rain is pouring down. This is exactly the time to think about inflation, because we can be certain that the problem will return to beset us. Only the most persistent counter-pressures will keep prices where they belong. As usual, the Advertising Council has anticipated the need, and you are well under way on your sound-dollar campaign. I congratulate you on your foresight, and wish you every success on this latest of your important undertakings.

Turning to the international situation, I note that Mr. Herter has just given you a briefing on this subject, so my own remarks will be short. But I would like to leave with you this thought:

We are up against a problem that has no fixed or definitely foreseeable termination. As long as the Communists insist that their aim is to dominate the world, we have no choice but to adopt measures that will prevent this from happening. So we follow the only sound course open to us. We hold up a military shield and from behind that shield we strive to build a world that is decent, a world that is rewarding to people.

If we can do this indefinitely, as to time—and confidently throughout the free world, then the Communist threat will tend gradually to shrink because the possibility of growth will be denied to it. Remember, two-thirds of the world's people, and the great preponderance of its productive resources, are on our side of the Iron Curtain. The need of America, of the free world, is to develop this great unrealized potential for peace, justice, and freedom.

This is going to take a long time. The vital requirement is not by any means exclusively a matter of military strength—the free nations urgently need economic growth and the free communication of ideas. The mainspring of this effort will be our American economy with our body of progressive traditions, knowledge, and beliefs.

We are challenged to prove that any nation, wherever it is—whatever its strength—can prosper in freedom, that slavery is not necessary to economic growth even in the atmosphere of a cold war of conflicting ideologies. We will have to show that people need not choose between freedom and bread; they can earn both through their own efforts. We must prove to other peoples what we have already proved to ourselves: that in providing for man's material needs private enterprise is infinitely superior to Communist State Capitalism.

America must demonstrate to the world—even under the conditions of a global struggle—that personal liberty and national independence are not only cherished dreams, they are workable political concepts. Broadly stated—the test before us is an exercise in living—living in the presence of danger. We can recognize the danger, in potential aggression, and provide against it. But security is only one of the requirements of society. Our ability to go on existing as a free nation is the product of several factors, all interdependent. For example, such matters as solvency and security are natural complements in a free society. Over the long term we either provide for both, or we will discover that we have provided for neither.

This is why it is so important that we do not become unhinged by tension and by crises; why we have such a direct concern in the long range results of our educational process in the nation; why we should concern ourselves with the trade problems of other free countries. This is why a stable dollar and a sound fiscal policy are so essential. Orderly, meaningful economic expansion cannot take place if inflation rots away the value represented in loans, insurance, pensions, and personal savings.

Economic expansion is an absolute necessity if we are to find jobs for our growing labor force, meet the Communist economic challenge, and pay for our costly armaments. Always we must act in the concept that we are building for the future—for the world of our children, and those who come after them. We are the trustees of an ancient and noble inheritance which embodies the conviction of our forefathers that all men are endowed by their Creator with certain rights, rights that spell human dignity. We owe to those who will come after us the most responsible stewardship of these priceless values that we know how to provide.

So it is that we need a Continuing Confidence Campaign—one to be practiced by all who believe in America. We need people who can look beyond today's tensions and tomorrow's troubles to see us as we really are: a powerful, peaceful nation, in whose continued growth and strength are found the one great hope of the world.

Thank you—and goodbye.

NOTE: The President spoke at the District Red Cross Building. His opening words "Mr. Gray" referred to Gordon Gray, Special Assistant to the President for National Security Affairs, who served as chairman of the conference.

77 ❡ Remarks at the Dedication of the Robert A. Taft Memorial Bell Tower. *April* 14, 1959

Mr. Chairman, President Hoover, Mr. Vice President, Mr. Speaker, Members of Congress, Ladies and Gentlemen:

It is not my function in this program to eulogize the memory of Robert A. Taft. I have been given the privilege in my capacity as Honorary Chairman of the Robert A. Taft Memorial Foundation to present this memorial to the Congress of the United States. But in doing so, I would feel remiss if I failed to give some expression to the very great admiration and affection I formed for the Senator in the very late weeks of his life.

I met him officially and in close cooperative political work only after the Inauguration in 1953. But in the remaining months with him, I and all members of the administration learned how much we depended upon him.

In his long career of public service, he was many things to many people. Numbers here today knew him as a colleague—either a trusted leader or a formidable opponent.

All knew him as a commanding figure on Capitol Hill. To the people of the United States he was a liberal in his championship of individual rights and opportunity, but he was also the very symbol of informed and responsible conservatism in everything affecting the Nation's economy. He was, by his own definition, a politician. An admiring nation now acknowledges that he was infinitely more.

To me, Senator Taft was the vital link between the legislative and the executive branches of our Government in the early period of this administration. During those days, whenever I needed him most, he was there, with all his vast knowledge of government—all his wisdom and experience. For the good of all America, no one gave of himself more unstintingly, more generously than did Robert Taft. And, doing these things, he gave, also, to me and to my associates in the Cabinet, the priceless gift of friendship. For all this, I am humbly, eternally grateful.

He made a remark one day to me that has made a very great impression on my memory. We were discussing two projects in which he took a somewhat more liberal attitude than did I. And we went over the factors in discussing this for a little while, and finally I said to the Senator: "I do not understand why you are always labelled in the newspapers as a conservative and I, at least sometimes, am called a liberal." He said, "Mr. President, in politics you will learn that the newspapers give labels to political figures, and there is not necessarily any direct connection between a man's convictions, beliefs, and purpose and what is stated in some of the columns of those papers."

But I repeat—those last weeks, brief though the experience was, have left with me a very great feeling of gratitude to his memory.

So it is with a sense of high distinction and honor that I dedicate this memorial to one of the Senate's illustrious members—and by the symbolic presentation of these keys to the Vice President and the Speaker of the House, I hereby turn over its custody to the Congress of the United States.

NOTE: The dedication ceremony was held at the site on the Capitol Grounds at 10:00 a.m. Representative B. Carroll Reece, President of the Robert A. Taft Memorial Foundation, served as Presiding Officer, assisted by Representative Clarence J. Brown, Chairman of the Founda-

tion's Subcommittee on the Physical Memorial.

A complete report of the dedication is published in House Document 121 (86th Cong., 1st sess.).

Mr. Taft served as United States Senator from Ohio from 1939 until his death on July 31, 1953.

78 ¶ The President's News Conference at Augusta, Georgia. *April* 15, 1959

THE PRESIDENT. What I have to say concerns Secretary Dulles.

Q. What was that, Mr. President?

THE PRESIDENT. It concerns Secretary Dulles. I had a conversation this morning with him, and in view of the findings the doctors have made—yesterday—and which were not yet reported when I met him day before yesterday, he has definitely made up his mind to submit his resignation.

The formal letter of resignation will reach me in a day or so. I will then reply to it.

I want to make one or two things clear. The findings are not of the kind, so far as I am aware, that make him helpless. He is, nevertheless, incapacitated, so far as carrying on the administrative burdens of the office, as well as doing the thinking for it over there.

Q. You say he is absolutely incapacitated?

THE PRESIDENT. I am saying incapacitated for carrying on the administrative load, in addition to assisting in the making of policy. So I have asked him to remain as my consultant, and I will appoint him to some office that makes it possible for him to be useful both to the State Department and to me; because I think all of you know my opinion of Secretary Dulles. I personally believe he has filled his office with greater distinction and greater ability than any other man our country has known. He is a man of tremendous character and courage, intelligence and wisdom. Therefore my determination to keep him close where he can be useful, both to the State Department and to me and indeed in considering everything that may affect our foreign relations, I think is a very wise and proper thing to do.

With respect to a possible successor, no final decision has been made, and I will let you people know as quickly as this is practicable.

Now I believe there is no other particular additional information that I can provide, but if there are any questions on this particular subject, I would be glad to entertain any of them.

Q. One thing, Mr. President, is there anything that you would care to say as to the effect of this necessary action on the coming meeting of the foreign ministers?

THE PRESIDENT. Well, yes; I think I should say something about it. As you know, both Foster and I have kept in close communication on this matter. He has developed a team over in the State Department of which he is very proud and in which he has great confidence. And we believe that whatever the decision is, that there will be no damage to the, you might say, effectiveness of our presentations in the next conference.

Q. Would you expect the Secretary's successor to come from within the Government?

THE PRESIDENT. I wouldn't want to say so at the moment.

Q. Mr. President, does this mean that Mr. Herter will attend both the April 29 and May 11 foreign ministers conferences as our representative?

THE PRESIDENT. I would say this: no matter who the appointee is, yes. He would be going to both, no matter who the successor. He would be going almost as a matter of necessity, I think, because he is familiar with it.

Q. Mr. President, does this mean that the Secretary will become a member of the White House staff and not a State Department employee then?

THE PRESIDENT. I haven't even thought of the exact status, but it will be on a consultative basis. As you know, in each department, and for me, there are allowed certain consultants, but he will be there on that basis. And this, by the way, is something that I know that he wants to do, as well as knowing that I want him to do it.

Q. Mr. President, can you give us an idea when you might be able to make up your mind about his successor?

THE PRESIDENT. Well, I can just say this: it will not be long delayed. It will be a matter of days.

Q. Mr. President, as you know, it has been rather taken for granted,

I guess in Washington, that Mr. Herter would succeed Mr. Dulles if he had to resign.   Does your announcement that you will make the announcement later suggest that it might be somebody else when you make the decision?

THE PRESIDENT. Well, there are a number of people, I think, in Government, or at least a few, who have particular talent in this field, and there are all kinds of considerations to be studied.   And indeed, I shall talk—before I make final decision—to Foster himself about this thing. But I just don't want to imply either an intention to appoint a particular man or any refusal in that direction.

Is there anything else, gentlemen?

I can't tell you how much regret I feel about this.   I am quite sure that the United States will share that feeling.

Goodbye, and thank you.

NOTE: President Eisenhower's one hundred and fifty-sixth news conference was held in the Colonial Room of the Richmond Hotel, Augusta, Ga., at 9:35 a.m. on Wednesday, April 15, 1959.   The attendance was not recorded.

79   ¶ Letter Accepting the Resignation of Secretary Dulles.   *April* 16, 1959

Dear Foster:

I accept, with deepest personal regret and only because I have no alternative, your resignation as Secretary of State, effective upon the qualification of your successor.

In so doing, I can but repeat what the vast outpouring of affection and admiration from the entire free world has told you.   You have, with the talents you so abundantly possess and with your exemplary integrity of character, employed your rich heritage as well as your unique experience in handling our relations with other countries.   You have been a staunch bulwark of our nation against the machinations of Imperialistic Communism.   You have won to the side of the free world countless peoples, and inspired in them renewed courage and determination to fight for freedom and principle.   As a statesman of world stature you have set a record in the stewardship of our foreign relations that stands clear and strong for all to see.

By this letter I request you to serve in the future, to whatever extent your health will permit, as a consultant to me and the State Department in international affairs. I know that all Americans join me in the fervent hope that you will thus be able to continue the important contributions that only you can make toward a just peace in the world.

With affectionate regard,

As ever,

D. E.

NOTE: Secretary Dulles served as Secretary of State from January 21, 1953, through April 21, 1959. His letter of April 15, released with the President's reply at Augusta, Ga., follows:

Dear Mr. President:

It is apparent to me that I shall not be well enough soon enough to continue to serve as Secretary of State. Accordingly, I tender my resignation to be effective at your convenience.

I am deeply grateful for the opportunities and responsibilities you have given me.

I was brought up in the belief that this nation of ours was not merely a self-serving society but was founded with a mission to help build a world where liberty and justice would prevail. Today that concept faces a formidable and ruthless challenge from International Communism. This has made it manifestly difficult to adhere steadfastly to our national idealism and national mission and at the same time avoid the awful catastrophe of war. You have given inspiring leadership in this essential task and it has been a deep satisfaction to me to have been intimately associated with you in these matters.

If I can, in a more limited capacity, continue to serve, I shall be happy to do so.

Faithfully yours,

JOHN FOSTER DULLES

80 ¶ Remarks Following Announcement of the Vice President's Visit to Moscow To Open the American National Exhibition. *April* 17, 1959

I AM PLEASED that the Vice President will be able to go to Moscow and represent the American people. These exhibitions are designed to achieve a broader understanding between our two peoples—the kind of mutual understanding upon which our peaceful future depends. It is a hopeful approach. We welcome it wholeheartedly.

NOTE: This statement, released at Augusta, Ga., was part of a White House announcement relating to the exchange of exhibitions with the Soviet Union. The release stated that the Vice President would open the American National Exhibition in Sokolniki Park, Moscow, on July 25. It also noted that the exhibition was being held in accordance with the December 29, 1958, agreement with the Soviet Union for exhibits to be held in New York and Moscow during the summer of 1959 (see Department of State Bulletin, vol. 40, p. 132).

Later, on May 21, the White House released the names of 51 leaders in the fields of industry, science, education, and the arts who had been appointed to serve as a citizen advisory committee for the American National Exhibition. The release noted that the group had met with the President at the White House on January 23 to discuss preliminary plans for the exhibition, and that individual members had been assisting George V. Allen, governmental coordinator of the exhibition, and Harold C. McClellan, its general manager.

81 ¶ Letter to Nikita Khrushchev, Chairman, Council of Ministers, U.S.S.R., on the Discontinuance of Nuclear Weapons Tests. *April* 20, 1959

[Released April 20, 1959. Dated April 13, 1959]

Dear Mr. Chairman:

Today the Geneva negotiations for the discontinuance of nuclear weapons tests are resuming. During the recess I have considered where we stand in these negotiations and what the prospects are for the successful conclusion which I earnestly desire. I have also talked with Prime Minister Macmillan, who reported to me of his frank discussions on this matter with you.

The United States strongly seeks a lasting agreement for the discontinuance of nuclear weapons tests. We believe that this would be an important step toward reduction of international tensions and would open the way to further agreement on substantial measures of disarmament.

Such an agreement must, however, be subject to fully effective safeguards to insure the security interests of all parties, and we believe that present proposals of the Soviet Union fall short of providing assurance of the type of effective control in which all parties can have confidence: therefore, no basis for agreement is now in sight.

In my view, these negotiations must not be permitted completely to fail. If indeed the Soviet Union insists on the veto on the fact finding activities of the control system with regard to possible underground detonations, I believe that there is a way in which we can hold fast to the progress already made in these negotiations and no longer delay in putting into effect the initial agreements which are within our grasp. Could we not, Mr. Chairman, put the agreement into effect in phases beginning with a prohibition of nuclear weapons tests in the atmosphere? A simplified control system for atmospheric tests up to fifty kilometers could be readily derived from the Geneva experts' report, and would not require the automatic on-site inspection which has created the major stumbling block in the negotiations so far.

My representative is putting forward this suggestion in Geneva today. I urge your serious consideration of this possible course of action. If you are prepared to change your present position on the veto, on procedures for on-site inspection, and on early discussion of concrete measures for high altitude detection, we can of course proceed promptly in the hope of concluding the negotiation of a comprehensive agreement for suspension of nuclear weapons tests. If you are not yet ready to go this far, then I propose that we take the first and readily attainable step of an agreed suspension of nuclear weapons tests in the atmosphere up to fifty kilometers while the political and technical problems associated with control of underground and outer space tests are being resolved. If we could agree to such initial implementation of the first—and I might add the most important—phase of a test suspension agreement, our negotiators could continue to explore with new hope the political and technical problems involved in extending the agreement as quickly as possible to cover all nuclear weapons tests. Meanwhile, fears of unrestricted resumption of nuclear weapons testing with attendant additions to levels of radioactivity would be allayed, and we would be gaining practical experience and confidence in the operation of an international control system.

I trust that one of these paths to agreement will commend itself to you and permit the resuming negotiations to make a far-reaching response to the hopes of mankind.

Sincerely,

DWIGHT D. EISENHOWER

NOTE: This letter was released at Augusta, Ga. In the first paragraph the President referred to talks with Prime Minister Macmillan, held in Washington, March 20–23.

82   ¶ Remarks at the Swearing in of John Foster Dulles as Special Consultant to the President With Cabinet Rank.   *April* 23, 1959

YOUR willingness to continue to contribute your abundant talents and unique experience to the service of the United States and the free world is but one more example of your magnificent spirit and devotion to the Nation's welfare.

It is highly gratifying not only to myself and the Secretary of State— but indeed to the people of the Nation—to know that we both shall continue to have the benefit of your advice and counsel.

NOTE: The President spoke immediately after Mr. Dulles had taken the oath of office at Walter Reed Hospital.

Mr. Dulles replied as follows:

"Mr. President:

"For six years and more I have served as your Secretary of State. The relationship has been one of intimate understanding and effective cooperation which has afforded me deep satisfaction. Unhappily, my health no longer permits me to continue with the manifold responsibilities of that great office. Yesterday, my trusted friend and second in command, Mr. Herter, took over. I am proud that he and his associates in the Department of State and Foreign Service constitute a team that is highly qualified to carry on your basic policies. You, I know, share the same pride and confidence.

"I now assume, at your request, the position of Special Consultant to the President. I am grateful to you for wanting me to serve in this capacity. I accept in the hope that I shall thus be able to assist you and the Secretary of State in the solution of problems which will continue to confront our nation in its quest of a just and honorable peace."

Others attending the ceremony included the Vice President, the Secretary of State, Mrs. Dulles, the Director of Central Intelligence, and the Under Secretary of State for Economic Affairs.

83   ¶ Remarks at the Meeting of the Board of Directors of the National Association of Manufacturers.   *April* 23, 1959

Mr. Chairman, Ladies and Gentlemen:

It is a pleasant duty to welcome you here to the Nation's capital. I have been looking forward to the opportunity to come here, one reason being that I wanted to thank you in person for the work you have done in helping cut down Federal expenditures, and therefore sustaining a sound and good American dollar.

This business of trying to keep expenditures down and the budget balanced is of course criticized by some as meaning that an administration or a legislator or any other official is exhibiting more concern about a dollar than about some particular activity that the critic believes is far more important.

Now, a balanced budget in itself is not a sacred word, but on the other hand, it is not a bad word. And if it means that we are living within our means it gives, first of all, confidence to our people, the feeling that if the Government has to spend this much money, at least they are getting in that much in the coffers, and we are not going deeper in debt, paying more interest or putting out more money into circulation.

It also has a great effect on our friends. The Secretary of the Treasury told me, when he came back from New Delhi a couple of months back, that he was questioned by twenty-one different governments as to our ability to pay our bills and therefore to keep the dollar as sound as it needs to be if we, America, are to be secure in our alliances, and do our part in making certain that communism will make no inroads into the free world.

So in thanking you for the work you have done along this line, I want to make also a special request of you. You are employers of men and women, and I think one of the most important problems that the United States has today in its leadership—whether that leadership be political, whether it is business or it is labor, professional or anything else—is to have people that really understand the considerations and factors that come into the matter of fiscal integrity and to have the compulsion within themselves of informing others.

The strongest force in a democracy is an informed public opinion. And if that public opinion is informed, then that force will be exerted wisely. I can't conceive of a better and finer occupation, really a vocation rather than an avocation, for anyone who is employing others and dealing with others and advising with others than to use his influence in making certain that these basic considerations and factors of our great fiscal problems are understood.

I feel that it is not necessary for me to dwell upon the need today for our national security against the threat that is constantly posed, that I do not need to plead for support in making certain that our alliances are sound, that we do our proper part in making certain that we keep the opportunities open for trade, to defend ourselves, and to raise the standards of living that make for that kind of morale that freedom needs to have, if it is going to defeat communism.

I think those matters are understood well by you. And I merely want to say again, the fight that I am making for a balanced budget, for the soundness of the dollar, for combating inflation, is merely to make certain that one of the foundation stones of all of these necessary activities is there—that it is not destroyed—and thus makes it possible for us to build in this world intelligently and soundly, for ourselves and for our future.

And so I bring again not only thanks but congratulations and my very best wishes for a fine and enjoyable meeting while you are here.

NOTE: The President spoke at the Sheraton-Carlton Hotel, Washington, D.C. His opening words "Mr. Chairman" referred to Milton C. Lightner, Chairman of the Board of the National Association of Manufacturers.

84   ¶ Remarks at the 40th Anniversary Meeting of the International Chamber of Commerce.
April 23, 1959

Mr. President, Mr. Chairman, Ladies and Gentlemen:

First let me express the hope—and the conviction—that this great meeting, the 40th anniversary of the International Chamber of Commerce, has been a useful and rewarding experience for every one of you. I am quite sure it is going to have some interest for some of you. Just seeing this panel makes me think I have got a lot of questions I would like to ask. I'm sorry I'm not so privileged. Now glancing at the scope and searching character of your program and at the names of the men who have taken part indicates that it could scarcely have been otherwise.

The coming together, anywhere, of businessmen from more than 50 countries—men of high competence and common purpose—must surely benefit them all. It proves again that the whole can be greater than the sum of its parts. That this Congress should have taken place in the United States is a circumstance of which I and all my countrymen are proud indeed. We trust you have sensed the warmth and sincerity of your welcome here.

Some of you perhaps are visiting us for the first time. Others are old friends. In either case, while you are here, we want you to see all you can of our country because in gaining an understanding of a region and its people there is no substitute for personal visitation and observation. You will not be pleased with everything you see. Neither are we. But you will see us as we are; you will form your own opinions, and you will gain in knowledge and in understanding. Along this road—and it is of course a two-way road—lies international understanding and the hope for peace.

The theme of this Seventeenth Biennial Congress—"Today's Challenge to Businessmen—Their Responsibilities in Domestic and World Affairs"—is of universal interest. Probably every one of the subjects you have considered so carefully in your sessions is also a concern of governments. Sound money, high employment, rising standards of living, the movement and marketing of goods and services—all these and more present problems that face both men-of-business and men-of-government. And I break no government security when I say we hope that businessmen will come up with some of the solutions.

Your actions, your discussions, your decisions—not only in this Congress but more importantly in your day-to-day commerce with each other—hold the free world's hope for progress toward greater unity and firmer mutual strength. For our strength must come from growth. Perhaps you will permit me to repeat to you what I said to another group meeting here in Washington just 10 days ago. I said:

"The free nations urgently need economic growth and the free communication of ideas. . . . We are challenged to prove that any nation wherever it is—whatever its strength—can prosper in freedom; that slavery is not necessary to economic growth even in the atmosphere of a global cold war of conflicting ideologies.

"We will have to show that people do not need to choose between freedom and bread; they can earn both through their own efforts. We must prove that in providing for man's material needs, private enterprise is infinitely superior to Communist state capitalism."

So I believe that this is today's challenge to businessmen: the challenge to prove that the free market economy which the International Chamber of Commerce has championed so long and so well can out-produce any other kind of economy known to man.

Since the days of Marco Polo, the march of civilization has tramped down the trade routes of the world. Commerce between peoples moves more than products. It distributes ideas and technologies. It develops mutual understandings, and cooperative efforts toward common goals.

And never has this been truer than it is today. The old saying was that "trade follows the flag." Today, in a very definite way, "the flag follows trade." But the flag of which I speak is an international banner, that of freedom and peace.

As you return home from these meetings to plunge once again into your business activities, I trust that you will hold firmly in your programs and policies to the basic thought that the trade routes of international commerce are also the paths to peace.

Thank you—good fortune, and goodby.

NOTE: The President spoke at the Sheraton-Park Hotel, Washington, D.C. His opening words "Mr. President, Mr. Chairman" referred to Edmond G. d'Estaing, President of the International Chamber of Commerce, and Philip Cortney, Chairman of the U.S. Council of the International Chamber of Commerce.

The panel to which the President referred consisted of 11 Members of Congress who had been invited to answer questions submitted by the national committees of the International Chamber of Commerce concerning U.S. tariffs, U.S. foreign economic policy, and related matters.

85 ¶ Message to the Congress Transmitting the Final Report of the National Advisory Committee for Aeronautics. *April* 27, 1959

To the Congress of the United States:

In compliance with the provisions of the Act of March 3, 1915, as amended, which established the National Advisory Committee for Aeronautics, I transmit herewith the Forty-fourth and Final Annual Report of the Committee for the Fiscal Year 1958. This report covers the activities of the Committee through the close of business September 30, 1958, when it was superseded by the National Aeronautics and Space Administration.

The National Advisory Committee for Aeronautics is to be commended for its many contributions to the progress of aeronautical science in the United States and for the spirit of teamwork in aeronautics it has inspired among leaders in science, the military and industry. I wish also to acknowledge at this time the excellent work and dedication of the Committee's research staff who, over the years, have given unstintingly of their talents in a manner which reflects credit upon them and all other civil service personnel of the United States.

Dwight D. Eisenhower

NOTE: The report is published in Senate Document 6 (86th Cong., 1st sess.).

86 ¶ Veto of Bill Concerning the Loan Approval Authority of the Administrator, Rural Electrification Administration. *April* 27, 1959

To the United States Senate:

I return herewith, without my approval, S. 144, "An Act to modify Reorganization Plan No. II of 1939 and Reorganization Plan No. 2 of 1953."

The bill provides that, in the approval and disapproval of loans, the Administrator of the Rural Electrification Administration (REA) shall not be subject to the supervision, direction or other control of the Secretary of Agriculture. In all other respects the functions and activities of the REA would be exercised within the Department of Agriculture under the general direction and supervision of the Secretary.

Were S. 144 to become law it would mark a major retreat from sound administrative policy and practice. Twenty years ago the REA, then an independent agency, was by Reorganization Plan placed within the Department of Agriculture and under the general direction and supervision of the Secretary. The President, in his message transmitting Reorganization Plan No. II of 1939, said that the proposed reorganization was for the "sole purpose of improving the administrative management of the executive branch".

That action of twenty years ago accords entirely with the later finding of the first Commission on Organization of the Executive Branch that: "There must be a clear line of authority reaching down through every step of the organization and no subordinate should have authority independent of that of his superior."

Because S. 144 violates this sound injunction I am compelled to disapprove it.

338

Moreover, there is nothing in the recent history of the REA which affords any basis for concluding that the best interests of the agency or the public would be served by removing the Administrator's loan-making authority from the general direction and supervision of the Secretary of Agriculture.

The REA since its inception has moved steadily in the accomplishment of its mission. When the agency was established, only a small percentage of the nation's farms had central station electric service. Today 96% of our farmers have such service and about ½ the increase has been provided by REA financed facilities.

In the past six years the REA financed systems have made their greatest progress. Loans of more than a billion dollars have been made in this period, nearly half as much as was loaned by the agency in the previous seventeen and one-half years of its existence. Power sales have more than doubled since 1952, loan delinquencies have been reduced to the vanishing point and the net worth of electric borrowers has more than tripled. Plant investment for these systems has more than doubled in the past decade. The REA telephone loan program, authorized in 1949, has resulted in loan approvals which now total approximately $500 million and modern dial telephone service is rapidly being extended to the nation's rural areas.

The REA has been working well and progressing efficiently under the existing administrative arrangements. The change in those arrangements proposed by S. 144 would be contrary to the public interest.

DWIGHT D. EISENHOWER

87 ¶ Remarks at the Annual Meeting of the United States Chamber of Commerce. *April* 27, 1959

Mr. McDonnell, Delegates, Members of the United States Chamber of Commerce, and Guests:

May I first join you in a sincere tribute to your distinguished former President, Harper Sibley. With you, I deeply regret his passing.

It is a privilege to meet with you at this annual convention. It is particularly gratifying that in such meetings you, leaders of the business community from all parts of the country, concern yourselves with the broad range of problems of great importance to our Nation's life. In this way you demonstrate the deep sense of civic responsibility which characterizes modern American business.

On our part we of government look to the business community because of the vital role that this great force plays in contributing to American thinking and decisions, in helping to build America's security, and in expanding her economy.

To sustain the Nation's position in this world, sharply divided as it is between the values of freedom on one side, and the aggressive purposes of a communistic and atheistic dictatorship on the other, is a many-sided task.

At the outset, we must recognize one incontestable truth: in the face of the announced Communist intention to dominate the world, isolation for America is a futile and fatal policy. The fortunes of the free world are the fortunes of America. Our free society and our prosperity will flourish if freedom and progress flourish elsewhere. Our fortunes, our liberty and, indeed, our lives will be imperiled if the independence and welfare of other free nations are imperiled. Consequently, it is for us imperative that if international communism is to be frustrated in its drive for world domination, that there be a system of nations in which liberty, justice, and human dignity are the permanent pillars of society.

We have first to assure our own Nation's defensive and deterrent power. Beyond this, we know that the over-running of any free nation would transfer the resources of that nation to communism and by that much, weaken the free world. Should this step-by-step process be allowed to continue indefinitely, even our great Nation would face eventual encirclement and the result would be catastrophic.

We live in a climate of tension and challenge. We confront world communism in a protracted struggle in which we are menaced by political, economic, and military resources. As long as the Communists pursue their basic goal along broad and diverse fronts, we have no choice but to meet the challenge wherever or however it may be presented.

Now in the complicated problem of protecting freedom, one of America's essential requirements is to maintain an expanding national economy based upon a sound and stable dollar.

A strong economy is the physical basis of all our military power. A sound economy is proof to ourselves and to all others that we have the capacity to do indefinitely whatever we need to do in protecting our basic interests. Such an economy also provides the working proof that it can produce a standard of living which a regimented economy cannot remotely approach.

But there is still another reason for us to make certain of the health and growth of the American economy. Nations, less developed and smaller than ourselves, and which are more nakedly exposed to the Communist threat, cannot support their independence and liberty without some assistance from our economy. Whether the main weight of the Communist threat, applied at any given point, be military, political, or economic, the threatened area requires help from the more fortunately situated nations. Among these we are pre-eminent. And now that the Communists are adding to their threat of military force an increased threat of penetration through economic methods, the need for our economic strength and soundness and our assistance to others becomes even clearer.

Recognizing, then, the community of interest among the free nations to sustain our collective and individual safety, we must strive to make our cooperative associations stronger and more effective. The strongest tie that binds us together is a spiritual one—our common belief that the human values we support and defend are priceless beyond life itself.

Because we all—regardless of differences in religion, race, and culture—are dedicated to the protection of these values, we have devised organizational mechanisms through which we may more closely cooperate in the common effort and, through unity, achieve greater strength to assure success.

Each of the free nations so associated supplies what it is best able to provide for the common defense. The contribution of our Allies in numbers of men in the armed services far exceed our own. Not always, however, can they, alone, maintain these numbers and at the same time provide even the minimum standard of living necessary to sustain health, hope, and morale. In these cases we see that it is to our advantage to provide some financial help.

Clearly, mutual security and the Nation's security are synonymous.

I cannot re-emphasize too strongly that in our struggle against Soviet imperialism we must have firm friends and willing allies. We must, through patient work, promote collective growth and strength. Aside from the material assistance we may provide through weapons, and private and public loans, we must help to produce a freer flow of world trade. We must do this without prejudice to our national security and without inflicting undue hardship on our local producers.

Especially among the less-developed countries we must use every available means—political, technical, professional, and material—to assure that these people not only add to the free world's strength, but eventually become valued participants as both sellers and buyers in the markets of world trade.

Such examples as these are those of what we Americans can do, and are doing, to promote our security and to build a new fraternity of peace-loving nations. There are, of course, many others.

Of one thing I am sure. Our investments in this work are the most fruitful we can make or do make. Our returns are earned in terms of greater security, stronger and sturdier friends with which to live and to work and to trade, and in more enthusiastic supporters in the search for peace and security.

Wisdom, a nation's wisdom, is needed. There is no room in America for narrow selfishness, either personal or collective. We must look frankly at the problem as it stands now before us and as it will change and develop in the future. We must strive to eliminate stupidity, prejudice, arrogance, and ignorance from our thinking. We must, as a people, employ the greatest degree of wisdom that we can, as humans, achieve.

Many of the decisions to be made in this great effort belong to the businessman rather than exclusively or even primarily to the Government. In the fields of private investment abroad and in promoting a greater volume of trade, there is much you can do to increase free world cohesion and strength.

Moreover, I hope that each of you in America's business community will work tirelessly for a better national awareness of the challenge before us and the character of the response we must make both in our own interests and in those of all humanity. Success demands the force of an informed public opinion to strengthen the instruments of freedom in the free world community. As business, community, and national leaders— leaders who do not panic under threat or grow complacent in apparent success—you have a priceless opportunity to help promote the understanding through which the needed public opinion can be produced.

At this point I mention with deep gratification the resolution of support for the Mutual Security Program passed by this Chamber a few short months ago. I am quite certain that all America applauds your forward-looking and decisive action.

Each year will bring new problems—always demanding the very best that is in us. And there will be no stopping, or resting, or turning back. We face a future of building and living, patiently and unflinchingly, in the shadow of danger—yet for all this, a brightly hopeful future for a nation and its friends which keep themselves strong, solvent and free—and who fight basically, and who fight only, for peace—a peace with justice for all.

Thank you very much.

NOTE: The President spoke at the opening session at Constitution Hall. His opening words "Mr. McDonnell" referred to William A. McDonnell, President of the U.S. Chamber of Commerce.

88 ¶ Telegram to the Governor of Mississippi Concerning Assistance by the Federal Bureau of Investigation in Pearl River County.
April 28, 1959

[Released April 28, 1959. Dated April 27, 1959]

The Honorable J. P. Coleman
Governor
Jackson, Mississippi

Thank you for your wire expressing the appreciation of the people of Mississippi for Federal Bureau of Investigation assistance in Pearl River County. These agents will of course continue to provide full facilities to help in any way in this matter. It is my earnest hope that there will be swift apprehension of the guilty persons.

DWIGHT D. EISENHOWER

NOTE: The Federal Bureau of Investigation assisted in the Mack Charles Parker case for the purpose of ascertaining if there had been a violation of the Federal Kidnaping Act.

Governor Coleman's telegram follows:

The President
The White House

The people of Mississippi appreciate the assistance of the Federal Bureau of Investigation in the Pearl River County occurrence and I am deeply grateful. I trust that these trained men will be allowed to pursue their investigations until the guilty persons shall have been apprehended.

J. P. COLEMAN

89 ¶ The President's News Conference of *April* 29, 1959.

THE PRESIDENT. Good morning. Please sit down. I have no statement of my own.

Q. Marvin L. Arrowsmith, Associated Press: Mr. President do you think Mrs. Luce should go on to Brazil as Ambassador, or if she should follow the advice of her husband and offer to resign? [*Laughter*]

THE PRESIDENT. Well, let's look at a little background.

Mrs. Luce was our Ambassador in Italy for a long time and operated very successfully there. Actually her work in helping to bring about a settlement on the Trieste question, I think was brilliant.

She resigned for reasons of health and personal reasons some time back; and a few—I suppose two or three—months ago, Secretary Dulles came to me and suggested that we ought to get her back. He said he thought he would like to send her into Brazil, because he thought her talents would be useful there.

I have always known her as a dedicated and useful public servant. As a matter of fact, I knew her really only as an ambassadress.

Now, she had some difficulties as you know, about confirmation and there were attacks made upon her.

Then she made a remark.

Now that remark, as far as I am concerned, was not meant as any disparagement of the Senate of the United States. She was unquestionably in a sort of heated type of disposition and temperament at the moment, and she said something that was perfectly human, even if she probably would have hoped it had never been published. [*Laughter*]

But what I am saying is this: even if ill-advised, it was human and she did not mean it as a disparagement of the United States Senate. I don't think she meant it that way and I don't think the Senate thinks of it as that way. So I see no major impairment of her usefulness for the post we intended.

Indeed, I had a survey made so far as it could be done by telephone yesterday afternoon in Brazil, and the answer there is quite clear that she is welcome in the post.

Q. David Sentner, Hearst Newspapers: Have you received her resignation or any communication from her since yesterday?

THE PRESIDENT. No, I have not been in direct communication with her at all, and she has not submitted any resignation.

Now, she did, back about March 3d or 4th, the time of that Time article about Bolivia, she came in and said if we thought, in the State Department, that her usefulness had been impaired, she was quite ready to withdraw in spite of the fact that she was quite anxious to undertake that task. I was told then that Brazil, in spite of that article, welcomed her presence.

Q. Merriman Smith, United Press International: Mr. President, in Augusta on April 15, in announcing the resignation of Secretary Dulles, you told us that you would name a successor within a matter of days. And then you were asked whether this meant that you might be considering someone other than Mr. Herter, and you said that there were a number of people in Government who had particular talent in this field; and there were all kinds of considerations to be studied.

Well, in the period between your press conference down there and the morning of April 18, when you announced the selection of Mr. Herter, there was a degree of speculation and interpretation in Washington that this had been a delay damaging to Mr. Herter and indicative, possibly, of some reluctance on your part to appoint him.

Now, what is your reaction to that sort of thing, sir?

THE PRESIDENT. Well, I think it was a lot of unnecessary speculation and unprofitable speculation.

From the very beginning of his illness, Foster Dulles, whose mind has not been impaired in the slightest—and I visited him only Monday afternoon—took up with me voluntarily the identity of his successor, should this become necessary. He thought that we should—no need for jumping into this thing with haste—that we'd look over the whole field and see what we had better do.

He and I both came to the conclusion that when this, if this ever came about, this necessity for replacement, that Mr. Herter should do it. But we didn't want to start any great speculation because I did not know, neither did the Secretary know, whether he would experience a period of upturn in his disease, or whether there would be no improvement and he would have to withdraw.

Now, the one thing that concerned us very definitely was Mr. Herter's health. And so when I got the final, definite notice—well, I don't know the exact date; let's say the 14th, something like that—and the doctor said that it would be better for him to resign, and he decided he should resign, then Mr. Herter was sent over to a clinic that had nothing to do with Government and where it would be not his own doctor, to be an objective examination, and the report came back. That was a report that needed to be read, but it nevertheless gave him, in my opinion, clear health certificate for going ahead, certainly for 2 years.

At this time it was merely a question of how to get hold of Mr. Herter now to make certain that I could give him his appointment in a dignified way. And I asked him to come see me. I believe he was traveling that day. So instead of getting him for Friday morning, why, I got him for Saturday morning.

He and Secretary Dulles and myself were completely agreed as to how this should be done, and let's not forget this: so far as I'm concerned, in such a serious matter as this, when you're losing a public servant of the stature and standing of Mr. Dulles, you don't try to hold a wedding until the other man has at least left the house. I think it was done decently and properly, and that is all there is to it.

Q. Thomas N. Schroth, Congressional Quarterly: Mr. President, last January, in your State of the Union Message, you said you planned to set up a committee that would draw up a set of national goals. As of now, no such committee has been set up. Could you tell us what the delay is for?

THE PRESIDENT. Well, it's to get exactly the right, proper people, the people that can give the time, and the people of the quality and standing that can do it; that's what the question is.

Q. Jules Witcover, Newhouse Newspapers: Rear Admiral Nunn, the senior U.N. delegate to the Military Commission in Korea, has demanded that the Communists disclose the fate of 2147 allied prisoners who were never accounted for.

Do we know now how many of these are Americans, and are we making any new efforts to recover them?

THE PRESIDENT. You bring to me news about this report from the Admiral.

Now, I recall, from memory, that there were a great number of people that we could not account for, and we have had long, serious, and even continuing discussions with the Chinese Communists trying to make them disclose where our prisoners were held.

At that time they gave us identifications in certain numbers and of those, we have gotten back a few and there are still some left there. But the details of this I would have to have looked up for you, and you could get it from Mr. Hagerty.

Q. William McGaffin, Chicago Daily News: Mr. President, I noticed in the newspaper this morning that Mr. Dulles, the Director of the CIA, calls the situation in Iraq the most dangerous in the world today.

Sir, do you feel that the fact that that situation has become so dangerous is a reflection on the foreign policy which has been pursued in your administration?

Is there any way of recouping the situation now before it slips behind the Iron Curtain?

THE PRESIDENT. Well, let's say this: we always recognized Iraq as a friendly country. So did the preceding administration. We have always met its request, at least so far as possible and certainly always in a reasonable manner, for the assistance that it needed. It had been one of the most progressive of the countries in the region. After the great difficulty that came about, after the revolution or revolt there that removed the King and the Prime Minister—now, from that time on there is also another feature that has come into the thing, and that is certain cross-currents of antagonism within the Mideast.

We are trying and have been trying to be friends with everybody in the Mideast. We are very concerned about Iraq. We do our best not only to sustain but to promote our better relationship with that country, but that is complicated by—well, you know from the newspapers about the connections with communism and the difficulties with Egypt. This is not one of the easy problems.

I don't know that I would classify it as the most dangerous, but I would say this: it is one of those things that requires attention every single day on the part of our Government, and if there is anything we can do to promote better relations with this country without making other

347

enemies in the same region, why that is a good policy to follow. And we do follow it.

Q. Ronald W. May, Madison (Wis.) Capital Times: Mr. President, the United States is about to fall behind Russia in the field of high-energy physics.

In Madison we have the Midwestern Universities Research Association that some years ago developed an atom smasher of very much more power than anything in existence, and they have been coming to the Atomic Energy Commission for years, asking for money to build this smasher, and have been consistently turned down.

Now, it has been reported that your Special Committee in this field is going to recommend that Stanford University get about the equivalent amount to build, to rebuild an old-fashioned type smasher, and this worries people in the Midwestern Universities. And they have learned now that the Russians are building the great advanced machine which was developed in Madison.

I wonder if there is any explanation for this.

THE PRESIDENT. Well, it sounds a little bit like a pressure group presentation. [*Laughter*]

Now, I didn't know that Madison was seeking this particular mechanism there. Naturally, I wouldn't, but I do know this: I have had a very long presentation on the building of a—what you call an atom smasher—accelerator, I think, is the word they use when they talk to me.

They showed me the pictures of the biggest and presumably the best machine the Russians have, and I believe it is a half mile in diameter, but our people have come to the conclusion that a linear accelerator is better than any other.

They also told me, because I said, "Let's put this on a reservation somewhere and hide it," they said it has to be on the university; and they said because of past experience in this kind of thing they were putting on, they thought it should go in the Stanford locality.

Now, this is far from being old-fashioned. I am told by the scientists that this is the most extraordinary thing that has yet been attempted, will put us way ahead of where we are now, and will take about 5 years to build, I understand.

Q. Mary Philomene Von Herberg, San Francisco Call-Bulletin: Just supposing that everything goes well with this foreign ministers conference so that the summit conference is held, we are wondering, out in San Francisco, if you would not like to hold that summit conference there.

The city is very excited about it.

THE PRESIDENT. Well, as a matter of fact, that is the kind of question, the timing and the site and composition of the conference, that will be decided, certainly taken up by the foreign ministers. So I couldn't possibly give an answer to it at the moment.

Q. Miss Von Herberg: No, but we wondered if you would be interested in going out there.

They liked you when you were there before. [*Laughter*]

THE PRESIDENT. Well, I always like to go to San Francisco.

Q. Charles S. von Fremd, CBS News: Mr. Hagerty indicated yesterday that you might have some comments that you would like to make about the labor bill which was passed by the Senate and is now going to the House. Would you care to, at this time?

THE PRESIDENT. Are you asking a question or do you want me to volunteer something?

Q. Mr. von Fremd: No, I'd like to——

THE PRESIDENT. Well, the fact is that this whole labor situation, which has been characterized as worse than malfunctioning, even racketeering in some few labor organizations and among certain individuals, been highlighted by the McClellan committee report, this whole thing was studied by the administration last fall and winter, and we put it on a program.

Now, in the Senate bill as it has come out and passed and sent to the House, we think there are very definite weaknesses. I don't mind saying that I am very much disappointed, particularly in three fields: the secondary boycott is not dealt with properly and effectively; blackmail picketing the same way; and then the field of clarifying the relationships of States to those areas where the NLRB has refused to assert any jurisdiction. We believe there ought to be a definite law here to confer or to recognize that authority of the States to meet those particular problems.

Now, in those three areas I think the bill should be strengthened, and I am very hopeful that the House will do so.

Q. John Scali, Associated Press: Mr. President, your old friend,

Marshal Montgomery, seems to be at it again.

He seems to be taking a rather dim view of American leadership at the moment. He says that it is not as good as it might be, and that it lacks decision at the top.

I was wondering if there was any observation you care to make.

THE PRESIDENT. I think that about all I can say you will find in the British newspapers of this morning and last night; and I think if you will read those, that all the answers are there.

Q. Robert J. Donovan, New York Herald Tribune: Mr. President, it has been some time since you talked with us about the situation in Germany. Could you tell us how you think it is shaping up now that the talks are getting under way, and what your hopes are for the next few weeks, or any plans we have.

THE PRESIDENT. As you know, we have had some very serious conferences, Mr. Herter and indeed with Secretary Dulles and myself on the developing scene.

The only, you might say, *sine qua non* in our policy is this: we will not desert two million free people to some kind of domination that they would rebel against. We are going to maintain our rights to discharge the responsibilities that are still ours.

Now, after we stand on that flatfootedly, on that principle, I should say there are a great many approaches as to what might be done to ease the situation a little bit, to make certain that it will grow no worse from the standpoint of either side, and which will give some hope of improvement and more stability so that we will not be constantly facing a new so-called crisis or reason for tension.

Mr. Herter has gone over with our friends of the West to concert the kind of papers we will either separately or together table in this foreign ministers meeting. And thereafter we will see whether we can get anything that indicates hopefulness in the way of getting Germany in one— put it this way: make one little step toward a position where it could begin to think of negotiating a peace treaty.

Q. Mrs. May Craig, Portland (Maine) Press Herald: Mr. President, some high Air Force officials want strategic control of the missile-shooting submarines. What is your position on that?

THE PRESIDENT. Well, I think I would be with the submarines.

I hadn't heard this charge before. I would think that here is something that the Secretary of Defense could control and direct and coordinate without any difficulty.

Q. Roscoe Drummond, New York Herald Tribune: Mr. President, could you give us your view of the British compromise proposal which has been laid on the conference table at Geneva, and which the Soviets seem to be interested in, having to do with the inspection of possible suspicious blasts?

THE PRESIDENT. Well, Mr. Drummond, here is the basic issue there, as I see it: that proposal was made on the theory that the veto would be removed, that there would be no Eastern insistence upon the veto, and therefore the only problems to solve would be how many of these free inspections could be made. But so long as the Soviets insist upon the veto with respect to the composition of the committees, inspecting teams, their right to go inspect within the number, then there is no sense whatsoever, as I see it, of talking about the number that will be allowed.

Now, the difference between that and what we propose and with the British concurrence was—let us stop atmospheric tests, tests in the atmosphere, because the simplest kind of system could assure that our present methods could be reinforced with only a few stations, and there would be no teams driving around.

But until you have the authority to do this without the veto, then the number thing doesn't come in at all.

Q. Mr. Drummond: May I ask a related question, Mr. President?

THE PRESIDENT. Yes.

Q. Mr. Drummond: Do we rightly understand that the British proposal is that there should be an agreed number of inspections that each side could make in the country of the other without veto, and then there would be a veto over additional inspections?

THE PRESIDENT. Well, Mr. Drummond, as submitted to me and, as a matter of fact, as discussed with me in personal discussions, it didn't go into this detail. It was trying to find some way that would circumvent or get around the strict, unequivocal veto; and this would be, therefore, in their opinion, some advance if we could get that promise.

Now, the matter ought to be studied very intelligently and carefully. But each of these, you see, has some action and interaction and reaction, and it is very difficult to make, you might say, a shooting-from-the-hip answer to that kind of thing.

Q. Laurence H. Burd, Chicago Tribune: Mr. President, if there is a summit conference, would you expect Vice President Nixon to attend it with you?

THE PRESIDENT. Well, it is quite early to be talking now about the composition of such a meeting, because the meeting itself has not yet been established. But I would say this: if the Vice President were to come, he and I would never be there at the same time, I would be quite sure of that.

Q. Joseph A. Loftus, New York Times: Mr. President, a further question about the labor bill, with particular attention to this bill of rights which is now in there to protect members from autocratic officers.

Would you, do you believe that this offsets in any degree the absence of some of the items that you asked for?

THE PRESIDENT. The bill of rights, as I saw it introduced and read it as introduced by Senator McClellan, I thought was a very fine thing.

There have been amendments made that withdraw from that position; and I would not believe, as it stands now, that it was a real substitute for the kind of things that I think should be done and that I specified.

Q. Sarah McClendon, Manchester (N.H.) Union Leader: Sir, on January the 3d the Russians made a claim that they had sent a rocket to the moon, and you, I believe the record of the Senate investigators showed, congratulated them on that very day, although our scientists did not seem to pick up a signal until the following day, and later there was great doubt among our scientists as to the claims by Russia.

Now, some people have thought that maybe your quick congratulations may have aided Russian propaganda in their claim to accomplishment. Would you——

THE PRESIDENT. Well, if I did, I will say this, it was strictly unintentional.

Now, I made a statement on the advice of the scientists who believed it was an advance, and it would be, since it was supposed to be in the peaceful field of space exploration, it would be really wrong not—to withdraw recognition of that accomplishment.

Now you say I did it before it was accomplished. Not as far as the scientists told me.

Q. Mrs. McClendon: Could you tell us who those scientists were? Were they in Government or were they outside Government? Who advised you to go ahead with that?

THE PRESIDENT. I'll say this: in my opinion, some of the finest in the country.

Q. Richard L. Wilson, Cowles Publications: Mr. President, your statement about Vice President Nixon could leave the implication that you might not remain at a possible summit conference for the entire duration. Is that a logical——

THE PRESIDENT. I didn't mean to leave the implication that this was a probability of any kind, but I do remind you people always of some of the constitutional limitations that are placed on me, if you have to go out of the country for any considerable time.

Now, how would you have someone acting as the head of the state, or in his position, in a delegated position? Remember, the Secretary of State and his aides are working every day in the details with the foreign ministers; then you meet in the afternoon with the heads of state; someone has to be able to meet there who is not involved in the details all day long.

So I would have to find, I should think, if I did find it necessary to come home 2 or 3 days, somebody else. I just suggested that was one way that we might solve the difficulty. There's been no planning, I assure you; no plans of any kind.

Q. James B. Reston, New York Times: Mr. President, Senator Fulbright, the chairman of the Foreign Relations Committee, has suggested an amendment to the Mutual Security Act under which for 5 years a billion five hundred million would be appropriated each year for the Development Loan Fund.

What position are you now taking on that proposal?

THE PRESIDENT. Well, I have not had any studies yet. As to the beneficial effect of a rigid kind of a commitment of this kind, I believe this: here is something that requires the very finest brains we have all the time. Nothing that I deplore so much as the fact that in certain quarters this subject seems to become a political one, and we expect to get political advantages out of using slogans such as "Giveaway" and that kind of thing.

Now, I do believe that unless the United States is prepared to carry forward a program of higher appropriations than we are now using— I say that because we have been using up from the carryover something around 8 billion; we are down now to I think 1.8—we have got to carry forward a program that each year is going to be something stronger than what we are now doing, if we are going to serve our own interests in this world.

I am quoting such opinions as that of Admiral Radford and Mr. McCloy and Mr. Webb and Mr. Draper, the people that have been studying this very searchingly, and with no partisan or governmental or, you might say, administrative responsibility in the whole thing, and I think there we must listen very seriously to their words.

Q. Mr. Reston: Mr. President, could I clarify one other point about that? Do you accept the principle of the long-range commitment?

THE PRESIDENT. Yes, yes.

Q. Mr. Reston: As I understand the argument is, you can save money if you can commit for 5 years.

THE PRESIDENT. Yes, I'd agree with that, I'd agree with that. I haven't talked to Senator Fulbright directly on this, but this has been an argument that Secretary Dulles and I put forward when we first asked for the development fund, because we asked for "no year" money to be put in there, to be used so far as possible in the long run, to be used as a revolving fund, but in the meantime to keep it at the level where you could do the job.

Q. Ruth S. Montgomery, Hearst Newspapers: Mr. President, what do you think about the type of attack that some Senators have made against Admiral Strauss, as well as Clare Luce, and what is back of it, do you think?

THE PRESIDENT. Miss Montgomery, I am not and I do not intend to question anyone's motives and therefore to ascribe to them any particular reasons for why they do things. But there are at this moment before the Senate 76 nominations made by the President, to say nothing of a thousand postmasters that are down there waiting confirmation. Of those 76, there are 47 I think that are classed as major appointments: 1 Secretary, 4 Assistant Secretaries, a number of judges, 10 U.S. attorneys. All of these people as a matter of fact—judges, including one Supreme Court Justice—all these people are important to the functioning of the United States Government, and some of them are wondering now whether they are going to be here for a month and what they should plan to do, or whether they are going to be here after the Congress adjourns.

Every one of these men, so far as I and my advisers can discover, is not only well qualified for his job or her job but they are people that we think are pre-eminently qualified.　So therefore I know of no reason for keeping this matter in abeyance so long.　I do not criticize at all, legitimate research into ability, record; and any kind of fact that can be brought out, should be brought out; but we should get at it and do it and not just to defer the thing.

I think that Secretary Strauss is one of the finest public servants I have known.　I have known him in a number of capacities, I have known him in private life, and I have never heard one single word against his character, against his honesty and his ability.　And, therefore, I am really puzzled as to why this delay should occur.

Marvin L. Arrowsmith, Associated Press: Thank you, Mr. President.

NOTE: President Eisenhower's one hundred and fifty-seventh news conference was held in the Executive Office Building from 10:30 to 11:03 o'clock on Wednesday morning, April 29, 1959.　In attendance: 252.

90　¶ Letter to the President of the Senate and to the Speaker of the House of Representatives on the Recommendations of the Committee To Study the U.S. Military Assistance Program.　*April* 29, 1959

Dear ——————:

In my Mutual Security Message last month, I stated that the bipartisan Committee to Study the United States Military Assistance Program would soon render an interim report, and that after study of this report I would submit to Congress such recommendations thereon as I should deem appropriate.

The Committee, composed of eminent Americans, has made an excellent study of the grave perils inherent in Communist military, economic and political activities throughout the world.　It has pointed out that without a continuing and effective Mutual Security Program our single and unthinkable alternative is "to seek survival in isolation—a state of siege—as the world continues to shrink."　The Committee has highlighted the necessity for a truly mutual effort, and after first-hand observation by its members has noted the important strengthening of the free world through our assistance—assistance which strengthens us as it strengthens our allies.

Rightly the Committee has emphasized the need for modernization of free world military forces, particularly in the NATO area. It has recommended a substantial increase in the level of commitments in Fiscal Year 1960, pointing out that such an increase would not involve a significant increase in expenditures during that year. I believe, with the Committee, that NATO force modernization must go forward as rapidly as sound decisions permit.

The unanimous findings of the Committee in its interim report confirm the imperative need for Congress to authorize and appropriate the full amount requested for both economic and military assistance in the Mutual Security Program for Fiscal Year 1960. With this full amount available, I shall, in support of the Committee's recommendations, direct full use of the flexibility which Congress has wisely provided in the Mutual Security Act, including the Contingency Fund. Progress to implement the Committee's recommendations can be made in this way. Nonetheless, even including these measures, as well as our continuing efforts to improve the operational efficiency and economy of the program, it may well be that the carrying out of essential equipment and training programs, including the force modernization recommended by the Committee, will require additional authority to obligate funds in Fiscal Year 1960. Undoubtedly more funds will be required should the Congress fail to appropriate the full amount already requested.

Late this fall, I shall review the then-current status of our efforts to implement the Committee's recommendations. This review will encompass then-existing world conditions as shaped by developments over the next few months, the rate of force modernization, particularly in the NATO area, and, of course, the progress of 1960 procurements for NATO and other areas. In the light of this review, I will make appropriate recommendations to the Congress. This review will enable me to take full account of the Committee's recommendations also in the formulation of the military assistance budget for Fiscal Year 1961.

I again emphasize that the program already before the Congress is the minimum required to support our own nation's security and the common defense of the free world.

I enclose the Committee's Interim Report for the earnest consideration of the Congress.

Sincerely,

DWIGHT D. EISENHOWER

NOTE: This is the text of identical letters addressed to the Honorable Richard M. Nixon, President of the Senate, and the Honorable Sam Rayburn, Speaker of the House of Representatives.

The interim report referred to by the President was entitled "Preliminary Conclusions of the President's Committee to Study the United States Military Assistance Program." Submitted to the President on March 17, this report is published in the Congressional Record of March 18, 1959 (vol. 105, p. 3963). For subsequent reports by the President's Committee see Items 136, 137, 170, 183.

91   ¶ Letter to Dean Sayre Concerning United States Participation in the World Refugee Year. *April* 30, 1959

[Released April 30, 1959. Dated April 28, 1959]

Dear Dean Sayre:

I will certainly be happy to sponsor a White House meeting for a discussion of the role which the American people and their government should play in the World Refugee Year beginning in June 1959. I have set May 21 and May 22 for such a meeting, to be held in the Indian Treaty Room of the Executive Office Building under the direction of Deputy Under Secretary of State Loy W. Henderson. It is my plan to invite to it a representative group of private citizens whose interests and experience should prove of utmost value in considering all aspects of this important matter.

It is most gratifying to me that the United States Committee for Refugees has been willing to assume a major responsibility for mobilizing the private resources of this country to meet the objectives of the World Refugee Year. Your efforts, I know, will do much to insure that the response of the American people will be generous, and that the traditional American leadership in the refugee field will be maintained. I will be unable personally to participate in the meeting, but I hope that it will assist in the formulation of specific plans for the World Refugee Year, as I am sure it will assist the government.

I assure you that this Administration will support the World Refugee Year, and will continue to cooperate with our own citizens' groups and with other governments of the free world to help resolve the grave humanitarian problem of refugees.

Sincerely,

DWIGHT D. EISENHOWER

NOTE: This letter was in reply to one from The Very Reverend Francis B. Sayre, Jr., Dean of the Washington Cathedral and Chairman of the Board of the United States Committee for Refugees. Dean Sayre's letter, in part, follows:

"No time can be lost in planning for United States participation. Accordingly, I was directed to ask you whether you would sponsor a rather informal White House meeting at which members of our Committee and other invited participants could discuss and plan for an American contribution to the Refugee Year. Such a meeting would seem to us to be of equal service to the members of your government and to the American people in general."

World Refugee Year was established by resolution of the United Nations General Assembly, adopted December 5, 1958, calling upon the member nations to cooperate in promoting World Refugee Year as a means of securing increased assistance for refugees throughout the world. On May 19, 1959, the President issued Proclamation 3292 (24 F.R. 4123) providing for United States participation and designating July 1, 1959–June 30, 1960, as World Refugee Year.

92 ¶ Remarks Upon Receiving the 1958 World Peace Award at the AMVETS Luncheon. *May* 1, 1959

Mr. Chairman, Commander Burdine, the Democratic Senator from Maine, distinguished guests, my fellow veterans and friends:

Any man privileged to receive from his fellow veterans an award signifying their respect for his efforts to promote peace should indeed be proud. Moreover, he should be very humble.

Any man who was part of the war must understand and must forever have engraved in his heart the truth that our opportunity to promote peace and to develop peaceful mechanisms was earned for us in the war by the sacrifices of thousands—of millions. When I think of the bravery and courage of men at war, for some reason I don't think so much of the bombardments or of the critical or dramatic moments that occurred to every one. Instead, the picture I get is one of endurance, faithfulness, duty, loyalty—the soldier slogging his way toward the front in the rain, in the mud, blue-lipped, often muddy-faced—drenched—miserable, with never the thought crossing his mind that he should lay down his burden or his task.

There is, of course, one thing he should always have: the knowledge of why he is fighting, and the knowledge that his great country, signified by this lovely flag, is always behind him.

We have too often forgotten our responsibility for doing that for the soldier. Sometimes we have not told him why men have been called to sacrifice everything, including life, for the cause of freedom which means the cause of peace.

Freedom means to live and to let live. Freedom does not seek to dominate. It wants no sway of power over others. It wants the right for each individual to develop himself to the full power of the rights and opportunities that our God has given us. This is what freedom wants, and the boy should, from babyhood, be taught that; all of us should be taught that.

Freedom has been defined as the opportunity for self-discipline. Other forms of discipline are imposed, but in freedom we must have self-discipline. Therefore, a soldier goes to his task because he feels within himself the duty to do it, to discipline himself, not to respond merely to the methods of tyranny and dictatorship.

So, as I think of the soldier, struggling, lying in the mud to get some rest, I think sometimes of ourselves.

Have we the courage, the stamina, the sense of duty, and the understanding of what freedom and peace truly mean? Have we got the courage and the stamina to continue everlastingly to carry on the search for peace, a peace with justice?

There is nothing jingoistic in America's ambitions. She seeks only for others the rights, the privileges, and the freedoms that she maintains for herself and will defend with everything she has.

This, it seems to me, is the one thing we must keep always in our understanding and in our hearts.

Freedom is not something that we keep just because this flag is so beautiful. As the commentator said in the beautiful description of the flag, the flag is what we make it.

Peace is what we make it.

Are we ready to sacrifice for it? Are we ready to dig in our pocketbooks? Are we ready to give our efforts, our intelligence and everything we have to create the conditions under which all men can enjoy the fruitfulness of the earth, under the kind of conditions that we think of when at Christmas time we say "Peace on earth to men of goodwill everywhere"?

I cannot tell you how proud I am to have this emblem. I wish I were worthy of it.

Thank you.

NOTE: The President spoke at the May-flower Hotel, Washington, D.C. His opening words referred to William H. Ayers, U.S. Representative from Ohio, Dr. Winston E. Burdine, National Commander of AMVETS, and Edmund S. Muskie, U.S. Senator from Maine.

The award, a silver helmet mounted on a silver base, was inscribed as follows: "AMVETS Peace Award presented to the Honorable Dwight David Eisenhower, President of the United States of America, in recognition of exceptionally courageous and devoted contributions to honorable world peace that all peoples might live with freedom and dignity. May 1959."

93 ¶ Remarks of Welcome to Sir Winston Churchill at the Washington National Airport. *May* 4, 1959

Sir Winston:

This is a great honor indeed to welcome you once more to the United States. I do so not only as my dear friend of wartime days but as one who is, after all, half American himself. We think it is only fitting that you should come and visit this country which—after all—claims at least the maternal side of you.

So, welcome again, and we do hope you enjoy your trip here to this country.

NOTE: Sir Winston responded as follows:

Mr. President, Ladies and Gentlemen:

I am most happy once again to set foot in the United States—my mother's country. I always think of it and feel it.

I have come here on a quiet visit to see some of my old comrades of wartime days. I am indeed sorry that the brevity of my stay makes it impossible for me to go to Canada or to see as many of my friends as I should like.

I always love coming to America. But I shall not say, as most people who are traveling nowadays about the world seem to do, everything I think.

It will suffice me to thank you all for your welcome, and to bring you the assurance of our lasting friendship.

94 ¶ The President's News Conference of *May* 5, 1959.

THE PRESIDENT. Thank you. Please sit down.

This morning, or maybe it was yesterday, hearings were starting again for a mutual security program. I don't want to take up too much of your time, for the simple reason that everyone here has heard expressed time and again my views about mutual security, its need for real support if we are concerned about our Nation's security, and our Nation's position in the international world. And, I repeat, it is not a partisan question; it's one of those things that should be discussed and debated on the basis of need and of logic and of good sense and fact, and not considered at all in any partisan attitude.

As I repeat that, you people know the dependence that I place upon it in assuring the security of the United States, and as a tool in our battle for a lessening of tension and some advancement toward peace.

Any questions?

Q. Merriman Smith, United Press International: Mr. President, from the conference that you directed Ambassador Thompson to undertake yesterday in Moscow with Mr. Khrushchev, and from other reports to this Government, do you have any reason to believe that Russia is holding any American fliers as prisoners?

THE PRESIDENT. No. I have no reason to believe anything of this matter. Actually we are unaware of the fate of these individuals other than, of course, the six that were returned after their death. But I did, on a very personal basis, direct the Ambassador to take this issue again to Mr. Khrushchev.[1]

Q. Ray L. Scherer, NBC News: Mr. President, Mrs. Luce resigned because she said she felt her usefulness had been impaired in view of the bitterness involved. Do you think that Admiral Strauss would be well advised to do likewise?

THE PRESIDENT. I do not. I have told you again and again that I think here is a man who is not only a valuable public servant, but who is a man of the utmost integrity and competence in administration. And if we've got to the point where a man, because of some personal antagonisms, cannot be confirmed for office in this Government, then I must say we're getting to a pretty bad situation.

Q. William McGaffin, Chicago Daily News: Mr. President, to get

---

[1] On May 4, the Press Secretary to the President released the following statement in reply to a question concerning the conference Ambassador Thompson had with Nikita Khrushchev:

On instructions from the President, the United States Ambassador to the Union of the Soviet Socialist Republics, Llewellyn E. Thompson, today had an interview with the Chairman of the Council of Ministers of the U.S.S.R., Nikita Khrushchev, in connection with the case of the United States Air Force C–130 transport plane that was shot down by Soviet fighter aircraft over Soviet Armenia on September 2, 1958. The Ambassador's representation dealt particularly with the President's concern for the fate of the eleven members of the crew who are still missing and unaccounted for.

back to mutual security for a moment, some Senators feel that you are taking too timid an approach in your request for the mutual security program, and also that you are spending too much on military foreign aid and not enough on economic.

THE PRESIDENT. Well, with respect to this timid approach—I think I am correct, although I am speaking only from memory, and if I have to correct my statement I shall do so at my next meeting with you— I think that each time I have made recommendations on mutual security it has been cut down by the Congress. I therefore think that it has not been carried forward as vigorously as it should be.

Now, with respect to the military portion of this thing, I would remind you that if we are going to hold Korea, Taiwan, and one or two other areas where we are really committed under basic policy to protect, a large portion of this military aid goes there.

The Draper Committee found that we must do more to modernize the armies in NATO, and recommended very strongly that we have an increase in this part of the thing. This is where we stand at this moment.

Q. Mr. McGaffin: Well Mr. President, however, there has been considerable criticism that we have not been too wise in allocating military aid to, for instance, Pakistan. That aid is regarded by India as something hostile, and one reason why India's second year, second 5-year plan is in difficulties is that India felt it necessary to buy arms herself to counter the arms we are giving Pakistan.

THE PRESIDENT. I want to tell you that such questions that you are now raising have been studied hours and weeks and months, literally, by this Government, this administration, calling in often legislative leaders of both parties in the effort to get a reasonable and, as nearly as possible, correct answer about this whole thing.

Of course there is criticism. Everybody in this field has his own particular beliefs. But I say this: so far as I know, there has been nothing that is done here except on the basis of supporting the free world and America's position in that free world.

Q. Carleton Kent, Chicago Sun-Times: Mr. President, Mr. Truman told the Senate yesterday that the 22d amendment automatically makes the President a "lameduck" when he enters his second term.

In the last 2 years, have you felt that you had one hand tied behind you by the amendment, as he said?

THE PRESIDENT. I haven't sensed that particular feeling. I find this, that it seems to me I am more bombarded with requests for help of all kinds, whether it be administrative, altruistic and charitable, or political, than I ever have in my prior years in the Presidency.

I have commented on this amendment in terms of a bit of, let's say, indecision in the meaning that I'd see some advantages and disadvantages on both sides. I think the first time I said I didn't think much of the amendment; the second time, as I recall, I said I rather believed that, after some study, on balance the amendment gives greater assurance to America than its repeal would.

But again I say it is something I am perfectly ready to submit to the convictions and opinions of the people of the United States because I don't feel too strongly about it.

Q. John Scali, Associated Press: Mr. President, the foreign ministers meeting begins in 6 days. In advance of that, could you tell us how you regard prospects for settling specific differences with the Soviets at this meeting; and could you also tell us, sir, how much progress you would believe necessary in order to justify a summit meeting?

THE PRESIDENT. Well, I couldn't talk to you very much in specific terms. We don't know what will come out.

Certainly I hope that there will be some progress, and actually, all of us do know that within the Soviet regime there is only one man who can talk authoritatively.

Therefore, if there is anything that gives enlarged hope for decreasing tensions in the world, then I think a summit meeting would become almost a—its occurrence would be a foregone conclusion.

Now, there is no point, at this moment, of trying to lay out in detail what will be our approach. Secretary Herter on Thursday night is making a report to the Nation in which he will discuss our propositions and proposals and attitudes in some detail, and I think that it would be best to wait for that.

Q. Thomas N. Schroth, Congressional Quarterly: Sir, in 1951, on July 3d, in London you made a strong plea for the free nations of Europe to unite. You referred to it, you said it was difficult to overstate the benefits that would accrue to NATO and the nations of Europe recruited to unite, and you referred to Sir Winston's desires in that same regard.

Would you care to assess what has happened since 1951 in Europe in this regard, and do you feel that it is still as urgent as ever?

THE PRESIDENT. I believe in it, really, with all my heart. I would never have gone to SHAPE in January of 1951 unless I believed that the interests of the whole free world would be served and that the advantages to be obtained by the free world were almost decisive, unless I believed thoroughly in this proposition that Western Europe must unite more closely.

Now, I never tried to establish a pattern, although in that particular talk I did urge a more dramatic and, you might say, precipitant move than I thought Europe was ready to take. But I did it for a very definite reason.

I knew from conferences with many governments that the leaders realized this was something that had to come about someday, and I wanted to do my part in helping people, the people of Western Europe, to understand the value.

Since then of course, I remind you we have had Euratom, we have had the Common Market developing, we have had the Steel and Coal Community developed and coming along; and so there have been many steps. By no means am I discouraged in this.

Frankly, I think there is no talk in my whole life that I worked on as long and as seriously as I did that one, because I believe it thoroughly.

Q. Robert G. Spivack, New York Post: Mr. President, I believe it was a week or so ago that you expressed your indignation over the kidnaping by a Mississippi mob of a Negro prisoner and according to the news reports the FBI now has found the body.

I wonder if, as you review this episode, you feel that it emphasizes a need for stronger civil rights legislation, or if you have any other specific conclusions you draw from this affair?

THE PRESIDENT. Well I hadn't thought even about the idea that it needs new law in this particular case.

The State authorities got on the job immediately, they called in the FBI, they have been working in cooperation. Law has been violated, and I don't know how you can make law stronger except to have it— when you make certain that its violation will bring about punishment.

Now I know the FBI is on the job and I have every confidence that they and the State authorities will find some way of punishing the guilty, if they can find them.

Q. Lloyd M. Schwartz, Fairchild Publications: Mr. President, United Steel Workers are demanding that the steel industry base their wage settlement on first quarter profits which were at a record high. Is there any possibility, in your opinion, of economic controls if an inflationary contract comes out of these wage negotiations?

THE PRESIDENT. I don't know whether this high was a record or not, because I am told that in the first quarter of either '57 or '58 they were $2.03 a share and this year they were $1.86. But there is no use of taking just the technical argument as to whether there was greater or less profits. I say this, and I say it and emphasize it: here is something in which not only Government but the whole public, 175 million people, are involved; and their interests are going to be preserved or damaged or possibly even advanced by decisions reached by the employees and employers in this field. It is a basic industry and whatever is done affects all the rest of industry. I can say only this: that we must look to them for some good sense and some wisdom, I mean real business-labor statesmanship, or in the long run the United States cannot stand still and do nothing.

I say this: I deplore the possibility of putting the Government into this field, either as a party in negotiations and certainly in establishing laws to fix the levels of profits and of wages and prices. Once we do that, I believe we have gone to a route that is going to hurt the American system, as we know it, when we are going to do it in peacetime.

So therefore, I would again insist that the whole 175 million of us ought to make clear that we are concerned about this matter and this is not something where we are standing aside and seeing ourselves hurt.

Q. Edward P. Morgan, American Broadcasting Company: Another point on mutual security, sir. A number of people, Mr. Nixon and Senator Kennedy among them, have just recently made recommendations for massive increases in aid to India. Do you share this view, and do you see anything pertinently urgent about it, in view of Peiping's mounting attacks on India?

THE PRESIDENT. Well, I wouldn't want to answer precipitately here.

I will say this: from the beginning, India has been one of our great concerns. We have shown, I think, a very sympathetic and understanding attitude toward her government and its representatives in asking for our help in both the first and second 5-year plans. But when we say "massive" I get fearful about adjectives, and if I were going to discuss that question further, I would want to go again now into details of what we think they need and what we are prepared to give. It's certainly, there, one of the countries that we are, I'd put it this way, massively interested in, in order that the best interests of the free world will be served.

Q. Mr. Morgan: Just one additional point, if I may, sir.

Do you have any comment on Peiping's tactics of massive increase of attacks—propagandawise, at least—on India?

THE PRESIDENT. Well, no. For the moment, I merely say that I can quite understand Mr. Nehru's astonishment and maybe his sense of apparent indignation that these attacks would be made upon a nation which has tried so hard to be peaceful and neutral.

Q. Charles H. Mohr, Time: Mr. President, do you think that the situation in Iraq offers us an opportunity to improve our somewhat strained relations with President Nasser of the United Arab Republic? And if so, what steps are we taking? For instance, should the Russians withdraw any of their support at the first stage of the high dam, would we be willing to step back into that situation, or——

THE PRESIDENT. I discussed this Mideast situation and some of its intricacies last week, and I doubt that at the moment I am prepared to take any specific thing like stepping in to help with the Aswan Dam, and indeed, to do anything other than to say we are trying to be fair with everybody. We are not trying to promote personal quarrels or personal prestige, as such. We are trying to be fair in our relationships with these nations and to get every single one of them to recognize that in freedom and independence they have got a greater chance to go ahead in the realization of their own aspirations, rather than if they try to accept too closely an association with the Soviets.

Q. Sarah McClendon, El Paso Times: Sir, Speaker Rayburn said yesterday that the housing bill lacks only one Republican vote of coming out of the House Rules Committee. And he said this was rather strange that they couldn't get one Republican vote in view of the fact that you were for this bill, or at least for a housing bill.

I wondered if you have had any trouble with your—if your legislative aides have reported having any trouble persuading these Republican members of the Rules Committee to vote for the bill?

THE PRESIDENT. Well, of course this is a matter for the Republican leadership in the House, and I am not in the business of getting legislative aides to go around and get a particular vote for a particular bill in a particular committee.

My method is to work through the Republican leaders, and then my legislative aides help them, always in coordination with the leadership program.

Now, there is no question of where I stand on the housing bill. As you know, I put in an emergency bill where I asked for $6 billion worth of authorization for insuring home loans. I have asked for $200 million additional in housing loans for colleges; and a hundred million dollars extra in another field where it escapes me for the moment—what is the other hundred million? [*Confers with Mr. Hagerty*]

Well, I have forgotten—oh, urban renewal, where the funds are exhausted—urban renewal.

Q. Spencer Davis, Associated Press: Could you give us some insight into your talks with Sir Winston Churchill and whether or not any mention of Field Marshal Montgomery has come out in the discussions?

THE PRESIDENT. Well I think that we tried to talk about important things. [*Laughter*]

I found him, like all the rest of us, showing some of the wear and tear of advancing years, but he was alert. We had a nice talk at a family dinner about numerous questions around the world, both personalities and issues. Then I suddenly remembered that at that moment by London time he was up until 3 o'clock, and so we terminated the visit until I see him again at luncheon today.

Q. Robert C. Pierpoint, CBS News: I am wondering, sir, if you have the feeling possibly that Mr. Truman is avoiding or evading some of your invitations to meet with you at the White House?

THE PRESIDENT. I'll make one thing clear: when I send in a personal invitation, as differentiated from an ordinary formal state invitation, I always make it quite clear in the notes that I write that anyone with any reason, or that finds it inconvenient coming to that meeting, has the right to do so without question, and that I understand.

Now, with respect to any other connection or invitations of that sort of thing, I'd say now we're getting into the strictly personal field and that there is nothing to be said about it.

Q. Frank van der Linden, Nashville Banner: Sir, Mr. I. Lee Potter, who is chief of the Republican campaign to carry more votes in the

South, recently predicted that the Republican candidates for President in 1960 would win as many Southern States as you carried in '56, largely because of another Democratic split.

Do you feel confident that either Mr. Nixon or Mr. Rockefeller will do as well as you did in the Southern States?

THE PRESIDENT. Have you got any other candidates? [*Laughter*]

By your question, you see, you are putting me in the position of saying there can be only two possible candidates, and I say the Republicans have got a lot of good men.

Q. Mr. van der Linden: Let's say a Republican——

THE PRESIDENT. I'll put it this way: I hope that whoever is the Republican candidate carries far more States in the South than I did.

Q. Harold P. Levy, Newsday: Mr. President, Senator Symington says that contrary to the testimony of General Twining, we have no IRBM's ready to go in England. The Senator calls this, and I quote, "part of a deliberate policy to conceal from the people the weakness of our position."

Would you comment on this, sir?

THE PRESIDENT. No.

Q. Lowell K. Bridwell, Scripps-Howard: There are some indications that the Congress is rather reluctant to pass the penny-and-a-half-per-gallon gasoline tax increase which you requested, and instead, is showing some signs of wanting to transfer excise taxes from the general fund to a highway trust fund in order to keep the highway program going. Would you comment?

THE PRESIDENT. I think that everything that we need to do in this country, we ought to pay for.

They are talking now about, saying, "Well, we'll continue to build roads." But by this method that you describe, you would not be paying for other programs which the Congress obviously feels to be essential.

So, if they don't want to put in the cent-and-a-half additional tax on gasoline that I think is necessary to carry forward this road program effectively, then they ought to find the revenue to make good the deficits they would create in the general fund.

Q. David Kraslow, Knight Newspapers: Would you care to comment, sir, on a proposal to abolish military assistance to South America and Latin America and use the money instead to create a hemispheric police force under the auspices of the OAS?

THE PRESIDENT. Well, I hadn't seen it put forward in exactly that way.

We have, as you know, a very great interest in the OAS, particularly in its economic development of that region. As you know we have gone into the International Fund, World Bank, recommending greater amounts through which those countries would benefit. We have advocated, and as a matter of fact have been engaged in helping to set up, the Pan American financial institution with one billion capital. All of that sort of thing we are trying to do.

Now, when it comes down to building up a common defense system, really of military units, you have got a lot of headaches and difficulties; and I would say it would have to be studied very thoroughly before any plan could possibly be accepted by anybody.

Q. S. Douglass Cater, Reporter Magazine: At the 2-day conference now being held on India, with Mr. Eric Johnston sponsoring it, the point has been made that India's present rate of progress is really not fast enough, particularly in view of the undeclared competition with Red China just to the north.

Have you given any thought to what kind of impact program, combining public and private aid, might spur India to make the necessary progress?

THE PRESIDENT. Might do what?

Q. Mr. Cater: Spur India to make the kind of progress that will——

THE PRESIDENT. Well, of course I have given a lot of thought to it, and everybody in this particular branch of Government has done the same. We have, after all, limited means.

Now, we are a rich country, and I believe that we will be richer as we are very generous but very selective and very wise in the programs we adopt to help other countries. One of these is India. But, since everybody wants more than you can give, you have got a problem that is never quite to be solved. I didn't know that Eric Johnston had a symposium on this matter, but I know that everybody in the State Department, the ICA, Defense, and everybody of that group in Government is always interested in it. I assure you this: I believe that India's progress should be more rapid, but I don't say that we have a sole responsibility to make sure that it is.

Marvin L. Arrowsmith, Associated Press: Thank you, Mr. President.

NOTE: President Eisenhower's one hundred and fifty-eighth news conference was held in the Executive Office Building from 10:32 to 11:02 o'clock on Tuesday morning, May 5, 1959. In attendance: 211.

95 ¶ Message to President Echegoyen on the Flood Disaster in Uruguay. *May 5, 1959*

[Released May 5, 1959. Dated May 4, 1959]

Dear Mr. President:

The American people join me in expressing to you and the entire Uruguayan nation our sympathetic concern over the tragic losses resulting from the calamitous floods in your country. We hope that the relief operations, in which we have been glad to participate, have already helped to alleviate the distress caused by this disaster and that the unfortunate people affected by the floods will soon be able to reestablish their homes and regain their livelihood.

Sincerely,

DWIGHT D. EISENHOWER

His Excellency Doctor Martin R. Echegoyen
President, National Council of Government
Oriental Republic of Uruguay
Montevideo

96 ¶ Remarks at the Dinner in Honor of Sir Winston Churchill. *May 6, 1959*

Sir Winston, and Sir Winston's Friends:

We are gathered here to honor a man who has been not only our friend but who has given to each of us something intensely personal. Here is a man who may not be described merely as a spokesman of the United Kingdom in war and in peace, but an individual who makes on all who meet him an impression that is unforgettable.

Some of you have known him in the wartime days, when he was our inspired leader along with our own President. Some of you have known him in the diplomatic circles when you have been Ambassadors to the

Court of St. James or officials of our own Government. You have known him in many ways, but always as an individual who stands out in your consciousness, in your memories.

There are several men here this evening who said to me when I asked them to come to this party, "I have some very important engagements, but to see Sir Winston once again is one of the greatest things that could happen to me. I have broken the important engagement in order to do so."

Now, for me, there is a certain coincidence between this meeting and the circumstance that initiated my friendship with Sir Winston. I met him in this house—and this was something for a newly commissioned Brigadier—in the same room that he is now occupying is where I met him. I had seen him from some distance at a December 1941 conference in the War Department; but as I said, I was a Brigadier, and in that first meeting I didn't get close to the head of the table.

But soon after this, I was ordered to London, along with General Clark, on a mission, and he was there. At about this time Tobruk had fallen. The fortunes of the Allies seemed never at lower ebb. This was on our minds when we were admitted to his room. It is trite to say that Sir Winston took it in his stride. But it was true. He said, "Well, we have lost Tobruk." We had pinned our hopes on Tobruk holding out to impede the eastern advance of Rommel. He said, "All right, we shall have to correct it." And they did—at El Alamein and later.

So throughout this friendship, beginning in early 1942, I have had a great privilege which has come to only a few men: to be exposed to a great mind, to a great leader, to hear an eloquent tongue, to know him as a leader, a statesman, a political leader, a politician. And also to know him as an American. As to this last, a specific incident!

One night I was riding with him on a military train in the South of England. We were on an inspection trip, and among a dozen Americans, there was only one other Britisher in the car. We were having dinner. Someone inadvertently used the old expression, "Shoot if you must this old grey head." Sir Winston smiled and began and finished the complete poem of "Barbara Frietchie." So all of us agreed he was a little bit more American than we were.

I think, though, of all the things he has known and done in war and peace, his proudest boast is this: that he is the subject of Britain's monarch. Of that I know he is proud. And as a matter of fact, I am proud for him. Because I, too, respect and admire the Royal Family.

Now, observing the requirements of protocol, I am not allowed, on this occasion to propose his name for a toast. But I know that Her Majesty the Queen would be proud to know that each of us, in drinking a Toast to the Queen, is thinking of one of her most brilliant, loyal, and greatest subjects: Sir Winston Churchill.

Gentlemen, the Queen.

NOTE: The President spoke at a stag dinner in the state dining room at the White House at 9:00 p.m. Sir Winston responded as follows:

Mr. President and Gentlemen:

I am grateful to you for allowing me to have the honor to be associated with the Toast of the Queen.

It is remarkable how much you have contributed to using this new link of the Crown to bring together these vast populations which are on either side of the Atlantic to await development of the world. It is a most remarkable and most encouraging thing.

I am very much complimented that our host, the President, should have invited here tonight so remarkable a gathering of many of the most distinguished figures of the United States of America. It is a great honor to meet you all, I can assure you that I deeply feel it as such. To come across the Atlantic and to see so many friends and so many elements in the union of our peoples has been a great and memorable joy to me.

Here at this table, to look around, sit those whose decisions can perhaps influence the destiny of mankind more deeply than any other group of men you could find.

We are all of us here today faced with complex and difficult problems. They are perhaps harder to resolve than those which confronted us in the last war, in the days of our closest comradeship. And yet, in a way, you did not run the risk of making mistakes, of slipping here or there in minor matters such as we sometimes experience nowadays in time of peace.

I would suggest to you that the solution today is the same as it was then. I feel most strongly that our whole effort should be to work together. It resounds in my mind, a precious and hopeful thought. That anyone should cast aside as "only another country" is ridiculous. We have got to work together. I think that it is in close and increasing fellowship, the brotherhood of English-speaking peoples, that we must work.

It is that that I look at, first and foremost, and I was very pleased indeed to have the opportunity of coming over here and telling you, late in the day, what I have always lived up to, namely: the union of the English-speaking peoples. I am sure that it is in a close and increasing fellowship with you, our American friends and brothers, that our brilliant future rests.

Consider, broadly speaking, there's a very large mass of people—we are small, but we are 80 millions, with Canada, Australia, and New Zealand brought in. You are 175 millions—well, how does that add up? It seems to me, adding it up, it's more or less 300 millions, pretty near. Anyhow, a few more years of your tenure of office will easily see that raised three million a year and building up, and there you will be.

And let us be united. Let us be united, and let our hopes lie in our unity. Because we understand each other. We do really understand each other. We understand when things go wrong, or things are said, or anything like that, we really can afford to pass them by.

We understand each other, and we hope that the realization of this truth will continue to increase on both sides of the Atlantic, to the lasting benefit of the free world—and above all, the peoples of Britain and America.

I earnestly hope that an effort will be made, a fresh and further effort forward, to link us together. Because it is really of the utmost importance that we, who think so much alike, as well as speaking, who think so much alike, should see clearly before us the plain road onwards through the future.

Now, Mr. President, I have detained you some time, but I must ask this distinguished company to join me in drinking the health of the President of the United States, which I now propose.

97 ¶ Statement by the President on the Death of Donald A. Quarles, Deputy Secretary of Defense. *May 8, 1959*

I AM deeply shocked and saddened to learn of the sudden and tragic passing of Donald A. Quarles, Deputy Secretary of Defense. As Deputy Secretary—and prior to that as Secretary of the Air Force—Mr. Quarles devoted his extraordinary talents to the service of his country. His contribution was of inestimable value to the security, not only of the United States, but of that of the entire free world.

I share with his associates in the Government a keen sense of personal loss. Mrs. Eisenhower and I extend our deepest sympathies to Mrs. Quarles and to the family.

NOTE: In addition to the foregoing statement, the President issued Executive Order 10817 (24 F.R. 3779), which provided that, as a mark of respect to the memory of Mr. Quarles, the flag of the United States should be flown at half-staff on all Government buildings, grounds, and naval vessels until interment.

98 ¶ Special Message to the Congress on the Establishment of the Inter-American Development Bank. *May 11, 1959*

To the Congress of the United States:

I herewith submit to the Congress the Agreement for the establishment of the Inter-American Development Bank together with a Special Report of the National Advisory Council on International Monetary and Financial Problems recommending United States participation as a member of such Bank. Representatives of the United States took an active part in the inter-American meetings which formulated the Agreement. I urge that the Congress enact legislation authorizing the President to accept membership in the Bank for the United States and to assume the subscription obligations prescribed in the Agreement.

The establishment of the Inter-American Development Bank and our participation in it will be a most significant step in the history of our economic relations with our Latin American neighbors. It will fulfill a long-standing desire on the part of the Latin American Republics to have an Inter-American institution specifically designed to promote the financing of accelerated economic development in Latin America. At the Buenos Aires Economic Conference in August and September of 1957, the United States supported a resolution calling for a study of possible solutions for the problems of financing economic development. In August of 1958 the United States indicated that it would be prepared to consider the establishment of a development institution for Latin America and in September of that year an informal meeting in Washington of the Foreign Ministers of the American Republics recommended that a specialized committee of governmental representatives negotiate and draft an instrument for the organization of such a development institution. A Specialized Committee, thereafter established by a Resolution of the Inter-American Economic and Social Council, was convened at the Pan American Union in Washington on January 8, 1959, and devoted three months of continuous effort to the preparation of the Agreement which I now lay before the Congress for its approval.

The proposed institution is well designed to serve the needs of the Latin American Republics on a sound financial basis. The bulk of its assets, $850 million, which are subscribed for the capital stock of the Bank, are to be used to make or facilitate loans on banking terms, repayable in the currency in which the loan has been made. Each member republic is called upon to make a significant subscription to the capital of the Bank. Of the $850 million in authorized capital stock, $400 million is for paid-in shares to be paid for in installments over a period of approximately three years. Half of each installment is payable in gold or dollars, and half in the national currency of the members. The United States subscription to the paid-in capital is $150 million. The Latin American subscriptions for such capital total $250 million.

The balance, $450 million of callable capital, will constitute a guarantee of borrowings by the Bank in capital markets and would only be actually expended if the Bank were unable to meet its commitments. It is planned that the Bank will rely heavily on raising funds from private sources for the financing of sound economic development projects in Latin America. The United States portion of the callable capital is $200 million.

It should be noted that the Agreement expresses the intention of increasing the capitalization of the Bank by an additional $500 million after September 30, 1962, if the increase is approved by a three-fourths vote in the Board of Governors. The increase would be in the form of callable capital and the United States share would be approximately $200 million. This arrangement was included in recognition of a deep conviction on the part of the Latin American representatives that definite provision should be made in the Agreement for an increase in the capital of the Bank at an early date. The United States representatives agreed that such an increase would be desirable but believed that it would be wise to have an initial period of experience with the Bank's operations before the additional capital was subscribed. Accordingly, if the Bank's operations are established on an effective basis in accordance with expectations, the United States will in good faith be committed to vote for the increase and subscribe to its share of the increased capital.

The Agreement also establishes a Fund for Special Operations to be financed by specified contributions by all of the member countries, half in gold and dollars and half in the national currencies of the members. Its initial resources will be $150 million. The United States contribution of $100 million is payable in installments, the first of which will be $50 million. The Fund is established for the making of loans on terms and conditions appropriate for dealing with special circumstances arising in specific countries or with respect to specific projects, where normal terms of lending would not be appropriate. Loans by the Fund may be made repayable in whole or in part in the currency of the borrowing country. The Agreement carefully segregates the resources of the Fund from the capital resources of the Bank so as not to jeopardize, in any way, the financial soundness of the institution and its ability to raise funds in the capital markets.

It is proposed that the funds necessary to meet the initial portion of the United States subscription to the Bank be provided by a no-year appropriation, to be expended at such time after its enactment as may be desirable taking into account the active role which the United States has played in formulating the proposal for the Bank.

The Charter authorizes the Bank to provide its members, and private entities in the territories of the members, with needed technical assistance. Particular attention is given to technical assistance in the fields of preparation, financing, and execution of development plans and projects, and the training of personnel specializing in the formulation and implementation of development plans and projects. These are two areas where there has long been a need for additional assistance and the facilities which will be provided by the Bank should be very helpful to member countries in utilizing their international borrowing capacity for the development projects most essential to their economies.

Throughout the Agreement emphasis is given to the promotion of private investment in Latin America. It is recognized that only through the increased flow of private investment can the desired rate of progress be attained, and that public institutions such as the one now being created, must complement, rather than substitute for, private investment.

In the preparation of the Agreement careful attention has been given to the experience of other institutions for international financing. The representatives of the Latin American countries, as well as those of the United States, have demonstrated an awareness of the necessity of making adequate provision for safeguarding the resources of the institution in order that its future existence as an important factor in the development of the hemisphere may be assured. In this respect the Agreement follows, in many aspects, the charter of the International Bank for Reconstruction and Development. It is anticipated that the new Bank will work closely with existing sources of public credit, including the International Bank for Reconstruction and Development, the Export-Import Bank, and the Development Loan Fund.

The Special Report of the National Advisory Council, submitted herewith, describes the Agreement creating the Bank in greater detail.

I am strongly of the opinion that because of the following general policy considerations the United States should support the creation of this Bank for Latin America:

(1) The special relationship, historical, political and economic, between the United States and the Latin American Republics;

(2) The pressing economic and social problems in the area resulting

from a rapid rate of increase in population and widespread desire for improved living conditions; and

(3) The desirability of an institution which will specialize in the needs of Latin America, which will be supported in large part by Latin American resources and which will give the Latin American members a major responsibility in determining priorities and authorizing loans.

I urge the Congress to enact promptly legislation enabling the United States to join with the other members of the Organization of American States in establishing the Inter-American Development Bank which will foster, in a sound and efficient manner, more rapid advance by the people of the nations south of our border as they strive to improve their material well-being.

DWIGHT D. EISENHOWER

NOTE: The text of the agreement for the establishment of the Inter-American Development Bank and the Special Report of the National Advisory Council are published in House Document 133 (86th Cong., 1st sess.).

99 ¶ Remarks of Welcome to His Majesty Baudouin I, King of the Belgians, at the Washington National Airport. *May* 11, 1959

Your Majesty, Ladies and Gentlemen:

Speaking on behalf of the American people, Your Majesty, I assure you of a very warm welcome to this country.

Our people have long admired and respected Belgium. We have sympathized with her in her adversity during the periods of war. We have greatly admired the way that she has rallied from the distress and destruction of such wars and has taken her place in the ranks of those nations marching toward peace and cooperation among themselves.

So, when you travel about our country, our people first of all will be trying to show their feelings of affection to the Head of State of Belgium. But they will be trying also to show their feeling of friendship and real close association with the people of your great—even if relatively small from our standards—country.

So again, from all of us, to you and to your people, a warm welcome.

NOTE: King Baudouin responded as follows:

Mr. President:

My heartfelt thanks for your gracious and warm welcome.

Forty years ago, my grandparents and my father enjoyed a wonderful welcome which was accorded them at their arrival and throughout their journey across this great country. Eleven years ago, I came to this country on a private and much too short visit. Ever since I have had the desire to know it better. I am grateful to you for your kind invitation and for the opportunity given me to travel in the United States.

Today, on my arrival to this Capital, the heart of the free world, I should like to leave with you a special message of friendship from the people of Belgium. The two countries have been closely united in war and in peace. Their joint destiny is now ensured by historical alliance. We are indebted to the United States for their assistance in the hours of grave peril when our very existence was at stake. But we owe them so much more: our faith in justice and our hopes for a better world.

May this great country of yours, supreme in its dignity, ever conscious of the rightfulness of its cause, continue to march forward in the service of peace and freedom.

100 ¶ Toasts of the President and King Baudouin.   *May 11, 1959*

Your Majesty, Mr. Vice President, President Hoover, and My Friends:

We are met here this evening to extend a welcome to the King of the Belgians. When my mind goes to Belgium, when I think of it in an historical sense, I think of it as a country of strife and conflict. Back and forth across its highways have marched hundreds and thousands of soldiers responding to the demands of war. Its cities and streets have known the names of Europe's most famous soldiers—Caesar, Marlborough, Napoleon, Wellington, and in more recent times in our two latest great wars, His Majesty's distinguished father and grandfather.

Belgium has felt the heel of a ruling tyrant—the Duke of Alba still bears a name that is excoriated in his country. But from all these conflicts and from all these disasters, the Belgian people have always responded with renewed effort to live in peace and to help preserve the peace. And they are peaceful people.

Thousands, literally thousands of Americans went last year—among them many of you—to see the great Fair at Brussels. You could not help but sense that here is a people devoted to the arts, who think of the spirit of man more than simply his material needs for advancement—a people who, with us, both officially and in spirit are bound together in the search for peace with justice.

Our own people have had a history something of this order. Born in war, we suffered the tragedies and agonies of succeeding wars, with never once losing our dedication to peace, to the dignity of man, his liberty, his freedom, his opportunity to pursue happiness.

I think it is because of this similarity of experience that we recognize a basic kinship between our two peoples. That spirit and kinship inspired the warm welcome that was extended in the streets today to our guest of honor by thousands of people who carried tiny Belgian flags. They were trying to say "Here is a representative—the head—of a people that we love, admire, and respect and with whom we are proud to be partners in defense of freedom as we are in NATO."

Moreover, and finally, we know that these two peoples have the stamina and the courage to stand for this purpose of seeking and defending peace.

So it is with an unusual sense of distinction that I ask this company to rise in order that we may drink a Toast to the King of the Belgians, His Majesty King Baudouin.

NOTE: The President proposed this toast at a state dinner at the White House at 9:45 p.m. King Baudouin responded as follows:

Mr. President:

When I took off from Brussels last night, I felt I was truly entrusted with the good wishes of nine million people. So my first thought tonight is to convey them to you personally and through you to the people of the United States.

You have referred, Mr. President, to the ties uniting our two countries. These ties have brought us ever closer together for many generations. For us, America may have been a distant land in the past. It has never been an alien country, and my compatriots have never had the feeling of being strangers in your midst.

Today we are not only good neighbors, we stand together in peace, and for peace, the way we stood together in war.

May you and Mrs. Eisenhower enjoy many long years of good health and happiness. And may this great country continue its march forward in the service of mankind.

Ladies and gentlemen, I invite you to raise your glasses to the President of the United States.

101 ¶ Special Message to the Congress Transmitting Reorganization Plan 1 of 1959. *May* 12, 1959

To the Congress of the United States:

I transmit herewith Reorganization Plan No. 1 of 1959, prepared in accordance with the Reorganization Act of 1949, as amended, and providing for transfer of certain functions from the Secretary of the Interior to the Secretary of Agriculture.

Both the Department of Agriculture and the Department of the Interior now have responsibilities with respect to certain land or timber exchanges and land sales involving Federal lands. Also, the Department of the Interior is responsible for the use and disposal of mineral materials from acquired lands which are under the jurisdiction of the Secretary of Agriculture. By placing certain functions pertinent to these matters in the Department which administers the lands, Reorganization Plan No. 1 of 1959 will bring about simplification of the work of the two Departments relating to such matters, more expeditious and economical performance of such work, and clarification of responsibilities concerning the work.

The exchange act of March 20, 1922 (42 Stat. 465), as amended, authorizes the exchange of national-forest land or timber for other lands within the boundaries of the national forests. The national forests are administered by the Department of Agriculture. Under this law and the seven other land exchange statutes cited, the Secretary of the Interior must make determinations as to whether a transaction is in the public interest, must review and accept titles, and adjudicate appeals. With exceptions indicated in the transmitted reorganization plan, including exceptions with respect to the issuance of patents to lands, the plan provides for the transfer of the functions of the Secretary of the Interior under these exchange statutes to the Secretary of Agriculture, who administers the national forests. The Secretary of the Interior also has the responsibility under the act of April 28, 1930 (46 Stat. 257) to reconvey lands under the jurisdiction of the Secretary of Agriculture not accepted in exchange transactions. These functions either are duplications of those performed by the Department of Agriculture or can be more easily performed by that Department as it administers the lands involved and has detailed information and records.

The Tongass Timber Act of August 8, 1947 (61 Stat. 920) authorizes the sale of tracts of national-forest land found reasonably necessary for the processing of timber from the Tongass National Forest. Under the act, the Secretary of the Interior must appraise and sell such lands, with concurrence of the Secretary of Agriculture. The Department of Agriculture administers the land involved, has personnel on the ground, and can perform this function most expeditiously and economically.

Section 10 of the Weeks law of March 1, 1911 (36 Stat. 962) authorizes sale of small tracts of acquired national-forest land found chiefly valuable for agriculture. Under the act the Secretary of the Interior must join in the promulgation of joint regulations. Such lands are administered by the Department of Agriculture and sale of them is not related to programs of the Department of the Interior. This function can be most easily and economically performed by the Secretary of Agriculture.

Under the act of July 31, 1947 (61 Stat. 681), as amended, the Secretary of Agriculture can dispose of common varieties of sand, gravel, stone, pumice and other materials from lands reserved from the public domain which are under his jurisdiction. With respect to these materials in acquired lands under the jurisdiction of the Secretary of Agriculture such disposal must be by the Secretary of the Interior. The reorganization plan will place in the Secretary of Agriculture the same authority in regard to such materials in acquired lands under his jurisdiction as he now exercises for other lands. Such activity most efficiently and economically can be performed by the Secretary of Agriculture in conjunction with other management activities on lands he administers.

By providing sound organizational arrangements, the taking effect of the reorganizations included in the accompanying reorganization plan will make possible more economical and expeditious administration of the affected functions. It is, however, impracticable to itemize at this time the reductions of expenditures which it is probable will be brought about by such taking effect.

After investigation, I have found and hereby declare that each reorganization included in the reorganization plan transmitted herewith is necessary to accomplish one or more of the purposes set forth in section 2(a) of the Reorganization Act of 1949, as amended.

I recommend that the Congress allow the reorganization plan to become effective.

DWIGHT D. EISENHOWER

NOTE: Reorganization Plan 1 of 1959 is published in House Document 140 (86th Cong., 1st sess.).

102 ¶ The President's News Conference of
May 13, 1959.

THE PRESIDENT. This morning I would like to talk for a moment about some very badly needed legislation. I called attention to this in January.

The first of these is to increase the lending authority for the FHA for insuring mortgages. I asked for 6 billion. I think it is needed. And if we don't get action soon, there is going to be a bad situation in the housing field.

Then I asked for legislation that would make it possible to carry forward the highway program. This is a very necessary activity. It is one which now has a great momentum, in which thousands of people are working, and to stop it because of the failure to provide the revenues would, in my opinion, be very bad for our country.

Now, we can't go any faster than the money comes in, for the simple reason that the amendment in the original bill says you must build only according to the amount of money you have to spend during that year.

And the other thing is this problem about wheat. We now have in storage over $2\frac{1}{2}$ times of our yearly consumption of wheat. I think we have something on the order of $3\frac{1}{2}$ billion, or will have by the end of June, at least, $3\frac{1}{2}$ billion invested in this wheat surplus. It is costing a quarter of a billion dollars a year just to store it, take care of it, carrying charges. And the situation gets worse. It isn't just enough to quote the figures of the money we have spent in the past. The fact is that all the money as spent has made the situation worse rather than better.

I am making a request of the Congress to speed up action on these three items, so that the country will not suffer because of inaction.

I think there will be sometime—at noon, after the message has gone to the Congress, you people will have a copy of it.

That is all I have to say.

Q. Marvin L. Arrowsmith, Associated Press: Mr. President, how do you size up the Russian tactics so far at the foreign ministers conference, their efforts to seat East Germany, Poland, and Czechoslovakia?

THE PRESIDENT. Well, Mr. Arrowsmith, it is very difficult to see behind someone else's forehead, and you are not quite sure what they are thinking.

For ourselves, we have been very anxious to have any negotiations that might be called to be fruitful, to avoid using them as propaganda platforms and merely as ways and means of repeating our story or anybody else's story to the world. And this struggle, of this particular kind, does seem to have some of that purpose behind it. However, I am very hopeful that we can get some of this behind us now very quickly and get to the business of fruitful negotiations on the problems that both sides have agreed are important.

Q. Merriman Smith, United Press International: Mr. Smith— [*Laughter*]——

THE PRESIDENT. Maybe you're just a recruit.

Q. Mr. Smith: Sir, some of your recent and higher ranking appointees seem to be running into steady and increasing trouble in Congress. I wonder if you could give us your thoughts on why these appointees are encountering difficulty in being confirmed, and whether you think there is any pattern to this opposition to them.

THE PRESIDENT. It is rather baffling to contemplate a situation and try to determine what is behind it. As I have told you people so often, one of the tasks I set before myself 6 or 7 years ago in this job was to try to find people for appointive positions who were real public servants, who had records that would give promise of their competence in the public service, and then who were men of character and integrity and, where possible, proved even in the Government service.

A number of the appointees that I have recently made are of that character, like Mr. Strauss, Mr. Rothman, Mrs. Luce. All of these people, I went over them with advisers and with people outside the Government, trying to select for very important positions the finest I could get.

Now, the kind of delaying tactics, the kind of attacks made upon them, upon their integrity, is something that must have some kind of purpose other than mere searching into their competence.

For example, Mr. Strauss was secretary for Mr. Hoover, starting way back in the wartime days—Mr. Wilson's administration. He has occupied very important positions in Government since that time. And for them he always has been confirmed when they were appointive positions. He has interspersed that career, that governmental career, with business ventures that have earned for him the reputation of being one of the fine businessmen of our country and a man of integrity and ability and capacity. Why he cannot, after all these months, be confirmed is something that is completely beyond me—unless there is, you might say, a delaying thing there out of which they think some benefit will accrue. I don't know what it could be.

Q. Garnett D. Horner, Washington Star: We haven't heard a great deal from you lately, sir, about your program for a balanced budget and fight against what you have called reckless spending. Does this indicate any lessening of concern on your part?

THE PRESIDENT. Mr. Horner, I can't thank you too much for asking that question. [*Laughter*]

I have gone back to my last two or three conferences and I said, "These people have been conspiring to keep me from insisting that this country is hurting itself by too much spending."

We are on an upturn in our economy. And at this very time we are talking about balanced budget like it was something evil.

Ladies and gentlemen, my attitude is entirely different. I say a balanced budget is the minimum target that we are looking for. At this kind of time we ought to be getting some surpluses, we ought to be paying off something on our debt. If we could have these surpluses and begin gradually, even if a little at a time, reducing this debt, we would first of all be cutting down our expenditures for interest—in this year we are, I believe, allowing $8.1 billion and we hope we can keep it down to that.

This is almost unconscionable. Instead of that, we talk about something to be gained by spending more money, piling the debt up bigger and bigger. I simply can't understand it, because today you—I think I have told you before my definition of inflation: when you take a market basket full of money to the grocery store and bring back your pocketbook filled with groceries. Now, that is the kind of thing that we don't want to happen. And yet, as we look back at the history of the value of our own dollar over the last 20, 30 years, we have seen prices going up and up and up.

The Federal Government simply must do its duty if we are going to preserve the kind of economy that we like to call a free competitive economy.

If we can preserve the values of our insurance policies, our bonds, if we can again make the Government bond something that commands a premium and is the very finest investment that the small saver can make, that is the kind of thing we must do. And we are going to do it only if we have got fiscal responsibility.

And if we, all of us, don't demand from labor, from business leaders, and from the Congress the kind of sensible, reasonable, needed action that all of us know to be necessary here, each one of us—not just "some other person"—each one of us is going to be hurt immeasurably.

Q. William McGaffin, Chicago Daily News: Mr. President, along this line—I apologize for my voice. Can you hear me, sir?

THE PRESIDENT. Yes, I can.

Q. Mr. McGaffin: Along this line, it has been suggested that some money could be saved in the Pentagon if there were less missile duplications, such as that between the Bomarc and the Nike-Hercules. Your Secretary of Defense the other day suggested that he had been unable to do anything about it, and that perhaps Congress should put the Pentagon's feet to the fire.

Do you feel, sir, that this is within your own province as Commander in Chief?

THE PRESIDENT. Well, I did not know about any statements made by Mr. McElroy. He hasn't informed me of that particular incident.

But I will tell you this: here is a matter that from the very beginning has been of the most critical concern to everybody in the administration. And only within the last 5 days, I think, I had again a large group of the scientists in my office, whose job it is to analyze each of these developments, not only on the possibility that they are duplicating missions, duplicating capacities for performance, but whether or not they are duplicating the very guidance, propulsion, and other weight-carrying systems, you see; because if doing it, again, we have to have a better coordination.

Indeed, one of the big reasons that I fought so hard and, fortunately, successfully for reorganization of the Defense Department was to get this whole scientific field into better control. And I think that with the new Space Agency and with the ARPA, together, and under the Secretary of Defense, progress is being made.

But I will tell you, it is very difficult, because over the years many, many contracts have been made where this coordination has not been had prior to the making of the contract; so that you now have to study, is it more economical and more efficient to stop some of these things in their tracks, or have you gone so far that you almost have to spend some more money to see about this thing?

It is a very important thing, and I believe that it really belongs in the executive department. We cannot duck our responsibility in this particular place.

Q. Kenneth M. Scheibel, Gannett Newspapers: Mr. President, on the Pentagon again, Congressman Kowalski of Connecticut claims that the Defense Department is wasting $250 million a year through assigning service personnel to jobs as cooks and drivers, waiters. How does his report compare with the information you have on this subject?

THE PRESIDENT. Well, I have had no report on this subject. People are used for this kind of work; for example, all of the chauffeurs in the White House, except for my own Secret Service chauffeur, are from the Army. And then there is, in the White House—there used to be a yacht, a big yacht, and the crew for that yacht was used for mess purposes here in the White House. The yacht is no longer in commission, but those people carry on that mess.

Now, that kind of thing, I assume, goes in big headquarters every place, in the Pentagon and so on down the line. So I have no report. But I imagine this: if we just got these things all done by civilians, you probably would have to pay a lot more money.

Q. Lloyd M. Schwartz, Fairchild Publications: Mr. President, about 3 weeks ago three New England Governors came in and spoke to you about setting up an interagency committee on textile industry problems, and I believe at that time you expressed some reservations and suggested perhaps a broader sort of committee might be authorized.

Have you reached a decision on this, or have you decided not to authorize it?

THE PRESIDENT. No. What we have done, there are so many possibilities in the line that it turned out to be much more of a comprehensive study than I thought, and I just had a report within the last few hours that they are not quite ready for their final recommendation. But I tell you this: we will certainly make sure that this particular thing is followed very closely.

Q. Mrs. May Craig, Portland (Maine) Press Herald: Mr. President, since Vice President Nixon is opening the American exhibit at the Moscow Fair, would you look favorably on Mr. Khrushchev coming to open the Russian exhibit in New York? Has it been suggested to you and if so would that open the door to a summit meeting in this country with Mr. Khrushchev present?

THE PRESIDENT. You are really getting into the field of speculation.

No, I have not been contacted by anyone about the possibility of Mr. Khrushchev coming here on his own. I have heard of messages from some cities in this country who are very anxious to have a summit meeting, and they are sending invitations to everybody in the world, including me, to come to this country. But there has been nothing official whatsoever about it. As a matter of fact, one of the purposes of these foreign ministers is to decide, if there is to be a summit meeting, what will be its location and its timing.

Q. Mrs. Craig: But sir, the fair is different.

THE PRESIDENT. I beg your pardon?

Q. Mrs. Craig: The fair is different, perhaps.

THE PRESIDENT. Well, the fair is there. But as I said, on that one, no one spoke to me about it, no one has spoken to me until you have about it.

Q. Felix Belair, New York Times: Sir, I think you have expressed yourself on two or three occasions about the 22d-amendment-repeal proposal about 3d terms for the President. Just to straighten it out, I wonder if I might ask, if called upon for your opinion by members of Congress as to how they might vote, what would be your suggestion to them?

THE PRESIDENT. Well, I'll tell you. As I have explained to you people, here is one of those old questions where you can say a lot and you can argue very plausibly on both sides.

If I were called on to testify on this one, because that is all I can do—I have no function, of course, in the business of amending the Constitution—I would say at this moment I would not make any mistakes in a hurry. I think the Constitution is something that ought to be amended only after careful thought, not with any other purpose in mind except that of what over the years and over the long term is good for the United States.

So, as of now, I would say, let's let it lay on the shelf for a while and see how it works.

I just don't believe we should amend it, the Constitution, just every time we think a new law ought to be passed. We had that in the prohibition business, and I don't think we ought to have it so often.

Q. William H. Lawrence, New York Times: Mr. President, in the brief interval since Secretary Quarles died, have you had an opportunity to talk with Mr. McElroy about whether or not he will stay on as Defense Secretary and, if not, in what direction you might now be looking for a successor?

THE PRESIDENT. Mr. McElroy and I have had, as you would suppose, a number of conversations. We are not asking for completely fixed commitments on anybody's part. What we are trying to figure out now is, what is the best thing to do to make satisfactory replacement for Mr. Quarles.

Q. Don Oberdorfer, Knight Newspapers: Mr. President, this Sunday will be the fifth anniversary of the Supreme Court's decision striking down school segregation.

From your vantage point here in the White House, would you assess the Nation's response to this challenge of a great legal and social change?

THE PRESIDENT. Well, you are asking what has happened as a result of that decision; of course there has been much acclaim and there has been much resentment that up until that moment had not been created.

I believe that the United States as a government, if it is going to be true to its own founding documents, does have the job of working toward that time when there is no discrimination made on such inconsequential reason as race, color, or religion.

And I think we ought to, all of us, work at this. But I continue to say the real answer here is in the heart of the individual. Just law is not going to do it. We have never stopped sin by passing laws; and in the same way, we are not going to take a great moral ideal and achieve it merely by law. What we must do, all of us, is to try to make a reality in this country the great aspirations voiced by our Founding Fathers.

Q. Pat Munroe, WTVJ (Miami, Fla.): Mr. President, the Republican Party in Puerto Rico is making an all out drive for statehood, although Governor Munoz is opposed. Do the Republicans there have your support, sir?

THE PRESIDENT. Well, they didn't contact me on that question.

One time, as you will recall, I suggested that if Puerto Rico wanted independence, they should ask for it, and I would appear before Congress the following day to ask them to grant it. That they declined.

Now, this is the first time I have heard that they are making a drive for statehood, and certainly, as you say—on a partisan basis—I would be rather astonished that any such drive would be made on a partisan basis.

Q. Rowland Evans, New York Herald Tribune: Mr. President, in connection with your request for housing legislation, did you mean to imply that you are thinking of the bill the Senate has passed and that is now stuck in the House Rules Committee?

THE PRESIDENT. I most certainly did not.

Q. Mr. Evans: I wondered, sir, if you did.

THE PRESIDENT. No. I said I asked for $6 billion additional authority for the FHA to insure mortgages for the building of homes. That is what I asked for. Now, this is a long ways from great big public housing programs and things of that kind.

Q. Mr. Evans: That is what I wondered, sir. In other words, you are not in sympathy particularly with the Senate bill.

THE PRESIDENT. You don't have to say "particularly." [*Laughter*]

Q. J. A. O'Leary, Washington Star: Mr. President, in connection with the highway program, if Congress is unwilling to give you the gas tax increase that you asked for, would you rather see the pay-as-you-go amendment suspended for a while than no action?

THE PRESIDENT. What I would like to ask them is this: to provide the revenue then that will do the job. I say in this time, when in our first quarter, our GNP, 465 billion, and by this last quarter, I don't know how far it will be, but it is going to be approaching 500 billion very soon— if at that time we can't pay our bills; when are we going to pay them? Are we just going to let prices go on up and never pay them? Are we going to be a bankrupt nation? I don't think we have to be. So if they don't put that kind of revenue in—we ought to continue the road program, because of its great necessity, and we ought to pay for it.

Q. Sarah McClendon, Camden Courier-Post: Sir, I wonder if it is legally possible for you to delegate the power to, the decision-making power, to drop the nuclear bomb?

THE PRESIDENT. Well, the nuclear bomb was dropped long before my time.

Q. Mrs. McClendon: I mean in a future war, of course that's different. I mean in the future, could you delegate the power, the decision-making power?

THE PRESIDENT. I would have to see what the emergency was. I would say this: here is a thing that has to be done by the authority of the President as the Commander in Chief. There can be many, many circumstances or situations of emergency that we can't even conceive of right now, and you might suddenly—to make delegations of all kinds.

I would not ever say I should delegate authority to drop the bomb or not to drop the bomb. What I say is you have to run a war according to the necessity of the situation, and I wouldn't further predict.

Q. Robert L. Riggs, Louisville Courier-Journal: Returning to your appointments, sir, there have been reports published that a year ago Admiral Strauss came to you and advised you not to reappoint him to the Atomic Energy Commission because he feared the Senate would not confirm him. Is that true, sir?

THE PRESIDENT. Well, first of all, I think that conversations between me and my individual advisers become very personal, and I really don't believe it is a question I should answer.

But I will say this: Admiral Strauss has had one attitude toward me from the very beginning, back in 1953, and this, indeed, applies to the other members of my Cabinet. In essence, you can say their readiness to remove themselves when they thought they were an embarrassment to me or a debit, rather than an asset, to the administration, has always been perfect. They have never sought, as far as I know, any kind of advantage that would keep them, or tried to exercise any influence that would keep them in this particular post or in another post.

Q. Rutherford M. Poats, United Press International: Mr. President, several weeks ago, as I recall, you expressed some doubt about the wisdom of adopting Prime Minister Macmillan's plan for a limited number of inspections of a nuclear test ban. Now the reports from Geneva suggest that the Russian version of that idea is making some progress and that we perhaps may be on the threshold of an agreement there.

Can you give us your assessment of the prospects of an agreement, and tell us whether you have revised your original judgment as to the wisdom of adopting the limited method?

THE PRESIDENT. Well, I am not going to try to recall my exact words, but I did say here would be something that needed real study, because it is a difficult one, and I had not heard it until, well, a few weeks back.

We have been studying this thing, and we say that any limitation of the inspections would have to be conformed to the necessities required by scientific data. I am giving you exactly the advice given me by my scientists; they say until this thing is examined in all of its elements, you cannot possibly state or fix the number of these examinations that would be necessary, because how many stations, where they would be, how they are situated, what their instrumentation and everything else, all that has to be done before you can figure out at all any reasonable or any, you might say, appropriate number of on-site inspections.

So, my ability to make an estimate of what is going to be agreed or not agreed is just nil.

Q. Ray L. Scherer, NBC News: Mr. President, again on the Khrushchev visit, if he should express a desire to come here, would he be officially welcome?

THE PRESIDENT. You people love to ask "if" questions, don't you? [*Laughter*]

I think that you ought to wait until we hear something about it, and then see what the situation is.

Q. Edward P. Morgan, American Broadcasting Company: Mr. President, one of the most difficult, indeed tragic, problems of your administration has been the health of many of its members.

Mr. Quarles died last week, Secretary Dulles is fighting cancer, and yesterday General Twining had a serious operation.

Have these events inclined you at all, sir, to think in terms of the increased importance of basic medical research and the possible concomitant importance of Federal assistance in such projects?

THE PRESIDENT. The mass of my scientific conviction and opinion in this field is that we are doing quite a remarkable job.

There is one conflict here that most people don't think of. If we take too many medical men, scientists, physicists, and chemists out of current work and put them just into future research, you are, by that much, limiting the people that are taking care of the population right now or taking care of their jobs. Frankly, one of our great problems today, and we need research on, is how are we going to meet these mounting costs— let's say $25 in the hospital a day for a room, and some maybe $60 a day for nurses, to say nothing of the operational and the loss of income and all that sort of thing. Here is another problem in health that has to be studied.

Now, as I recall, in NIH appropriations since 1953 we have quadrupled them, and in the last 2 years—since 1956—we have doubled them. I think it is $259 million, the Federal share this year. To my mind, you cannot possibly expand more rapidly than that and do a good job, because you have to look for the facilities and talent and everything else that you are looking—as I say, at the same time that you are taking the day-by-day practice and jobs we have. So, much as I agree with the thought implicit in your question, that the more we can do to keep these people healthy and prevent these things the better, still I think we are doing a pretty good job.

Marvin L. Arrowsmith, Associated Press: Thank you, Mr. President.

NOTE: President Eisenhower's one hundred and fifty-ninth news conference was held in the Executive Office Building from 11:01 to 11:32 o'clock on Wednesday morning, May 13, 1959. In attendance: 225.

103 ¶ Remarks at the Semiannual Conference of State Civil Defense Directors. *May* 13, 1959

I CAME in to get a chance to thank each of you for what you have been doing, in a responsibility that is one of the serious ones resting upon the Nation.

I am particularly pleased with the legislation that makes us partners, the Federal Government with the States and localities, well recognizing that the main responsibility for implementation of responsibility rests with the locality which is to be protected.

But just to thank you for taking part in a responsible job is not quite enough. This is the job that means the greater assurance for America of its security—our national security. It is a very essential part of our security arrangements and activities. And it is because of my great concern about this that I am anxious to receive you.

Now, having thanked you collectively, Governor Hoegh says that I may have the opportunity of meeting each one of you so that I can say thanks to you in person as you come by. And I assure you again that my appreciation of your work and my recognition of its importance could not be deeper.

NOTE: The President spoke in the Conference Room at 11:45 a.m. In his closing remarks he referred to Leo A. Hoegh, Director, Office of Civil and Defense Mobilization.

104   ¶ Special Message to the Congress Urging
Timely Action Regarding the Highway Trust
Fund, Housing, and Wheat.   *May* 13, 1959

To the Congress of the United States:

In making my legislative recommendations in January of this year I called to the particular attention of the Congress three matters requiring urgent consideration and action.   It is now some four months since I made these recommendations and to date the Congress has dealt finally with none of them.   On one, it has taken no action at all.

These recommendations were as follows:

1. To avert a serious disruption of the Interstate Highway Program due to an impending deficit in the Highway Trust Fund, I recommended a temporary increase in the Federal tax on motor fuels;

2. To avoid the possibility of a serious interruption in homebuilding, I recommended an increased authorization for the insuring of home mortgages by the Federal Housing Administration;

3. To halt the accelerated build-up of surplus agricultural commodities and to reduce those stocks and their ever mounting cost to the taxpayer, I recommended corrective legislation.

Since these recommendations were made, time has grown steadily shorter and the problems occasioned by the lack of action in the Congress increasingly critical.

Highway Trust Fund

In setting up the Interstate Highway Program in 1956, the Congress provided that it be conducted on a "pay-as-you-go" basis and, to accomplish this purpose, established the Highway Trust Fund.   Motor fuels and other highway user taxes are paid into this Fund, and Federal grants, amounting to 90% of the cost of building the Interstate Highway System, are paid to the States out of the Fund.

Legislation enacted last year, however, has increased the rate at which money is being spent from the Fund and nothing has been done to put more money into the Fund.   Because the law wisely requires that the Fund's expenditures not exceed its receipts, it will be impossible this year, without Congressional action, to apportion funds so that the States may make commitments for future highway construction.   Apportionments in the following year would also be far below those needed to carry forward the road building schedule now contemplated by law.

To keep the Highway Trust Fund on a "pay-as-you-go" basis and to maintain the planned construction schedule, I recommended a temporary increase of 1½¢ a gallon in the Federal tax on motor fuels, effective July first of this year.

The recent suggestion that receipts from the manufacturers' excise tax on automobiles be earmarked for the Trust Fund is an unsatisfactory alternative. The transfer of those receipts, running about a billion dollars a year, from the general fund to the Highway Trust Fund would mean only that the problem would then be to raise new taxes to replenish the loss to the general fund.

An even more unsatisfactory alternative, proposed by some, would be legislation to waive the "pay-as-you-go" requirement. This would only be a refusal to face reality—one that the Congress would be hard put to explain. Less than three years ago, as a matter of legislative policy, the Congress declared in the Highway Revenue Act of 1956 that if it ever appears that the Trust Fund's total receipts will be less than its total expenditures "the Congress shall enact legislation in order to bring about a balance of total receipts and total expenditures."

Less than two months remain for timely, responsible action by the Congress on my recommendation.

Housing

In January I urged the enactment of emergency legislation to increase by $6 billion the Federal Housing Administration's authority to insure privately extended home mortgages.

This recommendation has not been enacted. The height of the homebuilding season is upon us, builders must plan ahead and the agency's insurance authority is in danger of being exhausted.

The $6 billion increase in authority involves no Federal spending and FHA's operations are self-supporting.

Because it could see that its authority was running out, the agency late last year, where it could, began issuing agreements to insure in the future provided it then actually had authority remaining. By thus substituting provisional agreements for actual commitments, the agency has been able to avoid an abrupt halt in its operations due to a lack of insurance authority.

Although the agency may be able to continue on this temporary basis until June thirtieth, the end of the fiscal year, the situation grows more precarious every day. The agency's outstanding agreements to insure in the future now exceed $3 billion, more than twice the amount of the agency's remaining authority to make actual insurance commitments.

To avoid the possibility of a serious interruption in home-building all across America, sound Congressional action in this area is urgently needed.

Wheat

I have frequently requested legislation to deliver our farmers and tax-payers everywhere from the mounting failures and staggering excesses of the mandatory farm price support and production control program. Unless this pressing issue is squarely met and resolutely dealt with, the next few years will see the surplus problem, because of its staggering cost to increasingly frustrated and impatient taxpayers, crash of its own weight, carrying with it all that is sound and good in the support of agriculture by the Federal Government.

The most dramatic failure of all—and the problem requiring the most urgent attention—is the wheat program. Surplus wheat stocks are already two and one-half times our annual domestic consumption for food. By July 1 of next year these stocks are expected to reach 1.5 billion bushels and to involve an investment of $3.5 billion by the Federal Government. Wheat storage, handling and interest charges alone will cost the American taxpayer close to half a billion dollars in the next fiscal year. Final proof of the present program's utter failure to control production lies in the fact that the last wheat crop was the largest in history.

Because the Secretary of Agriculture is required by law to announce a continuation of this thoroughly discredited program by the fifteenth of May, in January I urgently recommended corrective legislation. The deadline set by law is now only two days away. No such legislation has been passed.

I understand that at this late hour the Congress has elected further to postpone its decision by briefly extending the deadline for announcing next year's wheat program. Having chosen this course, the Congress should use this added time to enact realistic and constructive legislation that will effectively avert the impending disaster in wheat.

I am compelled once again to call these particular matters to the special attention of the Congress because the orderly and efficient conduct of the people's business so requires. I urge the Congress to act expeditiously in these critical areas.

DWIGHT D. EISENHOWER

105 ¶ Toasts of the President and the King of the Belgians at the Belgian Embassy. *May* 13, 1959

Your Majesty and ladies and gentlemen:

It is a great privilege on behalf of the American people, sir, to salute you tonight as the head of the state of Belgium, one of the states that in all the dramatic vicissitudes of the past decades has stood firmly by the side of our country. It has earned and won not only our friendship but our great admiration and respect.

You are about to travel through other parts of the United States. Fortunately you will not be confined in your travels to the limits of New York City and Washington. And I say fortunately, because of the fact that you will see the United States as it is. I hope that you may be asked to dinner or for luncheon by a man who works with his hands, who probably will not wear a jacket and may have his sleeves rolled up when you arrive. But his invitation will mean that he shows to you America's respect for Belgium's courage, gallantry, stamina, and the capacity to recover from every kind of difficulty and catastrophe.

Because America loves Belgium, and you as its head, as a man that gives to the United States the image of Belgium, you will be welcomed warmly—more warmly, even, than you will in the joint session of the Congress or at any formal dinner that I could give.

I envy your opportunity to go back through this country and see such receptions. And when you go back, you will have brought America and Belgium closer together, and you will have bound them more firmly together in their love of freedom, their firmness in defense of justice, their determination that no atheistic dictatorship will ever dominate our right to think and work and worship as we please.

And so, as such a representative of your country, and as an individual who will bear back with him the great evidence of the affection of this country for your people and your person, I ask this company to join me in saluting the King of the Belgians.

NOTE: This toast, in response to a toast by King Baudouin, was proposed at a dinner at the Belgian Embassy in honor of President Eisenhower at 9:35 p.m. The toast proposed by King Baudouin follows:

Mr. President:

For three days now, I have enjoyed the hospitality of your great nation. I have been deeply touched by your personal welcome, and the greetings I received everywhere have found spontaneous echo in my heart.

In this short time, I have captured many visions that will accompany me throughout this land. Many visions I will bring back to Belgium. My pilgrimage to the shrines of Arlington and Mount Vernon, the reception given me by the Members of Congress, the friendly response of the representatives of the press, are all part of my own treasure-house, never to be forgotten.

In a way this party is a goodbye party, because I shall not be able to retrace my steps and to return to this Capital City. It is also the opportunity given me to

thank you, and through you the American people, for the privilege your invitation afforded me to visit the United States. To this expression of gratefulness on my part, I should like to add a message of good wishes on the occasion of the happy anniversary Mrs. Eisenhower is celebrating with Mrs. Doud today.

For me, this is a moment of keen anticipation. I am about to see at close hand your largest cities, your latest factories, your wide-open fields. I will meet with your industrial and labor leaders. I will come to know better the great American people, with generosity in their hearts and fearlessly striving for a better world. The might, the majesty of your country, will unfold before us. Such is the great adventure that awaits me.

Mr. President, you have found an everlasting place in the heart of Belgium. Not only did you lead us out of darkness into the light of freedom, but you have lived to personify the fearlessness and the equanimity of the American people.

Ladies and gentlemen, will you now raise your glasses with me to the President of the United States.

106 ❡ Remarks at the Ground-Breaking Ceremonies for the Lincoln Center for the Performing Arts, New York City.   *May 14, 1959*

Mayor Wagner, Governor Wilson, Commissioner Moses, Mr. Rockefeller, and Friends and Supporters of the Lincoln Square Project, Ladies and Gentlemen:

Before I begin, may I be permitted to express my own personal appreciation to the artists who have performed here this morning for the pleasure of this great audience.

Of course, their performance does raise one question: if they can do this under a tent, why the Square?

Lincoln Center for the Performing Arts symbolizes an increasing interest in America in cultural matters, as well as a stimulating approach to one of the Nation's pressing problems: urban blight.

Here in the heart of our greatest metropolitan center, men of vision are executing a redevelopment of purpose, utility, and taste. It is a cooperative venture in which Federal and local government, artistic groups, large foundations, and private citizens are joining forces. And the satisfaction that all of us feel in this splendid enterprise is enhanced by the fact that paralleling this development—in another part of the Lincoln Square project—is a great new educational undertaking: Fordham University, under the leadership of my old friend and colleague, Father McGinley, is proceeding here with the establishment of a new campus in the midst of this great city. All of us salute this magnificent effort.

At Lincoln Center, Americans will have new and expanded opportunities for acquiring a real community of interest through common contact with the performing arts.

American technology, labor, industry, and business are responsible for the twentieth century freedom of the individual—making free a greater portion of his time in which to improve the mind, the body, and the spirit. To them we are likewise indebted for the capacity to establish this Center. The lives of all of us will be enriched.

The beneficial influence of this great cultural adventure will not be limited to our borders. Here will occur a true interchange of the fruits of national cultures. From this will develop a growth that will spread to the corners of the earth, bringing with it the kind of human message that only individuals—not governments—can transmit. Here will develop a mighty influence for peace and understanding throughout the world. And the attainment through universal understanding of peace with justice is today, as always, the noblest and most shining ideal toward which man can strive and climb.

And so, as we break ground for the first of your great halls, the concert hall, the new home of New York's Philharmonic Symphony Orchestra, I pay sincere tribute to your vision, your effort, your energy that is creating the Lincoln Center for the Performing Arts.

And now I understand we proceed with the ceremony by turning over the first shovel of earth.

Thank you very much.

NOTE: The President's opening remarks referred to Robert Wagner, Mayor of New York City, Malcolm Wilson, Lieu-tenant Governor of New York, Robert Moses, Commissioner of Parks of New York City, and John D. Rockefeller 3d.

107   ¶ Address "Science: Handmaiden of Freedom," New York City.   *May* 14, 1959

Dr. Bronk, Mr. Sloan, fellow innocents in the field of science, Ladies and Gentlemen:

It is a great privilege to be present at this meeting with so many Americans actively interested in basic science.   Equally it is for me a unique experience.   I have no professional competence in searching out nature's secrets and out of my own knowledge I can make no professional suggestions, on the substance of science, to which you could possibly accord the slightest validity.

Nevertheless, I hope that in a fairly long life, punctuated here and there by promotions of various types, that I have not reached the state of exalted position and complete uselessness that was achieved by one of the hunting dogs I heard about, trained by a northern woodsman.

Their master, who had long enjoyed a warm acquaintanceship with a university community, had the habit of naming his dogs for faculty members that he admired.   But when a few wives became a little indignant over the practice, he decided to name his dogs for various academic ranks—instructor, assistant, and professor, and so on.

One hunting season, a man from Chicago hired for two dollars and a half a day a dog he liked very much.   And the following year, asking for the same dog, was told the price would be five dollars a day.   When he protested the steep inflation and insisted that it was the same dog, the owner agreed but said that the dog had been promoted to assistant professor and was now worth the added money.

Well, next hunting season, the price jumped to seven dollars and a half because the dog had then achieved the rank of associate professor.   And the year after, it was raised to ten dollars, the reason being that the well-trained canine had reached the noble status of full professor.

The following year, when the hunter returned to rent the same dog, he was turned down.   "Why not?" demanded the hunter insistently. "Well, I'll tell you," said the old woodsman, "I can't let you have him at any price. This spring we gave him another promotion and made him the president of the college. Now all he does is sit around and howl and bark, and he ain't worth shooting."

Now, even though my scientific education is limited, I think there may be some usefulness in considering together certain aspects of the relation of government to science and the conditions under which the work of scientists and scholars will best flourish.

In our lifetime greater advances have probably taken place in science and technology than in all prior history, and these advances have profoundly affected, and will continue to affect, our manner of living. These advances and changes have also had a profound effect on Government and on national policy. In my public service I have found myself increasingly involved in dealing with problems and policies affected by the growth and impact of science and technology. Out of this experience in dealing with these matters and my close and cordial relationships with increasing numbers of scientists and engineers arise such observations as I shall make tonight.

First, I must congratulate the Sloan Foundation, the National Academy of Sciences, and the American Association for the Advancement of Science, for sponsoring this conference on basic research. The Nation cannot help but feel a profound satisfaction in seeing so many leading representatives of education, industry, and Government participating in a symposium concerned with such a vital effort.

And I derive special satisfaction from the fact that this conference is sponsored by private interests. Too often we have tended to look unduly to the Federal Government for initiative and support in a multitude of activities, among them scientific research. We must recognize the possibility that the Federal Government, with its vast resources and its increasing dependence upon science, could largely pre-empt the field or blunt private initiative and individual opportunity. This we must never permit.

Too much dependence upon the Federal Government may be easy, but too long practiced it can become a dangerous habit.

Yet, Government's role in research and its responsibility for advancing science must be large and there must be a persistent partnership between Government effort and private effort. Our science and technology are the cornerstone of American security, American welfare, and our program for a just peace. For the Government to neglect this would be folly. But the strength, growth, and vitality of our science and engineering, as in every other productive enterprise, hinge primarily upon the efforts of private individuals.

Private institutions, foundations, colleges and universities, professional societies and industry, as well as all levels of Government, have a vital role to play in promoting individual leadership and in striving for excellence and the achievements of a high level of creative activity. Thus is created increased opportunity to pioneer, to initiate, and to explore untrodden areas.

Now, through the growth of scientific knowledge we in America have profited immeasurably.

We have done so because we are free.

Freedom is the central concept of our society, and this freedom of each to try, to fail, and to try again is the mainspring of our progress.

Freedom is both cause and effect; by sustaining it we preserve the essential condition of learning, while the benefits that flow from knowledge work to keep us free.

As we have long known, freedom must be earned and protected every day by every one of us. Freedom bestows on us the priceless gift of opportunity—if we neglect our opportunities we shall certainly lose our freedom.

Our immediate task—America's first responsibility—is to see that freedom is not lost through ignorance, complacency, or lack of vigilance. And this applies to our domestic problems and to those abroad. It is important that in our daily lives at home we so conduct ourselves in politics, in business, in education that liberty is not impaired. Equally we must be alert to our duty of assuring that neither we, or other free nations, succumb to an ideological system dedicated to aggressive force and governed by fear.

That we succeed in this task—that we successfully preserve freedom amidst an uneasy climate of disquiet and tension—depends more than ever upon the readiness of each of us to advance American science and engineering.

It is in this strong conviction that I particularly stress the freedom of the scholar and the researcher.

From the very outset of our Republic, the Government of the United States has sought to encourage science and learning. Our early statesmen, Washington, Jefferson, Franklin, and Adams, all sought to find ways by which the new Republic could sponsor learning and promote the progress of science and the useful arts.

The founders of the American political system clearly believed that the secrets of nature must be better known so that they might be used to advance the welfare of all our people.

But while, under the stimulus of practical need, the application of science to problems of production and growth became accepted practice in our young, vigorous, and rapidly growing society, the uninformed often referred in slurring terms to what we called the "impractical scholar." Fortunately, we have come far from that point. We have done much in overcoming this misunderstanding. We have learned that the apparently visionary researcher is likely to produce unexpectedly practical results. Witness the work of such scientists as Faraday, Pasteur, Gibbs, Einstein, Fermi, and Von Neumann.

Basic science, of course, is the essential underpinning of applied research and development. It represents the frontier where exploration and discovery begin. Moreover, achievements in basic research, adding as they do to man's fundamental understanding, have a quality of universality that goes beyond any limited or local application or limitation of time. Eventually, those discoveries benefit all mankind.

Today, the American record in basic research is becoming no less brilliant than in applied science. The past 50 years have seen a remarkable growth of graduate schools of science and other types of research institutions. Since World War II scientists working in the United States have won more than half of all the Nobel Prizes awarded in the physical sciences. If we can continue to cultivate our strength and achievement in this field of basic research, we shall greatly enhance our capacity to defend ourselves, and simultaneously advance our economic and cultural strength.

Vigilance and effort are required.

I am told that fewer than 30,000 scientists and engineers, or less than two hundredths of one percent of our population, are now engaged in basic research. Only about four percent of our scientists and engineers are engaged in basic research. Educators and scientists warn us that we need to step up this effort, if we are to move forward on the broadest scientific front.

And I think, my friends, this has to be a studied effort. Although we have long known that necessity is the mother of invention, we cannot depend upon accident to bring about these advances that we need.

All of us know the old story of finding that cooked meat was much better than raw meat, when the ancient Chinese had his barn burned down and a bunch of pigs were in it. Well, he found out about crackling, that it was very good.

Another accident, and for this story I am indebted to a friend of mine here who is far too shy and modest to want me to identify him. And it was about a hearing aid, Mr. Sloan. This man needed a hearing aid, and he went to the store and he found that the cheapest one was two hundred dollars and when they ran up to eight hundred, he decided this was clear outside his pocketbook range, so he decided to make one himself. Which he did. And he worked it with pretty good effect.

Well, finally, a man said to him, "Now tell me, Bill, does this thing really work?"

He says, "Of course not, but it makes everybody talk louder."

We cannot afford to look for our advances in this kind of result, even if the result was, in this case, only psychological.

In seeking out and educating the necessary talent we need to insure, as we have done in the past, that the search for fundamental knowledge can best be undertaken in areas and in ways determined primarily by the scientific community itself. We reject a philosophy that emphasizes more dependence upon a centralized approach and direction. Regimented research would be, for us, catastrophe.

The progress and growth of America depends upon many qualities of our people. Clearly these include curiosity, imagination, educational preparedness, and tireless stamina. Without these we could not be a people of true creative genius. We must search out the talented individual and cultivate in all American life a heightened appreciation of the importance of excellence and high standards; not only in specialized fields, but in individual dimensions of diversity as well.

It is very much worth noting, I believe, Tocqueville's comment of 125 years ago in some notes just published for the first time, that what makes the American such an intelligent citizen is that he does a little of every-

403

thing. This he thought was an important reason for superiority of the American in the ordinary business of life and the government of society.

But while today we require a high degree of specialization, it remains vitally important for the specialist in every field to understand that his first responsibility to himself and to his country is to be a good citizen.

Above all, the specialist must comprehend how his own work fits in effectively in promoting the national welfare.

———

Twenty years ago, Federal support of science was about 100 million dollars annually. Today, this annual investment, by the Federal Government, in applied and basic research, together with pilot development, has grown to over five billion dollars. A large fraction of these Federal funds is spent in laboratories owned and operated by private groups. Much of this expenditure is to meet the current and practical needs of the Federal Government. The size of these Federal expenditures and the policies and practices of the Federal Government inevitably have a substantial effect on the Nation's private scientific institutions. But again we remind ourselves that the whole program would be self-defeating if it were allowed to limit the freedom of its own research.

During recent months we have made many moves to strengthen the management of your Government's scientific activities. These include a number of advisory committees and several new legally authorized agencies. All of them are designed to point up and enhance and coordinate scientific research.

And now, let me cite one example which illustrates an appropriate way for the Federal Government to further our basic scientific research effort. Incidentally, when I quote the cost, George Humphrey will hurt.

Recently the General Advisory Committee to the Atomic Energy Commission and my Science Advisory Committee, under the chairmanship of Dr. Killian, appointed a special panel of scientists to undertake a comprehensive review of the Federal Government's participation in the high-energy accelerator physics field.

On the basis of this report, I am recommending to the Congress that the Federal Government finance the construction as a national facility of a large new electron linear accelerator. Physicists consider the project, which has been sponsored by Stanford University, to be of vital importance. Moreover, they believe it promises to make valuable contributions to our understanding in a field in which the United States already is strong, and in which we must maintain our progress. Because of the cost, such a project must become a Federal responsibility. This proposed national facility, which will be by far the largest of its kind ever built— a machine two miles long—has the endorsement of the interested Government agencies—including the Treasury. Construction of the accelerator will take six years, at an over-all cost of approximately $100,000,000.

———————

By such means the Government labors to advance our scientific knowledge and to further the free use of science for healing, for enriching life, and freeing the spirit.

In emphasizing these objectives and needs, I am deeply aware that they are inseparable from the broader goal of enriching the quality of our society and enhancing the excellence of our intellectual life.

We cannot improve science and engineering education without strengthening education of all kinds. America must educate all the varied talents of our citizens to the limit of their abilities.

Here what we seek is talent of the first rank.

We do not ask of a man his race—his color—his religion.

In the field of intellectual exploration, true freedom can and must be practiced.

The dignity of man is enhanced by the dignity and freedom of learning. How well the learning is accomplished depends upon the competence and devotion of those to whom the training is entrusted: the teachers and educators at all levels, everywhere, throughout our land.

So let us cultivate more respect for learning, for intellectual achievement, for appreciation of the arts and humanities. Let us assign true education a top place among our national goals. This means that we must be willing to match our increasing investments in material resources with increasing investments in men.

For my part I have long urged and supported the idea that there should be established a hall of fame for the Arts and Sciences. Membership would be an honor to which every American boy and girl could aspire.

Talent and quality are vital to our national strength—they are the ingredients needed to carry us onward and upward to higher peaks of achievement in science as well as in the non-material world of the mind and the spirit.

Science, great as it is, remains always the servant and the handmaiden of freedom. And a free science will ever be one of the most effective tools through which man will eventually bring to realization his age-old aspiration for an abundant life, with peace and justice for all.

Thank you very much indeed.

NOTE: The President spoke at a symposium on basic research sponsored by the National Academy of Sciences, the American Association for the Advancement of Science, and the Alfred P. Sloan Foundation, which was held at the Waldorf-Astoria Hotel in New York City. His opening words referred to Detlev W. Bronk, President of the National Academy of Sciences, and Alfred P. Sloan, Jr., of the Alfred P. Sloan Foundation, Inc.

The report of the President's Science Advisory Committee and the General Advisory Committee to the Atomic Energy Commission was made public by the White House on May 17.

108 ¶ Statement by the President Upon Approving a Joint Resolution on Wheat Acreage Allotments and Marketing Quotas. *May* 15, 1959

I HAVE today approved the Joint Resolution which extends the date for announcing the 1960 wheat acreage allotments and marketing quotas from May 15 to June 1, 1959. It is my hope that these additional two weeks will be used by the Congress to enact realistic and constructive—not stopgap—wheat legislation.

The wheat program, which the present law has forced us to administer, is a failure. It has failed to prevent recurring surpluses and has resulted in excessive costs to the taxpayer.

If the wheat program is not soundly changed both surpluses and costs will continue to increase.

I pointed out the urgency of the wheat situation in my agricultural message of January 29, 1959 and again in a special message on May 13, 1959.

The Joint Resolution, signed today, affords an additional two weeks for making corrective changes in time for farmers to plan for the 1960 wheat crop.

NOTE: As enacted, the Joint Resolution (S. J. Res. 94) is Public Law 86–27 (73 Stat. 25).

109 ¶ Remarks to the Cadets at the United States
Air Force Academy, Colorado Springs, Colorado.
May 16, 1959

General Briggs, Colonel Adamson, and Cadets:

This is a privilege to which I have long looked forward. I had some
connection with this Academy from its very beginning. I was on the
Board, as a matter of fact, that decided there should be an Air Academy,
and behind the scenes clandestinely and not saying anything about it, I
was very anxious that the Academy be in this State that I love so much.
So, to receive honorary membership in the Class of 1959 is an honor that
I assure you I shall not forget. This is something that I had not thought of
receiving, and for the thought that prompted it, I am truly appreciative.

And now, if you will permit an old soldier, I would like to say one or
two words or express one or two thoughts—possibly you have heard them
often, but it won't hurt to repeat them.

The two older Academies are rich in tradition and very proud of them.
To you men has been given the opportunity to create tradition. Everything is, with you, a first. The first graduation of this Academy, this
proud Academy, which through the years will be prouder, will be something you will be looking back on all your lives, and indeed those that
come after you will remember, the incidents, the customs, that you will
create. Even the minor aspects of that graduation—its procedures, its
little incidents—its customs—throwing caps or turning somersaults on
graduating—even such things will be traditional. And people, 50 years
later, will be doing the same thing. There's a very fine thought about
tradition because through it we keep things that are worthy; they give
us inspiration in our hearts. They keep us, sometimes, from going off the
deep end in faddism—as we remember that our own spiritual forebears
did not do it quite that way.

So later classes will improve upon and enrich tradition, but the basic
soul of what you establish now will live on.

One little thing in connection with this thought is this: a very great
man, my classmate, was your first Superintendent, and I have just been
told by General Briggs that one of the major buildings here is to bear his
name. This building will long remind you of the high ideals that he

exemplified, and the great service he rendered to this Academy, as well as to his country.

And so it is in that spirit that I wish to all of you the very best, the very best of luck through the years—good fortune.   The one admonition I would give you for this: make sure you get enjoyment out of every day. Life should be a thing to enjoy.   Make certain that your face doesn't grow longer as the day grows older.   Go to bed with a smile and remember a very fine day.   And with that custom, I am quite sure you will find a long, happy, and fruitful life, fruitful to yourself, to your country, and to humanity.

Thank you, and good luck to all of you.

NOTE: The President spoke in the Cadet Dining Hall at 12:30 p.m.   His opening words referred to Maj. Gen. James E. Briggs, Superintendent of the U.S. Air Force Academy, and Colonel of Cadets Herbert A. Adamson.   Later in his remarks the President referred to the late Lt. Gen. Hubert R. Harmon, Superintendent of the Academy until July 31, 1956.

110   ¶ Letter to Nikita Khrushchev, Chairman, Council of Ministers, U.S.S.R., on the Discontinuance of Nuclear Weapons Tests. *May* 16, 1959

[Released May 16, 1959. Dated May 5, 1959]

Dear Mr. Chairman:

I have your reply to my communication of April thirteenth in which I suggested ways in which we might move more rapidly toward the achievement of a lasting agreement for the discontinuance of nuclear weapons tests under adequately safeguarded conditions.

I do not disagree with your statement of the need to conclude a treaty which would provide for the cessation of all types of nuclear weapons tests in the air, underground, under water, and at high altitudes.   This is the objective I proposed last August, which my representatives at Geneva have sought since the beginning of negotiations there, and which in my most recent letter I reaffirmed as the goal of the United States.   I sincerely hope that your affirmation of this objective will prove to mean that you would now be willing to accept the essential elements of control which would make this possible.

You refer to the possibility mentioned by Prime Minister Macmillan for carrying out each year a certain previously determined number of inspections. I have also been informed that your representative at the Geneva Conference has formally proposed that agreement be reached on the carrying out annually of a predetermined number of inspections, both on the territory of the Soviet Union and on the territories of the United States, the United Kingdom and their possessions. In keeping with our desire to consider all possible approaches which could lead to agreement for discontinuance of nuclear weapons tests with effective control, the United States is prepared to explore this proposal through our representatives in the negotiations at Geneva. In particular it will be necessary to explore the views of the Soviet Government on the voting arrangements under which this and other essential elements of control will be carried out, the criteria which will afford the basis for inspection, and the arrangements which you would be prepared to accept to assure timely access to the site of unidentified events that could be suspected of being nuclear explosions. It will be necessary to know, also, the scientific basis upon which any such number of inspections would be determined and how it would be related to the detection capabilities of the control system. I have noted your understanding that these inspections would not be numerous. The United States has not envisaged an unlimited number of inspections, but adheres to the concept that the number should be in appropriate relationship to scientific facts and detection capabilities.

As I stated in my last communication, if you are prepared to change your present position on the veto, on procedures for on-site inspection, and on early discussion of concrete measures for high altitude detection, we can proceed promptly in the hope of concluding the negotiation of a comprehensive agreement for suspension of nuclear weapons tests. I hope that your position on these basic issues will change sufficiently to make this possible.

There are reports that your representative in Geneva has given some reason for thinking the Soviet Government may be prepared to modify its approach regarding these questions. If this should prove not to be the case, however, I could not accept a situation in which we would do nothing. In that event I would wish to urge your renewed consideration of my alternative proposal. It is that starting now we register and put into effect agreements looking toward the permanent discontinuance of all nuclear weapons tests in phases, expanding the agreement as rapidly as corresponding measures of control can be incorporated in the treaty. I would again propose that toward this end we take now the first and readily attainable step of an agreed suspension of nuclear weapons tests in the atmosphere up to the greatest height to which effective controls can under present circumstances be extended.

In my communication of April thirteenth, I suggested that the first phase of such an agreement should extend to the altitude for which controls were agreed upon by the Geneva Conference of Experts last summer. We would welcome discussions of the feasibility at the present time of extending the first phase atmospheric agreement to higher altitudes and our representatives in the present negotiations at Geneva are prepared to discuss the technical means for controlling such an agreement.

It is precisely because of my deep desire for a complete discontinuance of nuclear weapons tests that I urge again that you either accept the measures of control that will make such agreement possible now or, as a minimum, that you join now in the first step toward this end which is within our reach. Such a step would assure that no time will be lost in setting up the elements of the system already substantially agreed and in stopping all tests that can be brought under control. While this is being done our negotiators would continue to explore the problems involved in extending the agreement to other weapon tests as quickly as adequate controls can be devised and agreed upon.

Sincerely,

DWIGHT D. EISENHOWER

NOTE: For the President's communication of April 13, see Item 81, above. Mr. Khrushchev's reply, dated April 23, appears in the Department of State Bulletin (vol. 40, p. 705). The present letter was released at Denver, Colo.

Following receipt of Mr. Khrushchev's April 23 reply, the White House released the following statement:

The President and the Secretary of State are disappointed that Mr. Khrushchev has not been willing to take the practical and immediately feasible measure of nuclear test suspension proposed in the President's letter of April thirteenth.

Contrary to the impression given in

Mr. Khrushchev's letter, the United States does want a complete test ban. That is what President Eisenhower proposed in August 1958 and what we have been trying to get agreement on for five months in Geneva. The Soviets have thus far, however, been unwilling to accept the controls which would make such agreement possible.

The Soviet suggestion does not address itself to the key point—the veto—which has thus far blocked agreement. The President and the Secretary of State hope that when clarified, the Soviet position may reflect a change in attitude on this question so that progress can be achieved.

111 ¶ Letter to Secretary Gates Designating Him To Act as Secretary of Defense. *May* 18, 1959

Dear Mr. Secretary:

In the event of the absence of the Secretary of Defense during the next thirty days or until the appointment of a Deputy Secretary of Defense pursuant to law, you are, under the provisions of Part V of Executive Order 10820 dated May 18, 1959, designated to act as Secretary of Defense, and authorized and directed to perform the duties of that office, during his absence.

Sincerely,

DWIGHT D. EISENHOWER

NOTE: The Honorable Thomas S. Gates, Secretary of the Navy, was subsequently appointed by the President as Deputy Secretary of Defense and assumed his new duties on June 8, 1959.

112 ¶ Letter to the Governors of New Hampshire, Rhode Island, and Massachusetts on the Establishment of a Special Inter-Agency Committee on Textile Problems. *May* 19, 1959

[Released May 19, 1959. Dated May 18, 1959]

Dear Governor _____:

It was a pleasure to meet with you and with Governors _____ and _____ on April twenty-fourth.

I have reflected considerably on the difficulties of the textile industry, the subject of our conference.

There is, of course, no single cause for the problems of this industry. High production costs, competition from abroad, and other problems, are all important. Nor is there any single solution. Adjustments in farm price supports, which the Administration has sought and partially obtained, will tend to equalize raw material costs. Area development, vocational training, and Federal employment services can also help in meeting the problems of the New England area. There are, moreover, the safeguards of our trade agreements legislation as well as voluntary limitations abroad on the amount of textiles shipped into this country. While the economic problems of this industry do persist, this many-sided program has been of considerable help.

You recommended the establishment of a special inter-agency committee on textile problems. After consultation and reflection, I think it would be wise to set up such an inter-agency committee on an ad hoc basis. I am proceeding with this plan. As I visualize it, this committee would concern itself with a number of the important problems affecting the textile industry. It would obtain various views including those of the advisory committee consisting of three representatives respectively from management, labor, and the public, which the Secretary of Commerce is setting up. After careful study, and to conclude its responsibility, the committee would make its views known, informally, to the Secretary of Commerce.

I appreciate your sincere interest in the welfare of the textile industry, which I share, and I value your counsel as to how our efforts can be made more fruitful.

Sincerely,

Dwight D. Eisenhower

NOTE: This is the text of identical letters addressed to Governor Wesley Powell of New Hampshire, Governor Christopher Del Sesto of Rhode Island, and Governor Foster Furcolo of Massachusetts, following their meeting with the President at the White House.

113 ¶ Letter to Secretary Strauss on the Establishment of an Inter-Agency Textile Committee. *May* 19, 1959

[Released May 19, 1959. Dated May 18, 1959]

Dear Lewis:

I have given considerable thought to the formation of an inter-agency textile committee, such as recommended by the Special Subcommittee of the Committee on Interstate and Foreign Commerce, headed by Senator

Pastore. This proposal has also been recommended to me by Senator Saltonstall and Governors Powell, Del Sesto and Furcolo.

I think an ad hoc committee, chaired by the Department of Commerce, would be appropriate. The committee would address itself to a number of important problems affecting the textile industry. The committee should be composed of Assistant Secretaries or men of equivalent rank from the Departments of Agriculture, Commerce, Defense, Labor, State, and Treasury, and from the Council on Foreign Economic Policy. The committee should report informally to the Secretary of Commerce. Studies should be undertaken soon so that the committee could give its counsel to the Secretary of Commerce before the 1960 session of the Congress.

Please undertake the formation of this group as soon as you conveniently can.

Sincerely,

DWIGHT D. EISENHOWER

114 ¶ Letter to John Foster Dulles Awarding Him the Medal of Freedom, and Accompanying Citation. *May* 20, 1959

[Released May 20, 1959. Dated May 19, 1959]

Dear Foster:

It is an honor and a privilege to award you this Medal of Freedom. Inadequate though it is to express my gratitude and the gratitude of the Nation you have served so well, it does stand as a small token of the affection and esteem that the people of America and of the world hold for you and your tireless efforts on behalf of freedom.

With warm regard,

As ever,

D. E.

CITATION TO ACCOMPANY THE AWARD OF

THE MEDAL OF FREEDOM

TO

JOHN FOSTER DULLES

To JOHN FOSTER DULLES for contributions of the highest order to the security of the United States and to the peace of the world.

During more than six years as Secretary of State, in a time of international stress and national peril, he met problems of the gravest import with wisdom, judgment and courage.   Tirelessly striving for the ideal of peace, he has steadfastly insisted that true peace can exist only with justice.

He worked and lived in the conviction that freedom will prosper only as men are willing to devote the same supreme endeavor to the waging of peace that they have given to the works of war.   No man could do more than John Foster Dulles to exemplify this belief.   His faith and his vision inspire all who love freedom.

He has served his country well.   His belief in the ideals of America has been deep and strong.   Those ideals will be kept secure so long as our country has men of the mold of John Foster Dulles.

In recognition of a lifetime of service to his country, and in profound gratitude, I deem it a high privilege to award him the Medal of Freedom.

DWIGHT D. EISENHOWER

NOTE: The President's letter and the medal and citation were delivered personally to Mrs. Dulles for her husband at Walter Reed Hospital by the President's son, Maj. John S. D. Eisenhower, Assistant Staff Secretary in the White House Office.

115   ¶ Statement by the President for the White House Conference on Refugees.   *May* 21, 1959

[Read by Gerald D. Morgan, The Deputy Assistant to the President]

IT IS a pleasure to welcome you to the White House Conference on Refugees.   At the same time, I want you to know how gratified I am that so many of you have been able to arrange your busy schedules to participate in this meeting.   From it, I am sure, will come a clear concept of our country's role in the World Refugee Year.

To such a group as this it is not necessary to describe the daily problems of the millions of dispossessed people around the world whom we call "refugees". You are well aware of their problems. In fact, you and the organizations which many of you represent deserve the highest praise for what you have done and what you are now doing to help these refugees and to keep alive their hope for a better way of life.

The response of the American people to the needs of the homeless and the outcast has always been generous and timely. Since the early days of Nazism, and even more particularly since the end of World War II, Americans have opened their hearts and land to thousands of such people.

With charity and understanding, the American people have welcomed these refugees to our shores. Here, immigrants have traditionally exchanged their despair for confidence, and their fears for security. Today they are citizens; many of them own their own homes; some of them own their own businesses; their children are in our schools; and they, as families, are making a full contribution to our national life.

Much has been done, but the refugee problem remains—acute and chronic—and it will remain so long as the world suffers from political unrest and aggression. And as long as there are refugees, we cannot ignore them.

That is why the United Nations, with the close and immediate support of the United States, sponsored the World Refugee Year. This is a year to focus the concern and the ingenuity—and the generosity—of the world on the continuing problem of refugees. Perhaps, with such a mobilization of effort—as in the International Geophysical Year—but for the advancement of humanity rather than science, it may even be possible to resolve some particular refugee problem. This would be a great step forward, and we can all hope for such progress. In any event we must further our efforts to create lasting international understanding of and concern for this problem, which I fear will be with us for a long, long time.

Now, I have asked you to come together to share with the government your experience, your judgment and your insight regarding the things which should be done and how best to do them. The task of refugee care is not one for governments alone. It can be done only with broad and devoted citizen support. As leaders in your own communities, as officers of private groups, I know you will want to assume the greatest possible personal responsibility in this humanitarian cause.

Working together, I am confident this can, and will be, a useful and promising meeting.

DWIGHT D. EISENHOWER

NOTE: The conference was held in the Indian Treaty Room of the Executive Office Building. (See also Item 91.)

116 ¶ Remarks at the Dedication Ceremonies at the Francis Scott Key Memorial Auditorium, St. John's College, Annapolis, Maryland. *May 22, 1959*

Mr. Cleveland, Governor Tawes, Governor McKeldin, President Weigle, Members of the Faculty, Members of the Student Body, Mr. Mellon and Professor Van Doren, Friends of St. John's, Ladies and Gentlemen:

First, may I be permitted to express my congratulations to all those who were participating in this program of enlarging this College, and establishing here these two splendid buildings which will mean so much to education and to the future of St. John's College.

I can conceive of no nobler avocation of the good citizen than to be a supporter of those whose business it is to educate our youth.

And so to each my heartiest congratulations—indeed, my gratitude and thanks.

And now I am commissioned to convey a message of some delicacy, and I hope I can do the job well. The message is brought about by a problem that is experienced by Midshipmen of the Academy just across the way. They have tried, it seems, without success, to get a very unfeeling military administration to give them the time after their "hops" that are held there, to take their lady friends to the proper transportation conveyances and to their hotels, and to get back to their quarters in time to avoid punishment.

And they therefore send this message to the male part of the student body of St. John's College. They have asked me especially to ask you to avoid post-dating their dates when they are on the way home. I confess I wasn't long aware of this problem, but it seems to be a very acute one with them, and they are my good friends.

Francis Scott Key, the author of our national anthem, is enshrined in the hearts, of course, of all Americans. As a distinguished graduate of St. John's, he is doubly honored on this campus. So I am happy to join in dedicating this new auditorium to his memory.

The colleges of civilization remind us that the affairs of the human community are continuous and are indivisible. Your own Great Books program, organized around the masters of thought for thirty centuries, convincingly demonstrates the interdependence of human activities.

Today is merely the forward edge of history. From Homer to Einstein, through politics and poetry to philosophy and physics, the past instructs the present, ever revealing the continuity of the human adventure.

I note with real interest that among the aims of your educational program, special emphasis is given to the development of understanding and, quoting, "by persistent questioning and discussion of the basic problems that face all men at all times."

Now I am told that this school year marks the coming of age—the twenty-first year—of the Great Books concept at St. John's. At the same time that Professors Barr and Buchanan were instituting on this campus this tribute to the unity of knowledge, an official of the League of Nations was calling our attention to the unity of politics in a series of lectures given to another eastern college. He was a diplomat-philosopher from Spain, and he had this to say to the students of Swarthmore in 1937:

He said, "Now it will be impossible for any government to make a success of foreign affairs until it realizes that to a great extent, perhaps to a complete extent, there are no longer, really speaking, foreign affairs; there are only world affairs. All the ministers of foreign affairs should be rechristened ministers of world affairs, if only from the educational point of view, to drive into public opinion this view, that it is now the world that matters and not merely those foreigners who do not belong."

Now today, how meaningful for us—these words delivered nearly a quarter-century ago. For us indeed there are no longer "foreign affairs" and "foreign policy." Since such affairs belong to and affect the entire world, and to which each locality is part of that world, they are essentially local affairs for every nation, including our own.

We have discovered that we cannot separate what we do abroad from what we do at home. We have found that our efforts to promote a freer flow of world trade are hurt wherever there exists an unreasonable demand for protectionism among our own people. We have learned that our interest in stable world markets is compromised by an outdated farm program which stimulates and subsidizes a tremendous farm surplus which overhangs the exchanges of the world; we have learned that unnecessary spending at home may foreclose our essential spending abroad. We have learned that the fate of our own nation is bound up with the fate of others.

Our whole position in world economic affairs is determined by the health of our economy and the soundness of our money. If we should neglect these at home we could soon become powerless abroad—our prosperity, our security, our freedom would be jeopardized. The concerns of "foreign" policy are not something remote and apart from the rest of our activities; they are deeply rooted in the very center of our local, personal pursuits day by day.

This is why the college and its product, the educated citizen, are so supremely important. It cannot be too often repeated that there is urgent need for the citizen to grasp the relationship between his own actions and attitudes and those of the nation of which he is a participating member. For only when these relationships are clearly seen, can we be sure that our Republic is performing as it should, and as indeed it must, if self-government is to prevail.

Questions, fundamental in their significance, must be answered by an informed citizenry—not merely by ambitious politicians.

How does a free society organize effectively to prepare for an indefinite period of armed uneasiness; how, within a framework of free decision-making, can our economy be best developed to meet this challenge; how can our educational and other social institutions be best shaped to develop mind and spirit; how can individual initiative be nurtured within a framework of national determination for survival—in short, how can we meet the world challenge while still preserving our way of life and enhancing the opportunities for all?

This then, is the true measure of the challenge—and the opportunity—before us. Never was the opportunity of the educated citizen to contribute to greater understanding more evident, and more to be taken advantage of. To you at St. John's I offer a respectful salute as you prepare to make yourselves worthy of this challenge. Moving side by side with sister academic institutions across our land, may you carry our nation to ever higher planes of achievement.

Again, my warm congratulations upon the completion of this fine new building, and best wishes for your continued success.

Thank you very much.

NOTE: The President spoke following the dedication of buildings housing the Auditorium, the Mellon Laboratory, a library, and the Theodore R. McKeldin Planetarium. Among those present at the ceremony were 25 descendants of Francis Scott Key, a graduate of St. John's College in 1796.

The President, in his opening words, referred to Richard Cleveland, Chairman of the Board of Trustees of St. John's College, J. Millard Tawes, Governor of Maryland, Theodore R. McKeldin, former Governor, and Richard Weigle, President of the College. The President also referred to Paul Mellon and Mark Van Doren, who were awarded honorary fellowships. Later in his remarks the President referred to Frank Stringfellow Barr and Scott Buchanan, former President and former Dean of the College, respectively, who instituted the Great Books program.

117 ⁋ Statement by the President on the Death of John Foster Dulles. *May* 24, 1959

JOHN FOSTER DULLES is dead. A lifetime of labor for world peace has ended. His countrymen and all who believe in justice and the rule of law grieve at the passing from the earthly scene of one of the truly great men of our time.

Throughout his life, and particularly during his eventful six years as Secretary of State, his courage, his wisdom, and his friendly understanding were devoted to bettering relations among nations. He was a foe only to tyranny.

Because he believed in the dignity of men and in their brotherhood under God, he was an ardent supporter of their deepest hopes and aspirations. From his life and work, humanity will, in the years to come, gain renewed inspiration to work ever harder for the attainment of the goal of peace with justice. In the pursuit of that goal, he ignored every personal cost and sacrifice, however great.

We, who were privileged to work with him, have lost a dear and close friend as all Americans have lost a champion of freedom. United, we extend to Mrs. Dulles, to her children and to all members of the Dulles family our prayers and deepest sympathy, and the assurance that in our memories will live affection, respect and admiration for John Foster Dulles.

NOTE: In addition to the foregoing statement, released at Gettysburg, Pa., the President issued Proclamation 3295 (24 F.R. 4199) which provided that, in grateful tribute to Mr. Dulles, the flag of the United States should be flown at half-staff on all Government buildings in the United States and in foreign countries until interment.

On July 15 the President issued Executive Order 10828 (24 F.R. 5735) designating the airport being built in Fairfax and Loudoun Counties of Virginia as the Dulles International Airport.

118 ¶ Statement by the President on the Report of the President's Science Advisory Committee, "Education for the Age of Science." *May* 24, 1959

THIS REPORT makes clear that the strengthening of science and engineering education requires the strengthening of all education. As an excellent statement of educational goals and needs, I hope it will be widely read and that it will stimulate a wider understanding of the importance of excellence in our educational system.

One subject discussed in the report warrants special emphasis—the importance of raising the standing of our teachers in their communities. Higher salaries are a first requirement, but we need also to recognize the great importance of what teachers do and to accord them the encouragement, understanding, and recognition which will help to make the teaching profession attractive to increasing numbers of first-rate people.

NOTE: The report, dated May 24, 1959, was published by the Government Printing Office.

119   ¶ Memorandum Concerning Proposed
Agreement With Germany for Cooperation on Uses
of Atomic Energy for Mutual Defense.
May 26, 1959

[Released May 26, 1959. Dated May 4, 1959]

Memorandum for:
   The Secretary of Defense
   The Chairman, Atomic Energy Commission

In your joint letter to me of May 1, 1959, you recommended that I
approve a proposed Agreement between the Government of the United
States of America and the Government of The Federal Republic of
Germany for Cooperation on the Uses of Atomic Energy for Mutual
Defense Purposes.

The Federal Republic of Germany is participating with the United
States in an international arrangement pursuant to which it is making
substantial and material contributions to the mutual defense and security.
The proposed Agreement will permit cooperation necessary to improve
the state of training and operational readiness of the armed forces of The
Federal Republic of Germany, subject to provisions, conditions, guarantees, terms, and special determinations, which are most appropriate in
this important area of mutual assistance, in accordance with the agreement in principle reached in December 1957.

Having considered your joint recommendations and the cooperation
provided for in the Agreement, including security safeguards and other
terms and conditions of the Agreement, I hereby

(1) approve the program for the transfer of non-nuclear parts of
atomic weapon systems involving Restricted Data under the terms and
conditions provided in your joint letter and the proposed Agreement;
however, types, quantities and conditions of transfer of such parts are
subject to my further approval;

(2) determine that the performance of this Agreement will promote
and will not constitute an unreasonable risk to the common defense and
security of the United States; and

(3) approve the proposed Agreement and authorize its execution for

the Government of the United States in a manner designated by the Secretary of State.

After execution of the Agreement, I shall submit it to the Congress.

I am forwarding a copy of this memorandum to the Secretary of State.

DWIGHT D. EISENHOWER

NOTE: Similar memorandums relating to agreements with the Netherlands and Turkey were sent to the Secretary of Defense and the Chairman of the Atomic Energy Commission. Other memorandums relating to agreements with specific countries were released by the White House and published in the Congressional Record as follows: France and the United Kingdom (May 26, vol. 105, pp. 8160, 8163, respectively), Canada (June 9, vol. 105, p. 9240), and Greece (June 17, vol. 105, p. 10030).

120 ¶ Special Message to the Congress Transmitting Proposed Agreements With Germany, the Netherlands, and Turkey for Cooperation on Uses of Atomic Energy for Mutual Defense. *May 26, 1959*

To the Congress of the United States:

In December 1957 the Heads of Government of the nations members of the North Atlantic Treaty Organization reached agreement in principle on the desirability of achieving the most effective pattern of NATO military defensive strength, taking into account the most recent developments in weapons and techniques. In enunciating this agreement in principle the Heads of Government made it clear that this decision was the result of the fact that the Soviet leaders, while preventing a general disarmament agreement, had left no doubt that the most modern and destructive weapons of all kinds were being introduced into the Soviet armed forces. The introduction of modern weapons into NATO forces should be no cause for concern on the part of other countries, since NATO is purely a defensive alliance.

It is our conviction and the conviction of our NATO allies that the introduction into NATO defenses of the most modern weapons available is essential in maintaining the strength necessary to the Alliance. Any alliance depends in the last analysis upon the sense of shared mutual interests among its members, and by sharing with our Allies certain training information we are demonstrating concretely our sense of partnership in NATO's defensive planning. Failure on our part to contribute to the improvement of the state of operational readiness of the forces of other members of NATO will only encourage the Soviet Union to believe that it can eventually succeed in its goal of destroying NATO's effectiveness.

To facilitate the necessary cooperation on our part legislation amending the Atomic Energy Act of 1954 was enacted during the last session of the Congress. Pursuant to that legislation agreements for cooperation have recently been concluded with three of our NATO partners; all of these agreements are designed to implement in important respects the agreed NATO program. These agreements will enable the United States to cooperate effectively in mutual defense planning with these nations and in the training of their respective NATO forces in order that, if an attack on NATO should occur, under the direction of the Supreme Allied Commander for Europe these forces could effectively use nuclear weapons in their defense.

These agreements represent only a portion of the work necessary for complete implementation of the decision taken by the North Atlantic Treaty Organization in December 1957. I anticipate the conclusion of similar agreements for cooperation with certain other NATO nations as the Alliance's defensive planning continues.

Pursuant to the Atomic Energy Act of 1954, as amended, I am submitting to each House of the Congress an authoritative copy of three agreements, one with the Federal Republic of Germany, one with the Kingdom of the Netherlands and one with the Government of Turkey. I am also transmitting a copy of the Secretary of State's letter accompanying authoritative copies of the signed agreements, a copy of three joint letters from the Secretary of Defense and the Chairman of the Atomic Energy Commission recommending my approval of these documents and copies of my memoranda in reply thereto setting forth my approval.

DWIGHT D. EISENHOWER

NOTE: The text of the agreements and related documents is published in the Congressional Record of June 9 (vol. 105, p. 9241).

Similar messages to the Congress concerning agreements with other countries were made public by the White House. Together with the text of the agreements and related documents they are published in the Congressional Record as follows: France and the United Kingdom (May 26, vol. 105, pp. 8159, 8161, respectively), Canada (June 9, vol. 105, p. 9238), and Greece (June 17, vol. 105, p. 10028). The agreement with the United Kingdom is an amendment to the agreement of July 3, 1958 (Senate Report 2041, 85th Cong., 2d sess.).

121   ¶ Statement by the President Following a
Meeting With Paul F. Foster, U.S. Representative
to the International Atomic Energy Agency.
May 28, 1959

I HAVE just conferred with Paul F. Foster, the new United States Representative to the International Atomic Energy Agency in Vienna, Austria.   The acceptance of this important assignment after a lifetime of public service is characteristic of the devotion to duty which has marked the career of this outstanding American.

I know that Admiral Foster will well represent the United States in Vienna and will continue to manifest those qualities of leadership which are so necessary in the International Agency.

As one of the principal supporters of the "atoms-for-peace" program, Paul Foster has notably furthered the cause of peace and worldwide understanding.

I told Under Secretary of State Douglas Dillon and Mr. John A. McCone, Chairman of the Atomic Energy Commission, who accompanied Paul Foster, that I attached the highest importance to the continued growth and development of the Agency and, accordingly, I instructed them to provide complete support to the new United States Representative.

We all should be gratified that the United States will be represented in the Agency by a man such as Paul Foster, and I wish him Godspeed in his new duties.

122   ¶ Statement by the President Concerning the
Wheat Surplus.   *June* 1, 1959

AS REQUIRED by law, the Secretary of Agriculture has today announced the 1960 wheat program.   Subject to farmer referendum vote on July twenty-third this will be a continuation of the existing discredited wheat legislation.   This legislation has piled up well over $3 billion worth of wheat, a supply equal to two-and-one-half times our annual domestic needs. Storage, handling, and interest charges for this wheat will cost the American taxpayer close to half a billion dollars during the next fiscal year. Continuation of this legislation for another year leads the wheat program one step closer to disaster.

Six separate times during the present session of the Congress I have called this matter to the attention of the Congress.

Despite widespread agreement that the present wheat program, if continued in effect, will ultimately end in disaster, five months have gone by, including the two-week extension especially provided to remedy the situation, with no conclusive Congressional action.

Even at this late date I urge upon the Congress changes in the law which would provide a workable program at a lower cost, applicable to the 1960 crop. The means of accomplishing this purpose, as outlined in my special message of January twenty-ninth, is to reduce the incentives for excess wheat production. Difficulties of the present program should not drive us to legislation involving even greater difficulties.

123 ¶ The President's News Conference of *June* 3, 1959.

THE PRESIDENT. I have no statement to make.

Q. Merriman Smith, United Press International: Mr. President, when the Big Four foreign ministers were here last week, you expressed the hope for what you called a measure of progress at the Geneva foreign ministers meeting as being necessary for a later summit conference.[1] And against that background, I would like to ask you a two-part question:

---

[1] On May 28, after the President's meeting with the foreign ministers who had recessed the Geneva Conference to permit them to attend former Secretary Dulles' funeral, the Press Secretary to the President issued the following statement:

This morning the President, with Secretary Herter present, received the Foreign Ministers of France, the United Kingdom, and the Union of Soviet Socialist Republics. The President said that he had followed the Geneva Conference proceedings with close attention, remaining in constant contact with Secretary Herter. He expressed the hope that the thorough exchange of views that are taking place there would lead to a better approach to the solution of the problems that confront us in Europe. He, of course, stressed the necessity of finding peaceful solutions to our problems.

The President likewise expressed the hope that on their return to Geneva the foreign ministers would be able to achieve that measure of progress which would make a subsequent meeting of heads of government desirable and useful.

One, sir, whether you have detected from Geneva any evidence of this progress which you feel is necessary as a prologue to a summit meeting; and second, whether from Geneva or the statements recently by Premier Khrushchev, whether you sense any cooling off by the Russians toward the idea of a summit meeting?

THE PRESIDENT. Well, the first answer is no, there has not been any detectable progress that to my mind would justify the holding of a summit meeting.

Now, I think I have expressed before my readiness to interpret satisfactory progress or define satisfactory progress rather liberally, because it would be unrealistic to believe that the foreign ministers could make a number of agreements that would be significant to the world and would of themselves promote a much more peaceful situation in the world. This is because these foreign ministers are, after all, acting for someone else, delegates of their governments, and these matters have to be brought back and studied carefully.

Nevertheless, I think that as the very least, we should expect, as Mr. Herter said in his opening statement, that we could see where we are apart on issues, whether we could narrow these gaps, and whether we could define the areas where it was going to be worth while for us to confer; that is, at the summit.

This would be, say, at least a decent working paper. But at the same time this crisis was brought about, the crisis that called for a summit meeting or which was used by some to call for a summit meeting was by the unilateral action of the Soviets with respect to Berlin. Therefore, there certainly should be some agreement that until a reunification of Germany could, in the future, be brought about, there should be a clear commitment that we will not be impeded in exercising our rights and privileges with respect to West Berlin; things of that kind. That, I would say, is specific.

Now, there are other ways, of course, in which there could be progress in the way of opening up contacts, exchanges of persons, of ideas, of books, and press comments, and all that kind of thing, some of the gaps into the Iron Curtain, back and forth.

Now, with respect to the speculating as to what the Soviets want, whether or not they want a summit meeting more or less than they did some months back, I don't know.

I will say this: some of the statements made by Mr. Khrushchev were certainly not calculated to ease tensions and to promote, you might say, a relaxed atmosphere for the conduct of negotiations at Geneva.

Q. J. Anthony Lewis, New York Times: Mr. President, at a meeting here the night before last, the question of the ceiling on interest rates on Government bonds was discussed with congressional leaders. I wondered whether you had come to a decision yet, Mr. President, on asking for a raise in that ceiling.

THE PRESIDENT. I said in my State of the Union Message that because of the very facts of that particular fiscal year, there would have to be a raise of some kind effected in the debt ceiling. There was a conference with the congressional leaders present, with two or three of my own staff, with Secretary Anderson. There was a general discussion of this whole problem, the problem of the debt and the management of our governmental finances.

The purpose of the meeting was not to reach decisions then, but to see whether we could concert our thinking so that the Treasury Department would be in position to make specific proposals and give them to the Congress. This has not yet been done, and no specific decisions made.

Q. Lloyd M. Schwartz, Fairchild Publications: Mr. President, the steel wage negotiations appear to be stalemated with a strike probable at the end of the month. Would you consider invoking the Taft-Hartley Act's cooling-off provision if a strike appears to be imminent?

THE PRESIDENT. I would have to wait for the time to come before I would make a decision of this kind.

Q. Robert C. Pierpoint, CBS News: Mr. President, do you agree with the charge of some of the Republican congressmen that anti-Semitism may be a factor in Admiral Strauss' confirmation difficulties on Capitol Hill?

THE PRESIDENT. Well, I didn't know that this charge emanated from Republicans.

I will say this: if it is brought forward seriously, this is indeed tragic. We have here a man of the highest type of character, ability, devoted many years of his life to public service; and to see such a false charge thrown at him in order to belittle him or hurt him would be very, very sad, I think.

Q. Sarah McClendon, El Paso Times: Sir, in these discussions on raising the interest rate that were held here the other night, will you please tell us what was said about the impact that this might have on the people generally?

THE PRESIDENT. I don't know that this particular point came up for discussion at that meeting, for the simple reason that the impact ought to be well understood, I should think, by all our people, if the Nation cannot borrow money.

As of now, the rate is fixed for any money except below 5-year money, and if you put the total $283 billion or $288 billion finally in short-range money, then the people will be so badly hurt that we have just got to do something.

Q. Frank van der Linden, Nashville Banner: Sir, John L. Lewis and Jimmy Hoffa both said they don't think Congress should pass any labor law at all this year. This looks like it may slow down the passage of the bill in the House somewhat.

Do you think the Congress should go home this year without passing a real labor reform bill?

THE PRESIDENT. I most certainly do not. You know, I am disturbed by what seems to be becoming habit in this country, to adopt certain theories that Marx advanced. One is that there is inevitable a bitter and implacable warfare between the man that works and the man that hires him. To my mind this is absolutely and completely un-American. It is not the way a free country must work. Every last workman, down to the lowliest, the most menial task you can think of, is just as important as any manager or any capitalist that invests in a company.

We have got to talk about cooperation, how do labor and management and capital cooperate to produce the wealth that this country needs? That is what we mean by an expanding economy.

These new labor laws, as I see it, are simply to protect the man that is working with his hands to help create this wealth. This is not any kind of punitive law, it is simply—well, Senator McClellan himself put in a "bill of rights." This is one of the things that I approved of. I was sorry to see it watered down. And it is protecting the laborer from the racketeering practices on the part of a few men in the labor field. That is the kind of thing it is for, and I would certainly like to see American thinking be directed toward 177 million people that are trying to get ahead, and not with some internecine warfare that is useless and futile and destructive.

Q. Raymond P. Brandt, St. Louis Post-Dispatch: Mr. President, have you a reply to Mr. Lewis' charge that you are against labor in the steel negotiations and have interfered before the negotiations have really begun?

THE PRESIDENT. Well, of course that charge is completely untrue. I have never interfered with anyone. Now, I have, before this body and others, stated that I believe that both sides have to exercise self-discipline or this country is in a bad time. I have talked to businessmen urging that their products be priced just as low as they can make them, and if there were places where they could reduce prices I would be delighted. I do not want to see, though, this so-called wage-price spiral continue until we get to the point that something drastic has to be done.

Now, Mr. Brandt, I must tell you this: so far as any interest of mine with respect to the relatively few in management and in the big capitalist class, it is very, very little as compared to what I think about the mass of people that do work with their hands and minds and at their type-writers and everywhere else to produce this wealth. But I do say this: they mustn't do things that damage themselves.

This is a very serious problem that requires the finest thought that can be developed, and we shouldn't be talking about it politically with any thought for the advantage that an individual is getting for his own per-sonal political ambitions, or a party for the furthering of its political fortunes. It should be a very serious thing because it means America, be we Democrats or Republicans or Independents or anything else.

Q. George C. Wilson, Congressional Quarterly: Mr. President, since your 1959 Federal aid to schools proposals have not received much atten-tion on Capitol Hill, would you support your 1957 school aid proposals as an alternative to the Democratic——

THE PRESIDENT. You are expecting my memory to be a little bit more perfect than it is at this minute. For 6 years I have been—7 years, I guess, now—putting in something on the educational bill. The details of your question, let Mr. Hagerty answer.

Q. E. W. Kenworthy, New York Times: Mr. President, in 1957, when you asked Congress to create the Development Loan Fund, you stressed the need of having long-term availability of funds. Senator Fulbright has now suggested that this need be met by Treasury borrowing author-ity. Would you support that?

THE PRESIDENT. I do not believe in borrowings for any purpose for this Federal Government in times of prosperity unless there is a great emergency facing us. I believe we must pay our way and, as I have said to you before, we should begin reducing this debt. If we don't, we have almost unsolvable problems confronting us all the time.

Now, I do believe in the authority for making long-term commitments if you are going to administer the Development Fund properly, efficiently, and effectively. Exactly the way the money is going to come out through it, get into it and so on, has got to be studied. I would not favor just borrowing without going through Appropriations Committee for that system.

Q. Mrs. May Craig, Portland (Maine) Press Herald: Mr. President, did you have any indication during the visit of the foreign ministers or since that Mr. Selwyn Lloyd might soon leave his post?

THE PRESIDENT. No, indeed. As a matter of fact, I think that Mr. Macmillan's forthright statement on this in the House of Commons was not only sincere, but I think it was a very timely statement that he has made in view of the rumor that was published in one of the London papers. I think there is nothing to it whatsoever.

Q. Chalmers M. Roberts, Washington Post: Mr. President, a moment ago, when you were discussing the Berlin situation, I believe you said that you felt there should be a clear commitment on the Soviet part, as to Western rights in West Berlin. Do you mean, sir, that this commitment should be made as part of the agreement to have a summit meeting, or do you mean that this commitment should be made without any time limit and not merely to get to the summit, so to speak?

THE PRESIDENT. I say that until the Germans participate themselves, as a whole, in settling these problems we ought not to have any more questions or difficulty about the Berlin question, that's what I mean.

Q. Mr. Roberts: Well, may I ask, then, do you mean that this commitment should be given before—as a condition, in your mind, for having a summit meeting?

THE PRESIDENT. Well, I don't like to call it condition. I would just say this: I don't see how the head of any self-respecting government can go to an international conference in response to any kind of thing that can be interpreted as a threat.

Q. William Knighton, Baltimore Sun: Mr. President, has the inter-service dispute over the merits of the Army's Nike-Hercules versus the Air Force's Bomarc reached the point where you as Commander in Chief have to step in and make a decision?

THE PRESIDENT. I don't think it necessarily has to come to me in a specific decision. I am not sure whether I told you before, but at least it is public property, that the Defense Secretary is now making a complete and exhaustive study of the missile field. These problems are not as simple as they may sound. You cannot take the capabilities of one weapon and compare it with the capabilities of another and necessarily say that the one that you think is going faster, further, and higher is a better one. You have a whole—it is more than a family, it is a whole bevy of these missiles; and with supporting aircraft and other forms of defense, these have to integrate.

Now, this overall study which is, I think, scheduled for very soon—I would say within 10 days certainly—it will try to correlate all these factors and give any conclusions that they up to this point have been able to make.

As of now, I am standing behind the defense system and plans that I recommended to the Congress some time back in January or February. But if this study shows the need for some modifications, I am quite ready to assist in making them.

Q. Ruth S. Montgomery, Hearst Newspapers: Mr. President, follow-ing up on that same question, several Senators said that lately you have spoken out rather sharply to them about what you have termed the muni-tions lobby which you feel has been bringing some pressure on some of the Congressmen to try to change your defense program and plan.

Could you comment on that?

THE PRESIDENT. Well, I don't know who has a right to carry outside the White House any remarks I have been making, and to make those re-marks public property. That is supposed to be a little bit of a private place over there, although maybe not always.

I don't think I have used that word, Miss Montgomery, in public. I may have; I am not saying I didn't, but I don't believe I have.

I do say this: obviously political and financial considerations get into this argument—rather than merely military ones—that is produced when people have to advertise very strongly about a particular thing companies do; obviously something besides the strict military needs of this country are coming to influence decisions.

Q. Edward P. Morgan, American Broadcasting Company: Mr. President, the political experts have been wrong before, but some of them are speculating that there is a very real possibility that the Republicans can take the Presidency again in 1960 and again lose the Congress.

Would you have any counsel to your successor of either party in dealing with a Congress of opposition, and what do you think about this apparently increasing American political phenomenon of splitting tickets?

THE PRESIDENT. Well, Mr. Morgan, I would be glad to discuss that question sometime when we have got about 2 hours by ourselves— [*laughter*]—because it is very serious. Personally, I detect a more vocal support for some change, even in basic constitutional change, so that we could incorporate into our system some of the features of the parliamentary system. But, as I say, this is a very long thing and we will have to do it a little more at our leisure, I think.

Q. John Scali, Associated Press: Mr. President, if there is satisfactory progress at a foreign ministers level at Geneva, what would you think of the concept of a series of summit meetings at which the world leaders could get together and try to ease world tensions?

THE PRESIDENT. Well, I have no opinion about this because it would be entirely on the basis of results and the promise of further results. I have put myself on the record, as often as I was asked the question, that I am ready to go anywhere, any time, where I am quite certain that tensions will be lessened and where the confidence of people will rise rather than be decreased.

Now, I see, after you go to one meeting, it could very well be the kind of results to say, "Well, this is profitable; all right, we will go another time." I have no objection as long as there is improvement and progress.

Q. John Herling, Editors Syndicate: Mr. President, you and Secretary of Labor Mitchell have recently been receiving bouquets from the leaders of the railroad unions for signing the railroad benefit legislation which now extends unemployment insurance to 52 weeks, and the question that some other members of organized labor are asking is, if it is good for railroad workers, why isn't it good for unemployed workers generally? I wonder whether you have any comment on that, sir.

THE PRESIDENT. For a long time I have been arguing that the States should have more uniform standards, and that those that had such short periods for unemployment insurance should be extended. Most times this has been set at 26 weeks, and I think that is the figure that I have taken in the past.

Now, I signed a bill that was about as closely balanced between advantages and disadvantages as I have ever had to study. I kept it on my desk until the last minute to see whether I could get any new information.

I finally decided on balance it should be signed. But let's remember this: this is a group that is not under OASI. It is a different group, and I am not sure that I would—well, I am quite certain I would not take all of the features of that bill and make them part of my own particular plan for solving this problem in a broader base.

Q. Carleton Kent, Chicago Sun-Times: Mr. President, it was reported yesterday that at your conference with Republican leaders you expressed yourself as disturbed over the polls which have shown that the Republican Party is experiencing some kind of a decline. If that is true, can you discuss your plans with us for improving the Party's position?

THE PRESIDENT. Well, I don't know as there is any news about this, because I have been disturbed about this for the last 6 years. [*Laughter*]

Even in a very overwhelming vote given to the national ticket in '56, when we lost both Houses, it pointed the way to a very serious study and you might say revolutionary effort. I think there are plans afoot that will bring improvement, and I think they can be discussed a little bit later when the committee that we have got working on this will report.

Q. Marvin L. Arrowsmith, Associated Press: Mr. President, there have been some contentions that the usefulness of Lewis Strauss will have been hopelessly compromised even if the Senate should confirm him. Do you believe he will be able to operate effectively, particularly in his relations with Congress, in view of this bitterness that has developed?

THE PRESIDENT. I have seen no criticism whatsoever of his work in the last 8 months, when he has been filling this post. And therefore, I see no reason whatsoever that he can't do it efficiently, no matter how long he stays there.

Q. Lambert Brose, Lutheran Layman: Mr. President, in this connection, may I ask do you feel that all these attacks on Mr. Strauss by the Democrats, and even by Senator Langer of your own party, are motivated solely by political considerations, or do you see the possibility of perhaps some honest difference of opinion on his qualifications?

THE PRESIDENT. Well, here and there I should think that it would be a strange thing if any individual in the world commanded the complete respect and admiration and affection of every other individual. So I suppose there is some room for honest differences of opinion.

Q. William M. Blair, New York Times: Mr. President, there has been pending in the Congress proposals for putting a ceiling on price support loans to individual farmers. Do you favor a ceiling such as the $50,000 suggested, sir?

THE PRESIDENT. I have recommended it before, and I am not so sure as I was as high as 50,000.

Q. Robert G. Spivack, New York Post: Mr. President, at the time of the lynching in Mississippi of Mack Charles Parker, you voiced your deep concern and you said you were going to follow the investigation very closely. In view of this expressed interest, I wondered if the Justice Department consulted with you when the FBI was withdrawn from the case.

THE PRESIDENT. Well, they were informed through—the Attorney General's Office informed me; they felt it was necessary.

Q. Laurence H. Burd, Chicago Tribune: Mr. President, in connection with divided parties in the Presidency and Congress, you spoke of some people thinking in terms of a constitutional change. Have you looked into that yourself, and do you lean in that direction?

THE PRESIDENT. Strangely enough, this is one thing that, when we had a leisurely hour, Secretary Dulles and I often talked about. We decided that it was better, from our own opinion, our own conviction, to stick with what we have, but try to make it work a little bit better.

I believe that if we come into the business of parliamentary government, it would be so strange for us we just wouldn't know how to work it probably as well as some of the others do. But on top of that, I think there are many advantages of ours. The only thing we ought to do, I think, is make it work a little better.

Q. Earl H. Voss, Washington Star: Mr. President, when the Geneva negotiations on nuclear tests resume next Monday, are we planning to press for your latest April 13 proposal, for the first phase, banning of atmospheric tests, or are we ready to discuss the Soviet Union's latest proposal?

THE PRESIDENT. Well, you will remember, in that letter I said that what we are aiming for is a much broader agreement that would contemplate control of all types of bans—above the atmosphere, in it, and under the surface.

Now, what I did propose: I said, could we not make a start in the atmospheric thing, which would have two or three things. One, there would be no increase in the pollution of the air, such as it is, and it would be rather simple to detect. Therefore there would be very, very minor arrangements in inspectional systems as compared to what you would have to have in a broader base. But just exactly what turn the June the 8th opening will have, I don't know.

Marvin L. Arrowsmith, Associated Press: Thank you, Mr. President.

NOTE: President Eisenhower's one hundred and sixtieth news conference was held in the Executive Office Building from 10:32 to 11:01 o'clock on Wednesday morning, June 3, 1959. In attendance: 207.

124 ¶ Remarks to a Group of Business Magazine Editors in the Conference Room. *June* 4, 1959

Ladies and Gentlemen:

I do not feel qualified, particularly, to talk to you about your business. You study the whole gamut of business activities in our country and on them you express your own conclusions and convictions.

But I might express a few ideas on two things: first, tell you some of the things that I believe about the work in which you are engaged; second, it might be useful for a moment to talk about some of the responsibilities that fall upon me and my associates in Government.

To start, there is an old military saying, "You can do nothing positive except from a firm base."

This means that if you don't have a region or a place or an area from which you can replace your casualties, supplies, ammunition, and all the rest—no matter how well you may start out on any expedition—you are in the long run lost. Even Hannibal, after thirteen years in Italy, could not finally win because he had no firm base on which to depend.

The great base today on which America must stand is a sound, expanding, healthy, and vigorous economy.

We must have that. If our economy is to develop properly, we must have something else: we must have an enlightened, informed public opinion. In any free country the great motivation which makes the whole thing operate is public opinion. If that opinion is well-informed respecting the vital issues of our day, then Congress and the Executive, heedful of that kind of opinion, are going to act with more wisdom than they otherwise might if they were thinking only of the next election.

We must have, then, an informed public opinion and a sound economy, and we must recognize their value not only to us but our standing in the world, including our security from any threatened attack, no matter of what character.

In these fields you people here this morning have a tremendous responsibility and a great opportunity. You can help enlighten America about the issues of our economy, its nature, its character, how it can be vigorous and expanding, more useful to us as a people, more effective in preserving and enhancing the position of leadership that has been forced upon America in the whole effort of advancing the cause of peace with justice.

Now a word, too, about the Executive responsibility to avoid unnecessary expenditures so that we may begin, no matter if even in moderate fashion, to reduce the national debt that this country is carrying.

That debt is important because we are taking today more than eight billion dollars out of your pockets for interest payments alone, with no reduction of the debt itself. That eight billion dollars of interest is going up. This is so because in this time of great prosperity, every kind of economic activity is seeking new money. There are new demands for new machinery in our productive processes, for building every kind of home and industrial facility, for roads and communications—for everything. The demand for money by municipalities, States, school districts, irrigation districts, and all the rest is unprecedented.

America—the Federal Government—has to compete with that kind of demand, not only for the eight billion dollars in interest payments on our national debt, but we have to compete in the market place in selling our bonds, which must be kept sound.

There is one method which is too often advocated for keeping the bonds at a nominal par value. That is to force them upon a central bank—make the central bank purchase them. Well, that's a very fine system, if you can make it work. But since the effect of the buying of our bonds by the central bank (Federal Reserve) increases the amount of credit, the result is inflationary. No country ever has made such a plan work over a long period. You don't have to go farther back in history than a year or two to find where these unfortunate results were experienced in one great European country.

But, if the United States Government is not to be in a position to compete with every business and every worthwhile economic activity for money in managing our 285-billion-dollar debt, we are going to be in trouble, particularly if we are denied the right to bid on a business basis—that is, at realistic interest rates. We cannot resort to artificial, forced methods and still keep our own confidence, and the confidence of the world in the American dollar.

Now every time—at least I found this when I was on the political stump—I used the expression "sound dollar" I was charged by my political opponents as being against the man of modest means.

To my mind, such a charge makes no sense at all. I would think that you people could do much to convince all our people that the sound dollar is their own real economic salvation.

Here we need an informed public opinion. In our Nation we have become what I call a pension society.

When I was a boy, it was thought we could live our lives on a little piece of ground in the West, and the older folks—grandfather and grandmother—could live in the same home, after their days of hard work were ended. That's the way we took care of ourselves and our older people. Today, through the changes in our industrial system, we as a people have become dependent for old age security, more and more upon pensions, insurance policies, savings bonds, and savings accounts. These are the people that are particularly hurt by depreciation of the dollar.

People who get a dollar one year and spend it that or the next year are not as much hurt even if there develops a sort of creeping inflation, or cheapening of the dollar. But the man who makes a living today and puts away his savings to be used 40 years from now can receive some startling lessons over that 40-year period.

My wife and I decided, in 1916, to get married. Since I, like all other second lieutenants, was always overdrawn at the bank, I decided that I ought to show a little more sense of responsibility. So I began to buy a small insurance policy.

437

Well, I gave up smoking ready-made cigarettes and went to Bull Durham and the papers. I had to make a great many sacrifices to buy that small insurance policy. Then 30 years later the company came around to pay it off. And I had even forgotten about it. It was so small that I would have been ashamed to ask my wife to exist on it for 6 months.

Yet, I still think of the fun we had in working for our own future. Indeed it was easy to make little sacrifices because I was young and of course very much in love.

But today, think of the man at the lathe, the drill press, who is earning money which he is putting away in his pension with his company or into an insurance policy. If we today cannot assure him that 40 years from now he is going to be able to have a good living left, then I say, sooner or later, he will quit buying insurance policies; he will not have any confidence in the Government bond; and he will not think very much of his pension.

These are some of the facts that I think you people know about and undoubtedly you teach them. But I think we don't teach them strongly enough.

Our economy, if it is going to be competitive and a free economy, must be just that. It's the only way we are going to be strong and expanding. If we are going to live as a free people, we must not be a controlled people, and we must not start controlling prices in times of peace.

We are living in a time of prosperity that looks like it is assuming boom proportions. If now, today, we can't pay off some of the Federal debt, then our financing is going to have to be done under very unsatisfactory methods, to the damage of all of us. In the long run there will be inflation, there will be a further cheapening of our money, and it won't be the rich that will be suffering. Instead it will be all those millions who with their hands and brains, typewriters, shovels, and all the rest, are producing the wealth of the United States, and depending upon insurance and pension plans for old age security.

So as I leave you, I thank you for your patience in listening to a very homey exposition of some of my own views and convictions on this subject. They may not be very erudite but they are earnest and firm.

125 ¶ Message Transmitted Via the Moon to the Prime Minister and People of Canada Upon the Opening of the Prince Albert Radar Laboratory. *June 6, 1959*

I AM delighted to greet you, Mr. Prime Minister, and the Canadian people on the occasion of the opening of the Prince Albert Radar Laboratory. The completion of this laboratory constitutes another major advance along the road of cooperative ventures between our two countries in defense research and other fields. The transmission of this message by way of the moon—a distance of almost half a million miles—emphasizes the technical importance of your new laboratory and is a specific illustration of the scientific cooperation between Canada and the United States. The work of this laboratory cannot fail to make a significant contribution, in future years, toward the solving of mutual problems.

NOTE: The message was recorded on tape and transmitted from the Millstone Hill Radar Observatory of the Massachusetts Institute of Technology Lincoln Laboratory to the Prince Albert Radar Laboratory, Prince Albert, Saskatchewan.

126 ¶ Special Message to the Congress on the Management of the Public Debt. *June 8, 1959*

To the Congress of the United States:

Successful management of the debt of the Federal Government is one of the most important foundation stones of the sound financial structure of our Nation.

The public debt must be managed so as to safeguard the public credit. It must be managed in a way that is consistent with economic growth and stability. It must also be managed as economically as possible in terms of interest costs. The achievement of these goals is complicated today by several factors, despite the fact that United States Government securities are the safest investment in the world. Our growing prosperity, combined with Government programs to support mortgages and other types of debt obligations, has strengthened the position of these mortgage and other investments with which the Treasury must compete when it sells Government securities.

In addition, the rapid growth in borrowing demands of corporations, individuals, and State and local governments (which issue tax-exempt obligations) tends to diminish the amount of funds available for investment in direct Federal Government securities. Furthermore, the market for all fixed dollar obligations has been affected by a recent preference among some buyers for common stocks.

The achievement of a fiscal position that allows our revenues to cover our expenditures—as well as to produce some surplus for debt retirement—will improve substantially the environment in which debt management operates. Greater flexibility of debt management action is required, however, under present-day conditions if a reasonable schedule of maturities is to be maintained and the safeguards against inflation strengthened.

I am, therefore, asking the Secretary of the Treasury to transmit to the Congress today proposed legislation designed to improve significantly the Government's ability to manage its debt in the best interest of the Nation.

The legislation provides principally for:

(1) Removal of the present 3.26% interest rate ceiling on savings bonds. This, together with other changes, will reinvigorate the savings bond program.

(2) Removal of the present 4¼% interest rate ceiling on new issues of Treasury bonds. The present ceiling seriously restricts Treasury debt management and is inconsistent with the flexibility which the Secretary of the Treasury has on rates paid on shorter-term borrowing.

(3) An increase in the regular public debt limit from $283 billion to $288 billion, and an increase in the temporary limit from $288 billion to $295 billion. These increases are essential to the orderly and prudent conduct of the financial operations of the government, even with expenditures covered by revenues in the fiscal year 1960, as the Budget proposes.

Savings Bonds

Removal of the present 3.26% maximum limit on savings bond interest, together with certain other changes, will permit the Treasury to improve the terms of savings bonds. This will strengthen the contribution

440

of the program both to habits of thrift throughout the Nation and to a better structure of the public debt.

The Treasury is proposing the following revisions in the savings bond program, subject to approval of enabling legislation: A 3¾% interest rate to maturity for all Series E and H Savings Bonds sold on or after June 1, 1959; an improved interest rate on all Series E and H bonds outstanding and continued to be held; and improved extension terms for outstanding Series E bonds when they mature.

4¼% Maximum Interest Rate on New Bond Issues

There is no statutory maximum on the interest rate which can be paid by the Treasury for marketable borrowing of 5 years or less (bills, certificates, and notes). The Secretary of the Treasury should have similar flexibility with regard to Treasury bonds (which run 5 years or more to maturity).

The Treasury always tries to borrow as economically as it can, consistent with its other debt management objectives. But in our democracy no man can be compelled to lend to the Government on terms he would not voluntarily accept. Therefore, when the Government borrows, it can do so successfully only at realistic rates of interest that are determined by the supply and demand for securities, as reflected in the prices and yields of outstanding issues established competitively in the Government securities market.

I am aware of the fact that many proposals have been made which are designed to produce lower interest rates. However, any debt management device which would seek to interfere with the natural interaction of the competitive forces of our free economy and produce unnatural reductions in interest rates would not only breach the fundamental principles of the free market, but under current conditions could be drastically inflationary. The additional cost to the Government alone from increased prices of the goods and services it must buy might far exceed any interest saving. The ultimate harm to the entire Nation of such a price rise could be incalculable.

Market yields on a number of Treasury bonds are already above 4¼%. With one exception all bonds which have 5 years or more to run to maturity have market yields above 4%. The Treasury recently has done substantial short-term borrowing. But it must avoid undue shortening of the public debt and therefore should continue to sell intermediate and longer-term bonds whenever market conditions permit. It should not be prohibited from doing so by the existence of an artificial ceiling which under today's conditions makes it virtually impossible to sell bonds in the competitive market.

Debt Limit

The Treasury's current estimates, assuming that revenues cover expenditures for the fiscal year 1960 as a whole, indicate the need for an increase in the regular (or permanent) statutory public debt limit from $283 billion to $288 billion. The $288 billion figure is $13 billion above the permanent limit of $275 billion in effect at the beginning of the fiscal year 1959. This $13 billion increase is approximately equal to the Federal Government deficit during the current fiscal year, as estimated in the Budget submitted in January.

The Treasury expects the debt to approximate $285 billion on June 30, 1959, leaving about $3 billion leeway under the proposed $288 billion regular ceiling—a leeway which is essential to protect the Government in case of unforeseen emergencies and to provide necessary flexibility in debt management operations.

Even with budget receipts covering expenditures in the next fiscal year the debt is expected to rise considerably above $288 billion next fall and winter as the Treasury borrows to cover seasonal needs. This seasonal borrowing can then be repaid before the end of the fiscal year. I am asking, therefore, for a temporary increase of $7 billion in the public debt limit beyond the $288 billion permanent ceiling to cover those seasonal borrowing needs. This temporary limit would expire June 30, 1960, and can be reviewed prior to that time.

Certain other technical proposals to improve the management of the public debt are also included in the proposed legislation.

The enactment of this program is essential to sound conduct of the Government's financial affairs. It will contribute significantly to the Treasury's ability to do the best possible job in the management of the public debt. I urge, therefore, that the Congress give prompt consideration to this request.

_____

There is another matter to which I wish to call your attention, quite apart from the legislative program discussed above. When I submitted my Budget to you in January interest costs on the public debt for the fiscal year 1960 were estimated at $8 billion. The increase in interest rates that has taken place since that estimate was made is now expected to add about half a billion dollars to this figure.

At the same time, however, I am informed that, because of the strength of economic recovery and growth beyond our earlier expectations, our revenue estimates for fiscal year 1960 will be sufficient to offset the increased interest cost on the public debt.

DWIGHT D. EISENHOWER

127 ¶ Remarks and Address at Testimonial Dinner Honoring Republicans in Congress. *June 8, 1959*

[The President spoke first to the guests who dined with him, then to a group in another dining hall upstairs]

Chairman Wayne, Senator Goldwater, Mr. Martin, Distinguished Guests, Ladies and Gentlemen:

I am scheduled to make a speech—upstairs. Here, I am supposed to say just Hello. But, being a good Republican, in front of good Republicans, I don't think I can stop just there.

I want to explain about this speech. When they told me maybe it would be an idea for me to extend a few words of greeting, Barry Goldwater said, "Why don't you just give the same speech over that you are going to do upstairs?"

"Well," I said, "It has neither weight, nor inspiration, nor logic, and I see no reason for inflicting it on anybody twice, even the people at this head table."

But I am going very briefly to express a hope. I hope the Republican Party transforms itself into one gigantic recruiting service. We need recruits. We need them from among Democrats—discerning Democrats, that is—from Independents, from people that have never voted, or people who have just failed to vote.

To get new recruits, we have got to have real morale. We have got to have a morale that comes from the belief in a cause. Whenever I think

443

of a great service, or a great accomplishment brought about by morale, I often think of Cromwell's army. His Roundheads marched into battle singing hymns, and never once were they shaken. Because he had told them—he had drilled into them that they had a cause for which to work.

Ladies and gentlemen, the cause of good government, sound, stable, progressive government for this country is the greatest cause that we could possibly have today on God's footstool.

We need management. And this you will have from your several chairmen—the National Committee and the senatorial and congressional committees, and with the hierarchy of leadership reaching on down to the last man.

We will need money. You are providing some now. Money, as Barry Goldwater said, will not do the job, you have got to give yourselves, if you are going to be real recruiters. So we have to have these men and women with them believing as we do: that the United States must stand proud and strong before the world as the champion of freedom and decency, and peace with justice.

We can do that only if we are strong at home. And we must follow those policies that logic, good sense, history itself, are good for this country, to keep our economy strong, our dollar sound, and ourselves spiritually inspired to do our duty—each single one of us.

And about this speech upstairs, I should have said I tried to get Mrs. Eisenhower to make it for me, but she wouldn't do it. I found that I might as well just—well, I don't know—have asked her to vote the Socialist ticket. Experiencing defeat there, I will say goodnight, good luck to you, and keep a-going.

SALUTE TO THE REPUBLICANS IN CONGRESS

Chairman Wayne, Congressman Martin, Senator Goldwater, Senator Dirksen, Distinguished Guests, and My Fellow Republicans:

It is a great pleasure to join in this salute to the distinguished Republicans whose presence in the Congress gives real lustre to both the Senate and the House of Representatives. I pay tribute also to those former Members who, because of the accidents of politics, are not now voting members, but who, we hope, will soon be recommissioned for this duty.

And further, I have looked forward to this opportunity to thank these Republican Senators and Congressmen for the splendid job they are doing to forward our Republican proposals in the 86th Congress. Your solidarity and loyalty in so many important tests now are a good omen for the great test coming in the fall of 1960.

Just a word about this solidarity to which Senator Goldwater referred. After the 1952 campaign, one of the expert political analysts came into my home and told my wife, I thought very unwisely, that she was responsible for 74 of the electoral votes that the ticket received that fall. I have never before this moment admitted to her that I thought that was an underestimate. But anyway, that's what the expert said.

Now, in 1956, as the campaign was going on, my wife was sitting with me one day, when a man came in with what was obviously a rather preposterous proposal, but he urged it with great vehemence. And finally she said to me, "My boy, if you do that, I'll take my 74 electoral votes and walk out."

Now we are not going to have any lack of that solidarity in this next campaign.

Clearly, the Republicans in the Congress have proven they have not been afraid to stand up and be counted. Next time you hear it said that there are no differences between our parties, you might point out this: except for the support of some discerning Democrats, it is the Republican Party that fights for responsible, sensible, and progressive policy in Government, as urged in the recommendations of the administration.

I am grateful to you Members of both Bodies. And I have come here to tell you so.

By the way, I sometimes hear of this support being measured in terms of percentages. I am gratified that in the records the grade is something more than a passing mark, and I hope by the end of this session everybody will be getting an A-plus.

With our minds on the next election, I want to emphasize four ingredients of successful organization: Morale, Men, Means, and Management.

This applies, of course, to political organizations.

First, Morale.

Above all else, it involves belief in a cause.

The will to win is always important—but alone it cannot long inspire a group to its best efforts. Only through the intensity of our belief in political principle and our pride that together we are creating increasing progress in America can we have a successful political party for the long pull.

Morale is created by many things. It comes from faith in leaders; from conviction in their sincerity, integrity, and above all, in their selflessness. Morale is not something to be sold—it is something to be generated. Though an organization might be impoverished as to means, and though it might be decimated in strength, it will never despair so long as its morale is high. Morale can stand acknowledged setbacks, but it will never recognize defeat. Morale is the seed of future victory.

The next two ingredients are Men and Means.

Politics has changed much within our lifetime. There was a time when Republicans in the north could win elections no matter how lacking their candidates might be in qualifications. Those days are gone. Our elections must be won by nominating bright, personable, vigorous candidates of character who are natural-born recruiting officers. To make their efforts truly effective, we need to give them enough money to tell the full story to the electorate.

All of us with a devotion to the Republican Party have a duty—and it is a joyful duty—to do everything within our power to choose and encourage candidates of the highest caliber, and to see that they have the means to wage successful campaigns.

Finally, I turn to Management. Management requires organization. Management is the function of orchestration. It makes certain that we all play the same tune at the same time, on the proper instruments, and with such effect that we will daily gain new listeners by the thousands.

No one person can possibly create from many millions of individuals an effective team or teamwork. This has to be done by a hierarchy of leadership, operating through many workers in successive echelons of responsibility. It has to be done intelligently and thoroughly. It has to be done with the single purpose of influencing the individual—and this means the individual in the remotest precinct of America.

It must be businesslike; above all, it must be spirited. It requires positive and abhors negative attitudes. As Republicans we should always assert that something is "half full" rather than to moan that it is "half empty."

Republican legislators are leaders in the management team. Today they are showing their mettle by battling actively for the major tenets in the Republican faith. At this moment we are engaged in a highly important battle for a sound dollar.

This is not a fight to balance the budget as an end in itself. This is not a fight just to pinch pennies.   This is a fight to keep our Nation fiscally strong so that we may maintain the forces we must have for the security of ourselves and the free world.   This is a fight to promote an expanding economy and domestic prosperity.   This is a fight to make sure that a dollar earned today will tomorrow buy for the housewife an equal amount of groceries.

You in the Congress—all Republicans—all recruits from the Democrats, and I must say discerning Democrats, and Independents that we can get—are battling to protect the worker as he earns his pension, and to protect the retired man who must live on it.   This is a fight to prevent prices from impoverishing every man, woman, and child in the Nation.

As you, my friends—my colleagues, wage this fight without ceasing, you will demonstrate your worthiness of victory at the polls.   As the Nation comes to recognize this, you will win.

Thank you very much indeed.

NOTE: The dinner, held in the Sheraton-Park Hotel, Washington, D.C., was sponsored by a committee consisting of Representative Joseph W. Martin, Jr., Chairman, Senator Barry Goldwater, Chairman of the Republican Senatorial Committee, Representative Richard M. Simpson, Chairman of the Republican Congressional Committee, and Lewis T. Breuninger, Chairman of the Republican Finance Committee of the District of Columbia. The actor, John Wayne, served as master of ceremonies.

128   ¶ Remarks at the National Conference on Civil Rights.   *June* 9, 1959

Mr. Chairman and My Friends:

I came over here this morning primarily to thank you for your undertaking of a work that in my opinion is one of vital, prime importance to the United States and to its future.

Because the problem in which you are involved is an emotional one, it is certain that you have to have qualities of courage to undertake it. But above the quality of courage it is quite necessary that we have within our breasts, if we are to do this work, those feelings of compassion, consideration, and justice that derive from our concepts of moral law.

I say moral law rather than statutory law because I happen to be one of those people who has very little faith in the ability of statutory law to

447

change the human heart, or to eliminate prejudice.

I think that the Congress was wise in establishing this Commission because the very purpose of the Commission is conciliatory, fact-finding, and giving examples to us. Indeed at times I think it holds up before us all a mirror so that we may see ourselves, what we are doing and what we are not doing, and therefore making it easier for us to correct our omissions.

There can be no doubt that America has not reached perfection in attaining the lofty ideals laid down for us in our founding documents and in the amendments that have been made to our Constitution. The important thing is that we go ahead, that we make progress. This does not necessarily mean revolution. In my mind it means evolution. This is what we are talking about.

We are saying that the concept of equality among men is equality in their opportunities, that we do not deny them that opportunity. I think no one could find complete equality between any two individuals in the world, if we wanted to take absolute values in all of their spiritual, intellectual, and physical connotations. But we can talk about equality of opportunity, guaranteed to each person in this Nation.

Just as the members of that commission have undertaken a job that is difficult, so each of the State commissions has done the same. The progress that you are going to help achieve is that of education, promoting understanding to see that we come nearer to achieving our ideals without necessarily, or maybe not even wisely, trying to place on our statute books too many punitive laws.

If I may digress from the exact subject of which I have been speaking, and which, of course, is occupying your thoughts and efforts while you are here, I should like to talk about the word "understanding" for just a moment.

The Federal Government in both its legislative and executive branches is involved in many problems that are most difficult of solution. In fact, some of them, under the particular conditions of the present, seem almost to defy solution: all we can do is to hold the line and wait for some change in either material or, let us say, mental conditions in which people are living. But the big, the strong thing, that must be behind the whole effort of the United States is understanding at home on the basic issues. This is needed to bring about higher standards of living in our own country, to make certain that free areas in other parts of the world do not go under the domination of communism, to make certain that our alliances are stronger through the intellectual, spiritual and material development of those countries with which we are allied.

We are too often swayed by slogans. For example, in the fields in which the United States is attempting to help other free countries so that together we may be safer and stronger and more confident, we use the slogan "give away." I submit, any intelligent man that will look at the world today and can find it in his heart to condemn America's purpose and her efforts to bring other free nations into a higher level of sturdier, better allies, more effective allies, then he is following a line of reasoning which I cannot follow.

All of our domestic problems, including the one now before you—the equality of opportunity of all men regardless of inconsequential considerations—comes in the same category of demanding understanding. This is so whether it be the farm program, the debt program, the need for reducing Federal expenditures, how we want to expand in one direction and contract in another. All demand understanding.

None of these problems, when you come down to it, can be dealt with in a vacuum. They are not mutually exclusive. In almost all cases, you will find them interdependent.

As we achieve a better level of equality of opportunity in this country, our own national prestige and leadership is enhanced. Our economic problems are involved often with this same subject with which you are now dealing. Therefore, not only by developing a better understanding in these basic issues can we help solve the problem with which you are specifically concerned this morning, but by bringing your own minds and hearts into focus on this particular question you help to develop better understanding through the whole of the United States.

Remember, in a democracy, the only motivating, energizing force is public opinion. If that public opinion is well informed, then the United States will act wisely and strongly and fairly at home and abroad.

So you are not solving, or helping to solve, just one problem. You are working for America. I say to you, in my opinion, there can be no better thing to do.

Thank you very much.

NOTE: The President spoke at the Statler Hilton Hotel, Washington, D.C. The national conference, consisting of members of State advisory committees on civil rights, was sponsored by the Commission on Civil Rights, established by Public Law 85–305 (71 Stat. 626). The President's opening words "Mr. Chairman" referred to Dr. John A. Hannah, Chairman of the Commission.

129   ¶ Address at the Annual Meeting of the American Medical Association, Atlantic City, New Jersey. *June 9, 1959*

Dr. Orr, Dr. Gundersen, Distinguished Guests, and Ladies and Gentlemen:

I am honored in this opportunity to extend greetings and felicitations to you and your colleagues in the medical profession. The American Medical Association, representing physicians in general practice and specialties in many fields, has brilliantly earned the high position it holds in the Nation. In making this statement, I cannot logically be accused of self-flattery—because even though I am exceedingly proud of belonging to the College of Surgeons, I assure you that my credentials of membership in the College are not the kind that entitle me to wield a knife upon my fellow man.

Because health, including bodily and mental vigor, is an essential asset in everything we do, all national progress is facilitated by progress in health. Whether it involves healing the sick, guarding the public against quackery, evaluating drugs or helping to maintain high hospital standards, the medical profession is steadily promoting better health among our people.

Indeed, Lord Bryce observed, on one of his last visits to the United States, that "medicine is the only profession that labors incessantly to destroy the reason for its own existence."

By working toward this end the medical profession promotes broad national progress.

Today, as every schoolboy knows, diseases like diphtheria, scarlet fever, and smallpox, which brought such tragedy to so many American families a few generations ago, have all but disappeared.

In our country medical science has virtually eliminated typhoid, pellagra, and malaria, and is well on the road to conquering tuberculosis and poliomyelitis.

Even more dramatic have been the gains of modern medicine against deaths among infants.

Forty years ago, 10 percent of the babies born in this country died before their first birthday; today the figure is below 3. During the past decade alone, deaths of mothers in childbirth dropped 65 percent. Happily also, the Nation has experienced a steep decline in deaths from childhood diseases.

For all this the Nation is profoundly grateful.

Only a century ago the average physician in America was a man with rarely more than a high school education. He learned about the treatment of diseases as an apprentice to another man who was called a physician, but who was likely to be as poorly educated as his pupil. We are told that sick people in great numbers avoided physicians as much as they sought them out, since it was uncertain whether they would profit or lose from the encounter.

But the need for better medical education could not long be ignored. And it was no accident that as medicine advanced and professional medical skills developed, in the United States, as in Europe, they were associated closely with the great universities where the spirit of inquiry and instruction were at the forefront. For in medicine, as with all scientific discovery, professional progress flourishes best in an atmosphere of scholarly inquiry.

In reflecting upon the well-nigh unbelievable advances of medicine during this past century, we do not forget the nursing profession and our hospitals, which developed side by side with the medical sciences.

It was not until the War Between the States that, in America, any sizeable number of volunteer women—and I stress the word volunteer—recognized that care could help bring the sick and the injured back to health. The help they gave was in doing only the simple things—keeping the patients clean, feeding them, changing their bandages. Nurses were not then expected nor were they trained to do more. But today the leaders of the nursing profession are college graduates. Many hold Masters', others Doctors' Degrees. Within half a century, the nurse has been transformed from a sympathetic attendant to a thoroughgoing professional.

Even as late as 1911, when I joined the military service as a cadet at

West Point, the presence of a trained nurse in any military hospital was a rarity. Trained nurses were on duty in only four military hospitals in the United States.

Moreover, more than a hundred years ago, when your organization was founded, our hospitals were, all too frequently, places that individuals did their best to avoid—for their chances of coming out alive were not encouraging. As for the unfortunates with contagious illnesses, they were merely sent into isolation so that they would not endanger the lives of other citizens.

Today, about 35,000 new hospital beds—all in modern and efficiently equipped hospitals—are being added to our national resources. One out of ten Americans enters a hospital each year, and most of them quickly return to their normal activities.

———

You men and women of the medical sciences bring to all our people healing and disease prevention practices through your cooperation with many organizations—including hospitals and universities, voluntary health organizations, industry and Government.

This all thoughtful Americans applaud. For the real measure of our strength—our Nation's strength—lies in the diversity, extensiveness, and interdependence of the American system.

The advances achieved by the medical profession are an inevitable reflection of American life. A rising living standard has contributed materially. Every day we have better food, better sanitation, higher standards of housing, better water supply systems, and vastly extended education. Each of these factors underscores the intimate link between a productive and expanding economy, and high standards of medical and health care.

We see, then, that our economy, like our bodies, must be vigorous.

In this sense the relationships between the balanced diet and the balanced budget are easily understood. Neither is an end in itself. There are some useless items of food all of us crave and often eat, no matter how unwisely, just as there are always products and services for which we the Federal Government thoughtlessly spend, often to our own detriment. But in each instance we must conduct ourselves with a wary eye on the consequences. Habitual violation of the requirements of a balanced diet can lead to ruined health; deliberately to unbalance the Federal budget in time of huge indebtedness and rapidly increasing prosperity can bring about an enfeebled economy. The choice, therefore, is ours, and we must act with clear mind and resolution in either case.

In the management of our governmental activity one simple need is for judgment, frugality, and restraint.

The Federal Government can be, with some accuracy, likened to a bank which uses the money deposited in the form of taxes by the American people to finance many businesses—some necessary, some not so necessary. In these Federal operations are involved, in one way or another, all the banks' depositors—every man, woman, and child in this room, and in the United States.

If a bank—in this case the Government—should persistently use its funds foolishly, or too lavishly, because of a yielding by its directors to the demands of specially favored or powerful groups of depositors, the result would be exactly the same as in the case of a commercial bank following the same reckless course. The bank would finally go bankrupt, the businesses financed by it would be destroyed and the depositors would be impoverished. Now, of course one advantage enjoyed by the Government over a commercial bank is that, when the Federal Government spends its money foolishly it can, by law, call upon its depositors—all the people—for more and more funds in the form of taxes. Worse, the Government can inflate your money. Finally, all prices would go out of sight and everybody would go broke.

We must live within our means if we, as a people, are to prosper. Unless both responsible officials—and by this I mean the Congress and the Executive—and all our citizens begin to insist that we make significant annual payments against our burdensome national debt, we will weaken the credit of the Nation.

The medical profession, as much as any other, has a vital interest in preventing inflation. Certainly it wants to provide its services for a fee within the range of what people can reasonably pay.

If the time ever comes when large numbers of our citizens turn primarily to the Government for assistance in what ought to remain a private arrangement between doctor and patient, then we shall all have suffered a tremendous loss.

For, my friends, the cost of inflation is not paid in dollars alone, but stagnated progress, lost opportunities, and eventually, if unchecked, in lost freedoms for doctor and patient, and all the rest of us.

For those who will take the trouble to look, there is no difficulty in seeing a connection between fiscal responsibility and a successful, meaningful life for all in a climate of freedom. I am confident that you doctors, as community leaders in great urban centers and in the villages and farm areas of America, can do much to promote greater understanding of the importance of this vital relationship.

So I believe that, as you show us how better to preserve our own health, you can do a great service to yourselves, and to the Nation, as you teach that the future of the Republic and the free world depends upon our ability to maintain fiscal soundness in Government, a robust economy, and a stable dollar.

Impressed as we are by progress in the medical sciences, including miracle drugs, miracle operations, and breakthroughs in eliminating heretofore incurable diseases, we sometimes forget that this progress deposits new problems on our doorstep.

Familiar conditions, even perspectives, have a disturbing habit of changing profoundly over a short period of time. For example, some of you may recall a remark made by your distinguished fellow professional, Sir William Osler, at the turn of the century. In his farewell address at Johns Hopkins University in 1905, he said:

"My second fixed idea is the uselessness of man above 60 years of age and the incalculable benefit it would be in commercial, political, and in professional life, if, as a matter of course, man stopped work at this age."

By 1905 I was 15. And it is quite likely that I then, and others here of a comparable age, would have agreed with Sir William. But certainly we now repudiate the thought.

Nonetheless the sober fact was that half a century ago, relatively few people reached the age of 60. The average life expectancy for a person born in 1900 was 48. Today it is over 70. In 1910 there were 3 million men and women 65 years of age and over; today there are more than 15 million.

This shift in the age pattern of our population has been accompanied, of course, by revolutionary changes in our social and economic structure.

We are no longer an agrarian society. Industrial and technological changes have centered our population in cities and large towns, bringing far-reaching alterations in our living habits.

Thus most of our senior citizens of today no longer can enjoy the relative security which their pioneering parents or grandparents provided for themselves individually as farmers or as small independent shopkeepers or professional workers. Our older people largely live, today, on fixed retirement income represented in pensions, insurance policies and savings. To this group, inflation is not merely a threat—it is a robber and a thief. It takes the bread out of their mouths, the clothes off their backs, and it limits their access to the medical care and facilities they need.

So here is a situation that calls for true team effort among the medical profession, industry, Government, and the broad body of our citizenry.

We must work together to make possible for our senior citizens, meaningful activity so that they can become—as they all hope to—independent, useful, and creative members of our society.

I learn that the American Medical Association has embarked upon a program to orient our thinking about the place of elder citizens in modern society and to help them meet their health care needs. I am indeed gratified to know of this program. In health as elsewhere in American life, our summons to greatness calls for a lively partnership of individual effort, with action by voluntary agencies and private enterprise and, where necessary, Government action at appropriate levels.

As civilization expands, of course, there are many other kinds of challenges—to medicine and to society.

In the beginnings, at the time of Homer, activity and good habits meant good health. We read from a Roman author about those times "that with no aids against bad health, health was generally good because of good habits which neither indolence nor luxury had vitiated." It seems like one of the doctors' prescriptions would be hard work and lack of indolence.

So—we are constantly called upon for new assessment of our environment, imagination, and effort to force and prevent, or to recognize and conquer, these changing problems.

And three thousand years later, an American physician, Dr. George Miller Beard, was writing about diseases that today we would call neuroses. He observed—this was in 1830, by the way:

"They all occur under similar conditions, and in similar temperaments. They are all diseases of civilization, and of modern civilization and mainly of the nineteenth century, and of the United States."

455

Today, increasing speed of transportation has forced us to revise immigration practices to protect against certain contagious diseases.

Here at home the rising curve of highway deaths and injuries is another reminder that progress on one front is overlaid by tragedy on another. More than 2,800,000 Americans were killed or injured in 1958 alone. Since the automobile first coughed and crawled onto the road, the ranks of its injured and dead have included more than 60 million of us.

Elsewhere new industries present new health hazards in the form of occupational diseases. Millions are exposed to new health risks brought on by an exploding urbanization bringing with it contamination of the air and pollution of our streams.

In an age of ceaseless challenge our society looks to, and understandably expects from, the medical profession a dynamic response. Accelerated progress must lead to the mastery not only of the newer threats to human health and vigor, but the age-old scourges of cancer, diseases of the heart and mind, and disorders of the central nervous system.

And let us not forget the common cold. Medicine provides one field in which all humankind can unite against a common enemy—disease. And beyond and above this battle, we must still tirelessly work to overcome the most menacing of all our maladies, the social sickness of war and the untold suffering it brings upon us.

Members of the medical profession, peace and enoblement of the human spirit are the common aims of free societies. True to our country, to the cause of freedom and to our God, we shall pursue these aims, without ceasing or tiring. So doing, we shall one day establish a durable world community of peace-loving nations in which suffering born of strife will be known no more. In bringing about this happy result no one can or will do more than the doctors of medicine.

Thank you and goodnight.

NOTE: The President spoke at the Traymore Hotel, Atlantic City, N.J. His opening words "Dr. Orr, Dr. Gundersen" referred to Dr. Louis M. Orr and Dr. Gunnar Gundersen, President-elect and retiring President of the American Medical Association, respectively.

130 ¶ Remarks at the Graduation Exercises of the Foreign Service Institute. *June* 12, 1959

Secretary Dillon, Mr. Hoskins, Members of the Graduating Class, Distinguished Guests, and Friends:

To ask anyone whether or not he would like to say some words, if that person has had any experience in political life and omits such an opportunity or ignores it, is truly, if not miraculous, at least an error.

In the years that Secretary Dulles and I served together, he often spoke about the lack of opportunity among high officers of Government, and indeed of high officers in any profession, for contemplation. He felt so strongly about this that he believed that there should be some reorganization in the very highest echelons of the Executive departments so that there could be more time to think about the job.

As a matter of fact, before I leave this Office, I hope to lay before the Congress a plan that I believe will do something of this kind.

Mr. Dulles spoke about this school in the same terms. In keeping with that idea of contemplation, he once said such a school will give some of our foreign officers the opportunity to contemplate their own profession, to think about it not merely as cramming of more information into your heads or talking about new techniques or even possibly any plans or policies or ideas, but of providing the opportunity, under guidance, to contemplate your profession and all it means to the United States.

I would like to voice my own tremendous interest in this school and my support for the idea that a few of our officers should be taken out from the normal activities of their offices, no matter where they are— as secretaries, counselors, or whatever—and be given this opportunity.

Not only can our Government afford this; my belief is it cannot afford to ignore it. So, if I am guilty of lobbying for an appropriation for this particular activity, I plead guilty with the greatest of enthusiasm.

The program that you are undergoing is of course terrifically important. One of the things that I would like to bring out is this: today we are exploring space, trying to expand our universe—but all the time we are contracting our own world.

We are so tied together now with communications that when a man has a bad temper in Moscow or in Bucharest or any other place in that

457

region, we look at our reports to see whether it's going to have any effect before tomorrow morning.

When I was 3 years old—that was 1893—the first ambassador of the United States was appointed. Today there are 77 ambassadors representing the United States abroad. We have representations in 86 different countries, and I think we have large groups or at least representation in something like 285 separate cities.

With each of these ambassadors the State Department is in daily communication—often in communication to the extent of what should be described as trans-Atlantic essays. But these have to be digested. And the next day there must be some kind of action taken on them very shortly. In other words, this world is not only small but it is extremely complicated, and these messages are necessary. Every kind of factor in human existence comes in—psychological reactions, political reactions. There are economic, military requirements to be met, and to think about.

If people are not going to get the kind of opportunity that this school is giving them, then the inevitable result will be to do them in keeping with the past—either by preconceptions or routine or habit.

We must have men who are capable of thinking—thinking objectively on the problem that is before them—who can give the best information with the best interpretation and the best advice they can provide to the State Department.

I would make one other observation: what we call foreign affairs is no longer foreign affairs. It's a local affair. Whatever happens in Indonesia is important to Indiana. Whatever happens in any corner of the world has some effect on the farmer in Dickinson County, Kansas, or on a worker at a factory.

Now this means that even our news is no longer properly called foreign news. It's local news, because it is so important to us. All this means that everyone who is charged with foreign affairs or anyone that has any direct or indirect responsibility concerning them—indeed, I think, every citizen—should think of the oneness of the world.

We cannot escape each other, certainly not until the day we can emigrate to Mars. We just can't escape each other. We must understand people. We must make it our business to know what they are thinking, and why—and what it means to us.

Because no nation, even one so directed and operated as is the Soviets', can dominate all and be the controlling factor. Of course, a democracy would not even attempt it because it would be completely antithetical to their own conceptions and doctrines.

So while I was complimented that the Acting Secretary of State would think it worthwhile to quote from me, I think that expression "soldiers of peace" is a pretty good one. I go back to it to say this: you are soldiers of peace, but you must be soldiers of peace for all men. As long as any man, any significant sector of our world cannot enjoy the blessings of peace with justice, then indeed there is no peace anywhere.

That is the reason that again I express my feelings about the terrific importance of this kind of operation. I extend to each of the graduates my congratulations on your expanded capacity and opportunities for service, and my best wishes for good luck to each of you.

NOTE: The President spoke at the Foreign Service Institute, Arlington Towers, Arlington, Va. His opening words "Secretary Dillon, Mr. Hoskins" referred to C. Douglas Dillon, Under Secretary of State for Economic Affairs, and Harold B. Hoskins, Director of the Foreign Service Institute.

131   ❡ Remarks at the Opening of the National 4–H Club Center.   *June* 16, 1959

Miss Hollmer, Mr. Secretary, Distinguished Guests and Friends:

It is truly a great privilege for me to come here for these few moments to be with the 4–H'ers and the people who have brought about the development of this Center.

I am here just because I like the 4–H'ers. I have liked them ever since I first met them. I have met them in every kind of hamlet, city, place, and under every possible condition, and never yet found one who seemed to demonstrate any trait or characteristic that I found unpleasant. I like them.

One reason I like them is because they are young. They are America. They are America of tomorrow and next year and the decades to come. And since every true American is dedicated to America's future as well as to the solution of any of its current problems, we must look toward these young people and say here is a representation or the focus of our dedication.

Next, I like 4–H'ers because they are dedicated to excellence. They want to do things better. They do so many things. One I am interested in is that they always bring up fatter steers and nicer looking ones.

459

The next thing I like about them is their example to other young people. They are doing useful things. They are leaders. They lead us to greater dedication to our country, a greater expression of the love for our country that we all feel. They are, by their work, indeed making this country a better one.

There are dozens of other reasons why I like these people. In the rural areas they are agents for bringing to everybody everywhere some new knowledge, new information, and certainly new inspiration. They do the same in the cities.

As long as we have young people of these characteristics, devoted with their hearts and their heads and their hands and their health to doing these things, America cannot be anything but successful.

And so, as I have the honor of cutting the ribbon which is the symbol of the dedication of this building, I pledge to all of 4-H my continued support, admiration, respect—and I say again, affection.

Thank you very much.

NOTE: The President's opening words referred to Anita Hollmer, New York delegate to the National 4-H Conference then meeting in Washington, and Ezra Taft Benson, Secretary of Agriculture.

132 ¶ The President's News Conference of *June* 17, 1959.

THE PRESIDENT. I have no announcements.

Q. Marvin L. Arrowsmith, Associated Press: Mr. President, Senator Morton told us a couple of days ago that you are considering going directly to the people, perhaps make a few speeches, on behalf of your legislative program, mutual security and labor legislation, for example, and I wondered, could you elaborate a bit for us on just what you have in mind and what you think the necessity for such a procedure is?

THE PRESIDENT. Well, there is no specific program or schedule in mind.

What I have said, there are certain features that I have recommended to the Congress that I believe are vitally important for the welfare of the country, and I shall do what I can to inform the country so that we can have a strong public opinion supporting that kind of thing; some of them, as you have mentioned, mutual security, balanced budget, reducing

Federal expenditures, and so on. There was no specific schedule developed at all.

Q. Merriman Smith, United Press International: In view of the recent developments in Geneva, sir, do you feel that the prospects for a summit conference have grown dimmer since we last discussed this with you 2 weeks ago?

THE PRESIDENT. Well, certainly they have grown no brighter, unfortunately. There seems to be, if not an impasse, an unreadiness to discuss things that could be classed as giving us possibilities for fruitful negotiations at the summit, and therefore I'd say the prospects are no brighter at this moment.

Q. Chalmers M. Roberts, Washington Post: Mr. President, assuming that the foreign ministers meeting does recess or break down without the kind of agreement you refer to, do you consider that Vice President Nixon's trip to Moscow next month might offer a new channel of negotiation with the Russians on these problems?

THE PRESIDENT. Well, I hadn't thought of it as that, as a mechanism for reopening negotiations.

I would say this: we would never lose any opportunity that would arise through the contact of any responsible official of any government with his opposite number or with the other government to bring about some advance. I understand, for example, Mr. Kozlov is asking to see me, and I certainly shall make an engagement some way so he can come to see me.

Q. Charles W. Bailey, Minneapolis Star and Tribune: The Senate and House conferees yesterday agreed on a new wheat bill that would raise price supports 5 percent and at the same time cut acreage allotments by 20 percent. Could you give us your comments on this last approach?

THE PRESIDENT. No. I don't think I can comment very much on it this morning because it just came in to my desk, and I have not yet talked to the Secretary of Agriculture on this particular thing.

As you know, we still do not believe in raising price supports in any kind of a formula, because we just believe it's not good for the farming industry or for the country.

Q. Peter Lisagor, Chicago Daily News: Mr. President, back to foreign policy for a moment.

Have you been in direct communication with Mr. Khrushchev in recent days in an effort to end the stalemate on the nuclear test ban talks in Geneva?

THE PRESIDENT. I think I have said several times that my communications with heads of state or heads of government are never made public by me unless there is mutual agreement, or unless someone else has done it. Therefore, I don't advise publicly whether or not I have communicated with any other head of government.

Q. Don Oberdorfer, Knight Newspapers: Mr. President, a congressional committee investigating what some people have called a munitions lobby is looking into the employment of high-ranking, former high-ranking officers by defense contractors. Do you think that improper pressures are exerted when former high-ranking officers take jobs with companies which solicit defense contracts?

THE PRESIDENT. Well really, I don't know anything about it. No one has certainly ever tried to do it to me, and anyway, I don't have anything to do with the contracting business.

I think there is justification for the Congress informing itself as to exactly what connections, not necessarily with former officers of the Government, but with the contracting officers of the present Government. I think it's all right to look into these things because we must be careful. I think anyone that is acting in good faith would have nothing to fear of such an investigation.

Q. Charles H. Mohr, Time Magazine: Mr. President, this is also a question about nuclear test cessation. The Berkner report on new seismic techniques for detecting underground blasts contained a section that suggested that there were muffling or decoupling techniques available to the Russians which would allow them to possibly reduce the seismic signal from a 10-kiloton blast to a 1-kiloton sound level. And in view of that, in view of the fact that we have already offered to inspect only 20 percent of events below 5 kilotons, do you still think it will be safe to conclude and sign a cessation agreement with the Russians without danger of cheating or evasion?

THE PRESIDENT. You've asked a question that has about as many technicalities in it as I can imagine.

Now, this decoupling is, as you know, the possibility of setting an explosion off, the full effect of which is not communicated to instruments that are related around the whole country.

Now, what we have done, we have filed these reports and I believe that there is a fixed date when they will come out for the public.

Isn't that so? [*Confers with Mr. Hagerty*] Yes.

Everybody will have a chance to take a look at them and the conclusions of the panel.[1]

Coupling with those reports is the production of a new technique that makes the possibility of detecting now very much better than it was when we made the first settlement at Geneva.

Now, this means that the very time when you have found out that some of the possibilities of concealment have grown up, the possibilities of detection have gone up at about an equal rate, apparently, so that you have a tremendously difficult technical problem to solve if you're going to get equality in this business.

But I do say this: we would be foolish if we expect 100 percent from any system. There is no system, whether it be defensive or detection or intelligence or planning or anything else, that is 100 percent perfect. What we do have to do is to refine the process to the point where we minimize risks and indeed bring them down below the level where they could be truly dangerous to our country.

Q. Robert J. Donovan, New York Herald Tribune: Mr. President, in thinking about your heavy responsibilities with nuclear warfare, I have often wondered, have you ever seen a hydrogen bomb?

THE PRESIDENT. They won't allow me. I have seen the bomb, yes, I mean they won't let me see the test, they want me not to go.

Q. Mr. Donovan: You have actually seen the hydrogen bomb?

THE PRESIDENT. I have seen the bomb, I haven't seen the test.

Q. Mr. Donovan: An atom bomb, too?

---

[1] These documents were submitted by the United States Government on June 12 in Geneva to the Conference on Discontinuance of Nuclear Weapons Tests. They were released in summary form by the State Department on that date; the full report, entitled "The Need for Fundamental Research in Seismology" was published by the Department of State in July.

The report was prepared by the Panel on Seismic Improvement, under the chairmanship of Dr. Lloyd V. Berkner, which had been appointed December 28, 1958, by the Special Assistant to the President for Science and Technology, at the request of the Department of State. The Panel reviewed the feasibility of improving the system, recommended by the 1958 Geneva Conference of Experts, to detect and fully identify underground nuclear explosions.

THE PRESIDENT. Oh, yes. Oh, I have seen the bomb, I have seen all the weapons, I just haven't been allowed to go to the tests.

Q. Mr. Donovan: You couldn't give us any details on your visits——

THE PRESIDENT. No.

Q. Felix Belair, New York Times: Mr. President, with respect to a meeting at the summit, you made it quite clear in our last meeting, I think, that no head of a self-respecting government could go into a negotiation with other heads of government under any kind of ultimatum such as the Soviets have imposed on Berlin.

I wondered, does the Soviet failure to withdraw that ultimatum mean to you that you could not go into a summit negotiation on other questions such as disarmament, nuclear test suspension, or any others?

THE PRESIDENT. Mr. Belair, I don't recall that I put my conclusion and my statement of a couple of weeks ago on the basis just of Berlin. I said that if a foreign ministers meeting made such progress as to give to any reasonable person the belief that that progress would make a summit meeting fruitful, then I would be glad to go; because certainly I am not going to indulge just prejudice or preconceived notions or anything else to such an extent that it will stand in the way of some kind of tiny step toward easing tensions in the world.

So, if I did tie that directly to the Berlin bit, I did it only as an example. If there is any kind of reasonable progress that justifies a summit meeting, why of course I would never decline the opportunity.

Q. Edward P. Morgan, American Broadcasting Company: Mr. President, your political opponents have accused you on a number of occasions of lack of leadership. But now the shoe is on the other foot.

The Democratic Advisory Council, by implication anyway, is criticizing its own leadership in Congress, or the lack of it.

Could you give us the Eisenhower definition of leadership in Government, and could you spell out for us, sir, a little more your concept of the role of the Presidency now?

THE PRESIDENT. I think you have just quoted some things which give the best definition of what leadership is not. And I think I'll content myself with that statement.

Q. John Scali, Associated Press: Mr. President, there appears to be some sentiment in Britain for a summit conference, even if the Geneva foreign ministers meeting winds up without any substantial progress of easing the Berlin and other problems.

What do you think of this idea?

THE PRESIDENT. I sometimes hesitate to speak at too great length here because I have always a feeling I've spoken to you before so often on these things that I'm just putting on an old record.

What I want to point out is that there is developing in the world sort of an idea that heads of government can take themselves away from their normal posts and go and do a lot of things that cannot be otherwise accomplished.

Now, the foreign ministers of free countries are people who go to conferences clothed with a very great deal of authority. The governments involved normally try to establish limits within which their foreign minister can negotiate. He communicates with his own government every single night. There are exchanges of telegrams and cables to keep him informed and to keep the government informed so that from the standpoint of traditional diplomacy the foreign minister provides the mechanism—either he or the government's ambassadors—provide the mechanism through which these agreements are supposed to be obtained.

Now, everybody knows that when you are dealing in a dictatorship, there is only one man, finally, that can make the decision, a firm decision, final decision. Therefore there has grown what I believe to be a false doctrine that we should revamp our entire diplomatic procedures in order to go to a summit meeting every 30 days or so.

Now, from my viewpoint, the dictator can give his foreign minister just as much flexibility in dealing with these troublesome and tough questions as can a democracy. Therefore, I think to assume that foreign ministers have now become useless, they are no good, throw them away, and make every single head of government or head of state to spend his time in work that has been the function of specialists in this line, I think is a step backward in diplomacy. This is like Alexander and Napoleon meeting on a raft in a river and settling the fate of the then world.

You can't do that. To my mind, if these foreign minister meetings cannot prepare the ground and sow some of the seed for accord, then I see no use whatsoever for trying to have a harvest when there is no planting and no tilling.

Q. Garnett D. Horner, Washington Star: Reports this morning are, sir, that the crew of the Navy bomber plane, Navy patrol plane, that was attacked by MIG fighters say that most of the guns on the plane would not work so they could shoot back, because of missing parts.

I wonder if you have anything to say about that angle or if you have new information about who were the attacking planes?

THE PRESIDENT. No, I have no new information. But I will say this: that such a report as this is, well, one that would cause anyone great concern, particularly myself because I have been a military man through my life. I have sent that whole report to the Navy Department, through the Defense Establishment, to get a complete report. I would expect that the Navy at the proper time will make it public.

Q. Raymond P. Brandt, St. Louis Post Dispatch: Mr. President, both the steel management and the steel unions are issuing self-serving statistics which are in great conflict. Is there any way that Government can bring out some impartial figures on profits and wages and productivity so the people can understand the issue and make their own decisions?

THE PRESIDENT. Well, I think you have asked about the most intelligent question on this particular matter; and I haven't thought about it in this particular way, to put these statistics together, you might say in columns right down the line and seeing what the judgment is. I don't know whether this would be helpful or not, but I'll take your suggestion and I'll have it studied. It's one that I just wouldn't want to shoot too rapidly on for the simple reason that they are tough questions, they are people that are bargaining right now, and it's not my business to try to influence them. But I do say, this is a matter that affects the public, and I do have a public duty to do what I can, as long as I don't get into the business of the bargaining itself. Therefore if I can do anything, why you can bet I will.

Q. Pat Munroe, Chicago American: Mr. President, going back to the wheat problem, assuming that there is no way to stop the flood, have you an alternate plan which would involve the destruction of the wheat in order to save tremendous storage costs or perhaps would you advocate a "crash" giveaway program, worldwide?

THE PRESIDENT. Well, no. You can't advocate that, because then you hurt all the other producing countries; Canada, Argentine, Australia, Turkey, everybody that produces wheat now find themselves in a very bad spot, and their market has gone to pot.

I would not advocate destruction. Possibly this is the Pennsylvania Dutch in me that when something has been produced for the use of people, and it's been produced by the sweat and toil of those people, I just find there's something rebels in me against advocating destruction as a cure.   I believe there is a better one than that.

As far as storage is concerned, of course, originally I think it was hoped that all this storage would be done right on the farms.   I will say this: just the carrying of these surpluses and the storage costs are getting to the point that it's itself such a burden that it is one the Government ought to be getting out of as far as it can.

Now, the only plans that we have so far are those that have gone in my messages to the Congress.   By and large, their central feature is, get these support prices down so you get this kind of incentive out, get products to be in the classes that the market itself gives reasonable prices for them.   I think that by and large must be done.

Q. Jerry O'Leary, Washington Star: Mr. President, a Democratic Senator has complained that the executive branch is lobbying to get support for Mr. Strauss.   If that's true, do you see anything wrong with it?

THE PRESIDENT. There are a number of things that I have recommended to the Congress, and when my conscience tells me they are right, I'm going to use every single influence that I can from the executive department to get the Congress to see the light.   If that's lobbying, I'm guilty, but I don't think there's anything else to do about it.

Q. James B. Reston, New York Times: Sir, I wondered if you would talk to us a bit about the apparent misunderstandings that have grown up with France, and the relations of those misunderstandings to the defense of NATO.

And, second, do you have any plans to see General de Gaulle about them?

THE PRESIDENT. Well, I think the only part of your question that I can answer in detail is the second part.

I think all of you know that from the time of his election there has been a standing invitation, more than once repeated, to President de Gaulle to come over here.

In the meantime, I have made plans that if any errand takes me to Europe, I'm going to make a special effort to meet him, because there are differences of opinions between our two governments; and I think he believes and I believe that a personal conversation between the two of us might ease some of the rough points in these arguments and possibly solve them.

He and I are old friends, comrades of the war and since, and I would be hopeful that here would be one place that because of the special character of the problems, so many of them having to do with defense, that maybe two heads of government who both by coincidence have been old comrades-in-arms, we might have some solution that wouldn't otherwise be apparent.

Q. Warren Rogers, Jr., New York Herald Tribune: Mr. President, yesterday Assistant Secretary of State Walter Robertson said that he thought this attack on the Navy patrol plane was deliberately timed at the time of the Geneva foreign ministers conference to create tensions.

Do you agree with that, sir, and have you yet determined who did it?

THE PRESIDENT. Well of course, I always try to get away from motives.

Now, we don't know who did it, don't know who did it. And while you might say it is more than coincidence that such a thing has happened, to supply a motive where you are not sure is just some kind of wisdom that I don't have. So I would say that it does seem a strange coincidence, and I'll let it go at that.

Q. J. F. Ter Horst, Detroit News: Sir, there seems to have been a trend in Congress in the last few days for the Democratic leadership to approach legislation in the view that half a loaf is better than none, in order to get your signature on what they might propose.

Do you think this falls within the definition of constructive legislative work, as far as you are concerned? Does this meet your legislative goals?

THE PRESIDENT. By the Constitution, I am part of the legislative process. I think that the American public expects its President always to exercise his best judgment in giving his approval or disapproval or qualified approval or disapproval in such cases. That's exactly what I do.

Now, whenever any legislative program is put before me, I have to decide whether, in principle, it agrees with the basic beliefs by which I conduct my office, and whether in amount or quantity or quality it comes within the reasonable range of what I am trying to get at. And if it does these things, I think it is a disservice to veto anything merely because it has failed in some detail to go along with the expressed views of the President.

On the other hand, as quickly as it gets out of line I think the President is not doing his duty unless he does express disapproval.

Now, what is happening right now in the Congress, I will know only when the bills of which I speak are laid on my desk and then I know what the program is. I don't think it's profitable to begin to guess what their views are in what they are doing. I'll just have to wait until I get the bills.

Q. Earl H. Voss, Washington Star: Mr. President, you probably noticed in the papers this morning General Creasy's statement about nerve gases.

I am wondering if you can tell us what you think about the possibility of persistence of a balance of terror, even if we were to get a nuclear disarmament such as we are seeking.

THE PRESIDENT. You say we get nuclear disarmament. I think that always we have—that is, the Western World has coupled nuclear disarmament with a degree of general disarmament. Now there are many ways of bacteriological war, nerve, or gas warfare. There are other terrible weapons of mass destruction that are now in the, well just let's say they are capabilities that anybody could use, along with the nuclear terror.

So, I would think that when we talk about nuclear warfare, we shouldn't talk about it alone, we should talk about its results, and what is done with it rather than merely on nuclear warfare. So, I would think that disarmament is a matter that has to be dealt with pretty well across the board.

Q. Spencer Davis, Associated Press: Would you comment, sir, on the action of the International Olympic Committee in expelling Nationalist China from its ranks and refusing to recognize it under the name of Republic of China?

THE PRESIDENT. Well, of course, it's been known by this for years, even after it had to occupy Taiwan as what it considers a temporary abode. I believe there are some 40 or 45 nations now recognize it under that name. Frankly, it seems to me that the Olympic Committee has gotten into politics rather than merely into international athletics.

Q. John Herling, Editors Syndicate: This relates to the steel problem, sir.

There is just about 10 days left before steel companies start banking their furnaces, and without intervening in actual negotiations, as you have declined to do, do you believe, sir, it would be useful if you were to invite union and industry representatives to the White House to establish a kind of a climate of accommodation within which they might hammer out an agreement?

THE PRESIDENT. Well, I will tell you on that one: you have got a historical incident, and I believe the outcome was an attempt to seize the steel plants when exactly that kind of method was adopted.

While I would urge again, personally and directly or indirectly and through press and press media, for each side to recognize the great dangers that come about in inflation and in price rises, I believe for the Government directly to go into this thing further, in trying to apply political or other pressure, then we are getting inevitably into the beginning of a process that could be more hurtful than helpful.

And so, to take a publicized meeting of this kind where everybody would have to be talking to his own constituency, I would doubt that you would get as much advance as you would by keeping insisting that these people in their bargaining must remember the public, the public of the United States, because in the long run, 175 million is so much more important than either side of this steel industry that we should take that as the main target, the advance and welfare of the public, and to put their own selfish or personal desires and ambitions in that context before they make their conclusions.

Marvin L. Arrowsmith, Associated Press: Thank you, Mr. President.

NOTE: President Eisenhower's one hundred and sixty-first news conference was held in the Executive Office Building from 10:32 to 11:03 o'clock on Wednesday morning, June 17, 1959. In attendance: 229.

133 ¶ Remarks at the "Industry Salute to the Federal Housing Administration" Dinner. *June* 18, 1959

Mr. Chairman, Distinguished Guests, My Fellow Americans:

My part in this program is a very simple one—to say Happy Birthday to the Federal Housing Administration and to thank the members of that organization and all of those people of the industries who cooperate with the FHA in producing homes for America.

But in this word of thanks, I would like to be, with your permission, just a little bit more specific. First, because of the degree of enjoyment that I felt in hearing the glee club of VMI, I would like to thank that club by paying to its school, its alma mater, a little tribute. Here is a school which cherishes in its traditions the fact that Stonewall Jackson was one of its instructors.   It is a school—and the only school I think in history—where the entire student body marched to the battlefield and conducted itself gallantly in such a battle.   I am not too sure of my memory, but I think it was the battle of New Market.

It is a school that has given to the United States and to the Armed Services many of its most distinguished members.   Among these distinguished members is one man who in World War II stood out as one of the great soldiers, and later one of the great statesmen in our time: George Catlett Marshall.   He was both a patriot, a distinguished soldier, and the most selfless public servant that I ever met.   Any school that can boast of products like General Marshall and all his associates who were so valuable in the wars and, indeed, in peacetime service to this country, is indeed a distinguished institution, and one that we certainly will nourish as long as there is an America.

Now, I want to make my word of thanks a little bit more specific to you people here tonight.   I was impressed by the financial statement that Dr. Saulnier gave us about the financial record of the FHA.   He said it was remarkable.   I say in a Government like this, it was miraculous.   And, if there is one special word of thanks that I could then extend to the FHA, it is for doing this job in a way that it wasn't the taxpayer who had to carry the bill.

But to you people, who have carried your own enterprises within the field of competitive free enterprise, you have done a great service.   I am told that before the time of the FHA, the typical purchaser of a home put about 40 percent of the purchase price as a down payment, and normally financed his debt with at least a 6½ percent interest.   During the period since the change in those conditions has taken place, we have become truly a nation of home owners.   A home owner owns part of the public street in front of his home, part of the village square and the village park, part of the school.   He is indeed a citizen of the United States, and a man who owns in his own right a part of it.

I believe that we can measure the strength of the United States in the same tempo as we see this percentage of home ownership by its citizens go up and up.   Indeed I think there is no more valuable purchase that any man could make except a home—with one single exception. That exception is, for the man, the purchase of a wedding ring.   That wedding ring is the inspiration for the home and for purchasing it.

So, because of these feelings, I express to each of you, personally, and as far as I am able officially as part of the Government of the United States, appreciation for what you are doing in cooperation with the FHA to make us more and more and more a nation of home owners—happy home owners.

Thank you.

NOTE: The dinner honoring the Federal Housing Administration's 25th anniversary was held at the Sheraton-Park Hotel, Washington, D.C. The President's opening words "Mr. Chairman" referred to Aksel Nielsen, President of the Mortgage Investments Co., Denver, Colo., and chairman of the sponsoring committee, which represented 15 industrial organizations cooperating in the work of FHA. Later in his remarks the President referred to Raymond J. Saulnier, Chairman of the Council of Economic Advisers, who also addressed the group.

134 ¶ Statement by the President on the Rejection of the Nomination of Lewis L. Strauss as Secretary of Commerce. *June* 19, 1959

LAST NIGHT the Senate refused to confirm the nomination as Secretary of Commerce of Lewis Strauss—a man who in war and in peace has served his Nation loyally, honorably and effectively, under four different Presidents.

I am losing a truly valuable associate in the business of government. More than this—if the Nation is to be denied the right to have as public servants in responsible positions men of his proven character, ability and integrity, then indeed it is the American people who are the losers through this sad episode.

135 ¶ Message to Members of All Scientific Expeditions in the Antarctic. *June* 19, 1959

ON BEHALF of the American people, I extend best wishes to the members of all wintering expeditions in the Antarctic on the occasion of midwinter's day 1959. Everyone appreciates the great strain under which you work—the restricted daily routine, environmental hardships, the separation from families and friends and the isolation from familiar scenes. I salute you all in the name of science for the work you are performing and the sacrifices you are undergoing for the benefit of all mankind. You are participants in a unique venture of peaceful cooperation toward the enrichment of human knowledge. May you have a most productive winter season in Antarctica.

DWIGHT D. EISENHOWER

136 ¶ Letter to the President of the Senate and to the Speaker of the House of Representatives Transmitting Report "The Organization and Administration of the Military Assistance Program." *June* 24, 1959

Dear Mr. —————:

I transmit for the consideration of the Congress a report on the Organization and Administration of the Military Assistance Program, submitted to the President on June 3, 1959, by the President's Committee to Study the United States Military Assistance Program.

I am in full agreement with the basic concepts enumerated by the Committee in its letter, and urge that the Congress provide for continuing authorizations for the Military Assistance Program, and hereafter make appropriations for military assistance to the Secretary of Defense under a separate title in the Department of Defense budget. In addition, I believe that legislative action along the lines suggested by the Executive Branch is necessary to clarify the responsibilities of the Departments of State and Defense in the administration of the Military Assistance Program.

The remainder of the principal recommendations in the Committee's letter largely pertain to administrative actions which could be taken within the Executive Branch without additional legislative authorization. These proposals as I interpret them are acceptable to me, and the appropriate executive agencies are now studying them and will make appropriate recommendations for my early consideration and approval with respect to their implementation.

Sincerely,

DWIGHT D. EISENHOWER

NOTE: This is the text of identical letters addressed to the Honorable Richard M. Nixon, President of the Senate, and to the Honorable Sam Rayburn, Speaker of the House of Representatives.

The Committee's letter and report of June 3, 1959, are published in House Document 186 (86th Cong., 1st sess.). This is the Committee's second interim report; see also Items 90, 137, 170, and 183.

The basic concepts in the Committee's letter, to which the President refers, are quoted in Item 137, below.

137   ¶ Letter to William H. Draper, Jr., Regarding the Second Interim Report of the President's Committee To Study the U.S. Military Assistance Program.   *June 24, 1959*

Dear Bill:

I want to thank you and the other members of your Committee for the thoughtful Second Interim Report of the President's Committee to Study the U.S. Military Assistance Program, which was summarized in the letter of June 3, 1959, submitting the report.

Let me say first that I fully concur in your Committee's judgment as to the high importance of assuring that the Military Assistance Program is organized and administered as efficiently and effectively as possible. Your exploration of these aspects of the program has been most useful and timely.

Your Committee in its June 3 letter unanimously recommends acceptance of two basic concepts:

(1) The strengthening of the position of the State Department on the policy level of military assistance planning and an increased assurance of the conformity of the Military Assistance Program to foreign policy and to related assistance programs.

(2) The focusing of responsibility on the Department of Defense for planning, programming and execution of military assistance within the framework of policy guidance laid down in the National Security Council and by the Department of State.

I am fully in agreement with these concepts.

I also consider the principal recommendations outlined in the letter of the Committee for effectuating these basic concepts to be valuable and well reasoned. Two of these recommendations, providing for a continuing authorization of military assistance and appropriating for military assistance as part of the Department of Defense budget, require legislative action. In transmitting copies of your report to the Congress, I am indicating my support of these proposals. I have also approved the substance of a legislative proposal to clarify the respective responsibilities of the Departments of State and Defense in the Military Assistance Program.

The remainder of the principal recommendations contained in your letter of transmittal largely pertain to administrative actions which could be taken within the Executive Branch without additional legislative authorization. These proposals as I interpret them are acceptable to me, and the appropriate executive agencies are now making a detailed study of these proposals and will give to me, for my early consideration, recommendations with respect to their implementation.

I am in complete accord with your conclusion as to the necessity for continuing reappraisal and critical evaluation of our military assistance programs to assure that such programs do not tend to continue simply through their own existing momentum beyond the period of their real need.

May I once again thank you and the members of your Committee for the earnest study of and constructive suggestions about our vital Military Assistance Program. In these troubled times I can think of no more important problem upon which the devoted attention of outstanding citizens is needed. As I have noted many times, our Military Assistance Program is a vital part of our total security effort.

Sincerely,

DWIGHT D. EISENHOWER

NOTE: See note to Item 136.

138 ¶ Statement by the President on the Financing of the Interstate Highway System. *June* 25, 1959

I HAVE consistently requested the Congress to maintain the pay-as-you-go principle which was embodied in the Highway Act of 1956. With this in mind in January I recommended a temporary increase of 1½ cents in the gas tax to provide revenues to meet anticipated deficits beginning in fiscal year 1960.

I am deeply concerned that no action has yet been taken on this proposal. As matters now stand, no apportionment of Interstate funds can be made to the states in July or August of this year for fiscal year 1961, and only a small apportionment next year for fiscal 1962. The only serious alternatives now being considered by the Congress—waiving the Byrd "pay-as-you-go" Amendment or diversion of other taxes—would solve nothing. They would either increase the size of the Highway Fund deficit by further postponing the pay-as-you-go principle, or reduce the general revenues available for other essential programs. Either of these alternatives would be unacceptable to me.

There is attached hereto a report from the several State Highway Commissioners. They have been queried as to the effect of no new apportionments of money in July or August of 1959, which is the present likelihood. As this report indicates, the Federal Highway Administrator has been informed by the several State Highway Departments that 10 states will have to cease issuing any new contracts for the Interstate System this summer, and that 15 additional states plus the District of Columbia will be forced to suspend contract-letting by about the end of this year. An additional eleven states will have run out of Interstate funds for new work by July 1960.

This is a critical situation in our national road-building program, and one which should give great concern to every motorist. We are on the verge of a stalemate in the orderly development of our vital Interstate road network.

NOTE: Telegraphic reports from the State Highway Commissioners and the Federal Highway Administrator's "Report on the Interstate System Program, June 23, 1959," referred to by the President, are published in the Congressional Record of June 25, 1959 (vol. 105, p. 10777).

139   ¶ Veto of Bill Relating to the Wheat Program. *June* 25, 1959

To the Senate:

I am returning herewith, without my approval, S. 1968, a bill "To amend the Agricultural Act of 1949, as amended, the Agricultural Adjustment Act of 1938, as amended, and Public Law 74, Seventy-seventh Congress, as amended."

This bill seeks to enact temporary wheat legislation. It would require wheat producers to reduce their acreage by 25 percent and at the same time would provide for increases in price supports on wheat to 90 percent of parity.

On May 15 when I approved the Joint Resolution for extending the date for announcing the 1960 wheat acreage allotments and marketing quotas I said, "It is my hope that these additional two weeks will be used by the Congress to enact realistic and constructive—not stopgap—wheat legislation."

The proposed legislation embodied in H.R. 7246 [1] is stopgap. It is not realistic. It is not constructive. It goes backward instead of forward. It is not in the interest of the wheat farmers of America.

The bill disregards the facts of modern agriculture. The history of acreage control programs—particularly in the case of wheat—reveals that they just do not control production. Under acreage controls in the 1954–58 period, acreage was reduced by over 25 percent but at the same time yield per acre was increased by about 30 percent. The same situation would be likely to happen in 1960 and 1961. The poorest acres would be retired from production and all the modern technology would be poured onto the remainder.

Hence the bill would probably increase, and in any event would not substantially decrease, the cost of the present excessively expensive wheat program now running at approximately $700 million a year.

In my January 29, 1959, special message on Agriculture, I recommended that price supports be related to a percentage of the average market price during the immediately preceding years. In this message I also stated that if in spite of the tremendous increases in yields per acre the Congress still preferred to relate price support to existing standards then the Secretary should have discretion in establishing support levels in accordance with guidelines now in the law.

Contrary to the recommendations I made, this bill prescribes for a sick patient another dose of what caused his illness. The proposed return to the discredited high, rigid price supports would hasten the complete collapse of the entire wheat program.

While the hour is late I feel that this Congress still has the opportunity to adopt realistic wheat legislation beneficial to all segments of our economy.

DWIGHT D. EISENHOWER

---
[1] House companion bill to S. 1968.

140   ¶ Veto of Tobacco Price Support Bill.
June 25, 1959

To the Senate:

I return herewith without my approval S. 1901, "An Act to amend
Section 101(c) of the Agricultural Act of 1949 and the Act of July 28,
1945, to stabilize and protect the level of support for tobacco." This bill
fails by a wide margin to do what should be done if the best long-term
interest of the Nation's tobacco farmers is to be safeguarded.

The bill's merits are few. For the first time in many years tobacco
prices would be supported at less than 90 per cent of parity—in the first
year, for example, at 88 per cent for flue-cured tobacco and at 87 per cent
for burley. Supporting tobacco prices as provided in S. 1901, rather than
at 90 per cent of parity under a continuation of present law, would result
in a saving to the United States Government in the first year of
$14,000,000.

The bill's demerits, however, are fundamental and far reaching. The
bill takes a long step backward by resurrecting 90 per cent of "old
parity" as one basis for determining the support level for tobacco. The
Congress itself discarded the "old parity" formula years ago. Because the
bill actually can result in the support level being set at 90 per cent of
"old parity," the American tobacco farmer in such circumstances could
very easily be misled into believing he would receive 90 per cent of parity,
as parity is computed for all other commodities.

But more importantly, I cannot approve a bill that holds out hope to
the tobacco farmer that it will help him solve his problems, when such is
not the case. United States growers of many types of tobacco are heavily
dependent upon exports. Yet we have been fast losing our fair share of
foreign markets. The deterioration in our tobacco sales abroad can be
directly attributed to the high level of price supports that are required
by existing law. And while prices have been supported at these high
levels, and would continue to be under this bill, the law has required
severe cuts in tobacco acreage in the United States at a time when
acreage and production abroad have been expanding. The best that can
be said about S. 1901 is that it might slow down the rate at which we
are losing our fair share of foreign markets. It would not prevent further
losses. It certainly will not regain any lost markets, because the level

of price supports it requires would still be too high.

I believe the bill's demerits far outweigh its merits, and accordingly I am returning it without my approval.

The Congress has a pressing responsibility to enact realistic legislation designed to meet the problems of tobacco farmers—legislation such as that recommended in my Special Message of January 29, 1959.

DWIGHT D. EISENHOWER

141 ¶ Remarks at the Formal Opening of the St. Lawrence Seaway. *June 26, 1959*

Your Majesty, Your Royal Highness, Mr. Prime Minister, Mr. Roberts and Mr. Castle, Distinguished Guests, and Citizens of Canada and the United States:

It is a great personal privilege to be a part of the ceremony of the official opening and dedication of the St. Lawrence Seaway. The occasion gives to me the opportunity to express again to Your Majesty the lasting respect, admiration, and affection of the citizens of the United States for you, and for all the people of Canada for whom you reign as their gracious Queen. Moreover, I prize this renewal of my friendly contacts with your eminent Prime Minister who was so warmly hospitable when I visited Ottawa last year.

And because we are in this beautiful part of Canada where French is principally spoken, will you permit me a single halting sentence of my Western Prairie brand in that language:

Je suis très heureux de me retrouver parmi vous au Canada où, il y a un an, j'ai fait un si agréable séjour.

This waterway, linking the oceans of the world with the Great Lakes of the American continent, is the culmination of the dreams of thousands of individuals on both sides of our common Canadian-United States border. It is the latest event in a long history of peaceful parallel progress by our two peoples.

Side by side we have grown up together. Long ago we found solutions for many of the problems characteristic of pioneering peoples. We have built nations out of vast stretches of virgin territory and transformed a wilderness into one of the most productive areas on earth. We are still developing better means of production and communication and supporting measures needed for the welfare of our respective peoples.

A notable spirit of cooperation has been responsible for major steps in our past progress. That spirit animates both countries today. We enjoy between us a larger volume of reciprocal trade than do any other two nations in the world. Our peoples move freely back and forth across a boundary that has known neither gun nor fortress in over a century. Our citizen-soldiers have three times fought together in the cause of freedom and today we are as one in our determination to defend our homelands. We have lived in peace with each other for nearly a century and a half. We cherish this record.

There have been and are still problems to solve between us. But in the past, as now, we have never faltered in our conviction that these problems must be settled by patient and understanding negotiation, never by violence.

So today, our two nations celebrate another triumph in peaceful living. The St. Lawrence Seaway presents to the world a 2300 mile waterway of locks, lakes, and man-made channels. Its completion is a tribute to those far-sighted and persevering people who across the years pushed forward to their goal despite decades of disappointments and setbacks. We pause to salute all those who have shared in this task, from the architects and the planners to the artisans and the workers who have spent countless hours in its construction. Included among those who made possible this great development are statesmen and political leaders of the major parties of both countries, beginning with the administrations of Prime Minister Bennett of Canada and President Herbert Hoover of the United States.

The parade of ships already passing through the Seaway on their way to and from the heart of the continent, strikingly demonstrates the economic value of this new channel. But the Seaway is far more than a technical and commercial triumph. It has more significance than could just the successful construction of even this notable aid to commerce and navigation. It is, above all, a magnificent symbol to the entire world of the achievements possible to democratic nations peacefully working together for the common good.

So may this example be never forgotten by us, and may it never be ignored by others. For in the reasonable resolution of the acute international problems of our time rests the single hope for world prosperity and happiness in peace, with justice for all.

Thank you very much.

NOTE: The President spoke at ceremonies held in an area bordering the approaches to St. Lambert lock near Montreal following Queen Elizabeth's remarks. B. J. Roberts, President of the St. Lawrence Seaway Authority of Canada, and Lewis G. Castle, Administrator of the Saint Lawrence Seaway Development Corporation of the United States, referred to in the President's opening words, participated in the ceremonies.

Queen Elizabeth's remarks follow:

Mr. President:

I am delighted that this occasion which marks the inauguration of a great joint enterprise between our two countries should afford me the first opportunity of welcoming you and Mrs. Eisenhower to Canada. It is with the warmest feelings of friendship that I do so on behalf of the Canadian people, myself and my husband. The President of the United States will always be welcome here, but today there is an added pleasure and a special warmth in our greeting. You will always be remembered as one of the great military leaders who brought the free world through the most severe crisis of modern times. The soldiers, sailors and airmen of the Commonwealth, including many thousands of Canadians, were proud to serve under your leadership until the ultimate victory was won. We welcome you here as a President of a great and friendly neighbouring State; but we have a special welcome for you as General Eisenhower. Today Canada and the United States are celebrating a victory of another kind. This distinguished company has come together from the two great countries that border this waterway to mark the completion of a combined operation that ranks as one of the outstanding engineering accomplishments of modern times. We can say in truth that this occasion deserves a place in history. This is nothing new to the St. Lawrence River which from the times of Cartier and La Salle, of Wolfe and Montcalm, has been the scene of so much of North America's history.

Depuis le jour où les intrépides explorateurs et colons français ont jeté les fondements du Canada sur les rives de ce fleuve, des hommes prévoyants ont rêvé d'une voie navigable en eau profonde depuis le port à marée de Montréal jusqu'à la tête des Grands Lacs. Plusieurs générations de Canadiens tant de langue française que de langue anglaise ont travaillé à la réalisation de ce projet grandiose. Même au 17ième siècle, il y eut déjà des projets visant à contourner les Rapides de Lachine. Ces rapides doivent, incidemment, leur nom à la croyance générale de l'époque qu'ils bloquaient la route vers la Chine. Dollier de Casson, dès mille six cent quatre vingt, avait déjà envisagé la possibilité de surmonter cet obstacle. Sa tentative hardie était cependant vouée à la défaite, car il était bien en avant de son siècle. Il demeure cependant le pionnier de la canalisation du Saint-Laurent et nous nous devons aujourd'hui de lui témoigner notre reconnaissance.

Since the time of Dollier de Casson men have dreamed and worked for two and a half centuries to make this river navigable, and now at last it is a reality. This waterway will carry ocean shipping from tidewater to the very heart of the continent, a distance of more than two thousand miles. It will affect the lives of many generations of our peoples; and it is bound to exercise a profound influence on the maritime trading nations of the world. It is right that we should acknowledge the foresight of those who first conceived this great plan. But we should also acknowledge the courage and persistence of those men in public life, in both countries, who brought about the political agreement essential to putting the project in hand. When their work was done, it rested on the engineers to design these vast and complex works, which finally began to take shape in the hands of the men who drove the trucks, poured the concrete and performed all the other tasks to complete the Seaway. To each and every one of them I offer my congratulations and the congratulations of their fellow citizens. Just ninety-nine years ago my great-grandfather, King Edward VII, then Prince of Wales, came to open the Victoria Bridge. In those days that bridge was regarded as a tremendous feat of engineering. It was obviously a good bridge because nearly one hundred years later it is still in use. In fact I shall sail under it shortly. It was also the final link in a new railway line more than two thousand miles long.

So in 1860 people thought of the Victoria Bridge as a striking symbol of Canadian progress and achievement. Today, within sight of the spot where the Prince of Wales stood in 1860, we are opening a project with exactly the same significance for our own age. In the context of a much larger and stronger Canada this enterprise reflects the same confidence and determination. The same creative vision has conceived and built a highway which will open the middle of this continent to the commerce of the world.

Je vois dans l'achèvement des travaux de la canalisation du Saint-Laurent, une signification qui dépasse les avantages économiques qui en découleront. Cette réalisation ouvre, en premier lieu, un nouveau chapitre de l'histoire de la Confederation en établissant de nouveaux liens entre les deux principaux groupes ethniques dont la présence donne à la

nation canadienne un caractère particulier. Le succès de cette entreprise démontre, en outre, qu'il est possible pour deux états voisins de coopérer dans un esprit de confiance mutuelle à l'édification d'une oeuvre commune. Enfin, cette nouvelle route fluviale facilitera la rencontre de milliers de citoyens du nouveau et l'ancien monde, contribuant ainsi à dissiper les malentendus et à renforcer l'entente et la paix entre les nations.

This vast undertaking has been a co-operative effort of Canada and the United States, of the Power Authority of the State of New York and the Hydro-Electric Power Commission of the Province of Ontario. The two nations built it together and the two nations will share its benefits. Power will flow from the new turbines to drive factories on both sides of the River. Ocean-going ships will go up and down this waterway, taking goods to and from American and Canadian ports, and exchanging the products of North America for those from the rest of the world. More than all this, it is a magnificent monument to the enduring friendship of our two nations and to their partnership in the development of North America. That partnership is most agreeably symbolized, Mr. President, in the fact that you and I have joined together to perform this ceremony today.

142 ¶ Letter to David J. McDonald, President of the United Steelworkers of America.
June 27, 1959

Dear Mr. McDonald:

I have your June twenty-fifth letter suggesting I appoint a board to hear evidence and determine all relevant facts in the negotiations between your Union and the Steel Industry.

As you know, Congress in the Taft-Hartley Act authorized the President, in emergencies affecting the national health or safety, to appoint boards of inquiry for fact finding in labor and management disputes. In limiting this authority to emergencies, Congress, in my opinion, acted wisely, and I do not believe it would be in the national interest for me to follow your suggestion. Congress has also provided for conciliation and mediation through the Federal Mediation and Conciliation Service, and that Service stands ready at any time to assist the parties to reach agreement.

I suggest to both parties to this dispute that they continue to bargain without interruption of production until all of the terms and conditions of a new contract are agreed upon. Acceptance of this suggestion, I am sure, will be in the interest of the steel workers, the steel companies, and the public.

It was reassuring to note the statements in your letter that the "Federal government should not interfere with the actual bargaining process" and that "the final settlement should be and will be made by the parties themselves." I think that you and I are in agreement that free voluntary collective bargaining is an integral part of the American democratic way of life.

With best wishes,

Sincerely,

DWIGHT D. EISENHOWER

NOTE: Mr. McDonald's letter was released with the President's reply.

143 ¶ Statement by the President Upon Signing Bill Amending the Federal Airport Act.
June 29, 1959

I HAVE today approved S. 1, "An Act to amend the Federal Airport Act in order to extend the time for making grants under the provisions of such Act, and for other purposes."

The Administration has strongly recommended that Federal money should be used exclusively for airport development projects which contribute to the increased safety of air travel. S. 1 takes a major step in this direction by prohibiting the commitment of Federal money for parking lots and airport building bars, cocktail lounges, night clubs, theatres, private clubs, garages, hotel rooms, commercial offices or game rooms.

The bill is not as conclusive, however, with respect to those parts of airport buildings intended for any other use. Federal money may be committed for their construction if, in the opinion of the Federal Aviation Administrator, they are essential for the safety, convenience or comfort of persons using airports for public aviation purposes. The dimensions of this latitude accorded the Administrator are supplied by the debate on this bill and by the whole history of this legislation. Thus viewed, the Administrator's discretion is very broad.

It is important that the bill and its legislative history do accord this breadth of discretion to the Administrator. The Administration recommended the expenditure over the next two years of $120 million devoted exclusively to projects designed to increase the safety of air travel. S. 1 authorizes the expenditure over the same period of $126 million, much of which might be required for projects unrelated to safety if the Administrator did not have the discretion that he does.

One other feature of the bill requires prompt corrective action by the Congress. Because Alaska is treated as a territory under the bill, it will be entitled to less than half the funds it should receive as a State.

NOTE: As enacted, S. 1 is Public Law 86–72 (73 Stat. 155).

144   ¶ Statement by the President Upon Making Public the Interim Report of the Cabinet Committee on Price Stability for Economic Growth. *June* 29, 1959

THE INTERIM Report submitted to me by the Cabinet Committee on Price Stability for Economic Growth, of which Vice President Nixon is chairman, contains recommendations for checking inflation that are important to all Americans. I am therefore making the Report public and sending copies of it to all members of the Congress. I urge that the Congress consider anew the Committee's three recommendations, all of which require legislative action. Each of these recommendations has been previously submitted by me to the Congress.

The Committee is continuing its work and will issue statements from time to time to inform the public on questions related to economic growth and price stability. A sound public understanding of the facts bearing on these questions is needed if we are to find constructive answers to them.

NOTE: Plans for the establishment of the Committee were announced in the State of the Union Message (Item 6) and in the Economic Report (see Item 15). On January 31, the White House announced that the Vice President would serve as Chairman, and that members would include the Secretary of the Treasury, the Postmaster General, the Secretaries of Agriculture, Commerce, and Labor, and the Chairman of the Council of Economic Advisers. On March 18 it was announced that W. Allen Wallis, Dean of the University of Chicago Graduate School of Business, would serve as the Committee's Executive Vice Chairman.

The interim report (13 pp., mimeographed) recommended (1) recognition by Congress of reasonable price stability as an explicit goal of Federal economic policy, (2) a balanced budget and a reduction in the debt, and (3) removal of the present limitation on the interest rate on long-term Government bonds. The report stated that, for the purpose of developing positive, long-run recommendations for increasing efficiency, productivity, and maximum economic progress, the Committee was conducting further studies in the following areas: tax reform, U.S. competitive position in foreign markets, Government regulations affecting industry, farm price support programs, labor and business practices, and public understanding of the problem of economic growth and price stability.

As a means of informing the public on these matters the White House released the following Committee statements in mimeographed or pamphlet form: "What Do We Really Want From Our Economy?" (August 17), "The Record of Prices" (September 7), "Managing Our Money, Our Budget, and Our Debt" (October 25).

145 ¶ Citation Accompanying the Distinguished Service Medal Presented to General Maxwell D. Taylor. *June* 30, 1959

[Text read by Brig. Gen. Andrew J. Goodpaster, White House staff Secretary]

The President of the United States of America presents the Distinguished Service Medal (Second Oak Leaf Cluster) to:

GENERAL MAXWELL D. TAYLOR

UNITED STATES ARMY

for exceptionally meritorious service as set forth in the following:

CITATION:

For exceptionally meritorious service and distinguished achievement as Chief of Staff, United States Army, from 30 June 1955 to 30 June 1959. In this position of great responsibility, General Taylor demonstrated outstanding professional competence, selfless devotion to duty, and leadership of a high order. As a member of the Joint Chiefs of Staff, advising the President and the Secretary of Defense on matters of the greatest consequence to the nation's security, he has brought his wide experience and deep insight to bear on the deliberations of that body. He has made a major contribution to the work of the Joint Chiefs of Staff in providing for the strengthening of unified planning and operational direction of the Armed Forces. Within the Army, he has with foresight and determination put into effect far-reaching new concepts of military organization and devoted great effort to the modernization of the Army and to the readiness of Army forces as a powerful and effective component of our military establishment. Dedicated to the advancement of mutual security of the community of free nations, General Taylor has made an outstanding contribution to the high degree of combat readiness of other armies of the Free World. In the performance of his duties, General Taylor has rendered service of the highest value to the nation and has reflected great credit upon himself and our Armed Forces.

DWIGHT D. EISENHOWER

NOTE: The President was presented at the ceremony held in the Conference Room at the White House.

146 ¶ Statement by the President Upon Signing Bill Relating to Veterans' Home, Farm, and Business Loans. *June* 30, 1959

I HAVE today approved H. R. 2256, "An Act to amend chapter 37 of title 38, United States Code, to provide additional funds for direct loans; to remove certain requirements with respect to the rate of interest on guaranteed loans; and for other purposes."

Under present law the Government can guarantee the repayment of a loan made by a private lending institution to a veteran for the purchase of a home only if the rate of interest on such a loan does not exceed 4¾ per cent. Because of this statutory interest rate ceiling, private lending institutions are today finding these guaranteed loans to veterans less and less attractive and are investing their funds elsewhere. So without the increase in the interest rate ceiling to 5¼ per cent, which H.R. 2256 provides, eligible veterans would be virtually unable to obtain the benefits of Veterans Administration loans guaranteed by the Government.

It would have been preferable, as the Administration recommended, to have accorded the Veterans Administration the same flexibility in interest rates as the Federal Housing Administration already has for comparable programs. The Veterans Administrator would then have a wider latitude within which to set the interest rate and, as a result, veterans would have a greater assurance that they would be able to purchase a home under the guaranteed loan program.

H. R. 2256 also authorizes an additional $100 million for direct Federal housing loans to veterans. Loans of this variety are to be made, according to the basic law, only in those areas where private capital is not generally available for the financing of veterans guaranteed home loans. In keeping with this purpose, therefore, the Veterans Administrator will exercise maximum caution in making direct loans until it can be determined whether the increase in the allowable interest rate for guaranteed loans will draw sufficient private capital to that program.

NOTE: As enacted, H.R. 2256 is Public Law 86–73 (73 Stat. 156).

147 ¶ Letter Accepting Resignation of Secretary of Commerce Strauss. *June* 30, 1959

[Released June 30, 1959. Dated June 27, 1959]

Dear Lewis:

Because of the rejection of your nomination by the United States Senate, you have expressed to me a fixed conclusion that it would be in the interests of efficiency in the current operations of the Department of Commerce for you to resign as Secretary, which post you have held since last November under a recess appointment. Your reason for making this decision, in spite of the meager opportunity for winding up the many affairs which have commanded your personal interest and effort, is in keeping with your unfailing practice of placing the public interest above your own.

I have frequently expressed my conviction that the charges leveled against you were totally unjustified. These could have destroyed a less sturdy individual. But I know that in your heart you cannot fail to take with you, as you leave office, a profound satisfaction in the extraordinary services you have rendered to the country and which, over the years, have been acclaimed by eminent leaders in American life. Certainly you will clearly have the admiration, respect and affection of your close associates in government. To them you have typified patriotism, diligence and wisdom, as you have borne the responsibilities devolving upon you in the several posts of trust that you have occupied.

Personally and officially I feel keenly the loss that your resignation imposes upon me, and I assure you that I accept it, as of June 30th or at such later date as you may find more convenient, not only with personal sadness but with the belief that the citizens of the nation will share this feeling with me. I assure you also that there is no one whose character, qualifications and selflessness I respect more highly.

With warm personal regard,

Sincerely,

DWIGHT D. EISENHOWER

NOTE: Mr. Strauss served under a recess appointment as Secretary of Commerce from November 13, 1958, through June 30, 1959. His letter of resignation, dated June 23, was released with the President's reply.

148 ¶ The President's News Conference of *July* 1, 1959.

THE PRESIDENT. We will start the questions.

Q. Merriman Smith, United Press International: We are well aware, sir, of your disinclination to discuss personalities, but we wondered if you would make an exception today; this being the day it is, we wonder if you would give us your formula for 43 years of successful marriage. [*Laughter*]

THE PRESIDENT. No, I haven't any formula. I can just say it's been a very happy experience and speaking from the advantage of my years, I would say this: that a successful marriage I think gets happier as the years go by; that's about all.

Q. William McGaffin, Chicago Daily News: Mr. President, do you see any solution to the quarrel between Congress and the executive branch of the Government over the question of freedom of information?

THE PRESIDENT. Well, I don't know exactly what you are adverting to when you say freedom of information.

This question, from the time of Washington, has been a live one.

When the Executive determines that something will damage the security of the United States or its vital interests, then it withholds information that possibly could be put out. But, I don't know of any specific thing which you are talking about at this moment.

Q. Mr. McGaffin: Mr. President, if I could just spell it out briefly: Congress seems perturbed over various instances where they feel that the executive branch has misused the claim of Executive privilege and denied them information which they feel they should have. For instance, there are evaluation reports made by the ICA on certain countries which have received mutual security, Formosa, Laos, Brazil, Guatemala, a whole string of them, and Congress has raised the point where they are going to try to pass a law which would compel ICA to turn that information over to them.

THE PRESIDENT. Well, there are certain things, particularly in the security field that, if you reveal, are very obviously damaging the United States; and I think anyone of good sense will see that. You simply must take measures to see that those things are not revealed.

For example, suppose you have a method of getting information. Now, that particular information can be obtained only in one way. Therefore you reveal it. Instantly, you can topple an entire system of getting information. So, there are all sorts of things that simply cannot be revealed.

There is nothing new about this. There seems to be a sort of a congenital built-in mutual opposition that I don't know why it occurs, I don't particularly feel it personally, but I know it's there and at times it comes to my attention in one form or another.

But, I am using my own conscience on the matter and when such things as these come to me for decision, I shall continue to do so.

Q. Thomas N. Schroth, Congressional Quarterly: Now that the new fiscal year is upon us, do you have any plans for a special message to the people regarding the fiscal problems?

THE PRESIDENT. Not for the moment, not for the moment; no.

Q. Robert C. Pierpoint, CBS News: Mr. President, in view of some recent statements by British statesmen indicating that they feel that a summit conference may already be justified by the Geneva talks, I wonder if you could reconcile the apparent differences between ourselves and the British?

THE PRESIDENT. Well, you say the differences between ourselves and the British. There are just as many opinions in Britain as there probably are in our country about the wisdom of many of the procedures contemplated in this field of negotiation.

Now, we have always taken the attitude here that there was no use to convene, or to go to a summit meeting, unless there was some ground discovered or prepared by the legitimate diplomatic agencies of governments which give some kind of promise to this summit meeting.

Now, this was the opinion and conviction of the foreign ministers as they came back from Geneva, when they arranged the recess, and I think it still is.

Q. Mrs. May Craig, Portland (Maine) Press Herald: Mr. President, the House Un-American Activities opened a hearing this morning on the type of art that we are sending to the American Exhibit in Moscow. More than half the artists have some record of Communist affiliation—with the movement.

One picture, for instance, depicts an American general in the most unflattering way, and the artist has said that generals of the armies are a continuation of the class struggle.

Would you review our presentation there to make sure that it truly represents Americans to the Russians?

THE PRESIDENT. No. I will say this: this is exactly the way the thing is done. The authorization for this fair, which is a very huge affair, and this furor about the art is really a relatively minor sector, as those of you who have been up to the Russian place—my goodness, the art is down in two fairly small rooms and the exhibition is all over two floors.

Now, in the same way, in our place, the artistic representation is only a minor part of this business. But no one in the Government had a single thing to do with it except Mr. Allen, as the official responsible for this kind of thing, appointed a committee. Now, who he got to advise him on appointing the committee I don't know; but this committee was made of curators of art museums, and I believe one of them was a president, and I believe another one was an artist, and so on.[1] They

---

[1] As announced by the White House on February 24, the committee members, designated by George V. Allen, governmental coordinator of the exhibition, included Franklin C. Watkins, instructor of painting at the Pennsylvania Academy of Fine Arts, Philadelphia, Pa.; Lloyd Goodrich, director of the Whitney Museum of American Art, New York City; Henry Radford Hope, chairman of the Fine Arts Department of Indiana University; and Theodore Roszak, distinguished American sculptor.

did make this rule—now this, I don't know why they told me after the event, because naturally there were details of which I know nothing—the detail is that there would be no art, no piece of art or painting that went over to Moscow except those produced since 1918, since the First World War.

Now this one of which you speak was produced in 1946. It looks like a lampoon more than art, as far as I am concerned. But I am not going, I assure you, I am not going to be the censor myself for the art that has already gone there. Now I think I might have something to say, if we have another exhibition anywhere, to the responsible officials of the methods they get the juries. Possibly there ought to be one or two people that, like most of us here, say we are not too certain exactly what art is but we know what we like. What America likes is after all some of the things that ought to be shown.

Now there are one or two artists, for example I think one of the artists in the classical sense like Andrew Wyeth—there is his picture; it was a woman, I believe, just a bust of a mother. I have had photographs taken of all of these because of this quarrel, or secured them from another source. I have nothing to say about them because I am not an artist, but I am describing to you what happened and why I am not now going to be any censor, or make myself, at this moment.

It seems strange—all of the editorial opinion I have seen on this is defending the committee very strenuously, and so I don't know what's right.

Q. Edward T. Folliard, Washington Post: Mr. President, in January, when you called for a balanced budget, there was a good deal of skepticism. Now, thanks to the business upturn, it looks as if the Treasury will get more revenue than has been expected, and Senator Lyndon Johnson and others, answering Charlie Halleck's crack about budget busters, say that Congress is going to appropriate less money than you have asked for.

In view of these things, Mr. President, do you look for a balanced budget and possibly a surplus in fiscal '60?

THE PRESIDENT. As you know, I am earnestly working for that; and not only the balanced budget that I have said before should be our minimum objective, we should be starting to pay something on our debt. And you can see that the sentiment of Congress is that we should, because they do not make the permanent debt $295 billion, they make it $285 billion and $10 billion temporary, which means you have got to get back by June 30th, back again on the balance. I don't know what's going to happen in that field, but it does show that Congress itself expects us to get in the business of paying off some of these great obligations. And I think we should.

So, my expectation is that we are going to do just that. I will be delighted when Congress can find proper ways to cut any of my particular recommendations, as far as their money is concerned, but I'll say this: merely because they are cut in one place doesn't mean that I haven't got a big concern about any increase anywhere else.

Q. Kenneth M. Scheibel, Gannett Newspapers: Mr. President, speaking of that exhibit and Russia, some people have the idea that you are sending Vice President Nixon over there to build him up as a presidential candidate for 1960 over Governor Rockefeller. Would you comment?

THE PRESIDENT. Well, I suppose there is nothing that you can do in the last 18 months of any President's term that touches on any individual where there won't be some interpretation that he is trying to be political about it.

Mr. Nixon just happens to be the Vice President of the United States, which I think makes him a logical choice for someone to go over in high position and open our exposition.

Actually he has asked my brother to go, and I don't think anyone accuses my brother of having political ambitions, and there are two or three others in the party. Then, I believe, there is another planeload of newspaper people and so on.

But in any event, if they can find any political effect out of such a choice, why, I don't know how they find it.

Q. Ruth S. Montgomery, Hearst Newspapers: Mr. President, why is it that we are able to build submarines that will go under the North Pole and we can build—we can send mice and apes into orbit, but we can't find anybody who can air-condition this room? [*Laughter*]

THE PRESIDENT. Well, you know, I'll tell you frankly, I think you people can make yourselves one pressure group that I'd have great sympathy with. [*Laughter*]

Q. Edward P. Morgan, American Broadcasting Company: Mr. President, last night former Secretary of State Acheson in a speech charged your administration's military spending policies are endangering the security of the country, and he called for an additional $7.5 billion in annual defense expenditures, not necessarily deficit, for 4 or 5 years, boosting ground forces and an immediate crash effort to bridge the missile gap.

Now, you may not want to comment on your policy, on that speech, but would you say how much you think defense is going to be an issue in the 1960 political campaign?

THE PRESIDENT. Well, I think if defense is an issue, it will at least show this: in the last 6½ years, it has been able to keep anybody else from attacking us.

Q. Robert G. Spivack, New York Post: Getting back to Vice President Nixon's visit to Moscow, at the same time that your brother's visit was announced, there were some newspaper stories and some interpretations that sending your brother along was an attempt to minimize or knock down the significance, political significance, of the Vice President's trip, and just now you said that the Vice President had asked your brother to come along.

THE PRESIDENT. That's correct.

Q. Mr. Spivack: I wonder if you can tell us how it all came about.

THE PRESIDENT. Well, because he just asked my brother to go along and they both asked me whether I thought it would be a good idea, and I said sure. Period.

Q. Ray L. Scherer, NBC News: What sort of an impression did you get of Mr. Kozlov and his place in the Russian scheme of things from your visit to New York?

THE PRESIDENT. Well, of course in most of the personal visits with representatives of the Soviet Government, you find that you have had a rather pleasant personal experience. They are outgiving, they apparently like to have fun, they appreciate a joke, they see humor in a number of things and so, by this standard, and I mean in this, you might say in this habit, I found a man that was very friendly; and frankly I enjoyed the visit I had with him.

It was entirely personal, it was not political. He showed me with a great deal of interest and I think justifiable pride the many items they had to show in their exhibition, and I think it will attract the eye and interest of anybody.

I am looking forward to my visit with him this morning, I think it's at 11:15. I don't know what we are going to talk about—it's a meeting without agenda; but whatever we talk about, I am sure it will be a little bit more serious than that one.

Q. J. F. Ter Horst, Detroit News: Sir, this week the Supreme Court ruled out of bounds the Nation's industrial security clearance program on the grounds that neither Congress nor the executive branch had authorized it. I wonder, sir, if you could tell us whether you feel the continuation of this program is vital to the country, and also whether you would prefer to have Congress initiate the authorization or whether you will do so?

THE PRESIDENT. As quickly as that decision was handed down, our people were directed to begin a study of it. It is one of those things, because they made it on these sole grounds that authority had not been delegated. I don't know what further decisions would be made if we did so delegate it or did attempt it. So I think it will have to be studied and then an answer reached.

Q. Frank van der Linden, Nashville Banner: Sir, in view of the Senate's rejection of Admiral Strauss as Secretary of Commerce, after this long ordeal, are you having much trouble finding a successor in his Cabinet post?

THE PRESIDENT. Well, I'll just say this: that anyone having gone through what Mr. Strauss has gone through stands as sort of an example to someone else, and someone else may take a long look.

I have not been one of those people that has found any difficulty in getting people to take positions merely because of financial sacrifice. I have found a great readiness, and I have heard, just, you might say casual comment of the kind you are now discussing, but that's all.

Q. Stewart Hensley, United Press International: A little more on Mr. Kozlov. You said you expect your talk with him in a few minutes to be a little more serious than the New York visit. He said when he arrived here yesterday that he hoped his talks with you and with others here would lead to getting rid of some of what he called the abnormalities in the Russian-American situation.

Do you have any suggestion for him as to how this can be done, or is the ball on his side of the court?

THE PRESIDENT. I suppose that in such a situation, each side rather thinks the other has some new or additional responsibility. We have, as our position, that described by Mr. Herter here a few nights ago after he came back from Geneva, when he said there are only two or three basic principles which mark a minimum position in, you might say, our readiness for negotiation; everything else, we try to be flexible in and we certainly will attempt to promote and develop some ideas that we hope will be fruitful.

But, of course, in this one or two basic things which I have so often repeated, why, of course, we cannot recede.

Q. Sarah McClendon, Manchester (N.H.) Union Leader: Mr. President, sir, I wonder what we are going to do about this arms situation down in Cuba and the Dominican Republic, in view of the fact that we probably have supplied the arms and ammunition that they may be getting ready to shoot at each other, and also in view of the fact that there seems to be ample argument for the claims that there is Communist infiltration in some of these armed forces.

THE PRESIDENT. Well, I think that if America is going to be true to itself and to its pledges, that it must depend primarily upon the Organization of American States to take cognizance of these difficulties; and if they can find any reason for action, that they are the ones that must recommend it.

The United States, as I have so often said, tries to maintain friendly relations with friendly governments. There is no sense of closing our eyes to some of the situations of the current time in Central America and in the Caribbean. But we do look primarily to the Organization of American States to take the initiative, otherwise we again would be called the dollar imperialists or something else of that kind.

Q. John Scali, Associated Press: Soviet Foreign Minister Gromyko a few days ago denied that Russia had any ambitions to annex West Berlin. He professed to see some evidence at Geneva that both sides were getting closer together, and he again reiterated the need for a summit conference. What do you think of these views?

THE PRESIDENT. Well I think he said this before, and until there is something that you can identify as either progress through deeds or a readiness of presenting an agenda which, in itself, would be negotiated by, let's say, heads of state, I don't quite see the reason for his conclusion.

Q. Richard L. Wilson, Cowles Publications: You referred, sir, to the growing interest in the nominations for candidates for President in 1960——

THE PRESIDENT. No, someone else referred to it. [*Laughter*]

Q. Mr. Wilson: I wondered if you considered yourself neutral in this discussion?

THE PRESIDENT. Well I think it would be too much to think that a man's sentiments and ideas were completely neutral. I have said time and again that the Republican Party, in my opinion, has brought forward a group of able, capable men of vigorous years and that any could be selected with honor to himself and to the party.

But, I certainly shall never, so far as I am able, indicate publicly to anyone, or privately, to the details of the procedures well, that will bring about some nominee, because I don't think it is correct or right.

Q. Raymond P. Brandt, St. Louis Post-Dispatch: Do you agree with Vice President Nixon that the main issue in the 1960 campaign will be inflation?

THE PRESIDENT. Well, I didn't know he had said that, but certainly it will be one of them. Of course, I tried to bring it to the Congress in 1958, and I said we simply couldn't go on with irresponsible spending. I gave instance after instance of bills that I thought would have required just unconscionable spending. The decision at the polls was not one, at that moment, to lead me to believe that people were too much concerned by inflation. But I think they have changed their minds.

Q. Mr. Brandt: There has been a written report, a newspaper report, that there is a secret or confidential Government document that prices will increase 3 percent during 1960.

THE PRESIDENT. What's that?

Q. Mr. Brandt: There has been a confidential Government report that the price index will rise 3 percent in 1960. Have you seen such a report?

THE PRESIDENT. No.

Q. Spencer Davis, Associated Press: In this connection, sir, the Senate Foreign Relations Committee has cut down the size of the military assistance which you have requested rather considerably and at the same time increased the amount of economic assistance to other countries, saying that $500 million will be sufficient for the critical areas of Formosa,

Korea, and Viet-Nam and the rest could more or less take care of itself. Would you say what you believe, what you think of this?

THE PRESIDENT. Well, I can say only this: I agree with the idea implicit in their recommendation, which is that the struggle has become far broader than it was in the early days when we thought of the matter merely as the use of force or the threat of force to throw us off balance. They have got into the economic and the cultural and propaganda fields I think very much more strongly than was formerly the case. But with respect to this matter of military assistance, I sent the question very recently again to the Chiefs of Staff and I said, "I want to know whether you, with your combined military opinion, believe that this sum that I put in, $1.6 billion, is sufficient."

I can't remember the exact words in which the reply came back, but the $1.6 billion in their opinion was not only the minimum that we dared to use if we were really concerned about the security of our country, but they implied that since that sum would necessarily have to be augmented by what is left of the once big pipeline, that we would have to do more in 1961.

Marvin L. Arrowsmith, Associated Press: Thank you, Mr. President.

NOTE: President Eisenhower's one hundred and sixty-second news conference was held in the Executive Office Building from 10:02 to 10:29 o'clock on Wednesday morning, July 1, 1959. In attendance: 177.

149 ¶ Letter to the Secretary, Western Association of State Highway Officials, on the Interstate Highway Program. *July* 2, 1959

[Released July 2, 1959. Dated June 30, 1959]

Dear Mr. Sherard:

I was very happy to receive your telegram of June twenty-fifth informing me of the action of the member states of the Western Association of State Highway Officials assembled in annual meeting last week.

As you know, this Administration sponsored the interstate road building program several years ago, and has since supported it on an urgent and pay-as-you-go basis. I am in full agreement with you on the desirability of continuing the program on schedule and without interruption. It was, of course, for this purpose that I proposed a 1½ cent increase in the gas tax in my budget message submitted to the Congress on January 19, 1959.

To date my continuing efforts to receive favorable Congressional consideration of this proposal have been unavailing, and the deadline for the 1961 apportionments draws near. I would hope that the Western Association of State Highway Officials would join me in urging the Congress to support an appropriate proposal to bring new revenues into the Highway Trust Fund. Only in this way can we continue the pay-as-you-go principle which was embodied in the Highway Act of 1956 and keep the interstate program on schedule. I should add, however, that diversion of revenues from the general fund would not be an acceptable answer to this problem.

I am enclosing a copy of a statement which I made on this subject last week which may possibly be of interest to your members.

Sincerely,

DWIGHT D. EISENHOWER

NOTE: The statement referred to by the President in the closing paragraph of this letter to T. D. Sherard appears as Item 138, above.

150 ¶ Letter to Governor Egan Concerning the Presentation to Alaska of the First 49-Star Flag. *July 2, 1959*

Dear Governor Egan:

This morning I presented to Senator Hugh Scott the first 49-star flag. This flag, which was made in Philadelphia at the Quartermaster Depot, U.S. Army, was used in the ceremony at the White House on January 3, 1959, when I signed the proclamation admitting Alaska as a State into the Union. Senator Scott will present this flag to the Mayor of Philadelphia on July fourth for display over Independence Hall on that day. From there I understand it will be carried to you to be flown over your State Capitol, after which it will be deposited in the Alaskan State Museum.

I should like to express my great pleasure at being able to convey through you to the people of Alaska the first flag of new design in forty-seven years.

With sincere best wishes,

> Sincerely,

> DWIGHT D. EISENHOWER

The Honorable William A. Egan
Governor of Alaska
Juneau, Alaska

151　❡ Remarks at the Cornerstone-Laying Ceremony for the Extension of the United States Capitol. *July* 4, 1959

Mr. Speaker, Mr. Stewart, Members of the Commission, Distinguished Guests, and Ladies and Gentlemen:

We are here today for the ceremonial laying of a cornerstone—a ceremony that has twice before marked the history of this building, the Capitol of the United States of America.

By this symbolic gesture we do more than to recognize and provide for the expanding needs of the Congress, resulting from national growth. We rededicate ourselves to the principle of representative government. We reaffirm our devotion to the values upon which this Republic rests.

These values, unequivocally stated in the Declaration of Independence, in our Bill of Rights, and in other parts of that remarkable document, the American Constitution—are both the hallmarks and the hand tools of freedom. In a free society they must be prized and they must be used, lest freedom wither.

In the collision of ideas between freedom and despotism, freedom is neither won nor held in a climate of spiritual stalemate. Its preservation is a many-sided and never-ending task.

Complacency today speeds the erosion of liberty tomorrow. Inertia will destroy it; dynamic dedication assures its lasting vitality.

On this Fourth of July, 183 years since our Nation embarked on its course of independence, we are reminded that our Declaration of Independence did more than galvanize the idea of freedom for our own people.

"The generation that produced our Declaration of Independence," said Lincoln, "meant to set up a standard maxim for free society which should be constantly looked to, constantly proximated, and thereby constantly spreading and deepening its influence and augmenting the happiness and value of life to all people of all colors everywhere."

Now each of these three cornerstone ceremonies has marked stages of America's evolution.

In 1793, when President Washington laid the cornerstone of the original Capitol building, a young but vigorous nation was struggling into political existence.

Fifty-eight years later, when President Fillmore laid the cornerstone of the House and Senate wings, the Nation was no longer in its infancy.

On that day a proud Daniel Webster extolled the progress of the United States since 1793—from 15 States to 31; from 209 Post Offices to 21,000; from 35 colleges to 694—and why it had become necessary to enlarge the Capitol building.

Again this ceremony represents growth. America has come a long way since the laying of the 1851 cornerstone.

Yet it is somehow unnecessary to commemorate this occasion by reminding ourselves of the bare statistics of cultural and material growth.

Rather, we come here today to remind ourselves of our responsibilities—to the world and to ourselves.

We come here to rekindle our faith that this building, the central home of America's representative government, will house wisdom, understanding, and compassion for all people.

Finally, we gather on this Fourth of July—as our forefathers did at Independence Hall—more than 9 score years ago—to emulate them as they pledge their common adherence to basic principles, and their common obligation to uphold these principles regardless of differences of opinion, even of policy.

Today, so long as we never waver in our devotion to the values on which these men began the building of this new nation, no differences of political policy or partisan feeling can cause America to falter on her upward course.

As we now lay this new cornerstone in the United States Capitol, we are grateful for the courageous beginnings of a new nation, represented by the first stone; for the pioneering effort and the bountiful growth represented by the second; and for the confidence that we, if we make ourselves worthy, that this third stone will forever symbolize America's unending purpose, under God, to lead along the path toward peace, with justice for all peoples.

Thank you very much.

NOTE: The President spoke at 12 noon from a stand erected on the plaza at the east front of the Capitol. His opening words referred to Sam Rayburn, Speaker of the House of Representatives, and J. George Stewart, Architect of the Capitol, both of whom were members of the Commission for the Extension of the United States Capitol. The other members were Vice President Nixon, Senator Dirksen, Minority Leader of the Senate, and Representative Halleck, Minority Leader of the House of Representatives.

152 ¶ Message Recorded for Broadcast to Americans Overseas. *July 4,* 1959

My Fellow Americans:

One hundred eighty-three years ago a dramatic event took place in our country—the proclamation of our independence and the establishment of our Nation.

Today I speak to each of you—American citizens abroad—first, to convey the greetings of all of us at home on this special occasion; and second, to acknowledge a keen appreciation of your important role as our representatives to the rest of the world.

Approximately two and a half million of you are outside the United States today, all guests in foreign lands. Whether you are overseas in an official capacity, serving at one of our diplomatic missions or consular posts; or in uniform, helping to secure the common defense of freedom; or studying or teaching at a foreign school; or contributing knowledge to help improve the health or productivity of one of the world's newly developing lands; or working as a correspondent of our free press; or engaged in commerce; or traveling as a visitor to enhance your understanding of our neighbors on earth—you are, in foreign eyes, guests of those nations in which you reside. I trust that your hosts may ever consider you welcome representatives of the United States and of everything we cherish.

On this national holiday, I take this opportunity to talk to you directly about what you represent.

First of all, the significance of July fourth. This date annually commemorates and renews our dedication to the principles of freedom, of government elected by the people, of equal opportunity for all.

These are not static principles. What began in 1776 was a continuing, dynamic experiment. Let us look at the United States today, to see what we have accomplished, since 1776, in carrying out the American experiment. In these 183 years we have developed an industrialized society while maintaining our personal freedoms. Despite the predictions of Karl Marx, our economy has developed swiftly through unprecedented teamwork on the part of those who toil and those who invest and manage. During this development, the working man has obtained an increasingly larger share of the fruits of his labors. We live under the rule of law, which jealously guards our freedom from illegal restraint. It guarantees our freedom of information, our freedom of movement. I do not suggest that all of these achievements exist constantly or uniformly throughout our land. The goals for which America strives are not always easy of attainment.

But we have an abiding determination to reach those goals without sacrifice of principle, and to further the cause of freedom at home and abroad.

We have grown in the realization of interdependence among nations as well as among individuals.

We helped establish and steadfastly support the United Nations in applying the concept of collective security to preserve freedom and integrity.

We felt it our duty to extend help to those who need and desire it. In the forms of economic, scientific, technological, and defense assistance, we try to help other peoples realize their legitimate aspirations.

Our major goal is the achievement of a lasting peace with justice.

This, then, is what you represent abroad. You can be proud of the American experiment, dynamic, vital, constructive, hopeful. I ask you to tell that story. But let the facts speak for themselves. It is traditional with us not to impose ideas on other peoples. And in those countries engaged in social experiments of their own, let them know that we wish them well in their efforts toward the peaceful enhancement of the individual. Give our encouragement to all nations to solve their problems in their own way, in accordance with their own traditions—as we do ourselves. If my message to you on this Fourth of July could be put into one sentence, it would be this:

State the facts of freedom and trust in God, as we have ever done. Thus, we know that truth will triumph.

God bless you all.

NOTE: The message was broadcast over the Government's international radio network (Voice of America); highlights of the message were broadcast in other lan- guages. In addition, tapes of the broadcast were sent to U.S. embassies for use in connection with Fourth of July ceremonies.

153 ¶ Veto of Bill Relating to Housing and Urban Renewal. *July 7, 1959*

To the Senate of the United States:

I am returning herewith, without my approval, S. 57, "An Act to extend and amend laws relating to the provision and improvement of housing and the renewal of urban communities, and for other purposes."

For many months I have been looking forward to approving a sound and constructive housing bill. New homes are now being built at near record rates. I had hoped to receive from the Congress legislation that would further advance the cause of better housing for Americans within the limits of fiscal responsibility.

To my disappointment, the Congress has instead presented me with a bill so excessive in the spending it proposes, and so defective in other respects, that it would do far more damage than good.

First, the bill is extravagant and much of the spending it authorizes is unnecessary. Its spending authorizations total a minimum of $2.2 billion—all of which would be available for commitment without further Congressional or Presidential action. The comparable budget recommendations of the Administration totaled $810 million.

Its authorizations of $900 million for urban renewal—telescoped into two years—are excessive.

Even though we have over 100,000 previously authorized public housing units as yet unbuilt, the bill would authorize 190,000 more.

A new program of direct Federal lending is authorized for housing for elderly persons when needs in this area can be adequately met by private funds invested under the protection of Federal insurance. The college housing loan program would be continued with increased authorizations at interest rates below the cost of money to the Treasury and a new program for college classrooms and related academic facilities at the same subsidy interest rates would be started. Although the amounts initially authorized for the latter program would be relatively small, the eventual demand for these loans would reach staggering proportions. To the extent that these and other programs merely displace private financing they lead to Federal spending that is entirely unnecessary.

Second, the bill is inflationary. The spending authorizations of S. 57, taken together with other seriously objectionable provisions would be inflationary and therefore an obstacle to constructive progress toward better housing for Americans. One of the most damaging effects of inflation is that it dries up the sources of long term credit. There is perhaps no industry in the nation more heavily dependent for its operations on long-term funds borrowed at reasonable rates of interest than the housing industry. We have made good progress in the fight against inflation but we cannot win that fight if we add one spending program to another, without thought of how they are going to be paid for, and invite deficits in times of general prosperity. No one can gain from a fiscal policy of this inflationary type—least of all, the housing industry.

Third, the bill would tend to substitute Federal spending for private investment. Many provisions of the bill, instead of stimulating private investment, would drive private credit from areas where it is urgently needed.

The requirement that the Federal National Mortgage Association buy mortgages at par under its special assistance program, regardless of the price that these mortgages command in the open market, would have this effect.

So also would the provision of the bill limiting the fees that FNMA may charge when purchasing mortgages.

The provisions authorizing college housing and college classroom loans at subsidized interest rates, additional Federal purchases of cooperative housing mortgages and a new program of short-term loans by the Federal Government on the security of mortgages would similarly substitute public for private financing.

Fourth, the bill places needless limitations on the FHA program and contains provisions that would impair FHA's soundness. Instead of removing the wholly unnecessary limit on the amount of the mortgage insurance authority of the Federal Housing Administration, the bill would continue these important programs on an uncertain, hand-to-mouth basis.

Through lower downpayments and longer maturities the bill would introduce underwriting provisions of questionable soundness into a number of FHA's loan insurance programs.

Fifth, the bill contains provisions which are discriminatory and unfair. The way the bill is written a few large cities, by making early application, could tie up all the funds available under the Urban Renewal Program. The Administration would be specifically prohibited from preventing this discrimination against our smaller cities which have not yet entered the program or which do not have large planning staffs.

Under present law cities can count streets and other local improvements, which they had already intended to construct, as a part of their share of the costs of an urban renewal project. S. 57 would extend these credits retroactively to include such improvements made by cities up to five years before commencement of the project. As it is, the local cash contribution has averaged only about 14 per cent of the cost of acquiring and preparing a project site for development. S. 57 would reduce such contributions even further.

In view of these defects, I have withheld my approval from this bill.

There remains, however, a need for the enactment in this session of the Congress of legislation, such as I recommended last January, which will carry forward our important housing programs on a sound basis:

1. The insurance authority of the Federal Housing Administration, which does not involve the lending of Federal funds and does not cost the taxpayer a cent, is nearly exhausted. Additional mortgage insurance authority should be granted by eliminating the ceiling on this authority.

2. The Federal Housing Administration program for insurance of property improvement loans, which expires September 30, 1959, should be extended at least through this fiscal year.

3. The Federal Housing Administration program for insurance of Capehart military housing loans expired on June 30, 1959, and should be extended for 1 year.

4. The Voluntary Home Mortgage Credit Program, which expires July 31, 1959, should also be continued.

5. Authorizations for urban renewal grants should be replenished, the

local share of the costs should be increased, and the college housing program proposed in the Budget Message should be enacted.

6. The statutory interest rate ceilings governing mortgages insured under the Federal Housing Administration's regular rental housing and cooperative housing programs should be raised.

Legislation along these lines will help make private housing funds available for investment in housing and related construction, will promote the effective use of the resources and energies of State and local governments in housing and urban renewal activities, and will allow the Federal Government to play its part in a truly constructive and non-inflationary manner. This is the way to provide more and better housing for the American people.

DWIGHT D. EISENHOWER

NOTE: See also Item 208 and note.

154 ¶ The President's News Conference of July 8, 1959.

THE PRESIDENT. Good morning. I have no announcements of my own.

Q. Marvin L. Arrowsmith, Associated Press: Mr. President, the situation in the steel wage talks remains stalemated as you know, with the new strike deadline just a few days off. Do you plan any new move, anything to try to avert such a strike?

THE PRESIDENT. No, other than to continue to urge both sides to continue negotiations to find a reasonable answer. This suggestion was made in my letter that I sent to both sides some days back.

There is one misapprehension I think I should clear up. Someone reported to me that they thought I had personally requested a continuation of work for 2 weeks. I took no such action. I simply asked that they continue to negotiate until a solution was reached.

Q. Merriman Smith, United Press International: Mr. President, there is a story from Moscow this morning that Premier Khrushchev told the American Governors who visited with him yesterday two things: that he is available for travel—[*laughter*]—and that he would like very much to visit the United States.

But, a new and somewhat significant point is that he thinks, he told them that he thinks a visit by you to Russia would be very beneficial to relations between both countries.

I wonder what your feelings on this same subject are?

THE PRESIDENT. Well, I certainly have not reached any conclusion about the suggestion you just bring to my attention because this is the first time I have heard of it.

There are very many questions, very serious, in such a meeting because, after all, the United States is a member of a group of nations that try to work together in defending their own interests for promoting peace and their own security. So, for one head of such a government to make anything that could be called a negotiation or an agreement would rather be difficult, and I would say possibly misunderstood.

Now, if you have a meeting of the kind that takes place between the heads of government when they come here, or I go somewhere else, then you'd say that's more social—it has a social aspect—ceremonial, and that sort of thing, a gesture of good will. But I assume that we are now talking about real tough negotiations; it would have to be studied very thoroughly before you would make any move in that direction.

Q. John Scali, Associated Press: Mr. President, Averell Harriman reports that on June 23, Premier Khrushchev told him, "Your generals talk of maintaining your position in Berlin with force. That is bluff. If you send in tanks, they will burn and make no mistake about it. If you want war, you can have it, but remember, it will be your war. Our rockets will fly automatically."

What do you think of talk such as this?

THE PRESIDENT. Well, I don't think anything about it at all. I don't believe that responsible people should indulge in anything that can be even remotely considered ultimatums or threats. That is not the way to reach peaceful solutions.

Q. Peter Lisagor, Chicago Daily News: Mr. President, Mr. Harriman also reported that he thought it would be a good idea if Mr. Khrushchev were invited to the United States, to rid him of some of his misconceptions. I know we have talked about this before, but what do you think about an invitation to him at this time, inasmuch as Mr. Mikoyan and Kozlov have already come here?

THE PRESIDENT. Here is something that I would never rule out of the realm of possibility. But we have, as I say, very tough questions to settle. We have to concert our positions with our friends and allies. So if this man were to make just a ceremonial visit, I'd say there it would be a matter of his own, let's say, reception that would be important in the country.

Q. Henry Taylor, Scripps-Howard: Sir, in the NATO Council in Paris this morning, the United States has formally told France that we intend to withdraw our fighter bombers from France, due to the absence of nuclear warheads there. Do you have any plans to talk to General de Gaulle about this, and do you think this is an intention which will have to actually take place?

THE PRESIDENT. As I understand it, some of these movements are taking place. And, of course, General de Gaulle and I have agreed long since that at the first opportunity we would talk together about many things that are of interest to both countries. This particular one had not been specified, but we have agreed that all of the matters where we don't see quite eye to eye, why, we should talk over and see if we can do anything about it.

Q. Ray L. Scherer, NBC News: Mr. President, about your veto power, some of your Republican friends are saying that if you should use your veto a good deal, it could perhaps boomerang and result in a kind of negative public image of the Presidency. I wondered if you had considered this fact in your calculations.

THE PRESIDENT. Well, I'm not thinking so much of public images as I am the public good.

I call your attention, again, that I cannot be running for anything; I am finished with political life when my next, I guess it's 18 months, are over.

It seems to me if any man has almost the compulsion to think only of the United States of America and its citizens rather than any political image or political ambition, then I should be, or any President who is in his second term today should be, such an individual.

So the veto is used by me not lightly. I don't enjoy having to say that these things are bad and to explain the reasons why I think they are bad. What I'm trying to do is to get legislation passed that will benefit the United States and keep us solvent at the same time.

Q. Chalmers M. Roberts, Washington Post: Mr. President, the

foreign ministers are going to be back at Geneva again on Monday. I wonder if you could tell us if you see any change in the prospects of agreement on Berlin and thereby the possibilities of a summit, whether you have given Secretary Herter any new instructions this morning?

THE PRESIDENT. I think there has been no change in our attitude from that reported by Mr. Herter shortly after he returned from Geneva from his prior visit.

We continue to say that the firm position we have is that of respecting our responsibilities and making certain that we retain our rights with respect to Berlin. From there on, and with that solid conviction as the unmovable stone in the whole structure, we are ready to talk and discuss anything because we certainly do want to find some way of reaching a solution that will not keep the whole world on edge—for example, as evidenced by the number of questions that are properly brought up on this matter right here in meetings such as this. I concede that under the present conditions they are proper, and they are newsworthy. But we are trying to get to a place where that will be a little less than that. We must do it, in my opinion, if we are going to do a real service for the citizens of the world.

Q. William H. Lawrence, New York Times: Quite apart from the legalisms of the situation, Mr. President, have you any opinion as to whether racial segregation is morally wrong?

THE PRESIDENT. Myself?

Q. Mr. Lawrence: Yes, sir.

THE PRESIDENT. Well, I suppose there are certain phases of a segregation—you are talking about, I suppose, segregation by local laws——

Q. Mr. Lawrence: In public facilities.

THE PRESIDENT. ——in other words, that interfere with the citizens' equality of opportunity in both the economic and the political fields?

Q. Mr. Lawrence: Yes, sir.

THE PRESIDENT. I think to that extent, that is morally wrong, yes.

Q. Laurence H. Burd, Chicago Tribune: Mr. President, you had rather a long talk last week after you saw us, with Mr. Kozlov. Was anything produced out of that talk that would give any new hopes, any new elements raised?

THE PRESIDENT. I saw nothing new. Of course there was a great protestation of friendly intentions; just as I say, on my side, that we want to be friendly, that we recognize that there is a basic friendship between the Russian people and our people. Everybody that comes back and reports this, reports the interest of the Russian people in what we are doing, how we live. They seem to feel that it will be a great service to mankind when the feelings of those people are allowed to be influential, let's say. And I say the same thing.

I would say I think the American people basically like the Russian people, as they know them. So therefore I think there ought to be some way of exploiting that natural almost affinity between the two peoples and see whether we can't get somewhere.

Q. Mrs. May Craig, Portland (Maine) Press Herald: Mr. President, the laws say that only the President can order the release of nuclear bombs. I am told there is no provision for the President to delegate that power.

Do you think in the exigencies of modern war that there should be such an authorization? Do you think that your informal agreement with Mr. Nixon on assuming the Presidency if necessary carries the authorization to use nuclear bombs?

THE PRESIDENT. Well, you sound to me a little bit like a lawyer, Mrs. Craig, because I'm not so sure; I don't see how you could first of all deny any Commander in Chief, as a matter of fact, of exercising the responsibility for some delegation when it needs to be done. That's just his job, that's the way he would run things.

If in an emergency Mr. Nixon would succeed to my responsibilities, I would think that he would take them over *in toto* for whatever period he was there, and that there would be no reason for him not doing so. He would, in fact, be the acting President; and of course, in the case of a fatality, why then he'd be the permanent President.

So I think there would be no question about that at all.

Q. Lloyd M. Schwartz, Fairchild Publications: Mr. President, are you at all apprehensive that a steel strike might upset this recovery tempo which we seem to be enjoying at the moment?

THE PRESIDENT. I don't know exactly what would be the effect. It would depend upon the recovery and its duration.

I do say this: I really believe that it's a pity that we can't all act in accordance with our basic conceptions as to what is good for the country, and therefore not have a strike. I think that in the industrial field a strike is the last action that can ever be taken that is possible to take. We ought to negotiate and keep negotiating until we have gotten somewhere. And I really believe that it can be done if people will just keep before their eyes what the United States needs, rather than just each side.

Q. Lambert Brose, Lutheran Layman: To pursue the subject of visits of officials from Russia to this country a little further, the Mayor of Detroit refused to meet Mr. Kozlov but the business executives of that city, including Henry Ford II, gave him a warm welcome; and similarly, business executives in California did likewise.

Do you see a danger that the peoples of Eastern Europe might think we are sort of glossing over Russia's takeover of both countries and other crimes, and perhaps lose heart and despair of ever regaining their independence?

THE PRESIDENT. I think that's one of the things that you have to consider when you think about such visits back and forth. But, on the other hand, I think that the citizens of the United States are accustomed to paying to the head of any country that comes here, or one of their high officials, the deportment that is expected from civilized people. They show that kind of deportment, and I don't think that they are necessarily showing any approval.

Now, I admit that such things are possible of misinterpretation, and that's one reason I say we must be very careful indeed when we do these things.

Q. Sarah McClendon, Camden (N.J.) Courier Post: Sir, we have here a very strange thing. When you started this session of Congress, you were at somewhat of a disadvantage in your second term, and you had a big Democratic majority in Congress. It looked for awhile as if Congress might wag the White House but now it looks as if you have the power, not only in the veto and in the bills that you are able to get passed to work your will on Congress, it also looks as if you were winning the propaganda war, sort of, between the Democrats and the Republicans.

Would you give us some idea of how, what system you employed to do this? [*Laughter*]

THE PRESIDENT. Well I guess everybody would have their own, but I don't admit for a second all of the allegations you make in your premise—[*laughter*]—to be fact. I am having really a very busy, hard time because I think there are too many people that are not looking at many of these problems in the broadest possible way. When you come down to it, I stick by that; I am trying to do what I believe will be good for the country, and I repeat, as I said this morning, I don't enjoy vetoing bills. I don't believe that there is any validity in such expressions as "government by veto."

I am part of the process of legislation and when I, who am the only official, along with the Vice President, who is voted into office by all the people, I think I have got a special responsibility to all the people. So I try to tell them and explain to them what I am doing. If they approve, that ought to have some effect.

Q. Raymond P. Brandt, St. Louis Post-Dispatch: Mr. President, you say you are still having trouble with your foreign aid bill.

THE PRESIDENT. Yes.

Q. Mr. Brandt: One reason, the Congressmen tell us and we as newspapers know, we cannot get the facts about the foreign aid program: the foreign aid program cites what they call the Dworshak amendment which says there shall be no propaganda about the foreign aid.

Have you discussed with Director Riddleberger about changing that amendment so that the people and the Congressmen can learn something about the foreign aid program?

THE PRESIDENT. I knew that none of their appropriations could be used for propaganda purposes, or what we would prefer calling educational purposes, but I did not know that this barred newspaper people in visiting these offices from getting facts, and I will look into it. Certainly, when I go on the television, and I have done it several times on this mutual security business, I tell the facts right down the line as far as my time will allow me to do so. And I think it should be done. Pardon me, just let me take a minute of time, now.

I think the number one problem for the United States, and even for the world today, is this: for all Americans to understand the basic issues confronting us. Public opinion is the only motivating force there is in a republic or in a democracy, and that public opinion must be an informed one if it is going to be effective in solving the problems that face this poor world internationally and in many instances domestically.

Therefore, I think that any trouble we take to keep people informed, as long as we are not damaging in any way the national security, I think we ought to do it, and there ought to be some way.

I didn't know about this particular—well, I suppose I've been told about it, but I didn't think of it at the time, and I'll look into it.

Q. Mr. Brandt: May I say something more on that, sir?

THE PRESIDENT. Yes.

Q. Mr. Brandt: You had a Mr. Hollister in there who did not have a press conference

You had a Mr. Smith in there who did not have a press conference. Hollister, I think, had one.

Now, you have a new man now, Riddleberger, and have you discussed it with him?

THE PRESIDENT. No, I haven't discussed with him this particular point, no, because I really didn't realize that the law was this strict and specific.

Q. Mr. Brandt: We did have very pleasant relations with Paul Hoffman.

THE PRESIDENT. Yes.

Q. Mr. Brandt: But in recent years we have not had access——

THE PRESIDENT. [*Addresses Mr. Hagerty*] You look at it for me.

I'll look it up.

Q. Rutherford M. Poats, United Press International: Mr. President, speaking of the foreign aid bill, the Senate has very heavily reduced the appropriation bill, the authorization for military aid, and has done it in such a way as to allocate a much smaller amount for Asia and the Middle East, particularly. In view of your support of the Draper committee report, in which you have stated that a big cut would be disastrous for those countries along the periphery of the Communist areas, can you give us your views as to what effective action you may take or are thinking of taking to head off this disaster, as you have seen it?

THE PRESIDENT. Well, there are a number of things. Of course I can use every bit of persuasive power that I have to make these people see that they are, to my mind, ignoring some of the basic considerations in the security of this Nation and in the security of our vital interests in other areas. Next, if we haven't enough of the means to carry out the responsibilities we believe to be ours, there is always the possibility for deficiency bills. And if you don't have that, if you can't do it because of the lack of authorization, law, then you could have only one other recourse and that would be a special session.

But in any event, I am never going to give up the basic fight for the

Nation's security and for protecting our vital interests, as I see them. I asked here what I thought was a minimum sum, $1.6 billion. The Draper committee thought we ought to go $400 million more, and I agree that in the '61 budget there has to be more than 1.6.

Now, they are cutting this 1.6, and I just personally believe that they are not taking into account the tremendous responsibilities that the United States has in these areas, if we are going to protect our own interest, and to keep our own expenditures down to the minimum in this whole area of national and free world security.

Q. David Kraslow, Knight Newspapers: Mr. President, do you feel there is any reason why a Catholic should not be elected President of the United States?

And, secondly sir, do you feel that a Catholic could be elected President?

THE PRESIDENT. Well, the first one is simple. Of course there is no reason. As far as I am concerned, it's a perfectly extraneous question. I think it's like asking a man whether he is a Methodist or a Presbyterian or something of that kind. I do not agree at all with the theory that prejudice, religious prejudice, should rule our choice of candidates and officials in this Nation.

Now whether he could be elected, whether it could be done, I have no opinion whatsoever.

Now, there was only once, of course, Al Smith was nominated, and he was defeated. I don't know whether the thinking of the country has changed, but I'll say this: if I saw any man that I thought was really a qualified responsible individual running for office, my vote would never be changed on the basis of his religion.

Q. Spencer Davis, Associated Press: Mr. President, have you received reports that Communist China now has rockets capable of the destruction of the 7th Fleet and of attacking Formosa and——

THE PRESIDENT. You are referring to the statements made by Mr. Khrushchev?

Q. Mr. Davis: Yes, sir.

THE PRESIDENT. Well, that's the only written word on this that I have seen, reading the accounts of his own statements.

Q. Edward P. Morgan, American Broadcasting Company: Khrushchev also told those Governors yesterday that the Soviets envied and admired American bigness, riches, and strength. This does not seem to be altogether a wistful observation. We are told repeatedly of the long-term planning that the Russians have and that one of the main objectives of these long-term plans is to overcome us.

This Government, on the other hand, seems unable for a variety of reasons, to plan its programs more than from year to year in sort of pieces.

Are you concerned about this, sir? Is it possible that if the Russians are overtaking us, that they are doing so partly because they are out-planning us?

THE PRESIDENT. One of the reasons, Mr. Morgan, that I have made such strenuous efforts to get properly organized and supported what I call the National Goals Commission—for the simple reason that I think we are doing too much of our thinking, indeed of our operations in political Washington on the basis of just "one time," of the one trip of the earth around the sun, and this to my mind makes no sense whatsoever.

We have got to look ahead and we ought to see today, when we pass a law, what's going to be its effect 5 years from now. A bill, for example, that cost you $15 million now, as you look and begin to analyze it, well, in 5 years it will be $75 million, and that kind of thing. In the same way, everything we do of a constructive character, where is it going to lead us, what's it doing? We've got to do the same thing whether it's trying to increase our GNP, of course which is going up now, but I mean if we're going to have a steady growth instead of a sort of a cyclic thing that is all dips and ups. We don't want that, we want a steady growth. And I am for it.

Q. Mr. Morgan: Mr. President, what has happened to your plan for the Committee on National Goals?

THE PRESIDENT. Well, there is a great deal of work in getting it all organized and financed, because I am determined it will not be done by the Government. It's going to be done privately.

Q. Roscoe Drummond, New York Herald Tribune: Mr. President, in light of the tenor of the questions here this morning on West Berlin, and in light of Mr. Khrushchev's provocative remarks to Governor Harriman, do you feel that the American people are adequately alerted to the consequences that might flow from failure to get an agreed solution on this problem?

THE PRESIDENT. I think they are, Mr. Drummond. It seems to me we have been talking about both the near- and far-term consequences of failure to get some kind of an agreement. We are constantly plagued with this, that we are putting more of our substance, more of our sweat, our toil, and our man-hours into these negative things we call armaments for no reason whatsoever, no constructive thing. They're just to hold on what we have. We are, even our minds are atmosphered in the thought of destruction. We think in terms of atomic bombs and missiles. The world is suffering a terrible loss, I think spiritually and materially, in every way, in this failure. But I'm quite sure that the people are alerted to what could be the eventual consequences of this failure, and that's the reason we must never stop trying, and that's the reason I say I am personally ready to go any place where I think any good can be done, and at any time.

So, if they are not alert to it, then I don't know where they are, because I do meet a good many types of people from the soldiers and the people that are working around me, and I know that their understanding is quite clear that this is a tough situation all the time.

Marvin L. Arrowsmith, Associated Press: Thank you, Mr. President.

NOTE: President Eisenhower's one hundred and sixty-third news conference was held in the Executive Office Building from 10:30 to 11:00 o'clock on Wednesday morning, July 8, 1959. In attendance: 191.

155 ¶ Veto of Bill for Relief of Harry H. Nakamura. *July* 8, 1959

To the Senate:

I return herewith, without my approval, S. 611, "For the relief of Harry H. Nakamura."

The bill would allow Mr. Nakamura, within a one-year period, to file a claim under a 1948 law entitled "An Act to Authorize the Attorney General to Adjudicate Certain Claims Resulting from the Evacuation of Certain Persons of Japanese Ancestry under Military Orders."

It is alleged that Mr. Nakamura lost approximately $113,000 when liquidation of his business was forced by the evacuation in 1942 from California of him and his family.

Although the deadline for filing claims under the 1948 law was January 3, 1950, Mr. Nakamura's claim was not filed in time because of the illness of his attorney.

After the enactment of the 1948 law, a considerable effort was made by the Department of Justice to acquaint potential claimants with the necessity for presenting their claims on time. Despite these efforts, a number of claims were not presented prior to the filing deadline.

The record on this bill furnishes no valid basis for distinguishing Mr. Nakamura from others who similarly failed to file timely claims. The relief proposed by S. 611 would, therefore, be discriminatory and would create an undesirable precedent.

For these reasons, I am constrained to withhold my approval from the bill.

DWIGHT D. EISENHOWER

156 ¶ Memorandum to Federal Agencies on the United Givers Fund Campaign in the National Capital Area. *July* 9, 1959

To the Heads of Executive Departments and Agencies:

This fall, the United Givers Fund of the National Capital Area will conduct its fourth annual campaign among us. This appeal seeks our voluntary support for nearly 150 local and national agencies which provide health and welfare services to the people of Washington and nearby Maryland and Virginia. As citizens of this area, your personnel will be asked to contribute to this Fund.

Among its many participating agencies are the American National Red Cross and its six metropolitan area chapters, the United Service Organizations (USO), the Salvation Army, the Boy and Girl Scouts, and others which meet many varied human needs. These voluntary health, welfare and character building agencies contribute much to the strength of our community.

The Honorable Neil H. McElroy, Secretary of Defense, has accepted the task of serving as Chairman of the Government Unit for the 1959

United Givers Fund Campaign. I know his fellow workers in Government will want to join in making this campaign an outstanding success.

DWIGHT D. EISENHOWER

157 ¶ Letter to the President of the Senate and to the Speaker of the House of Representatives Transmitting Report on Mass Transportation in the Washington Region. *July* 11, 1959

[Released July 11, 1959. Dated July 10, 1959]

Sir:

I herewith transmit for the consideration of the Congress the report of the National Capital Planning Commission and the National Capital Regional Planning Council on the Mass Transportation Survey of the Washington Region.

The report, the end result of several years of intensive study and research by the Planning Commission and Council, aided by experts drawn from public agencies and private concerns, points out the present and future problems of transportation of people and goods in the Region. The report also proposes a plan to meet the transportation problem and makes recommendations for organizing and financing the creation of the proposed transportation system.

The actions which may be taken in the years ahead to meet the problems of transportation will have a profound effect on the economy of the entire area, the welfare of its people, and the status of Washington as the Nation's Capital. Accordingly, I am requesting the various Government agencies to make a detailed study of the Mass Transportation Survey report and the Planning Commission and Council's recommendations. Such recommendations as are warranted will then be made to the Congress.

Sincerely,

DWIGHT D. EISENHOWER

NOTE: This is the text of identical letters addressed to the Honorable Richard M. Nixon, President of the Senate, and to the Honorable Sam Rayburn, Speaker of the House of Representatives. The report "Transportation Plan—National Capital Region" (87 pp.) was published by the Government Printing Office.

158 ¶ Exchange of Messages Between the President and President Diem of Viet-Nam on the Occasion of His Fifth Anniversary as National Leader. *July* 11, 1959

[Released July 11, 1959. Dated July 4, 1959]

Dear Mr. President:

I extend to you my congratulations and sincere good wishes on the occasion of your fifth anniversary as national leader of Viet-Nam.

The world has watched with admiration the progress made by Viet-Nam in the five years since you assumed leadership. It is now a country strong in its determination to preserve its freedom and active in promoting the development of its economy. We in the United States are aware of your own indispensable role in bringing about this remarkable progress. It is a task in which we are proud to have been associated with you.

I wish you, Mr. President, and the people of the Republic of Viet-Nam, continued success in advancing toward your goal of a better life in freedom.

Sincerely,

DWIGHT D. EISENHOWER

NOTE: President Diem's reply of July 9 follows:

The President
The White House
Washington

I greatly appreciate your thoughtful message of congratulations on the fifth anniversary of my accession to office. On this occasion we in Viet-Nam remember with deep gratitude the warm friendship and active support of the United States during the darkest days of our struggle against colonialism and communism and are looking forward to an ever closer friendship and cooperation between our two countries in the years to come. Please accept my heartfelt thanks for your kind message and my most sincere wishes for your personal happiness and wellbeing and for the prosperity and welfare of the great American nation.

NGO DINH DIEM

159 ¶ Memorandum to Federal Agencies on the United Fund and Community Chest Campaigns. *July* 14, 1959

To the Heads of Executive Departments and Agencies:

United Funds and Community Chests will make their annual appeals this fall throughout the country and among Federal civilian and military personnel. Many of these campaigns will include such national agencies as the American National Red Cross, the United Service Organizations (USO), as well as others working to eliminate disease and secure the health of us all. They will be seeking to raise more than $425,000,000.

We, in Government, want to assume our full citizen's share of this great charitable work. The United Fund and Community Chest campaigns provide us with an opportunity for doing this.

The Honorable Neil H. McElroy, Secretary of Defense, will serve as Vice Chairman of the United Community Campaigns for the Federal government throughout the country. I am confident everyone will cooperate gladly with him in these campaigns. It is my hope that employees of your department—in each community where it conducts its operations—will give thoughtfully and generously to these campaigns.

DWIGHT D. EISENHOWER

160 ¶ Statement by the President on the Strike in the Steel Industry. *July* 14, 1959

I AM SURE the Nation shares with me a keen disappointment in the failure of the steel companies and the Steel Workers Union to reach agreement on a new contract.

The fact that the contract expired without agreement having been reached does not in any way relieve the parties of responsibility to continue to bargain without interruption.

The services of the Federal Mediation and Conciliation Service have always been available, and I recommend that the parties immediately call the Director of the Federal Mediation and Conciliation Service for assistance.

I am confident that with good will on both sides of the bargaining table, agreement can be reached without undue delay. The American people have a deep concern in these negotiations and will rightly expect steady progress toward a just and responsible settlement.

NOTE: The strike began at 12:01 a.m. on July 15. On July 13 a statement by the Press Secretary to the President pointed out that there was still time for settlement before the strike deadline, and added that in the interest of the union members, the steel companies, and the public, "the President hopes that the union and the industry will continue to work for a settlement."

161   ¶ The President's News Conference of *July* 15, 1959.

THE PRESIDENT. Please sit down.

Good morning. I have no announcements.

Q. Merriman Smith, United Press International: Mr. President, from what you know of steel stockpiles and the requirements of the Government, could you estimate roughly how long it would be before the steel strike interferes with defense production?

THE PRESIDENT. No. I wouldn't want to make an accurate estimate of the length of such a period. Manifestly, if all our steel that's now in inventories is used up, why, you get into a very serious situation.

Q. William McGaffin, Chicago Daily News: Mr. President, looking back, do you feel that you could have done anything more to avert a steel strike? Would it have been wiser, perhaps, in retrospect, to have appointed a fact-finding board, or to invoke the Taft-Hartley processes?

THE PRESIDENT. No, I don't think so. If I had thought it was better, I would have done something else. I believe that we have got thoroughly to test out and to use the method of free bargaining, and the second that we try to bring the free bargaining, collective bargaining, about by pressure of Government that is too great under the circumstances, then I believe it's not free.

Now, the law says—the Taft-Hartley Act—that under conditions, certain conditions, why, the President can invoke this 80-day cooling-off thing, but those conditions are certainly not here at the moment.

As far as a fact-finding board is concerned, I believe that all the facts are pretty well known. There was a question asked me here a couple of weeks ago whether the Government had anything in this line, and I find that in all our reports, in the Labor statistics and the Commerce and the other figures that are published, some quarterly, some monthly, they are all there. So the facts are there and the public knows them, if they want to take the trouble to read them.

I do believe that I have done what should be done, which is to keep urging on both sides statesmanship and a readiness to negotiate, and I will still continue it. I believe that now they should do so, and I had requested and suggested they ask for the assistance of the Federal Mediation Service, and they have done that and are meeting today under that method.

Q. David P. Sentner, Hearst Newspapers: Mr. President, can you give us your reaction to the testimony yesterday before a Senate subcommittee, of Major Díaz, a former Castro Air Force chief, charging that Premier Castro was a willing tool of international communism?

THE PRESIDENT. Well, of course, he says that; there is no question that's what his testimony said.

Now such things are charged, and they are not always easy to prove. The United States has made no such charges. The United States is watching the whole area. The Caribbean area is in a state of unrest. The OAS has moved in to the extent of asking for a meeting for the foreign ministers to go all through this situation and see what should be done. The United States expects to cooperate with the OAS. That's our stand today.

Q. David Kraslow, Knight Newspapers: Mr. President, could you tell us if General Swing was called to the White House within the past few days to discuss the handling of the Díaz y Lanz case?

THE PRESIDENT. He was there twice in the last few days, but I don't think once that the Lanz case was mentioned, not as I recall.

Q. Lloyd M. Schwartz, Fairchild Publications: Mr. President, a Senate Labor Subcommittee has just reported out a $1.25 minimum wage bill with extended coverage, and Secretary of Labor Mitchell has called this bill inflationary. I wonder whether you share this opinion of the bill?

THE PRESIDENT. I agree with the Secretary absolutely.

Q. Rowland Evans, Jr., New York Herald Tribune: Do you recall, sir, in 1954 your warning about a possible outbreak of partisan conflict if the Democrats won Congress, and you amended that later?

But, I wonder against that backdrop whether you would discuss your relations with the Democratic Congress today, and tell us, sir, whether you are still finding time for an occasional visit with Speaker Rayburn and Senator Johnson, the two leaders in Congress.

THE PRESIDENT. Well, I don't know—you say "finding time."

Whenever there seems to be an occasion I am always ready and have in the past invited them to come see me.

Now, so far as I know, there has been no damage to the personal relations between the three of us, and therefore there is no reason why we shouldn't have personal meetings.

Now, when it comes down to the relations of any President with a Congress controlled by the opposite party, I just say this: it is no bed of roses. [*Laughter*]

Q. Frank van der Linden, Nashville Banner: Sir, for the last 4 years you've asked Congress to pass a bill allowing the Tennessee Valley Authority to issue its own bonds to expand its power facilities.

Now, the two Houses of Congress have finally passed such a bill, but Senator Dirksen has said that if he were President, he would veto it.

I wondered, sir, does that represent your thinking or do you think you would sign that bill?

THE PRESIDENT. No. I never have made any predictions about that kind of thing.

I will say this: the failure to give what I believe a proper restriction on the expansion, and the failure to make provision for the TVA's financing to come through the budgetary process are both serious defects.

Q. Sarah McClendon, San Antonio Light: Sir, there seems to be a sort of a slow move on the part of the National Wool Growers Association and now aided by the American Meat Institute, to get Secretary of Agriculture Benson to take quality grading off of all meat, particularly the lamb that the American people eat.

I wonder if you think this would be wise?

THE PRESIDENT. Well, now, there is one—you know I raise beef— [*laughter*] and I don't know anything about this lamb problem at the moment. I'll look it up. But the wool and the importation of wool, that problem I've gone into very deeply. I didn't know about this, but I'll talk to the Secretary about it.

Q. Raymond P. Brandt, St. Louis Post-Dispatch: Senator Truman had a labor expert on his staff, John Steelman. Who in the White House is watching the steel strike for you, what organization have you got for that?

THE PRESIDENT. Well, you have two people; three people, really. You have got, first of all, the Secretary of Labor who keeps in touch with it and talks with me every day. You have the Chairman of the Economic Advisers, who is deeply immersed in this thing. I've got Mr. Paarlberg, who is my economic adviser within the White House itself, and then, of course, you have Mr. Morgan, who has been in this field with the labor committees and so on of the Congress for a long, long time. So all of those people—as a matter of fact, usually as a group—come to see me.

Q. Richard Harkness, NBC News: Mr. President, going to your discussion of last week with us about your vetoes, do you fear a period of stalemate where there can be no legislation, no advance in the vital fields of welfare, housing, and farm bills, necessary legislation?

THE PRESIDENT. I'll give you just a few statistics on vetoes.

Now, I've been accused of trying to govern by vetoes.

President Cleveland, in 8 years in the White House, had 584 vetoes.

President Roosevelt, in 12 years, and who never had a Congress ruled by the opposition, had 614 vetoes.

There were others that were quite large.

I believe so far my record is 140, and so far as I know, not a single one of them has been on partisan basis. So I'm still hopeful that there will be enough commonsense, meeting together between the Executive and the Legislature, that we will get the necessary bills passed.

Q. John Herling, Editors Syndicate: Mr. President, some time ago I believe you stated that wage increases should reflect productivity increases in the economy and that anything beyond that is apt to be inflationary.

Have any recent developments changed your mind in regard to that principle?

THE PRESIDENT. No. As a matter of fact this is a generalization that I made. I said I believed that wage increases, if they go beyond the increase in individual productivity, then you begin to have something that compels rising costs and, that means, has an inflationary effect. But, I still believe that.

Q. Ray L. Scherer, NBC News: Since Mr. Nixon's visit to Russia is somewhat ceremonial, and since it's been stated he will not negotiate, can you give your hopes for his visit?

THE PRESIDENT. Well, first of all, of course it's a return courtesy. The First Deputy came to this country to visit the Russian exhibition up in New York, and then to make a visit around our country.

Mr. Nixon is going over to open our exhibit, and I am very hopeful that his schedule will be so arranged in cooperation with the Soviets that he gets exactly the same kind of privileges and opportunities that were shown to Mr. Kozlov.

Q. Edward P. Morgan, American Broadcasting Company: Mr. President, I beg your pardon in advance for a long question.

A serious public health situation which in fact has existed for a long time seems to be just coming to general attention. It involves the disposal of radioactive waste from commercial plants.

For example, the Public Health Service confirms that several thousand people living on a river in Colorado are exposed to radioactivity at levels far above those acceptable for human safety, from soil, from crops, from water, and from the air, due to the dumping by a uranium-processing company of waste in the river. Even the fish have disappeared.

Some remedial action seems to be now about to be taken. Has the Atomic Energy Commission explained to you any reason why there has been such a delay on this problem, and do you have any comment on this problem in general?

THE PRESIDENT. Oh, no. Here is the point: the Atomic Energy has a special section that has to deal with all of this matter of radioactive fallout and so on, and I have been briefed on this from time to time. This is one incident of which I have not heard; and the only thing I can say on this one, I will look, I will make inquiries right away.

Q. Clark R. Mollenhoff, Des Moines Register and Tribune: Mr. President, several committees of Congress have charged recently that departments of your administration have used secrecy and so-called executive privilege to hide imprudence, mismanagement, fraud, and in some cases material that has later resulted in indictments. And the Comptroller General, Mr. Campbell, has also said that these departments have violated the law, the Budgeting and Accounting Act, in withholding information from him in violation of this law which says that all material shall be made available.

I wondered if you have taken any steps to correct this, or how you reconcile this withholding with the Budgeting and Accounting Act which says it must be put forth to the Comptroller General, and your own constitutional requirement that you faithfully execute the laws.

THE PRESIDENT. I think you had better put that question in written form and let me take a look at it because you start off, right off the bat with the premise or implication that someone is guilty of fraud and I don't believe it.

I will see your letter, if you would like to submit it.

Q. Robert G. Spivack, New York Post: Mr. President, the other day Democratic National Chairman Paul Butler urged congressional opposition to your proposal for increasing the interest rate ceiling, and in doing that he said this. He said, "The Democrats traditionally favor high wages for workingmen and salaried employees. The Republicans favor high wages for money," which is the way he defines interest.

Do you consider this a valid statement of a basic difference between the major parties?

THE PRESIDENT. I'd say it's ridiculous.

What we are trying to do, to make what a man earns today buy an equal amount of groceries or what else he needs, tomorrow. In other words, we are trying to combat and to stop this constant price rise that we know as inflation, the cheapening of our money and the excessive costs in the production of the things that we have to have. These are the things that we are trying to do.

One of the important parts of this is the handling of the Federal financing. And Federal financing today, I remind you, means the handling of a 280-plus billions of dollars of debt all the time.

When we get to the point that we cannot borrow money for longer than 5 years without the interest limit, we've got an increasing amount of this money that has to be turned over all the time and drying up all of the sources, private sources of investment in this country. We simply have got to get this debt scattered out through the years up, say, to 30 ahead. We cannot do that with this limit, because today, the last time we put out some bills on an auction basis, what will the market pay, we had to pay at that moment 4.7. That, to my mind, is showing what the trend is. We are demanding too much short-term money right now, all the time.

To make such a statement shows—to my mind, at the very least, and the kindest thing I could say—its ignorance.

Q. Charles H. Mohr, Time Magazine: Mr. President, you have said that before leaving office you hope to lay before the Congress a plan to do what you call reorganize the highest echelons of Government, and we realize you probably have not been able to make a final policy determination, but I wonder if you could tell us your tentative thinking on such a reorganization and especially whether you would favor the so-called three Vice Presidents plan that was discussed in 1958, informally, in the administration.

THE PRESIDENT. Well, I'll just tell you this much, one negative feature. I would not favor the use of the term of "Vice President." That has a constitutional, traditional meaning, and I don't think we could use the term "Vice President" in any other way.

I believe this: the Government should have some reorganization. It constantly remains a bit antiquated, and it puts certain burdens upon higher officials of Government that become practically, you might say, not unbearable but unsolvable under the present system.

Now, I've got my plans all set up, but I'm not going to put it before the Congress until the final session when I'm here, because I'm not going to do it with any thought that it is I who will profit, but somebody else that will come after me and will have the benefit of a better organization. That is exactly what I expect to do.

Q. Robert J. Donovan, New York Herald Tribune: Mr. President, have you any comment on the new talks at Geneva—any comment on the resumed talks at Geneva?

THE PRESIDENT. No, they seem to be off to a very slow start. At the first session, when it was suggested that they resume these private talks which seem to be more productive than the plenary talks, Mr. Gromyko insisted that the Germans come into this particular type of meeting. I believe the final agreement was they'd have to go back to plenary sessions, and I believe it's on, I think it's Friday, maybe it's Thursday, the next one. The 15th, wasn't it? [*Confers with Mr. Hagerty*]

I think it is.

But in any event, there doesn't seem to be any bright, hopeful rift in the clouds at the moment, but we are still plugging away.

Q. William H. Lawrence, New York Times: Mr. President, has Secretary Herter discussed with you his hopes to bring Mr. Bohlen back into a high position in the State Department as an adviser on Soviet affairs? Do you have an opinion on it?

THE PRESIDENT. Twice he suggested this to me—I mean, he brought up the subject, because he had seen stories in the paper that this was going to be done. And he said as far as he was concerned, he had done nothing about it and didn't intend to at that moment. So he wasn't even discussing it. So, in other words, his report to me was completely negative.

Q. Mr. Lawrence: At a press conference since then, he has——

THE PRESIDENT. I don't care what he may have said——

Q. Mr. Lawrence: ——he has not discussed——

THE PRESIDENT. He told me and that's the last time I've seen him.

Q. Peter Lisagor, Chicago Daily News: About Geneva again, do you believe that the Russians are seriously trying to reach an agreement at Geneva?

THE PRESIDENT. I didn't understand the question.

Q. Mr. Lisagor: Do you believe that the Russians are seriously trying to reach an agreement at Geneva?

THE PRESIDENT. Well, I think they'd like an agreement which was all in their favor; there's no question about that. Of course they would.

But are they ready—I think a better question, if I could rephrase it for you—are we ready to see concessions made, some of them on both sides, that will ease the situation there and give everybody a confidence that we are making some kind of a step toward peace?

Q. Donald H. Shannon, Los Angeles Times: Yesterday at the Senate Rackets Committee talk with the President of the Teamsters he acknowledged that he is planning a merger of the Teamsters and the Longshoremen, and I wondered how you viewed the prospect of a national transportation union headed by Hoffa and Harry Bridges?

THE PRESIDENT. Well that's one I had better not comment on here. Thank you very much. [*Laughter*]

Q. Henry N. Taylor, Scripps-Howard: Mr. President, in this Geneva tangle at the present time there has been some discussion of the possibility of leaving the Berlin issue unsolved without any further easement on it, if the Soviets won't permit it, to go forward to a summit conference on other issues entirely. I wonder if you could give us your views on that.

THE PRESIDENT. Well, I don't know exactly what you mean. Do you mean that you would go to a summit conference under an ultimatum of time, or under a statement that we were going to be thrown out at a particular time, whether it's 1 year, 2 years, or 3 years? I don't know exactly what you mean.

Q. Mr. Taylor: Well, this presupposes——

THE PRESIDENT. In other words, let me answer it this way: there has to be some clear understanding of our rights and our responsibilities before you can go ahead and negotiate.

Now, I am not adverse, along with my associates or this Government's associates, in negotiating about ultimate fate of Germany, Berlin and all the rest of it, but in the meantime there has got to be clear recognition of our rights and responsibilities.

Q. Frank Bourgholtzer, NBC News: Can you tell us whether you have given Secretary Herter sufficient authority to commit you to a summit conference or can he only advise you for a final decision on your part?

THE PRESIDENT. Secretary Herter and I are completely in agreement with all the rest of the Government as far as I know, almost unanimously with the American people, that we are not going to surrender our rights or to make a retreat that could be clear evidence of weakness on our resolution, and weakness in the West.

Now, if that matter is settled clearly, we have that kind of progress, why then Secretary Herter has the authority to make any kind of a plan, subject of course to final approval as to detail, but he knows that he can go ahead from there and negotiate.

Q. John R. Gibson, Wall Street Journal: Mr. President, on the subject of interest rates for Government bonds, there is considerable discussion these days on the Hill and within the administration on the so-called Metcalf amendment which would say that the Federal Reserve should buy bonds as a manner of increasing the money supply. What is your view of this amendment and would you favor perhaps no bill at all rather than have this amendment tacked on or would you go along with it?

THE PRESIDENT. Well, I wouldn't here announce a final decision. I say this, these two amendments, there are two of them that are very bad we think: one, the 2-year limit; and the other one that implies that we should embark on what we would, and I think the Federal Reserve would call unsound financial operations. And the first thing that I believe that's in the Federal Reserve Act is that it's duty is to see that the finances of the United States are handled on a sound basis.

So, we are concerned deeply about these two amendments. Now I cannot give you any prediction on what I will do.

Q. John Scali, Associated Press: Mr. President, over the weekend Averell Harriman suggested that it might be wise to give some form of diplomatic recognition to East Germany. What do you think of such an idea?

THE PRESIDENT. Well, I don't know how you can give some form of diplomatic recognition as of now. We certainly have no such thought in our heads.

Q. Gordon White, Chicago American: Mr. President, when Mr. Mikoyan was here some time ago you said that you didn't believe it would be possible to have Premier Khrushchev under the same terms formally visiting the United States. But some people now seem to believe that Mr. Khrushchev is a prisoner of his own propaganda and perhaps does not really understand the situation in the United States. Do you feel now that it would be worth while for the Russian Premier to visit the U.S.?

THE PRESIDENT. Well, we discussed that question last week quite thoroughly here, as I recall, and while here is one of those things again that I don't reject out of hand, because I have constantly stated that any time I believe that we can promote the interests of the United States and its standing in the world and the cause of freedom, then I will do anything. And if it ever should come up that I believe this would be a good thing, well, then, I, of course, I'm not going to refuse. But we did discuss last week the pros and cons and we thought the cons, for the moment, sort of had the day.

Q. Milburn Petty, Oil Daily: Mr. President, do you think a compromise is possible on highway financing that would keep the highway program on schedule, and if so, in what areas of compromise would be acceptable to you.

THE PRESIDENT. Well, of course, all legislation, all government, almost, is compromise. Now, I think this: it would be difficult to have the highway program on its current schedule without providing the revenues for which I asked, for the simple reason that it was on this basis we asked the amount—the 1½ cents. Therefore, if there is any compromise, there would have to be a slowup in the schedule, as I see it.

Q. Peter Edson, Newspaper Enterprise Association: Mr. President, the West German Government has apparently suggested, with regard to Geneva talks, that a commission be created to handle the German question similar to the commission that settled the Austrian peace treaty. Does this seem to offer a reasonable approach for ending the Geneva talks or transferring their problem to a body that could make a settlement that is not a summit conference?

THE PRESIDENT. You mean that we'd just—

All they have done, as I recall, the West Germans did suggest we might have a meeting of the four High Commissioners with German advisers from both sides, and then make this their special problem.

Now, these were not four foreign ministers; these were four representatives of special commissions. I believe that that idea was suggested even publicly, and I think that there was a rejection of that idea from the other side.

Marvin L. Arrowsmith, Associated Press: Thank you, Mr. President.

NOTE: President Eisenhower's one hundred and sixty-fourth news conference was held in the Executive Office Building from 10:31 to 11:00 o'clock on Wednesday morning, July 15, 1959. In attendance: 201.

162 ¶ Exchange of Messages Between the President and Frol R. Kozlov, First Deputy Chairman, Council of Ministers, U.S.S.R. *July* 15, 1959

[Released July 15, 1959. Dated July 14, 1959]

Dear Mr. Kozlov:

Thank you for the thoughtful message which you sent to me on your departure from the United States. I hope that you enjoyed your stay in this country and that you have returned to Moscow with a better understanding of our people, our institutions, and our way of life. It is gratifying to know that you have been impressed with the desire of the American people for peace, a desire which represents their strongest mandate to their Government. This ardent desire is also inseparably linked with our firm belief in the rights of peoples everywhere to enjoy peace with justice and freedom.

I share the hope that the increasing contacts between our two countries, which your visit to us and the forthcoming visit of Vice President Nixon to the U.S.S.R. so well symbolize, will lead to a greatly improved mutual understanding between our peoples.

Sincerely,

Dwight D. Eisenhower

NOTE: Mr. Kozlov's message of July 13 follows:

Dear Mr. President:

On leaving the United States I wish to express to you and all Americans who extended to us such a warm welcome, my heartfelt gratitude for the possibilities accorded us to get acquainted with your great country. We are leaving with confidence that the American people want peace just as our Soviet people. We are profoundly convinced that the expanding contacts between our countries, including those concerned with the Exhibition as well as meetings between statesmen of the USSR and the USA promote the improvement of our relations and will undoubtedly have favourable influence on reaching an agreement on international problems, the settlement of which is so eagerly expected by all peoples who so unswervingly stand for the preservation and strengthening of peace throughout the world.

F. Kozlov

163 ¶ Letter to President Meany Acknowledging AFL–CIO Support of the Government's Position on West Berlin. *July* 16, 1959

[Released July 16, 1959. Dated July 15, 1959]

Dear Mr. Meany:

Thank you very much for your letter of yesterday. For a long time I have been keenly aware and appreciative of the firm stand taken by the AFL–CIO in support of the government's refusal to abandon either the free people of West Berlin or our rights and responsibilities respecting that city.

Your present letter should convince everyone, including the Soviets, that in the United States labor is free—and because it is free, it is part of the decision-making process in our country. When free citizens form their conclusions and convictions on matters that affect America's international position, they cannot be divided on the basis of vocation, creed or partisan politics. The efforts of any outsider to divide America are bound to fail when the basic beliefs and the vital interests of this nation are at stake.

I am grateful for your letter because even though I have had no doubt in my own heart or mind of AFL–CIO solidarity in this matter, I salute your entire membership for reaffirming this solidarity before the entire world.

With warm regard,

Sincerely,

DWIGHT D. EISENHOWER

164 ¶ Remarks to the American Field Service Students at the Interdepartmental Auditorium. *July* 16, 1959

THANK YOU very much. A warm welcome to the boys and girls that are visiting our country under the auspices of the American Field Service.

I have been meeting with groups of visitors brought here by the American Field Service since 1948. The first group I met was on the steps of Columbia University where I was then President. I think they numbered something on the order of 30 possibly 35.

Every time that I have been able to meet with you since then, your number has grown. This is the first time, incidentally, wherever I have met them, that we have had to come indoors. You at least have found that there's one thing not perfect about America, and that is the predictions of the weather service, because they told me we were going to have a rainstorm. But I am so hopeful that your number will increase to the extent where no enclosure could possibly hold you, that I personally would be willing—and I hope you would—to endure a little bit of rain while I had the chance to say to you a word of greeting.

There is nothing that I can think of that could more improve this project sponsored by the Field Service than to multiply your numbers. I hear that this year there are more than 1,100 of you. I would hope that I can live until the day I see 11,000 of you.

One reason that I would like to talk to you for a moment is because you are young. I like to think of the years—how much of the future you hold in your hands. As the years stretch out ahead of you, everything is a vital problem. There is an element of promise, a belief, a faith, that things are going to be better, and you are going to help make that true. And in the measure that you help make it true will be your true happiness and your true enjoyment out of the years that you have ahead of you.

Your journey to this country has certainly in many respects been an adventure. You must have wondered, when you were in your homeland, what your welcome would be. Would the people in the family with which you lived truly be interested in you? Would America show to you that courtesy, that hospitality, that we wanted to show but you could not be sure of it? And have you seen anything about our country that will help you, as you try to improve your portion of the world in these years that you have, just as we in America are trying to do the same thing?

I meet your counterparts from America quite often. I meet the young Future Farmers of America, the 4–H boys and girls, and from them I get exactly the same kind of inspiration that I do in meeting with you. Because through youth it seems to me is the best chance we have to make this a better world. You, like all the boys and girls you have met in the United States, want peace. You want a just peace. You want a peace that will give to each of you the right to stand up as a dignified being, as one who is not a creature of someone else's will, but is entitled to expand and develop himself according to the dictates of his own conscience.

These are the things that our young boys and girls want. They are the ones you want. The more you meet together, the more the very factor of that meeting makes this dream come true. As you get to know us, as you carry back understanding of us, our Field Service visitors—800 this year going over to visit your countries—bring back better understanding of you. As a result of these visits reasons for conflict, argument, or at least for attempting to solve problems in any spirit except that of negotiation, and peaceful and friendly attitude, are gone. You can't know each other and be enemies between yourselves.

These are the things that people want, that you want, and will continue to want. The point is: I believe you will be better equipped than the average to help bring about understanding.

One of the greatest ambitions that I have had, both as a soldier and later as a political figure in this country, is to develop more of what I call the people-to-people programs. The Field Service is one of the most successful. But the whole people-to-people movement—whether it is in the areas just of teen-age youngsters, or as young executives, lawmakers, scholars and professors—as that grows and grows, the world itself will be better.

So I congratulate you for the opportunity that is yours, to help make

534

your part of the world—and therefore the whole world—better.

As I give you my confidence that you are going to do this, I say to you Godspeed as you prepare soon to go home.

I hope that each of you, whether you be a whole deputation or a single individual, will carry back with you an expression of America's hope that we will be friends—your country and ours—that we will be bound together by this same appreciation of the high values of personal liberty, freedom, and dignity—and that you bring with you the good wishes of every single American for rising living standards, greater educational opportunities—all of those things that make life worthwhile—just exactly the things that we in this country are seeking.

God bless you all—goodbye.

165 ¶ Statement by the President on the Death of Eugene Meyer. *July* 17, 1959

IN THE passing of Eugene Meyer, the nation and the news profession have lost an outstanding newspaper executive. As publisher and later as Chairman of the Board of the Washington Post and Times-Herald, and before that as a Government official in a number of major posts, Mr. Meyer was known as a distinguished citizen.

Mrs. Eisenhower and I extend our deep sympathies to Mrs. Meyer and her family in the personal loss they have sustained.

166 ¶ Statement by the President on the Death of Admiral William D. Leahy. *July* 20, 1959

IN THE passing of Admiral William D. Leahy the nation has lost an outstanding American and I have lost a close personal friend. As a Naval Officer and a diplomat, Admiral Leahy dedicated his life to the service of his country in war and in peace. Mrs. Eisenhower and I join with the people of America in mourning his death.

NOTE: In addition to the foregoing statement, the President issued Executive Order 10829 (24 F.R. 5817), which provided that, as a mark of respect to the memory of Admiral Leahy, the flag of the United States should be flown at half-staff on all Government buildings, grounds, and naval vessels until interment.

167   ¶ The President's News Conference of July 22, 1959.

THE PRESIDENT. Please sit down.

Good morning. Ready for the questions.

Q. Marvin L. Arrowsmith, Associated Press: In Warsaw yesterday Premier Khrushchev professed to be puzzled about why Vice President Nixon is going to Russia and he apparently linked this puzzlement with criticism of your proclamation on the captive nations. Do you see this attitude as a sort of strike against the Nixon visit even before it starts?

THE PRESIDENT. Well, no. I wouldn't think of it in that way. The Nixon visit was of course proposed quite awhile back, and it's really an exchange of visits between Mr. Kozlov and Mr. Nixon. It's a good will gesture and we wanted to have a prominent American to officiate at the opening of our exhibit.

Now, as far as the resolution about the captive nations, this was a resolution by the Congress, asked me to issue a proclamation, which I did; and asked the United States to conduct ceremonies in memory of the plight of such peoples.[1]

But I don't think there is any specific relationship between the two things.

Q. Merriman Smith, United Press International: In the same connection, sir, what do you think, quite aside from the Nixon visit, of the proposition of the Russians through Pravda, in a three-column article this morning, and through statements by Khrushchev, literally criticizing the proclamation by you of a week of prayer for the captive people?

What do you think of their basic criticism of you for proclaiming a week of prayer?

THE PRESIDENT. Well, of course they don't admit there are any captive nations. They have their own propaganda. They present a picture to their own peoples, including the world, so far as they can, that we know is distorted and is untrue.

---

[1] The Joint Resolution (S.J. Res. 111), designating the third week of July as "Captive Nations Week," is Public Law 86–90 (73 Stat. 212). On July 17 the President issued Proclamation 3303 "Captive Nations Week, 1959" (24 F.R. 5773), urging the people of the United States "to study the plight of the Soviet-dominated nations and to recommit themselves to the support of the just aspirations of the peoples of those captive nations."

This, to our way of thinking, is quite important not only because it is a matter of simple justice and human concern for all these people, but when you come down to it this country is made up of a great many of those people. We have relatives and people of the ethnic derivation of all those captive nations, and it becomes sort of a personal thing with us and would be almost unusual for us to be silent all the time and just acquiesce, presumably in their right to express themselves in the form of their government.

Q. Ray L. Scherer, NBC News: Do you see any danger that continued stalemate at Geneva might bring about an erosion in the Western position, in the effort to get something settled?

THE PRESIDENT. Once in a while you see such hints, because there is implied that there is a weakening of the strength of will of our delegation.

Well, knowing Mr. Herter and some of the others, I'm quite certain, on his part, at least, that this is not taking place, and I'm confident with respect to the others and the allies. So that while these things are very wearing, and sometimes physically wearing as well as mentally, intellectually, I think there need be no fear that they are standing firmly on principle.

But I do insist always, we are ready, they are ready, to undertake any negotiation on any suggestion or any offer that, recognizing our basic rights as the starting point, still offers some promise to easing what we call world tensions.

Q. William McGaffin, Chicago Daily News: Mr. President, is it correct that you, yourself, are the source of some stories which have appeared the last couple of days expressing your views on domestic and foreign affairs——

THE PRESIDENT. You mean did I have some people at my house for dinner from the newspaper world, and I say yes.

Q. Mr. McGaffin: Mr. President, in view of some of the restrictive practices which have been followed by your administration, I think it's a very good sign that you, yourself, have decided to increase the flow of information——

THE PRESIDENT. Thank you for the comment. [*Laughter*]

Q. Mr. McGaffin: Mr. President, there is considerable curiosity about this new departure as, for instance, why you decided to restrict your audience to a chosen few, and why you did not let the correspondents refer to you directly as the source of the stories.

THE PRESIDENT. That I didn't what?

Q. Mr. McGaffin: That you did not let the correspondents refer to you, yourself, as the source of the stories.

THE PRESIDENT. Well, this was an experiment, for one thing.

Secondly, I wanted to show a courtesy to a number of people that have been with me very closely, and I'm referring now to the men who have covered the White House, covered me wherever I've gone, day in, day out, when they go on good trips, bad trips, or anything else. And I have felt toward those particular people a peculiar feeling of closeness, and I wanted to show them a courtesy.

Naturally, I knew if I did they were going to talk about matters of current interest, and I said merely that there would be no quotes.

Now, so far as I'm concerned, that was an experiment, and I'm looking at it now. The stories, I will say, are more detailed than I ever anticipated they would be. [*Laughter*] And I am not so certain that it possibly is good practice, but I'll probably try it again.

Q. Kenneth M. Scheibel, Gannett Newspapers: About those reports, you were quoted as saying you could support either Vice President Nixon or Governor Rockefeller for the presidential nomination in 1960. Now, you have——

THE PRESIDENT. I don't think anyone stated it in that way, that they were quoting me. I have stated that, and I've stated it here.

Q. Mr. Scheibel: Well, now, you have spoken to us many times about the experience and abilities of Mr. Nixon. I wonder if you would give us your assessment of Governor Rockefeller's qualifications for the Presidency?

THE PRESIDENT. Well, I don't think that we are in the same relationship. One man has been working with me for 8 years, definitely as my close associate in Government, and I can speak, I think, authoritatively. There are a number of others, and if I should try to assess all others, I could probably be verbose, but wouldn't offer much to the clarity of the picture. As a matter of fact, these things are still far off in the future, and they are not too interesting at the moment.

Q. Robert J. Donovan, New York Herald Tribune: Roy Wilkins, if I am quoting him right, said in a speech before the NAACP the other day that the Negro voters may have to go to the Republican Party next year because of what he calls the big fat zero, I think, of the Democratic record on civil rights.   Do you have any comment on that?

THE PRESIDENT. Well, I didn't read that comment. I have often reviewed with you people what, as a practical matter, this administration has tried to do in recognition of its responsibility to see that all individuals in our country had equal opportunity, in both the economic and the political fields.

There is no need to go into that record. You people know it from the services, and here, and one bill that had to do with voting which, to my mind, was the most important of all of the legislation proposed. There has been progress and it's slow and I never can fail to say this progress is not going to be made entirely by law, it's going to have to be by our own education and understanding and our own regard for moral standards in this world.

Q. Mrs. May Craig, Portland (Maine) Press Herald: Mr. President, in the stories written after the Monday dinner you were represented as feeling that because of the overwhelming nonnuclear power of the Soviet Union in Europe, if war came there we might be forced to resort to nuclear warfare.

My question is: would you use nuclear weapons over the territories of our friends and allies in the captive countries, or would you return to your original policy of massive retaliation directly on the Soviet Union?

THE PRESIDENT. I don't recall, myself, of that question having been asked, and I don't recall it having been answered.

Now, I think that there has been no change in my convictions and policies for 4 or 5 years and you are implying something about our friends; I don't have any intention of going out and destroying friends anywhere and under any provocations.

Q. Michael J. O'Neill, New York Daily News: Mr. President, do you feel that the time has come when the West should break off the negotiations at Geneva?

THE PRESIDENT. That's something that has to be determined, of course, mostly by people on the spot.   In spite of the daily telegrams and conversations with State, there are all sorts of things come up, and you never know when another proposal, with a slightly different cast or character, is proposed.

What I say again is, I don't think that that is so terribly important, the exact time of when these things have to cease because of finally patently failure to progress.

But I do say we do not want to weaken the very basic purpose of our stand.

Q. John L. Steele, Time Magazine: Sir, a bipartisan group in Congress this week introduced a resolution to provide out of the Navy's mothball surplus ships a mercy fleet which would have the function of going around the world and meeting disasters such as flood, famine, and disease.

I wonder if you could comment generally on this person-to-person approach and if it will receive serious study by the administration.

THE PRESIDENT. Well, I think, of course, that it will—I know that it will receive earnest study.

There is one ship you may know about, the *Hope,* that the Navy already had agreed to recommission so long as private money found the way to stock it, staff it, and make it possible to go around on this kind of an experimental and helpful mission.

Everybody, of course, is concerned about the health and well-being of peoples, and this might be, of course, a very good idea.

I would say this: I'm always suspicious of helpful plans that are just originated in the country that thinks its—I say "suspicious"; I shall go back and say I like to look very closely at plans that originate solely within the helping country. I like to think of everything from the Marshall plan, and since then, it's been a scheme or an arrangement whereby the underdeveloped country or the country needing help presents its own plan, its own idea of what should be done and where can we be helpful.

Now, this doesn't mean that we are not consultants in developing these plans.

I think the whole matter should be studied very closely to see its usefulness and exactly how it would be received. In the meantime, as I repeat, there is one; the ship, I think, is about ready to sail next January or something like that.

Q. Edward T. Folliard, Washington Post: Mr. President, Secretary of Labor Mitchell announced yesterday that he was going to make an investigation or a study of the steel strike, said he would report to you from time to time on his findings.

What would you expect to result from Mr. Mitchell's inquiry or study, Mr. President? What would you hope to——

THE PRESIDENT. Well, Mr. Folliard, the law says that Mr. Mitchell must do this.

Now, as I told someone here—I believe it was Mr. Brandt asked the question—there are a number of places where the actual facts of profits and labor costs and the number of people employed and number of tonnage and all the rest of it are all available. But the law says that in a specific instance, something that breaks out, as I believe it calls it, a labor dispute—although I don't want to be quoted exactly, I think that's what it says—now, he has a little different function. Now he has to look at all of the facts that are pertinent to that dispute, even though they go beyond the facts of profit, of labor costs, investment and all the rest.

Here are facts that he must try to find out, and I think indeed has been trying for a long time, because the law has still been there a long time. But he did say that he wanted to be sure that he was getting the cooperation and the assistance of the Chairman of the Economic Advisers and the Commerce Department and one or two others to make certain that he was doing this in accordance with what I should like.

Q. David P. Sentner, Hearst Newspapers: Mr. President, would you tell us at least one question you would like Vice President Nixon to seek an answer to from Premier Khrushchev?

THE PRESIDENT. We should be careful to understand one thing about the Vice Presidential position in this Government of ours.

He has a position of his own. He is not a subordinate of the President, and he is not a part of the diplomatic processes and machinery of this country. He cannot be sent out on a special mission except as he agrees to go as a special agent of the President.

Now, he is going here this time on a good will gesture. He is seeking, and I have forgotten but I think he has been already accepted as a caller on Mr. Khrushchev and there will be a chat with him.

Now, that chat will be determined I should say in its character by Mr. Khrushchev. He is the head of their government, he is the man who is being called on, and Mr. Nixon will be able, I hope, to show the temper and feelings of the American people more accurately probably than a casual visitor here could do it. He knows all about government, he knows about the attitudes, he can impart information, but he is not negotiating anything.

Q. Lloyd M. Schwartz, Fairchild Publications: Mr. President, in the stories in the morning's papers you were represented as believing that a tax cut is impossible during the rest of your term of office. Could you expand on the basis for such a decision?

THE PRESIDENT. Well, I think there is only this one statement to be made. I believe that we should start paying off something on this big debt of ours. Already the estimates are that the interest alone on our debt for 1961, and we are already working on that budget, will be 8,700,000,000. Now when you are getting to this kind of cost just for interest, it would look to be the part of wisdom to start getting the debt down a little bit, thereby creating the kind of confidence that will make a tax cut more justifiable.

Now, because of the short time remaining, as you get these things happening and to pay something on the debt has not yet been done, I would hope it would be.

Q. Harold R. Levy, Newsday: Sir, your thinking on a summit conference appears to have hardened since last week's news conference. On the basis of what has been said since then, are we to conclude that you have now virtually written off the possibility of such a meeting?

THE PRESIDENT. I think that I have said this: as the Geneva Conference has gone on, I have lost some of my earlier hopes for really productive progress on this side. I have not hardened in the slightest degree in my opinion and my conviction that if we see anything, any kind of a suggestion or arrangement that looks like progress, as long as our own basic rights are respected, then I say the road is open to a summit meeting. But it's merely on what comes out of this conference; that's the real measure of the probability.

Q. Sarah McClendon, El Paso Times: Sir, this book written by Drew Pearson and Jack Anderson, "U.S., Second-Class Power," has inspired the munitions investigation on Capitol Hill, sparked by Mr. Santangelo and now being conducted by Mr. Hébert.

In this book there are some allegations that way back yonder when you were Chief of Staff that you turned down the intercontinental ballistic missile and that this put us back, in a defensewise manner, some 10 years.

I wonder if this is true and if you had it to do over again, would you do differently?

THE PRESIDENT. Do you know anything truthful in any such allegations? I don't.

Q. Raymond P. Brandt, St. Louis Post-Dispatch: This time of the year the President usually announces the bills that he thinks are most desirable or essential.

Have you made up such a list that you think this Congress, this session of Congress, should pass?

THE PRESIDENT. Well, as a matter of fact, this time I haven't gone to the trouble of making my list. But I do remember this: one of the very first things, and one I made one of the first orders of business, was to try to get a bill with the necessary machinery set up by us that would curb all of the abuses that were brought out by the McClellan committee. That's one that I'm quite sure of.

There are others, of course, along the line of getting the necessary revenue for road construction, and a decent farm bill, which I think is terribly important to the United States, even at this late date.

There are a number and I could make up a little list and be prepared. But I just for the moment—I talk legislation so often I forget the ones that are passed and about to be passed.

Q. Richard L. Wilson, Cowles Publications: Mr. President, in the event of any interference with access to Berlin, are we in a position to supply Berlin with enough to keep the city alive and keep industry going?

THE PRESIDENT. Well, if you're talking about an actual blockade of Berlin, you must remember this: West Berlin has become a very prosperous industrial city, and much of the raw materials they draw upon come from East Germany. They are a very fine customer of raw materials in that region and they deal very greatly also with West Germany in commerce made out of these raw materials. So you now have a very complicated and very large industrial activity going on that could not possibly be supplied, I should think, by air. If that's what you're thinking of—in the terms of ground blockade—I would think there would have to be some other arrangement.

Of course, there might be no blockade of the economic production in the city. I don't know.

Q. Mr. Wilson: May I ask one other question on that, sir?

THE PRESIDENT. Yes.

Q. Mr. Wilson: Would this mean that we would only try to supply Berlin by air, or would we try to supply it by land?

THE PRESIDENT. Oh, no, I don't see how you could draw that inference at all. I was taking the premise that you postulated, that was that we were blockaded, now, what were we going to do about it.

Q. Mary Abbot, Charleston (W. Va.) Gazette: Sir, increasingly there are men being replaced by machines, particularly in the coal mines; and small communities that have a large percentage of these displaced workers are becoming areas of economic blight.

I wonder if you have discussed with your economic advisers the possibility of a program to do something about these technologically unemployed?

THE PRESIDENT. As a matter of fact, we call it the depressed area bills. I think that they have been up every year for oh, 3 or 4 years.

Yes; as a matter of fact, one of the men that is very expert in this field is the man I just nominated as Secretary of Commerce, Mr. Mueller. He has made long studies of what can be done between the Federal Government in cooperation with the States, and I think his studies are very valuable.

Q. Lillian Levy, National Jewish Post and Opinion: What assurances do we have that a rearmed and restored Germany soon to be given the added power of American nuclear know-how and weapons will not turn against the West as it has done twice in a generation? In any event, sir, with the background of history is such a calculated risk justified?

THE PRESIDENT. Well, you are asking for quite a study and analysis rather than just a simple question that can be easily answered.

I would say this: if you have a struggle with any two people or any group of people, it behooves you, I think, to decide where your greatest danger is, and there is where you should give your attention at that moment.

Now this doesn't mean you shouldn't have your eye on future potentialities, but particularly when those potentialities look as low as I think they are along the lines that you were suggesting about a hostile Germany, and rearmed, I would say I would rather have Germany strong and my friend today.

Q. John Herling, Editors Syndicate: As you know, sir, there are more than 15½ million Americans over the age of 65, the vast majority of whom can't afford to get any medical care, governmental or nongovernmental.

Could you tell us what you would think of a Government-financed program under the Social Security System, to take care of the medical needs of such people without disturbing the normal private relationship between doctor and patient?

THE PRESIDENT. Well, I think you ought to take the question, in the first instance, to the Secretary of Health, Education, and Welfare. He has talked to me about this problem, but just exactly what I would think now about undertaking a new program, I would wait until I talked to him. So I would take the question to him.

Q. Spencer Davis, Associated Press: You were reported last week, sir, to have felt that the press misinterpreted your feelings and your consideration of Mr. Bohlen for a position as a consultant on Soviet policy. Would you care to clarify that?

THE PRESIDENT. No, I didn't say they had misinterpreted. I said it turned out we were talking about two different things.

The question was, had I been considering approving a movement of Mr. Bohlen to Washington, and I said no. And having asked that question twice of Mr. Herter, he had said no; but it turned out that he, in a press conference, had talked about this matter. But he talked about it, of conversations of some time back, had come to the conclusion that Mr. Bohlen was so preoccupied with important negotiations now, he should not be disturbed and therefore had dropped it as of now. Now, I don't know whether Mr. Herter will ever bring this up again. Then I took the occasion, I believe I saw a headline saying that I was cool toward Mr. Bohlen, I wanted to make clear that here's a man I've known since 1942 and I consider him one of the intelligent, fine, dedicated men in the State Department. And I still think so.

Q. Thomas N. Schroth, Congressional Quarterly: Could you give us some of your thinking on the use of the veto as an administrative device?

Do you agree with Woodrow Wilson that it is perhaps the strongest weapon in the hands of a President, to use it reluctantly, and how bad does a bill have to be before you'll resort to a veto?

THE PRESIDENT. You're asking a question in a generality that can't be answered accurately except in specifics.

The bill has to be in front of you. What does it do to the United States? What does it purport to do for a particular group, or what else does it do?

I have said time and again that it is clear that I am, or the Presidency is, a part of the legislative process, so stated by the Constitution; it states just exactly how he may act and then what Congress can do.

And if he didn't exercise his own judgment as to what is best for this country in this case, I think he'd be derelict of his duty; that's what I think he is.

Q. William M. Blair, New York Times: Tomorrow, wheat growers vote in a national referendum on their control and price-support program for the next crop year. Do you have any advice, sir, for them on the eve of their voting, or for Congress?

THE PRESIDENT. Well, I think they have a hard choice, because there was not any satisfactory legislation passed. So they have now the choice between taking the program as it is now, which last year piled up again these tremendous surpluses and which is, to my mind, detrimental to the country as a whole; or, the other alternative they have is no program at all.

So I think, because of the failure to have something that they could vote on that was a little bit more meaningful, it's a sorry choice they have to make.

Marvin L. Arrowsmith, Associated Press: Thank you, Mr. President.

NOTE: President Eisenhower's one hundred and sixty-fifth news conference was held in the Executive Office Building from 10:31 to 11:01 o'clock on Wednesday morning, July 22, 1959. In attendance: 224.

168 ¶ Statement by the President on the Death of Douglas McKay. *July* 22, 1959

I WAS saddened to hear of the news of the passing of Douglas McKay. As former Governor of his State and former Secretary of the Interior, Mr. McKay devoted much of his life to public service. In his passing the nation has lost a distinguished citizen and an American of outstanding character. He was a loyal and valued friend.

Mrs. Eisenhower joins me in extending our deep sympathies to Mrs. McKay and her family on the great personal loss they have sustained.

169 ¶ Remarks to Members of Future Farmers of America. *July* 22, 1959

THANK YOU—thank you very much. First of all, let me thank you for the gifts. They are most attractive and certainly will be useful back in Gettysburg when the winters come around.

I always get a kick out of meeting with a bunch of young people. This is especially true when I find that you are interested in agriculture, are taking the vocational courses in your high schools, and are here for a program to improve your leadership abilities in your own communities.

I can't think of anything more important. First of all, if you are a farmer and know the relationship of the farm and its products to our economy and to our place in the world, you have to have a broad understanding of the United States, its citizenship, its economy, and its relationship with the other countries. Because of your capacity, as future leaders as well as future farmers, you have the potentiality of influencing many, many thousands out and beyond the confines of just your own organization.

Then, being young, you have got many years to do it. Every once in a while I look at one of my grandchildren—about the age of that little girl over there—and I say to myself: when she is my age it will be the year 2011, or something like that. That sounds an awfully long way ahead. But if you can look at your own school histories and look back, say 50 years, as to the situation that then existed, in farming, in transportation, in communications, in our thinking, and in our relations with the world, you will see that a veritable revolution has already taken place.

You have got to be prepared for even a more rapidly developing revolution in all of these things, for the simple reason that the speed of acceleration has gone up so fast. In 50 years since man first flew—the Russians sometimes say something else, we say that the Wrights flew 50 years ago—but from that airplane to the jet, the jet fighter, that goes two or three times the speed of sound is no greater progress than you are going to see between what you know today and in that year 2009, 50 years ahead.

You people are going to be the ones to influence it. You are going to shape it, and you are going to make it the kind of world in which you want to live—and indeed in which in many respects you must live, if you are going to live at all.

This is the kind of thing that is in front of you. I don't like the word "challenge" particularly, I like to think of the prospects, the opportunities that lie out ahead of an individual, no matter what his age. How rich those opportunities are, how vast they are, when they are put in front of the imagination of youngsters. That is the kind of thing I hope for you. It is the kind of thing that I believe you will be doing, and I certainly assure you of my confidence that you will do it well.

547

Now, as to farming itself, I just talked to Mr. Hester, your president, and he is a dairy farmer. I am interested in beef. They are both good industries, and as far as I can work at it, I am going to be trying to improve the beef industry. No one will notice it, of course, but it will still be fun to try. I can imagine the fun each of you gets out of the thing you are trying to do in agriculture that is your specialty for the moment, and maybe for your life. But I say this: agriculture is a part of this great complex we know as America, and a part of America's relationships to the whole world. As America is the leader, so you must be.

I can't say in words sufficiently emphatic to convey my full meaning when I say God bless you all. I hope for you all the luck, and the happiness, the enjoyment and the satisfaction that life can possibly bring to you.

Goodbye—good luck.

NOTE: The President spoke in the Rose Garden. The gifts to which he referred were a blanket and a gold paperweight bearing the FFA insignia. Later, he referred to Adin Hester, President of Future Farmers of America.

170 ¶ Letter to the President of the Senate and to the Speaker of the House of Representatives Transmitting Report "Economic Assistance: Programs and Administration." *July 23, 1959*

Dear ————:

I transmit for the consideration of the Congress a report on "Economic Assistance: Programs and Administration," submitted to me on July 13, 1959, by the President's Committee to Study the United States Military Assistance Program. This report analyzes the objectives of economic assistance, reports on the operations of present programs, and makes recommendations for future programs and organizational arrangements.

I have transmitted copies of the report to the Executive Agencies concerned, so that the Committee's recommendations may be carefully considered and, where appropriate, taken into account during the formulation of next year's mutual security program.

Sincerely,

DWIGHT D. EISENHOWER

NOTE: This is the text of identical letters addressed to the Honorable Richard M. Nixon, President of the Senate, and to the Honorable Sam Rayburn, Speaker of the House of Representatives. The report (71 pp.) was published by the Government Printing Office. This is the Committee's third interim report; see also Items 90, 136, 137, 170, and 183.

171 ¶ Statement by the President Upon Approval of Bill Amending the Mutual Security Act of 1954. *July 24, 1959*

I HAVE today signed H.R. 7500, a bill amending the Mutual Security Act of 1954. Three amendments made by the bill concern disclosure by the Executive Branch of information, documents, and materials relating to the Mutual Security Program or certain of its aspects.

I have signed this bill on the express premise that the three amendments relating to disclosure are not intended to alter and cannot alter the recognized Constitutional duty and power of the Executive with respect to the disclosure of information, documents, and other materials. Indeed, any other construction of these amendments would raise grave Constitutional questions under the historic Separation of Powers Doctrine.

In this connection, I am constrained to emphasize once again that it is established policy of the Executive Branch to provide the Congress and the public with the fullest possible information consistent with the public interest. This policy will continue to guide the Executive Branch in carrying out the Mutual Security Program so that there may be a full understanding of the program and its vital importance to the national security.

NOTE: As enacted, H.R. 7500 is Public Law 86–108 (73 Stat. 246).

On the same day the Press Secretary to the President released the following statement concerning appropriations for mutual security:

The President is disappointed by the action of the House Appropriations Committee on the Mutual Security Bill. The accumulative cuts made are deeply below the minimums he considers necessary for the security of our nation and the free world.

The President most earnestly hopes that the ultimate action of Congress will be to restore the appropriations to the full amounts authorized.

172 ¶ The President's News Conference of July 29, 1959.

THE PRESIDENT. Good morning. Please sit down.

One little announcement has to do with the election in Hawaii.

Now, I don't take the occasion just to express any gratification about those winners in my party, but I do express certain gratification about the people that have been elected—individuals. One of them, I notice, was a Chinese-Hawaiian, another a Japanese-Hawaiian, and I believe others of Hawaiian ancestry.

I think this is a very fine example for democracy at work, in operation. I believe it's a good example for the whole world and I am, for that reason, highly gratified with the results.

Of course, I don't want to say that I'm unhappy that we got a Republican Governor and at least one Senator. I believe all the other races are still undecided, although favoring the other party.

That's my announcement.

Q. Sterling F. Green, Associated Press: I would like to ask a two-part question concerning Vice President Nixon's visit to Russia.

The first is whether you think the Vice President has so acquitted himself as to ease the tensions between this country and Russia, and the second is a request for comment on reports from the Nixon party that the Vice President has discussed with Premier Khrushchev a possible visit to the United States.

THE PRESIDENT. Well, with the first one, I think that all of us could agree from reports and from the television performance that the Vice President has acquitted himself splendidly and in accordance with what you'd expect from a man in his high office and representing this Government.[1]

Now, as to whether or not that has actually reduced the tensions, I think only time can tell. But this thing is clear: again we have reports of the readiness of Soviet populations to welcome Americans. This has been noticeable since the early days, certainly during the war and since,

---

[1] On August 1, the Press Secretary to the President announced that the President had sent a personal message to the Vice President expressing his admiration and respect for the manner in which he had conducted himself throughout his tour of the Soviet Union.

and it seems to be a continuing manifestation of the people's friendliness toward America.

On the second part, about the reports that come out from associates with and people accompanying the Vice President, I think here you have got a subject that has been bandied back and forth in many countries and here in our own. I saw not long ago a poll that was taken on the advisability of inviting Mr. Khrushchev here. I think it is one of those things that is a perennial question that will be talked about a lot all the time, and not merely because of this visit of the Vice President's.

Q. Frank van der Linden, Nashville Banner: Sir, Congressmen Landrum of Georgia and Griffin of Michigan are co-sponsoring a new labor bill which seems to meet most of your requirements in regard to secondary boycotts and other matters. Is it your hope, sir, that other Republicans and discerning Southern Democrats may combine in the House to pass that bill?

THE PRESIDENT. You are asking now to comment on the specifics of a bill. I have not studied every proviso, or every clause of that bill, but I understand—because I had reports both from the Congress and from the Secretary of Labor—that the bill comes a long ways closer to meeting the request that I made upon the Congress last January than any other that has been seriously studied. It particularly makes progress toward these three areas I thought so important—blackmail picketing, secondary boycotts, and the "no man's area." So in those general areas they have certainly come a long ways and so, without quoting specifically on all of the provisions, I would say the bill is a tremendous improvement and I commend the people that have gotten together to put it on the calendar.

Q. Robert C. Pierpoint, CBS News: In light of the record profits announced by steel yesterday, and in view of the study that Secretary of Labor Mitchell has made on the steel situation and the information that you have received from him, do you feel, sir, that steel might be able now to grant some wage increases without necessarily increasing the price of steel?

THE PRESIDENT. We are talking on a subject now that I have stated repeatedly I'm not going to talk about when the negotiations were still going on. I don't believe that you can take any of these subjects, take it and discuss it, you might say, in a vacuum or by itself in isolation from all other pertinent facts, and be doing anything except to appear to be favoring one side or another. I think that the minute that the Government does that, it is in trouble.

So, as I say, I have constantly argued that we must have a solution that does not create or incite inflation and that it must be by free bargaining and not under pressures.

Q. David Kraslow, Knight Newspapers: Mr. President, a Gallup poll released over the weekend reports the American people believe that Democrats are more interested than Republicans in holding down prices.

Do you feel, sir, that this indicates the Republican Party has failed to convince the American people that the Democratic Party is a party of spenders?

THE PRESIDENT. I think that there has not been as good a job done in telling the story of the last 7 years as should have been done. For example, today, in the headlines in the newspapers you will see the cost of living has gone up to new highs. Well, of course, it was a new high when we started, but the curve of increase has been so much less than what it was in the preceding 7 years; we don't take that fact into consideration. I have forgotten exactly the percentage for the last 7 years just before I came in—I think it was something over 30; here the cost of living has been about 7 percent in the last 7 years. That kind of comparison is just not made because the headline says the cost of living is at a new high; and if you put one-tenth on a past high, why, of course, that's a new high!

In many ways, from cutting budget, reducing expenses, keeping down, for example, in every field that I know, we have tried to be on the conservative, middle-of-the-road side. But that has not apparently been publicized sufficiently.

Q. Sarah McClendon, Manchester (N.H.) Union Leader: Sir, back to the labor bill. We are now witnessing some of the greatest lobbying I guess we will ever see in Washington, pro and con on this bill that comes up next week, and I have heard Democratic and Republican Congressmen say the last 2 days that they want to vote for a strong bill but feel that if they do they'll be labeled "antilabor" back home, and they feel that at this time that it would be very helpful if you did come out and make an appeal to the voters to ask Congressmen to vote for a strong bill.

THE PRESIDENT. Mrs. McClendon, if you go back to my State of the

Union Message, and even beyond that, last fall I said the first order of business that I was going to present before the Congress in 1959 was a bill, or a program in this field that would meet all of the defects that were uncovered by the McClellan committee. I still believe we should do it and I just, discussing this bill, I said I think it comes a long ways and it sounds to me in their main provisions they are trying to do just that; and of course, therefore, I'm for it.

Q. Edward V. Koterba, United Features Syndicate: Sir, there have been published in the last few weeks two accounts speculating about your personal plans after leaving the White House in 1961. One account stated that you and the First Lady are planning to take an apartment in Washington; and, another states that you have had offered to you the presidency of a Gettysburg college.

Sir, even though you still have 542 days to serve in the White House—[*Laughter*]——

THE PRESIDENT. Sounds like a plebe at West Point.

Q. Mr. Koterba: ——could you at this time give us a hint about what you would like to do, or hope to do after you leave the White House?

THE PRESIDENT. Well, about any apartment in Washington, I should think that would be left, that decision, to the distaff side of the family, and you had better get some of your lady reporter friends to go and talk to her about it.

Now, this is the first I have ever heard about the presidency of Gettysburg College. As a matter of fact, there is a man there now that I respect and who is younger than I am, so I don't know why I should be thinking of that.

I have expressed to numbers of people my desire to do some traveling and particularly in the areas where I have not been before. I have had dozens, and literally hundreds, I think, of invitations from governments and from private people and I would like to go through really a rather good tour of all Latin America and of Africa and of the Far East again. While I have lived a great deal in the Far East, I haven't been in the Indian Ocean area where I'd love to spend a lot of time. Now that is what I'd like to do.

The only thing I promised is, after I am out, that when we go together, I will use some transportation other than an airplane. [*Laughter*]

Q. Charles L. Bartlett, Chattanooga Times: Mr. President, everyone who is talking about the TVA self-financing bill has come away with the impression that it is your intention to veto it. In that event, I was wondering if it would be your intention also to submit a request for appropriation funds to build the needed generating capacity down there.

THE PRESIDENT. Well, people are talking in impressions.

Now, I am studying this bill I think more earnestly and with more lawyers and that kind of thing than almost any other bill I've seen in a long time.

This bill does three or four things that I think were absolutely necessary, and they are things that I have fought for since 1953.

There is one provision in this thing that seems to me does not conform with the balance of powers between the three branches that must be maintained if this country is to stand in the form that it has in the past. This is so serious that this is the item that causes me my anxiety. I would like to get that bill without this very—I think—unwise proviso. I would like to have the bill come back to me without that on. I don't know whether yet that is sufficiently strong, or whether my views are sufficiently crystallized, because I have still got a little more conversing to do.

Q. J. A. O'Leary, Washington Star: It looks as though the House today will vote to cut about 700 million off your foreign aid. What will that do to our position in the world?

THE PRESIDENT. Well, it will damage it seriously. Of course, I'm not going to take all the specific items, and I am not discussing the details of a bill that is still yet to be passed, but I would be very, very hopeful that the other side would restore a lot of those amounts.

Q. Lambert Brose, Lutheran Layman: Mr. President, on another aspect of our position in the world, Secretary of Defense McElroy testified that Russia now has intercontinental ballistic missiles capable of hitting our country, somewhat less than 10 of them.

On the other hand, Lieutenant General Schriever yesterday said that our first intercontinental missile will be ready for combat use September 1st.

Do you feel that Russia's superiority over us in this one phase of armament at the moment gives her an advantage over us presently in Geneva, at the bargaining table, and that she can practice blackmail diplomacy until we do catch up in the missile field?

THE PRESIDENT. No, I don't think so at all. After all, we fired last night very successfully an operational—that is, a Series C—Atlas; and it fulfilled every single test and was fired at long range. What I would like to get at is this: I must tell you once again, the Russians have been working on long-range ballistic missiles since 1945. We started in 1954. Now, I think that our scientists and our services have done an extraordinary job in catching up as fast as they can. They are going at a very satisfactory and in my opinion about the maximum rate that it is possible to go.

In addition to that, you must remember that this is a period of transition. You cannot "off with the old" immediately, and go all to the new until you have tried it out. Therefore, our strength that is counterbalancing some of these other strengths—of which I don't have any idea of the exact numbers although the Secretary of Defense, I believe, did say that fewer than 10; in any event, that part I don't argue about—I just say this: we have other means and other methods that are fully counterbalancing during this transition period, in my opinion.

Q. William McGaffin, Chicago Daily News: Mr. President, could you tell us what you talked about at dinner Monday night with another group of correspondents?

THE PRESIDENT. Everything I could think of! [*Laughter*] At least everything that I was asked, and I think it would be too long to recite the list.

Q. Raymond P. Brandt, St. Louis Post-Dispatch: Can you tell us what specific point it was in the TVA bill? I didn't get it clear in my own mind.

THE PRESIDENT. Well, there is a specific point that says this, that the budget or the proposed expenditures of this corporation, this governmental corporation, can go to the Congress and in spite of Presidential recommendations, he has no executive power to do anything about the amount of those expenditures. Therefore, since it says Congress can modify this amount in any way it sees fit, it can increase it or decrease it, the President has not the veto and therefore he must accept the will of Congress without the process of saying, "You must do this over my judgment by a two-thirds majority."

And this—an extension of my remarks: no matter how beneficial any bill may be temporarily, in doing the things we want to do now, any time that a bill purports, with the consent of the President, to encroach on one branch of our coequal branches and give an advantage to one or the other, then we have made a very, very serious mistake and one where the long-term effects can be serious indeed.

For my part, this provision couldn't possibly in my period of service affect me, but I must say my successors in this office, whoever they may be, and whatever party, could have a very, very tough time unless this thing is batted down every time it comes up.

Q. Rutherford M. Poats, United Press International: Sir, in view of your understanding of the situation at Geneva today, and of your reports from Vice President Nixon, can you tell us whether there is any point in continuing the Geneva foreign ministers conference?

THE PRESIDENT. Well, I wouldn't go to the point of saying there is no point of continuing. I would say this: there is not yet any progress, at least that's been reported since last evening; there has been no progress that would justify the calling of a summit meeting.

Q. Kenneth M. Scheibel, Gannett Newspapers: You have been criticized in the past for not spending enough money on the space program because the Russians were ahead of us, but the other day the House cut $68 million out of your budget for the space program. I wonder what your reaction was to that?

THE PRESIDENT. Well, I talked to Dr. Glennan about it. He thinks it's quite serious. The program, of course, that is already set up is, to my mind, a rather—well, indeed it *is* quite generous. I think it's on about the third year it gets close to a billion dollars just in space.

Now, remember, Glennan and his crowd are supposed to have the peaceful uses; this, therefore, is not involved, except you might say psychologically, in our defending the United States. This seems to me to be quite a splendid program; I mean, a very well supported one.

Now, this $68 million, he gave me the details of what this would do to him, and he thinks it's very detrimental to success.

Q. Mrs. May Craig, Portland (Maine) Press Herald: Mr. President, without taking sides either with the steel industry or the steel workers, can you not take sides with all of us and urge the steel industry, in view of its very large profits, to cut prices?

THE PRESIDENT. Well, of course, this has been suggested for a number of years. Again, you ask me while this thing is going on, by implication, to say their profits are too high.

I don't know whether you or anybody else in this room has taken a complete analysis of all profits, expenses, investments, and all the rest of the things. We just know that there is reported by the U.S. Steel Company—not the other companies, U.S. Steel—a very large profit.

Well, now, they put this thing on the record. I should not comment on it as having any effect whatsoever on these negotiations. When they are done, by that time I should think I may have something to say about the whole arrangement, not just one thing.

Q. Andrew F. Tully, Jr., Scripps-Howard: Sir, without mentioning any names, I wonder if you'd give us your impression of the men so far who are running for President on the Democratic ticket.

THE PRESIDENT. I think they have enough troubles of their own; I'll not try to add to them.

Q. E. W. Kenworthy, New York Times: On Geneva again, sir, a hindsight criticism that was made of the 1945 agreement on Berlin was that it did not make explicit the Western rights in the city. The latest dispatches from Geneva state that our most recent proposal for a 5-year interim agreement again allows our rights to flow implicitly from the proposed arrangements.

Don't you think it would be preferable to have those rights stated explicitly?

THE PRESIDENT. As I recall what the arrangement is, our rights that we now have will not be changed in any way at the end of any interregnum that may ensue, except by the unanimous consent of all; and if there is no change that comes by such common agreement, then you are right back to where you were just at this moment.

Q. Edward W. O'Brien, St. Louis Globe-Democrat: Mr. President, while the Russians talk peace and friendship, do you detect any slackening in Communist internal subversion within this country.

THE PRESIDENT. Within this country?

Q. Mr. O'Brien: Yes, sir.

THE PRESIDENT. Well, here is something that I get periodic reports on and in detail, from committees properly set up. But I wouldn't at this moment be able to say that I detect any diminution of these efforts. On the other hand, I certainly couldn't say that I detect any increase. But in the matter of—it seems to me now it will be the next 2 or 3—months, I will have another very detailed report and an exhaustive investigation of this thing.

Q. Clark R. Mollenhoff, Des Moines Register and Tribune: Yesterday the House passed an amendment by an overwhelming vote which would shut off the funds from the ICA if certain reports and communications, evaluation reports, Inspector General reports, are not made available to Congress and the GAO, and there was some criticism of the administration by those who sponsored this. I wonder if you consider this a personal criticism of the administration's secrecy policies, and if in the light of this you will make available the ICA evaluation reports, Inspector General reports, and other communications as the Congress desires.

THE PRESIDENT. You start your question with an implied fact that is not a fact. You say the administration's secrecy policies. There has been no administration—please sit down—there has been no administration since my memory, and I have been in this city since 1926, who has gone to such lengths to make information available as long as the national security and the national interest of this country is not involved. So, whatever secrecy policies they are, they are policies that are not as severe, certainly no more restrictive than those of the predecessor. Now, with respect to the kind of amendment you were talking about, there was in 1954, I remember, an Attorney General's opinion given to the effect that this kind of a movement or attempt on the part of Government is a direct invasion of Executive responsibility and authority and therefore could not be anything but unconstitutional.

Now, I do not believe that this amendment in this form will ever get to my desk, because I believe that each branch of the Government must be respectful of the authorities and the responsibilities of the others if we are going to make this Government work. It has done so in the past, and I don't believe that any branch is going to be so careless in this direction.

Q. Chalmers M. Roberts, Washington Post: In regard to the Vice President's discussion of a Khrushchev visit, does Mr. Nixon have any authorization from you to proffer such an invitation to Mr. Khrushchev?

THE PRESIDENT. Of course not. But he has got every right to listen and converse and discuss it as you and I might right here, as to whether it has advantages or disadvantages or anything else; but he has no right to proffer an invitation.

Q. Thomas N. Schroth, Congressional Quarterly: Mr. President, Vice President Nixon is reported to have been embarrassed by the timing of the "captive nations" declaration. Do you have any second thoughts as to whether you and Congress should have timed it at this particular time?

THE PRESIDENT. I have no particular feeling about it, for this reason:

I have stated this since the very first time that I thought it was proper for me to mention such things in public. I resigned from the Army in 1952, in July. I then became a citizen and during the 1952 campaign I said frequently that the United States would never believe and never accept the idea that a true peace had been established in the world until every single nation had a right to express its own views about its own destiny. I said the United States would always use whatever peaceful methods were available to it to bring about this opportunity.

Q. William J. Eaton, United Press International: Has Secretary of Labor Mitchell given you any indication when the steel strike will be settled?

THE PRESIDENT. Well, I don't think he has because I don't think he knows. [*Laughter*]

Now, what he does, he sees me every day. As I have pointed out frequently, there is a lot of information of course that is possibly important to our labor relations business that is available to everybody. In the meantime, he is keeping in touch with everything he can, assembling every fact; as a matter of fact he is analyzing all of the historical events of past strikes and giving to me that kind of information.

By the way, just before you start—[*laughter*]—there was one thing here in connection with one question, in connection with the Geneva Conference.

There is a conference called for August 12th in Santiago, Cuba [Chile], and there is a possible conflict with Secretary Herter's schedule because it's one which I have long ago told him I'd expect him to go to because of its importance in trying to settle pan-American affairs and difficulties in the Caribbean. So, that one fact should be remembered in connection with any speculation on what might happen in—[*Confers with Mr. Hagerty*]

Oh, I mean Santiago, Chile, I am sorry.

Q. Mr. Eaton: Does that put a deadline on it?

THE PRESIDENT. No, I don't put a deadline. They might have to make some arrangements for a few days, but I do want him to go to it, that's all.

Sterling F. Green, Associated Press: Thank you, Mr. President.

NOTE: President Eisenhower's one hundred and sixty-sixth news conference was held in the Executive Office Building from 10:31 to 11:01 o'clock on Wednesday morning, July 29, 1959. In attendance: 226.

173 ¶ The President's News Conference of *August 3, 1959.*

THE PRESIDENT. I asked this morning for this special press conference on the subject of the impending exchange of visits between Mr. Khrushchev and myself.

Now, while in Europe this has been for the past few days one of the worst kept secrets of a long time, still I think there may be enough special interest in the matter as to justify you people taking your time to come here this morning.

First of all, a little bit of the history:

Some time back, I suggested to the State Department that I believed in the effort to melt a little bit of the ice that seems to freeze our relationships with the Soviets, that possibly a visit such as I now have proposed would be useful. We studied this thing, and in early July I initiated the correspondence that finally brought about an agreement. Some of the details, exact details, are yet to be agreed between the diplomatic agencies of our separate, several governments.

Now, at this identical time, an identical statement is being issued in Moscow. The statement is as follows—and there will be copies at the door when you leave, so that you don't have to take the time to write it down:

[*Reading*]   The President of the United States has invited Mr. Nikita Khrushchev, Chairman of the Council of Ministers of the U.S.S.R., to pay an official visit to the United States in September. Mr. Khrushchev has accepted with pleasure.

The President has also accepted with pleasure Mr. Khrushchev's invitation to pay an official visit to the U.S.S.R. later this fall.

Mr. Khrushchev will visit Washington for 2 or 3 days and will also spend 10 days or so travelling in the United States. He will have informal talks with the President, which will afford an opportunity for an exchange of views about problems of mutual interest.

On his tour of the United States, Mr. Khrushchev will be able, at first hand, to see the country, its people, and to acquaint himself with their life.

President Eisenhower will visit Moscow and will also spend some days travelling in the Soviet Union. This will provide further opportunity for informal talks and exchange of views about problems of mutual interest with the Chairman of the Council of Ministers of the U.S.S.R.

On his tour of the Soviet Union, President Eisenhower likewise will be able at first hand to see the country, its people, and to acquaint himself with their life.

Both Governments express the hope that the forthcoming visits will help create better understanding between the U.S. and the U.S.S.R. and will promote the cause of peace. [*Ends reading*]

That is the end of the quoted statement.

Now, one or two other items.

We have, of course, been consulting for a couple of weeks through the foreign ministers about this possibility—our Western foreign ministers; they have, of course, agreed.

And then, the heads of state were notified just recently about this impending visit, and some of them have been able to answer. All of them have agreed—I think all of them have been able to answer; all have agreed that the matter is one that should produce plus rather than negative values. In other words, on balance, they think it's a very good thing to do.

In the meantime, I might tell you that this morning I have taken considerable trouble to inform some of the leaders of Congress, and those that I've heard from have been quite favorably disposed toward this plan.

I want to make this clear: by no means am I intending to be or can I be any spokesman for the Western powers in my talks with Mr. Khrushchev. I can be a spokesman only for America and for its Government. Nevertheless, I have already suggested that prior to these meetings, I go to meet our friends in Europe and to discuss with them problems of mutual interest.

The visit itself has no direct connection with any possible later summit meeting. I of course would hope that the mere announcement would inspire the foreign ministers to a greater activity, and probably some greater effort at conciliation, so that there might be results before Wednesday, when they temporarily adjourn at least, that would justify the scheduling of such a later meeting, at what time I don't know.

But in any event, even if they have to reassemble, I would hope that they could do that, if they found it reasonable and proper.

So, I merely want to make clear that this is a personal visit for the purposes that I have outlined and are given in the statement, but with the hope that it will do something to promote understanding and possibly progress toward peace in the world.

Now, as long as we talked on this one subject, because this is a special conference, I am perfectly ready to take 10 minutes or so for questions.

Q. Edward T. Folliard, Washington Post: Mr. President, Governor Meyner, who is one of the nine Governors who called on you the other day after their return from Russia, was talking about the possibility of a Khrushchev visit and he said there was the possibility of what he called "incidents," brought on by refugees in this country, and he thought that Premier Khrushchev should be told that there are such people, and that we didn't try to stifle people in this country.

Have you given some thought to the possibility of incidents, Mr. President?

THE PRESIDENT. Naturally, because this is always a possibility in our country, as is evidenced by the fact that we found it so necessary to provide protection for the members of the President's family.

Now, we do have these uncontrolled individuals, and of course we talked about that, and they know it. We have not failed to point out this fact to the U.S.S.R. representatives. I am certain, however, that we can control this matter.

Q. Robert J. Donovan, New York Herald-Tribune: Do you know, sir, whether Mr. Khrushchev will come directly to Washington first, or will he go to New York and then here, or how?

THE PRESIDENT. I can't tell you a thing about details. I can't give you the exact dates, the exact times, the exact schedules, or exactly how he will come here.

Q. Chalmers M. Roberts, Washington Post: On this schedule, sir, do you know when you will go to Europe——

THE PRESIDENT. No—oh, excuse me. Finish your question.

Q. Mr. Roberts: ——to see the allied heads of state?

THE PRESIDENT. Sometime later in this month I would like to; that is my suggestion.

Q. Mr. Roberts: And then you will come back here?

THE PRESIDENT. That is right.

Q. Mr. Roberts: And Khrushchev will come here?

THE PRESIDENT. Yes.

Q. Mr. Roberts: Will you accompany him in the United States as he, you, in the Soviet Union?

THE PRESIDENT. Well, I don't think it would be feasible for me to go all the way through the United States with him. But certainly, there might be some visiting around. I don't know, the details are just something I just don't know anything about yet.

Q. Mr. Roberts: But you do expect to get to Russia yourself before winter closes in there? [*Laughter*]

THE PRESIDENT. Well, there, I don't know. I would say, the fall doesn't end until December 22d, so if I stick with my schedule it will have to be before that, but that's about all I can say.

Q. Felix Belair, New York Times: The impression has somehow been received, Mr. President, that in considering a possible visit by Mr. Khrushchev to the United States, that before you would issue an invitation to him, there would have to be some evidence of give. I mean in the sense of give and take on the part of Mr. Khrushchev, on Western principles. May we take it that there has been some such indication?

THE PRESIDENT. No, I don't think you can say that, Mr. Belair.

This is what I have said: the holding of a summit meeting and negotiation, that that would be, to my mind, absolutely impractical and as the State Department says, counterproductive unless we could count on some positive results.

But I would say these, so far as our discussions of mutual problems, are exploratory rather than any attempt at negotiation.

Q. Mrs. May Craig, Portland (Maine) Press Herald: Mr. President, were the Vice President's hints in Russia that a visit is possible, with or without your permission; and were they possibly part of your plan for laying the ground for your announcement today?

THE PRESIDENT. Well, they were only to this extent: that I told the Vice President the day he left here—before he left, I guess—that these negotiations were in progress in written form and that the prospects were they would take place.

Now, I told him, I said, "so that you will not be astonished or surprised and feel let down by your Government, should they be opened up by the other side; you are not, yourself, and of course will not open this subject." But these offhand remarks about what would be a good thing, that of course was on his own initiative. There was certainly never any prohibition, because everybody else that's gone over there has said whether or not this would be a good thing, and I guess he had the same opportunity.

I think I'd better get over here.

Q. Spencer Davis, Associated Press: Would you spell out a little further, sir, what you hope to accomplish through your meeting with the allied powers before your meeting with Mr. Khrushchev?

THE PRESIDENT. I think coordination with the allied powers has been remarkably good in the past weeks, but I do think this: that there are a number of problems, some of them not even affecting the U.S.S.R., but some of them touching upon it, that ought to be talked out between heads of government, and since I am to see the other member of the four powers that undertook the control of Germany after the war, I thought it would probably be a good thing to see the other two.

So I am ready in this month to go over and to see these people, if this is acceptable to them. Already I have heard from one, Mr. Macmillan, who will be delighted, so I am quite sure I will be going to Europe sometime in the latter part of the month.

Q. William J. Eaton, United Press International: How long will you stay in Russia?

THE PRESIDENT. Well, I would doubt that I could give the same amount of time he gives here, but I wouldn't know any details. I'd have to talk about it.

Q. Richard Dudman, St. Louis Post-Dispatch: Do you intend also to talk to the West Germans?

THE PRESIDENT. Oh, I'm quite sure that somewhere along the line, if I get over there, I'll see Mr. Adenauer.

Q. Mr. Dudman: I mean in advance of the visit to Russia?

THE PRESIDENT. Oh, yes, yes. I would, of course. When I go over there in August, certainly I will hope to see Mr. Adenauer somewhere along the line, it may not be in Bonn. After all, it takes time to go to each of these places and to go through the certain preliminaries for each talk; therefore, you don't know what the details will be.

Q. Fletcher Knebel, Cowles Publications: Could you say, sir, was it just two items of correspondence, you invited him and he accepted, or was there more than that?

THE PRESIDENT. Well, I'd say it is a little bit more complicated than that. [*Laughter*]

Sterling F. Green, Associated Press: Thank you, Mr. President.

NOTE: President Eisenhower's one hundred and sixty-seventh news conference was held in the Executive Office Building from 10:30 to 10:45 o'clock on Monday morning, August 3, 1959. In attendance: 139.

174 ¶ Message to the Governors' Conference in San Juan, Puerto Rico. *August* 3, 1959

[Read by Under Secretary of State C. Douglas Dillon]

IT IS an honor to send greetings, for the first time, to forty-nine State Governors at this Annual Conference. And I will shortly sign a proclamation officially admitting the fiftieth State. I am equally pleased that you are assembled in San Juan, heart of the great Commonwealth of Puerto Rico.

We Americans introduced to the world a new concept by which local and national interests form a partnership for self-government. The admission of Alaska and Hawaii to the Union reaffirms our belief in this Federal system. It is further strengthened by our unique and special relationship with the Commonwealth of Puerto Rico, which stands as a shining symbol of friendship and cooperation.

A gathering of the Governors of our States is an occasion on which to voice our pride in the wisdom of our Founders. It should also be a time to look ahead to present and future problems, searching for solutions that are in accord with our great heritage.

Last October 16th the population clock in Washington registered 175 million people. As each second is ticked off we have new lives to think of; with each year we, in effect, admit to the Union another State whose population is about that of Kentucky.

We are dedicated to meeting the governmental needs of this expanding nation within the finely balanced Federal framework. We know that heavy-handed centralization, the loss of local responsibility, leads to the loss of local authority and finally of individual freedom. In your efforts to guard against this centralizing tendency, and to lead the way to ever-rising standards of governmental excellence, I again extend my fraternal cooperation to you, the Chief Executives of the forty-nine States of the American Union, the Commonwealth of Puerto Rico, and the Territories that are represented at this Conference.

DWIGHT D. EISENHOWER

175 ¶ Statement by the President Upon Signing a Bill Amending the Tennessee Valley Authority Act. *August 6, 1959*

I HAVE TODAY approved the bill, H.R. 3460, an act to amend the Tennessee Valley Authority Act of 1933, as amended, and for other purposes. This measure meets basic requirements of major importance to the future of the TVA—a program of self-financing; a program of repayments to the government of the major portion of its investment plus interest; and a limitation upon future geographical expansion of the TVA service area. While the provisions of the bill in respect to these matters vary in certain details from what I should have preferred, they broadly conform to the purposes I had in mind in originally proposing this legislation.

One part of this bill, however, is wholly unacceptable. It attempts to divorce TVA's construction program of new power-producing projects from effective Executive review and allows the Congress to modify the Authority's program without regard to the views of the President and without opportunity for the President to exercise his Constitutional role in the legislative process.

TVA is, however, part of the Executive Branch of the Government. Therefore, this particular provision would be a clear invasion of the prerogatives of the Chief Executive. Accordingly, I have conferred with Leaders of both parties in the Senate and House of Representatives; we are in full agreement that the independence of the Executive and Legislative Branches must be preserved. I have been informed by these Leaders that legislation will be passed swiftly by both Houses deleting this objectionable feature. In accordance with that understanding, I have approved H.R. 3460.

NOTE: As enacted, H.R. 3460 is Public Law 86-137 (73 Stat. 280).

176 ❡ Radio and Television Address to the American People on the Need for an Effective Labor Bill. *August 6,* 1959

[Delivered from the President's Office]

My Fellow Americans:

I want to speak to you tonight about an issue of great importance to every man, every woman, and every child in this Nation. It is above any partisan political consideration. It affects every American, regardless of occupation, regardless of political affiliation.

I speak of labor reform legislation.

In these few minutes I hope to place before you some salient facts affecting this matter so that all of us may more fully understand what is at stake.

This Nation needs a law to meet the kind of racketeering, corruption, and abuses of power disclosed in many instances by the Senate Investigating Committee headed by Senator McClellan. For 2 years, I have advocated such a law.

For many months, newspapers have carried extensive accounts of racketeering and corruption in labor-management matters. Many of you have actually witnessed disclosures of this corruption on television in your own homes. It is a national disgrace.

The legislation we need has nothing to do with wages—or strikes—or problems we normally face when employers and employees disagree. Nor am I talking of any new approach to collective bargaining. Nor about any new labor-management philosophy. I am talking solely about a reform law—a law to protect the American people from the gangsters, racketeers, and other corrupt elements who have invaded the labor-management field.

You know, a great deal is being said and written about this subject. We hear one bill called a "weak" bill—another, a "strong" bill—and so on. The American people are not interested in adjectives—or in labels. They are interested in a law which will eliminate the abuses.

I want only effective protection from gangsters and crooks for the people of America—for the men and women who labor with their hands, their minds, their energies, to make America a better place for themselves and for their families.

We all know that only a small minority of individuals among unions and employers are involved in corrupt activities. We know that the vast numbers of employers and union officials are honest, and deplore corruption as much as you and I deplore it.

But any corrupt minority is too large.

The damage that such a minority does to working men and women, and to the American public cannot be tolerated.

After all—employers and unions operate in this field under the sanction and protection of Federal law. The people very properly look to their Government to pass effective laws to stop abuses.

To date, legislation to correct these deplorable conditions has not been enacted. Meanwhile, the evidence of abuses has continued to mount before congressional committees. Chief among the abuses from which Americans need protection are the oppressive practices of coercion.

Take a company in the average American town—your town. A union official comes into the office, presents the company with a proposed labor contract, and demands that the company either sign or be picketed. The company refuses, because its employees don't want to join that union. And remember, the law definitely gives employees the right to have or not to have a union—clearly a basic American right of choice.

Now what happens? The union official carries out the threat and puts a picket line outside the plant—to drive away customers—to cut off deliveries. In short, to force the employees into a union they do not want. This is one example of what has been called blackmail picketing. It is unfair and unjust. This could force the company out of business and result in the loss of all the jobs in the plant.

I want that sort of thing stopped. So does America.

Take another company—let us say, a furniture manufacturer. The employees vote against joining a particular union. Instead of picketing the furniture plant itself, unscrupulous organizing officials, in this case, use another scheme. They picket the stores which sell the furniture this plant manufactures. The purpose is to prevent those stores from handling that furniture.

How can anyone justify this kind of pressure against stores which are not involved in any dispute. They are innocent bystanders. This kind of action is designed to make the stores bring pressure on the furniture plant and its employees—to force those employees into a union they do not want. This is an example of a "secondary boycott."

I want that sort of thing stopped. So does America.

The blackmail picket line and the secondary boycott cannot possibly help the working men and women of America.

Another important problem is that of the so-called "no man's land." Under existing law, the States have practically no authority over labor cases, according to Supreme Court decision.

Here is a typical example of what can happen in this situation. A labor dispute occurs at a small plant. The union—or the employer— goes to the Federal Labor Board. The Board says the case is too small for Federal action—because it has only a small effect on interstate commerce. Then, the union, or the employer, goes to State officials, but they can't do anything because the States have no authority. That leaves the worker and his employer in this "no man's land"—cut off from Federal or State help.

What is the result? The disputing parties have no recourse to law. So, all too often, the dispute is "settled"—if we can use such a word—by force, with a test of strength between them, with damage to one or both, and to the community.

I want the "no man's land" abolished, because I believe that small unions and small businessmen have rights, just as everyone else. I want to give the States authority to deal with cases the Federal Board cannot and should not handle and, by all means, we must not bring every case to the Federal level, as some have proposed. In this kind of situation the States can act more promptly and more effectively than can the Federal Government.

Now any reform bill worthy of the name must also protect the individual rights of union members—within their unions. It must assure them of fair elections. It must assure them of honest handling of their money—money made up by dues often collected under auspices of Federal law. It must also give to the Government effective authority to investigate and enforce these provisions. Unless it does these things, and deals effectively with the problems of coercive picketing, boycotting, and the "no man's land," it is not a reform bill at all.

Now let us examine what Congress has done so far this year. Has its action measured up to the minimum requirements I have outlined to protect the American people? I regret to say that, as yet, the answer is no—definitely no.

The bill which passed the Senate in April is not effective. It does not deal with or curb the picketing or boycotting practices I have described. And while it purports to deal with the "no man's land," it gives no real relief.

In the House of Representatives, the Labor Committee bill is even less effective than the Senate bill. It, too, fails to deal with picketing and boycotting practices I have described. Its provisions relating to the "no man's land" go precisely in the wrong direction. And it actually exempts about 70 percent of all unions from reporting on their finances. It even removes criminal penalties against those who violate the rights of union members.

Neither the Senate bill nor the House Committee bill will really curb the abuses the American people want to see corrected.

However, Congress need not limit itself to such a choice.

The Administration bill is still before the Congress. There is also before the House a bipartisan bill jointly sponsored by two Members of the House Labor Committee—Mr. Landrum of Georgia, a Democrat, and Mr. Griffin of Michigan, a Republican. The Landrum-Griffin bill is a good start toward a real labor reform bill, containing many of the corrective provisions I have urged.

Again I emphasize: labor reform is not a partisan matter. Further, I don't come before you in any partisan sense. I am not a candidate for office—in this or other issues. I do not seek the support of any special interests. I am only trying to make sure that American workers and the public get the kind of protection that Americans deserve.

Nearly one hundred years ago Abraham Lincoln in his memorable Address spoke of the sacrifices made so that, in his words: "government of the people, by the people, for the people, shall not perish from the earth." That was the question he posed to our Nation in his generation.

In our lives and actions, the people of America, in private and public sectors, daily face millions of choices with this continuing question always in the background.

As the Congress prepares to vote on labor reform, this great question is still, as always, with us. In the basic sense, the issue is: shall the people govern? If they do not, crooks and racketeers could prevail.

This business of government, including this question of labor reform, is your business. It is every citizen's business.

Americans want reform legislation which will be truly effective. It is my earnest hope that Congress will be fully responsive to an overwhelming national demand.

Thank you, and good night.

177 ¶ Remarks to Members of the National Rural Letter Carriers Association.
August 11, 1959

Mr. President, Ladies and Gentlemen:

When I realized that I was to have the privilege of meeting so many of the rural letter carriers, it was inevitable that my mind should go back to the farming community where I was raised as a boy. It was there I first met people of your profession—people who had the duty and the responsibility, and indeed the privilege, of keeping our rural families in touch with the rest of the world.

Now, in those days, it was not so easy. So far as I can recall, I never saw a paved road in my youth. My small town of Abilene—as the Kansas representatives here will probably know—didn't have a paved street, even in that town, until somewhere along about 1906. But back in 1898, when I was a young boy—starting down to the Smoky Hills to fish, or shooting rabbits and quail in the fields—the one vehicle, the one activity that you could count on was the rural mail deliverer. He came along with a one-horse wagon, always with the top up, because the weather was bad. In rainy weather he was down to his axles. I often wondered just exactly when his day ended, because he had quite a route— an assignment of a dozen miles or so—and it really took time, this dozen miles or so, down a Kansas gumbo road in a rainy season.

So you have come a long way, not only in numbers, but in the type of service or at least the exact character of the work that you are required to do. With automobiles and with paved roads, it's a different thing. But the job is still the same—to make certain that our rural population is not cut off from the same privileges of mail delivery and in touch with the rest of the world exactly as the urban population is kept in touch.

Of course now with the television and the radio and your mail carrier, we think of the country home, the country family, as just as well informed—possibly better informed—than a lot of our urban families.

I lived among those farm families, and I know how difficult it was to keep in touch, in the old days. Beyond the crops and the condition of the cattle, and the hogs, and the rest of it, we didn't know, often, what was going on. Although as a boy, I must tell you, particularly those of you who are Democrats—very few, I hope—that I did carry a torch in a McKinley torch parade in 1896 in Abilene, Kansas.

So I congratulate you today, one reason being that you have become so numerous, your importance is more recognized, and because you have so organized that you can make your own sentiments and your own feelings and your own convictions expressed through your officers and through your organizations.

Someone told me that your organization was very much on the side of keeping down rising costs, keeping down inflation, and above all, unnecessary Federal expenditures. If that is your doctrine, ladies and gentlemen, I would like to be an honorary member of your organization.

Thank you and good luck.

NOTE: The President spoke at the south portico of the White House. His opening words "Mr. President" referred to Charles R. Larson, President of the National Rural Letter Carriers Association.

178 ¶ Statement by the President Upon Signing Bill Concerning the Promotion of Naval Officers. *August* 11, 1959

I HAVE TODAY signed H.R. 4413, "An Act to provide improved opportunity for promotion for certain officers in the Naval service, and for other purposes."

One provision of the Act repeals, effective November 1, 1959, a 1925 law which, as amended, requires upon their retirement, the honorary advancement to the next higher grade of Navy and Marine Corps officers who were specially commended for performance of duty in actual combat prior to January 1, 1947.

The November 1 deadline poses a serious problem for those active duty

˙officers who are presently eligible for honorary promotion upon retirement. A number of these officers are, of course, on sea duty or at stations abroad.   In a very short time they must decide either to effect their retirement by the November 1, 1959 deadline, or to continue on active service beyond that date in the hope that they will receive a regular promotion in due course.

This decision is made more difficult by the principal provisions of H.R. 4413 which will bring about the forced retirement of many officers in order to prevent a stagnation in the promotion of their juniors.   I believe that it would be only fair to officers, who by their noteworthy combat service, have shown their dedication to our country, that they be allowed an additional period of time during which to make what is for them a momentous decision.

Out of consideration for the service which these officers have rendered, I hope the Congress will promptly accord them such additional time.

NOTE: As enacted, H.R. 4413 is Public Law 86–155 (73 Stat. 333).

179   ¶ The President's News Conference at Gettysburg, Pennsylvania.   *August* 12, 1959

THE PRESIDENT. Good morning.   This is one way to get some of you people to come up to see the famous battlefield, isn't it?

I have no announcements.   We'll go to questions.

Q. John M. Hightower, Associated Press: Mr. President, what results do you hope to achieve in your talks with Premier Khrushchev?

THE PRESIDENT. Well, I would hope for a bettering of the atmosphere between the East and the West.   I do not by any manner of means intend or plan that this meeting can become a real negotiation of basic problems between the West and the East, because I have no intention of attempting to be the spokesman for the West.

You will recall that Mr. Adenauer has gone to Moscow, Mr. Macmillan has gone to Moscow, and there have been these private talks between these several countries—Mr. Khrushchev and the Prime Ministers of these two countries.   I am trying to do my best to see whether we can't bring about a somewhat better situation in the relations between the two and maybe he can learn a little bit more about our country as certainly I can about his.

Q. Charles W. Roberts, Newsweek: Sir, in that connection despite the fact that Mr. Khrushchev has said he does not want to see military installations in this country, several Members of Congress are insisting that he should be shown our missile bases and our military might, so that he won't miscalculate in the future. What is your reaction to their demands?

THE PRESIDENT. When you ask someone as a guest to your country, you do not attempt to regiment the guest and force him to do things whether he wants to or not. He was, or will be, invited; I have instructed that he be invited to see some of our installations. If he doesn't want to, that is that. And I didn't ask any *quid pro quo,* I might say, for it.

Q. Edward T. Folliard, Washington Post: Mr. President, at your last press conference you were asked whether on your European trip you would see Chancellor Adenauer of Germany, and your answer was "Somewhere along the line . . . it may not be in Bonn."

Since then, of course, you have announced you will go to Bonn.

THE PRESIDENT. That is right.

Q. Mr. Folliard: Is there any story behind that, Mr. President?

THE PRESIDENT. Not at all. I, of course, was trying to make the thing as easy on myself as I could, and I had understood that the Chancellor had already been invited by Mr. Macmillan to come to London, and therefore it seemed to be a very natural thing to do. But he was not coming to London at that particular time. I want to see him, and so I am going to see him.

Q. William Knighton, Jr., Baltimore Sun: Mr. President, since the foreign ministers have failed to produce any progress on anything, do you now have a new criteria for your attendance at a possible summit meeting?

THE PRESIDENT. Well, at least this, I still have this: progress.

Now, I would like to, in my conversations with Mr. Khrushchev, see and ask him at least why he will not allow such progress. My criterion is still progress that I can see as measurable progress.

Q. Robert C. Pierpoint, CBS News: In recent weeks, sir, we have been invited, or many of us have been invited, to share your hospitality at the White House, and to speak with you personally about many of the matters that concern all of us; and also you have now instituted or are going to institute a new form of diplomacy by travel around the world.

You have set a very heavy schedule for yourself. And you are participating with great vigor in domestic affairs.

And I was wondering, sir, if you could explain to us whether this apparent new departure for you is due to perhaps a new concept in your own mind of the Presidency, or whether you are just feeling much better physically, or why all of this activity?

THE PRESIDENT. Well, I think it is perfectly simple. I have told you people several times that I believe the Presidency should be relieved of detail and many of its activities by proper officials who can take delegated authority and exercise it in his name. But when you have a situation that has gone on, as we have had this cold war since 1945, and certainly since 1953 when the Korean War ended, it becomes the kind of a stalemate that has in it—well, it has the element of almost hopelessness for people, and finally becomes something there must be no gun unfired and no individual effort spared in order to break that kind of a stalemate. So the only thing here is that I am trying to end the stalemate and to bring people together more ready to talk.

Now, when you talk about in the domestic field, the situation is somewhat different. But let us remember that if I live to finish my tour, there will only be 25 percent of that tour in which I have had a Congress of the same political party as myself. Therefore, it becomes more and more difficult, I think, as time goes on, to get understandings and to get progress in legislation that will be helpful for the country. And I think it takes, therefore, possibly more personal activity than I think would be normal in more normal circumstances.

Q. Edward V. Koterba, United Features Syndicate: Mr. President, back in 1953 you made an observation regarding Milton Eisenhower's ability, stating that if it were not for his name, he would have had a high Government job at that time while you were President. And now there has been some talk that Dr. Eisenhower could well be considered by the Republicans for the post of Vice President or even the Presidency.

In view of the high regard that you and many others have towards your brother, would you not consider him excellent vice presidential material in 1960?

THE PRESIDENT. Well, I don't recant one single word about my admiration for my brother. But I couldn't think of anything that would be worse for any political party to take people so closely related as my

575

brother, who is 9 years younger than I, of course, and make it look like an attempt at establishing a bit of a dynasty. I would have none of that. And I tell you much more emphatically, he wouldn't have it.

Q. Stewart Hensley, United Press International: Mr. President, you spoke of instructing that Mr. Khrushchev see military installations if he wished to. Aside from that—

THE PRESIDENT. I said they would invite him.

Q. Mr. Hensley: Yes. Aside from that, sir, would you tell us what you would particularly like him to see in the United States, either specifically or in general categories?

THE PRESIDENT. I would like for him, among other things, to see this: the evidence that the fine, small or modest homes that Americans live in are not the unusual or exception as he seemed to think the sample we sent over to Moscow was.

I would like him to see, for example, Levittown—the town surrounding the Fairless plant—see this town universally and exclusively inhabited by its workmen, and to see what those homes are.

I would like to see him have to fly along in my chopper and just make a circuit of the District, to see the uncountable homes that have been built all around, modest but decent, fine, comfortable homes—all around this country.

I would like to see him go into our great farmland and see our farmers, each one operating on his own, not regimented.

For example, I would like to see him go in the little town where I was born and pick up the evidence—of course there are some still alive when I was there, you know—and let them tell him the story of how hard I worked until I was 21, when I went to West Point. He said in one of his conversations to Mr. Nixon, "What do you know about work? You never worked." Well, I can show him the evidence that I did, and I would like him to see it.

Now, I want him to see our great industrial plants and what we are doing.

I want him to see a happy people. I want him to see a free people, doing exactly as they choose, within the limits that they must not transgress the rights of others.

Q. Laurence H. Burd, Chicago Tribune: Mr. President, do you plan to go with Mr. Khrushchev anywhere outside of Washington, show him around?

THE PRESIDENT. No, not unless there would be some unusual or abnormal sort of a little trip that I don't think of at the moment.

Q. Mr. Burd: Do you think he will be coming up here?

THE PRESIDENT. No, I don't. It is possible that he might want to come up to Camp David or possibly even Gettysburg. I don't know. I don't know what the details are. As a matter of fact, I believe there has been only one conference between my representative and his on the details, and there has been no answer yet received from them. So I can't give you any details. I am just telling you the kind of thing I would like to have him see of America.

Q. Felix Belair, New York Times: Mr. President, if we can leave Mr. Khrushchev for a minute, could you tell us anything at all, Mr. President, about your plans for participation in the next campaign, the presidential campaign—if you have had time to even think about it.

THE PRESIDENT. Well, by that time, of course, after the nominations, I will be a little bit of a bystander, as far as contests are concerned. I will, of course, have to carry on my own official duties. So I would say what I would be in would be those activities that are suggested and requested by the people running the campaign and where I can fit them in with my own work schedule.

Now, I will say this: no one could be more concerned than I am in the opportunity for preserving and strengthening what I call moderate government, sound, middle-of-the-road government in this country. I am completely dedicated to it, and I shall do what I can as long as it is requested by the people who at that time will be responsible for that phase of the activity.

Q. Lewis W. Shollenberger, CBS News: Mr. President, up on the Hill Congress is getting ready to go home. I wonder if you have any ideas, any priorities, if you will, of what you would like to see them pass before they went home.

THE PRESIDENT. Have you got any authority for that first statement you made? [*Laughter*]

As you know, I believe that it is vital to this country that we have an adjustment in the interest rate law. I believe that our prosperity and the soundness of our money demands it. I believe that a reasonable labor bill that will stop the kind of secondary boycott, blackmail picketing that I have before described must be enacted, should be enacted certainly.

I believe that the road bill should be financed so that it can go on for the benefit of this country on a pay-as-you-go basis, instead of asking our grandchildren to pay it for us.

And finally, I think that a sound civil rights bill should be enacted.

Now, there are some others. I should still like to see something in wheat, and some of the others that have been already rejected. But those would, I think, really be something the Congress should certainly consider very earnestly.

In addition, I should say, I would like to see a revised housing bill, one that I believed was sound.

Q. Edward W. O'Brien, St. Louis Globe-Democrat: Mr. President, when the Vice President was in Russia, he was challenged repeatedly by the Russians on the point of our bases abroad. If Khrushchev raises that same question, would you, sir, indicate the line of your answer?

THE PRESIDENT. Simply this: this country disarmed unilaterally after 1945 to a level that I think every military man certainly thought was unwise. And when we began to see what we had done to ourselves, and we began to restore our defense arrangements, it was also clear that there were a lot of nations in the world, feeling as we do, wanted to associate themselves together. Therefore, it was only logical and proper that these bases should be established. And I am quite sure every statesman or political leader of the world knows that they are only defensive.

As I have pointed out so often, how can a democracy make a surprise attack—for the simple reason that we have to engage in war by the will of the Congress. At the very least—let us say like in a war with Spain, the people were inflamed by the Maine incident—the fact is that the matter has to be debated and decided in the Congress. Nowadays a surprise attack can be made in minutes. There would be no time for such debates.

A free country, in my opinion, is absolutely helpless when it comes to launching a surprise attack.

These bases and our armaments are not meant for aggression and they will never be used that way.

Q. William H. Lawrence, New York Times: Mr. President, to revert back to Mr. Belair's question, in terms of the 1960 campaign, do you regard your role as party leader, and President, as one in which you will exercise purely a veto power over a prospective Republican nominee who would be unsatisfactory in terms of your foreign and domestic policies? You have told us, too, that you would not express a preference.

Is this because you feel that the 8 or 10 men that you have mentioned as a group, without identifying them——

THE PRESIDENT. Yes.

Q. Mr. Lawrence:——are so evenly matched in terms of the Presidency that you have no real preference as between one and the other?

THE PRESIDENT. No, I don't think it is that completely, Mr. Lawrence. Very naturally, we know that every individual is different from all others, and therefore the reaction on me is different to each of those individuals than it would be on you.

Now, what I'm saying is this: you want a candidate who is vigorous, who is straightforward, hard-hitting, who really honestly believes in the philosophy that would hopefully be expounded in the national platform of that year. And then a man who has a real standing in the minds of the public for experience, honesty, integrity, and character.

Now, if you have got these things, I would think that the worst thing that could happen would be any attempt to interfere with the free choice of the Republican Convention. And consequently when I say I would not interfere, this is just as strongly as I can make the thing. I shall not interfere with the choice they make. But, as I said, merely that if the choice falls among those people that I have indicated, but in an anonymous fashion, I will do whatever I possibly can to help in the election.

Q. James B. Reston, New York Times: Mr. President, would you talk to us about the kind of personal papers that you have kept of an historical nature over this remarkable period you have been in office.

THE PRESIDENT. Unfortunately, I think some of them at times are not quite as complete as they could be. However, there are records which by long custom and I suppose by law become the personal records of the President, and those go to this repository in Kansas, the library that is now under development.

The records, by and large, of course, are found in your correspondence, in the papers that you have to approve—those are in your own personal files, that is, a copy of them—and finally, such records as you have in the results of all of the conferences and meetings that you have weekly in the White House.

So that, embellished by a few memorandums—a good many memorandums and recommendations, are the records that I think will be finally stored at that place.

Q. Mr. Reston: Is it your intention to do some personal writing yourself, or have you put in train any orderly procedure for writing the history of this period?

THE PRESIDENT. I haven't. I have tried my best to keep everything orderly in the way, in the keeping of the records, because I believe they belong finally to the public and to posterity, because every era is another milestone in effect in American history, and they will belong to them.

Now, for my own part, frankly, I can quote only General Somervell when he left the Army, and they asked him what he was going to do. He said, well, first he was going to sit on the back porch, and then he thought that after about 6 weeks he would start to rock slowly.

Well, now, after that, I don't know exactly what I will do. But I will say this: I will certainly have an interest, a very vital interest, even if I don't participate, in the work that you people, this collective group, what you do every day, because to my mind it is more important today to educate the United States almost, than it is to do anything of a spectacular nature abroad or great trips or anything of that kind. And I believe that everybody that has knowledge and conviction on both our domestic and our foreign affairs ought to be trying to put these things in the way so that America can understand the basic issues, because that is the strength of this country—understanding of those issues.

Q. Spencer Davis, Associated Press: Mr. President, the State Department has warned several times of its concern over the situation in Laos, and indicated that this has the backing of Moscow and Peiping in stirring up tensions in southeast Asia. Do you intend to talk to Mr. Khrushchev about this in your effort to ease the cold war?

THE PRESIDENT. I think it would be only natural for me to say this. Each of us talks about his hopes for peace, a better understanding. And where we see incidents, even if not necessarily inspired in Moscow, but inspired certainly by Communists, well, then of course, I think such specific instances will have to be part of such conversations.

Q. Frank Holeman, New York Daily News: Mr. President, you have told us what part of the United States and what areas you would like to show Mr. Khrushchev. Could you tell us now what parts of the Soviet Union you would like to see and what particular things you would like to see?

THE PRESIDENT. Well, I would like to have a few days to see people more than anything else. And that is a thing that is a little bit born of necessity. You see, any so-called VIP going around to see anything is inevitably surrounded by very large groups. He really can't take a good look at the facade of a building. How can you stand in the middle of ten thousand people and look up here at the Empire State Building? You just don't do that.

Now, you do have, as you go around such trips as the Vice President did, people who are knowledgeable; he was very experienced in this kind of thing, and he had people looking into educational facilities, medical facilities. He had Admiral Rickover along. He had people that were actually observing for him more searchingly than he could possibly observe. So I would say I would like to see people because, as I say, I have to do it.

Q. John Edwards, American Broadcasting Company: Mr. President, some of those who have been criticizing the invitation to Mr. Khrushchev have called this a reversal of Mr. Dulles' policy. Will you discuss this point, and also will you tell us when the decision was made that the time was now ripe to invite Mr. Khrushchev, and when you first issued that invitation?

THE PRESIDENT. This is far from a reversal. Mr. Dulles and I used to discuss this thing often with others of the State Department, one or two, but never in large groups, and the possibility of what might come out of it.

Now, just as I would feel today, I would be foolish to say that I expect everything about such a trip or such a visit to be on the plus side. There will be some minuses, no question.

Now, finally, I think in the later months of 1958, we began to feel that the methods that we were pursuing had to be reinforced by something differently than we had been doing up to this moment. Now, he and I never got around to a decision, but we watched very closely the first session of the foreign ministers meeting in which at that moment I had hopes, but very little expectation. So we began to work on this thing, and I gave this subject to two or three of my trusted associates in the State Department and said, "Now let's try to tot up the balance."

And so when it came into the beginning of July, this decision was made, and I invited him.

Q. Raymond M. Lahr, United Press International: Mr. President, the steel strike is 4 weeks old today. Has there been any change in your attitude about the role of the Federal Government in this dispute?

THE PRESIDENT. Not in the slightest. There was an act called the

Wagner Act enacted many years ago, and its greatest and first premise was that the bargaining between management and labor should be free and untrammeled. And personally, I think, except for the use of the Federal Mediation Service, that until there is a national emergency discernible, a national requirement, a need for action, I couldn't think of anything more objectionable than to put the Federal Government constantly in the business of settling these major strikes.

Now, just the other day, I believe it was yesterday, someone told me that there was a feeling that this strike had to be settled before Mr. Khrushchev got here.

Well, don't we want Mr. Khrushchev to see this country as a freedom-loving place? Why should we worry too much about the fact that people can strike in this country? I think that this is a shallow kind of thinking.

Now, I will say this: democracy is the strongest when there are among the different individuals and groups cooperation rather than strife, when there is self-discipline rather than just too intense competition. So the strength would be seen, but only if it is done on a free basis. Because if we are going to do it on a regimented basis, then we are a different type of country than I think we want.

Q. Donald H. Shannon, Los Angeles Times: What is the status of your National Goals Commission?

THE PRESIDENT. I think we have not yet, still, finished the complete arrangements for its financing. I have absolutely refused to go to the Federal Government. I am not going to be a pressure group of one, asking the Federal Government for money. The financing is going ahead, and when that is completed—so that the work doesn't have to stop right in the middle—it will get going.

Q. Garnett D. Horner, Washington Star: Mr. President, you mentioned a while ago, sir, you would like to see a sound housing bill passed by the Congress. There is a considerable difference of opinion, it seems, on Capitol Hill, as to whether you would find acceptable a substitute bill that has been worked up by a subcommittee of the Senate committee. Could you tell us whether it would be?

THE PRESIDENT. There was, as a matter of fact, a number of quite objectionable features. But there were four, as I recall. One was a college classroom building put in a housing bill. Well, this seems to me to be sort of an abrupt change in policy. This is for housing. Then the special arrangements for the housing for elderly people, and one or two others that I thought were particularly objectionable.

I do not, by any manner of means, say that a bill has to conform in every detail to the desires or the convictions that I express. We all know that all bills that the President signs are normally compromises of some kind, and I am not one to refuse to compromise. I still won't back away from principle though, and when it runs into principle, including the principle of a sound economy and paying as you go, instead of going further in debt, then I will be very quick to object.

Q. Douglas B. Cornell, Associated Press: Mr. President, you mentioned the fact that you would like to see the Soviet Premier see some defense installations or military installations. What type do you have in mind—missile bases, for example?

THE PRESIDENT. No—now, I am not going to make a great point of this. He was invited on the theory that he might like to see some of our defense establishments to get an idea of their strength and their modern character, and I am not going to push and press it. So let's not put in my mouth words that I think he should do it. This is just his privilege, and if he doesn't want to do it, okay.

Also, I would give him a fairly wide choice in the character of installation, if he wanted to see it.

Mr. Cornell, Associated Press: Thank you, Mr. President.

NOTE: President Eisenhower's one hundred and sixty-eighth news conference was held in a gymnasium adjacent to the temporary White House Office in the Hotel Gettysburg from 10:00 to 10:30 o'clock on Wednesday morning, August 12, 1959. In attendance: 95.

180 ¶ Statement by the President Following the Adoption by the House of Representatives of the Landrum-Griffin Labor Reform Bill.
August 13, 1959

WITH, I am sure, millions of Americans I applaud the House of Representatives for its vote today in support of the Landrum-Griffin Labor Reform Bill which would deal effectively with the abuses disclosed by the McClellan Committee. I congratulate all those who voted in support of this legislation.

This action gives cause for real hope that the Congress will ultimately pass a good Labor Reform Bill.

NOTE: This statement was released at Gettysburg, Pa. The President approved the Labor-Management Reporting and Disclosure Act of 1959 (Public Law 86–257, 73 Stat. 519) on September 14, 1959.

181 ¶ Statement by the President Upon Signing the Labor and the Health, Education, and Welfare Appropriations Bill. *August* 14, 1959

I HAVE TODAY approved H.R. 6769, which makes appropriations for fiscal 1960 for the Departments of Labor and Health, Education, and Welfare, and for certain other agencies.

I have taken this action despite concern with regard to the appropriations for the Department of Health, Education, and Welfare.

First, with respect to medical research, every American is of course deeply interested in the improvement of health. This interest is reflected in the Administration's progressive record of support for health activities. But there is a limit to the rate at which medical research can grow and yet grow soundly. Appropriations to the National Institutes of Health have increased fourfold in the last six years. H.R. 6769 would add a further increase—from $294 million to $400 million—or 36% in a single year. This increase gives me cause for concern on three grounds. I am concerned lest it should:

(1) Lower the quality of the projects supported by increasing the flow of grant applications more rapidly than the procedures for their careful appraisal can be effectively adapted;

(2) Cause too great a diversion into research of the manpower and other resources needed for equally vital teaching and medical practice;

(3) Substitute Federal funds for non-Federal support of medical research and training and discourage further expansion of such support.

Such effects would work against the very goal being sought—improved health for all the American people. Indeed, the Congress itself apparently felt concerned about the possible lowering of research quality which might result from the level of funds it approved, since the conference report on H.R. 6769 states that "there should be no reduction in the high standards for determining the acceptability of research projects for financing from these appropriations."

Because the American taxpayer is entitled to have his tax money spent wisely and efficiently, I am directing the Secretary of Health, Education, and Welfare and the Surgeon General of the Public Health Service to take appropriate steps to satisfy themselves that the following criteria will be observed in the review of any new research project or training program:

(1) That it is of such high priority and great promise that its deferment would be likely to delay progress in medical discovery;

(2) That it will not result in the harmful diversion of manpower and other resources needed for teaching and medical care services; and

(3) That it will not bring about the substitution of Federal for non-Federal sources of support for medical research and training.

Second, in the category of construction grant programs—grants for the construction of sewage treatment plants, facilities for medical care and research, and schools in Federally affected areas—the appropriations made in the bill would provide for program levels which seem to me to be entirely too high in relation to other essential Government programs.

I do not doubt that worthwhile construction projects can be found in each of these areas which will absorb the funds appropriated. But the mere fact that money is spent for some identifiable need does not mean that it is wisely spent, or that it must be spent by the Federal Government. With respect to the waste treatment construction grant program, I am requesting the Secretary of Health, Education, and Welfare to urge the States, in their various State plans, to make every effort to give first priority in the approval of projects by the States to those which involve interstate stream pollution or affect downstream communities.

A national budget demands hard choices just as does a family budget. The recognition of a need is the beginning, not the end, of any budget-making process. I recognize, however, that in reconciling competing demands within the total framework of a sound fiscal policy, the Congress, as well as the Executive Branch, has responsibility for the exercise of judgment. Therefore, even though I disagree in this instance with the manner in which that judgment has been exercised, I do not feel that I should withhold my approval of this bill.

NOTE: As enacted, H.R. 6769 is Public Law 86–158 (73 Stat. 339).

182 ¶ Veto of Bill Relating to Oil and Gas Leases or Options in Alaska. *August 17, 1959*

To the House of Representatives:

I return herewith, without my approval, H.R. 6940, "An Act to amend the Mineral Leasing Act of 1920 in order to increase certain acreage limitations with respect to the State of Alaska."

An unrestricted doubling of the present maximum allowable holding of oil and gas leases or options—which H.R. 6940, in the case of Alaska, would authorize—would not, in my judgment, be in the best interests of Alaska or the Federal Government.

Rather than providing an inducement to the development of oil and gas resources in Alaska, the bill would tend to produce an excessive concentration of control over such potential resources, and there is no assurance provided by the bill that the interests so held would at any time be developed.

Development contracts and unit agreements already provide relief from acreage limitations when circumstances justify their approval.   Any additional concentration of ownership would among other things deter participation in these existing and successful programs which are designed to provide specific assurance of the expenditure of funds for exploration and development work.   The need is for further progress under existing programs, not just speculative or control holding of excessive acreages, if the development of oil and gas resources on public lands is to occur and the interests of Alaska and the Nation are to be served.

I am aware that allowing increased acreage holdings might be of immediate financial importance to our 49th State, but I believe this to be a shortsighted goal for it eventually could well result in depriving both the Alaskan and Federal governments of substantial revenue.   Sacrificing sound principle and the long-run public interest in order to achieve a limited immediate gain does not seem to me to be wise.

DWIGHT D. EISENHOWER

NOTE: This veto message was released at Gettysburg, Pa.

183   ¶ Letter to the President of the Senate and
to the Speaker of the House of Representatives
Transmitting the Final Report of the President's
Committee To Study the U.S. Military
Assistance Program.   *August* 20, 1959

Dear Mr. ——————:

I transmit herewith for the consideration of the Congress the Final
Report of the President's Committee to Study the United States Military
Assistance Program, with the several studies which are Annexes thereto.

Together with the Committee's three earlier Reports, of March 17,
June 3 and July 13, which I have previously sent to the Congress, this
Report and the annexed studies provide us with an extremely valuable
analysis of the Mutual Security Program.

Over a period of nine months, this group of eminent citizens has made
the completely independent, objective, and non-partisan analysis for
which I asked in appointing the Committee.   This penetrating examination will, I believe, furnish invaluable guidelines, both to the Congress
and the Executive Branch, for these programs which are of such critical
importance to the defense and foreign policy of the United States.

The members of the Committee have given many months of careful
study to these problems and have made a collective personal appraisal,
based on their own experience in activities closely related to the program
and on recent visits to the areas receiving assistance.

I call your special attention to the comments of the Committee concerning the dangerously low level of appropriations authorized for the
Military Assistance Program for fiscal 1960.   I agree with their analysis,
and, as indicated in my letter to you of April 29, this fall I shall review
the effect on the program of the final Congressional enactment for fiscal
1960. Following that review, I will make appropriate recommendations
to the Congress.

The basic concepts of the Committee's plan for reorganizing the administration of the Military Assistance Program, embodied in its second
Interim Report, were approved by me, and I am gratified that the Congress has already taken legislative measures toward putting some of these

recommendations into effect. Work is under way on implementing by executive action other recommendations of this Report.

The present Report, like the Third Report which dealt with economic assistance and its administration, covers fields so extensive as to require correspondingly extended consideration. I have submitted copies of this Report to the Executive Agencies concerned, and shall later communicate with the Congress concerning recommendations requiring legislation which are embodied in both the Third and Final Reports.

Sincerely,

DWIGHT D. EISENHOWER

NOTE: This is the text of identical letters addressed to the Honorable Richard M. Nixon, President of the Senate, and the Honorable Sam Rayburn, Speaker of the House of Representatives.

The report dated August 17, entitled "Conclusions Concerning the Mutual Se-

curity Programs," and the annexes are published in House Document 215, Parts 1 and 2 (86th Cong., 1st sess.). For releases concerning the reports of March 17, June 3, and July 13, see Items 90, 136, and 170, above.

184   ¶ Remarks Upon Signing the Proclamation Admitting Hawaii to the Union and the Executive Order Changing the Flag of the United States. *August 21, 1959*

Gentlemen:

I think that we shall recognize that this is truly an historic occasion because for the second time within a year a new State has been admitted to the Union. It had been a long time since any State had been admitted, so to have this 49th and 50th membership of our Union in such a short space is truly a unique experience.

All forty-nine States will join in welcoming the new one—Hawaii—to this Union. We will wish for her prosperity, security, happiness, and a growing closer relationship with all of the other States. We know that she is ready to do her part to make this Union a stronger Nation—a stronger people than it was before because of her presence as a full sister to the other forty-nine States. So all of us say to her, "Good Luck." And to each of her representatives, a very fine tour of service in the public domain. We know that they will find their work interesting and fruitful for all of us.

———————

The Speaker just reminds me of one fact that has great historic significance. Next Monday will be the first time in 158 years there has not been a Delegate in the membership of the Congress of the United States. The Delegates are gone and in their place we have Senators and Congressmen.

NOTE: The ceremony was held in the Cabinet Room at the White House at 4:00 p.m. Among those present were the Vice President, Speaker Sam Rayburn, Secretary of the Interior Seaton, Edward Johnson, former Secretary of the Territory of Hawaii (representing Governor-elect William F. Quinn), Senator-elect Oren E. Long, Representative-elect Daniel K. Inouye, Lawrence Lau (representing Senator-elect Hiram Fong), and Lorrin Thurston, Chairman of the Hawaii Statehood Commission.

The new 50-star flag, to become official on July 4, 1960, was unfurled immediately after the President signed the documents.

Executive Order 10834 "The Flag of the United States" and Proclamation 3309 "Admission of the State of Hawaii into the Union" are published in the Federal Register (24 F.R. 6865 and 6868, respectively).

185 ¶ Message Recorded for the American Bar Association Conference on the Law and the Layman at Miami Beach, Florida. *August 24, 1959*

Ladies and Gentlemen:

I want you to know that I am not simply indulging in formalities when I tell you how pleased I am—personally and officially—that you are undertaking this Conference on the Law and the Layman.

I am delighted with your interest in our judicial system, and especially our traffic courts. It may be a trite observation, but nevertheless a true one, that the traffic courts give most citizens their only first-hand contact with the judicial process.

These courts, then, need to be well conducted by qualified judges. An atmosphere of dignity is essential. The purpose at all times must be to safeguard the constitutional rights of all defendants, while serving the best interests of the public.

When these conditions exist, the people who appear in court respect the law, and realize that law exists for their protection. When courts do not come up to these standards, people become disillusioned and cynical.

It is inevitable, then, that traffic courts can foster respect for all courts.

Certainly your Conference is timely, coming when the Nation faces the depressing possibility of a new record traffic death toll of around forty thousand.

I believe most people do not realize—I learned it, myself, only recently—that violations of the law are involved in two-thirds of our fatal accidents. It seems to me that if this fact could be brought home to every driver, it would do a great deal to stimulate voluntary law observance.

My own observation has been that laws, most of the time, seem somewhat remote and abstract to the average person. He figures that other people make the laws; other people violate them. He is a law-abiding citizen himself.

Yet, this same law-abiding citizen may be violating traffic laws because he doesn't know what the laws are. Or he may cheat on what he considers minor violations because he feels it won't do any harm. It is a sort of game. What he doesn't realize is that this is why accidents happen.

So, you are here for an important purpose, and your opportunity is great. You can furnish the leadership that will stimulate all citizens to know the law and to obey it—for their own good as well as for the good of others.

You can also create the public demand that will give us the right kind of traffic courts everywhere and the public support which these courts must have if they are to cope with the critical accident problem.

186 ¶ The President's News Conference of *August* 25, 1959.

THE PRESIDENT. To start this morning's conference I will read a short statement about my forthcoming visit to Europe.

[*Reading*] I am about to embark on a journey which I wish could be extended until I had visited the capital of every nation on this globe that, like ourselves, is dedicated to individual liberty and dignity, and wants only to live under a government established by the consent of the governed. The fulfillment of such a wish is not now possible, but my itinerary does include the Federal Republic of Germany, Great Britain, and France, all of which are, with us, immediately concerned with problems involving our relations with the Soviets. I shall have conversations with the head of government of each of these countries and of Italy, and with the President and Secretary General of the NATO Council.

The trip has several purposes:

To pledge, once again, in the several capitals I shall visit, America's devotion to peace with honor and justice; to support Western unity in opposing, by force if necessary, any aggressions; and to preserve the defensive strength required for our common security.

To suggest to each of the responsible officials whom I shall meet that we, together, restate our readiness to negotiate realistically with the Soviets on any reasonable and mutually enforceable plan for general or special disarmament; to make a real beginning toward solving the problems of a divided Germany; and to help in reducing, otherwise, tensions in the world. In pursuing these purposes, to reiterate jointly that regardless of pressure or inducement we shall never retreat from our ideals or principles or weaken in our resolution to remain secure as we continue the search for peace.

To discuss with each head of government problems common to that nation and ours.

To reassure, through the President and Secretary General of NATO, the dedication of the United States to the North Atlantic Treaty and to say again to every free nation with which our country is associated in bilateral or multilateral treaties that we seek to be a loyal partner in our common enterprise, which is the advancement of freedom and human standards and the furthering of a just and lasting peace.

To suggest to each of the several heads of government that we, together, explore ways and means in which our governments may equitably and effectively cooperate in helping solve one of the most pressing problems of our time, that of assisting to advance the cultural, health, and living standards of the almost two billion people in the world who are citizens of the newly developing or underdeveloped countries. [*Ends reading*]

With respect to this last purpose, I want to say that this, today, if not merely one of the most pressing problems, could easily be the most.

Two billion people are going to find some way of expressing their convictions that they do not have to live in conditions that are completely unsatisfactory by any minimum standard that we set up for humans. Unless the civilized world, not just ourselves, but the civilized world is willing and ready to share in the burdens of making it possible for these people to achieve progress in this area, this world is going to have tough going.

It is because of this deep conviction of mine, not only that I am going to present this matter to my associates and to others, because some of it, of course you know, is performed also in the United Nations, but it is one reason that I am pleading so earnestly with the Congress to look at this terrific problem and consider very seriously before they cut down further the appropriations made for mutual security.

Q. Merriman Smith, United Press International: Mr. President, there is some criticism in the morning papers of your going to Russia. Now, in this connection, sir, I would like to ask a two-part question:

Do you think that Mr. Khrushchev would have agreed to come to this country if you had not agreed to exchange the visit; and, secondly, should Mr. Khrushchev, while he is here, engage in some of his typical attacks on the United States, would that affect your plans for going to Russia? In other words are there any conditions attached to your trip to Russia?

THE PRESIDENT. First of all, take your first part of your question: I invited Mr. Khrushchev to come to this country because of several reasons. The first of them is that I wanted to explore for myself whether this man personally was ready or had any intention of making a suggestion that the free world could study and possibly accept, and in doing so put us all on a better path toward, first of all, reducing tensions and, secondly, to the development of greater programs in the future.

Secondly, I wanted to make certain that he was in no doubt—not as to America's strength in the industrial sector or military sector, he knows all that; but I wanted him to see with his own eyes a free people living and working. I think this is a tremendous lesson for anyone who has any sense of responsibility. The mere fact that a number of people have opposed this idea publicly and through advertisements, that to my mind is one of the lessons he can learn. We don't resent it. Everybody in this country is able to make his own convictions and his own opinions and he is certainly at liberty to express them. I think it is one of the fine lessons that he can learn, and it may have some effect.

Now, without going further into that part of it, I think it would be unrealistic to say that circumstances could not alter a part of a decision already made.

In my original invitation I suggested that he come and that at some time later I would make a visit to him. Now, there could be circumstances arise that would make such a thing unrealistic. I don't know. But as of now, and assuming that the visit here at least does no damage, then I would think that I have committed myself, as I say, in the absence of unforeseen circumstances, to make a short visit to Russia.

Q. Peter Lisagor, Chicago Daily News: Mr. President, to follow up that question, part of the criticism is that your visit to Russia somehow or other will erode the Presidential prestige to a ceremonial visit of that kind.

Would you care to comment on that?

THE PRESIDENT. Someone might say that it might erode my prestige; I think here it would be farfetched to say it erodes Presidential prestige because the next President is certainly free here to make his own decisions. But I tell you this: what we are talking about now is finding some little break, some little avenue yet unexplored through which we can possibly move toward a better situation. It seems to me that everybody is forgetting what we are doing to ourselves. We are putting now, just in the engines and the training and preparations of war something on the order of $41 billion every year. No one seems to stop to think about what that is doing to this country.

We have got to get before the Congress right now the most serious problem in debt management that you could possibly imagine. These expenditures are the things that are making this problem, and it has to be handled intelligently, in turn, or we are going to be in trouble.

Finally, if this thing goes on and on indefinitely into the future, where is the explosion point?

These are the things, it seems to me, that the facile critics ought to stop and think about. This is a serious business. I think any President that refused finally to use the last atom of prestige or the last atom of his energy, by failure to do this, to do this discovery if it is possible to discover, then I think he indeed ought to be condemned by the American people.

Now, that is what I am trying to do, and I get a little bit weary about people that just say, "Well, this would be a terrible blow to Presidential prestige," or any other prestige. We are talking about the human race and what's going to happen to it.

Q. Thomas N. Schroth, Congressional Quarterly: Mr. President, in connection with this debt problem, would you give us your views on the veterans pension bill which is now before you, and on which you are expected to act before you leave for Europe?

THE PRESIDENT. Well I don't know that I have to act; I think I have got 4 or 5 days yet. I don't have to be here when I have to act.

Q. Mr. Schroth: I just said you were expected, you don't have to——

THE PRESIDENT. Oh, you don't! [*Laughter*]

The whole study just came to my desk this morning. I've had a legislative meeting, and that took almost up to this moment, so I haven't had a chance to study its final arguments pro and con.

Q. Mrs. May Craig, Portland (Maine) Press Herald: Mr. President, when Senator Johnson was asked about a possible invitation for the Soviet Prime Minister to address Congress, either together or separately, he said that such an invitation was up to the State Department and the White House. Would you think it useful to include an address in either one or both Houses in Mr. Khrushchev's program?

THE PRESIDENT. Well Mrs. Craig, I never, myself, heard of any intervention by the State Department, and certainly I've never made any, in recommending, even, action on the part of the President as to inviting a particular person before them. I would think this is completely in their hands and no one else's.

Now, in the Foreign Relations and Foreign Affairs Committees, they might ask the State Department to say, "Do you think this is a good thing or not a good thing," but as far as I know, there has never been any intervention by the executive department on this.

Q. Edward T. Folliard, Washington Post: Mr. President, there is to be a World Fair in 1964. Some business leaders would like to see it staged here in Washington, D.C. Would you favor the idea?

THE PRESIDENT. Well, showing how little I know about the factors that would even allow me to make a guess rather than a prediction, it occurred to me that the town of my birth, Denison, Texas, might be a good place to have one. [*Laughter*]

Q. Robert C. Pierpoint, CBS News: Mr. President, on the subject of the Communist invasion of Laos, the SEATO Pact I believe has a clause which would allow any of the former states of Indochina to ask for help from the SEATO nations in case of Communist invasion.

I would like to ask, first of all, has Laos asked for help against the

Communists; and, secondly, are we considering giving that help, whether they have asked or not?

THE PRESIDENT. I don't know whether they have asked the head-quarters of the SEATO; they have asked us.

But you make a premise: you say "a Communist invasion." Now, I do not know that the State Department has yet given me any declaration that this is, in fact, invasion. The fact is, though, that the Laotians are in such a fix that they want some help to reinforce their police forces and the units they keep for internal order. We have got it under study as a matter of urgency. Indeed, again I should like to request all of those people that have to make some decisions about our mutual security program, right today and tomorrow, whenever it's coming off, that they better look at this kind of a system which is a thing that doesn't give you many, let's say, full sleeping nights.

Q. William Knighton, Baltimore Sun: Mr. President, would it be possible for you at this time to clear up for us the apparent mystery surrounding the alleged hint by Mr. Khrushchev of a new proposal on Berlin pertaining to a corridor to be controlled by West Germany, and whether it was conveyed to you by Dr. Milton?

THE PRESIDENT. Well, the last part first: no, to that one. Milton hasn't said a word to me about it.

I have heard of such a suggestion. I have never discussed it with the State Department, with any of our allies; I do not know whether any implication could fairly be made from any remark that Mr. Khrushchev has made that this is even in his mind as a hint. But I have heard of it; and I think, indeed, at one of the little dinners I had we chatted about it awhile, but never anything further than that.

Q. Andrew F. Tully, Jr., Scripps-Howard: Sir, there has been a lot of discussion in recent days about the kind of official reception Mr. Khrushchev is going to receive here. Are you going to meet him at the airport?

THE PRESIDENT. As of today, yes; and the reason I say it today is, of course, we naturally assumed that he was head of government and not head of the state. We were informed as of last evening by the Soviet Foreign Ministry, and I should say that this is their decision which we would respect, that Mr. Khrushchev as Chairman of the Council of Ministers is in effect their Head of State; or at least is coming in his visit here as the head of the state. As head of state, I shall meet him at the airport.

Q. Mr. Tully: Does that mean a state dinner too, sir?

THE PRESIDENT. Well, I don't know about that. I never thought of it as a state dinner. I would, of course, have to give him a dinner. Now, I never thought of it as a state dinner—and I would expect—[*laughter*]—

But the character and details of these things have not yet been worked out. I don't know exactly what he would like to do yet.

Q. Roscoe Drummond, New York Herald Tribune: Mr. President, in your opening statement you gave assurances to several allies and others that certainly in your discussions with Mr. Khrushchev there is going to be no departure from ideal and principle.

THE PRESIDENT. That is correct.

Q. Mr. Drummond: I thought I observed that you made no reference to the question of the captive nations, and I wondered if this point applies equally on that aspect of policy.

THE PRESIDENT. Mr. Drummond, since 1952 I have been making talks of more or less public nature about this point. I stated then, and I have stated a hundred times since, while I am here America will never concede that there has been a sound, durable or working peace that could be called global until these nations have had the right to express their own convictions, their own opinions and desires about their own fates; and then as far as the United States was concerned, it would never cease to use every peaceable means—and I have always emphasized that word "peaceable"—peaceable means to give them such an opportunity.

Q. Lambert Brose, Lutheran Layman: Mr. President, when Mr. Khrushchev comes over here and sees how obsessed many Americans are with the material things of life, swimming pools, expensive cars, short work hours, easy educational courses, some people feel that instead of going back impressed with our strength, he will get the idea that we will be easy to defeat in an economic or political, or even military war, and I'm just wondering, do you think that contention has any merit?

THE PRESIDENT. I think that the strength of America is in its people. We can put it this way: I do not believe it's necessarily true for each of us that we could get up and, with Patrick Henry, say "As for me, give me liberty or give me death"; but I believe that basically this is what you might call our national spirit. I believe that the American Nation will never surrender its liberties to any kind of outside threat or aggression; rather, they would die.

596

I believe he is bound to see that. Of course, he is going to a number of cities. You may know I invited him to go to Abilene, Kansas; I thought he would certainly see something different than he would in big cities. He is going to see the big cities and he is going I believe to one small town, or fairly small town, Ames, Iowa; and of course he'll be in Des Moines. So that's the only place he really comes close to what you might call rural, and what I like to think often, thinking Americans.

Q. Henry N. Taylor, Scripps-Howard: Sir, you say that the Government of Laos has asked for reinforcements in their present difficulties. Have they asked for troops to help them?

THE PRESIDENT. No. I didn't say "reinforcements." I said they asked for assistance—in terms of money.

Q. Mr. Taylor: Money and equipment, sir, or——

THE PRESIDENT. Well, I didn't check up the details this morning. I knew of this request, I just got it this morning, and it's right in the midst of urgent study this morning.

Q. Charles E. Shutt, Telenews: Would you care to comment, sir, on the current steel strike, as to whether either side might need prodding a bit in the negotiations?

THE PRESIDENT. Actually, I have kept very clear of any alleged reports or alleged information as to the attitudes of each side. For that particular point I rely on the newspapers only, because I am not going to have my own convictions and opinions colored by this kind of thing.

Now, so far as the strike is concerned, for the moment at least, I repeat this one thing: I still insist that free bargaining means that these people must solve their own problems. I have urged all of them, both sides, not only in this strike but any other that is impending or even thought of, that negotiations must not contribute to inflation because here is a terrible enemy ready to pounce on us anytime we get unwary.

Finally, I say that when the national security or our national health is in danger, then and then only am I expected to act by the Taft-Hartley Act.

Q. J. F. Ter Horst, Detroit News: Sir, could you tell us whether in your conversations with the Republican legislative leaders this morning they gave you any clue as to the outcome of the labor reform bill?

THE PRESIDENT. I have a note. [*Laughter*] The reason of this note is because rather than to answer any question about a particular bill I just want to make one short statement about the legislative future as I see it, for the rest of this session. Rather than answering about one specific item, I prefer to comment on a number of items still pending before Congress which I most earnestly hope will be acted upon before this session adjourns.

On three of these I am today addressing a letter to the Vice President and the Speaker of the House. These items concern debt management, highway construction, and the FHA authorization. Each of these is a presently operating Government program. Each needs to be adequately handled before adjournment or there will be serious repercussions to the country.

In addition to these operating programs, I reiterate my earnest desire for passage before adjournment of a number of other key measures. These include an effective labor reform bill, a civil rights program such as I urged upon the Congress, adequate appropriations to carry forward the imperatively needed mutual security program. Finally, I stress my disappointment that the Congress has been either unwilling or unable to enact sound farm legislation as I have urged throughout this session.

There are, of course, many other important measures still before the Congress, and I would hope that these also would be passed. But those I have listed here clearly demand attention before the Congress closes its doors.

With respect to the labor bill, it was up for discussion and the hope was expressed very earnestly that the Conference would reach some kind of a conclusion within the next couple of days. If that happens, of course my hope is that it will be very close to the House version.

I want to talk about another bill just for a moment; that is to ask all of you, and everybody else that has given any thought to this problem of debt management, to understand and to do your best to make others understand the very serious implications of failure to act.

Our savings bonds—40 million people own them. It is completely unfair that they are now compelled to get an income off their bonds, that many bought as a patriotic duty, that is completely out of line with what the market today will give for bonds of equal security and validity.

I want to point out especially the tremendous inflationary effect of putting all of our financing in the short-term area. If we do this, we are going to so increase the money supply that the inflationary effect will be really great.

Finally, what you might call our sense of responsibility in our fiscal management is being watched not only by our people, by the bankers and everybody else that understands what is happening, but it is being watched very closely abroad. These countries have very great investments in our stocks, or in amounts of our reserves that are earmarked, that they have earned and are theirs; and if we don't show the kind of sense of responsibility in our management, then these people will begin to question whether or not our money should be now the standard, or practically the standard, for the whole world that it is.

Q. Frank van der Linden, Nashville Banner: Sir, regarding the labor reform bill, AFL–CIO Vice President James Carey has sent a letter to 229 members of the House who voted for that bill, and says that some of these members have accused him of in effect political blackmail because he said that his people would urge all the working people to cast their lot against them and take appropriate action.

What do you think of that kind of a tactic?

THE PRESIDENT. Well, I am not going to say anything at all about his action because that is done on his own responsibility. I would say this: I assume that every Congressman who has voted on this has voted his own conscience, and I don't think any man is going to surrender his conscience because of any kind of threat or implied threat that involves the polls.

Q. E. W. Kenworthy, New York Times: Mr. President, the nuclear test negotiations are expected to recess this week. If this recess continues beyond October 31st, do we intend to continue the tests?

THE PRESIDENT. The decision—no decision concerning the continuation of our voluntary abstention until after this recess has been accomplished, and until the last item of the records have been studied and looked over.

Q. Raymond P. Brandt, St. Louis Post-Dispatch: Is this debt management question serious enough for you to call a special session of Congress if this session does not pass adequate legislation on the subject?

THE PRESIDENT. Of course, Mr. Brandt, there could be some measure that might make it less than mandatory to look at this thing again; but if nothing at all is done, then I think this becomes a question of the gravest import and I would have to get all my financial advisers, the Chairman of the Economic Advisers and the Chairman of the Federal Reserve Board and the Secretary of the Treasury and all the rest of us, and just really get down on it.

Q. Frank Bourgholtzer, NBC News: Do you think, Mr. President, that with regard to Laos that Premier Khrushchev has sufficient authority to put a stop to whatever form of Communist activity there is in Laos?

THE PRESIDENT. That is one of the questions that bothers lots of people. I simply could not make a really intelligent estimate.

I would think that a country as large as Red China, and their, you might say, the little appurtenances hanging around them would not be, could not be controlled as to details of their actions from Moscow; but I should think Mr. Khrushchev's influence would be an important factor.

Q. Sarah McClendon, Manchester (N.H.) Union Leader: Sir, recently you approved the Secretary of State's appointment of Mr. Charles Coolidge to a position where he will review the disarmament policy of this country on behalf of Defense and State Departments.

I know that he has been appointed to jobs in the past by both Mr. Truman and yourself of high position, but I wonder if you took into consideration this time the fact that in 1950 he was a member of this Dover group in Boston that approved the armistice terms of the Chinese Communists, and that those terms are still part of the Communist international program?

THE PRESIDENT. I did not know that.

Martin L. Arrowsmith, Associated Press: Thank you, Mr. President.

NOTE: President Eisenhower's one hundred and sixty-ninth news conference was held in the Executive Office Building from 11:28 to 12 o'clock on Tuesday morning, August 25, 1959. In attendance: 233.

187 ¶ Special Message to the Congress Urging Timely Action on FHA Mortgage Loan Insurance and on the Interstate Highway Program.
August 25, 1959

To the Congress of the United States:

On Wednesday of this week I shall leave for Europe on a mission important to the security and welfare of the American people. This mission will require my absence from the country for about ten days. Unavoidably, it comes while the Congress is in what may be the concluding days of a session, and while important items of legislation are under consideration.

Before I leave I should like to comment on two matters that involve Government programs now in progress which would be seriously hampered in the absence of appropriate action by the Congress.

1. FHA LOAN INSURANCE AUTHORIZATION

The Congress is well aware of the important services performed by the Federal Housing Administration in insuring mortgage loans for Americans who wish to buy homes. Not all homes are purchased under FHA, but a large number are, and it is important that there be no forced reduction in its activities. Yet this is exactly what will happen if additional loan insurance authorization is not available to FHA at an early date.

The Administration has repeatedly requested the Congress to grant FHA an increase in its loan insurance authority. I renew this request, and suggest that it be passed in a separate piece of legislation. An increase in FHA's loan insurance authority should not be made contingent upon the possibility of approval by the President, after the Congress has adjourned, of legislation which contains features that the Administration finds seriously objectionable and that are entirely unrelated to FHA's home loan insurance program.

2. HIGHWAYS

As I have repeatedly stated, there is an urgent national need for legislation to allow the Interstate Highway Program to proceed at a steady rate. Both the Congress and the Executive are justly proud of the vast highway construction program enacted in 1956. A good beginning has been made on this program, and it is inconceivable that it should be allowed now to come to a halt. For traffic safety and convenience, as well as to meet the requirements of a growing economy, it is essential that we continue to build new, modern roads.

Last January I recommended a temporary increase of 1½¢ in the Federal tax on gasoline in order to maintain the planned highway construction schedule on a pay-as-you-go basis. The recent action by the Ways and Means Committee of the House of Representatives in approving an increase of 1¢ for two years represents a step in the right direction. Although it would mean some slowing down of present construction rates, a 1¢ tax increase would allow a reasonable rate of progress to be maintained.

A small increase in the tax on gasoline is the best way to put the Interstate Highway Program on a self-supporting pay-as-you-go basis. I must express again my objection to proposals that would, in the absence of foreseeable budget surpluses, divert receipts from the General Fund of the Treasury that are collected from various excise taxes on automobiles. The transfer of these receipts to the Highway Trust Fund would only shift the fiscal problem from the Highway Trust Fund to the General Fund, which is already in precarious balance. I should also make clear that I do not favor proposals that would finance anticipated deficits in the Highway Trust Fund over the next several years by the issuance of bonds.

DWIGHT D. EISENHOWER

188   ¶ Special Message to the Congress Urging Action on Debt Management Legislation. *August 25, 1959*

To the Congress of the United States:

On June 8, I transmitted to Congress a message requesting legislation that would (1) remove the artificial limitation which the law now imposes on the interest rate at which the Treasury is allowed to borrow money for more than five years, and (2) remove a similar limitation on the rate the Government can pay on Savings Bonds.

Last week, the Committee on Ways and Means of the House of Representatives voted to suspend consideration of these proposals for the remainder of this session. This action was a grave disappointment to me.

The American people have a tremendous stake in this proposed legislation. Failure to enact it means that—

—millions of thrifty Americans cannot be fairly treated, since the Treasury will be unable to pay a fair rate of interest on Savings bonds;

—the cost of living may rise further, as the Treasury will be forced to manage our $290 billion debt in a way that adds to pressure on prices;

—responsible people at home and abroad can only conclude that we have not yet determined to manage our financial affairs as soundly as we should.

I would like to make two things absolutely clear:

First, the Administration is willing to assume full responsibility for managing the Federal Government's debt if it is allowed to do so free from artificial restrictions and on a parity with other borrowers.

Second, if the requested legislation is not enacted, those in the Congress who are unwilling to pass it must assume full responsibility for the possibly serious consequences.

This country's outstanding public debt of almost $290 billion is held by our citizens and financial institutions, and by foreign central banks and investors who have accumulated dollars as part of their reserves. Each investor has his own investment requirements. He buys different kinds of securities in order to meet those needs. Common to all investors, however, is the requirement that the rate of interest paid on the securities be fair and equitable in the light of other investment opportunities and, secondly, that the purchasing power of their invested dollars will not be impaired.

These considerations apply directly to the way in which the Government handles its debt. There can be no question as to the Government's obligation to deal fairly and justly with the millions of its citizens who invest a portion of their savings, sometimes as a patriotic duty, in Government bonds. And there should be no question as to our determination to manage our debt soundly and in the best interests of all of the people.

We have worked tirelessly for a balanced budget. We need this balance so that we can avoid the deficits that lead to higher prices, to a rising cost of living, and to an eating away of the value of the billions of dollars that thrifty and far-sighted Americans have saved. But Congressional inaction on our debt management proposal could do much to offset the progress we have made toward fiscal responsibility.

To manage the public debt in a sound manner the Treasury must be able to borrow money for long as well as short periods of time. A 1918 statute now prescribes, however, that we cannot pay more than 4¼ percent for long-term money. So long as the present prosperity contributes to a strong demand for credit, and thus keeps the cost of new long-term borrowing higher than 4¼ percent, we will not be able to borrow for periods longer than five years.

Let me suggest one simple parallel to show why the Treasury should be able to borrow for longer periods. Suppose that an individual had a mortgage on his home that had to be renewed every few months. He would be exposed to every shift in the economy and to every change in financial conditions. Yet, the Congress in effect is forcing the Treasury into this type of exposed position. It is saying to the Treasury, "When you have any borrowing to do, do it all on a short-term basis."

Within the next twelve months the Government must borrow $85 billion to cover maturing securities, redemptions, and seasonal cash needs. This Government, with its great financial resources, can normally carry a sizeable amount of short-term debt. But it cannot afford to rely exclusively on borrowing that must be continually renewed. Yet, if the Congress insists that we continue to finance wholly with short-term securities, the whole $290 billion debt will grow shorter and shorter. This will make it even harder to handle in the future.

The vital interests of all Americans are at stake because excessive reliance on short-term financing can have grave consequences for the purchasing power of the dollar. The issuance of a large amount of short-term Treasury debt would have an effect not greatly different from the issuance of new money. Because these securities are soon to be paid off, their holders can treat them much like ready cash. Moreover short-term securities are more likely to become lodged in commercial banks. When a commercial bank acquires a million dollars of Government securities, bank deposits rise by a million dollars. This is the same as a million dollar increase in the money supply. When the money supply builds up too rapidly relative to production, inflation is the result. The piling up of an excessive amount of short-term debt poses a serious threat that may generate both the fear and the fact of future inflation at an unforeseeable time.

Now, while the Nation is enjoying a period of rapid economic advancement, we want to keep the cost of living steady. And, if we act wisely, we should be able to do so. We must live within our means and we must exercise all the necessary precautions in the use of credit. We have made good progress toward preventing excessive Government spending. But we may fail in our efforts to keep prices from rising if we do not handle our debt in the proper way. This is why the Treasury must have the capacity to finance the Government's requirements in free credit markets without artificial restrictions.

The need for sound debt management stems not only from domestic considerations. Foreign investors have substantial holdings of our securities, as well as other claims on this Nation. With so large a financial stake in our economy, these foreign central banks and other foreign investors have a very practical interest in the manner in which we handle our affairs. It is essential that they, too, continue to view the American dollar as a strong and stable currency. In a free market economy, confidence is not the simple result of legislation. It is earned by adherence to sound practices.

Let me state as plainly as I can that this is *not* legislation to increase interest rates. This Administration is *not* in favor of high interest rates. We always seek to borrow as cheaply as we can without resorting to unsound practices. The Treasury already has the authority to borrow at any rates of interest on obligations up to five years. What we are seeking is the authority, already possessed by all other borrowers, to obtain funds for longer periods as well. To prohibit the Treasury from paying the market price for long-term money is just as impracticable as telling the Defense Department that it cannot pay the fair market price for a piece of equipment. The result would be the same in either case: the Government could not get what it needs.

The need for Congressional action with respect to the existing 3.26 percent interest rate ceiling on Savings Bonds is equally pressing. The Government occupies a dual trusteeship position with respect to the 40,000,000 Americans who own Savings Bonds and the 8,000,000 people who purchase them regularly. The average holder looks to the Government for a fair rate of return, reasonably competitive with other savings opportunities. The Treasury has announced that when the ceiling is removed, it will immediately raise the rate from 3.25 percent to 3.75 percent on all newly issued E and H Bonds, if held to maturity. Whenever legislation is enacted, this rate increase will be made retroactive to June 1, 1959. In addition, the future return to the investor on Savings Bonds purchased before June 1 and held to maturity would be increased by ½ of one percent. These actions would result in fair and equitable rates of return on Savings Bonds.

The second part of the trusteeship relationship of the Government with respect to holders of Savings Bonds involves the purchasing power of the dollars invested in the bonds. The Savings Bond holder expects the Government to try to insure that the future value of his savings will not be eaten away by progressive erosion of the dollar. To help assure that the value of the dollar will be protected, the whole debt management proposal should be enacted.

Each of these trusteeship considerations is vital; the thrifty American is entitled to both.

The issue with respect to our legislative proposals is whether we are going to demonstrate responsibility in the management of our Federal debt. Ours is the richest economy in the world. We have a large public debt, but we can certainly handle it soundly and efficiently if we remove the artificial obstacles to borrowing competitively in the free market. By adopting the Administration's proposals, the Congress would be demonstrating to people at home and abroad that we have the determination to preserve our financial integrity and to protect our currency.

No issue of greater importance has come before this session of Congress. In the best interests of the American people, I urge the Congress to enact the Administration's proposals at this session.

DWIGHT D. EISENHOWER

NOTE: For the President's message of June 8, see Item 126.

189 ¶ Annual Message to the Congress Transmitting Report on U.S. Participation in the International Atomic Energy Agency.
August 25, 1959

To the Congress of the United States:

I transmit herewith, pursuant to the International Atomic Energy Agency Participation Act, the second annual report covering the United States participation in the International Atomic Energy Agency for the year 1958.

During 1958 the Agency, in addition to making major strides toward completing its organizational and staff structure, achieved a significant though modest amount of progress in establishing its substantive program of bringing the benefits of the peaceful uses of atomic energy to the peoples of its members.

In particular, increasing attention was given to the needs of the less developed countries. This involved development of the Agency's fellowship and training program and its information and technical assistance activities. Such programs are designed to meet the more basic needs of the less developed members for highly trained specialists, for knowledge of the latest developments in the various fields involved in the peaceful uses of atomic energy, and for an understanding of the needs and resources of such members for the establishment of meaningful national programs in this field.

The Agency also began to make a significant contribution with respect to the more technical aspects of the peaceful uses of atomic energy—particularly in the fields of radioisotopes and health and safety—through a variety of activities, including publication of a Manual on Practice on the Safe Handling of Radioisotopes. A Scientific Advisory Committee was established to advise the Agency on specific scientific and technical questions arising from the Agency's program.

Considerable progress was realized in 1958 in developing close and harmonious relations with the United Nations and other interested international bodies. Arrangements for cooperation with specialized agencies were formalized by the conclusion of relationship agreements with the International Labor Organization, the Food and Agriculture Organization, the World Health Organization, the United Nations Economic and Social Council, and the World Meteorological Organization. The Agency also was admitted to full participation in the United Nations Expanded Program of Technical Assistance.

In September the Government of Japan requested the Agency's assistance in procuring some three tons of natural uranium for Japan's first research reactor. This may well be the most important single event in the Agency's short history of striving toward fulfillment of its objectives—particularly if the positive response made by the Agency to the Japanese request should lead to the making of similar requests by other members. By the end of 1958 the Agency was making considerable progress with this request and also with the negotiation of general supply agreements with the United States, the United Kingdom and the Soviet Union—the members that had offered quantities of fissionable material to the Agency.

The United States participated fully in the work of the Agency and made major contributions to its progress in 1958. Consultants were provided for various Agency programs. Technical information was rendered. A considerable number of fellowships were provided and a substantial sum of money was given for the Agency's fellowship program. In addition, the United States contributed to the Agency's regular budget and made an advance to its working capital fund.

In these ways the United States continues to meet its pledge to make every effort to assist the Agency in achieving its high purpose.

DWIGHT D. EISENHOWER

NOTE: The second annual report is printed in House Document 221 (86th Cong., 1st sess.).

190   ¶ Remarks Upon Arrival at the Airport in Bonn, Germany.   *August 26, 1959*

Mr. Chancellor, Ladies and Gentlemen:

I am deeply grateful to you, Mr. Chancellor, for your words of welcome and indeed for the warm welcome that your fellow citizens here at this airport have accorded to me and my party.

In my country, the name Adenauer has come to symbolize the determination of the German people to remain strong and free. In the implementation of that determination, the American people stand by your side, and they send through me to you the German people, their very best wishes for your successful efforts in this matter.

And the American people stand by your side in insuring that the loyal, free people of free Berlin will, like yourselves, continue always to enjoy that great privilege.

Like you, Mr. Chancellor, I look forward to the talks we shall have. It is indeed for me a great honor to come back to this land to meet your elected leader, and with him discuss some of those matters that are so important to both our countries.

To all of you, God bless you.

NOTE: Chancellor Adenauer's remarks of welcome (through an interpreter) follow:

Mr. President:

On behalf of the Federal Republic of Germany, I have great pleasure to welcome you on German soil. I have always been deeply moved by the sight of that great monument to freedom at the entrance to New York harbor, the Statue of Liberty. It has been my privilege on previous occasions to assure you, Mr. President, that in these dangerous and trying times, all my countrymen regard the United States more than ever as the standard-bearer of freedom.

I wish to thank you for coming to visit us during your present journey to Europe.

I am convinced that the exchange of views which you will be having in the next few days with some European statesmen will further the cause of peace and security in the world.

191   ¶ The President's News Conference at Bonn. *August 27, 1959*

THE PRESIDENT. Ladies and gentlemen, before we start the conference proper, I should like, through you, to express to the German people my grateful thanks for the warmth of the welcome you accorded me last evening, one I assure you that was almost overpowering in its intensity and its volume.   And I want to make quite clear that I am aware of the fact that this is not a welcome given by a people to an individual, no matter what the importance of the position he might occupy.   As I see it, this is an attempt on the part of the German people to say to the American people that with you the words liberty and freedom mean exactly the same thing as they do to us, and that we both stand to support the concepts that are implied by those two words, with all our strength and with all our lives.

I shall now try to answer any questions you may have.

Q. Marvin Arrowsmith, Associated Press: Mr. President, can you tell us whether, in your first round of talks with the Chancellor, you have agreed on or discussed any new proposal to settle the Berlin problem?

THE PRESIDENT. No, there has been no new proposal advanced.   We have had only a brief 2 or 3 hours for these conversations on many subjects, and in fact, because of the importance of the questions being discussed, I am trying to delay my departure to the last minute that I can have with the Chancellor.

Q. Merriman Smith, United Press International: Mr. President, do you think there is any lesson that Mr. Khrushchev might possibly draw from the enthusiasm the German people showed you when you arrived here yesterday?

THE PRESIDENT. Well, I don't know whether he will get a lesson, but I am quite sure he cannot miss the meaning of one people trying to say to another people: "we believe in individual liberty, human dignity, and freedom."

Q. John L. Steele, Time Magazine: Are you able to tell us, sir, some of the subjects that you have discussed with the Chancellor?

THE PRESIDENT. I should think, so far as talking with you about details of conversations, that whatever the informal communique will have should be the answer, and I should not try to discuss them at this moment. After all, I have stolen this half-hour right from the very middle of these conversations and it wouldn't be proper for me unilaterally to tell what they are about.

Q. Charles W. Roberts, Newsweek: Sir, I wonder if you can account for the fact that allied unity seems to have weakened since the announcement of your proposed exchange of visits with Premier Khrushchev, and whether you discussed ways of strengthening unity among the Western allies with the Chancellor this morning?

THE PRESIDENT. Well, I haven't been reading the European press, but I have seen some comments or speculation in the American press that our unity has been weakened. I have seen no evidence of it, that is certain. And there has certainly been no evidence of it in the conversations I have had with the Chancellor and with his associates. On the contrary, I haven't heard one single dissident word when we come to the subject of the readiness of all free people, and particularly those of the NATO group, to stand firmly behind the principles that are stated in the charter of that alliance.

Q. Felix Belair, New York Times: We understand, Mr. President, that in view of the Chancellor, the field which offers the greatest prospect in the conversations with Mr. Khrushchev is that of disarmament. Do you share that view, sir?

THE PRESIDENT. I did not quite understand—what did you say?

Q. Mr. Belair: The impression here is that the Chancellor believes that that field of discussion offers the best hope for progress.

THE PRESIDENT. I did not hear him express it in those words. There is no question that he, with the rest of us, believes that the general subject of disarmament is one that has got to be discussed very seriously by us, by the United Nations, and everybody else who believes there is any prospect of lessening tensions. Because only as you go along with the progress of disarmament can you really produce with confidence in the world.

May I make a remark here? I notice that almost everybody that has asked a question so far are people I talk to in Washington all the time. So far I haven't heard a question from a stranger.

Q. Robert C. Young, Chicago Tribune: Mr. President, on the basis of conversations so far with the Chancellor, could you tell us, does he share your hope that the forthcoming exchange of visits with Mr. Khrushchev will, as you put it, help to melt some of the ice in this cold war?

THE PRESIDENT. I think so. Certainly that was the impression I got.

Q. (In German; as translated): Mr. President, have you also discussed with Federal Chancellor Adenauer any French problems?

THE PRESIDENT. I should like to say this: if I start to answer questions about detail, then I necessarily have to go into every one. Now of course we have to talk about France because we are talking about NATO, and France is a very important factor in the whole NATO complex, so I assure you that France has been talked about considerably.

Q. (In German; as translated): Mr. President, have you been discussing with the Federal Chancellor the adherence of Spain to NATO?

THE PRESIDENT. No, that was not—that has not been suggested at all. But let me again please ask this, not to go into details of my conversations which are not completed, and indeed may I remind you, the Chancellor can answer these questions for himself, for what he wants to say, so don't ask me what he said. I am ready to talk about problems and my slant on things, but I don't like to talk about conversations with another man who isn't here to answer them himself.

Q. Robert Pierpoint, CBS News: Mr. President, do you believe that resumption of disarmament talks with the Russians may come out of your trip to Europe?

THE PRESIDENT. Well, no, I couldn't say that. As you know, I have a special committee now organized within the State Department to review all of the issues that have been made in America, in order to achieve some progress in disarmament, and to criticize what we have done so far, both in sins of commission and omission, and to see whether we can get further along with the problem.[1]

Q. Ray Scherer, NBC News: Mr. President, in Washington on Tuesday you spoke of the strong feeling that we must do something to help underdeveloped nations. Would you indicate how West Germans might be brought into that effort?

---

[1] The President referred to a Joint Disarmament Study Group established for the purpose of conducting a review of U.S. disarmament policy on behalf of the Department of State and the Department of Defense. On July 29 the White House announced that with the approval of the President the Secretary of State had named Charles A. Coolidge of Boston to head the group.

THE PRESIDENT. It is a question we have so far adverted to, but I am quite sure we will speak about it more, more thoroughly. And I am certain of this, that the Chancellor himself feels exactly as I do about this necessity.

Q. (In German; as translated): Do you think, sir, that the time has come for certain changes in western policy toward east European states, especially Poland?

THE PRESIDENT. You are asking me a question that opens up a very vast field of discussion, and I assume that you are talking in terms of the suggestions that have been made in public print, time and again, that West Germany should seek some special relationships with Poland, or possibly one or two other countries. That, I would say for the moment is within the province of special problems for Germany, and I would not want to comment further on it.

Q. Charles H. Mohr, Time Magazine: This has to do with Poland, and could we have your slant on a special problem? In the demonstration yesterday there were signs appealing for your personal support regarding the lost German provinces behind the Oder-Neisse line. What is your feeling on that problem, in case unification does take place in the future?

THE PRESIDENT. Well now, again I must say, we are trying today, all of us, and not only among the conversations among allies, but with my forthcoming conversations with Mr. Khrushchev, to melt a little of the ice—an expression I used before in Washington. We are not, at this moment, complicating the matter by talking about the Oder-Neisse line or any other specific question that will merely complicate or draw the conversations down to a particular or detailed problem. We are trying to get a little bit better atmosphere.

Q. Roderick MacLeish, Westinghouse Broadcasting: Mr. President, would you characterize your trip and your talks with the European allied leaders as informative talks, or ones coordinating common Western policy?

THE PRESIDENT. It is not my function to coordinate Western policies. All the nations of NATO, now 15, have banded themselves together as equal partners, so far as their moral support of the principles for which we commonly stand is concerned. Now what is necessary—here you have certain countries, notably France, Britain, and ourselves, and Germany affected in a different way, that are particularly involved with problems that came out of World War II. Without any attempt at coordination, it is quite clear that only through detailed personal conversations, carried out in the utmost frankness and friendliness, can we be sure we are following the sum of the directions that are pointed out by our common dedication to that charter and to the problems that we have to solve as the result of World War II. So that is about as much detail as I can give in an answer to that question.

Q. John Edwards, American Broadcasting Company: Mr. President, pursuing Mr. Young's question just a little further, you said a moment ago that you felt Chancellor Adenauer agreed with you that there is some hope for melting the ice a little in the Khrushchev meetings. Can you say that you feel that the Chancellor has no misgivings about this exchange of visits?

THE PRESIDENT. You mean, you think the Chancellor feels that I am going to do something to weaken the German position or our common determination to stand for the principles that I have mentioned already several times this morning? I have certainly seen no indication of that. Now I did not say that, in terms of any expectation. Hope is a different thing from an expectation; certainly we hope that some good will come out of these conversations.

Q. (In German; as translated): Mr. President, may I come back again on the Polish question and ask you, in connection with the relaxation of tension you are certainly going to talk about with Mr. Khrushchev on his forthcoming visit, whether in that connection it would, according to your opinion, be a good thing and would be helpful to have diplomatic relations between Germany and Poland?

THE PRESIDENT. I attempted to answer that question a few minutes ago by saying primarily that this is a German question and one that I think I have no right to comment upon in detail.

Q. (In German; as translated): Mr. President, was the subject of the political integration of Western Europe touched upon in your conversations with Mr. Adenauer?

THE PRESIDENT. The integration of Europe has been a subject that the Chancellor and I have talked about for a good many years. I don't have to come back into this morning's conversation. It could not escape any conversation in which he and I are involved, because both of us believe that in the closer union of Western Europe is really the salvation of the world, almost. And while we did not discuss it at all, the political integration, we are certainly supporters of the economic and other types of union that are being developed within the area.

Q. (In German; as translated): Mr. President, has there been any talk about the vested German war assets in the United States, in your conversations with the Chancellor?

THE PRESIDENT. It has not been mentioned today. I suppose you are talking about the war assets that came into possession of the United States as a result of the war, and by the agreement in 1946? It is a live question in America. We have been doing our very best to solve it. It is not very easy, and we have not done it. But the subject did not come up this morning at all.

Q. Edward T. Folliard, Washington Post: Mr. President, in your talk at the airport yesterday, you said that the United States would stand by the side of West Germany, to see that the free people of West Berlin remained free. Do you think, Mr. President, that hostilities could grow out of what we call the Berlin crisis?

THE PRESIDENT. I believe that no one in the world wants general war. Now the problem of free Berlin, everyone can see, is a real problem. It is separated from the rest of West Germany by 110 miles, and it is something, of course, that annoys the Communist world very much. But when it comes to speculating as to whether that or any other specific problem is going to cause general war, certainly I am not going to be classed as a bomb-rattler. I just don't believe it. I don't believe anyone is stupid enough to want a general war.

Q. Robert W. Richards, Copley Press: Mr. President, you are on your way to London tonight, where Prime Minister Macmillan very much wants a Big Four summit meeting. The Chancellor and French President de Gaulle are reported to have opposed it. Have you discussed the possibility of a later summit, after the Khrushchev visit?

THE PRESIDENT. Well, we haven't got around to that, but I don't mind telling you, all of you, my conviction about this matter is exactly what I have stated time and time publicly. I believe any summit meeting so called would be a grave mistake unless there was confidence among all of us that real progress of some kind could be achieved. That progress, it seems to me, has to be promised by either further meeting or further consultation or conclusions of the foreign ministers, or in some other way that would give, certainly to the West, all of us, the belief that such a summit meeting could progress, and would not merely be a mill out of which would be ground new kinds of propaganda.

Q. Mr. Richards: I meant after the Khrushchev visit, if the Soviet Premier would give you some assurances that he was ready.

THE PRESIDENT. Well, I am sure of this, that if such assurance were given, it would be given publicly so that all could understand it.

Q. (In German; as translated): Mr. President, what do you think are the prospects at present of conclusion of an agreement on the final stopping of atomic tests?

THE PRESIDENT. Well, I am told that the report by the Geneva Convention was just made last evening or this morning—I am not sure. Is that correct? [*Confers with Mr. Hagerty*] As of this moment there seems to be no great progress.

There, as you know, all countries now have stated their voluntary abstention from testing. There are, of course, all kinds of testing. Some people believe there's nothing wrong with testing, as long as you do it above the atmosphere, or below the earth's surface, so that there would be no fallout. The whole problem is so complicated and so technical that I would merely say this: I see no reason that progress in the discussions should terminate, because they are extremely important to the world.

Q. Michael J. O'Neill, New York Daily News: In that connection, sir, is it our intention to continue the suspension of tests after October?

THE PRESIDENT. Well, as a matter of fact, there is being released in Washington a statement on the matter, and I don't want to release it now because I may "ball up" the time schedule.[2]

Q. (In German; as translated): Mr. President, before leaving Washington, you have demanded that a new start be made on the German problem. Do you expect, from your exchange of visits with Mr. Khrushchev, that new aspects will be brought into the picture which would effect the question of German reunification?

THE PRESIDENT. Well, I don't recall the statement that I said there should be a new start. What I believe I did say was that there should be hopefully a new attitude in which this whole problem could be considered.

---

[2] On August 26 the Department of State announced that the President had directed that the unilateral suspension of nuclear weapons testing by the United States currently in effect be extended through 1959. The release was published in the Department of State Bulletin (vol. 41, p. 374).

If there are, indeed, any propositions made that would seem to be appealing to our associates—America's associates—all those associates will be immediately informed, I assure you. Again I point out, I myself am not conducting negotiations for anybody else with Mr. Khrushchev. I am conducting conversations, trying to explore his mind, to see whether there's any kind of proposal, suggestion, that he can make, that would indeed make him a real leader in the search for peace in the world. If we can do that, that will be a tremendous achievement itself, and therefore specific plans are not something that I am particularly interested in so far as those conversations are concerned.

Q. (In German; as translated): Mr. President, in your Washington press conference, you mentioned special disarmament as distinct from general disarmament. Would it be possible for you to explain the meaning of the term "special disarmament"?

THE PRESIDENT. Possibly I did not use the word "special" very accurately, but there has been often discussed in the press and in political discussions, the possible separation of general disarmament from nuclear disarmament. And I said that no matter what reasonable proposals were advanced here, we would be prepared to discuss them, that was all.

Marvin Arrowsmith, Associated Press: Thank you.

NOTE: President Eisenhower's one hundred and seventieth news conference was held in the Conference Room of the German Foreign Ministry in Bonn, at 12 o'clock noon on Thursday, August 27, 1959.

192 ¶ Joint Statement Following Discussions With Chancellor Adenauer of Germany.
August 27, 1959

THE PRESIDENT of the United States visited the German Federal Capital on August 26 and 27, in order to confer with the German Federal Government. On the morning of August 27, President Eisenhower called on Federal President Heuss.

President Eisenhower and Chancellor Dr. Adenauer then had a private detailed discussion on world-wide political questions. Following this meeting, a larger meeting took place, including the President and the Chancellor and also the U.S. Secretary of State and the German Federal

Minister of Foreign Affairs, as well as advisers of both governments. The discussions were conducted in the spirit of frankness and friendship characterizing the close ties between the two countries.

The President and the Chancellor discussed disarmament, the problems of Berlin and German reunification, European integration, and the continued cooperation of the two countries in the Atlantic Alliance. They reviewed in detail the results of the recent Geneva Conference. In this context Western policy in relation to the Soviet Union was discussed.

President Eisenhower and Chancellor Adenauer restated their belief that pacts of collective defense in accordance with Article 51 of the United Nations Charter contribute to the maintenance of world peace. The mutual cooperation of both their countries within the Atlantic Alliance, which alliance is of utmost importance to world peace, will therefore continue to be one of the pillars of the foreign policies of the two countries.

The President and the Chancellor reaffirmed their resolve to continue their efforts to achieve a just and peaceful solution of the problem of the tragic division of Germany, a solution consistent with the desire of the German people and assuring peace and security in Europe. In this context President Eisenhower referred once again to the pledge given by the United States and its allies to protect the freedom and welfare of the people of Berlin.

NOTE: Because of the President's departure from Bonn immediately following the discussions, the White House release of this joint statement was made in London.

193 ¶ Remarks Upon Arrival at the Airport in London. *August 27, 1959*

Mr. Prime Minister and Ladies and Gentlemen:

I appreciate most deeply the kind words you have had to say, Mr. Prime Minister, about the task that falls to the lot of you and myself and our associates in these two governments, but I must say that my deepest reaction and sentiment at this moment is that of extraordinary pleasure—true enjoyment at being once more back again in this land that I have learned so much to love.

Here are some of my warmest and best friends, and with them I hope to renew friendships. And though I know that our primary purpose is to have these talks and conversations, which we hope will be fruitful in promoting the best interests of our two countries, let me say I did not have to come here to assure you or the British people that the American people stand with them, strongly, firmly, and determinedly, in the defense of freedom, liberty, and the dignity of man. You people know that we feel that way. But it is, I think, good that we can have the opportunity to view these changing problems as they are revealed to us, and to counsel together as to how we shall best meet them.

So, as I do myself the signal honor of going to pay my visit upon Her Gracious Majesty, as I speak to you and talk with you and your associates and my old friends, I count on this being one of the most enjoyable and I hope fruitful journeys that I have made to any country in the world.

Thank you very much, Mr. Prime Minister.

NOTE: The President spoke at 6:50 p.m. in response to the following remarks of welcome of Prime Minister Macmillan:

Mr. President:

It is my privilege to welcome you to British soil, on behalf of all the people of the United Kingdom, without any distinction of party or of creed.

You, sir, under the Constitution of the United States hold the office both of Head of State and of the Chief Executive Minister. Although you are primarily here in the second capacity for political discussions of great importance, we are glad to know that you are also to pay an informal visit to Her Majesty at Balmoral.

Mr. President, the programs which face our two countries, together with our allies, are difficult and complex. Your initiative towards their solution is a source of immense satisfaction to us all in Britain, and I think I may say throughout the Commonwealth. We feel them all the more, because you, sir, are a President whose name was a household word to all of us, even before you were elected to your high office. We entrusted to your charge in two theaters of war the most powerful forces which the British people ever raised, and worthily you discharged their task.

We have equal confidence that as leader of a great sister democracy, you will carry through your task with the same courage and the same success.

194 ¶ Veto of the Public Works Appropriation Bill. *August 28, 1959*

[Released August 28, 1959. Signed August 26, 1959]

To the House of Representatives:

I return herewith, without my approval H.R. 7509, a bill "Making appropriations for civil functions administered by the Department of the Army, certain agencies of the Department of the Interior, and the Tennessee Valley Authority, for the fiscal year ending June 30, 1960, and for other purposes."

This public works appropriation bill for Fiscal 1960 includes 67 unbudgeted projects estimated eventually to cost over $800 million. It ignores the necessity for an orderly development of America's water resources within the Nation's fiscal ability.

Without any of the unbudgeted projects provided for in this measure, 1960 expenditures for the Corps of Engineers and the Bureau of Reclamation will reach $1.1 billion—an all-time high and almost three-quarters again as much as the expenditure level in Fiscal 1955. Moreover, just to carry on construction currently underway will require by 1962 even higher expenditures—approaching twice as much as those of Fiscal 1955—and will ultimately cost $6 billion.

These future expenditure commitments result largely from the fact that in the last four years the Congress has added to budgeted construction over 200 unbudgeted starts, involving total costs of nearly $3.8 billion. In view of these commitments, I recommended in the January Budget Message that no funds be appropriated to start additional projects in 1960.

This tremendous expansion in government expenditures in just this one area in so short a period of time brings into sharp focus how Congress by action in one year builds increases into the Federal Budget in future years. For example, although the cost of the unbudgeted projects in H.R. 7509 will be relatively small in Fiscal 1960—about $50 million—their ultimate cost will be more than $800 million. This illustrates how easily effective control of Federal spending can be lost.

Overspending in respect to water resources is hurtful to the United States and to the proper development of these resources themselves. The American people are opposed to overspending no matter where it is attempted.

The unbudgeted projects provided for in this bill will, at the proper time, make an important contribution to the economic development of the areas in which they are to be built and to the Nation as a whole. But by any sound test of urgency, these projects should not be started this year if we are to have a responsible Federal fiscal policy. I believe that the American people look to the Government to see that their tax money is spent only on necessary projects and according to a priority as to urgency that does not weaken our financial structure nor add to the tremendous debt burden that posterity will have to pay.

I urge the Congress to enact a new bill appropriating funds only to finance projects now under construction and other going programs. If the Congress continues its refusal, in the case of the Trinity River project, to save $60 million of taxpayers' money through providing for construction of electric power facilities by non-Federal interests, such new bill should of necessity include funds to provide for Federal construction of such facilities, since the dam is now being built and it is essential that power facilities be in place when the reservoir is full.

Dwight D. Eisenhower

NOTE: See also Item 213.

195 ¶ Message to Mayor Brandt of West Berlin. *August 28, 1959*

[Released August 28, 1959. Dated August 27, 1959]

Dear Mayor Brandt:

I am grateful for your message of welcome.

As you know, the limited time available for my visits to Bonn, Paris, and London made it impossible for me to come to Berlin at this time. However, I should not want to let the occasion of my visit to Europe pass without conveying to you and to the stalwart people of Berlin my personal greetings and the expression of the admiration of the American people for the calm and resolute attitude which your city has shown in the face of the difficulties of the past year. It is my hope that we shall be able, in the discussions foreseen for the coming months, to bring to an end the present period of tension over Berlin. If we continue to face our common problem with fortitude, patience, and imagination, we may realistically expect that such an objective will be achieved.

As I stated at the time of my arrival in the Federal Republic, the Western Powers stand firm in their determination to preserve the integrity of Berlin and to foster conditions which will eventually permit the German people to be reunited into one free nation.

With warm personal regard,

Sincerely,

Dwight D. Eisenhower

NOTE: This message, addressed to the Honorable Willy Brandt, Governing Mayor of Berlin, was released during the President's visit in London.

196   ¶ Radio and Television Broadcast With
Prime Minister Macmillan in London.
August 31, 1959

THE PRIME MINISTER. Well, Mr. President, I want to start by saying how much we all welcome you here—hundreds of thousands of our people have seen you on the streets, and millions of our people will be watching you tonight.

In the 17 years of our friendship, which I think started in North Africa, we have had many frank talks together. And I think we can have a frank talk this evening. We have had good talks at Chequers, and here we are at Number Ten.

THE PRESIDENT. Well, Harold, let me tell you right away and tell to all of those good people out there who have been so kind to me and my party, that we are mighty glad to be back visiting again this lovely country.

THE PRIME MINISTER. Well, Mr. President, I thought we might start by saying a word about Anglo-American relations. In our lifetime we have been pretty close together, our countries. Of course there have been differences, there is no good denying them. There have been serious differences—before the war—after the war—2 or 3 years ago about the Middle East—sometimes about the Far East—but the great thing about it we never look backward, we look forward, I think. And you and I have tried to do that.

And now we are up against the biggest job in the world: how to keep peace and justice. And I want to say to you, if I may, that I think your visits to these three European capitals, and the interchange of visits that you are going to make with Mr. Khrushchev, are a very fine contribution to peace.

THE PRESIDENT. Well, Prime Minister, I would like to say a personal word about this business of Anglo-American relations. Except for the 2 years that I was in Columbia University, ever since 1941 I have been engaged in activities where one of my principal concerns has been the state and the strength of relationships between your country and ours. And I can say through that long personal experience that those relations have never been stronger and better than they are now. In this regard I would like to mention one country of the British Commonwealth that is our geographical neighbor in North America, and this is Canada.

Here is a border more than three thousand miles long that is defended by nothing but friendship. There is not a gun or a fort along it. This is the kind of thing that I think we must all strive to achieve, whether we are geographical neighbors or not, and I am quite sure that if Mr. Diefenbaker were here, he would say we are neighbors in the sense of the Biblical parable just as we are in the geographical.

And one other point, we have spoken of your country and ours in relationship with Canada, but we are neighbors in another great society, a society dedicated to peace and the defense of the West, and that is NATO. In that, we are all proud to be equal partners, and with all our other associated countries, we are dedicated to that one single objective of making ourselves secure and making peace more promising.

THE PRIME MINISTER. You said peace, Mr. President, and I agree with you. But of course a lot of our people, old people who have lived through two wars, and young people, are frightened of war. They fear war. And I have thought a lot about this, and read a good deal recently.

Now the first war, I feel, ought never to have happened. It happened by mistake. I believe if we had the same kind of international meetings as we have now, it wouldn't have happened.

The second war was different. I don't think that it could have been avoided. It was just when it happened and how it happened, because wicked men plotted it who were determined to achieve their aims.

Now we are in a situation I felt there was a danger that we might drift into something by mistake—bluff—counterbluff—lack of understanding on both sides—and drift into something. And that, I tell you frankly, when I read the Russian ultimatum in November about Berlin, I felt the danger of that drift. And that is why I set about my journeys last February. Some people thought that a bit odd, but we still in an alliance must all have a certain amount of play, and I think I am bound to say that they haven't turned out too badly.

I think now, the position you have created and your initiative, we are in a better position. I have never concealed from you, I always have wanted a summit meeting, and I believe your initiative will put us in a position to get it under the best conditions.

THE PRESIDENT. Well, Harold, I think there is one thing we should be very sure of: when we are talking about peace, we are talking about something now that is the imperative of our time. War has become so threatening in its capacity for destruction of our whole civilization that we—and I mean all people as well as statesmen—have the responsibility of making sure that our actions, the things we try to do, are all directed by this single purpose and directed with as much intelligence as we can marshal within such brains as the good Lord gave us. So that these different meetings we are having and the meetings that I am making in Western Europe now, the ones I expect to have with Mr. Khrushchev, they are always having as their background this sense: that peace is an imperative. We must all understand that. And indeed, if we are to have a summit, I am sure of this, Mr. Khrushchev must understand that exactly as you and I do.

If we do that, then—and I think there is real hope—we should have a summit and make something—I mean, if he does things that show that he recognizes that, just as you and I do, then I think a summit meeting would be profitable.

THE PRIME MINISTER. I agree. But of course we are talking now about the two great groups, the Communist group and our group. But there are lots of other peoples in the world too, countries outside, some of them not yet fully developed, some of them a bit backward. What about them, Mr. President?

THE PRESIDENT. I believe in a sense that the problem of the under-developed nations is more lasting, more important, for Western civilization than is this problem of the Soviet-Western differences and quarrel.

There are one billion, seven hundred million people that today are living without sufficient food, shelter, clothing, and health facilities. Now they are not going to remain quiescent. They are learning something about their own lot, and they are comparing their lot with ours, sitting here this evening. They are just going to have an explosion if we don't help. I believe the biggest cooperative job that all the world that calls itself civilized, including the Soviets, ought to address themselves to is this problem, and on a cooperative basis help to solve it, so that these people can achieve their legitimate aspirations. And that is the problem that every one of us must address himself to and see what we can do, what our proper part is.

THE PRIME MINISTER. I agree with you, because in a sense it is what we

have done in our own countries.   A hundred years ago there were deep
divisions between rich and poor—great cleavages.   The greatest of our
Conservative statesmen wrote a book called *Two Nations*.   We have
made one nation now.   There are still differences, of course, but not the
deep divisions.   The same as you have done in your country.   And I
think, like you, it isn't right that we, our people, should have all these
things—houses, health services and hospitals, and education—and there
should be these people in poverty and in misery.

And in a way we have a certain knowledge of this, because it is the
story of our Empire and Commonwealth.   I would like to take the
opportunity to say a word to you about that.   Now I know what colonialism means to Americans, because my mother was American.   It means
the Boston Tea Party and George the Third and all that.   But colonialism
had a good side too.   And now we are changing the old Empire into the
new Commonwealth.   We have got a lot of problems ahead of us—in
Africa, and so on, but we will solve them.   And you have only to look
around to see what is happening—India, Pakistan, Ceylon, Ghana,
Malaya—Nigeria soon—the West Indies—it's the road on which we are
traveling, and it isn't a sign of weakness, it's a sign of strength.

Don't let anyone in America think it's the sun setting on the British
Empire.   It's the dawn rising on the new Commonwealth, and it's all
part of the same story.

THE PRESIDENT. I agree.   I think you have expressed a very splendid
thought, not only for your Empire but for all of us who think about
these things.

I would like to point out that all of the political moves, all of the
educational moves you make, must be supported by trade.   We must
have better trade because it is through trade that all of us are going to
achieve better standards.   I know this is one subject that is dear to your
heart, and near to your heart, and it is one I think we should all think
about very thoroughly.

THE PRIME MINISTER. Well, Mr. President, we both believe the same
thing, I think, that these problems in the world can only be solved by the
expanding of the wealth and the trade of the world.   Of course we are
up against quite a lot of pressures.   You are, and I am.   And it is not
always easy to say, it is not always too easy to do.   So I think we have
done pretty well.   It's a great satisfaction to us to feel the enormous

increase in trade between Britain and the United States. You helped us very much with the heavy engineering. I wish you could do something for us on wool textiles—perhaps you will be able to do that. Still, broadly speaking, it is enormously increasing, and it wants to be in Europe, and with Europe, and the New World—all the world trading together.

And the old British pound sterling hasn't done too badly to help, because it's in good shape now.

THE PRESIDENT. Let me tell you this: we are concerned about it. We want to see it just as strong as you want to see it.

I would like to point out that supporting this kind of thing is the necessity for broadening our contacts in the world particularly, not only among ourselves but particularly with the Iron Curtain countries. I believe we have got to have a better exchange of ideas, the products, and the conclusions of scientific people; we have got to have more in books, but above all of people. I like to believe that people, in the long run, are going to do more to promote peace than our governments. Indeed, I think that people want peace so much that one of these days governments had better get out of the way and let them have it. And that is exactly the way we ought to think, if we are going to think correctly in this thing. It's those people that want these things, and long for them with all their hearts. We have got to make it possible for them to get them.

So the big way, one big way we are going to do it is by broadening these contacts. The people coming back here—some of them will be indoctrinated and we won't think they are too effective at first. But if we keep this thing up, there are going to be a lot of people that are not indoctrinated, and we know we won't indoctrinate our people—we can't—so the exchanges will finally bring truth and understanding to all people that will expand these contacts. So we become very much more understanding among ourselves; and understanding, in the long run, means peace.

THE PRIME MINISTER. I think we really are agreed, we have been agreed, and talked over these things for many years. We have got to be firm on the principles. We have got to maintain justice. But we have got to be flexible about the new conditions that arise and how to deal with each situation. I believe, like you, if we can keep the thing fairly steady over the generations—may take some time—but gradually the peoples of the world will demand, because of their contacts and friendships, what the governments—we—are trying to give them. It will take time. We must be patient with them.

THE PRESIDENT. I agree. In other words, you are saying strategic principle is immutable, tactics change according to armed weapons and the different changes.

THE PRIME MINISTER. Yes, and not only armed weapons, the psychological weapons—the contacts and the friendships of which you spoke.

THE PRESIDENT. But let us remember this one thing: when we say we are sustaining principle, once in a while something comes along that makes us state a principle, then seeing this affect a particular problem.

Now I refer you to West Berlin. We say freedom, if there is to be peace, is indivisible. Freedom is the possession, or should be the possession, of all men. Now we have got two million free West Berliners. Now we simply are not going to abandon principle. But here it seems to me principle says you cannot abandon two million free people and still be true to the statement that freedom is truly indivisible and the right of every man. So in that case, we have really got to be firm, in my opinion.

THE PRIME MINISTER. I agree with that. I agree also with your other principle, we have got to use the right tactical methods to achieve our purpose with a reasonable amount of adjustment that is necessary from time to time.

THE PRESIDENT. I agree, I agree. Well, this is something that lies so close to my own heart that any trouble there is for me to come to any capital in Europe, including Moscow, I am perfectly glad to do it, if it will advance something. I will not be a party to a meeting that is going to depress and discourage people. Therefore, we must have some promise of fruitful results. Except for that single exception, there is nothing they can't ask me to do that I won't try to do.

THE PRIME MINISTER. I know that, and I feel that what you are doing now will bring us much nearer to what we both want.

So let us run over what we said tonight, I think it's of some importance. Our own relations between our two countries are probably as close as they have ever been. We have got our NATO allies. There are difficulties, of course—no use pretending they don't exist. People take different points of view—they wouldn't be free governments if they weren't. We have to try and keep it all together.

We have got this problem of the underdeveloped countries which we really must work on—we I think are ready to do our part. We have got a stronger economy at home, so we are able to give more abroad.

And then, as you have said, you have got these contacts, the idea of developing movements between the countries which will make the background, and that will help the statesmen to do what the peoples really want.

And I think sometimes it's extraordinary, I think about it, and I expect you do. You and I sit in our rather lonely position sometimes, and think what is it the people want and can we give it to them and at the same time keep the principles we stand by—I call it peace and justice, and those are the two words.

THE PRESIDENT. You know, one Frenchman gave a definition of freedom I like. He said, freedom and liberty are merely the opportunity for self-discipline.

Now we know that there are certain things that great nations can do if they are organized, harnessed, as one, and go ahead to do it. In dictatorships, this is all done by the order and by the police that make the order effective, so there is a continuity of policy and a unity of effort that is quite remarkable, sometimes, in Western eyes. But let's remember this: our great strength is our dedication to freedom, and if we are sufficiently dedicated, we will discipline ourselves so that we will make the sacrifices to do the thing that needs to be done. And that is exactly what you and I, I think, are trying to teach ourselves, our friends, our own peoples, and we are hopeful Mr. Khrushchev.

THE PRIME MINISTER. Well, Mr. President, I think our time is rather drawing to an end, we mustn't go on too long, we have got some guests waiting. But I would like to say again how very glad—I know I speak on behalf of every single man, woman and child in this country whatever party or creed or anything—how glad we are to have you with us.

As I said when I met you at the airport, it was meant. It isn't only for what you represent—the great country you represent—of course it is that—but it is because we have known you all these years for what you are yourself. We have always known you from 17 years ago, when you took command of our great forces and carried them through to victory. And we welcome you here.

Now we have got our guests, and among our guests I am happy to say we have Sir Winston Churchill.

THE PRESIDENT. I must say you embarrass me, but I am delighted Sir Winston is going to be here.

Now, do you mind my saying one word directly to your people?

THE PRIME MINISTER. No, that's all right.

THE PRESIDENT. I want to thank everybody that has had a part in showing his kindness and British hospitality to me and to my party, and in doing so to show also that respect for the principles on which both our countries are founded and established and maintained—that we in our country so revere.

So finally, may I just say this one word: God save your gracious Queen and all her people.

NOTE: The broadcast was delivered from Number 10 Downing Street at 7:20 p.m.

197   ¶ Statement by the President Upon Signing the Supplemental Appropriations Act.
September 1, 1959

I HAVE today approved H.R. 7978, "An Act making supplemental appropriations for the fiscal year ending June 30, 1960, and for other purposes."

There has been considerable controversy about provisions for sewage disposal at the Dulles International Airport. I had recommended a tie-in with the District of Columbia sewer system. The Congress, however, by eliminating certain funds in the Federal Aviation Agency appropriation request, has implied that it desires the Agency to build a sewage treatment plant at the airport with the treated effluent being emptied into a tributary of the Potomac River. This procedure is objected to by the Federal Aviation Agency, the Corps of Engineers, the District of Columbia Commissioners, and local planning and pollution abatement agencies.

I am asking the Federal Aviation Administrator not to proceed with work on the treatment plant until this issue has once more been fully examined. I have asked the Administrator to report to me in this regard as soon as possible.

NOTE: As enacted, H.R. 7978 is Public Law 86–213 (73 Stat. 437).

198 ❡ Remarks on Leaving London.
September 2, 1959

Mr. Prime Minister, and Ladies and Gentlemen:

For me there is always a bit of sadness in my heart when I leave this country. I have had many experiences here, in war and peace. I have formed some of the most valued friendships that I have. So, whenever I leave, it is a goodbye that has with it and in it a bit more of sentiment than would seem fitting to express in such a spot and before such a machine as this microphone.

But as I go, I want to say one thing about Anglo-American relationships. We talk often about their warmth and their strength—their health. I would like for all of you to remember, and on our side of the water I should hope that we always remember, the value of these relationships. To my mind, if two nations such as ours, with common traditions and almost a common language, cannot together get basic agreement upon the principles, upon the general road we want to travel as we go side by side into the future, then indeed the future of the world is bleak.

We can, with the other nations of the British Commonwealth—on our side I am sure—do our part to make these things possible, so that all of us can gain the confidence that comes from having by its side a true ally, a true friend, friends that can express their differences without rancor, can discuss difficult questions without personal animosity, and between them find a way to advance the great causes for which we stand.

And so, once more I say goodbye—except that I have a little sneaking ambition for the next weekend where I am going to stop in Scotland. So although this is goodbye to you, sir, and to my friends here, I hope to have in that lovely spot a Saturday and Sunday where I might even get in a round of golf.

Thank you very much, and goodbye.

NOTE: The President spoke at the London Airport at 8:50 a.m. in response to remarks by Prime Minister Macmillan. In his closing remarks the President referred to his forthcoming visit to Culzean Castle, Turnberry, Scotland, where since 1953 a suite of rooms has been at his disposal as a testimonial of Scotland's appreciation for his services as Supreme Commander of the Allied Forces in World War II.

Mr. Macmillan's remarks follow:

Mr. President, in the 5 days that you have been with us, I think you will have realized the pleasure that your visit has given to every section of the country. I shall never forget, and I think you will not, your drive from this airport to London last Thursday night, and the hundreds of thousands, almost millions, of people who came out to greet you.

You were able to make an informal visit to the Queen at Balmoral, and in addition you came with your advisers to Chequers where we did do some work, although we also had some relaxation.

And I think that you will have understood the two great outstanding features of your visit here. First, the close friendship and alliance between two peoples with so much in common—their language, their origin, their belief in the rights of the individual, in the common law, and all those things which spring from the very roots of both of us. But also you will have realized the affection which we have for you personally. And

in that double capacity as the President of the United States, and if I may be allowed to say so, as General Eisenhower, you will have known how, from the real hearts of the people has gone out their affection.

We also hope that in the course of your visits to three European capitals, and your proposed interchange of visits with Mr. Khrushchev, we may be able to set out upon a road which will be fruitful for the world, and bring us that of which we spoke together two nights ago: peace and justice.

Sir, we wish you every possible success in your enterprise, and you will go from these shores knowing that you carry with you the good wishes of every man, woman, and child in the country.

199 ¶ Remarks Upon Arrival at the Airport in Paris. *September 2, 1959*

General de Gaulle, Ladies and Gentlemen:

I must tell you, Mr. President, that my heart is warmed by your very complimentary references to me, and more particularly to my country. I am delighted to be back in Paris. Indeed, there is an old saying in my country that for every American France is a second home. And certainly I feel at home in this country.

I am particularly delighted at the opportunity to have some conversations with my old friend and colleague General de Gaulle. He was, during the dark days of war, when freedom itself was at stake, he was the symbol of French courage, defiance, and dedication to those principles of peace and freedom.

Now we have an opportunity, in these troublous times, to talk together to see whether we can better concert all of our efforts toward the one single goal of peace with justice.

So again I say, thank you for your welcome, General de Gaulle, and my assurances that we will find ways to make our common efforts more effective.

Thank you very much, sir.

NOTE: The President spoke at Le Bourget Airport at 10:12 a.m. General de Gaulle's remarks of welcome, as published in the Department of State Bulletin (vol. 41, p. 410), follow:

Mr. President, we are very happy to see you, for we know you well.

You are the forever illustrious chief of the armies of freedom.

You are the President of a country which, among all others of the world, is dear to the heart of France, and, more, you are a man of intelligence, of courage, of honor.

In these difficult times it is quite natural that the United States and France must know each other and must agree together.

We will do this in complete friendship for the good of the nations that serve the same cause as we, and for the good of the whole world.

Mr. President, you are welcome.

200 ¶ Exchange of Letters Between the President and the Chief of State, General Franco, of Spain. *September 2, 1959*

[Released September 2, 1959. Dated August 31, 1959]

Dear General Franco:

Thank you for your cordial letter of August 24, 1959, delivered to me by your Foreign Minister, Mr. Fernando Maria Castiella, when he called on me in London on August 31.

I am of course pleased to know that you think well of the planned exchange of visits between Mr. Khrushchev and myself and that you clearly understand the basic thought that I have in mind in this connection.

I appreciate also your reference to the aid which we have extended to Spain in order to help our Spanish friends to assume certain responsibilities in defense of the west.

The agreements signed between our two countries in 1953 have produced good results for both of us. I am happy to have this opportunity to express to you my appreciation of the spirit of cooperation with which you have worked with us on the construction and operation of our joint bases. They are an important element in the common defense.

I should like also to congratulate you on the bold new economic program already auspiciously begun and on your membership in the OEEC. This constitutes another important link in forging the European unity to which you refer.

Your gracious invitation to Mrs. Eisenhower and me to visit your beautiful country so full of artistic treasures and historic landmarks is greatly appreciated. I hope that some day we shall have the opportunity to enjoy the friendly Spanish hospitality about which we have heard so much.

In the meantime, dear General, pleace accept my renewed thanks for your best wishes which are fully reciprocated.

Sincerely,

DWIGHT D. EISENHOWER

NOTE: This letter and General Franco's letter to the President were released during the President's visit in Paris. General Franco's letter follows:

Dear Mr. President:

Allow me, first of all, to thank you for your sacrifices and efforts to assist our western world and to lead it along the path of peace and understanding and in particular for the aid and benefits that Spain is receiving from the United States under your administration.

There are many people who do not fully realize that in the present circumstances, lack of action, inertia and an exclusively defensive attitude would lead, in no time, to defeat, and that in today's situation, all contacts are useful which seek to unveil the immediate aims of our opponents. As for the general and permanent aim of universal domination held by the Soviets, I know, that such a great soldier and strategist as you yourself are, always keeps it clearly in mind. For this reason, I reject the view of those who, forgetting your personal record, are fearful of the consequences of your meeting with Khrushchev.

When the late lamented Secretary of State, John Foster Dulles, visited us, we reached full agreement on our assessment of the general situation and on the needs of the hour. I have no doubt that the same identity of views will be reached at the forthcoming meetings of our Foreign Minister and Your Excellency and with your Secretary of State.

Your Excellency is well aware that western superiority based as it is, on the industrial power of the United States and its ability to adapt it to the needs of war, could be weakened, should the Soviet Union develop fully all its industrial potential and western Europe fails to reinforce its unity and its state of preparedness. The nations of our continent, as you well know, easily tend to disunite. I consider your presence here—your prestige—most useful in forging unity.

I cherish the hope, my Dear General, that whenever the international situation permits, you and Mrs. Eisenhower, will in the course of one of your journeys, visit our country.

With confidence in and sincere best wishes for the success of your great mission, I offer you, the assurance of my consideration and friendship.

FRANCISCO FRANCO

201 ¶ Remarks at the Hotel de Ville, Paris.
September 2, 1959

President de Gaulle, President of the Municipal Council—Parisians—and Citizens of France:

When the heart is full, the tongue is very likely to stumble. Should I try to express to you today the true feelings, the true sentiments that now inspire me, I should be completely unable to speak at all. I can say only that over the years, this city, this country, has become like it has for almost every American, something that is very dear, very real, and truly a part of the kind of world in which we want to live.

We have been allies for many years, from the days of Lafayette, back in the late seventeen hundreds. To this very moment America cherishes the friendship, the loyal support, the loyal cooperative efforts that have always been hers whenever she needed them from France.

To be more personal, let me speak for a moment about your great President, General de Gaulle. I met him in London more than seventeen years ago. Our acquaintanceship and friendship grew and developed in Algiers, and again we were in Britain; and then I met him again in France, as he began the process of reconstruction in this great country. And since that time I have kept in touch with him.

Now it is my great privilege to work with him again in the great purposes that he has just explained, those of finding a path to the peace and the security for all the world, so that you, your children, your grand-children, may like all of those in other parts of the world, in all the continents, live in confidence, can develop in themselves all their God-given qualities and become truly people without fear. People that love liberty will never let it slip away from them, either by neglect or under threat, and will march down the road to the future with all of the faith in their God and in themselves that will make everybody—all of us—a happy people.

And so, all I can say again to this throng, to all the people who lined the Champs Elysee, who were along the streets and the boulevards as I came down here, I have one small French phrase that I think expresses my feelings: *Je vous aimes tous.*

NOTE: The President responded to remarks by General de Gaulle at 6:42 p.m. The General's remarks, as published in the Department of State Bulletin (vol. 41, p. 410), follow:

"Here once again in Paris, welcomed by the ecstasy of an entire people, here is President Eisenhower. Although the years may pass, and with each one its problems, nothing can efface the memory of the great victory achieved under his command by the allied armies and, of course, in France, by the soldiers of France. The proof that we do not forget him, Paris has just supplied. But, Mr. President, you are here at a moment when America and France feel the necessity of bringing into agreement their views concerning everything that is occurring in the five parts of the world and that our two peoples consider each other as forming a unity.

"Be it that the world must face once again a period of threat and alarm or perhaps that we can hope tomorrow to take some steps along the road toward the relaxation of tensions as we wait for this path to lead to peace, is it not true that in any event our two peoples should renew not only their friendship, which is a basic truth, but the links that unite them, to safeguard together, and with other nations of the world, the sacred cause of freedom.

"Since this concerns the United States and since it concerns France, this adjustment of their objectives and of their actions, in effect, of their policies must be accomplished with mutual respect and confidence.

"But how much easier that is when the Chief of State and the French Government have to deal with President Eisen-

hower. Our people, our authorities, have the best possible reason to know who he is, what he has accomplished, and what he is worth. And I find in him, with the most profound joy, the good, the warm, the loyal companion beside whom I have marched in difficult times along the road of history. Which is why, to all of you, I can say that between us all has gone very well.

"Long live General Eisenhower! Long live the President of the United States! Long live America, forever the friend and ally of France!"

The President of the Municipal Council, Dr. Pierre Devraigne, presented the President with the keys to the city.

202 ¶ Joint Statement Following Discussions With President de Gaulle of France. *September 3, 1959*

THE PRESIDENT of the United States and the President of the French Republic have had during the day of the 2nd and 3rd of September meetings, during the course of which all the questions which are of interest to the two countries have been discussed. The Prime Minister of the French Republic and the two Ministers of Foreign Affairs took part in these meetings. The conversations between the former comrades-in-arms of the Second World War took place in the very friendly and cordial atmosphere which has traditionally characterized Franco-American relations.

President Eisenhower set forth to General de Gaulle his views on U.S.-USSR relations on the eve of Mr. Khrushchev's visit to Washington and in view of the expected visit of the President of the United States to Moscow. The two Chiefs of State expressed their complete agreement on the question of Berlin. They also agreed that a Summit Conference, useful in principle, should take place only when there is some possibility of definite accomplishment.

African problems in general and those which relate to North Africa in particular were discussed at some length. The President of the United States and the President of the French Republic stressed their devotion to the Atlantic alliance. They exchanged views with respect to means of assuring a more efficient functioning of this alliance.

The two Presidents reaffirmed the importance they attach to the resumption of negotiations on general and controlled disarmament as well as to the problem of assistance to the underdeveloped areas. They also examined the means of organizing better cooperation between the two countries in the world as a whole, especially through the expansion of consultations on all major problems, political as well as military.

NOTE: This joint statement was released in Paris.

203 ¶ Joint Statement Following Discussions in Paris With Prime Minister Segni of Italy. *September 3, 1959*

PRESIDENT EISENHOWER and Prime Minister Segni met today in the private residence of the United States Ambassador in Paris. Secretary of State Herter and Foreign Minister Pella were also present at the meeting, which lasted nearly two hours.

The international situation was carefully examined in the light of the conversations which President Eisenhower has had recently in Europe and in view of the exchange of visits which will take place in the near future with the Soviet Prime Minister.

The principal East-West problems were taken into consideration. Full identity of views resulted as to all questions examined.

Particular attention was devoted to the problem of disarmament and it was agreed that a controlled and balanced limitation of armaments represents the most appropriate means to guarantee peaceful relations between East and West.

The President and the Prime Minister stated once more that the West intends to pursue every effort to consolidate peace with justice.

They have also emphasized their firm determination to safeguard, through a common policy implemented in the framework of the Atlantic alliance and through further development of European collaboration, the freedom and security of the West.

In view of Italian interest in East-West problems and of the contribution which Italy can give to their solution, President Eisenhower and

Prime Minister Segni will resume their consultations in Washington, immediately after the visit of the Soviet Prime Minister to the United States, on the occasion of the official visit of Prime Minister Segni.

NOTE: This joint statement was released in Paris.

204   ¶ Message to the Fifth Annual Assembly of the Atlantic Treaty Association in Tours.
September 3, 1959

PLEASE convey my greetings to those participating in the Fifth Annual Assembly of the Atlantic Treaty Association. This annual meeting of distinguished citizens of the NATO countries reflects the democratic spirit of voluntary friendship and accommodation of national interests on which the strength of the North Atlantic Treaty Organization rests. The enlightened support of the people of these countries is vital to the organization in sustaining unity of purpose to maintain the common security. In the Atlantic Treaty Association and its constituent national groups they have an indispensable channel for demonstrating to all their intent to work together in the protection of their freedom.

As the Association meets again to confer on matters affecting NATO, it has my warm encouragement in its efforts to secure a fuller support and understanding of NATO as a partnership of free and peaceful nations.

DWIGHT D. EISENHOWER

NOTE: This message, dated August 31, London, was addressed to Frank Case, Jr., President of the American Council on NATO, Inc. It was released in Paris.

205   ¶ Remarks to the Permanent NATO Council at the Palais de Chaillot in Paris.
September 3, 1959

THERE IS really no important reason for me coming here this morning. I have no business to transact or any propositions to place before you. I come rather as one who wants to offer his own testimony to his own convictions and to my country's convictions as to the importance of the North

Atlantic Treaty Organization and to the importance of this Permanent Council in furthering the work of cooperation among the nations in that organization.

I am a representative of a large country, but I seek no position for my country in NATO other than that of an equal partner ready to do its part with all others regardless of size in the great work of assuring the security of the whole. I should like to point out that though one nation may have greater material resources, greater financial or economic or industrial strength than another, no nation in its spirit—in the moral force that it can exert in the world needs take a second place to any other.

NATO is really more a matter of spirit than it is just of strength. It is the strength of ideals, the strength of our determination to preserve those ideals, to work together as true partners, that make NATO a valuable, necessary, and constructive force in the world.

So I repeat, I come back—I come here again to this Council table not to offer anything new, merely to give you my testimony as to the value of this great group and the nations that you collectively represent.

I make only one prophecy: if we are firm among ourselves, if we refuse to retreat one inch from principle, if we remain flexible insofar as tactics, methods, and procedures are involved, and if we keep high our zeal and give to NATO the same patriotic passion and deep devotion that we each give to our own country, then there will be no war. We will be safe, we will progress together to a better world.

Thank you very much.

206 ⁋ Remarks at SHAPE Headquarters, Paris. *September* 3, 1959

General Norstad, and Members of SHAPE:

It is for me indeed a homecoming. As I look back over some 45 years of life since I graduated from school and think of the organizations to which I belong, the groups of which I have been a part, the duties that have been laid upon me, I can think of none which has such unique characteristics and has challenged my interest and my attention more than did my service in SHAPE.

Even the wonderful knowledge that you have won a victory in war cannot equal the experience, the feeling, the satisfaction that one has in saying, "I am doing something to promote better living for people—peace and security for humanity."

You are teaching and preaching and living the proposition that patriotism, love of country, can reach out beyond the borders, the geographical borders of a country and beyond the language that each of us may speak, and embrace the idea of freedom.

Because SHAPE and a member of SHAPE is engaged in far more than mere mastery of intricate staff practices and procedures, planning of logistics, and the operation and movement of troops. He is in the pursuit of an ideal that free peoples may, by joining themselves together, make more certain that peace will be for them, for their children, and their grandchildren a greater probability.

This, I submit, is a far worthier ambition in itself than merely to win a battle. For a battle is after all destructive. Its chief purpose is to gain and hold what we have. It does not obtain for us more freedom, greater opportunity, higher standards, greater aspirations.

So this job in which you are now engaged is one that I often feel is part of the work in which I am still engaged, with you, to pursue peace and a better future for all people everywhere, and particularly for those fifteen countries that are embraced in what we call SHAPE.

It has been a great privilege to come back to see you. I am proud of the invitation, because quite frequently I think there have been some places that haven't asked me back. Here they always do, and I am grateful.

Thank you.

NOTE: The President spoke at 4:30 p.m. His opening words "General Norstad" referred to General Lauris Norstad, Supreme Commander of Allied Forces in Europe.

207 ¶ Remarks on Leaving Paris.
September 4, 1959

Mr. Prime Minister and Gentlemen:

Again I say *au revoir* to this beautiful land. I must thank, on behalf of my party and myself, all the citizens of Paris and the surrounding area who were so kind as to come into the streets and give me a chance to greet them.

I particularly want to thank all the members of the government who have made my stay so pleasant and enjoyable.

And finally, I should like all of you to know that I feel that the visit of General de Gaulle and myself has been mutually profitable, and in my opinion will mark another further step in our cooperative effort to achieve a just peace.

Goodbye again—*au revoir.*

NOTE: The President spoke at Le Bourget Airport, Paris, at 9:00 a.m. He was accompanied to the airport by Prime Minister Michel Debre after taking leave of General de Gaulle at Rambouillet, where the President had spent the night as the General's guest.

208 ¶ Veto of the Second Housing and Urban Renewal Bill. *September 4,* 1959

To the Senate of the United States:

I return herewith, without my approval, S. 2539, "An Act to extend and amend laws relating to the provision and improvement of housing and the renewal of urban communities, and for other purposes."

On July 7, I returned an earlier housing bill, S. 57, to the Senate and set forth in an accompanying message of disapproval many of that bill's objectionable features. Although some of these features have been removed in S. 2539, and some partially corrected, in its most important provisions S. 2539 represents little over-all improvement over S. 57. In one respect—the setting of an expiration date next fall on the new loan insurance authorization of the Federal Housing Administration, with potentially serious disruptive effects on the building industry—S. 2539 is worse than the earlier housing bill.

Clearly this bill, like its predecessor, goes too far. It calls for the spending of more than 1¾ billion of taxpayers' dollars for housing and related programs over and above the vast expenditures to which the Federal government is already committed for these purposes. The history of the bill indicates that the Congress intends it to be a one-year bill. So regarded, S. 2539 calls for Federal spending at virtually the same rate as that provided for by S. 57—a rate far in excess of my recommendations to the Congress.

At a time when critical national needs heavily burden Federal finances, this bill would start two new programs, certain to cost huge sums in the future, under which taxpayers' money would be loaned, at subsidized interest rates, for purposes that could be better met by other methods.

One of the new programs would have the Federal government make direct loans to colleges for classrooms and related facilities and equipment by methods that would tend to displace the investment of private funds in these projects. This is Federal aid to education in a highly objectionable form.

The other new program would have the Federal government make direct loans for housing for elderly persons despite the fact that a program is already in operation and working well, at no cost to the taxpayer, and under which private loans for this same purpose are guaranteed by the Federal government.

Among its other objectionable features, this bill would authorize 37,000 new units of public housing while many thousands of previously authorized units have not been completed or occupied. These, too, would be subsidized, on a basis that would cost the taxpayer many hundreds of millions of dollars over the next forty years. The bill would also authorize 650 million dollars of Federal grants to cities for urban renewal projects. This sum considerably exceeds the first-year amount recommended by the Administration for these purposes.

This is not the kind of housing legislation that is needed at this time. It does not help the housing industry for the Federal government to adopt methods that in these times would increase inflationary pressures in our economy and thereby discourage the thrift on which home financing is heavily dependent. Nor does it make sense to purport to assist any group of citizens, least of all elderly persons living on fixed retirement incomes, by legislation that tends further to increase the cost of living.

There is still time for the Congress to enact a sound housing bill, and I once again urge that it do so. These things can be and ought to be done: (1) remove the ceiling on FHA mortgage insurance authority; (2) extend the FHA program for insurance of property improvement loans; (3) enact reasonable authorizations for urban renewal grants and college housing loans and adjust the interest rate on the latter; (4) extend the voluntary home mortgage credit program; and (5) adjust the statutory interest rate ceilings governing mortgages insured under FHA's regular rental and cooperative housing programs.

DWIGHT D. EISENHOWER

NOTE: On September 23 the President approved S. 2654 "An Act to extend and amend laws relating to the provision and improvement of housing and renewal of urban communities, and for other purposes" (Public Law 86–372; 73 Stat. 654).

209 ¶ Statement by the President: Labor Day. *September 7, 1959*

ON THIS Labor Day, Americans are firm in their dedication to the ideals of freedom, equal opportunity, and a just reward for their toil.

One cannot look back over past Labor Days without a compelling awareness of the broad and constant improvement in the condition of our people, in the real wages they receive, and in the benefits they enjoy. American labor has advanced continuously to new heights of accomplishment.

The rise in our level of living—the social and economic progress of American working men and women—gives promise of continuing achievement. My reasons for this confidence are threefold:

First, we have a political system based on a deep respect for eternal principles; recognizing the worth of individual initiative; and guarding the fruits of individual endeavor. Through this system we seek to release the energies and skills of our people for the benefit of all, without restricting opportunity to a chosen few.

Secondly, we recognize and protect the rights of employees to organize together and to bargain with their employers for an equitable share of the wealth they produce.

And finally, as a Nation we desire an honorable and productive peace for our neighbors around the world. We want and we are working toward that day when the creative energies of mankind may be fully employed in mutual advancement rather than in mutual annihilation.

This, for me, is the meaning and hope of Labor Day, 1959. It is a privilege to join my fellow citizens in honoring the success, the status, and the purpose of American working men and women.

DWIGHT D. EISENHOWER

210 ¶ Remarks at the Washington National Airport Upon Returning From Europe.
September 7, 1959

Mr. Vice President, Mrs. Nixon, My Friends and Ladies and Gentlemen:

Just as always, when one goes outside the country, for no matter what purpose, for whatever length of time, it is always good to be back, and it certainly is good to be back today to see my wife and all these good people.

There was a serious purpose to this visit. All of us—the heads of Government in West Germany, Britain, and France—we knew that we were united in basic principle and purpose and in our pursuit of peace.

But always there comes up among friends, who are necessarily separated at such distances, small details of procedures and methods and tactics in the pursuit of great programs. These have to be talked out. Every serious—indeed, I don't want to use the word serious—every troublesome little problem of this type has been talked out, and I am quite certain that for the moment at least everything is going splendidly.

Everywhere there was voiced governmental unity, but far more heartening than this was the evidence that can be seen in all of these countries of the deep friendship of these people for the American people.

There is nothing else, there is no other single fact of the modern world that is now so important, I think, as this: that the peoples of the Western World have for each other a very deep, abiding affection, mutual trust—and in this there is a tremendous personal, moral, and indeed a material and economic strength.

So I am glad to bring you that kind of news.

And now, just let me say again I am so glad to be back, and to every one of you who has come out here today to greet me: thank you.

211 ¶ Letter to the President of the United Steelworkers and to Representatives of the Steel Industry. *September* 8, 1959

Gentlemen:

Immediately upon my return from Europe I received another report from the Secretary of Labor concerning the negotiations between the steel companies and the United Steelworkers of America.

It is disappointing to me and disheartening to our people that so little apparent progress toward settlement has been made thus far. Tomorrow the strike will begin its ninth week. For this extended period a half million employees of the steel companies have been out of work. Over 85% of the steel-producing capacity of the Nation has been shut down. About 145,000 workers, who have no connection with the strike but whose jobs depend on steel, have been forced into idleness.

The preservation of freedom in America is not an exclusive responsibility of Government. Every individual to a greater or lesser extent shares that responsibility. In these times, when the continuing strength of the Nation is so paramount in this task, the responsibility that rests upon the Steelworkers and the steel companies is a heavy one. The American people have a right to expect a measuring up to this responsibility.

Disputes between labor and management must be settled by collective bargaining between the parties. It is only when the national safety and health are imperiled that Federal law should be invoked. All these weeks the Federal Mediation and Conciliation Service has been attempting to assist the parties to reach agreement. Secretary Mitchell has made available to the public an assessment of the economic facts bearing upon the dispute. The Secretary's report has demonstrated clearly that there is a reasonable basis for a settlement that will be responsive to the requirements of the public interest as I have previously outlined them in public statements.

This dispute is not a test of power. The people of the United States do not look to the economic strength of either side to govern the settlement. They will be satisfied only by a just settlement, voluntarily arrived at, that will serve the interests of all our citizens.

Half-hearted bargaining is not enough. Intensive, uninterrupted good-faith bargaining, with a will to make a responsible settlement is required. Compromising differences is a process with which I am familiar. I have seen far more difficult problems than the steel dispute resolved in far less time by people who spoke different languages and had diverse backgrounds. Everything in my experience leads me to believe that where there is a will to agree on both sides, there is a way to agree. The Steelworkers and the steel companies must find that way expeditiously.

Sincerely,

DWIGHT D. EISENHOWER

NOTE: This is the text of identical letters sent to the following addressees: David McDonald, President, United Steelworkers of America; Roger M. Blough, Chairman of the Board, United States Steel Corporation; Arthur B. Homer, President, Bethlehem Steel Corporation; Charles M. White, Chairman of the Board, Republic Steel Corporation; Avery C. Adams, President and Chairman, Jones and Laughlin Steel Corporation; J. L. Mauthe, Chairman of the Board, Youngstown Sheet and Tube Company; Ralph L. Gray, President, Armco Steel Corporation; Thomas E. Millsop, President, Great Lakes Steel Corporation; Jack L. Ashby, President, Kaiser Steel Corporation; Alwin F. Franz, President, Colorado Fuel and Iron Corporation; John L. Neudoerfer, Chairman of the Board, Wheeling Steel Corporation; Edward J. Hanley, President, Allegheny Ludlum Steel Corporation; Joseph L. Block, Chairman of the Board, Inland Steel Company.

212 ¶ Remarks to a Delegation From the National Council of Churches. *September* 9, 1959

Dr. Dahlberg and Ladies and Gentlemen:

My attitude toward one of the functions of the church in promoting peace is one of appreciation of the great service it can perform in uniting better the free nations of the world. I think we should never forget we are supporting principles which are after all religious in their derivation. And I mean politically speaking, as against a godless atheism—and because this is an atheistic ideology, denying all human rights, any kind of human dignity—we have an enemy operating under a dictatorship that has us always at a disadvantage.

We are a democracy. We achieve our decisions by debate, by a representative form of government. They have the great advantage,

644

whether it be economic or military, or any other kind of contest, of having in one mailed fist, all authority.

Now this is, I should hasten to say, not in the long run a particular form of efficiency. I believe it was Woodrow Wilson who said, "The highest form of efficiency is the spontaneous cooperation of a free people." And when the chips are down, that is exactly correct. If we declare a purpose to pursue an objective that will be costly, in sacrifice, in material sacrifice, maybe in suffering or in life, we will go on to the end. But when in a dictatorship that sacrifice and suffering holds more fear for the individual than his fear of the "boss," then chaos ensues. This happened in the last days of the Czars, and it happened in the last days of Hitler, and in other dictatorships—including Napoleon.

Now, to go back to my main thesis, that by reminding ourselves always in every free country, that every type of free government is a political expression of some form of religious belief, we have a great force of unity, and we achieve among ourselves, by spontaneous cooperation, the kind of power that the other fellow cannot, in the long run, command.

The Founding Fathers, when they wanted to explain to the world that this new form of government was united in America, and noted that they had a decent respect for the opinion of mankind, said that "We hold that all men are endowed by their Creator"—in other words, to explain our form of government you had to call upon the Divine Creator.

This, it seems to me, is the strongest link that we have among all the countries of the West. Indeed I think this even includes the Moham-medans, the Buddhists and the rest; because they, too, strongly believe that they achieve a right to human dignity because of their relationship to the Supreme Being. We must remember always that there are others that can have this same feeling of unity, because of their recognition of a religious destiny. So, what you are doing, what you are attempting to do is, to my mind, one of the finest things that you could possibly undertake.

Now I was going to talk for 10 seconds, and I have already for 10 minutes, but I will say one other thing: I have been giving my mind and heart to this business of foreign relations for a long time, long before I was President. And one thing is always clear—Jefferson spoke about it and many of our former statesmen: the need for an informed public opinion. Because since public opinion is the force that makes our country operate, makes it function, we must be perfectly sure that that public opinion is applied in the right direction, or we are not going on the right road.

I cannot tell you how much I have concerned myself about trying to take simple issues in the foreign relations field or indeed in the economic, and as I would like to suggest to you, the need for a sound dollar. I take these subjects when I can, right squarely into press conferences, on the television. I am going to talk about foreign relations tomorrow evening a little bit—15 minutes. But always I feel the necessity of trying to make the facts available to the American public. And sometimes, you know, you have to tackle them and hold them down to feed these facts to them. The man that plows a furrow in Dickinson County, or works on a Brooklyn dock, or drives a taxicab—when you begin to talk to him about the need for helping the people of Ghana, or of French Africa—well, he wonders what in the world you are talking about.

Now you give the facts, but it doesn't always penetrate, so there has to be education—sometimes almost spoonfed, and probably with the aid of a hammer. But we need it. We talk all the time in Government and the public print about the woeful ignorance of foreigners about America. One thing we must be very careful about, how fully does the average American citizen understand his country, its problems and its role in the world.

So, these two things: uniting the free world through this common respect for religion; and educating ourselves as to the type of problem that we must solve, if we are going to be true to those values that our religion teaches us.

These are two great works to which I should think all of us could dedicate ourselves full time.

Now just one more observation before I go out. I had a long talk with Cardinal Spellman on the phone. He is an old, old friend of mine—a good one. And I assure you that our Catholic brothers are joining you in these hours of prayer for peace—with the hope that those of Government that have to direct affairs in relationship with Russia and with others, can have some guidance that will come about because of this universality of prayer. He assured me in very emphatic manner on that, and I thought you might like to know it.

Thank you very much. It's good to see you—and good luck.

NOTE: The President spoke in the Conference room at the White House. His opening words "Dr. Dahlberg" referred to Edwin T. Dahlberg, President of the National Council of the Churches of Christ in the United States of America.

213 ¶ Veto of the Second Public Works Appropriations Bill. *September 9, 1959*

To the House of Representatives:

On August 28, 1959, I returned to the Congress without my approval H.R. 7509, a bill making appropriations for civil functions administered by the Department of the Army, certain agencies of the Department of the Interior, and the Tennessee Valley Authority, for the fiscal year ending June 30, 1960, and for other purposes.

H.R. 9105 which is now before me, is identical to H.R. 7509 in all respects (including the 67 unbudgeted projects which will ultimately cost our taxpayers more than $800 million), except that each individual project and appropriation item has been reduced by 2½ per cent. This only change not only fails to meet any of the objections I outlined in my message of August 28, 1959, accompanying H.R. 7509 but in addition could have the effect of impeding orderly work on going projects and result in an increase in cost instead of a saving.

Therefore, for the reasons outlined in such previous message, I am returning H.R. 9105 to the Congress without my approval.

Because the time before the probable adjournment of Congress may be too short to allow for deliberate reconsideration by the Congress of my objections, the Congress might well enact a continuing resolution, effective until January 31, 1960, so that work in progress may proceed in an orderly way.

DWIGHT D. EISENHOWER

NOTE: On September 10, the Congress passed the bill over the President's veto. As enacted, H.R. 9105 is Public Law 86–254 (73 Stat. 491).

214 ¶ Radio and Television Report to the American People on the European Trip. *September 10, 1959*

[Delivered from the President's Office at 7:30 p.m.]

Good evening, My Friends:

In these next few minutes, I should like to talk to you mainly about my recent European trip.

To give you first my most memorable impression—it is that the people of Europe have a deep liking for the people of America. This they made manifest in a number of ways. In the villages, towns, and in the big cities I could feel this message rushing across the Atlantic to you. Along the lanes and country roads the message was always the same. Even during a long automobile trip to make a courtesy visit to the Queen and to her family, there was scarcely a hundred yard stretch of road that did not have its little knot of people to send back this same greeting and this same sentiment to America.

During the past two weeks I have conferred, as you know, with Chancellor Adenauer of Germany, Prime Minister Macmillan of Britain, and President de Gaulle of France, all old friends of mine. I talked with Prime Minister Segni of Italy; also with Mr. Luns of Holland and Mr. Spaak of Belgium who are, respectively, the President and Secretary General of the NATO Council.

These men are statesmen. Like us, they are dedicated to preserving the security of free nations and to upholding the values we place above all others—freedom, equality of opportunity, human dignity, and peace with justice.

With them we reaffirmed our unity on fundamental issues and in support of the North Atlantic Treaty Organization.

There will be no retreat from the fundamental objectives to which we are collectively pledged. We agreed that the defensive strength required for our common security must continue to be maintained.

For the face-to-face reaffirmation of this faith and purpose, I am grateful and deeply gratified. I had the same feeling during my entire journey, in talking to President Heuss of Germany, and great numbers of other men and women in and out of government.

To our friends in Bonn, London, and Paris, I expressed America's concern over the aggressive actions of the Communists in Asia. Each believed that the United Nations should take official notice of the Laos situation and that we should support that body in seeking a satisfactory solution. Mr. Macmillan was especially emphatic on this point. I am happy that the United Nations has already designated a fact-finding commission of neutral observers. I hope that this prompt United Nations action will serve to halt the aggression that has threatened the freedom of Laos.

Quite naturally much of our discussion centered about our defensive alliance, NATO. All expressed approval of its growing capability to secure cooperation among member nations in political, economic, and scientific areas, as a supplement to its work in the security field. The Common Market and similar developments tending to knit more closely together the nations of Europe, also engaged our attention.

One subject involved in our discussions was that of the growing problems faced by the under-developed or newly-formed nations of the world. More than one billion needy people require real advances in education, health facilities, and living standards. There is an understandable ferment among them—an intense dissatisfaction with their present lot and an increasing determination to improve that lot. They must have greater technical assistance in all fields, large amounts of investment capital, and wider opportunities for trade.

Since all of us outside the Iron Curtain want such progress to be achieved in freedom, the highly industrialized free nations must find effective means to provide the needed help. Each of us has undertaken to study this vast problem which could eventually become a menace to our own freedom. No one nation alone should or can bear the burdens involved, we see again in this matter the need for cooperation and unity among ourselves so that, through equitable sharing, success can gradually but surely be achieved.

In connection with this world-wide issue, I had in Paris a unique and most interesting opportunity to learn many things about political developments in all parts of French Africa. To that city had been invited the prime ministers of the countries making up the French Community. Eleven came.

They were so anxious to express in some unique form their admiration, liking, and respect for the people of America that they sent through one of their number, Prime Minister Youlou, a baby elephant. The baby elephant, I understand, is on its way here now, and I shall have to find for it a home in one of our zoos.

The people of these regions who are, in local affairs, largely self-governing, are being helped by France in their economic, cultural, and political progress. They have been assured by France of the right to make their own final decisions as to their own political destiny.

The morale of all these men is high. They repudiate the false teachings of communism. They have a vision of progress and future greatness in freedom. They emphatically expressed to me their gratitude to France and General de Gaulle for the opportunities opening up before them.

It was in this kind of atmosphere that I talked with our Western allies about the impending visit of Chairman Khrushchev to the United States.

I outlined to them the reasons for my invitation to him, which are simply:

First, to give him the opportunity to see what America and Americans are like; to let him see and feel a great and thriving nation living in real freedom.

Second, to give him, face to face, the basic convictions of our people on the major issues of the day, including West Berlin, and to hear from him directly his own views on those issues.

I assured our allies in private conversations, as I have on other occasions publicly, that my invitation to Mr. Khrushchev does not contemplate merely a ceremonial visit—just as it does not suggest any purpose of reaching definitive negotiation. But it does imply the hope that serious exploratory efforts may reveal new opportunities for practical progress toward removal of some of the causes of world tensions.

Conversations with Chairman Khrushchev will not include any negotiation concerning subjects that directly relate to the interests of our allies or to any other part of the free world.

In this connection, I know that neither America nor her allies will mistake good manners and candor for weakness; no principle or fundamental interest will be placed upon any auction block.

This is well understood here and abroad.

Allied leaders expressed their understanding of the reasons that prompted the invitation to Mr. Khrushchev to visit America. While their hopes for progress revealed varying degrees of optimism, each was convinced that the effort was clearly one that had to be made.

Incidentally, I have every confidence that our people will greet Mr.

Khrushchev and his wife and family with traditional American courtesy and dignity. We cannot fail to accord him the same consideration which the Soviet public gave to Vice President and Mrs. Nixon.

Having just returned from France, it might be appropriate to recall a comment made about our nation over a century ago by that remarkable observer, Tocqueville. He said, "The great sustaining force of America is not simply to be found in its laws or institutions—but in the manners of her people, her habits of heart."

Each of the leaders with whom I talked is fully aware of America's conviction that any agreement to hold a summit meeting must be based upon the certainty that our status and rights in Berlin will be respected. In addition, we believe there must be some clear Soviet indication, no matter how given, that serious negotiation will bring about real promise of reducing the causes of world tensions.

Should a summit meeting on such a basis ensue:

We and our allies stand ready always to negotiate realistically with the Soviets on any mutually enforceable plan for a reduction in armaments.

We are prepared to make a real beginning toward solving the problems of a divided Germany.

We are hopeful of arranging for wider contacts in ideas, publications, persons, and information.

We are, in short, ready to negotiate on any subject within the limits dictated by the dedication of our Government and our people, to the cause of a just peace, and our loyalty to the United Nations and to its basic concept. That concept is that international disputes should be settled by peaceful means, in conformity with the principles of justice and international law.

I repeat, we shall not retreat from these ideals or principles or weaken in our resolution to remain strong in their defense. This means that we must be as concerned about the freedom of two million West Berliners as we are about the freedom of any part of our coalition.

We must be concerned about threats to freedom, no matter where they may occur.

Though specific problems may at times present such difficulties as to prevent immediate, practicable solution, yet we must all understand that wherever freedom is denied or lost—whether in Asia, Africa, the Americas, or in Eastern Europe—by that much is our own Nation's freedom endangered. Firmness in support of fundamentals, with flexibility in tactics and method, is the key to any hope of progress in negotiation.

The choice before world leaders is momentous.

In the past, conferences have all too often been characterized by suspicion, threat, and stubborn prejudice, and results have been barren and bleak.

But, could we create an improved atmosphere of mutual understanding and serious purpose, it would be possible to attack, with renewed hope, the problems that divide us.   If the Chairman of the Council of Ministers of the U.S.S.R. has constructive ideas and suggestions that could provide the basis for responsible negotiation on the issues that divide us, we would welcome the opportunity to study them with our allies.

It is my profound hope that some real progress will be forthcoming, even though no one would be so bold as to predict such an outcome.

Fellow Americans, we venerate more widely than any other document, except only the Bible, the American Declaration of Independence.

That Declaration was more than a call to national action.

It is a voice of conscience establishing clear, enduring values applicable to the lives of all men.

It stands enshrined today as a charter of human liberty and dignity. Until these things belong to every living person their pursuit is an unfinished business to occupy our children and generations to follow them.

In this spirit we stand firmly in defense of freedom.

In this spirit we cooperate with our friends, and negotiate with those who oppose us.

If the forthcoming visit of Mr. Khrushchev to this Nation should bring to him some real appreciation of this spirit and this conscience, then indeed the venture would be a thousandfold worthwhile.

I know that all America prays to the Almighty that this might come to pass.

Thank you, and good night.

NOTE: The baby elephant "Dzimbo," presented to the President by the Reverend Fulbert Youlou, President of the French Communities of the Congo Republic, was received by the National Zoological Park, Washington, D.C., on October 10, 1959.

215 ¶ Veto of Bill for the Relief of Eber Brothers Wine and Liquor Corporation.
September 14, 1959

To the House of Representatives:

I return herewith, without my approval, H.R. 2717, "For the relief of Eber Brothers Wine and Liquor Corporation."

The bill would permit income tax refund claims for this corporation's taxable years 1947 and 1948 to be presently determined even though applicable statutes of limitations have long since expired.

This special relief should be granted, it is said, because a January 29, 1951, decision of the Tax Court—holding that a certain form of income should be treated as a capital gain rather than as ordinary income—came at a time when the statutory three year period for claiming a refund had only six months to run on this taxpayer's 1948 return and only eleven months to run on its 1947 return. Despite the remaining time it did have in each case, this taxpayer failed to file for a refund on this new basis until July 14, 1952—a year and a half after the Tax Court decision. Nor did the taxpayer take any other timely action to protect its position. The 1947 and 1948 claims were disallowed because not presented in time.

A judicial decision modifying or overturning a previously held view of the law is not an unusual circumstance in the development of our tax law. Taxpayers and their counsel often must take action or otherwise adjust because of such changes.

The effect of the Tax Court decision here involved was to change the tax treatment of a certain kind of income. This, as always, meant different things to different taxpayers according to their individual circumstances, but the point is that as of the date of the decision everybody's rights—no matter how they may have varied—were fixed. This bill now seeks to alter those rights for one taxpayer.

The record on this bill discloses no valid reason for such special relief. The taxpayer simply failed to protect his position within the time allowed him by law. The very purpose of the statute of limitations is to achieve finality in tax administration. Special relief in this case would undermine this purpose, would discriminate against other taxpayers, and would create an undesirable precedent.

For these reasons I am unable to approve this bill.

DWIGHT D. EISENHOWER

216   ¶ Statement by the President Upon Signing the Equal Time Amendment to the Communications Act. *September* 14, 1959

I HAVE today signed S. 2424, which amends the Communications Act to make clear that a brief appearance of a candidate for public office on a bona fide news program or in the course of radio or television coverage of important news events will not require the station to provide equal time to all other persons who are candidates for the same office. This law will make possible the continued full participation of radio and television in the news coverage of political campaigns which is so essential to a well informed America.

The legislation makes reference to the continuing obligation of broadcasters to operate in the public interest and to afford reasonable opportunity for the discussion of conflicting views on important public issues. There is no doubt in my mind that the American radio and television stations can be relied upon to carry out fairly and honestly the provisions of this Act without abuse or partiality to any individual, group, or party.

NOTE: As enacted, S. 2424 is Public Law 86–274 (73 Stat. 557).

217   ¶ Remarks of Welcome to Chairman Khrushchev of the U.S.S.R. at Andrews Air Force Base. *September* 15, 1959

Mr. Chairman:

I welcome you, your family and party to the United States. I am especially happy that Mrs. Khrushchev and other members of your family are accompanying you. On behalf of the Government and of the people of America, I express the hope that you and they will find your stay among us interesting and useful.

I am looking forward to the talks we will have together. Although we shall not be negotiating any issues affecting the interests of other countries, I trust that a full and frank exchange of views on many subjects may contribute to better understanding, on both sides, of unresolved international problems.

During your stay here you will have an opportunity to see something of our country, our institutions, our customs, and our people. You will have a chance to speak with individuals and groups from all walks of life.

The political and social systems of our two countries differ greatly. In our system the people themselves establish and control the Government. You will find, I am sure, that they, like your people, want to live in peace with justice. Although they have built and maintain strong security forces, it is clear that because our people do want peace and because they are the decisive influence in basic actions of our Government, aggression by this Nation is an impossibility.

Just as I hope that I may later visit and learn more about your people, I know that you seek better understanding of our system, of our people, and of the principles which guide and motivate them. I assure you that they have no ill will toward any other people, that they covet no territory, no additional power. Nor do they seek to interfere in the internal affairs of any other nation.

I most sincerely hope that as you come to see and believe these truths about our people there will develop an improved basis on which we can together consider the problems that divide us.

After all, our common purpose should be, always, a just, universal and enduring peace. It is in this spirit, Mr. Chairman, that I greet you and welcome you to Washington and the United States.

NOTE: Chairman Khrushchev's remarks, as published in the Department of State Bulletin (vol. 41, p. 476), follow:

Mr. President, ladies and gentlemen:

Permit me at this moment, on first setting foot on American soil, to thank Mr. Eisenhower for the invitation to visit your country and everyone present for the warm welcome accorded us, representatives of the Soviet Union.

Russians say: "Every good job should be started in the morning." Our flight began in Moscow this morning, and we are glad that our first meeting with you on American soil is taking place on the morning of the same day. As you see, our countries are not so distant from each other.

I accepted the invitation of the President of the United States to make an official visit to your country with great pleasure and gratitude, and I will be glad to talk with statesmen, representatives of the business world, intellectuals, workers, and farmers and to become familiar with the life of the industrious and enterprising American people.

For our part, we will be glad to receive Mr. Eisenhower, his family, and those who will accompany him in the Soviet Union shortly. We will give the President a most cordial welcome and every opportunity to become familiar with the life of the Soviet people.

We have always considered reciprocal visits and meetings of representatives of states useful. Meetings and conversations between the statesmen of our two great countries, the Soviet Union and the United States of America, are especially important.

All the peoples are profoundly interested in the maintenance and consolidation of peace, in peaceful coexistence. War does not promise anyone any good; peace is advantageous to all the nations. This is the basic principle which, we believe, the statesmen of all countries should be guided by in order to realize the aspirations of the peoples.

We have come to you with an open heart and good intentions. The Soviet people want to live in friendship with the American people. There are no obstacles to having the relations between our countries develop as relations between good neighbors. The Soviet and the American people, like other peoples, fought well together in the Second World War against the common enemy and broke his backbone. In peaceful conditions we have even more reason and more possibilities for friendship and for cooperation between the peoples of our countries.

Shortly before our meeting you, Mr. President, the Soviet scientists, engineers, technicians, and workers filled our hearts

with joy by launching the rocket to the moon. Thus has been blazed a road from the earth to the moon; and a container of 390 kilograms with a pennant bearing the national emblem of the Soviet Union is now on the moon. Our earth lost several hundred kilograms in weight, and the moon gained in her weight the same amount of kilograms. I am sure that in this historic achievement of peaceful science rejoice not the Soviet people alone but also all those to whom peace and friendship among nations are dear.

Recently an atomic icebreaker has been completed in the Soviet Union. This practical embodiment of the desire of all peoples to see the nuclear energy put solely to peaceful use makes us happy. We are aware, Mr. President, that the idea of peaceful use of atomic energy is dear to you, and we note with gratification that your aims in this field coincide with ours.

We entertain no doubt that the splendid scientists, engineers, and workers of the United States of America, who are engaged in the field of conquering the cosmos, will also carry their pennant to the moon. The Soviet pennant, as an old resident of the moon, will welcome your pennant and they will live there together in peace and friendship, as we both should live together on the earth, in peace and friendship, as should live in peace and friendship all peoples who inhabit our common mother earth, who so generously gives us her gifts.

During these first few minutes of my stay in the United States permit me to extend hearty greetings and best wishes to the American people.

218 ¶ Joint Statement Following the First Discussions With Chairman Khrushchev. *September* 15, 1959

PRESIDENT Dwight D. Eisenhower and the Chairman of the Council of Ministers of the USSR, Nikita S. Khrushchev, met for nearly two hours this afternoon. They were accompanied by the Vice President, the Foreign Ministers and other advisers. The President and the Chairman reviewed the relationship between the two countries and exchanged views in general terms on international problems. They agreed on the general line of their further discussions, which will take place on all these subjects following the Chairman's return from his visit throughout the country. They plan to meet for this purpose at Camp David from Friday evening, September 25th, until noon on September 27th.

The atmosphere of the talk was friendly and frank with agreement that the discussions should continue in this spirit to seek ways to achieve a better understanding.

The following were present:

The President	Nikita S. Khrushchev, Chairman of the Council of
The Vice President	Ministers of the USSR
The Secretary of State	Andrei Gromyko, Minister of Foreign Affairs of
The United States Ambassador	the USSR
to the USSR	The USSR Ambassador to the United States,
Henry Cabot Lodge, Jr.	Mikhail Menshikov
Foy Kohler, Deputy Assistant	A. Soldatov, Chief, American Department of the
Secretary of State	Ministry of Foreign Affairs

219 ❡ Toasts of the President and Chairman Khrushchev. *September* 15, 1959

Mr. Chairman:

The ladies and gentlemen gathered at this board are here to greet you as the head of the Union of Soviet Socialist Republics, and to greet Mrs. Khrushcheva, your family and the members of your party. We trust that you will find your trip, your tour, of America both instructive and interesting and enjoyable.

It was a hundred and fifty years ago that diplomatic relations between your country and ours were opened. On November 5, 1809, John Quincy Adams, later Secretary of State, and later President of the United States, presented his credentials to Alexander I. And since that date there has been a history of many incidents of collaboration between your country and mine, and certainly a long history of friendship. In two World Wars we have been allies.

And now today, it seems to me that our two countries have a very special obligation to the entire world. Because of our strength, because of our importance in the world, it is vital that we understand each other better. You and I have agreed on this point.

I think that skillful debate is not now enough. We must depend upon fact and truth. And we must make it our common purpose, as I see it, that we develop for each other the maximum of fact and truth, so that we may better lead—between us—this world into a better opportunity for peace and prosperity.

And it is in that hope, sir, in that effort, in the hope that that effort will be successful, that I ask this company to join me in a Toast to you, Mr. Chairman, Chairman of the Council of Ministers, to Madame Khrushcheva, and to the people of the Soviet Union.

Ladies and gentlemen, Chairman Khrushchev.

NOTE: The President proposed this toast at a state dinner at the White House at 9:58 p.m. Chairman Khrushchev responded (through an interpreter) as follows:

Mr. President, Mrs. Eisenhower, ladies and gentlemen:

I wish to thank you, Mr. President, for the good wishes that you voiced, and to state on my part that we have come here on the invitation of the President with our intentions based on the need to come to an agreement on the improvement of our relations, because our countries are much too strong and we cannot quarrel with each other. If we were weak countries, then it would be another matter, because when the weak quarrel, they are just scratching each other's faces and it takes just a couple of days for a cosmetician and everything comes out right again. But if we quarrel, then not only our countries can suffer colossal damage but the other countries of the world will also be involved in a world shambles.

But I am sure that we can live in peace and progress together for peace.

You mentioned the fact that a hundred and fifty years have passed since diplomatic relations were established between the United States and Russia. I also want to say a few words on that example. I want to say that when your Ambassador was presenting his credentials to the

Emperor, Alexander I, I don't think the Emperor trusted your Ambassador too much, because after all the United States was a Republic and Alexander was a Czar, but all the same there did exist mutual understanding between the two countries, and contacts between them strengthened.

And our countries not only never fought with each other, but I don't think there were ever even any major quarrels between them. I don't pretend that I have too profound a knowledge of history, but I am sure that this was so.

Our countries have different social systems. We believe our system to be better—and you believe yours to be better. But surely we should not bring quarrels out onto the arena of open struggle. Let history judge which of us is right.

If we agree to accept this principle, then we can build our relations on the basis of peace and friendship.

You are a very rich and strong country. I read very many speeches made by many of the Senators and Representatives present here today, and so although I have made their acquaintance here for the first time today, in actual fact they are my old acquaintances by their speeches.

What we should now do is to strive together to improve our relations. We need nothing from the United States, and you require nothing that we have. It is true that you are richer than we are at present. But then tomorrow we will be as rich as you are, and the day after tomorrow we will be even richer.

But is there anything bad in this? After all, we are going to do this by our own forces—by our own strength.

I must say that the meeting I had today heartened me. When some of our journalists approached me after the meeting and asked me my impressions, I said that there was an agreed communique that was to be published and they should abide by what was said in that communique. But I could not help mentioning that I would inform my government that a good beginning had been made, and one could only hope that the final outcome would be even better.

And so I would like to raise my glass and propose a Toast to the President, to his wife, to all of you esteemed ladies and gentlemen.

220   ¶ Message to Dr. Adenauer on His 10th Anniversary as Chancellor of Germany. *September* 15, 1959

His Excellency Dr. Konrad Adenauer,
Chancellor of the Federal Republic of Germany,
Bonn

On the tenth anniversary of the assumption of your duties as Chancellor of the Federal Republic of Germany, I send most cordial personal greetings. On behalf of the American people I congratulate you for your historic contribution not only to the affairs of your own country but to those of the European community as a whole. Through your dedication and inspiring leadership, the Federal Republic has risen out of the chaos of war to a position of influence and responsibility in the community of free nations. Moreover, there has been developed in Germany a government guided by the principles of democracy and motivated by a sincere desire to play a positive role in the great movement toward European cooperation and integration. Your effective work in developing understanding between our two peoples has also been a contribution of major significance. It was a most valued and enjoyable opportunity to confer with you in Bonn recently, and I wish you many more productive years in the interests of your own country and those of the free world.

With assurances of my continued esteem and friendship,

DWIGHT D. EISENHOWER

221   ¶ Memorandum of Disapproval of Bill
Creating a Coal Research and Development
Commission.   *September* 16, 1959

I AM withholding my approval from H.R. 6596, "A bill to encourage
and stimulate the production and conservation of coal in the United
States through research and development by creating a Coal Research
and Development Commission, and for other purposes."

The Department of the Interior currently administers research and
conservation programs for coal, as well as for other mineral resources.
If an additional agency for this purpose were now to be created, the
Department of the Interior's established interest in such matters would
be diluted and the result could only be a blurring of the lines of
governmental responsibility in this important area of concern.

The first Hoover Commission recommended that the various functions
of the Government be grouped into major departments and agencies on
the basis of purpose. The creation of a new coal research agency by
approving H.R. 6596 would be a serious set-back in the progress that
has been made in following the Hoover Commission recommendations
for improving the organization of the Federal Government. The bill
is also undesirable because it could serve as a precedent for the creation
of other such special agencies.

One provision of H.R. 6596 would authorize the Secretary of the
Interior to contract for coal research. This feature of the bill is highly
desirable and I urge the Congress to enact legislation granting such
authority to the Secretary. H.R. 3375, or S. 1362, now pending in the
Congress, would accomplish this purpose, and have been endorsed by
the Administration to stimulate research, as well as production and
conservation of coal.

DWIGHT D. EISENHOWER

222 ¶ Remarks to a Group of Foreign Educators Participating in the International Teacher Development Program. *September* 16, 1959

Ladies and Gentlemen:

First of all, welcome to Washington, our Nation's capital. Now ordinarily, with such a group like this meeting in the Rose Garden, I should content myself with a few words of greeting and a few off-the-cuff remarks. But because of the importance of this group—representing as you do the teaching profession in so many different countries, and because of your tremendous interest in promoting understanding by coming to this country to see what you can bring to us and what you can take away from here—I decided to put my few simple thoughts, such as they are, on paper. So you will this morning get from me a bit of a precedent. I think never before in this Rose Garden have I read a speech—which is probably self-flattery. I don't mean to call it a speech; it's just an expression of some simple thoughts.

Dr. Hauck, Teachers and School Administrators:

I am happy to join with Dr. Hauck and others in his group in extending to you this welcome to our country. I hope in the coming months you will all have abundant opportunity to meet and talk with Americans in every walk of life. We of course want to show you our schools and colleges and our universities; our cultural institutions, farms, factories, and playgrounds. But most of all we want you to come to know our people; and what they think, and how they live, and what their aspirations for the future are. And I speak for all Americans when I say that we are tremendously interested in you and your ideas. We want to know better what you think, how you live and to what you aspire.

A little more than 30 years ago, I made my first trans-Atlantic crossing—it took 7 days. My latest crossing—early this month—took a little less than 7 hours. In the three decades between these trips, the world has experienced awesome changes. One of these is that 25 nations, with a population of nearly one billion, have achieved political independence. Each is struggling for stability, for a respected place in the family of nations, and for advancement in the well-being of its people. But to me the greatest change of all is the development of an exacting interdependence between free nations—an interdependence that involves the oldest and the youngest nations, the largest and the smallest, the most prosperous and the least developed of nations.

This interdependence calls for new thinking, new institutions, new vision. Above all, it calls for greater understanding among peoples—the genuine understanding of truth, which can dispel unfounded fears and suspicions, bars to true and lasting peace. People of good will everywhere have a tremendous job of communicating such understanding—and little enough time to do it. We need to pursue every possible avenue that can bring people together as friends and co-workers seeking solutions to their common problems.

As teachers and school administrators you enjoy an extraordinary advantage in this great task. You are the multipliers of knowledge; you serve to develop and disseminate thoughts and ideas, and to stimulate critical, creative thinking, and understanding in others. The educational institutions in which you work are the seedbeds of learning—and not merely of your own countries, but of all mankind.

Knowledge is or should be universal; it was meant to be shared; and it has the peculiar quality about it that when its parts are brought together, the result is a multiplication, rather than a mere addition of those values.

One of the powerful effects of teacher exchange is that the benefits are multiplied a thousandfold. A good teacher, given the opportunity to comprehend other cultures, is not just a transmitter of important facts about the language, economy, politics, science of the country he has visited. He becomes far more—a sort of ambassador-at-large, who brings to each one with whom he comes in contact, greater depth of understanding and greater toleration.

All of us surely agree that the exchange of students is valuable. Indeed, I would like to see a substantial increase in the almost fifty thousand foreign students now studying in the United States. But I emphasize that through teacher exchange we can open intellectual windows faster and in greater number, and thus more rapidly progress toward the greater understanding so desperately needed by our quarrelsome and shrinking world. A world of understanding will be a world of true freedom and peace.

We shall not be serving mankind well if we become obsessed with just the business of putting new satellites into orbit—so obsessed that we overlook the fact that we have some real problems left right here on earth.

We need to put new ideas—and more of them—into orbit. And we must use every resource at our command to see that people everywhere achieve greater understanding of each other before it is too late.

In this respect you of the teaching profession compose one of our most precious resources. As always with sound and enthusiastic teaching, we do not look for spectacular break-throughs. There are no easy solutions for the complexities that surround us. I confidently expect the teaching profession to write a new and one of the finest chapters in human history by developing the priceless commodity of genuine understanding. Only thus shall we ever achieve the kind of world we want.

I hope all of you will take home much of America in your minds and in your hearts. We certainly expect to get much from you.

Thank you very much. Goodbye.

NOTE: In his remarks the President referred to Dr. Arthur A. Hauck, Director of the Washington International Center. The International Teacher Development Program is administered by the International Educational Exchange Service, Department of State, and the Office of Education, Department of Health, Education, and Welfare.

223 ¶ The President's News Conference of September 17, 1959.

THE PRESIDENT. I have no announcement.

Q. Merriman Smith, United Press International: Naturally, sir, we are all very interested in your personal impressions of Mr. Khrushchev; but more particularly I would like to ask whether, from your conversations with him thus far and from your knowledge of his statements that he has made since he has been in this country, you see any concrete evidence of a change in his position on the issues that have been dividing the East and West?

THE PRESIDENT. Well, I think, Mr. Smith, it is a little bit early to talk about these things in detail. Mr. Khrushchev's attitude has been extremely friendly, but so far all the conversations have been confined to, let's say, agreeing on agenda items and to a restatement of general positions.

So I think that until after the conferences at Camp David have been held, it would be both undesirable and unwise to say much more about them.

I repeat that so far as manner and deportment is concerned, his whole attitude is one of seeking some kind of a position that could be agreed.

Q. David Kraslow, Knight Newspapers: Could you tell us, Mr. President, what the agenda will be for the Camp David talks?

THE PRESIDENT. No. No, we agreed to—there is no secret about it for my part, except that we did agree that there was no reason for specifying, because to specify is to limit, and there could be a number of questions that could come up in any case.

Q. Thomas N. Schroth, Congressional Quarterly: Would you please tell us, sir, how you feel Congress dealt with your program this year, and especially with the spending issue?

THE PRESIDENT. Frankly, I have been studying a little bit and actually doing a little drafting on a statement that I might issue in course of the next one or two or three days. I wouldn't mind making one or two comments.

You will have to recall, though, the atmosphere in which the session began. People in the majority, particularly, were predicting a very great prolongation of the recession, and therefore were advancing a number of projects that would be called pump priming in order to bring about recovery.

My own position was that the signs of recovery were all around us, that it was going forward rapidly, and that unnecessary spending should be completely curtailed.

Now there were a number of things that were done during the Congress that were largely in accordance with some of the views I had expressed. For example, I think that there has been a very fine step forward made in correcting abuses by people of evil intent in the labor movement. Things of that kind have been done.

I think the very flat refusal to take care of the matter of our long-range financing is one of the most serious things that has happened to the United States in my time.

This is something that causes great concern, and it must be in some way or other corrected because we are having too much short-term financing. All that paper is really money, and this means it puts a pressure on the interest rates and the cost of doing business. Also, it of course is another inciting cause for inflation.

One of my most personal, personal and official, disappointments was the disapproval of the nomination of Secretary Strauss.

But by and large there has been a great deal of good accomplished. But I do want to point out this again, that until there is a situation where both Executive and Legislature are controlled by the same party, I believe we cannot fix responsibility and there cannot be really the kind of leadership of the whole Nation that the Nation deserves. I believe it is unfortunate to have that kind of divided control in the Federal Government.

Q. Robert C. Pierpoint, CBS News: Mr. President, I wonder if you could give us your reaction to President de Gaulle's plans for the future of Algeria?

THE PRESIDENT. I read it, but I have not had the opportunity to give complete sympathetic study.

By the way, I wrote down a note on it. I think I would rather read it because this is a very important thing, I think. I had forgotten for a moment I had stuck it in my pocket.

[*Reading*] While I have read General de Gaulle's speech, I have not been able to give it the careful and sympathetic study it deserves. Therefore I do not want to comment on the details.

I might add that I am quite sure that there will be extremists at each fringe that will disapprove, but that is always the case with any constructive proposal.

It is a far-reaching declaration containing explicit promises of self-determination for the Algerian people and, as such, completely in accord with our hopes to see proclaimed a just and liberal program for Algeria, which we could support. I am greatly encouraged by General de Gaulle's courageous and statesmanlike declaration. It is our hope that it will lead to an early peace. [*Ends reading*]

And I might add it is a plan that I think is worthy of General de Gaulle's efforts.

Q. William McGaffin, Chicago Daily News: Mr. President, Mr. Khrushchev has said that he is going to make a proposal on disarmament at the United Nations tomorrow. You have expressed your views before many times on the basic essentials of any disarmament agreement which we could seriously consider. Could you restate those for us at this point?

THE PRESIDENT. Of course, the basic principle is that we are of the conviction, first of all, that mutual disarmament, universal disarmament, is really the one great hope of the world living in peace in the future years. We believe that no disarmament proposal can be considered as a practical one or as being contributory to progress toward peace unless it is self-enforcing, unless there is a regulatory kind of action that makes sure that everybody knows that the agreement is being observed.

Now within this particular limitation and the other one, that disarmament is mutual and equivalent or fair to both sides, we have no particular conditions to apply, because we have proposed several times general plans and special plans that we thought would have some effect or at least constitute a small step toward the ultimate objective. But within the limits that I just specified, we will talk about anything.

Q. Lambert Brose, Lutheran Layman: Mr. President, with millions of Americans seeing Mr. Khrushchev on TV, and noting his apparent conviction and sincerity when he speaks, and also at times his friendliness, warmth of personality, do you think that some Americans might get the idea, well, he is a pretty good fellow after all, and perhaps insidiously their general feeling of opposition to the whole idea of communism might become weak, and that they might become psychologically disarmed?

THE PRESIDENT. I think our whole civilization, the whole theory of free government, is based upon the right of anyone to present his views in any way he pleases to the American public.

I think the American public is strong enough to see and hear this man or any other man, and capable of making their own decisions.

Now, after all, when you are talking about communism versus freedom, you are talking down at the very depths of conviction in the hearts of free men. I do not believe that master debaters or great appearances of sincerity or anything else are going to fool the American people long.

Q. Edward T. Folliard, Washington Post: Mr. President, from time to time you have said that there is no alternative to peace, that a great war would be stupid, crazy. Mr. Khrushchev seems to be talking pretty much along the same line.

Do you think he really shares your horror of a great war?

THE PRESIDENT. Frankly, I believe that is the one thing that he does agree with us very fully. But you must remember what kind of a government we are and how responsive that government is to people, and people are the ones that are responsible for this great feeling of horror against this useless destruction.

So the mere fact that you agree with some particular obvious truth of this kind, of the futility of committing mutual suicide or something of that kind, the fact is that there is still room for a lot of misunderstanding, a lot of miscalculation which could be very serious.

But I must say that the understanding of this one great truth, you might say, in this temporal field we are talking about now, is sort of the beginning of all wisdom.

Q. Joseph A. Loftus, New York Times: Mr. President, I have a question about steel. Do you have any information to support the rumor that the steel companies are prepared to yield to further persuasion by you in the matter of appointing a board that would recommend settlement, and do you plan to take further steps?

THE PRESIDENT. What do you mean, "further persuasion"? I have used persuasion here through this microphone and every place I could. But now, lately, because I answered a letter, someone is making all sorts of misrepresentations or misinterpretations of what I said.

Now, if you are talking about the specific letter, I will comment.

Q. Mr. Loftus: Yes, sir, I am.

THE PRESIDENT. All right.

I had a letter and a man, Mr. Meany, not Mr. McDonald, Mr. Meany asked me to appoint a factfinding board. I have consistently stated I was not going to interfere in this strike, that it was a thing for free bargaining, and when the Government got into it, we could get into all sorts of arguments of delay and, I think, damaging effects upon the country, because soon people would be talking about the procedures that the Government was applying rather than the basic issues.

So I answered this letter; you will find a sentence, I believe, that says I still don't have any faith in this factfinding approach. But if both sides approach me and ask for a nongovernmental board, then I will cooperate with them in order to get it established, and then they themselves responsible for providing the financing, all the instructions, the terms of reference, and everything else.

That is the only thing I did—say that I would agree to that; because this, in my belief, is a continuation of free bargaining, and free bargaining is what I want to see. I want to see the basic issues discussed, not the argument as to whether or not there should be a Taft-Hartley Act or a fact board or anything else. I think the basic issues—they should understand them and they should get busy and determine them.

Q. Mr. Loftus: Mr. President, the industry said no. My question to you is, does that end it, as far as you are concerned?

THE PRESIDENT. My letter speaks for itself, absolutely. I am not going to take any part on one side or the other.

Q. Charles H. Mohr, Time Magazine: In reference to an earlier question, Mr. President, do you think that the fact that you are going to be allowed to go to the Soviet Union and speak in public to a people who seldom have much free interchange and to be seen by them as a representative of freedom means that we are getting the best of this bargain on the exchange, and do you also think that the Soviet Government can continue unscathed during a long period of free exchange of this kind?

THE PRESIDENT. Well, I think I have a great deal of faith in that one Biblical reference somewhere, where it it says, "Know the truth and the truth shall make you free."

Now, we have here, a system of government: it is a system of government, there is no question, that at least the dedicated Communists believe in thoroughly. They believe it is a step, it's a progressive step in the long march of civilization. We do not.

We do not have a real system; we have a way of life. We are concerned in giving every individual the maximum freedom to develop himself, and the Government is really a help, not the complete director of the individual.

So, since we believe that that feeling for freedom, that respect for freedom, love of freedom, is instinctive in men, we do think that the systematized order that is observed in Russia is a step backward, not forward.

Now Mr. Khrushchev believes that as one form of government has succeeded another in this world, he calls it socialism, but socialism or communism is the next step, and a progressive one.

Now whether or not my going there will help or will, let's say, stimulate thinking of people in that region along the lines that we believe in, I can't say.

But I do believe that in the long march of time—he is always saying this: history is going to decide between us.

I believe history, in the long run, is going to decide in favor of the free system.

Q. E. W. Kenworthy, New York Times: Mr. President, there have been reports that you will suggest to Mr. Khrushchev a joint effort, a joint attack on the problems of underdeveloped countries. Are these reports true?

THE PRESIDENT. No. No, that isn't exactly it. I have talked in a number of nations about the responsibility of civilization to see that these undeveloped and newly formed nations are helped, because this is a matter of self-interest for civilization; that unless these things are done, I believe that finally the ferment, the resentment, and finally the anger of such people can set up a very great global struggle.

As of now the United States is a party to a number of international organizations that are devoted to this purpose—the World Bank and the Development Association, which is to be a part of that Bank, under the Bank, the Monetary Fund, the Ex-Im Bank and a number of other things. I have suggested that each of the nations ought to take and study, specifically I asked the head of each of the governments that I just visited recently to study, the matter of cooperation in this matter so that each could take its share of the load.

Now, until there is some kind of peaceful solution of the political differences between ourselves and the Soviets, it is manifest that we couldn't ask them to be partners in any exercise of this kind.

Q. Marvin L. Arrowsmith, Associated Press: Mr. President, do you have any comment on the public reception that Mr. Khrushchev has received in this country so far?

THE PRESIDENT. No, not particularly. I thought there were very large crowds out. There were people that were naturally interested in seeing this person, this individual, the head of a government, and a man whose name has been a great deal in the headlines. But to my mind they did show a certain reservation, which is only natural, because all of us have had questions about this whole world situation that causes uneasiness; and I just do not believe that any extreme conviction ought to be expressed one way or the other.

Q. Sarah McClendon, El Paso Times: Sir, a lot of people are discussing Mr. Khrushchev's forum that he had yesterday for presenting his attacks on our governmental policy and our system and our basic philosophies.

Do you think when you go to Russia that you will get the same kind of forum, and do you think that, as a guest of that country, that it will be right for you to attack them similarly?

THE PRESIDENT. Well, I would hesitate to say I would attack anything in that country, for this simple reason. I believe the best way to present a message, if you have it, is to try to do it constructively, to show what America is interested in, what we would like to see the world be, what the issues are that we think are important, and the principles that are important.

I would not think it profitable even if, humanly, once in a while you would like to take that line; I think it would not be profitable to be in the position of attacking.

Q. Raymond P. Brandt, St. Louis Post-Dispatch: Mr. President, has there been time enough for you to study the De Gaulle statement to say whether it will change our position in the United Nations?

THE PRESIDENT. Well, I can't say it specifically; no. As a matter of fact, I haven't even discussed it yet with our State Department officials.

Q. Edward V. Koterba, United Features Syndicate: Could you tell us at this time, sir, whether or not Mrs. Eisenhower will accompany you on your tour of Russia?

THE PRESIDENT. Well, I hope so, but there's a number of factors that have to be taken into consideration. I couldn't make a definite statement one way or the other.

Q. James B. Reston, New York Times: When the Soviet Chairman was on the Hill yesterday, sir, he turned aside questions about Laos and other countries, on the ground that he had an agreement with you not to discuss third countries. Is there such an agreement as that?

THE PRESIDENT. Well, I think here there must be some kind of misunderstanding brought about by, possibly, faulty interpreting.

I said, I think in a speech and in my original letters, that we would not negotiate on matters affecting third countries or any part of the free world—my allies, I believe I said, or any part of the free world.

Now, manifestly, you cannot have a conversation between the Soviet Government and this Government that does not mention and discuss other countries. You have to. So I think there is some misunderstanding brought about by inadvertence. No, there is no such agreement, because we have to do it.

Q. Mr. Reston: We would be right then in inferring that questions such as Laos and Germany of course would be discussed at Camp David?

THE PRESIDENT. If we don't discuss Berlin, for example, I would have difficulty in seeing why we got together. No, of course we would have to talk about them.

Q. J. F. Ter Horst, Detroit News: Sir, at the same meeting between Premier Khrushchev and the members of the Foreign Relations Committee, one of the Soviet officials said that the State Department's proposed new draft of a program for mutual exchange in the cultural and personal exchange field with Russia was being scaled down by our side. Could you cast any light on that? We had gathered that you were rather in favor of that program, and that it would be expanded.

THE PRESIDENT. And everybody in the State Department that I ever talked to. If someone else is trying to scale something down, I have never heard of it. No, I have been trying to expand, not to scale down.

Q. Benjamin A. Franklin, American Broadcasting Company: Mr. President, Secretary of Labor Mitchell has been trying by administrative and rule changes in the Labor Department to improve the working and living conditions with some of the two million American migratory farm workers whom the Secretary himself has called forgotten people.

The farmers and growers associations are against the changes, and Secretary Benson backs them. The other day he told Mr. Mitchell in effect to mind his own business. Do you have any comments, sir, on this family quarrel?

THE PRESIDENT. Well, I can say this: I have listened to it a great deal. Actually I think it is one of those old cases where there wouldn't be so much talk except that there is so much to say on both sides. But there has been nothing done yet that I know of that can hurt anybody; it is still on the discussional stage.

Q. Carleton Kent, Chicago Sun-Times: Mr. President, I wonder if you can tell us something of what went through your mind when Mr. Khrushchev presented you a replica of the sphere that the rocket deposited on the moon the other day.

THE PRESIDENT. I think the fair thing to say is that he wanted this as a little memento.

They did make every announcement on the thing as early as they could. They said it was an exploration, a peaceful activity into space, and so he brought this thing along. I found it very interesting, how it was made up of what he called—again talking about this matter of interpretation—he used the word "pennant" all the time; it is a pennant sent up there.

Well, it is a little ball, as you photographers saw, at least, and it is made up of a series of surface pentagons each of which has a few initials on it.

Now, I suspect, in view of the speed with which it was running and hit, that the whole thing was probably vaporized; but nevertheless it was in there. [*Laugher*]

Q. John R. Gibson, Wall Street Journal: You spoke about the financing problem, the financing of the Government debt. Can you say what you intend to do about it, since Congress didn't act, without a special session or anything like that?

THE PRESIDENT. As you know, we fought very hard to get people to comprehend what these facts really mean to the United States, and we seem to have failed.

Now, they did do certain things, making it possible to pay better interest rates on our E and H bonds, and also to send out new E and H bonds that would bear a better interest rate. This ought to at least allay the fear of the holders, 40 million people, and stop any rush toward their cashing in. There are a few other little regulations, amendments, that were helpful.

But by and large, we simply have not been able to convince the Congress as to the vital necessity of this thing. I think that the financial community—insurance companies, the banks, and everybody else—has a job to do on educating our public, so that the Congress will feel the heat of truth about this matter and do something.

In the meantime, of course, we are doing everything that we can conceivably do to keep the difficulty from growing worse.

Q. Robert J. Donovan, New York Herald Tribune: Mr. President, is there any thought in your mind of a special session on this subject—of Congress?

THE PRESIDENT. It would be, of course, wrong to say I never have any thought about such things. I am saying that until we can explore this whole situation, I would be very careful in my moves.

And next I have this: it is only, now, a little over 3 months before the Congress is back here anyway; and by the time I think the proof is clearer and the educational process can grow a little further—in the original case, when we proposed this, many of the banks came down opposing it. Well, they have all been converted so far as I know, all that I have heard of, and they are now talking about supporting the administration view very strongly. If this happens, then the public and the Congress itself are going to get so educated that there will be no trouble about this.

Q. Charles W. Roberts, Newsweek: Now that you have talked to Chairman Khrushchev, sir, I wonder if you could tell us any more of your plans for your trip to Russia, when you plan to go, how long you expect to stay and what you want to see, and whether you plan to go to India on the way back?

THE PRESIDENT. It has not been discussed in the slightest degree, none of it, and so I just have to wait. I don't know when it can happen.

Q. Robert G. Spivack, New York Post: Mr. President, do you think it was wise of Congress to postpone action on civil rights to 1960, except for extending the life of the Commission?

THE PRESIDENT. Well, after all, I suppose we have got to take the practicalities into consideration. I, of course, put in a 7-point program at the very beginning of the congressional session, and I hoped that constructive action would be taken on it.

They finally had, in order even to get anything done, to agree on this firm date sometime in late January or early February; and so I don't think I'll comment further on it.

Marvin L. Arrowsmith, Associated Press: Thank you, Mr. President.

NOTE: President Eisenhower's one hundred and seventy-first news conference was held in the Executive Office Building from 10:59 to 11:30 o'clock on Thursday morning, September 17, 1959. In attendance: 220.

224 ¶ Exchange of Messages Between the President and President Tubman of Liberia. *September* 18, 1959

[Released September 18, 1959. Dated September 11, 1959]

Dear Mr. President:

Thank you for your most gracious message expressing sympathy for the victims of the recent earthquake in the western part of the United States.

I deeply appreciate the humanitarian ideals which motivated your message and express my gratitude to you, Mr. President, and to the Government and people of the Republic of Liberia.

With warm personal regard,

Sincerely,

DWIGHT D. EISENHOWER

NOTE: President Tubman's message follows:

The President
The White House
Washington

The distressing report of the devastating experience and results of the violent earthquake that struck the Pacific Coast of the United States has been received by me and the Government and people of Liberia with deep and sincere regrets and on behalf of the Government, people of Liberia, and myself, we extend to you, the Government, and people of the United States, especially the people of the affected areas, our most tender feelings of sympathy for this terrible disaster. Let us look to God in prayer for deliverance.

With assurance of my highest esteem,

W. V. S. TUBMAN

225   ¶ Statement by the President Following the Adjournment of the First Session of the 86th Congress.   *September* 20, 1959

THE 86TH CONGRESS is now half over, with some needed gains accomplished, but with many disappointing failures. In the second session I shall continue doing my best to assure responsible government for the American people.

When this first session began eight months ago, a greatly increased Democratic majority arrived in Washington apparently convinced, first, that there was still a recession; second, that it was bound to get worse; third, that heavy Federal "pump-priming" was our only salvation; and fourth, that they were mandated by the American people swiftly to enact these huge spending programs into law.

As a result, last January the majority in Congress sponsored many schemes to plunge billions of dollars into Federal programs which I opposed as unwarranted or excessive.

The American public at once and emphatically stepped in. By letters, telegrams, telephone calls and personal visits to their Congressmen, the folks back home demanded a halt to excesses being advanced in Congress. Before the session had been underway two months, the public had forced the majority to shelve at least temporarily its more lavish proposals.

This was an historic turnabout. It is high tribute to the good sense and political vigor of our citizens. To me it is the most gratifying and most promising aspect of the work of the session just ended.

I feel much the same about the work of my fellow Republicans in this Congress. In both Houses they were powerfully led; they were unified; they had great fighting spirit; they rejected compromise on matters of principle. Therefore their influence upon majority decisions in Congress went far beyond their numerical strength. I think Americans generally feel as I do—that these Republican Senators and Congressmen well earned the Nation's plaudits for their performance this year.

I pay my respects to those among the political opposition without whose cooperation our efforts against extravagance and legislative excesses would have been in vain. These men, though subjected to severe party pressures, had the conviction and courage to stand up and be counted on issue after issue basic to the welfare of the Nation. Sincerely I congratulate them for their good work for America this session.

Next I acknowledge, as I have each year, my appreciation to those members of both parties who have approached in a bipartisan manner most of the matters important to the Nation's security and the conduct of foreign relations. To this standard of being Americans first and Democrats or Republicans second when the Nation's safety and world peace are involved, all of us must steadfastly adhere. I am gratified that so many have done so.

Some important features of the Administration's legislative program, submitted last January, were enacted into law.

We were able at last to take an important step toward labor reform. Here again I congratulate, most of all, the American people, for it was due to their outspoken indignation that ineffective legislation was set aside and that reasonably sturdy barriers were erected against abuses that for years have injured the cause of American labor.

Hawaiian Statehood also was a notable achievement—a great event that the American people have eagerly awaited many years.

The Congress initially refused to support the national highway program, except on the basis of piling up large additions to the already huge public debt. It is gratifying that the Congress finally agreed to a partial support of the program, but at a lower rate than I recommended.

There were disappointments, of course, as in all sessions. Foremost was the refusal to establish the necessary authority for sound management of the public debt. This refusal, by forcing the Treasury to rely exclusively on inflationary short-term borrowing, may reduce the contribution to price stability that a balanced budget helps to provide and could make most difficult the maintenance of confidence both at home and abroad in our determination to manage our financial affairs soundly. I am gratified, however, now to be able to reinvigorate our savings bonds program by bringing more equity to the millions of patriotic Americans who own and buy savings bonds.

Again the Congress refused to put our Postal Service on a self-sustaining basis.

Mutual security was deeply slashed, with potentially serious consequences for us all. I deplore the shortsightedness that this unfortunate action reveals. In these times especially, Americans are entitled to expect better of the Congress than this.

Nor can I fail to mention again my disappointment that the majority in Congress seems to find it so difficult to wean itself from the porkbarrel. It is somewhat short of inspiring to see the Congress so insistent upon mushrooming the huge public works expenditures already being made at record levels throughout America. This action and others of a similar nature taken this session will surely make the difficult budgetary situation still more acute. For years to come heavier burdens will be imposed upon the taxpaying public.

The Congress again failed to make a realistic approach to our serious agricultural problems. Not only are taxpayers everywhere rightly troubled over the enormous and constantly mounting costs of present programs, but also our farmers have been waiting quite long enough for effective remedies. They are entitled to sensible legislation that will allow them to plan confidently for a secure future, with reasonable assurance that their lives will be free of oppressive governmental restraint. It must be distressing to millions of our people that the best the Congress could bring itself to do in this session was to attempt a return to programs discredited long ago.

There have been claims that the Administration's Budget, submitted last January, was cut by the Congress. The Congress distorted the shape of the Budget in many respects—cutting where they should not have cut and adding, particularly in long-term items, vast sums that not only add

676

to our financing difficulties but will also some day have to be paid by our grandchildren. Actually, the net effect of Congressional actions in this session is to increase, not decrease, Federal spending.

Finally, I remind everyone that the 86th Congress is only half over, and that it took an outspoken citizenry to divert it from its first purpose of having the Federal Government do new things it should not do—or more of the old than it should—at enormous cost to the public. The next session is only three months away. Should we again see extravagant proposals sponsored in the Congress, I shall continue to oppose them. I am confident of the continuing energetic support of the American people if such a struggle should develop. I believe that the American people can convert their gains for responsible government in this first session into a complete victory in the second.

NOTE: This statement was released at Gettysburg, Pa.

On September 23 the Director of the Bureau of the Budget submitted, in response to the President's request, a summary of the effect of congressional actions on the President's budget recommendations for fiscal year 1960. This summary (7 pages) was released by the White House.

In brief, the summary stated that the net fiscal impact of all congressional actions during the session was as follows:

1. Net expenditures for fiscal year 1960 (i.e. spending required by congressional action over the President's requests, plus revenues requested but not granted) were increased by $597 million.

2. Net expenditures over a period of years after 1960 were increased an additional $11.5 billion.

3. Pending legislation passed by one or both Houses and awaiting further action in the next session would cost an additional several billion dollars beyond the President's requests.

The Budget Director's summary contains an analysis of the tables in the Congressional Record of September 15, 1959 (vol. 105, p. D–926).

226 ¶ Statement by the President Upon Signing Bill Extending the Agricultural Trade Development and Assistance Act of 1954. *September 21, 1959*

I HAVE today approved H.R. 8609, a bill "To extend the Agricultural Trade Development and Assistance Act of 1954, and for other purposes."

Since 1954, this "PL 480" program has assisted in expanding our exports to higher levels and has helped to develop the economies of recipient countries. Its extension is desirable and I am gratified that this was accomplished without crippling barter amendments and other changes which would seriously have hampered its continued administration in the best interest of the United States and our friends abroad.

The omission from the bill of the Administration's proposals for further strengthening this Food for Peace program prevents the broader use of surplus commodities for food reserves and economic development which would have been desirable. Of more fundamental concern, however, are two new program authorizations in the enacted bill:

The food stamp plan it authorizes carries the implication that more surplus foods would be made available to the needy people of the United States. Actually the bill would not do this. Needy people received Federal surplus foods last year by direct distribution through State and local facilities. If implemented, this authority would simply replace the existing distribution system with a Federally-financed system, further increasing the already disproportionate Federal share of welfare expenses. The food stamp administrative mechanism would be much more complex, and it is extremely doubtful that it would provide any greater benefit to needy people than the present direct method.

The new authorization for 10-year supply contracts with foreign governments implies that our agricultural surpluses will be with us for many years to come. This implication is unfortunate and I can only urge again that the Congress act on Administration proposals to deal with the surplus problem. Any contracts developed pursuant to this authorization will need to be carefully administered to assure their conformity with efforts to solve this problem as well as with our international agreements.

NOTE: As enacted, H.R. 8609 is Public Law 86–341 (73 Stat. 606).

227 ¶ Statement by the President Upon Signing the Federal-Aid Highway Act of 1959.
September 21, 1959

I HAVE today approved H.R. 8678, the Federal-Aid Highway Act of 1959. In my budget message submitted to the Congress on January 19, 1959, I proposed a 1½ cent increase in highway fuel taxes for the purpose of keeping the Federal-aid highway program on schedule and continuing the self-sustaining features of the program established in 1956. Although the bill does not meet these objectives, I have approved it in order to avoid a serious disruption of the highway program with its attendant adverse effects on State finances, highway contractors and workers, and the economy generally.

Because the bill does not provide the level of revenues required for continuing the highway program on the schedule contemplated under existing authorizations, it will be necessary to make orderly use of these authorizations so that spending can be held within limits that will avoid future disruption of the program. This action will be required if the Federal Government is to meet promptly its obligations to the States and at the same time adhere to the self-financing principle upon which the highway program has been established. Of necessity, such actions may lead to some deferment or delay in the completion of the Interstate System as originally contemplated.

In this connection, at my direction there has been underway since July a comprehensive review of the interstate program's current policies, practices, methods and standards—including an examination of the relative Federal, State, and local responsibilities for planning, financing, and supervising the program. This study is being conducted by the Special Assistant to the President for Public Works Planning, General John S. Bragdon, in collaboration with the Secretary of Commerce and the Director of the Bureau of the Budget. If actions are needed to insure that our national objectives are being achieved at minimum Federal cost on a pay-as-you-go basis, it is expected that the necessary recommendations will be developed by this study.

NOTE: As enacted, H.R. 8678 is Public Law 86–342 (73 Stat. 611).

On September 9, a White House release stated that the President had requested the Congress to make a temporary advance of $359 million from the general fund to the highway trust fund, to be repaid before June 30, 1960. The release added that in prior years there had been large balances in the highway trust fund, but because of the higher expenditures resulting from the speed-up in the program authorized and directed by the Congress in 1958, and because pending legislation provided for a tax rate lower than the President had proposed, there would be a period beginning in October 1959 when the fund would be insufficient to permit reimbursement to the States when due. It was further stated that many States would be forced to delay payments to their contractors, and that the temporary advance from the general fund was requested in order to prevent such a situation from occurring. The temporary advance was authorized by Public Law 86–383 (73 Stat. 723), approved September 28, 1959.

228 ¶ Memorandum of Disapproval of Bill Amending the Federal Boating Act of 1958.
September 21, 1959

I AM withholding my approval from H.R. 8728, "To amend the Federal Boating Act of 1958 to extend until April 1, 1961, the period when certain provisions of that Act will take effect."

The Federal Boating Act of 1958 provides for the establishment of a new system of numbering small undocumented vessels. Under the Act, the part of the new system to be administered by the United States Coast Guard is to go into effect on April 1, 1960, at which time the authority for the existing system would be repealed. The bill would extend this effective date from April 1, 1960, to April 1, 1961.

This legislation was originally considered necessary because it had not been possible to obtain a supplemental appropriation for the Coast Guard to administer the new system. Since Congress passed the bill, however, the funds required for the implementation of the Federal Boating Act have been included in the Mutual Security Appropriation Act, 1960. Consequently, the extension of time provided in the bill is no longer needed.

DWIGHT D. EISENHOWER

229 ¶ Memorandum of Disapproval of Bill for the Relief of Peony Park, Inc., and Others.
September 21, 1959

I AM withholding my approval from H.R. 3096, entitled "An Act for the relief of Peony Park, Incorporated, and others."

The bill would direct the Secretary of the Treasury to pay the total sum of $100,706.50 to nine operators of ballrooms in Nebraska in refund of cabaret taxes paid by the claimants during the period September 1948 through October 1951.

By judicial decision the cabaret tax here involved has been held to have been properly collected from the claimants during the period covered by the bill.

680

Until January 1951, however, interpretation and enforcement of the applicable statute by the Internal Revenue Service were not uniform throughout the United States. Accordingly, until the interpretation of the law was clarified by judicial decision, and until enforcement of the law became uniform throughout the United States after January 1951, similarly situated taxpayers in many States were not required to pay the tax. The cabaret tax, however, was uniformly enforced within the State of Nebraska and was paid by establishments within the competitive area of the claimants. Moreover, during the years 1948 to 1950, the tax was enforced in at least seventeen jurisdictions, and during the major portion of the year 1951 was uniformly enforced throughout the United States against similarly situated taxpayers.

This bill not only would refund to the nine claimants a tax which was properly collected, but it would also discriminate against many other similarly situated taxpayers to whom no relief would be granted. Furthermore, the bill might unjustly enrich its beneficiaries by refunding the cabaret tax without regard to whether the ultimate burden of the tax was borne by the claimants or passed on to their patrons.

Under the circumstances, therefore, I am constrained to withhold my approval of the bill.

DWIGHT D. EISENHOWER

230 ¶ Letter to Secretary Anderson Approving the Increase in Interest Rates for Savings Bonds. *September 22, 1959*

Dear Mr. Secretary:

In accordance with legislation signed into law earlier today, I am returning with my approval your proposal to increase the interest return on all United States Series E and H Savings Bonds.

In approving your recommendation, I take this opportunity to reaffirm my enthusiastic support of the Savings Bonds Program. This is one of our country's finest and most worthwhile activities. It contributes to the sound management of the Nation's finances. It gives millions of American families the opportunity to save safely and regularly—while investing in their Nation's future.

To my mind there is no better way of saving, no more effective way of strengthening our power for peace, than to own United States Savings Bonds. To buy these bonds is to express faith in America. It helps provide the economic strength in both our Government and in individual families on which our freedom depends. I hope that the making of both old and new Savings Bonds even more attractive will serve as a renewed invitation to every citizen to buy and hold these "Shares in America."

Sincerely,

DWIGHT D. EISENHOWER

231 ¶ Statement by the President on the Increase in Interest Rates for Savings Bonds. *September 22, 1959*

THIS MORNING I signed a bill authorizing an increase in the interest rates on all United States Series E and H Savings Bonds.

Later, in approving the recommendations of the Secretary of the Treasury for a rate of 3¾%, I stated:

"To my mind there is no better way of saving, no more effective way of strengthening our power for peace, than to own United States Savings Bonds.

"To buy these bonds is to express faith in America.

"It helps provide the economic strength in both our Government and in individual families on which our freedom depends.

"I hope that the making of both old and new Savings Bonds even more attractive will serve as a renewed invitation to every citizen to buy and hold these 'shares in America.'"

NOTE: As enacted, the bill (H.R. 9035) is Public Law 86–346 (73 Stat. 621).

232 ¶ Statement by the President Upon
Approval of Bill for the Relief of the City of
Madeira Beach, Florida. *September* 22, 1959

I HAVE today approved H.R. 2390, "For the relief of the city of Madeira Beach, Florida."

The bill authorizes the payment of $12,828.35 in full settlement of the claim of the city of Madeira Beach for the Government's proportionate share of a special assessment levied to pay the cost of erecting structures for controlling erosion of shore property, including 500 feet of beach property of the Veterans' Administration.

Approval of this bill in no way alters the conviction I expressed on August 15, 1953 when I withheld my approval from H.R. 2750, "For the relief of the city and county of Denver, Colorado." At that time I stated that the question of modifying the Federal Government's constitutional tax immunity should be dealt with broadly and deliberately, rather than by a succession of piece-meal decisions on individual requests.

I believe, however, that the claim of the city of Madeira Beach is exceptionally meritorious.

If the city had not provided erosion protection, the Veterans' Administration would eventually have constructed its own erosion control devices at a cost probably greater than the amount claimed by the city. Since the Government would otherwise have incurred costs at least as great, it is only equitable that the Government now pay the nondiscriminatory special assessment levied on it by the city of Madeira Beach.

It is my hope that current consideration of the problems involved in payments by the Federal Government to State and local governments in lieu of taxes will result in soundly conceived general legislation which will make future private bills unnecessary.

NOTE: As enacted, H.R. 2390 is Public Law 86–353 (73 Stat. 627).

233 ¶ Memorandum of Disapproval of Bill for the Relief of the Estate of Nathaniel H. Woods. *September* 22, 1959

I AM withholding my approval from H.R. 2631, "For the relief of the estate of Nathaniel H. Woods, deceased."

The bill would direct the Secretary of the Treasury to pay the sum of $13,476.50 to the estate of Nathaniel H. Woods in refund of an estate tax which was erroneously paid.

The major portion of the estate tax in question was paid in December 1951 on the assumption that the first of two wills left by the decedent was valid. The second will, under which no estate tax was due, was admitted to probate on April 16, 1953 and, after prolonged litigation, was sustained as the valid will in December 1955. A claim for refund was not filed until June 1956. It was rejected by the Commissioner and the Federal courts because not filed within the period of limitations prescribed by law.

It appears that the three-year statutory period of limitations for filing a timely claim did not expire until April 16, 1956—three years after the executor qualified under the second will and more than four months after the conclusion of the litigation upholding the validity of the second will. A protective claim for refund could have been filed at any time during the three-year period after the qualification of the executor under the second will. It was not necessary to await the conclusion of the prolonged litigation concerning the wills. Even after the conclusion of the litigation, there remained more than four months in which to file a timely claim. The record in this case discloses no justification for the failure to file a claim until June 1956.

The statute of limitations, which the Congress has included in the revenue system as a matter of sound policy, is essential in order to achieve finality in tax administration. The limitation not only bars taxpayers from obtaining refunds, but also the Government from collecting additional taxes. Granting special relief in this case, where a refund was not claimed in the time and manner prescribed by law, would discriminate against other similarly situated taxpayers and would create an undesirable precedent.

Under the circumstances, therefore, I am constrained to withhold my approval of the bill.

DWIGHT D. EISENHOWER

234 ❡ Memorandum of Disapproval of Bill for the Relief of Mrs. Lourene O. Estes.
September 22, 1959

I AM withholding my approval from H.R. 6335, "For the relief of Mrs. Lourene O. Estes."

Mrs. Estes, on her income tax returns for 1952 and 1953, reported as income certain disability payments received from her employer. Prior to the time the taxpayer filed these returns, the Court of Appeals for the Seventh Circuit had held that such disability payments were excludable from gross income, although the Internal Revenue Service had ruled to the contrary.

On April 1, 1957, the United States Supreme Court decided that disability payments of the type here in question were excludable from gross income. On April 15, 1957, Mrs. Estes filed claims for refund for 1952 and 1953 based upon the excludability of the disability pay received by her. These claims were rejected because filed after the expiration of the 3-year period of limitations prescribed by law for the filing of such claims.

During the last Congress, I approved legislation designed to grant general relief, on a nondiscriminatory basis, to taxpayers who had received disability pay which was excludable from gross income under the Supreme Court decision. This general legislation does not provide relief for taxpayers, such as Mrs. Estes, who did not attempt to protect their rights by filing timely claims for refund.

The statutory period of limitations, which the Congress has included in the revenue system as a matter of sound policy, is essential in order to achieve finality in tax administration. A substantial number of taxpayers paid income tax on disability payments received by them and failed to file timely claims for refund. Accordingly, to grant special relief in this case, where a refund was not claimed in the time and manner prescribed by law, would be to discriminate against such other similarly situated taxpayers and to create an undesirable precedent.

Under the circumstances, therefore, I am constrained to withhold my approval from the bill.

Dwight D. Eisenhower

235 ¶ Memorandum of Disapproval of Bill for the Relief of Mrs. Mary D'Agostino. *September 23, 1959*

I AM withholding my approval from H.R. 1387, "For the relief of Mrs. Mary D'Agostino."

Mrs. D'Agostino's claim for gratuitous National Service Life Insurance benefits, filed April 20, 1956, was denied by the Veterans' Administration because it had not been filed within the statutory time limitation of seven years after the date of death of her son on December 22, 1940. The Veterans' Administration has also determined that, even if her claim had been timely filed, Mrs. D'Agostino would not have been eligible for the benefit because her son's death had occurred not in line-of-duty and did not meet the criteria specified in the law for such benefits. A subsequent statutory liberalization of line-of-duty criteria had no retroactive effect.

H.R. 1387, in addition to waiving the time limitation, would retroactively apply to this case the liberalized line-of-duty criteria enacted in September 1944. H.R. 3733 and H.R. 6529, 83d Congress, also sought retroactively to apply liberalized eligibility standards which, as a matter of law, had only prospective effect. In disapproving those measures I indicated that it seemed to me irrelevant and unwise to accept as justification for those bills the fact that an ineligible beneficiary could qualify under the then existing law which was never intended to have retroactive effect. My view has not changed and applies with equal force to the present case.

Approval of H.R. 1387 would be discriminatory and would create an undesirable precedent. Uniformity and equality of treatment for all who are similarly situated must be the steadfast rule if Federal programs for veterans and their dependents are to be operated successfully. Approval of H.R. 1387 would not be in keeping with these principles.

Dwight D. Eisenhower

236 ¶ Memorandum of Disapproval of Bill for the Relief of Mrs. Elba Haverstick Cash.
September 23, 1959

I AM withholding my approval from H.R. 1434, "A bill for the relief of Mrs. Elba Haverstick Cash."

This bill would pay to Mrs. Cash $5,000 as compensation for the death of her son as a result of maltreatment in a Veterans' Administration hospital in 1955.

Mrs. Cash's son entered a Veterans' Administration hospital in 1943 due to service-connected mental illness. He was hospitalized continuously in VA facilities until his death in 1955. During this entire period, Mrs. Cash received on her son's behalf service-connected compensation ranging in amount from $138 to $190 monthly.

It appears that in February, 1955, while attendants were changing his clothes, Mrs. Cash's son became unruly. In the ensuing struggle the attendants set upon him, causing serious injuries from which he later died. Although the attendants involved were found not guilty of criminal acts, they were either fired or otherwise rigorously disciplined for their part in this tragic affair.

In addition to receiving $5,000 under a National Service Life Insurance policy, Mrs. Cash, as a dependent parent, currently receives death compensation at the rate of $75 monthly. This is paid to her under general provisions of law which provide that, where a death occurs as a result of hospitalization by the VA, benefits are payable as if such death were service-connected. Mrs. Cash has no remedy under the Federal Tort Claims Act since that Act specifically bars claims based on assault and battery.

My strong feeling of sympathy for this mother in the unfortunate loss of her son is matched only by my distress that an incident of this kind should happen in a Government hospital. These strong feelings do not, however, alter the fact that there is a generous, comprehensive, and assured system of benefits provided for the survivors of veterans who die, in whatever manner, as a result of hospitalization by the VA. Mrs. Cash is currently a beneficiary of this system.

The situation here closely parallels that resulting when a serviceman suffers a service-connected death. In such cases, regardless of the manner in which death occurs, I firmly believe that the assured and general benefits to which survivors are entitled by law should be their exclusive remedy. This principle had led to the disapproval of other private bills granting special awards in such cases (see H.R. 1315, 85th Congress, "A bill for the relief of Mr. and Mrs. Charles H. Page," disapproved on September 7, 1957). I perceive no basis for reaching a different result under the analogous circumstances of the present case.

DWIGHT D. EISENHOWER

237 ¶ Memorandum of Disapproval of Bill for the Relief of Harold William Abbott and Others. *September 23, 1959*

I AM withholding my approval from H.R. 8277, "An act for the relief of Harold William Abbott and others."

The bill would direct the Secretary of the Treasury to pay $23,317.61 to eleven individuals in refund of transportation taxes collected after 1945 and before 1952 for transportation in connection with fishing parties. Refund of these taxes has been barred because claims for refund, and appeals from the rejection of such claims, were not filed within the time prescribed by law.

The relief sought in this bill is similar to that sought in a bill which I disapproved last year, H.R. 3193, "For the relief of Toley's Charter Boats, Incorporated, Toley Engebretsen, and Harvey Homlar".

On March 31, 1953, a Federal court held that the transportation tax did not apply to the type of transportation involved here. At the time of this decision, there remained a period of at least nine months in which to file timely claims for 1950 and a period of at least one year and nine months in which to file timely claims for 1951. Approximately $10,000 of the amount involved in this bill represents taxes collected during the years 1950 and 1951, which would have been refunded to seven of the claimants except for the fact that they filed their claims for refund more than two years after the date of the Federal court decision. The record in this case discloses no reason justifying this delinquency in filing claims.

Refund of a large portion of the amount involved in this bill was barred by the statute of limitations prior to the Federal court decision. The basic purposes underlying the statute of limitations continue to obtain in cases where a taxpayer, after having paid a tax, discovers that the interpretation of the law has been changed by a judicial decision. Granting relief in this case would discriminate against other taxpayers similarly situated and would create an undesirable precedent.

Under the circumstances, I am constrained to withhold my approval from the bill.

DWIGHT D. EISENHOWER

238 ¶ Statement by the President Recorded for the Opening of the United Community Campaigns. *September* 23, 1959

My Fellow Americans:

Tonight is the beginning of an enterprise which I believe is in the finest tradition of American generosity—the United Community Campaigns. In some 21 hundred cities and towns throughout the United States and Canada, the solicitors for the United Community Campaigns will shortly begin to ask for our support.

This campaign has many names across the country. Here in Washington we call it the United Givers Fund. In Gettysburg, it is the Community Chest. In my old home town in Kansas, it is the United Fund of Abilene. But whatever the name, the important word is "united." It means that in each community a great number of volunteer agencies are working together to raise money to advance the general welfare.

It would be hard to imagine American life without our volunteer charities and community organizations. These include many services for children, youth and families—services for the blind, the crippled and the handicapped—the Scouting movement, the Salvation Army, the "Y's"—hospitals, clinics, and medical research. It is a long and familiar and heartwarming list.

Some national agencies also take part in the United Campaigns. The American Red Cross, for example, will be a partner in more than a thousand communities. The USO also benefits and through the USO the members of our Armed Forces are served. This year, many of the United Campaigns will include requests for the new Medical Research Program, established by the National Fund for Medical Education.

There is a saying that he who gives is twice blessed, and this is certainly true of those who contribute to our United Community Campaigns. For the spiritual warmth and satisfaction of generous giving is matched by the fact that in helping our fellow Americans about us we are building better, safer, more decent neighborhoods and communities for ourselves and our children.

I hope you will help the United Community Campaigns to set a new record of service to America this year.

Thank you and goodnight.

239   ¶ Memorandum of Disapproval of Bill Increasing Retirement Benefits of Certain Policemen and Firemen.   *September 24, 1959*

I AM withholding my approval from H.R. 3735, "An Act to increase the relief or retirement compensation of certain former members of the Metropolitan Police force, the Fire Department of the District of Columbia, the United States Park Police force, the White House Police force, and the United States Secret Service; and of their widows, widowers, and children."

I am unable to approve the 10 percent increase in relief or retirement compensation which the first section of this bill proposes for its beneficiaries. Policemen and firemen who retired before October 1, 1956, are already receiving much more generous treatment than any other group of retired District of Columbia employees. This results from the Equalization Act of 1923 which provides for an automatic proportionate increase in pensions equal to any salary increases granted active duty policemen and firemen. The equalization feature has operated so effectively that a significant number of these retirees presently receive a larger pension than their annual salaries while on active duty. Also, under the 1923 law these retirees have forged far ahead of District Government annuitants subject to the civil service retirement program. In the interests of fairness, the present disparity should not be further increased.

I could readily accept the other provision of the bill which proposes to adjust and improve the benefits payable to the widows and surviving minor children of deceased policemen and firemen who retired prior to October 1, 1956. The circumstances of this group are different and I sincerely hope that the Congress, early in the next session, will enact the improved benefits which this class deserves.

DWIGHT D. EISENHOWER

240 ¶ Memorandum of Disapproval of Bill for the Relief of Howard F. Knipp.
September 25, 1959

I HAVE withheld my approval from H.R. 2068, "An act for the relief of Howard F. Knipp."

The bill would direct the Secretary of the Treasury to compute the income tax liability of Howard F. Knipp for the calendar years 1947 and 1948 so that his distributive share of the earnings of the John C. Knipp & Sons partnership, for its fiscal year beginning on February 1, 1947, would be determined on the basis of a full partnership taxable year ending on January 31, 1948.

The records of the Treasury Department show that Mr. Knipp, a calendar year taxpayer, was a member of a two-man partnership which had a fiscal year ending on January 31. The death of Mr. Knipp's partner on November 21, 1947, raised the question of partnership termination on that date. If the partnership terminated on that date, Mr. Knipp had to include in his income for the calendar year 1947 a much greater amount than would have been the case had the partnership continued until the normal end of its taxable year.

On June 2, 1953, the Bureau of Internal Revenue assessed a deficiency against Mr. Knipp on the ground that the death of his partner terminated the partnership and its taxable year. The Tax Court approved the Bureau's position on October 31, 1955, and that court's decision was affirmed by the Court of Appeals for the Fourth Circuit on April 10, 1957. On October 14, 1957, certiorari was denied by the United States Supreme Court.

The question of the partnership termination in this case has been litigated before the courts in an orderly manner. Approval of this bill would encourage demands for legislation overruling court decisions in individual cases and would create an undesirable precedent. The bunching of income in this case has admittedly worked a hardship on Mr. Knipp, but this is mitigated to some extent by the fact that for a number of years Mr. Knipp had the advantage of deferring payment of tax each year on eleven months of his firm's profits until the following year.

DWIGHT D. EISENHOWER

241 ¶ Message to the Governor General of Ceylon on the Death of Prime Minister Bandaranaike. *September 26, 1959*

His Excellency
Sir Oliver Ernest Goonetilleke,
G.C.M.G., K.C.V.O., K.B.E.
Governor General of Ceylon

Dear Governor General:

I was deeply shocked to hear of the passing of Prime Minister Bandaranaike. The world has lost a true friend of peace. Please extend my deepest sympathies to Mrs. Bandaranaike and to the people of Ceylon.

Sincerely,

DWIGHT D. EISENHOWER

NOTE: This message was released at Gettysburg, Pa.

242 ¶ Joint Statement Following Discussions With Chairman Khrushchev at Camp David. *September 27, 1959*

THE CHAIRMAN of the Council of Ministers of the USSR, N. S. Khrushchev, and President Eisenhower have had a frank exchange of opinions at Camp David. In some of these conversations United States

Secretary of State Herter and Soviet Foreign Minister Gromyko, as well as other officials from both countries, participated.

Chairman Khrushchev and the President have agreed that these discussions have been useful in clarifying each other's position on a number of subjects. The talks were not undertaken to negotiate issues. It is hoped, however, that their exchanges of view will contribute to a better understanding of the motives and position of each and thus to the achievement of a just and lasting peace.

The Chairman of the Council of Ministers of the USSR and the President of the United States agreed that the question of general disarmament is the most important one facing the world today. Both governments will make every effort to achieve a constructive solution of this problem.

In the course of the conversations an exchange of views took place on the question of Germany including the question of a peace treaty with Germany, in which the positions of both sides were expounded.

With respect to the specific Berlin question, an understanding was reached, subject to the approval of the other parties directly concerned, that negotiations would be reopened with a view to achieving a solution which would be in accordance with the interests of all concerned and in the interest of the maintenance of peace.

In addition to these matters useful conversations were held on a number of questions affecting the relations between the Union of Soviet Socialist Republics and the United States. These subjects included the question of trade between the two countries. With respect to an increase in exchanges of persons and ideas, substantial progress was made in discussions between officials and it is expected that certain agreements will be reached in the near future.

The Chairman of the Council of Ministers of the USSR and the President of the United States agreed that all outstanding international questions should be settled not by the application of force but by peaceful means through negotiation.

Finally it was agreed that an exact date for the return visit of the President to the Soviet Union next spring would be arranged through diplomatic channels.

NOTE: This statement was released at Gettysburg, Pa.

243 ¶ The President's News Conference of *September* 28, 1959.

THE PRESIDENT. I realize, ladies and gentlemen, that in the last few days the public and the press have been mostly preoccupied with questions of international import. But during this entire period, so far as I am concerned, there has always been in the back of my mind, and the subject of many conversations and discussions over the phone and otherwise about an important domestic problem, the steel strike.

As we start this conference, I want to read a little statement that I have written this morning on this matter:

"I have this to say to you today on the steel strike."

Incidentally, for your benefit, there will be the usual copies outside.

"I am not going to try to assess any blame, but I am getting sick and tired of the apparent impasse in the settlement of this matter, and, I think, so are the American people.

"Free collective bargaining—the logical recourse of a free people in settling industrial disputes—has apparently broken down.

"The long delay in coming to a reasonable agreement has already had a noticeable effect on our economy. Now, with negotiations abandoned, the prospects become serious for every individual in the Nation.

"This morning I shall not discuss specific governmental action but I tell you this: so far as governmental action can be brought to bear on this matter, I am not going to permit the economy of the Nation to suffer with its inevitable injuries to all. I am not going to permit American workers to remain unnecessarily unemployed. There are 500,000 steel workers out of jobs. There are 160,000 other workers in industry affected by the strike who are not receiving salary checks. This figure will continue to grow.

"This is an intolerable situation. It must not continue.

"It is up to both sides, labor and management, to recognize the responsibility they owe to our Nation and settle their differences reasonably and promptly. I shall use every conceivable personal and official influence available to me to break the impasse."

That is my statement, and I am ready for questions.

Q. Marvin L. Arrowsmith, Associated Press: Mr. President, could you give us a general evaluation of your talks with Mr. Khrushchev, and tell us specifically whether the renunciation of force mentioned in the communique means that Mr. Khrushchev now has withdrawn any Soviet threats or ultimatums with respect to Berlin?

THE PRESIDENT. Well, to have a little bit of outline, because this is a very involved subject, I think I had better try to keep straight on the track in this way:

First of all, I want to thank the American people. I think their restraint and their conduct on the whole was a credit to them. And if there is a better understanding on the part of Mr. Khrushchev of our people, of their aspirations, of their general attitudes about international questions, and particularly about their desire for peace, then that has been done by the American people.

I invited Mr. Khrushchev, as you know, to come here so that we might have a chance to discuss some of the obvious reasons for tensions in the world, and particularly between our two countries, because of the outstanding unsettled matters.

I did not ask him here for substantive negotiations, because those are impossible without the presence of our associates. But I thought that, through this visit of his and through these conversations, possibly I think as I have said to you before, some of the ice might be melted.

Now, if any of this has been done, again it's due to the American people; and I make special acknowledgements to the Mayors, Governors, the local officials who carried so much of the responsibility for making these visits possible, and for directing so many of the activities necessarily involved.

With respect to one other point, I think this: I think the American people have proved that they have an enlightened outlook toward these international problems; that they have got the strength in their own beliefs and convictions to listen to the other man politely, attentively, although reserving to themselves a right to oppose bitterly any imposition upon themselves of some of the practices, the beliefs, and convictions that are proposed and supported by another ideology; that they came through this with a very much better understanding, and proving that they themselves are very sophisticated, and if not sophisticated, let us say enlightened and understanding in these matters.

Now, the Chairman and I discussed the Berlin question at length. As you know, no specific negotiations can be carried out in such question as this without our allies, but you will have read the communique which brings up this point and says that negotiations are to be reundertaken, after making proper arrangements, in the aim to get a solution that will protect the legitimate interests of the Soviets, the East Germans, the West Germans, and above all, the Western people.

Over and above this, we agreed, in addition to what the communique said, that these negotiations should not be prolonged indefinitely but there could be no fixed time limit on them. I think that's perfectly clear and plain; and since it was the agreement of two individuals, I think that I should not attempt to go further in expounding on that point.

Q. Robert C. Pierpoint, CBS News: You seem to have a cold, sir. I was wondering, these have been very difficult and trying times for you, how have you borne up under this burden?

THE PRESIDENT. I think I have borne up all right. But you know, I think that I came back with the beginnings of a cold from Europe, and I always have trouble with bad colds. And with this kind of activity, with all the medicines the doctors can prescribe, and what sedations everybody takes for himself over and above what the doctors prescribe— [*laughter*]—I've done nothing, but I'll tell you this: if I can get 5 days out in the desert somewhere, in the dry desert, I am going, quickly. [*Laughter*]

Q. Laurence H. Burd, Chicago Tribune: Mr. President, Mr. Khrushchev has given his version of why you are postponing your trip to Russia. He spoke of the grandchildren making the decision. What is the actual reason for——

THE PRESIDENT. I assure you there is no sinister or no ulterior motive behind it. This has been a rather trying period, the last year, and we have both set up for ourselves rather large and full schedules. He is going to China, for example, the day after he gets back to Moscow. I have Mr. Segni here on Wednesday; I have the Ministers from the old Baghdad Pact here within a week; I have the President of Mexico I'm very anxious to have some long talks with; I have a number of heads of state coming along. It just looked like too much to put these things all together and get some of the other things that we want to do. So, I was personally the first one that said, "Well, maybe in the spring," because we were talking about the weather in Moscow and the temperature right now, how quickly it's going to be very bad, and how soon you could have snowstorms that would probably limit travel. Finally, you know, he said, well, he thought that would be very fine; and then is when he got in to the grandchildren, and what he told was perfectly true—they, the grandchildren, seemed to make this decision. [*Laughter*]

Q. Felix Belair, New York Times: Mr. President, can you tell us if the general subject of China arose during the talks and in what context?

THE PRESIDENT. To this extent, yes: it was raised, but the discussion was largely confined to this: a statement of our respective views which, you know, are diametrically opposed on almost every point; and it was agreed that it would be unprofitable to try to raise the China question in the matter of, you might say, the philosophy of action.

Now, he did, because of course our concern about prisoners and so on, suggest that he might find it possible as a friendly gesture, not because he feels he has any right to interfere in those things, to bring up the matter of our five prisoners we've been so concerned about.

Q. William J. Eaton, United Press International: Sir, do you plan to invoke the Taft-Hartley Act to halt the steel strike, or do you plan to invite industry and union leaders to the White House?

THE PRESIDENT. Well, I said that I didn't want to discuss this morning any proposed governmental action.

Actually, I am hoping to see a number of my own people, people that have been involved in this thing all the way through, today, discussing possible developments.

Q. Merriman Smith, United Press International: Mr. President, could you tell us, or give us some estimate as to when you anticipate a summit conference?

THE PRESIDENT. No, I can't guess. I can't guess because, first of all, I will report to all of my interested associates everything I can think of on this visit I just had, and I will seek their reactions. I wouldn't want to make any guess now, because there were just two of us talking and neither of us tried to fix any real time.

Q. Garnett D. Horner, Washington Star: Do you feel, sir, that the conditions you have previously mentioned for going to a summit conference have now been met or still are to be met in further negotiation?

THE PRESIDENT. I would say, for myself, this: the conversations have, so far as I am personally concerned, removed many of the objections that I have heretofore held; but again this is a matter for negotiation and consultation with our allies. And, as I say, the progress made—I can say that we have to consider, as long as we are going to negotiate, that there is progress because we are not on an impasse.

Q. E. W. Kenworthy, New York Times: Could you tell us what Premier Khrushchev indicated he was prepared to do in the matter of on-site inspections, the number of on-site inspections and the composition of the control post personnel in policing a nuclear test ban?

THE PRESIDENT. Well, I should make it quite clear, not only in answering your question but others that might be of that similar import, we couldn't possibly bring up among ourselves these detailed questions. It takes a long time to have a conversation, double the time that it does us because we don't have an interpreter; so this matter of composition of control posts and their numbers and the technical equipment and so on that would have to be used, those were not discussed at all.

Q. Charles H. Mohr, Time Magazine: Can we take it, sir, that your agreement that there is to be no fixed time limit on the negotiations over Berlin also means that there can be no fixed time limit on our occupation rights there, and our access rights to that city?

THE PRESIDENT. Well, of course there can be no fixed limit. We do say this, all of us agree that this is an abnormal situation, all the world does.

Here is a free city, sitting inside a Communist country, and a hundred and ten miles from the Western Germany of which it feels it is a part. Therefore, the only way you can get a solution is by negotiations that will probably take some time. We agree that these would not be unnecessarily or unduly extended, but we did say there is no fixed time to which they are limited.

Q. Mrs. May Craig, Portland (Maine) Press Herald: Mr. President, will you clarify for us the situation in regard to the credits the Soviets want, the money they still owe us, and will you need amendment of the law before you could give them more credits?

THE PRESIDENT. I had Secretary Dillon take the details of this question up with the Soviet delegation.

Now, he can give you most of the details. There is this about it: Mr. Khrushchev himself said they were ready to discuss the lend-lease matter and settlement, both sides expressed a desire for greater trade under proper conditions; but just exactly to what extent these are to go and what can be done now under the law, you will have to discuss with Secretary Dillon.

I can't quite go into all those details, but I will say this: I took Mr. Khrushchev, as you know, on several helicopter rides. He said his own Government had already, and for a long time, opposed his riding in such an instrument. But he said that he is interested in the purchase of one exactly like I used, and I believe he said he is going to ask Mr. Dillon to be his representative in seeing whether he cannot do so.

Q. Andrew F. Tully, Jr., Scripps-Howard: Sir, what did you think of Mr. Khrushchev?

THE PRESIDENT. Well, he is a dynamic and arresting personality. He is a man that uses every possible debating method available to him. He is capable of great flights, you might say, of mannerism and almost disposition, from one of almost negative, difficult attitude, to the most easy, affable, genial type of discussion.

I think that the American people sensed as they went around that they were seeing some man who is an extraordinary personality, there is no question about it.

Now, I thoroughly believe that he is sure that the basic tenets of the socialistic, or communistic, doctrine are correct. He has made great dents into the original concept of this doctrine. For example, he very definitely stated that he had made much better use of the incentive system in the Soviet economy than we. He knows all about our taxes and all the rest of it, but he talks in terms that if you do a better job you get a better house. He talked about some of the things they are providing for their people who really perform. So, in a number of ways, he shows how the application of the doctrine has been changed very greatly in modern usage in the Soviet region.

Q. Edward T. Folliard, Washington Post: Mr. President, to use your phrase, do you think that you and Mr. Khrushchev did melt some of the ice around East-West relations and if so, how much?

THE PRESIDENT. Well, I'd say this: the most that could be done here, Mr. Folliard, is a beginning.

I think that there are a number of people close to him that are quite aware of some of the problems that come about unless we do melt some ice. For example, he himself deplored the need for spending so much money on defenses. We tried, between ourselves, to talk for a little bit about our comparative costs, therefore how we could calculate just exactly how much of our wealth is going into these things that are, after all, negative and sterile and purely defensive. Well, this was an interesting exercise, but of course we got nowhere except his continued insistence they're just too expensive, we must find better ways.

The same way with the individual whose name I forget exactly, the man who was talking to Mr. McCone—well, Mr. McCone's opposite number. He pointed out their effort to develop this program of peaceful use of atomic energy; he said we must do it together because it is just too expensive for one country alone.

So, in a number of ways you find, if the ice isn't melted, an awareness on their part; not only the one that great wars are unthinkable, that's in the background, but in many ways, detailed ways, they are finding out we just have to do something that's a little bit more reasonable than what we have been doing.

Q. Charles W. Roberts, Newsweek: Sir, the most important of the three preconditions for a summit that we've made now seems to be the removal of threats to Berlin. I know you touched on that in the first question, but I wonder if you could indicate to us whether the Chairman did promise to ease the pressure or remove pressure somewhat.

THE PRESIDENT. I think the statement I have read answers your question; the reason that I don't want to say any more, we agreed exactly on that statement and I'm sure that he himself will make it, corroborate it. But to go further can be putting words in somebody else's mouth, that I don't think is fair.

I personally think that the question is answered right there: there is no fixed time on this. No one is under duress, no one is under any kind of threat. As a matter of fact, he stated emphatically that never had he an intention to give anything that was to be interpreted as duress or compulsion.

Q. Warren Rogers, New York Herald Tribune: When Mr. Khrushchev talked to your grandchildren, sir, did he tell them that one day they might live under communism?

THE PRESIDENT. Well, I don't think—no, I know he didn't. I think one of them might have thought he's old enough to know what he might have been saying. But he didn't; no, as a matter of fact, on the contrary, this was the kind of heartwarming family scene that any American would like to see taking place between his grandchildren and a stranger.

Q. James B. Reston, New York Times: Mr. President, Mr. Khrushchev used the phrase, talking about disarmament, "the strictest comprehensive control of disarmament."

I wondered two things: first, did he apply that to all disarmament or only to the total disarmament scheme he laid before the U.N.?

THE PRESIDENT. He said constantly, in talking about disarmament, "I want you to study the proposal I made." He did not add anything in the way of details to me. I did point out to him that we had allies, that we had made comprehensive plans and proposals of our own in the past, that Britain had just proposed another one in the United Nations, and that at this moment I had a very comprehensive committee under the chairmanship of Mr. Coolidge studying our whole past history in this matter and trying to discover whether we had anything new.

But in details of exact degree of strict control, I didn't go into it at all.

Q. Mr. Reston: Could I just get off one other point on that?

THE PRESIDENT. Yes.

Q. Mr. Reston: Did you try to indicate or set any goals that you would try to cut your budgets, for example, in the military field?

THE PRESIDENT. No. As a matter of fact, the reason I avoided budgets is a very simple one, because I don't believe there is any comparison of budgets between countries where everything is directed, and where costs really cannot be compared.

But I did say this: no nation could be more anxious than ours to get rid of some of this burden as long as we could with security, and with justice and honor, do it.

Q. Raymond P. Brandt, St. Louis Post-Dispatch: Mr. Khrushchev told us that his system would beat ours. Have you any plans to make the American people aware of their responsibility for their freedom?

THE PRESIDENT. Well, I would say this: I don't know how I can do this in terms of a plan; but I certainly was impelled, by some notes I made during these last 3 days, that every time I talk I am going to try to bring home to the American public the individual responsibility of the citizen.

As a matter of fact, I had to send out a message this morning, I forget on what group it was—"Know Your America Week," I believe that's it—and I said the American's rights and privileges are going to be maintained only if he exhibits a commensurate responsibility of his own to their maintenance—that is, self-discipline.

I think this applies again to the steel strike—all of us to think of it, get a proper judgment of our own, and really make these contending parties—again I say I am not assessing blame, but they've got to remember the country and what it stands for, freedom and human dignity. And we are going, one of these days, to have to look at this problem very, very earnestly if we are not by our own carelessness to damage our system.

Q. John Scali, Associated Press: Mr. President, when we move into these new negotiations on Berlin, could you tell us whether we will be guided by the same standards and principles that we had before, namely, that any solution must guarantee allied rights there, and protect the freedom of the West Berliners?

THE PRESIDENT. I can't guarantee anything of this kind, for the simple reason I don't know what kind of a solution may finally prove acceptable.

But you must start out with this: the situation is abnormal; it was brought about by a truce, a military truce, after the end of the war—an armistice—and it put strangely a number of free people in a very awkward position.

Now, we've got to find a system that will be really acceptable to all the people in that region, including those most concerned, the West Berliners.

Marvin L. Arrowsmith, Associated Press: Thank you, Mr. President.

NOTE: President Eisenhower's one hundred and seventy-second news conference was held in the Executive Office Building from 11:05 to 11:29 o'clock on Monday morning, September 28, 1959. In attendance: 288.

Shortly after the news conference was concluded the Press Secretary to the President issued the following statement in response to queries by the press:

The President, of course, did not mean that the freedom of the people of West Berlin was going to be abandoned or that allied rights were going to be surrendered by any unilateral action.

What he was referring to was that he could not now give in detail the ultimate solution of the Berlin question. Any agreement must be acceptable to the people of the area, including the most concerned—the people of West Berlin and the Federal Republic of Germany.

244 ¶ Remarks at Annual Meeting of the International Bank and the International Monetary Fund. *September* 28, 1959

Mr. Chairman, Governors, Distinguished Guests, Ladies and Gentlemen:

It is a real privilege and pleasure to extend again to the Governors of the International Bank, the International Monetary Fund, and the

International Finance Corporation a hearty welcome from the Government and from the people of the United States. We are honored by your presence in our midst and we anticipate fruitful results from your deliberations here this week.

We in the United States are fully aware that what happens in our economy can have significant effects on the well-being of the rest of the world, and that many other countries attach considerable importance to developments in our economic situation.

Happily, our economy today, despite the increasingly heavy impact of the interruption in steel production, is in a healthy condition. In recent visits abroad I could see at first hand the heartwarming evidences of a remarkable recovery and expansion in a number of European economies. By the same token, you will see here that the United States economy has long since completed its recovery from the 1957–58 recession, and is well advanced into a new period of growth. Although we have our problems, the recent growth of our economy has been of an orderly and balanced sort, and we confidently expect this trend to extend at a good rate into the future. We are gratified also that while recovery was being resumed, the overall level of consumer prices has been relatively stable and that a balanced Federal budget is in prospect for the present fiscal year. These are significant signs of the progress that can be made, if we pursue the right policies, in strengthening the financial bases of our economy and achieving inflation-free economic growth.

But the struggle to achieve these results is never over. We must use all of our forces, especially in fiscal and financial matters, to help keep the American economy sound and to avoid inflation. The same must be done, indeed, in all the world's economies. This is the one sure way to achieve truly dependable advances in human welfare.

It was only 15 years ago that many of the countries represented here today pledged themselves to the creation of cooperative international institutions to deal with basic international financial and economic problems. The result was the establishment of the International Bank and the Monetary Fund, the records of which have been impressive ones. The action recently taken by our governments to increase the resources of these institutions showed the great confidence there is in them and it should enable them to operate even more effectively in the future than in the past. Three years ago, the International Finance Corporation was added to this family of related international financial institutions to assist in financing productive private enterprise.

We are all aware of the general desire throughout the world for economic development and the need for international capital investment. While development is of course a natural and critical concern of the less-developed countries, it is important to all others as well. The improved economic position of the industrialized countries provides the means whereby they can better do their part in assisting development elsewhere, both directly, and through their participation in international institutions.

Clearly, by such actions, there will result a stronger and more stable free world, to the material benefit of every participating nation, both the helper and the helped.

It is recognized, however, that there are many development projects which, though economically sound, cannot be financed by existing international institutions. To meet this situation, the United States Governor of the Bank has proposed the creation of an International Development Association as an affiliate of the Bank. It is our belief that this new agency must be closely integrated with the Bank. Thus there will be assured the wise expenditure of its funds and the effective coordination of its activities with other institutions. In our view no other mechanism can perform this task for the free world as well as would the proposed IDA.

I congratulate the Bank, the Fund, and the IFC on their achievements and express my hope for an increasingly significant contribution on their part to the well-being of the world economy. To you, as the Governors of these institutions, falls the task of wisely directing policies toward the realization of these common and noble goals.

I express my complete confidence in your readiness and in your ability so to do. Thank you very much indeed.

NOTE: The President spoke at the Sheraton-Park Hotel, Washington, D.C. His opening words "Mr. Chairman" referred to Ambassador Fernando Berckemeyer of Peru.

245　¶ Statement by the President: Know Your America Week.　*September* 29, 1959

THE STRENGTH of America is centered in the idea—the concept of freedom. This concept is the most powerful and creative force on earth.

Freedom is power because it leads directly to and inspires the heart of every man. Freedom includes justice for all men, equal opportunity to work, and the right to worship according to one's conscience. In a free society, like ours, regimentation is repudiated, self-discipline is required. Consequently freedom imposes upon the individual responsibilities commensurate with the rights and privileges it guarantees to him.

I believe that the purpose of "Know Your America Week" is to revitalize in every citizen a determination to study and apply the principles on which our nation was founded. Thus he can make certain that representative government shall continue to serve each one of us and advance the general welfare of all.

The eyes of the world are upon free peoples and their governments as never before. Uncounted millions of people will look to us and other free nations to see whether we have still the determination, the wisdom and the spirit to insure that concepts of freedom and human dignity shall flourish, never wither, in the years before us.

We shall continue to hold ever higher the flame of liberty so that men everywhere may see clearly by its light and cherish its values.

Dwight D. Eisenhower

246   ⁋ Statement by the President After His Talks With Steel Industry and Labor Officials. *September 30, 1959*

I HAVE just completed talks with officials of several of the steel companies and of the steel workers union.

In view of the mounting impact of the strike on our nation's economy and on the jobs of hundreds of thousands of Americans, I sincerely hope that an agreement can be initiated before my return to Washington next week.

The purpose of the talks today was to help bring about a voluntary settlement of the steel strike which will be fair and just to all parties involved, including the public. I am persuaded that this is the kind of settlement that the American people want. It is the only kind that would be good for all Americans and for our whole economy.

247 ¶ The President's Toast at the Luncheon at the White House Honoring Prime Minister Segni of Italy. *September 30, 1959*

Mr. Prime Minister:

It is a very real pleasure for Mrs. Eisenhower and me to have you and Mrs. Segni in Washington as our honored guests. We have been looking forward to this occasion for some time and I am particularly glad we are able to renew our acquaintance so shortly after meeting in Paris earlier this month.

We are very pleased to have the opportunity which your visit affords us to exchange views with you and your colleagues on those important world issues which are before us today. These close consultations between allies which can be carried on in an atmosphere of candor and confidence are of great importance. Italy and the United States happily share the same beliefs and principles and, although our languages may be different, we understand each other when we talk of a world free from fear and secure in justice.

You, Mr. Prime Minister, are well known to us in this country as a statesman and a scholar. The important role you have played in your country, dedicated as you are to the welfare and self-respect of mankind, is an inspiration to all of us. We are truly delighted that you have been able to accept our invitation to come to the United States and we welcome this opportunity to greet you.

Ladies and Gentlemen, the President of the Republic of Italy.

248 ¶ Joint Statement Following Discussions With Prime Minister Segni. *September 30, 1959*

THE PRESIDENT of the United States, the President of the Council of Ministers of the Italian Republic, the Minister of Foreign Affairs of the Italian Republic and the Secretary of State met at the White House today and held two intensive discussions covering a wide range of subjects which are of mutual concern and interest to their two countries. The talks took place in a spirit of close friendship and mutual comprehension and were characterized by their frankness and their fullness.

In amplification of their meeting in Paris on September 3, the President and the Prime Minister reviewed in detail the current world situation. They discussed the developments of the recent visit to the United States of the Chairman of the Council of Ministers of the USSR and agreed that this exchange of views has proved useful in the cause of the peace.

The President and the Prime Minister and the Minister of Foreign Affairs and the Secretary of State restated their belief that all possible efforts should continue to be made to achieve a reduction of armaments throughout the world, within a framework of adequate controls and safeguards. The President expressed his gratification for the inclusion of Italy in the Committee of the Ten Powers which at the beginning of next year will handle the vital problem of disarmament. He stressed the contribution which Italy may be expected to make in this field and added that the United States Government will continue its support of Italian participation in the discussions of major world problems.

The President and the Prime Minister reaffirmed the dedication of their two countries to the United Nations, and to the principles on which it was founded. They also agreed that the present international situation does not yet permit relaxation in Western defense efforts. They reiterated their firm conviction that the combined strength and coordinated action of the free and sovereign countries in the North Atlantic Alliance are vitally necessary to assure peace and security and to protect the right of their people to live in freedom under Governments of their own choosing. They declared that the North Atlantic Alliance will remain the cornerstone of their foreign policies.

The President and the Secretary of State expressed the full recognition of the United States for the contribution which Italy is making in the development of closer political and economic association between the countries of Europe, and reaffirmed the support of the United States for such a policy.

The President and the Prime Minister also discussed the principles which guide the cooperative efforts of the free nations in their programs for assistance to the underdeveloped countries.

The President and the Prime Minister noted with particular satisfaction the opportunity afforded by this visit to carry on the consultations which are a continuing and regular process in the close relations happily existing between the United States and Italy.

The Prime Minister and the Foreign Minister will continue their discussions with the Secretary of State and other senior officials of the United States Government.

249 ¶ Statement by the President: The Jewish High Holy Days. *October 2, 1959*

GREETINGS to my fellow citizens of Jewish faith as they enter the season of their High Holy Days.

The teachings of your ancient belief have long sustained you and strengthened the communities in which you live. By constant repetition—in word and deed—of the commandments of God, you have nourished the noblest principles of mankind.

The demands of justice, the plea for mercy, the rights and the responsibilities of each individual; these should be uppermost in our thoughts at home and at work, when we sleep and when we awake.

DWIGHT D. EISENHOWER

250 ¶ Letter to the Attorney General Directing Him To Petition for an Injunction in the Maritime Strike. *October 7, 1959*

Dear Mr. Attorney General:

On October 6, 1959, by virtue of the authority vested in me by Section 206 of the Labor Management Relations Act, 1947 (Public Law 101, 80th Congress), I issued Executive Order No. 10842, creating a Board of Inquiry to inquire into the issues involved in labor disputes between employers (or associations by which such employers are represented in collective bargaining conferences) who are (1) steamship companies or who are engaged as operators or agents for ships engaged in service from or to Atlantic and Gulf Coast ports from Searsport, Maine, to Brownsville, Texas, or from or to other ports of the United States or its territories or possessions, (2) contracting stevedores, (3) contracting marine carpenters, or (4) other employers engaged in related or associated pier activities, and certain of their employees represented by the International Longshoremen's Association, Atlantic Coast District, ILA and Atlantic and Gulf District, ILA.

On October 7, 1959, I received the Board's written report in the matter. I understand you have a copy of that report.

In my opinion these unresolved labor disputes have resulted in a strike affecting a substantial part of an industry engaged in trade, commerce, transportation, transmission or communication among the several States and with foreign nations, which strike, if permitted to continue, will imperil the national health and safety and will affect the flow and utilization of necessary perishable products, including food for heavily populated coastal areas.

Therefore, in order to remove a peril to the national health and safety and to secure a resumption of trade, commerce, transportation, transmission or communication among the several States and with foreign nations, I direct you, pursuant to the provisions of Section 208 of the Labor Management Relations Act, 1947, to petition in the name of the United States any District Court of the United States having jurisdiction of the parties to enjoin the continuance of such strike and for such other relief as may in your judgment be necessary or appropriate.

Very sincerely yours,

DWIGHT D. EISENHOWER

NOTE: An injunction was granted on October 8 by the District Court for the Southern District of New York.

The Board's reports of October 7 and of December 7 and 23 were made available through the Federal Mediation and Conciliation Service. Final negotiations for the settlement of the strike were concluded on December 29.

This letter was released at La Quinta, Calif.

251 ¶ White House Statement Following the President's Discussion With Prime Minister Eqbal of Iran. *October 9, 1959*

THE PRESIDENT today had the pleasure of meeting with Prime Minister Eqbal of Iran, who represented his country at the Central Treaty

Organization Meeting which has just terminated. There was a very useful and interesting discussion concerning matters of mutual interest.

The President told the Prime Minister that Iran's courageous and unyielding stand in the face of the intensive and unwarranted propaganda attacks of recent months has evoked the admiration of all free nations. The President reaffirmed United States support for the collective efforts of Iran and other free nations to maintain their independence. In stressing the gravity with which the United States would view a threat to the territorial integrity and political independence of Iran, the President recalled the provisions of the Bilateral Agreement of Cooperation with Iran and the Joint Resolution to promote peace and stability in the Middle East.

252   ¶ Letter to Senator Gore Concerning the Interstate Highway Program.   *October* 9, 1959

Dear Senator Gore:

This is in further reply to your letter of September sixteenth concerning the Federal Aid Highway Program and the annual apportionment of funds to the states.

Since enactment of the 1959 legislation this whole question has been the subject of careful consideration in the Executive establishment. In addition, as you know, on several recent occasions members of the Administration have discussed this problem in great detail with various representative groups of Governors.

Last January I recommended that the Congress increase the gas tax by 1½ cents to be effective July 1, 1959. This additional amount of money would have been sufficient to allow the highway program to continue at the accelerated rate which had been authorized in the 1958 highway legislation. However, enactment of a one-cent increase in the gas tax, with an effective date of October 1, 1959, has resulted in smaller revenue to the Highway Trust Fund than would have resulted from my request, and is directly responsible for the problem with which we are confronted today.

I should like to emphasize that this Administration fully intends promptly to honor bills presented to it by the various states. In studying ways to achieve this objective while still adhering to the legislative directive establishing the "pay-as-you-go" principle in the Highway Act of 1956, it became obvious that if we were to be equitable to all of the states we would need to schedule the use of the existing unobligated authorizations. Without such scheduling, which will apply only to the letting of new contracts, we would face the untenable alternative of serious disruption of the program in the fiscal year 1961. In my opinion, any other course of action would be fiscally irresponsible and certainly would not be consistent with proper management of a trust fund which is established for a specific purpose, particularly in the face of a Congressional decision to limit the increase in trust fund revenues to two-thirds of the amount requested.

If, as you have suggested, Congress takes further action at its next session to provide, in an acceptable manner, additional revenues for the Trust Fund, the scheduling now contemplated will be adjusted to meet the new situation. Lacking such action by Congress, it is clear to me that the orderly scheduling of new contracts is the only prudent and equitable course to follow.

With warm regard,

Sincerely,

DWIGHT D. EISENHOWER

NOTE: The President's earlier letter (September 22) in reply to Senator Gore's letter of September 16 was not released by the White House.

253 ¶ Statement by the President Upon Signing Executive Order Creating a Board of Inquiry To Report on the Steel Strike. *October* 9, 1959

AFTER carefully studying the circumstances surrounding the thirteen-week-old steel strike, I have concluded that, if permitted to continue, this strike would imperil the national health and safety. The national interest demands an immediate resumption of production in this vital industry.

To bring about a resumption of production, I am invoking the statutory means which Congress has provided for that purpose. I have today issued an Executive Order appointing a Board of Inquiry to examine immediately into the issues of this dispute and to submit to me the report prescribed by law.

The strike has closed 85 percent of the nation's steel mills, shutting off practically all new supplies of steel. Over 500,000 steel workers and about 200,000 workers in related industries, together with their families, have been deprived of their usual means of support. Present steel supplies are low and the resumption of full-scale production will require some weeks. If production is not quickly resumed, severe effects upon the economy will endanger the economic health of the nation.

I profoundly regret that the parties to the dispute have failed to resolve their differences through the preferred methods of free collective bargaining, even though every appropriate Government service was available to them in support of their efforts. I have been advised by both parties that negotiations between them have broken down and that they see no hope for an early voluntary settlement.

Nevertheless, I want to emphasize that the action I have taken in no way relieves the parties of their grave obligation to the American people to resume negotiations and reach a just and responsible settlement at the earliest possible time.

NOTE: The Executive order required the Board of Inquiry to submit a report by October 16 (E.O. 10843, 24 F.R. 8289). This date was extended to October 19 by Executive Order 10848, issued October 14 (24 F.R. 8401). See also Items 264 and 265.

254 ¶ Remarks of Welcome to President Lopez Mateos of Mexico at the Washington National Airport. *October 9, 1959*

Mr. President:

The people of the United States extend a very warm welcome to you, to Mrs. Lopez Mateos, and to your lovely daughter.

We feel that we are more than merely your geographical neighbor. We are proud to call you our friend. And we devoutly hope that you feel in that same fashion toward us.

We have very much in common—more than a common boundary of sixteen hundred miles in length; we live by the same values; we believe in human dignity and human rights and human freedom. We have the same objectives in our countries, of protecting and furthering the interests of each citizen, the humble and the great.

Through the years there has developed between our two countries a greater understanding, a greater affection, and for these things we are exceedingly grateful.

Moreover, one of our great objectives is that in search for peace. We are determined between ourselves to handle our problems that inevitably occur between friends and neighbors, on the basis of fairness and justice to both sides.

Now, for you today, I hope as you start this visit, you will experience, every minute you are here, the same warm feelings of cordial friendship on every side that I experienced when I was your guest in Acapulco—one of the brightest and most cherished memories that I have in my entire tour in this Office—they are those days that I spent with you.

And if the American people can make you feel that same deep satisfaction that comes from being surrounded by cordial friendship, I assure you, sir, they will try—there is no question about that.

So again, *"bien venido."*

NOTE: President Lopez Mateos' response (as translated) follows:

Mr. President, distinguished friends:

Your Excellency's cordial welcome to the beautiful capital of the United States of America and the friendly words which with characteristic warmth you have addressed to Mexico, its people and its President, have moved me as a Mexican. As such, and Chief of State, I thank you for this kind reception.

Once again Your Excellency has shown your friendship toward my country. On your visits to Mexico you have had occasion to come into contact with the Mexican people. You thereby became better acquainted with the history of my country, its character and aspirations. You know, consequently, that the Mexican, through pride in his heritage and courage in the defense of his country's sovereignty, to him not merely a legal concept but an integral part of his historical make-up, has developed a mental attitude favorably disposed towards peaceful relations with the other peoples of the earth. Especially is this true with the United States of America for whom Mexico in this new era of mutual respect and of increasing reciprocal understanding has feelings of friendship in which we can justly take pride. It is a friendship untarnished, pure in its simplicity, free of the bitterness and misunderstandings of the past, free of burdening commitments in the present, and free to determine a future which shall be rich in joint accomplishments, all within the dignity and respect which enhance every truly friendly relationship.

Because of this existing friendship between Mexico and the United States of America, and because it is a living, tangible fact, you were able during your trips to my country—and especially in the course of your visit to Acapulco—to perceive that the people of Mexico appreciate and admire the great people of the United States, whose immense creative spirit and high moral virtues they fully recognize.

Thousands of Mexicans live in the United States. Two or three hundred thousand come every year to work temporarily in your agriculture. On my arrival to the United States, I salute them with affection.

Thousands of your citizens also live, study, work, and travel in Mexico. Both of these groups of Mexicans and Americans, through their cooperation, their efforts and labors, constitute living testimony that relations between our countries are an example of genuine good-neighborliness.

You know, Mr. President, and I know, that between us there are no secrets. This is because the friendship between Mexico and the United States is crystal-clear. No problem exists or can exist between our governments capable of weakening or jeopardizing this friendship. Our two countries surged into independence and live in freedom, inspired by identical ideals of justice and liberty.

We have problems, undoubtedly. No two countries as large as ours, with a common boundary of three thousand kilometers in length, and with so many and so diverse contacts, can fail to have problems. Some of these are intrinsically difficult; and others are made difficult by the conflicting interests involved. All of these problems are entrusted to diplomatic channels, and eventually, though sometimes after brief periods of stagnation, follow the course toward a solution in a normal manner.

I am ready to talk about these problems and about all matters which our advisers may consider appropriate to bring to our attention. I firmly believe that in the conversations between the Chiefs of State of the United States and Mexico, that is, in talks between friends, the most impor-

tant subject always will be: the United States and Mexico, our presentday relationships, our capacity for growth and our place in a world with respect to which the necessary economic and social changes should be foreseen.

Those who govern are in essence nothing more than the lookouts who during the dawn of Greek civilization manned the watchtowers of their primitive cities. From a height they were able to encompass a larger portion of the surrounding territory. Even if other factors were not present, this position by itself endows the meetings between Chiefs of State, as you have so successfully maintained, with great possibilities for fruitful progress.

It is particularly gratifying for me to assure Your Excellency that I return your visit in Acapulco with the greatest satisfaction. In fact, through me, the whole people of Mexico are returning the visit of the man they admire, as the soldier of World War II, who never knew defeat, and as the wise statesman who with clarity of vision has dedicated his best efforts to strengthening the bonds between our countries. They recognize you as their friend.

Being at the service of the people of Mexico, I ask Your Excellency to accept the expression of their friendship toward the people of the United States, and their best wishes for the prosperity and happiness of your country and its citizens.

255 ¶ Toasts of the President and the President of Mexico at the White House. *October* 9, 1959

Mr. President, Senora Lopez Mateos, our Distinguished Guests from our sister Republic across the Rio Grande, Chief Justice and Mrs. Warren, and My Fellow Citizens:

I assure you, Mr. President, that every individual in this company is proud to be here to have the opportunity to join with me and Mrs. Eisenhower in extending to you, your family and your party, and through you the people of Mexico, a warm welcome and expressions of our lasting friendship.

With you we feel a special feeling of affection. Despite our troubles, the troubles between us of the 1830's and the 1840's, the history of our true friendship begins in 1864. We in this country were then engaged in a tragic, fratricidal war, and at that moment a European monarch decided that by force and with a European soldiery he would take over and rule Mexico through a puppet government.

When our war was over—this internecine strife—our Commander-in-Chief sent down to the border trained, battlewise veterans, and with the statement and with the notice to the Europeans, "Get out or the United States will do something about it."

This, I am sure—and I have been so told by my Mexican friends—was of the greatest value to your great patriot, Benito Juarez, as he struggled so manfully to sustain the freedom of his people and the independence of his nation. And from that moment on, despite our difficulties, irritations and frictions of different kinds, we never have lost that feeling of friendship.

And happily, I think, in these recent years, more particularly since World War I, there has been a steady increase in those sentiments of friendship, mutual respect, and confidence between our two great countries.

To my mind, Mr. President, and if I may, permit me to pay you a compliment of a personal kind, as I have seen you and known you and listened to you, I think you are carrying on in the tradition of Juarez. I believe that other Americans, other citizens of this country, that know you, believe the same thing. For that reason they respect and love not only your country, but they respect and admire what you are doing for your country—dedicated as you are to the same ideals on which this country likes to feel it was founded, and the ideals which it attempts to sustain with its full strength, material and spiritual.

So you can understand, sir, why I deem it a special privilege this evening to ask this company to rise with me and to drink a Toast to the President of Mexico.

NOTE: The President proposed this toast at a state dinner at the White House. President Lopez Mateos' response (as translated) follows:

Mr. President, Mrs. Eisenhower, Distinguished Guests, Ladies and Gentlemen:
I would like to express my warmest thanks for the kind words that the President has spoken, that he has addressed to my country, to the people of my country, and to those who are traveling with me, to the members of my family and to myself. I am doubly grateful for these words, because I know they were spoken on the basis of warm friendship.

And another reason for which I am grateful, was the reference you made, Mr. President, to Benito Juarez, who on two occasions led his countrymen in the fight for freedom and independence, who taught the Mexican people how to fight in defense of these high ideals. And when one thinks of Benito Juarez, one invariably thinks also of Lincoln—the great admiration that Mexicans have for the many virtues which we see in this great figure of your history, and in thinking of him, the affection and admiration which we have for your people.

This afternoon, when I arrived in this most beautiful city, Mr. President, I expressed to you the admiration which the people of my country feel for you, and as a great statesman who after having fought for freedom on the battlefields of war, fights for freedom and peace and justice today on the battlefields of peace, and promotes the welfare of mankind.

For all of these reasons, Mr. President, I would like to ask all of those present to join me in raising their glasses to the happiness and prosperity of the great American people, to your personal good fortune, happiness, and prosperity, and that of your charming wife, Mrs. Eisenhower.

256 ¶ Toasts of the President and President Lopez Mateos at the Mexican Embassy. *October 11, 1959*

Mr. President, Senora Lopez Mateos, ladies and gentlemen:

It is indeed a great honor for me to be able to respond this evening to the gracious words and greetings of the President of Mexico.

While we stand here, may I ask all of you to turn to look at this wall, to see a picture from one of the most distinguished artists that is being placed in one of our art galleries. If you need any other evidence than a mere sight, to know that it is a work of art, I must tell you that the artist is a true one, because he is 84 years old, has one leg, and likes to go to night clubs.

I assure you, sir, that the American people will appreciate your very great kindness in making this work of art from this extraordinary individual—whose name, by the way, is Atl, which means "water"—in making it available to them in this way.

In the last few days, the friendship of the President and me has ripened. I am quite sure it is going to be, possibly, even a little bit closer, after tomorrow. He is experiencing one of the incidents of public life in Washington that I go through regularly—he is going to meet the press. I am quite sure that there will be even a warmer feeling of sympathy between us.

In any event, I join in his Toast to friendship—to friendship that makes both countries stronger, better, and happier, and will do that through the years.

So, will you please join now in a Toast to the President of Mexico.

NOTE: This toast was proposed in response to a toast by President Lopez Mateos at a dinner which he gave in honor of President Eisenhower.

The painting "Volcanoes and Clouds" by the Mexican artist "Dr. Atl" (Gerardo Murillo) was presented to the Smithsonian Institution's National Collection of Fine Arts.

The toast proposed by President Lopez Mateos (as translated) follows:

I wish to add very few words to the words that have already been spoken during our sojourn in the United States.

In the United States, every hour, and at every place, and with every person that we have met, we have heard repeated the word that you spoke at Acapulco: Friendship.

Due to the meaning that we Mexicans attach to this word, I invite you ladies and gentlemen to join in lifting your glasses to drink to the health and prosperity of the President of the United States, and to the people of his country.

257 ¶ Joint Statement by the President and the President of Mexico. *October* 12, 1959

DURING THE VISIT of President Adolfo Lopez Mateos to Washington, President Dwight D. Eisenhower and the President of Mexico renewed and strengthened the friendship which began at their meeting at Acapulco, Mexico, last February. Informally and without an agenda they exchanged views on general subjects of mutual interest to Mexico and the United States and on subjects of hemispheric and world concern in that atmosphere of cordiality and frankness which characterizes true friendship.

With regard to economic problems of much interest to public opinion in Mexico the two Presidents noted with satisfaction the recent strengthening of the Mexican economy. Special mention was made of the fact that although Mexico has had at its disposal since January of the current year a balance of payments credit from the Export-Import Bank in the amount of 100 million dollars, it has proved unnecessary to make use of more than a small part of this credit.

The Presidents were also heartened by the progress made towards resolving important commodity problems and consequent improvements in world market conditions with respect to basic commodities produced in Mexico and the United States, including the strengthening of cotton prices, the signature of the coffee agreement and the improved outlook for a better balance of supply and demand in world markets for lead and zinc.

The Presidents agreed that maintenance of the productive capacity of the Mexican mining industry is essential to Mexico's economic progress and to the security of the United States. Consequently, the Governments of both countries will continue to consult each other and the other lead and zinc producing countries with regard to the measures necessary to achieve these objectives.

The problems of the United States and Mexico regarding the exploitation and conservation of the economic resources of the seas were explored by the two Presidents, and they agreed that efforts should be made to provide for the orderly use of these resources.

It was agreed that the Mexican and American scientific communities should work more closely together.

The two Presidents also expressed gratification at the cooperation which has developed in seeking solutions to common health problems and they will instruct the health authorities of the two countries to broaden the area of joint action to the greatest possible extent. The excellent progress made in the eradication of malaria in Mexico was noted, and the hope was expressed that through international cooperation similar success could be achieved in the other countries of the hemisphere where malaria is still a significant problem.

At Camp David, the two Presidents chose the name Amistad Dam to designate the dam proposed to be constructed near Del Rio, Texas, and Villa Acuna, Coahuila, for flood control, conservation and storage of the waters of the Rio Grande, and possibly power generation.

Like the Acapulco meeting, the Washington visit demonstrated the firm resolve of the two Chiefs of State and of the two Governments to continue to examine their problems with understanding of and respect for each other's points of view in efforts to find solutions that are mutually beneficial to the peoples of Mexico and the United States.

The two Presidents are convinced of the value of continuing a personal relationship between the Chiefs of State of Mexico and the United States, not merely to provide an opportunity for cordial and frank exchanges of views on common problems, but more importantly, to sponsor the continued growth of friendship between the two countries and their Governments.

Lastly, the two Presidents expressed their belief that their personal friendship and the growing cooperation between their two countries in all fields of human endeavor will be an example to the world of how two nations can live independently side by side in friendship, cooperative effort and mutual understanding.

258   ¶ Address at the Ground-breaking Ceremonies for the Eisenhower Library, Abilene, Kansas.   *October* 13, 1959

Governor Docking, Mr. Fairless, Senator Darby, and Friends:

I am glad indeed to come again to Abilene.   Whenever I return here, I invariably sense, in these surroundings, an atmosphere of simplicity and peace.

This is not because Abilene is any less involved in the turbulent affairs of our interdependent world than are all other places my duties take me. Rather, it is because each homecoming causes my mind to go back, nostalgically, to the conditions I knew as a boy.   We did not then know the term "world tension"; life was peaceful, serene, and happy!

It was here that my parents spent most of their lives and my brothers and I grew to adulthood.   The years of our youth preceded the exacting interdependence of the world as we know it today.

Even more than the memory of those tranquil years, it was the abiding truths we learned at home that prompted my brothers and me some years ago to give our parents' home to a Foundation, organized initially by citizens of this town.   Later, as you know, the Foundation brought into being the beautiful museum we see across the street.   Their action and ours were not taken with any intention of glorifying a name, but an idea—an idea that visits by individuals to this simple home and this museum might serve to remind us all of some of the concepts that underlie the American way.

Our parents, like most American parents of the period, were concerned primarily with the cardinal features of their religious philosophy— beliefs which shaped their own lives and their guidance of their children. Love of God, fairness in human relations, independence and responsibility, concern for the welfare of others, and conviction that each free individual

719

could through his own efforts achieve a full life—these were all included in an idea which was as much a part of our home as the food we ate and the clothes we wore.

These concepts are foremost in my thinking now as I help break ground for this additional structure, a library.

In this library will be placed initially most of the written records of my military and Presidential service. As time passes, other documents pertaining to American development in this same period may gradually be added. One important addition already committed comprises many of the papers of John Foster Dulles during the years he was Secretary of State. All of these documents will, I hope, help to deepen understanding and demonstrate the application of the concepts that were basic to life in Abilene 50 years ago. In spite of the revolutionary changes that have come to us during the half century, I believe these fundamentals are as valid for today as they were then.

The generosity of the American people in providing the beautiful structure that will rise on this land is highly gratifying to me. No gesture could touch me more deeply than centering this meaningful enterprise in the heartland of America and having it bear my name. I feel a deep sense of obligation to my personal friends, and to all others who are cooperating in this enterprise, even though I realize that their participation is motivated by concern for the perpetuation of ideas, rather than the records of any individual.

Now we have no illusions that a mere study by research workers of the letters, messages, memoranda, and books deposited by many individuals here will miraculously endow their readers with wisdom.

Factual information must be energized by the force of reason, understanding, and interpretation. To the true historian, trends are more important than the recorded deeds of any period. A study of events of the past half century shows that the compelling forces have been at work, causing trends which will carry into decades ahead with persistent momentum.

We need not dwell on the disappearance of physical earth-bound frontiers and the opening of frontiers of outer space; or on the shattering of blissful self-sufficiency and the growth of exacting interdependence; or on the development of power so awesome that nations now have no logical alternative to replace coercion with honest negotiation and cooperation. These and other great changes are obvious, but whether they will lead us to disaster or to an era of hope and accomplishment will depend on the degree of understanding and wisdom we apply in solving a vast array of problems.

Because upon our powerful Nation the mantle of free world leadership has fallen, our responsibility in the search for solutions is inescapable. And, since in our country the basic social power is in the hands of all the people, each citizen bears directly a part of the responsibility for right action. Each of you here today must help make the fateful decisions of the future. Study of the past and the present will help to assure that these decisions are made wisely.

Think for a moment of the type of decision you will be forced to make in the light of just one obvious trend in the world scene.

When you of my age were youngsters, William Allen White was disturbed by the fact that Kansas was losing population. What would he say today about the rapid growth of Kansas and the swelling population of the Nation?

What would be his reaction to present estimates that while our country's population is increasing to two hundred seventy-five million in the next 30 years, the world's population will be nearly five billion people?

Many peoples of the world, once dominated and submissive, are now and will continue to be involved in a great ferment, explosive in its potential. Everywhere, knowledge and ideas, spread by modern communications, are routing centuries of ignorance and superstition. Peoples now know that poverty and suppression are neither universal nor are they inevitable.

Increasingly and insistently, they are demanding the elimination of the human indignities of starvation, ill health, and peonage. They want independence, individual freedom, and responsible government.

These increasingly numerous peoples of tomorrow's world will multiply those wants—and they will have at their disposal both more constructive and more destructive capacity than the world has known before.

Now how do you believe this capacity will be used? What decisions will you make in this regard?

These are sobering questions. They deserve your most earnest consideration.

For if the growing power of free men is wisely and skillfully applied toward the common aspirations of humanity, then a world of peace and plenty becomes a high probability. But if power is used recklessly, or is employed in the pursuit of false, selfish goals, then civilization will risk its own destruction.

You know that the free nations of the world have the capacity and can develop the will to overcome together the powerful, perplexing forces which for thousands of years have yielded hate, distrust, poverty.

Humanity's upward climb involves complex economic, educational, and political problems, all of which cry for wisdom as we seek solutions, as we search for world understanding.

I cite one homely example.

A common miracle is the telephone. You can speak into it and, with the speed of light, your words will be carried around the world. Yet, even this technological triumph encounters serious impediments to true, free communication among populations. Most people in the world do not have access to a telephone. This is an economic problem. Among those who do, you would not be able to understand many because of language barriers—an educational problem. And even if these difficulties were surmounted, almost a third of the world's peoples would be forbidden to talk with you—a political problem.

Obviously a program for peaceful progress calls for intelligent economic, educational, and political cooperation: economic cooperation which promises that peoples everywhere may, by concerted effort, conquer hunger and disease, and lift their levels of living; educational cooperation to develop that genuine human understanding on which all other cooperative activity must be based; and political cooperation, not only to settle disputes which continuously arise in an imperfect world, but also to build the social structures that encourage man in his striving for a better life.

Now, any reasonable person will recognize that no one nation, even with the legendary strength of an Atlas, could long support the world on its shoulders.

Each nation will progress only if its own people and leaders recognize that the major responsibility for improvement is theirs. Even if every other nation were as generous as the United States has been in recent years, this would still be so.

But this does not imply that we or any other fortunate people may be indifferent to the welfare of others. We cannot today live—either in domestic or international life—with the long-obsolete picture of the factory owner living on a hilltop in isolated riches and splendor, wholly indifferent to the aspirations and just demands of the oppressed multitudes in the plains below.

Clearly one objective of American foreign policy is and must be to help build a world economy in which each nation finds it possible to earn its own keep and to pay its own way, and do so in a manner which brings meaning and fulfillment to the lives of its citizens. Such a policy is crucial to our own prosperity and security; it is vital to the cause of a just and lasting peace.

I believe, and I trust you believe, that every free nation should have this policy. I further believe—and hope you agree—that the free nations of the world, motivated by both humanitarianism and self-interest, should cooperate voluntarily in a long-range program aimed at helping the presently less privileged peoples work step by step toward a better life.

Every nation should contribute to the common enterprise in whatever way it can. No nation should be deemed incapable of contributing in some fashion to the worldwide goal.

The ingredients of this assistance must be technical services, private and public loans, dependable, mutually helpful trade relationships, grants in emergency situations, security help in transition years, and, above all, continuing efforts to build true understanding among nations and peoples, without which all else will fail.

Foreign capital helped our own country make spectacular progress during the first three-quarters of the 19th century—capital which over a 40-year period we repaid with interest. So, too, can private and public capital, under the right conditions, now assist the less-developed nations make sound progress toward the achievement of their goals. Those "right conditions" must include both an honorable and responsible attitude within the nations needing the capital and intelligent trade relations among all free nations.

No other aspiration dominates my own being so much as this: that the nations of East and West will find dependable, self-guaranteeing methods to reduce the vast and essentially wasteful expenditures for armaments, so that part of the savings may be used in a comprehensive and effective effort for world improvement.

As the less developed nations succeed in establishing viable economies and raising their living standards, our own economy will soar to new heights and our technology will be challenged as never before. Burdensome surpluses—even those of wheat—will disappear. Indeed, the world may then be threatened with very real deficits—of food, energy, minerals. Enlarged demand throughout the world will have to be met by new methods, and more effective use of resources everywhere.

The world must learn to work together—or finally it will not work at all.

This is not a problem for the distant future. Within the lifetime of many of you here today, the global population will be five billion. You must now help determine how such a vast humanity may, in freedom, achieve stupendous increases in economic output, and increase the sum of human happiness on this earth.

The task ahead is not for the faint-hearted.

But does anyone of Central Kansas need to be told that our parents and grandparents who first worked this black soil were not faint-hearted? They had faith—faith in the religious concepts that dominated their beings, faith in the virtue and success of their own labor, faith in their neighbors and in the inexhaustible potential of free men.

If they were here today, they would, I'm sure, wonder whether we possess for our time, as they did for theirs, a comprehension of the concepts and basic principles which, universally applied, can lead mankind toward a world community of free nations, characterized by peace and justice.

Our forefathers who pioneered this land were concerned initially with individual family welfare. Soon, however, they developed allegiance to larger communities—the State and Nation—and in doing so they did not diminish their devotion to family or local community; indeed, they strengthened it. If they saw the world as it is today, they would be the first to realize that peoples everywhere must now achieve an allegiance to the wider, free-world community, and doing so they will thereby strengthen, make more meaningful, their devotion to family, to State, and Nation.

When this library is filled with documents, and scholars come here to probe into some of the facts of the past half century, I hope that they, as we today, are concerned primarily with the ideals, principles, and trends that provide guides to a free, rich, peaceful future in which all peoples can achieve ever-rising levels of human well-being.

Those who have so generously made possible the construction of this library do not seek reward or acclaim. Yet, I profoundly believe that they will feel deep gratification in the knowledge that thus they may have helped in some small measure to assure the Nation's eternal adherence to these simple ideals and principles as free men shape historic trends toward noble goals.

May God grant that this may be so.

Thank you very much.

NOTE: Participating in the ceremonies were Benjamin F. Fairless, chairman of the Board of Directors of the Governor's National Committee for the Eisenhower Presidential Library and of its Executive Committee, and Governor George Docking and former U.S. Senator Harry Darby, co-chairmen of the National Committee.

259 ¶ Remarks at the Luncheon After the Ground-breaking Ceremonies at Abilene. *October 13, 1959*

Governor Docking, Senator Darby, and distinguished members of this most distinguished audience:

I was warned by the remarks of Senator Darby that this was of course a nonpartisan meeting in every sense of the word. But I think there's nothing wrong, for me, in expressing a little bit of disappointment that Governor Docking could not have been Republican. And of course he is still a young man, and there's a chance—*(laughter)*. Certainly I for one would be on the threshold of welcoming him into the party ranks whenever he wants to change.

This is a most extraordinary privilege for me—a group of people made up largely of close personal friends, and representing in many ways various stages and phases of my own life. There is at least one individual here who was a member of my high school class that graduated in 1909 with me 50 years ago—when I tried to come out to the fiftieth reunion, it became impossible. There is here a classmate of mine from West Point, a man who became one of the most distinguished generals of our time; across the land there are individuals of every kind and of every class and every calling whom I have met—on the golf course, in business associations, associations with Columbia University, and in military and political life.

And we are all met in the town that has, for me, a very deep, sentimental meaning. I tried to express a little bit of this, this morning, but trying to speak into the teeth of a little wind and not knowing exactly which one of those many microphones I was supposed to be talking into, I was not very sure that I was getting over my point.

I spoke of a time 50 years ago when, we knew, our parents, my family and the people they knew lived a certain religious philosophy. I suppose that many of you believe that the name Abilene is an Indian name; it's out of the Bible. And in this simple community—that went through its heyday of, let's say, wild West hilarity, and even worse, and became a community of God-fearing, hard-working, simple people—it seems to me there's a sort of cross-section of the deep convictions that truly motivate the United States, when we stop and think what we are really trying to do.

Moneyed men are not really trying just to get more money. The professional, the teacher, the lawyer, the doctor, the man who is working with his hands to create the wealth of our country, those people are not thinking merely in material gain. There is a spiritual aspiration, spoken or unspoken, that may be articulate in their own minds, and may not be—but still, they are thinking of the future at least in these terms: my grandchildren, what am I going to leave to them? Or, if you have no grandchildren, the little tots you see around you, what is going to be the kind of world they are going to inherit, and that they are going, one day, to run?

This is the problem. This is the problem that is connected with this library. A group of people, with no selfish ends to serve at all, looking for nothing except to serve their fellow man, and not primarily just now but those people who can look and see this little segment in one particular phase of the development of the United States, from way back in 1607 in Jamestown to whatever hour that individual may be researching the records that these people have made it possible to accumulate, keep together, and make available for study.

So my pride is not because merely that I come down here amazed at what my own little town has done, because it was really the individuals of this town that had the idea about preserving the family home, and the museum. They had not then of course thought of a library, because they weren't thinking of any man being a President and accumulating the kind of papers to put in Presidential libraries. But they had the idea not merely to glorify the name of a soldier or a soldier's associates, but because even then they said, this institution is set up to promote good citizenship, and good citizenship means concern for the future.

So, as I see the physical development, the old ugly buildings that have been cleared away, the new structures and the big development that is going on around the museum and the home and the library, when I see what the town has done, it seems to me not a written record but a record in people's accomplishments, and in their faces, and in their friendships, that I sense as I come back here. These are the things that Abilene means to me.

So I thank each individual who had any part in making this library possible. And of course I am going to be long gone, one of these days. Most of us at my age have not too many years to think of the future. This means we are thinking of the future. My pride is that each one of you individuals is thinking of that future, and trying to make it a better place, a stronger America, standing always in the position of leadership to support freedom, the dignity of man, his rights, and an ordered existence in an orderly world of peace with justice.

Thank you.

NOTE: The President spoke at the Sunflower Hotel, Abilene, Kans., at 2:25 p.m., at a luncheon given by the Directors of the Governor's National Committee for the Eisenhower Presidential Library. In his remarks he referred to Paul H. Royer, a member of his high school class, and Gen. James A. Van Fleet, a West Point classmate, who were present for the ceremonies.

260   ¶ Statement by the President: National Newspaper Week.   *October* 14, 1959

To the Newspapers of the Nation:

It is a pleasure to take part in the twentieth annual observance of National Newspaper Week.

"Your Newspaper . . . Freedom's Textbook" is a fine theme for this year's observance. To me, it stands for the hopes and achievements of American journalism. As our editors report the daily affairs of their communities with zeal and accuracy, they help to supply our citizens with the lessons of history, together with the information which is required to make history move steadily forward in the direction of freedom and justice.

I am delighted to add my best wishes for the success of National Newspaper Week.

DWIGHT D. EISENHOWER

261 ¶ Statement by the President Regarding Appointment of Robert Cutler as U.S. Executive Director of the Inter-American Development Bank. *October 14, 1959*

THE SOUND organization and effective operation of this new international institution is of the greatest importance to the United States and the other nations of the Western Hemisphere.

Mr. Cutler, as Executive Director for the United States, will bring to the Inter-American Development Bank recognized competence and wide experience in economic and financial matters, supplemented by experience gained during his service in the Federal Government in which he was in continuous close contact with this Nation's foreign affairs.

My appointment of Mr. Cutler to this position evidences my deep personal interest in the successful carrying out by the Inter-American Bank of its important mission.

NOTE: The President's statement was made public as part of a White House release issued on the day the United States became a member of the Bank as authorized by Public Law 86–147 (73 Stat. 299). The release further stated that Secretary of the Treasury Robert B. Anderson would be appointed Governor of the Bank and that Under Secretary of State C.

Douglas Dillon would be named alternate Governor.

For the special message to Congress concerning the Bank, see Item 98. A report by Dr. Milton S. Eisenhower on U.S.-Latin American relations, strongly urging establishment of the Bank, was released by the White House on January 4, 1959.

262 ¶ Statement by the President on the Death of General Marshall. *October 16, 1959*

THE DEATH of General of the Army George Catlett Marshall at Walter Reed General Hospital today is cause for profound grief throughout the United States.

General Marshall long ago earned a place as one of the distinguished military and civil leaders of our century, an example of devotion to service and duty, an outstanding American.

For his wartime role as Chief of Staff of the Army, and for his subsequent service as Secretary of State and as Secretary of Defense, he has been honored as soldier and statesman. His courage, fortitude and vision, his selflessness and stern standards of conduct and character were an inspiration, not only within the Army, but throughout the Nation and among our allies. For his unswerving devotion to the safeguarding of the security and freedom of our Nation, for his wise counsel and action and driving determination in times of grave danger, we are lastingly in his debt.

Today these thoughts echo in the memory of a grateful Nation which joins with Mrs. Eisenhower and me in extending condolence to Mrs. Marshall and in mourning the passing of one of the Nation's most illustrious sons.

NOTE: In addition to the foregoing statement, the President issued Proclamation 3322 (24 F.R. 8477) which provided that, as a mark of respect to the memory of General Marshall, the flag of the United States should be flown at half-staff on all Government buildings, grounds, and naval vessels in the United States and in foreign countries until interment.

263 ¶ Message to the Newspaperboys and Girls of America. *October* 17, 1959

To the Newspaperboys and Girls of America:

Each year it is a pleasure to salute you. This year I must raise my salute higher than before in order to encompass you all. I understand you have enlarged your numbers by 100,000 since the last count.

Your present total of 700,000 represents a powerful force. In your work you strengthen two of our most cherished traditions: the freedom of the American press, and the opportunities of American citizenship. With your help, our newspapers are swiftly distributed to the homes and working places of our people. With your earnings and experience, you are better able to prepare yourselves for careers of your choice.

I am delighted to wish you well.

DWIGHT D. EISENHOWER

264   ¶ Statement by the President Following Receipt of the Report of the Board of Inquiry in the Steel Strike.   *October* 19, 1959

IT IS ESSENTIAL to the national interest that production be resumed immediately in the steel industry.

Free collective bargaining has not worked in this dispute despite the dedicated efforts of the Federal Government and the fact-finding Board of Inquiry, composed of eminent and impartial citizens.

In order to protect the interest of all of the American people, this leaves me with no alternative except to seek an injunction under the existing law.

America's hopes for a voluntary responsible settlement have not been fulfilled.   It is a sad day for the Nation.

265   ¶ Letter to the Attorney General Directing Him To Petition for an Injunction in the Steel Strike.   *October* 19, 1959

Dear Mr. Attorney General:

On October 9, 1959, by virtue of the authority vested in me by Section 206 of the Labor-Management Relations Act, 1947, I issued Executive Order No. 10843, creating a Board of Inquiry to inquire into the issues involved in a labor dispute between certain corporations or organizations in the United States producing or fabricating steel or the components thereof and certain of their employees represented by the United Steel Workers of America.   On October 14, 1959, Executive Order No. 10843 was amended by Executive Order No. 10848 so as to extend the time in which the Board was required to report to me.

This morning, October 19, 1959, I received the Board's written report in the matter.   A copy of that report is attached.

In my opinion this unresolved labor dispute has resulted in a strike affecting a substantial part of an industry engaged in trade, commerce, and transportation among the several States and with foreign nations, and in the production of goods for commerce, which strike will, if permitted to continue, imperil the national health and safety.

Therefore, in order to remove a peril to the national health and safety and to secure a resumption of trade, commerce, and transportation among the several States and with foreign nations and the production of goods for commerce, I direct you, pursuant to the provisions of Section 208 of the Labor-Management Relations Act, 1947, to petition in the name of the United States any District Court of the United States having jurisdiction of the parties to enjoin the continuance of such strike and for such other relief as may in your judgment be necessary or appropriate.

Sincerely,

DWIGHT D. EISENHOWER

NOTE: On October 21, the Attorney General sought and obtained in the District Court for the Western District of Pennsylvania an injunction against the continuation of the strike. The U.S. Supreme Court upheld the injunction in a decision handed down on November 7 (361 U.S. 39).

The terms of settlement were reached on January 4, 1960. The Board's reports of October 19, 1959, and January 6, 1960, were made available through the Federal Mediation and Conciliation Service.

266 ¶ Statement by the President on the Proposed Transfer of the Army Ballistic Missiles Agency to the National Aeronautics and Space Administration. *October* 21, 1959

TO STRENGTHEN the national space effort and provide for America's changing requirements in this field, I have concluded that the Army Ballistic Missiles Agency can best serve the national interest as an integral part of the National Aeronautics and Space Administration. The Army Ballistic Missiles Agency team has demonstrated its intense dedication in this field and has shown its high technical proficiency through splendid accomplishments under Army aegis.

The contemplated transfer provides new opportunity for them to contribute their special capabilities directly to the expanding civilian space program.

As part of this action, the development of "super-booster" space vehicles will be consolidated in the National Aeronautics and Space Administration, under the immediate direction of this team. I have directed that this program be vigorously pressed forward.

The specific plan and details involved in this transfer, including provision for continuation of military missile programs now assigned to the Army Ballistic Missiles Agency, will be ready to lay before the Congress when it reconvenes.

NOTE: This statement was released at Augusta, Ga.

267   ¶ The President's News Conference at Augusta, Georgia.   *October* 22, 1959

THE PRESIDENT. Good morning. Please sit down.

Merely because I thought I should come to a press conference in this unusual place, you are not to assume that I have any startling news to bring. As you know, I had established or scheduled a conference on Wednesday, and then when I decided suddenly, for my own convenience, to come down here, I thought it was only fair to carry out the chore that I gave myself. So that's the reason I am here this morning.

Q. Merriman Smith, United Press International: Mr. President, the Russian Ambassador to Paris says this morning that you have proposed a summit conference late this year, and that Mr. Khrushchev agrees. Now the British also seem to favor the idea of an early summit, and the French want to wait till spring. You have been in touch with the allied leaders recently, and today could you give us your position on this situation? Specifically, do you want a pre-summit Western meeting in the next few weeks, and do you think the big summit conference should be held this year?

THE PRESIDENT. I think the word "proposed" is not quite correct. I stated that I would be ready at any time from now on to go to a Western summit because I thought, preceding any meeting with the Soviets, there should be again an examination of our several positions together, so that we could have position papers, they are called; we want them coordinated.

Now I said I was ready to go any time from there on, and I said thereafter I would be ready to go to a major summit meeting—that is, with the Soviets—whenever we could all agree that we had a chance to study and get ourselves all prepared. In other words, I was thinking we could do this by the end of the year. But it was not a proposal, it was a statement of my position. That still remains my position. And I agree, as time is slipping by, the longer we postpone a Western summit, which I do think is necessary, why then that would have some effect on pushing back any other that we might agree upon, and might have some effect on the date that we might agree on.

Q. Charles Roberts, Newsweek: Sir, before General Medaris announced his intention to resign, he said that we are straddling the issue of whether we are competing with the Russians in space. I wonder if our position is that we are competing with the Russians, and if we are, if their recent successes in launching luniks and probes into space indicate that we must spend more money in this field in our next budget?

THE PRESIDENT. Well, you open a big subject with a lot of questions along with it. Here is a thing that has been studied ever since 1955 on a very urgent basis. I need not go again into the history of missile development within the Military Establishment, and the launching of at least our interest into the outer space field. But as early as 1953 or '54, we began to get the recommendations of certain scientific groups, and then I established my own, under Dr. Killian, which reported early in 1955. From there on, missiles and space vehicles began to take first priority in both defense and, you might say, in scientific research affairs.

Where we got into the outer space field was through the International Geophysical Year, if you will recall. Dr. Waterman was the one that proposed this to me, and we went into the Vanguard proposal.

Well now, as time went on, we began to do very well in the missile field. Now there was one reason that we could do pretty well in the missile field, and fairly early; it was this: we were ahead, it seemed clear, of anybody else in the development of efficient and still very powerful bombs. This meant that we did not have the same power in our engines or in our boosters that was required if those warheads had not been so efficiently designed and built.

So we have developed and we now have operational ICBM's. Therefore we have the certainty, the fact, that starting in 1955 until this moment we have done—our scientists have done—a remarkable job in bringing this about. But since we had no great interest at that moment in putting heavy bodies into outer space, we were going along with the engines or the boosters that were capable of handling our Thors, Jupiters, and Atlases—that kind of thing.

As the space exploration studies went further, it began to be obvious that we needed big boosters for this particular thing. We started, I believe, three projects—three routes, you might say—towards their designing. I think the scientists have come pretty well to the conclusion that one of these shows more promise than any other. The team that has had more experience in this field than any other is that headed by Dr. von Braun, a very brilliant group of scientists which was brought together by the foresight and the wisdom of the Army, in the original sense. They have done largely the work that they want to do for the Army. The Pershing, one of those other small items on which they have been working, has been largely completed. They are the ones now that we are looking for to get and develop this big booster.

But this great booster is of no present interest to the Defense Department. Its interest is in NASA, and that's the reason that we have decided to take this very competent team of scientists and this facility—the ABMA—and put it into the space department so that it can get the kind of booster that it needs.

Now, this statement that we are straddling as far as competition with the Russians is concerned: I don't know exactly what it means. I know this: we have established, and it has been published at least in outline, a program of space exploration; and Dr. Glennan has pointed out some of the major things we want to do. Our plan is a positive one, and I see no reason for thinking of it merely as competition with somebody else. It is something we intend to do.

And just one point about this transfer of ABMA I might point out is this: there are two separate facilities there. One of them is the Army Ordnance Center, I believe it is—Army Ordnance Research Center, some such thing. The Army projects stay right there, and their contacts and their coordination and the help that they get from the space agency will be no less than it has been before. Such little items, some finishing touches that remain on Redstone or one or two other programs, will be completed.

But at the same time, Dr. von Braun and his group are going over to the NASA because, I say, the big booster has its primary place in space exploration and not in our missile program.

Q. Art Barriault, National Broadcasting Company: Is any effort being made, sir, to retain General Medaris perhaps in a civilian capacity?

THE PRESIDENT. Well, as a matter of fact, I really don't know. I haven't seen his reasons for wanting to retire, but I understood, just a few days back, from the Army, that he was quite content and happy. I don't know exactly what his disappointments or his disagreements are, and I would like to hear them.

Q. Laurence H. Burd, Chicago Tribune: Mr. President, this is on the steel strike. Where do you think the major blame lies for this strike going on so long? And secondly, from the standpoint of the Government and the public, do you think the Taft-Hartley Act has proved adequate to deal with strikes of this kind, or do you think some other legislation is necessary?

THE PRESIDENT. Well, I don't think that Taft-Hartley has a very brilliant history, therefore I could say I do not believe it is necessarily good or adequate legislation. But on the other hand, I am not so sure that additional legislation is going to do exactly what we want.

Ladies and gentlemen, what we want: we want a growing and expanding economy, with fairness to everybody. But we don't want to try to control this or direct this by Government. And if we come to the point that we believe through the medium of controlling prices or any other compulsory type of action, then I believe we have hurt ourselves very badly.

Now as of the moment, I had no recourse except to resort to Taft-Hartley. Indeed, I am so concerned after 97 days of this strike as to what is happening to our country, that I have made a little memorandum. Mr. Hagerty will have some copies for you. It's just a short memorandum, a recitation of the brief facts of what has happened.

I put it this way: I don't think Taft-Hartley is necessarily presenting any cure for this thing. I believe that self-discipline, the setting up by all of us as our standard the welfare of the United States of America, is the only thing that ever will do it. Because if we can't settle our economic differences by truly free economic bargaining without damaging seriously and threatening to damage seriously the United States, we have come to a pretty pass.

That's the reason I said, on the day I asked the Attorney General to go and seek this injunction, it was a rather sad day for the United States.

Q. Edward T. Folliard, Washington Post: Mr. President, you have promised Premier Khrushchev to go to Russia next spring. Would it be possible for you to carry out that commitment and also attend a summit—

that is, the big summit conference—in the spring?   I have another thought in mind, sir, as I understood your earlier statement, your position still is that a big East-West conference should be held earlier than next spring?

THE PRESIDENT. No I don't—this is what I said, Mr. Folliard: I think that a Western summit must precede any other.   And then I think that one of the purposes of the Western conference will be to thrash out just what we should do, as to timing and subjects and our approach, and the positions we take.   I want to be very careful, always, to avoid the appearance even of trying to dominate any of our allies.   These allies are important.   They are equal partners.   And so I cannot state things before you as decisions and "We are going to do that."   They are matters that we have to discuss and see whether we can agree.

Now whether or not I could make a trip that would comprise both, let us say 7 or 8 days of a summit conference, and then 6 or 7 days of going around Russia, this would be quite long, and would be a time, you know, during which the Congress is in session.

Now normally, Congress, even if they passed any bills, if there were no emergencies of any kind, domestic or otherwise, would hold up bills so as to avoid embarrassment.   But it would be quite a long time to stay away at one time.

Q. Mr. Folliard: To follow that up, is it conceivable, Mr. President, that a big East-West summit conference might be held in Russia about the time you went there?

THE PRESIDENT. Well, I don't know.   The only thing I know about it, every time we have looked for a new spot, we come back to the things of the hotel accommodations and the technical apparatus that is always needed for simultaneous translation and all that sort of thing.   So nearly always we go back to Geneva.   I would personally have no objection to going anywhere.   I have said this time and again so you people get tired of it.   I would go any time and anywhere.

Q. Felix Belair, New York Times: The Development Loan Fund in Washington has indicated that any future credits granted by it to recipient governments in underdeveloped areas should be expended on materials or equipment within the United States.   It has also indicated lately that this policy, if it is a policy, might be made to apply to other foreign aid agencies.   I wonder if that would not mark a rather noticeable departure from your past policy?

THE PRESIDENT. We have always tried to make loans and grants on a basis that was free and where the recipient country could go and shop around, except in the case of one agency; that is the Export-Import Bank, which by law is required to make its loans requiring materials and machinery and things of that kind that were under such study be bought here.

Now I don't believe for an instant that we can make this law apply to the Development Loan Fund and everything else exclusively. I have said and it has been, I think, stated by one or two of my associates, we are going to make it a little less free. This is not a turnaround, a reversal, or going in another direction. It is simply to point out that when we are making this money available, it's dollars that's being made available; and where it is feasible and reasonable, we want that money to be spent here. It's not the abrupt reversal that your question might imply.

Q. Carleton Kent, Chicago Sun-Times: Mr. President, could you discuss with us your reasons for seeming to prefer an earlier summit meeting rather than a later one, as the French apparently do?

THE PRESIDENT. I would say this: I think an early Western summit would be very desirable. If you take four countries like Britain, France, and Germany—they would be there part of the time at least—and ourselves, there are bound to be important subjects come up that are viewed differently by each country. This takes a very great deal of study and work, and finally agreement, at the very head of government level.

Now I would prefer always, as I have told you people often, to do these things by diplomatic means, and then finally get head of government agreement. But fashions have seemed to change a little bit.

Now where you do have a dictatorship, there is only one man can make the decision, and although he can delegate as he chooses, it seems to be not popular with dictators to delegate too much. Therefore, if you are going to make agreements that are useful, I mean general and important agreements, with the Soviets, you are almost compelled to do it with the head of government. This means the Western heads of government must be coordinated among themselves, otherwise it would just be a Donnybrook.

Now I have no strong feelings exactly when the second one should be done. I said I would go there and make my proposals at the Western summit and we would talk it out and see what we should do. But I wouldn't predict any particular moment for the meeting with the Soviets.

Q. Paul F. Healy, New York Daily News: Sir, either as President or a TV viewer, do you have any strong feelings on rigged quiz shows?

THE PRESIDENT. Well, I am one of those that never saw them. So my interest has grown only as I have seen the reports in the papers. I think if it was done, it's a terrible thing to do to the American public. But I have made inquiry right away, and so far as I can see, up to this moment, the executive branch of the Government has had no responsibility or even no place to do anything. I have asked the Attorney General and one or two others to look into it. So as I say, my interest didn't develop until after I found out that there was apparently something a little questionable about the whole matter.

Q. Mr. Healy: You don't see any need for Federal regulation of any kind?

THE PRESIDENT. I would say this: I see no power in the executive department. This would be censorship. This would be a political agent. Now you do have the FCC; I am not so sure what their field would be here, but it's one thing that I think the Attorney General is studying for me. But not for executive department action.

Q. William H. Y. Knighton, Jr., Baltimore Sun: Mr. President, how's your cold?

THE PRESIDENT. Well, actually, almost 3 years ago I contracted a bronchitis which finally seems to have developed and become chronic. And so every slight cold has sort of a multiplied effect on me; consequently, I seek the warm weather and sun. [*Laughter*] However, you can't always be lucky on weather, and I am taking that rather philosophically. But it's really become a chronic condition, and when I went to California, to have an acute cold and flu attack on top of it, the reason becomes rather troublesome. So I take every day I can to get in the sun.

Q. Lou Harris, Augusta Chronicle: Mr. President, the National Cotton Council has petitioned the Department of Agriculture to invoke section 22 under the Agricultural Adjustment Act, because of what it believes is the increasingly large amount of importations from foreign countries in the textile field. Of course 3 years ago this agreement was worked out with Japan.

Do you anticipate, sir, that there is going to be any effort to work out a similar agreement with Hong Kong, Formosa, India, Pakistan?

THE PRESIDENT. The only thing I can say about those things is this: you get these reports, and instantly they go into the hands of the technical experts. A great deal of struggle goes on as to what should be done, because whenever you help somebody, you always seem to be hurting someone else. But finally, after all the technical studies are made and go through different types of organizations, it is brought to me to study; and that is always a tough decision to make.

I would say this: the last thing I heard—I am talking now with both foreign and domestic experts in the field—they said that they thought the situation was improving rather than deteriorating.

Q. Marvin Arrowsmith, Associated Press: Mr. President, we just want to make sure we understood you. Did you speak of an acute cold and flu attack?

THE PRESIDENT. I said an acute cold when I went to California, and that on top of a chronic bronchitis I said is annoying. I did have an acute cold then.

Q. Mr. Arrowsmith: Didn't you say something about a flu attack, sir?

THE PRESIDENT. I called it flu. Whether the doctor did or not, I don't think I ever asked him. [*Laughter*] Any time I feel as badly as I did that time, I call it flu, that's all. [*Laughter*] But as I say, my difficulty is a chronic bronchitis, which didn't originate until after my operation. I don't think it has any connection, but then is when it started—in 1956.

Q. Felix Belair, Jr., New York Times: Mr. President, just to perhaps quiet speculation on the point, can you conceive of a Western summit meeting without France's participation?

THE PRESIDENT. Oh, I wouldn't think so, no. Anything else?

Q. Russell Jones, CBS News: Sir, Mr. Khrushchev is reported to have backed the Chinese in taking Quemoy by force if necessary. Do you think this fits in with his conversations with you in this country and his expressed desire for a summit meeting?

THE PRESIDENT. I think I reported this before, but I am not sure. When the subject of Red China was brought up between Mr. Khrushchev and me, there was no further discussion other than the statement of our two separate positions. And it was then agreed only one thing, which was there was no sense in pushing the discussion any further because our viewpoints were so far apart.

On the other hand, I notice that as quickly as he went out to China, he made one or two speeches in which he put forth the generalization that all international disputes should be solved by peaceful means, in negotiation.

Now I think that both China and Russia argue that the Formosa-Red China dispute is from their viewpoint an internal one and not international. But after all, I believe there are 42 or more nations—I forget how many, but a great number of nations—that recognize the independence of Formosa, so I think certainly the rest of the world would take it as a threat to international peace.

Q. Marvin L. Arrowsmith, Associated Press: Mr. President, may I ask another question?

THE PRESIDENT. Yes.

Q. Mr. Arrowsmith: In connection with your remarks on Taft-Hartley, do they indicate that you are thinking about asking for new legislation when Congress comes back?

THE PRESIDENT. Not at this moment, for this simple reason. I am still hopeful that these people, both sides, will awaken to their obligations to the United States. I really believe, like I do in one or two other subjects, that punitive law, or law requiring compulsion against peoples' respected rights, is going to worsen the situation rather than better it.

Now, on the other hand, if people will not exercise the self-discipline that the whole concept of free government implies, then indeed this is going to be a time when we all have to study and see just exactly what may be done. Because we cannot allow the country itself to be damaged unconscionably.

Q. Robert H. Fleming, American Broadcasting Company: Have you heard anything from the Chinese Communists about the American fliers?

THE PRESIDENT. Nothing recent—nothing recent. It's one of those matters that is kept always on the agenda, and you make inquiry whenever you can; but we have heard nothing.

Q. Charles Roberts, Newsweek: If I may ask another question, I would like to return to the space situation. Do you plan to ask for more money in your next budget for space exploration?

THE PRESIDENT. Well, I have forgotten—was it 590 last year?

Q. Mr. Roberts: I couldn't tell you, sir.

THE PRESIDENT. Well—listen, why aren't you informed a little bit? [*Laughter*] As I recall, it became 590; I think they cut out about 68 million, and then put a little back, the way I recall. We will ask for something more than that, I am sure.

Q. Marvin L. Arrowsmith, Associated Press: Something more than——

THE PRESIDENT. Something more than we had last year.

Mr. Arrowsmith: Thank you, Mr. President.

NOTE: President Eisenhower's one hundred and seventy-third news conference was held in the Georgian Room of the Richmond Hotel, Augusta, Ga., at 10 o'clock on Thursday morning, October 22, 1959. The attendance was not recorded.

268 ¶ Statement by the President on the Effect of the Steel Strike on National Welfare and Safety. *October* 22, 1959

OBVIOUSLY, the steel strike threatens to "imperil the national health or safety."

We have had a 97-day shutdown in steel—the longest steel strike in this generation.

Steel is a national industry; it stretches from coast to coast. Its products move in interstate commerce. It employs over 600,000 people.

Steel is at the very base of any industrial economy. Especially it is basic to growth industries.

It is essential for repairs and maintenance.

It is essential for defense production.

Supplies are now below normal (10 million tons), and are nearing the exhaustion point. Some kinds of steel already are exhausted.

Even when the mills reopen, several weeks will be required to produce some kinds of steel, like special steel alloys for missiles, and steel sheets for automobiles. If iron ore shipments do not begin at once, there will not be enough iron ore at steel plants to maintain full operations next spring before lake shipments can begin again.

We must look to the future.

The national good requires that our space activities, our missile programs, and all our other defense programs go ahead without delay. They are now being delayed—and will be further delayed by this strike.

The National Aeronautics and Space Administration has informed me that shortages of steel are delaying the construction of test facilities and bases for this program, as well as the completion of parts for the space vehicles.

The Secretary of Defense reports delays in construction of bases or facilities for the Atlas, Titan, and Polaris missiles, and of the missiles themselves, because of the lack of special sizes and types of steel which are not made in mills that are now open.

Shortages of steel are causing widespread shutdowns and layoffs in other industries.

Over 57,000 employees were laid off just in the second week in October. That is over five times as many as were laid off three weeks ago. The total number of people idled by October 14 was 780,000, including the striking Steelworkers. Each week the situation is worse.

By the end of November, the Secretary of Labor estimates that a total of 1,775,000 employees (including the 500,000 strikers) would be idled.

By the end of December, it would be 3,000,000 if this dispute were permitted to continue. That means that some 9,000,000 citizens would be affected, including the men and their families.

The hardship which this strike has caused—and could cause—is tremendous. The National welfare is certainly affected when so many people are laid off and so much of an industry is stopped.

NOTE: This statement was released at Augusta, Ga.

269 ¶ Toasts of the President and President Toure of the Republic of Guinea. *October* 26, 1959

Mr. President, Madame Toure, Ladies and Gentlemen:

It is a distinct honor to welcome here this evening the new President of the newest independent nation in the world. I welcome not only President Toure of the Republic of Guinea, but his charming wife and the members of the party which have accompanied him to this country.

We are especially pleased that he should have chosen the United States to be the country that he should visit on his first official journey outside his own country, and amidst the preoccupations that are naturally his in the effort of leading a new country, establishing new customs, new procedures in government that are so important to his people.

I assure you, Mr. President, that the American people not only watch this new venture with great interest, but they extend to you and your people their very best wishes for a life in freedom, in justice, and in peace.

We want to be, with you, friends—we hope good friends, and we feel certain that this visit of yours cannot but help to inspire the peoples of both our countries to establish and maintain that kind of relationship.

So, ladies and gentlemen, it is a special honor for me this evening to ask you to rise to drink a Toast to President Toure, the President of Guinea.

NOTE: The President proposed this toast at a state dinner at the White House. President Toure's response (as translated) follows:

Mr. President, Mrs. Eisenhower, Ladies and Gentlemen:

In the name of the people of Guinea, I would like to express here the joy which all the members of our delegation have felt from the very moment they set foot upon the soil of the United States. There is no doubt in our minds that the friendly and brotherly invitation extended to us by the Government of the United States expresses in a very clear way the warm, friendly, sympathetic relationship which must exist between the United States and the peoples of black Africa.

No one can claim for himself the right to speak for all of Africa. But each man has the right, and the pride, to be able to attempt to express the hopes and the aspirations of the peoples of Africa. And the only ambition which fills us is that of making understood the aspirations and the hopes of Africa.

History is what it is—it includes the past, the present, and the future. There is an African proverb which says that the world rests on three pillars: in the present there is the past; in the future there is the present and the past. The past of Africa is heavy, but we hope that the future of Africa will be light indeed.

Our hope for freedom, for brotherhood, and for peace is a deeply felt aspiration, and a unanimous one. And we hope that all those who wish to build the world of tomorrow will look at what is happening and what will happen in the future, and forget those things in the past

which have divided the world.

As I told my brothers, who were here in this country and whom I met today, if one had to look back three centuries ago, no one at that time could have dreamed of the part that would be played today in the history of the world by the United States. In these three centuries, many States united and worked together to develop, on a gigantic scale, progress in the economic, political, and social sense.

These results which have been achieved are due to the faith which those Founding Fathers had in the future of their country. And the faith which we have in the present difficulties through which we are passing, we feel will build the future of the world.

And when we come here, we come not as the messengers of the sufferings of our people, but rather as the messengers of the future hopes of our people. Our present difficulties do exist. They are realities which we must face, but we feel that our courage will enable us to overcome them. And we are confident of the relations that will exist between our countries. We know that we came here in the first place to express our thanks for the kind invitation of the United States Government inviting us here; to express our confidence that the future will be built on the strong and close relationships which will exist between our peoples.

It is true that geographically and population-wise the Republic of Guinea is a small country, but that country would like to play a part in the relationships between nations in those things which bring nations together and bring about a collaboration of peoples and of races. In that field we would like to make an earnest. sincere, and dynamic contribution.

There are those who do not see the future of Africa the way we in Guinea see it, and they may believe that the policy of Guinea is a different one from that which is publicly expressed every day by those who are in charge—who lead the people of Guinea. If there is one small country in the world around whom more legends have been created than any other since 1958, we can say that that country is Guinea. But we thank God that we have acceded to full sovereignty over our own people under worthy conditions. And the pride and consciousness we feel of the part we must play does not allow us to have an attitude of disloyalty toward any party. because the ambition which fills us is to rehabilitate and rekindle the civilization of Africa. And these civilizations of Africa are in nowise in conflict or in contradiction to the civilizations and cultures of other countries, but will come as a valuable contribution and join with the contributions made by other peoples, so that the whole world may profit thereby.

We, as far as we are concerned, have faith in the equality of men. But the reality which we face has created a situation in which there is inequality in the means available to men. It is not an equality with other countries or an equality between the black man and the white man which God has ordained that we particularly seek. It is, rather, the equality in the technical and scientific fields— in the field of progress. Because it is only in these three fields that Africa lags behind the other civilizations of the world.

We are convinced that the Government of the United States will know how to assist Africa. And we know we are filled with confidence that Africa, which is an under-developed area, cooperating and collaborating with the United States, a highly-developed area, will be able to find the means to insure its own development in the social, political, and economic fields.

We are convinced that the rest of the century in which we live will see an Africa completely emancipated.

We are convinced that in a spirit of working together, in a spirit of collaboration, Africa will be able to find all the wealth of her soil and her subsoil, and not merely to locate this wealth but also to use it in such a way as to bring about a development and raising of the standards of living of all her peoples.

We ask you, therefore, not to judge us or think of us in terms of what we were— or even of what we are—but rather to think of us in the terms of history and what we will be tomorrow.

We ask, and we hope, that the friendship established between our peoples will grow ever stronger and ever closer. We ask that the United States, and particularly the Government of the United States, which bears such a heavy responsibility in the world, will continue its policy of direct cooperation with the peoples of Africa. And you may be sure that America's future and the African future will be preserved and safeguarded by this cooperation.

We would also like, in the name of all those whom we can legitimately claim to represent, to extend our warmest thanks and congratulations to the President of the United States, to his charming wife, and to all those who work with him, not only on behalf of the United States, but on behalf of all the peoples of the world.

We would like to speak here tonight with the young voice of Africa, which is not yet fully understood. This voice with which we speak has no place in it for any hatred against any people anywhere. I would like to speak with a message of brotherhood, a message of cooperation, and a message of solidarity— not because Africa stands to gain anything from this cooperation—but because the delay and the lag of Africa is something that is felt throughout the world in the international field. And similarly we are convinced that the progress of Africa will likewise have repercussions on the international scene.

America has always been known as the land of freedom. And there is no African who does not, every day, give thought to one of the great statements made by one of your great Presidents, Abraham Lincoln; that is, the greatness of men and people is created in the love of men and people.

We hope that the friendship between Africa and America will grow, and that it will aid mankind to find a happier future than we have known in the past.

And in thanking the Government and the people of the United States, I would ask you to join me in raising our glasses to the health and prosperity of the President of the United States, and his charming wife, and of the American people.

270 ¶ Remarks at the 55th Annual Meeting of the National Association of Postmasters. *October* 27, 1959

President Baker, Postmaster General, Ladies and Gentlemen:

It is always a privilege and an honor to meet with any group of Americans that are dedicated to service. You people are representatives of the great Postal Service which has meant so much to the United States.

Of course, I am not now going to recite anything of the history of your Service. You know it better than I do, unquestionably.

But I am struck by a few facts that stick in my memory. I think it's next spring that will mark the centennial of the inauguration of the Pony Express. On the inauguration of President Lincoln was the first time that Pony Express made the great record of 7 days and 17 hours to carry the message about the inauguration from St. Joseph, Missouri, to Sacramento, California. Never was that record broken until the building of the railroad and the construction of the telegraph lines across the continent.

I think if we contemplate for a moment the achievements of America over that hundred years, we can do it by talking about the achievements of the Postal Service in that same time.

I know that now in a matter of 5 hours and a half the mail can be taken all the way from New York to San Francisco. The Pony Express man waiting at St. Joseph got his message over the wires from Washington. Then when he reached Sacramento he put the mail on a river boat, and it went all the way to San Francisco. Now almost in a moment we have our telegraphic messages across the continent. But the actual letter that I put in this mail today can within a matter of just hours be delivered across the continent.

745

And, of course, there are projects in prospect—I hear the Postmaster General talking about them often—for getting letters into your hands in a matter almost of moments.

But still it is not just in this matter of speed of transmission that I think is the great service of the postmasters of this country—and I understand there are something of 33 to 34 thousand of them—it is not just in the matter of speed that this great service has shown its value to the United States and to the world. These post offices, particularly in the smaller towns, are centers of information. They are places where people get some understanding of the news as well as just the actual news itself.

But more than that, as members of—I believe it's called—the Universal Postal Union, the Association of Postmasters in the United States is helping to do something for the world that is extraordinary. Ninety-seven countries belong to that Union. It was founded in 1874, I believe.

Through this service of the Universal Postal Union, the delivery of a letter from Dickinson County, Kansas, for example, to some small village in Rhodesia, or in Egypt, or in the Philippines, is accomplished smoothly and quickly. Ninety-seven nations belonging to that one single service, dedicated to cooperation in helping humans—helping humans to send and receive messages of importance to them, to their families, and sometimes to their whole communities. There is only one other international organization that has as many members as yours has. In that accomplishment, in this record of a continuous improvement of accomplishment, is a lesson for the world that to my mind should be expanded in almost everything we do.

If the world needs anything, more than anything else it is better understanding of each other, a better readiness to deal with each other on a cooperative basis. Not merely to try to defeat somebody else in the accomplishment of any kind—to be the first with this or the first with that. Not merely to have greater armaments and a greater destructive power than another. Rather, instead, we should learn of humans and their aspirations and their hopes, their dedications to their communities and to nations to which they belong. We should be trying to make information available in every possible line of human activity.

In doing so, we will eliminate eventually the need for armaments. We will have to give less thought about our own security and our safety, and about the standing of our friends in the world community.

746

So, as you—each of you—takes the responsibility when you take your oath of office to help make certain that a piece of United States mail is sacred almost in its character, shielded from the knowledge of anybody else except the recipient, you make sure that America is tied more closely together. In the same way, we must make sure that the world itself is tied together more closely.

So, as you do this—do this service for the citizens of the United States— you are in a very definite sense doing it for the world; for the cause of a just peace, for the cause of greater mental ease, the lessening of tensions. In performing that kind of service, it seems to me you—all the people that you represent, people that are part of the Postal organization and other Postal organizations—are doing a tremendous thing for the world.

I submit again the great need for the world is that kind of understanding that comes about through the free exchange of information, from the very heart of Siberia to the heart of America, to the heart of Africa, and to all other places and locations in the world.

I congratulate you. I wish you an enjoyable as well as an interesting conference. I assure you of the pleasure that the Government and I personally have in welcoming you here to the Capital City of your own country.

Thank you very much.

NOTE: The President spoke at Constitution Hall. His opening words referred to Edward L. Baker, President of the National Association of Postmasters of the United States, and Postmaster General Summerfield.

271 ¶ The President's News Conference of
October 28, 1959.

THE PRESIDENT. This morning I have no announcements of my own.

Q. Marvin L. Arrowsmith, Associated Press: Mr. President, you have stated that you are ready to go to a Western summit conference at any time. Is there anything new on that? Has there been any progress towards setting up such a meeting?

THE PRESIDENT. Well, yes. As I have said a number of times, I have been holding myself available to go at any time, at any place most convenient to the Western people—I am talking about a Western summit at this time. General de Gaulle has explained some of his difficulties in scheduling and so on, but he will be ready sometime around mid-December to have a Western conference.[1]

Q. Edward P. Morgan, American Broadcasting Company: On a number of occasions, sir, you have spoken out emphatically in favor of increased world trade, even at some sacrifice. Nevertheless, the Development Loan Fund is now evolving a "buy American" policy and you yourself just the other day moved to increase rather substantially the tariff on some Japanese metal goods.

Could you discuss this problem, the seeming inconsistencies, and how they may be reconciled?

THE PRESIDENT. Well, I don't think there is any real inconsistency. You must remember this: with respect to goods from the United States, from what is called the dollar area, there are still a great number of restrictions, special restrictions, that are placed upon trade. I think that the entire Government, executive branch and obviously the Congress also, believes that in a freer trade is a better solution to many of the world's problems, and particularly the hope of raising living standards for the less developed people.

Now, at the same time, we are putting out on loans, grants, and other means to our friends, money that is used not only for purposes of trade but to make them secure, to make them more secure and to make the free world more secure against possible aggression.

What we say is that we are examining all of these procedures that we use in extending credit to the world to see whether or not we shouldn't have some arrangements whereby our own trade, our own exports are increased.

Now, as I explained the other day in Augusta, there is no countermarching of policy in the United States Government. We are looking at what we are doing all across the board and are making sure that we are doing something that is reasonable and proper, at the same time using every means like GATT and the rest of the agencies involved in foreign trade, to increase the volume of trade.

Q. Merriman Smith, United Press International: Could we follow up, please, sir, on your reply to Mr. Arrowsmith.

[1] On November 1 the White House announced that, at the suggestion of President de Gaulle, a 4-power Western summit meeting would be held in Paris beginning December 19 for the purpose of making a preliminary examination of questions for discussion later with the Chairman of the Council of Ministers of the Soviet Union.

One, are we to assume then, sir, that there will be a Western summit meeting in Paris in mid-December, with Mr. Macmillan and Chancellor Adenauer?

THE PRESIDENT. Everybody, just exactly like I have done, has expressed his readiness to go to a Western summit; the question of timing and the preparation for it, of course, is something else.

Now, when we speak of a Western summit and we speak of Mr. Adenauer, he, of course, would be there for the discussion of any question affecting Germany.

Q. Pat Munroe, Chicago American: Mr. President, in criticizing communism, you recently said that a systematized order is a step backward. Looking at the Soviet Union's economy and their hopes to improve it, is it your feeling that they will have to adopt some form of free enterprise or perhaps more incentive in the system, in order to become more nearly like our own?

THE PRESIDENT. Well, I will tell you of a little incident at Camp David.

We were talking about some of the changes, not necessarily in the Marxist doctrine, but some of the changes that the Soviets had adopted in operating their economy. We were talking also about some of the things that happened in our economy that were certainly a long ways from what we used to call laissez faire, and Mr. Khrushchev happened to make the point that actually they are using the incentive system to increase production far more than we are. He pointed out—and he is well read, I must tell you, about some of the things that happened here— he pointed out about our taxes, tax system, and so on. He said, "We give our incentives in things the people can feel and see and use; we give a better house, more rooms, another bath." He went on to tell the things that they do when a man has shown an increased productivity. "In many ways," he said, "you people stifle it; at least ours is more effective," or words to that effect.

Q. Chalmers M. Roberts, Washington Post: Related to this trade and dollar loss problem, does the re-examination that you mentioned earlier cover the largest single expenditure abroad, that is, our military expenditure? Is there any thought of cutting either troops or bases or expenses of that kind by some manner?

THE PRESIDENT. I think that it would be difficult to discuss this question, except on the basis of no word of it ever going outside this room.

[*Laughter*] Since that would be a rather difficult promise to exact and to implement, I would think we should not say too much about it, for this reason: every soldier, every base has been sent abroad by some agreements where people have a right to believe that there might be some different attitude expressed in American policy you might say, solely by confining a discussion just to the matter of troops abroad.   So I'd prefer not to talk about that.

Q. Frank van der Linden, Nashville Banner: Sir, former Governor Battle of Virginia recently left the Civil Rights Commission, and there are reports that you are seeking a similar Southern conservative to fill that place.   I would like to ask if that is the type of man you are looking for, and if it's true that you are considering former Governor Darden of Virginia and former Congressman Richards of South Carolina?

THE PRESIDENT. As you know, in the formation of the initial Commission, I studied a long time and searched and talked with a lot of people; many people frankly don't want to undertake a job that would normally bring about a great deal of criticism, and they just prefer to be out of it.

Now, I have no particular name yet.   I think Governor Battle feels that he has done his stint of public service in this area, and that is the reason he preferred to resign.   But I haven't got any new individual in mind at the moment.   When one is picked, why, it will be announced.

Q. Mrs. May Craig, Portland (Maine) Press Herald: Mr. President, are you pretty sore about reports that the Russians bugged our embassy in Moscow when the Vice President was there, and are you going to warn Mr. Khrushchev not to do that before you get there in the spring?

THE PRESIDENT. I didn't hear, I didn't understand the first part of your question.

Q. Mrs. Craig: The report is, at the return of our ousted Intelligence man from Moscow the report is that our embassy in Moscow was bugged in chandeliers and various other ways for Mr. Nixon's visit there. And I want to know if that annoys you and will you warn Mr. Khrushchev not to do that to you before you get there?

THE PRESIDENT [*laughing*]. Well, I will tell you, in 1945 when I was in Russia, I was told that if I had any really private conversation that we should hold it out in the yard—some place where we were away. So I suppose these reports that this man gives are the kind that has come over a long time. I think I can be discreet enough.

Q. Edward T. Folliard, Washington Post: Mr. President, do you want to comment on the behavior of Fidel Castro? What do you suppose, sir, is eating him?

THE PRESIDENT. Actually, I went over very carefully with the Secretary of State the statement that he made about the charges that have been made by Mr. Castro and our reply to it. I think that is about as full an answer as I can make at this time. I have no idea of discussing possible motivation of a man, what he is really doing, and certainly I am not qualified to go into such abstruse and difficult subjects as that.

I do feel this: here is a country that you would believe, on the basis of our history, would be one of our real friends. The whole history—first of our intervention in 1898, our making and helping set up Cuban independence, the second time we had to go in and did the same thing to make sure that they were on a sound basis, the trade concessions we have made and the very close relationships that have existed most of the time with them—would seem to make it a puzzling matter to figure out just exactly why the Cubans and the Cuban Government would be so unhappy when, after all, their principal market is right here, their best market. You would think they would want good relationships. I don't know exactly what the difficulty is.

Q. Laurence H. Burd, Chicago Tribune: Mr. President, at Camp David, what was your reply to Mr. Khrushchev when he told you that he thought their system was working better than ours?

THE PRESIDENT. Well, Mr. Burd, you can't answer those things categorically for this reason: there are very few places where the Soviets see anything superior in our system or in our accomplishments. Usually they say, "Well, maybe our bucket is not quite as full as yours now with respect to industrial development, but soon it will be just as full and soon ours will be running over." That's the kind of thing that goes on all the time, so the best answer is a smile, I think, for most of it.

Q. Felix Belair, New York Times: Sir, do you have anything you can tell us in reply or reaction to criticism that you should have appointed a factfinding board in the steel strike earlier than was done?

THE PRESIDENT. No, Mr. Belair, I haven't; and I will tell you why.

Every day, not merely after the strike began but every day from the time that we knew that there were developing rather hardened positions on both sides, I have had in my office or in other places people to advise me on this matter as to what would be the best way that might be useful in bringing about a conciliatory attitude.

My own concern, and the only concern that the Government has in this thing, is the public. I have tried to point out from the beginning that merely selfish interests of either the steel companies or the steel unions are not to be compared with the whole advantage, the whole benefits that come to America when we have full employment and full production. Now, if you try to move into this thing with the Government too seriously, to my mind, one side or the other thinks you are doing something they want; and I think of no better thing that Government can do than to abstain from any such action. So, until the matter became of the kind that seemed too serious to stand further, then is when I asked for the Attorney General to go and ask for an injunction.

Q. Lloyd M. Schwartz, Fairchild Publications: Mr. President, in that connection are you encouraged by the settlement that Kaiser has reached with the unions, and do you consider it an appropriate basis for a complete settlement of the strike?

THE PRESIDENT. Well, I am not going to say that I consider it a completely satisfactory basis for the settlement of the strike. I will say this: it is of course encouraging to know that steel production is, by this much, increased. I believe that, as far as the steel industry, Kaiser produces about 2 percent; in the aluminum area, I think they are almost 30 percent; so their agreement doesn't have a very vital effect upon the position of the country so far as production. But I do say that I think this should be a signal for both labor and management to find a basis in which we can get back into full production. To my mind the country not only needs it, but I think the country is more and more demanding it and I believe that these two sides should be ready to make the conciliatory moves that will make it possible.

Q. Ray L. Scherer, NBC News: Chancellor Adenauer intimated Sunday that he would be much happier if the summit would concentrate on disarmament and perhaps not take up the question of Germany at all. Do you think it's possible to have either a Western summit or a summit and not get definitively into the question of Germany?

THE PRESIDENT. Well, I'll tell you: first of all, I don't believe that it is possible to determine in advance exactly what the agenda is going to be. I agree with Mr. Adenauer, with Mr. Khrushchev, with General de Gaulle—and I think that I specifically brought this matter up, or the importance of this matter, with Mr. Macmillan—I agree that some kind of step toward disarmament would be almost the greatest thing that could now be achieved in the whole effort to ease the tensions and to bring about a better approach toward a just peace.

We are firm on one thing, any agreement for disarmament must include its own self-guaranteeing procedures, normally called inspection or controlled disarmament. With that one *sine qua non,* there is nothing that could more please me, and I am sure all of the United States, than some significant step toward disarmament. Now, I don't see how the subject can be discussed seriously without some mention being made of Germany.

Q. Robert C. Pierpoint, CBS News: Mr. President, to go back to this Castro problem, one of the things that seems to be bothering the Premier is the illegal flights of mysterious planes over Cuba, presumably from Florida, and apparently our FBI has confirmed that some of these flights are coming from Florida.

I wonder if you can tell us whether you have ordered any of our Federal agencies, for instance the U.S. Air Force, to try to put a stop to some of these flights?

THE PRESIDENT. I've gone through the civil angle rather than the military angle. The Attorney General doesn't just have orders, but he is really using every kind of reinforced means he can to make sure that there is no violation of this kind.

Now, this is not an easy task. There are more than 200 airfields in Florida, and most of them are crowded with private planes. And then you have to find what any individual is intending to do that may be illegal. This is not one of the easy problems to solve. But we are using every single facility that is available to the Federal Government, and we are getting, by the way, the cooperation of the State of Florida, too, so that we don't unnecessarily annoy our neighbors.

Q. Robert H. Fleming, American Broadcasting Company: Mr. President, with your estimate of the importance of a disarmament start, is there a chance of your travel calendar having an additional visit to Geneva if there is an agreement there on disarmament?

THE PRESIDENT. Well, I will tell you this: any engagement or any other kind of commitment I could have made would always be broken to go anywhere to make certain of the accomplishment of a single significant step in this whole field.

Q. Sarah McClendon, El Paso Times: Sir, in your State of the Union Message on January the 9th, you mentioned the need for national goals, and you described these as largely goals that might bring about better living, better education, and more teachers. I wonder if now after Khrushchev's statements on competition and the possibility that he might pass us, if we would need national economy goals?

THE PRESIDENT. Well, I didn't make any limits at all. As a matter of fact I think one of our goals is exactly what we want to be, let's say, in 1969—where we want to be with relation to the rest of the world. These goals ought to be international. As a matter of fact all of these goals are bound to be intertwined and interdependent. I don't see how you can have a prosperous economy without a proper relationship to other countries, and I don't think you can have strong relationships with your friends in defense against possible aggression except by having a strong economy here.

There is reciprocal action between all of these subjects, and there is nothing in my proposal that is self-limiting.

Q. Richard L. Wilson, Cowles Publications: Mr. President, the Russians claim that they are reducing the proportion of their government expenditures devoted to defense, the percentage devoted to defense. What is the outlook on the budget for the United States? Is there any possibility of reducing defense expenditures and increasing expenditures in other fields? What is the general outlook?

THE PRESIDENT. I would think that no significant reductions could be made this year.

Now, there is another subject Mr. Khrushchev and I talked about at considerable length. I think that there is no doubt that he has come to realize, as we have, that if we have to put into these, you might say unproductive armaments such sums as we now do—but I think it is necessary, I must interject that subject—then we are by that much barred from doing many of the things both at home and abroad that would bring about better living both for ourselves and for others; because if we produce it for others, then we produce it for ourselves again.

So, you may recall that about April 16, 1953, I was not only concerned about this matter, but I made a very earnest effort before the National Society of Editors, as I recall, pointing out the need for beginning to reduce military budgets, military armaments, and to use part of that money to produce a better world than we now have.

Q. James B. Reston, New York Times: Mr. President, is there a danger that if we tie our loans, that other countries like Germany and Japan will also tie their loans to purchases in their countries?

THE PRESIDENT. What I am saying is: each of these things is handled on a case by case method. So far as I know, there has been no suggestion yet that a policy be made that we will not make a loan unless x amount of it or all of it is used in purchases in our own country. The only place that applies is the Ex-Im Bank which was actually established in order to stimulate that kind of export business. But, it seems to us that we are merely, let's say, increasing the gold reserves of somebody else while we have to make good the resulting balance of deficit in our own receipts from abroad, and we want to take a look at it.

Now, you must remember, we have been very, very free about this, we have never had a restriction of any kind. But at that time, all the economies of Europe were in bad shape. There has been a great renaissance in their activity and in their prosperity. They are getting in position, as we see it, to help in this business of helping underdeveloped countries that we have been carrying so much by ourselves. Doing that, we can also take a look at our whole system of extending credit to see whether we can't, without damaging anybody else, require that certain of these amounts be used to buy our products.

Q. Mr. Reston: Would it be right to infer from that that this Government feels that they could do more than they have been doing in terms of defense aid and aid to the developing countries?

THE PRESIDENT. I don't know whether we have stated that as a conclusion. The very fact that I have asked them to study it, and I know that each of them is studying it, shows our concern, that we are not to be looked on just as an Atlas trying to carry the whole world, that this is a job for all of us. And those with increasingly efficient economies, we think, ought to be just as concerned about this matter as we are.

Q. John Scali, Associated Press: To follow up some earlier questions, sir, does the fact that you, General de Gaulle, and Prime Minister Macmillan stand ready to meet in mid-December with Chancellor Adenauer mean that such a conference definitely will be held in mid-December, and could you tell us where, whether the site will be Paris?

THE PRESIDENT. Oh, no, no. I can't say that, because there has merely been an expression of readiness, you might say, on everybody's part.

For myself, I haven't concealed my belief that we should have the Western conference possibly somewhat earlier. But we do have this: with the expressed readiness of everybody now to do something of this kind, I think our diplomatic processes can go to work and do a lot of the preliminary work toward preparing positions, and position papers, and then developing agreements that will tend to solidify the Western position. And I think that we don't have to remind ourselves that if we would ever visualize an East-West summit without the Western position in a good, strong coordinated position, this would be very bad, indeed.

Q. Charles E. Shutt, Telenews: Sir, has your recent diplomatic mail given any indication that the Red Chinese may be in a frame of mind to release our American prisoners that they are now holding?

THE PRESIDENT. No. I have seen nothing of that. As you know, I brought the matter up again, but I have heard nothing of it.

Q. Frank Bourgholtzer, NBC News: Mr. President, shortly after the Camp David meeting it was the impression that any East-West summit conference would deal principally with the subject of Berlin. You have indicated this morning that the question of Germany might come up only incidentally to a discussion of disarmament. Is this a change in our position?

THE PRESIDENT. You people apparently want to be right in the middle of this forthcoming summit meeting. [*Laughter*]

And I think you are being a little bit unreasonable.

Now, there are many ways in which we need progress.

What was achieved at Camp David was this: a statement that I made, later corroborated by the Chairman of the Council of Ministers of the Soviets, that any negotiations about Berlin would be not unnecessarily or needlessly, some such adverb, prolonged, but that there would be no time limit fixed upon it.

Now, the Berlin question was not discussed there except in that context. There was no attempt here for us to lay out a formula, or the other side to lay out a formula where the Berlin or German questions would be solved.

This matter we now can negotiate without the feeling on all the free world that there is not—without an axe hanging over our heads, that's all.

Q. Mr. Bourgholtzer: My question, sir, was whether this would be taken up at an East-West summit conference that would be forthcoming.

THE PRESIDENT. Oh! Sorry. Well I am almost sure you couldn't possibly in the East-West—now you are talking about the West conference?

Q. Mr. Bourgholtzer: No, the East-West that would follow the Western summit conference.

THE PRESIDENT. Well, I don't know what subjects are going to be brought up there, that's one of the reasons for having the Western conference.

Q. Mr. Bourgholtzer: Do you——

THE PRESIDENT. That's all.

Q. E. W. Kenworthy, New York Times: Sir, to return to Mrs. McClendon's question, there have been reports that——

THE PRESIDENT. Now wait a minute, what was it?

Q. Mr. Kenworthy: This is on the goals, on the national goals——

THE PRESIDENT. Oh, yes, yes.

Q. Mr. Kenworthy: ——in your State of the Union Message last January.

There have been reports that a chairman has been found for this committee, and that the committee will shortly start to work. Can you discuss that?

THE PRESIDENT. I have selected the principal members and I think there are one or two more that would probably be selected, with the advice and help of those others. But, they do not want to organize formally until after we are certain that this whole matter is understood, and that it is properly financed from the beginning by private sources.

We are particularly concerned right now in laying this whole matter out so that everybody will understand it. What we are really talking about, when you come down to it, is a coordination of an American policy for the future, international and domestic, because that is what goals mean—or put it this way: if you are concerned with that kind of a problem, then you must state within that whole broad area the goals the United States is trying to achieve.

Now that is really what I am talking about, and it is going to be a very difficult, it is going to take the very best brains that we have, and it must be adequately financed.

Marvin L. Arrowsmith, Associated Press: Thank you, Mr. President.

NOTE: President Eisenhower's one hundred and seventy-fourth news conference was held in the Executive Office Building from 10:30 to 11:04 o'clock on Wednesday morning, October 28, 1959. In attendance: 228.

272 ¶ Joint Statement Following Discussions With the President of Guinea.   *October* 28, 1959

UPON the conclusion of the visit to Washington of His Excellency Sekou Toure, President of the Republic of Guinea, the Governments of Guinea and the United States wish to set forth the following results of the conversations that took place between President Toure and his party, and President Eisenhower, Secretary Herter, and other officials of the United States Government:

1. The conversations took place in an atmosphere of cordial frankness and mutual understanding. President Toure expressed the hopes of the peoples of Africa for self-determination, economic and social development. Representatives of the United States indicated their understanding of these hopes and their desire to be of assistance wherever appropriate.

2. A Cultural Agreement between the two countries was agreed upon during the course of the conversations and was signed at 9:45 A.M., October 28th. It is the sincere hope of both Governments that this agreement will serve to increase understanding of each country and people by the other and form the nucleus of a lasting friendship.

3. The Government of the United States has decided, after the signature of a Technical Assistance Agreement, now under study, to put at the disposition of the Government of Guinea 150 scholarships for the training of Guinean students in the United States or elsewhere.

4. The facilities of the Export-Import Bank and the Development Loan Fund for specific development projects were called to the attention of the Government of Guinea.

5. The two Governments agreed to study the desirability of negotiating in the immediate future a commercial agreement as well as an investment guaranty agreement. As an initial step in developing closer commercial relations the Government of Guinea has agreed to receive a United States trade mission in the near future.

6. Representatives of the two Governments exchanged views on the growing importance of the African continent in the world of today. They

were in agreement that Africa's requirements and hopes should command the serious attention of the rest of the world, particularly the great powers.

NOTE: The text of the Cultural Agreement is published in the Department of State Bulletin (vol. 41, p. 722).

273 ⁋ Statement by the President on Receipt of the Fourth Annual Report on the Rural Development Program. *October* 29, 1959

I HAVE RECEIVED and reviewed the fourth annual report on the Rural Development program from the Department of Agriculture. The report again indicates progress in aid to small and low-income farm families and other rural people.

The report shows for the year:

Hundreds of projects to improve farms and farming;

New marketing facilities constructed and more profitable market outlets established;

Forests improved;

Wood finishing and processing industries expanded;

Thousands of new jobs due to industry growth; and

More income from a variety of other activities.

Activities are spreading beyond the initial pilot or demonstration areas. The program now includes thirty states and Puerto Rico.

This is essentially a peoples program. State and local people agree upon objectives and then move forward together. The programs are managed by state and local area committees—not from Washington. This is as it should be.

Particularly impressive are the initiative, leadership and hard work of various groups—farm, business, industry, civic, school, church, service clubs and others.

Existing state and Federal departments and agencies, with their existing authorities and responsibilities, lend their counsel and support. No new agency is required.

To expedite progress, I issued on October twelfth Executive Order No. 10847 officially establishing the Committee for Rural Development Program, which has been functioning from the start. The Order calls upon the various Federal departments and agencies to make the fullest possible contributions to area development programs and related activities.

The program is hitting at areas of greatest need. As the report states, eighty percent of farm families in typical rural development counties have yearly farm sales valued at $2,500 or less. Most farms in these communities gain little, if any, benefit from governmental farm price support activities.

Major emphasis has been placed on the future of rural youth through vocational training, new education courses, stay-in-school and education beyond the high school.

This program is successfully attacking the age-old and chronic problem of low incomes in widespread rural areas where there are fine farm families on small farms and poor soils. Rural families of such areas— non-farm and farm alike—need, and we are determined must have, more adequate incomes and greater opportunities.

NOTE: The 25-page report was made available in pamphlet form by the Department of Agriculture.

274   ¶ Remarks at the Economic Conference Breakfast.   *November* 2, 1959

Mr. Chairman, Mr. Palmer, and Ladies and Gentlemen:

I am afraid that your Chairman has promised more than I can deliver. I cannot talk by any manner of means on all of the influences, all of the pressures, that bring about inflation and just exactly what we should do about it. The matter becomes more difficult the more one studies it, because of its complexity and because of the intertwined pressures and influences that give it direction and intensity.

If I am allowed a few moments this morning, I would start off with the very simple proposition: this being a free Government, it is public opinion that runs Government and ourselves.

While I am certain I will repeat myself to a number of you, I want to use one definition of free government that has always meant a very great deal to me. It is a simple one. It is this: liberty is nothing but the opportunity for self-discipline.

Since there are many factors that are common to an economy and if they are not operated and devised correctly will ruin us, then public opinion must do it, which means self-discipline must do it. Otherwise, you will have control by Government and imposed discipline. In the long run, no matter how you cut it, imposed discipline is dictatorship.

Consequently, our problem is how to marshal public opinion. And the next thing we have to consider is this: what are the salient facts?

Some people come along and say "Well, this is too high." Or somebody demands too much here, or somebody else has pushed prices, or the Government's going in debt. Each one of these things is suddenly, in the mind of this particular person, the *"bête noir,"* the "evil genius" in the whole business.

But it is not. There are many things.

For the Government's part—and fortunately it has now been more well known than before—we believe that living within our income, putting something aside to pay off a huge and burdensome debt, and managing that debt intelligently in the best interests of people are some of the big things that the Government should be attempting to do.

But Government itself responds to public opinion, and since it was designed by our forefathers as a three-part Government, it is not necessarily going to be influenced always in the same direction, even with respect of this particular subject.

Of one thing I can assure you. The executive department is as determined as it possibly can be to preserve the value of the dollar, to prevent further inflation by means of living within its means, and to try to pay off something on the debt, and to manage this big debt intelligently.

Its responsibility doesn't end just with that effort. It has the job of helping to influence the legislature and the people—the people that have elected that Government—to see these facts, to exercise self-discipline where it is required, and by putting their full weight behind the soundness of our economy and the effort to expand it, to keep it growing on the basis of a sound dollar.

Consequently, the mere production of a budget, cutting the expenses here and there where it seems possible, trying to get the Congress to exercise its authority in the same direction, is not enough. The executive department also has to do its part in informing our people.

Now, going back again to simple things. Since public opinion is the only power, the only force, that keeps this country going, I say again that public opinion must be based on facts, must understand the relationship of these facts one to another, and then harness the emotional strength of people to bringing about the result that we need.

I came here this morning, not in any attempt to make this an unusual breakfast, I assure you, Mr. Chairman; I came here to assure you of my respect and my admiration for what you are trying to do, to assure you that I am enlisted with you in this great effort. I am not trying to find any particular "villain of the piece" but to find out what we have done—whether each of us by searching his own conscience feels that he has truly been a conservative, or whether inflation has been all right as long as it affects him, no matter how evil he thinks it is for someone else. We must try to find out how each of us is going to search himself, and then how, among us, we can achieve some understanding of the great basic directions in which we can move, and how we can make ourselves felt.

I for one hope that you will not forget what telegrams, letters, telephone calls coming in by the millions can do to help the Congress, and the President and the entire organization that he heads, in doing the right thing. This I would feel would be one of the great services you can now accomplish for the United States of America.

Along with that, when we think of the great diversity of our economy, and our industry and our agriculture, we must not waste our energy making somebody else angry, pointing the finger of suspicion at a particular individual. We must concentrate on how we are going to get everybody to understand that industry—made up of capital and management and labor—and insurance companies, and the farmer, and the working man, and the teacher, and everybody—how they have a stake in keeping our prosperity strong and growing. We must make certain that our growth is a healthy and a real one on the basis of a unit of exchange that stays sound, so that the individual earning his equity in his OASI funds, the individual who goes to the insurance company and buys a policy, the teacher who is on a pension, the people who put money in savings banks, everybody realizes we mean it when we say we can plan something for our grandchildren that is just as sound and just as stable as what we ourselves have inherited.

This, I feel, is a job for the United States. I am not going to talk about the necessary expenses of defense and what we have to do in research and science and space and some of these things. There are material and psychological and political reasons that require the United States to spend much more money than a little farmer boy from Kansas of 69 years ago would have ever thought possible. Let's take those things into account. Let's not be indifferent to them. Let's make certain that we get a hundred cents of value out of each of those dollars, whether it be for defense or circling the moon or any other kind of thing for which the Federal Government feels it must spend its money. Let's do these things for the present, certain that it will be to the benefit of our own grandchildren.

And now, before I end—because I was going to talk for one or two sentences and I seem to have pushed the wrong button—I was trying to write a letter a year ago, and never did get it written the way I wanted to. But I would just like to give you the idea and maybe some of you can do better.

I got the idea it would be good for me to write a letter to my own grandson and try to tell him that he should stop supporting me. I would like to get over the idea—I would like each of us to get over the idea to the younger generation, the people that are 30, 40, 50 years younger than we are, and say: "Whenever we add to the national debt one single more dollar, you are helping to support me, because I am living on debt which I am passing on to you. If I get a little bit bigger automobile or some other thing, you are the one to pick up the tab, whether it is done through the Government or through myself and my individual action."

If I could get over to all those younger people—which means our children that are only a few years younger than ourselves—and so on down, the idea that "we are just living on you," I think we would be doing a lot. I think that a great group of people, representing as you do so many influences and so much of our welfare and our activities in this country, could get your younger brethren and sisters really peeved and moving in the political direction, at least, that will help us.

So as I say, having rambled around this way, I think I could have said it all by this one simple statement: I should like to enlist with each of you in this great problem, this great effort that you have set yourselves to perform.

Thank you very much indeed.

NOTE: The President spoke at the Statler Hotel, Washington, D.C. His opening words "Mr. Chairman, Mr. Palmer" referred to D. Tennant Bryan, President of Richmond Newspapers, Inc., and of the American Newspaper Publishers Association, and H. Bruce Palmer, President of the Mutual Benefit Life Insurance Co., Newark, N.J. The conference of representatives of more than 40 national organizations was held for the purpose of considering ways in which these organizations could help contribute to economic growth and prevent inflation.

275 ¶ Exchange of Messages With President Lopez Mateos Concerning the Cyclone Disaster in Mexico. *November 2, 1959*

[Released November 2, 1959. Dated October 30, 1959]

Dear Mr. President:

I was shocked to learn of the cyclone, floods and landslide that are reported to have caused such havoc and loss of life in the vicinity of Manzanillo. The American people extend heartfelt sympathy to the Mexican people in this trying time. Although Ambassador Hill has already been in touch with officials of your Government, I want to inform you personally that this Government stands ready to cooperate in any manner it can in alleviating the hardships now being borne by the citizens of Mexico.

With warm personal regard,

Sincerely,

DWIGHT D. EISENHOWER

NOTE: President Lopez Mateos' reply, dated October 31, follows:

Highly Esteemed Mr. President:

I have received with sincere emotion the message in which you convey to me your regret over the havoc caused by the Pacific cyclone in a vast region of the Republic.

In name of the Mexican people, I deeply appreciate this evidence of solidarity which the people of the United States manifests to us in these unfortunate moments.

In the midst of the loss of lives and the destruction which the disaster has brought us, this government is controlling and progressively dominating the situation, and you may be assured that we shall not fail to remember the cooperation of our friends in case of need.

I send you affectionate greetings, with my cordial consideration.

ADOLFO LOPEZ MATEOS

276   ❡ Remarks at the Cornerstone-Laying Ceremony for the Central Intelligence Agency Building, Langley, Virginia.   *November* 3, 1959

Mr. Dulles, Secretary McElroy, Ladies and Gentlemen of the Central Intelligence Agency:

America's fundamental aspiration is the preservation of peace.   To this end we seek to develop policies and arrangements to make the peace both permanent and just.   This can be done only on the basis of comprehensive and appropriate information.

In war nothing is more important to a commander than the facts concerning the strength, dispositions, and intentions of his opponent, and the proper interpretation of those facts.   In peacetime the necessary facts are of a different nature.   They deal with conditions, resources, requirements, and attitudes prevailing in the world.   They and their correct interpretation are essential to the development of policy to further our long term national security and best interests.   To provide information of this kind is the task of the organization of which you are a part.

No task could be more important.

Upon the quality of your work depends in large measure the success of our effort to further the Nation's position in the international scene.

By its very nature the work of this agency demands of its members the highest order of dedication, ability, trustworthiness, and selflessness— to say nothing of the finest type of courage, whenever needed.   Success cannot be advertised: failure cannot be explained.   In the work of Intelligence, heroes are undecorated and unsung, often even among their own fraternity.   Their inspiration is rooted in patriotism—their reward can be little except the conviction that they are performing a unique and indispensable service for their country, and the knowledge that America needs and appreciates their efforts.   I assure you this is indeed true.

The reputation of your organization for quality and excellence of performance, under the leadership of your Director, Mr. Allen Dulles, is a proud one.

Because I deeply believe these things, I deem it a great privilege to participate in this ceremony of cornerstone laying for the national headquarters of the Central Intelligence Agency.   On this spot will rise a beautiful and a useful structure.   May it long endure, to serve the cause of America and of peace.

Thank you.

277 ¶ The President's News Conference of *November 4, 1959.*

THE PRESIDENT. In order to confirm some of the things that you have been reading in the papers, I want to give you an announcement, which may be of some interest.

I am planning to leave Washington on December 4th on a 2½ weeks' trip which will take me to nine countries.

In response to friendly invitations from the heads of state concerned, I plan to make brief informal visits to Rome, where I hope also to call on His Holiness the Pope, to Ankara, Karachi, Kabul, and to be in New Delhi for the inauguration of the American Exhibit at the World Agricultural Fair which opens on December 11th.

From India, I plan to visit Tehran and Athens en route to Paris to the Western summit meeting scheduled for December 19th.   On my way home from Paris, I shall stop briefly in Rabat.

When the detailed schedule of this trip is fixed in consultation with the several governments concerned, I shall, of course, make it known to you.

There are three critical dates.   December 3d, I think, or 4th is the very earliest date I could possibly go because there is all of the great work of developing the legislative program and the budget for the coming year.

December 11 is critical because that is the day when the Agricultural Fair will open.

December 19 is a critical one because that is the day I am to be in Paris.   So this doesn't leave a great deal of time for dallying along the way.

That is all I have to say.[1]

---

[1] On November 5 the White House released a statement concerning the composition of the party to accompany the President on his trip.   Noting that Secretary Herter would be unable to go because of duties connected with the NATO Ministerial Council Meeting in Paris on December 15, the statement announced that the ranking State Department representative would be Robert Murphy, Under Secretary of State for Political Affairs.   Other members of the party would include White House administrative Staff assistants and confidential secretaries.

Q. Merriman Smith, United Press International: I wonder, sir, if you could tell us generally your purpose for making such an extensive trip, what you hope to accomplish by it?

THE PRESIDENT. Well, first of all no President has ever visited Asia. I don't think it is necessary for me to go into the reasons why Asia is important, not only in view of American interest but as a great portion of the world's population and area. So I should like very much to visit the area, and I think I have expressed before this, to you people, my ambition to visit India, a nation of 400 million people that is struggling so hard to raise its own standards of living and to realize some of its own ambitions, human ambitions in that line.

Visiting India, I would feel it missing a chance if I didn't visit briefly at least some of our friends right in the area—Pakistan, Afghanistan, Iran, and of course on that route that I am following there are nations that are great friends of ours.

Frankly, I am hoping to build in that region of Asia and I hope in many other parts, a better understanding of the United States and good will for us.

I think this would be a great thing for us if there can be any success achieved in such a trip.

Q. Ray L. Scherer, NBC News: Could you say at this point, sir, whether most of the trip will be in one of the jet planes or would you perhaps take one of the prop planes, or would there perhaps be some sea travel involved?

THE PRESIDENT. I think that it will be largely in jet planes, that is what my schedule is concerned with.

Q. William McGaffin, Chicago Daily News: Mr. President, many persons contend that secrecy in Government has grown during your administration. They say this is because the doctrine of Executive privilege has been broadened and abused by some members of the executive branch since your May 1954 directive on this subject.

Sir, if you could be convinced of this, would you take steps to correct the situation?

THE PRESIDENT. Well, you say if I could be convinced of it. Frankly, I don't believe it. Now I want to make that very sure. Now I have tried——

Q. Mr. McGaffin: Well, why have——

THE PRESIDENT. I will try to answer your question that you have given.

Q. Mr. McGaffin: Pardon me.

THE PRESIDENT. I have done my very best to make certain that every department and agency of the United States Government makes available all information that is not obviously detrimental to the national interest if disclosed at that time.

Sometimes it is a matter of timing, but I see no reason for secrecy if it does not damage the United States, and I have tried to follow that policy. It is exactly what I meant when, somewhere about 1954, I put out a directive that gave the criteria by which these things should be measured.

This is a big Government, I have no doubt that errors are made. But that is at least my purpose, and I would think that if there are any more questions in detail, I believe the place to go would be the Attorney General.

Q. Garnett D. Horner, Washington Star: This would seem to be a very strenuous trip you are undertaking, and I wonder if you are likely planning some stop on the trip for some rest, or perhaps before that, of going somewhere for some rest, if you could get it.

THE PRESIDENT. I hope to go a few days sometime during November. I don't know when, but I shall not go so far away that I will not be in complete communication with the Government and all parts of it all the time.

Of course, it is customary that we do keep that kind of communication, I mean even where visits can be made; in other words, I do not believe I could go any further than Augusta, even if I got a few days, because there will be a lot of work to be done.

Q. Robert C. Pierpoint, CBS News: Could you tell us if you are planning to take Mrs. Eisenhower with you on this trip, or perhaps other members of your family?

THE PRESIDENT. Well, I hope to take some members of my family, but I don't think Mrs. Eisenhower will go. It is a little bit tough, I think, for her on that kind of a mission.[1]

Q. Marvin L. Arrowsmith, Associated Press: In light of your doctor's advice that you seek out a warm, dry climate whenever you can, I wonder if I could go back to Mr. Horner's question here. Is there any place that

---

[1] The President was accompanied by Major and Mrs. John S. D. Eisenhower.

you might be able to sit down for awhile on this trip abroad to get some of that climate?

THE PRESIDENT. Well, I would think most of the visit would be in the cooler countries. The only places I think it would be warm probably would be Karachi and New Delhi, and New Delhi, of course, I believe is some 4,000 feet and you might get a little bit of it there. Somewhere along the line, of course, I will have to take a break, but that will all be spelled out when I can give you the details of the plan.

Q. David P. Sentner, Hearst Newspapers: Would you care to give us your reaction to the House committee testimony dealing with fixed TV quiz shows?

THE PRESIDENT. Well, I don't mind, of course. I think I share the American general reaction of almost bewilderment that people could conspire to confuse and deceive the American people.

As quickly as I heard about it, I of course asked the Justice Department to get busy to see whether there were any laws violated and what we can do or whether we should propose any new laws.

The Justice Department tells me that they will be ready to present their conclusions before the first of the year. The Federal Trade Commission has moved into it because, tied to this matter seems to be that of—well, deceitful advertising; and they seem to have possibly some function in correcting this whole business.

I just think this: here is something that has grown up, everybody was astonished and almost dismayed when they heard about it, and I think everybody from the basic industry itself right on down to producers, performers, and actors and the public itself—nobody will be satisfied until this whole mess is cleaned up.

Q. David Kraslow, Knight Newspapers: Mr. President, the note delivered to the Cuban Government last week contained a general discussion on the menace of communism. Can you tell us, sir, why this was included in the note?

THE PRESIDENT. Well, I think it is a very obvious subject to bring up whenever there is a troubled area where the Communists might take hold.

We know that the Communists like to fish in troubled waters, and there are certainly troubled waters there.

Now I think the statement speaks for itself, but I would have personally thought it would have been rather missing an opportunity to say something about this matter if it had been completely avoided—I mean an opportunity to call attention to the seriousness of the Communist menace.

Q. Edwin A. Lahey, Knight Newspapers: Mr. President, do you have any plans for a special session of Congress in case you lose that injunction in the Supreme Court?

THE PRESIDENT. I don't believe I'd better answer any iffy questions on this. This is very emotional, it is very serious, and I think we will just have to wait and see what the answer is.

Q. Carleton Kent, Chicago Sun-Times: Mr. President, have you reached a decision yet on whether the United States will resume nuclear tests next year?

THE PRESIDENT. No nuclear——

Q. Mr. Kent: I believe that the prohibition period runs out December 31.

THE PRESIDENT. Yes, that is the prohibition, but we have implied, at least—I have forgotten, maybe we have stated—that we will not renew unilaterally the tests that have anything to do with the atmosphere.

Now, the whole matter of this business of tests, seems to have got a new impetus by the Russian statement the other day saying that they were ready to discuss, in conference, all of these technical difficulties and the technical implications of attempting to find out and identifying, you might say, undersurface disturbances and explosions.

This is itself not necessarily an advance, but it does show a willingness to discuss the thing in conference. Possibly this whole matter can be now discussed a little bit more intelligently than it was when there was denial that the road toward agreement is really beset with every kind of technical obstacle and difficulty that you can imagine.

It is a very tricky question and if we can get to a really intelligent discussion of the matter, we may make progress.

Q. Spencer Davis, Associated Press: Mr. President, would you say, sir, if there has been any recent communication from Mr. Khrushchev on the status of the American prisoners in China, and any hopes held out that China might renounce the use of force in its policy?

THE PRESIDENT. Well, I very often observed to this group that I try to avoid the discussion of communications that I receive from another head of state. And, as a matter of fact, unless it is already a matter of public record, I try to avoid an admission that one is received or not received.

I think it is not conducive to good relationships with such governments by making these things public.

I will say this: I do not believe that Mr. Khrushchev felt that he had any personal responsibility about this matter, even though he knows of the subject and knew of my interest in it. So far as the renouncing of force, he, himself, did say in a speech in China that he believes all nations should renounce force and should resort to negotiations in order to settle their differences.

Q. James B. Reston, New York Times: Mr. President, would you discuss the wider philosophical implications of this TV scandal? Is this something unique to an industry or is it something that perhaps reflects debasement of standards in the country?

THE PRESIDENT. I think to answer the last part of the thing, I do not believe it does, for this reason: the reaction of Americans seems to be so universal. Every one of them feels that not only he, himself—he may have a little sardonic chuckle when he realizes how he was taken in— but when he thinks about all America being deceived in this way I think he has a reaction immediately as expressed to me by my associates and friends and people I see. I don't think they are so much angry as they are bewildered; and it is like an old story, you know, of Joe Jackson in 1919 when they said, "Say it ain't so, Joe."

I think that is the way Americans feel about it. Now I do believe that every kind of industry that touches on the function of the distribution of news and entertainment on a mass basis, they have a responsibility just as I believe every other group does where the United States beliefs, convictions, and welfare are concerned; just as I believe that every economic unit should remember that self-discipline is the thing that will keep free government working on and on through the centuries to come. We must think of it all the time. So I believe that they have got a terrific responsibility, but I think that it does not imply that America has forgotten her own moral standards.

Q. Sarah McClendon, Burlington (Vt.) Daily News: Sir, I think everybody agrees it is a wonderful idea to have one space and missile agency but would you clarify for us why in picking this agency, you picked a comparatively new agency and an agency that was different from the one that had done much of the development in the missiles and in space?

THE PRESIDENT. Well, I think you should be making a difference between missiles, by which we normally mean weapons, and space and the rocketry that will be useful in exploring the space.

I cannot, for the life of me, see any reason why we should be using or misusing military talent to explore the moon. This is something that deals in the scientific field, and to give this to the Air Force or Army or Navy, it just seems to me is denying what really is a sort of a doctrine in America. You have given to the military only what is their problem and not anything else; the rest of it stays under civilian control. That is the reason for having this agency.

Q. Warren Rogers, New York Herald Tribune: Last week, Dr. von Braun and Roy W. Johnson said that the Saturn project should be developed on a crash basis to beat the Russians in space explorations. They said $140 million for fiscal '61 was not enough; it should be $100 million more. What do you think of that, sir?

THE PRESIDENT. Well, of course, I haven't had the studies placed before me yet as to what our people believe to be the proper thing, but I will say this: I have never seen any specialist of any kind that was bashful in asking for Federal money. [*Laughter*]

Q. Stewart Hensley, United Press International: You were speaking a moment ago about Cuba, and yesterday we had an attack on our Embassy in Panama.

Now, so many of these nationalist eruptions that keep coming over the landscape down there take on an anti-American tinge. Do you have any idea of anything new the United States can do to try to rectify the situation?

THE PRESIDENT. I think that no administration, supported by the Congress, I should say, has ever made more effort to develop better understanding between all of the countries below the Rio Grande than this one; and I think by and large there has been a very great measure of success achieved.

But there are in many of these countries an excitable group; people that are extremists and they start sometimes a mob action.

Now, as you know, or I think you know—I think the State Department gave you the statement, the protest, that our Ambassador made to the government of Panama—so you know exactly what our feelings are with respect to that, and that we confidently hope that every, not only in Panama, but every civilized government will make certain that law and order are preserved.

In a way it's a little bit puzzling to me. We have had some problems with Panama, and the treaty by which the canal was first built has been modified and revised a couple of times, each time giving a greater liberty or a greater degree or level of rights to the Panamanians.

Right today, we have been for, oh, a good time, several months, working with the Panamanians about the interpretations of the latest treaty, so that many problems that have come up to which they think they have not quite acquired all of the rights and privileges that they feel they should have, they have been studied in the effort to ameliorate all of the causes of these difficulties.

I do not know why this fact has not been brought out more, so that the feeling that causes such extraordinary performances would not be so acute.

Q. Paul Martin, Gannett Newspapers: Mr. President, I think you talked with Governor Rockefeller of New York for an hour and ten minutes last week and I believe that is the longest time you have spent in conversation with anyone since Khrushchev. [*Laughter*]

The Governor said you talked about some politics. Could you tell us anything about it?

THE PRESIDENT. Well, I would say this: this was a personal conversation and this is the first time that I knew that anyone was keeping a stop watch on me whenever I had a visitor.

It happens that I like Mr. Rockefeller. He served in my administration for a considerable time. And I will say this: I believe that a good portion of the time, I don't know whether more or most of it, but a good portion was about civil defense. It is a subject in which he and I have both been interested for a long time; and he, as Chairman of the Governors' Conference in this particular problem, wanted to talk to me about it.

Now we talked politics all across the board. You couldn't expect any two people that have political office to avoid that subject completely, and I could not possibly now remember any kind of conclusion we reached. We just found it interesting, that's all.

Q. John Scali, Associated Press: Mr. President, in discussions about a date for an East-West summit conference, the point has sometimes been made about the need to preserve the momentum resulting from your talks with Mr. Khrushchev.

The Russians talk about the need to preserve the spirit of Camp David.

In deciding upon a time and place, do you feel that there is a "Spirit of Camp David" to preserve or a momentum which you want to maintain?

THE PRESIDENT. I have heard this expression, "The Spirit of Camp David," and I don't know what it means.

Now I think this: possibly what is meant is that Mr. Khrushchev and I, particularly when we spoke alone in the car or in other places where we had opportunities, tried to talk in principle and in generality more; and there was, of course, in such areas, much more agreement, seeming agreement, at least, than there normally is when you get down to some specific and knotty problem which the ministers very likely will take up.

So I think the "Spirit of Camp David," as they use it, and I must say I have never used it, must simply mean that it looks like we can talk together without being mutually abusive.

Now, momentum. This is a word that's used very often in discussion of intangibles, such things as development of foreign relations and agreements just as we talk about a snowball rolling downhill.

I don't believe it is quite that simple. I think that's clear because one of the reasons for having a Western summit is to determine upon such details as timing and agenda and all of the rest of it.

Consequently, this momentum, if it is kept up, cannot just be rushing into something that is unprepared. We have got to be properly prepared for it.

Q. Edward P. Morgan, American Broadcasting Company: I'd like to follow up Mr. Reston's question on public morality, so called, Mr. President.

You have often expressed the importance of spiritual and other intangible values, but there seems to be some evidence that the country isn't keeping your counsel.

In addition to—certainly the spiritual values are not the determining factor in the long deadlock in the steel strike, the motivation of people, contestants and sponsors in the television quiz scandal, that's prizes and profits—and in contrast, only yesterday the voters of New York State turned down a half-billion-dollar bond issue for school construction.

Don't these things indicate a serious imbalance in values, in your opinion?

THE PRESIDENT. What you are getting at is that selfishness and greed—occasionally, at least—get the ascendancy over those things that we like to think of as the ennobling virtues of man, his capacity for self-sacrifice, his readiness to help others. So I would say this: the kind of things that you talk about do remind us that man is made up of two kinds of qualities, and I believe some psychologists say they have all had their roots in the instinct for self-preservation.

I am not so sure, because I am not a psychologist, but I do say this: the first two things you talk about are both disappointing to me. Now, I don't know anything about the $500 million bond issue; there may have been things here that I don't know anything about, so I wouldn't want to class that with the other two as implying that we have been a little bit indifferent to the country's moral standing or our own moral standing. I just would not comment on the school bonds issue.

Q. Mrs. May Craig, Portland (Maine) Press Herald: Mr. President, would you agree to the internationalizing of the Panama Canal, as has been suggested by some; two, are you considering our building another canal in that area; and if we did, could we hold that?

THE PRESIDENT. Well, I will say this, to your second question: here is one of those things that takes a lot of study, but for my part, for the last 14 years I have been in favor of building another canal, personally; but I would not say that this is something that I shall probably ever recommend.

Here is a thing that has to be studied from every possible angle with the other countries that might be involved and all the rest of it.

As to the internationalizing of the Panama Canal, that is something that, as of this moment, I would not even think of. We have got a specific treaty with Panama. We have scrupulously obeyed its provisions and indeed, for 50 years, most of our relationships with Panama have been a model. I believe that this particular incident that is so disturbing is really only an incident and should not be something that we should look upon as giving us a real reason for breaking up a relationship that has worked so well.

Marvin L. Arrowsmith, Associated Press: Thank you, Mr. President.

NOTE: President Eisenhower's one hundred and seventy-fifth news conference was held in the Executive Office Building from 10:30 to 11:00 o'clock on Wednesday morning, November 4, 1959. In attendance: 224.

278 ¶ Letter to the Chairman, Senate Foreign Relations Subcommittee, Concerning His Request for a Report Evaluating the Mutual Security Program in Viet-Nam. *November* 12, 1959

[Released November 12, 1959. Dated November 10, 1959]

Dear Mr. Chairman:

I am advised that on October 8, 1959, there was delivered to the Office of the Director of the International Cooperation Administration your written request that you be furnished with that agency's evaluation report of the program in Viet-Nam.

As I have stated on other occasions, it is the established policy of the Executive Branch to provide the Congress and the public with the fullest possible information consistent with the national interest. This policy has guided, and will continue to guide, the Executive Branch in carrying out the Mutual Security Program so that there may be a full understanding of the program and its vital importance to the national security.

At the same time, however, under the historic doctrine of the separation of powers between the three great branches of our Government, the Executive has a recognized Constitutional duty and power with respect to the disclosure of information, documents and other materials relating to its operations. The President has throughout our history, in compliance with his duty in this regard, withheld information when he found that the disclosure of what was sought would be incompatible with the national interest.

It is essential to effective administration that employees of the Executive Branch be in a position to be fully candid in advising with each other on official matters, and that the broadest range of individual opinions and advice be available in the formulation of decisions and policy. It is similarly essential that those who have the responsibility for making decisions be able to act with the knowledge that a decision or action will be judged on its merits and not on whether it happened to conform to or differ from the opinions or advice of subordinates. The disclosure of conversations, communications or documents embodying or concerning such opinions and advice can accordingly tend to impair or inhibit essential reporting and decision-making processes, and such disclosure has therefore been forbidden in the past, as contrary to the national interest, where that was deemed necessary for the protection of orderly and effective operation of the Executive Branch.

The ICA evaluation report which you have requested, which I understand is the August 15, 1957 report.entitled "Evaluation of Viet-Nam Program", is an internal Executive Branch communication comprising opinion and advice on official matters. It is one of a class of reports prepared by small teams of senior officers on the basis of extensive study in the field and in Washington. The purpose of each such report is to examine basic ICA program objectives and program content in a particular country from the standpoint of determining whether the ICA program in that country is effectively carrying out our foreign policy objectives. Such reports contain the candid personal opinions, suggestions and recommendations of the officers who prepare them, and are prepared for submission directly to the Director of the ICA for his information and use. Reports such as the one which you requested have been an important factor in the decision-making process within the agency, and requests for their release have consistently been denied.

Since the disclosure of the report requested by you would not be compatible with the national interest, I have forbidden that it be furnished pursuant to such request and hereby so certify in accordance with Section 111(d) of the Mutual Security Appropriation Act, 1960.

Although I have forbidden the furnishing of the evaluation report requested by you, I wish to make it clear that this has not been done for the purpose of preventing the disclosure of any facts shown by the report. Such facts will be made available to you as promptly as possible.

Sincerely,

DWIGHT D. EISENHOWER

NOTE: The President's letter was addressed to Michael J. Mansfield, Chairman, Subcommittee on State Department Organization and Public Affairs, Committee on Foreign Relations, United States Senate.

279   ¶ Message to Prime Minister Nehru of India
on the Occasion of His 70th Birthday.
November 14, 1959

Dear Mr. Prime Minister:

I am particularly delighted, on this occasion of your seventieth birthday, to send my congratulations and best wishes for continued health and long life.

This important milestone in your career offers me the opportunity to felicitate you on your many accomplishments during the long service that you have devoted to India and its people. Your leadership over many years, especially in the office of Prime Minister, has inspired your own people as well as millions outside of India. Through your writings, moreover, you have shared with others, including many Americans, your appreciation of India's noble past and the bright hope of its future.

Although any man could well be proud of this record of achievement, I know that your thoughts are not directed to the past but to the present and the future. You have devoted your life to the realization of a just and peaceful world order; but many problems remain to be solved before this goal can be reached.

I am looking forward to seeing you in a few weeks.

With warm personal regard,

Sincerely,

DWIGHT D. EISENHOWER

NOTE: This message was released at Augusta, Ga.

280   ¶ Letter to Secretary Flemming on
Receiving Report of the Federal Council on Aging.
November 16, 1959

[Released November 16, 1959. Dated November 12, 1959]

Dear Arthur:

I want to thank you and the other members of the Federal Council on Aging for your informative report on Federal action in assisting the aging.

Federal programs for the aged, including Social Security programs, have increased fivefold in the last decade and will total $15 billion in the fiscal year 1960. This is a substantial contribution to our national effort in this field, but the task is not done. The report suggests important areas for exploration. For example, I am sure we can do more to employ productively and utilize the skills and experience of our 15 million aged.

The creation of increased economic and social opportunities for the aged must clearly be a many-sided approach. It is important to emphasize the Council's observations that this will require the efforts of the individual, his family, his community, and the local and State governments, as well as of the Federal government.

The report merits study by the many groups now preparing for the White House Conference on Aging to be held in January 1961. I will look forward to future reports of the Council.

Sincerely,

DWIGHT D. EISENHOWER

NOTE: The report "Programs and Resources for Older People" (83 pp.) was published by the Government Printing Office. Secretary Flemming's letter of transmittal, dated September 30, was released with the President's reply.

For the President's letter of March 7 to Secretary Flemming reconstituting the Federal Council on Aging at Cabinet level, see Item 49.

281 ¶ Message to President Prasad Accepting His Invitation To Visit India.
November 16, 1959

[Released November 16, 1959. Dated November 14, 1959]

Dear Mr. President:

Thank you for your very kind message. I am happy to be able to accept the invitation of your Government to come to India, and thus to fulfill a long-standing wish on my part. I am looking forward with great pleasure to meeting you and to the opportunity for paying my respects to the people and Government of India.

DWIGHT D. EISENHOWER

NOTE: This message was released at Augusta, Ga.

779

282 ¶ Exchange of Messages Between the President and President Bayar of Turkey Concerning the President's Forthcoming Visit to Ankara. *November* 17, 1959

[Released November 17, 1959. Dated November 16, 1959]

Dear Mr. President:

Thank you very much for your kind letter regarding my forthcoming visit to Ankara. I am happy to have the opportunity to visit your country to pay my respects to the Government and people of Turkey.

I am looking forward to this opportunity to meet you again.

Sincerely,

DWIGHT D. EISENHOWER

NOTE: President Bayar's message follows:

Dear Mr. President:

I have been most happy to learn that you will stop one day in Ankara on your way to India on December 6, 1959. You may be assured that this news will be received with deep satisfaction by the whole Turkish nation.

Although the schedule of your trip does not, unfortunately, allow you to prolong your stay here, it will be, nevertheless, for us a real pleasure to meet you again and to talk to you, be it only for a short time.

Let me add that I am, of course, aware of the meaning of your trip, which constitutes a new proof of the great efforts which you display for the strengthening of the solidarity between the free nations and the realization of the ideals of peace and security.

Expressing, again, my happiness at the prospect of meeting you very soon on this occasion, I remain, with my best regards,

Yours sincerely,

CELAL BAYAR

The messages were released at Augusta, Ga.

283 ¶ Exchange of Messages Between the President and Prime Minister Menderes of Turkey Concerning the President's Forthcoming Visit to Ankara. *November* 17, 1959

[Released November 17, 1959. Dated November 16, 1959]

Dear Mr. Prime Minister:

It was kind of you to write about my forthcoming visit to Turkey.

I am happy to have this opportunity to pay my respects to the people and Government of Turkey.

780

I look forward to meeting you again and having another talk as we did on the occasion of your recent visit to the United States.

Sincerely,

DWIGHT D. EISENHOWER

NOTE: The message from Prime Minister Menderes follows:

My dear Mr. President:

It is with deep satisfaction that I have learned that you will give us the great honor of welcoming you to Turkey on December sixth.

This will be a great privilege for me, and the members of my Government. May I at the same time express to you,

once more, how sincerely we appreciate your tireless endeavours to strengthen the solidarity among the free nations, for the achievement of peace and security throughout the world.

Looking forward to meeting you soon, I avail myself of this opportunity to renew to you, my dear Mr. President, the expression of my highest consideration.

ADNAN MENDERES

The messages were released at Augusta, Ga.

284 ¶ Statement by the President Concerning the Antarctic Treaty. *December* 1, 1959

I AM gratified that The Antarctic Treaty is being signed today in Washington by the representatives of 12 nations. This Treaty is the result of the arduous and painstaking efforts of many people who for two years have worked to achieve this agreement of great importance to the world.

The Conference on Antarctica was convened October 15, 1959, as a result of a United States note of invitation, dated May 2, 1958, to those nations which had participated in scientific research in Antarctica during the 1957–1958 International Geophysical Year.

The spirit of cooperation and mutual understanding, which the 12 nations and their delegations exhibited in drafting a Treaty of this importance, should be an inspiring example of what can be accomplished by international cooperation in the field of science and in the pursuit of peace.

This Treaty guarantees that a large area of the world will be used only for peaceful purposes, assured by a system of inspection. Antarctica will constitute a laboratory for cooperative scientific research in accordance with treaty provisions. The legal status quo there will be maintained for the duration of the Treaty. Nuclear explosions are prohibited pending general international agreement on the subject.

The Antarctic Treaty and the guarantees it embodies constitute a significant advance toward the goal of a peaceful world with justice.

NOTE: The text of the Final Act and Treaty are published in the Department of State Bulletin (vol. 41, p. 912).

285 ¶ Letter Accepting Resignation of Neil H. McElroy as Secretary of Defense. *December* 1, 1959

[Released December 1, 1959. Dated November 30, 1959]

Dear Neil:

As I regretfully accept your resignation as Secretary of Defense, to be effective December first in keeping with your request, I wish to express my deep appreciation of your distinguished service these past two years.

Well I know that the responsibilities of members of the Cabinet are heavy and unrelenting; and I especially appreciate, with respect to the office you have so admirably filled, the extraordinary burdens imposed by its responsibility for day-to-day management of the huge national security complex encompassed by the Department of Defense. In recent years particularly, the tasks of reorganizing and modernizing our forces—always difficult at best—have had to be so met that we could confidently press our quest for a just peace from a foundation of sure strength at home.

What you have contributed personally to the solution of these and of a multitude of other pressing problems and to the general administration of defense affairs has been invaluable. I am indeed sorry that personal considerations compel your departure from the government at this time, but I am thankful that you leave to your successor a Department that will continue to reflect the very beneficial changes effected under your energetic leadership.

I am deeply grateful for the strong support you have consistently afforded not only to me but also to other Administration officials, and I shall not hesitate to call upon you as occasion may offer in the future. You know, I trust, that you take with you the lasting thanks of your governmental associates, the appreciation of the American people, and my own good wishes for continued success.

   With warm personal regard,

Sincerely,

DWIGHT D. EISENHOWER

NOTE: Mr. McElroy served as Secretary of Defense from October 9, 1957, to De-cember 1, 1959. His letter of November 27 was released with the President's reply.

286 ¶ Citation Accompanying the Medal of Freedom Presented to Neil H. McElroy. *December* 1, 1959

[Read by Brig. Gen. A. J. Goodpaster, White House Staff Secretary]

CITATION TO ACCOMPANY THE AWARD OF

MEDAL OF FREEDOM

TO

NEIL MCELROY

FOR EXCEPTIONALLY MERITORIOUS

SERVICE AND CONTRIBUTIONS TO THE

SECURITY OF THE UNITED STATES

   As Secretary of Defense from October 9, 1957, to December 1, 1959, Neil Hosler McElroy has held a major responsibility both for maintaining our armed forces as an effective deterrent to war during a period of far-reaching change in military technology and for strengthening collective security throughout the Free World by assisting friendly countries in their efforts to protect themselves against aggression. With outstanding success he has carried out these difficult assignments.

   Under his leadership, the armed forces effected an orderly introduction of many new weapons systems and expedited military research efforts essential to the security of our country in the years ahead. His experience in administering large organizations greatly contributed to the effective adjustment of our military organization to current needs, both at home and abroad. In negotiations with allied nations, he has further strengthened the bonds of friendship between them and the United States.

In recognition of his outstanding service to his country and his dedication to his task, I take great pleasure in presenting the Medal of Freedom to Neil Hosler McElroy.

DWIGHT D. EISENHOWER

NOTE: The presentation was made by the President at a ceremony held in the Cabinet Room following a meeting of the National Security Council.

287   ¶ Exchange of Messages Between the President and President Kubitschek of Brazil on the Establishment of the National Advisory Committee for Inter-American Affairs. *December 1, 1959*

Dear Mr. President:

I much appreciate your message of November eighteenth and share your hope that the National Advisory Committee for Inter-American Affairs will contribute positively to peace and understanding in this hemisphere, and to the economic betterment envisaged by Operation Pan America. The assessment of problems and needs which now is being undertaken by the Organization of American States at the request of eleven American nations will provide, I am confident, the cornerstone on which Operation Pan America can build to achieve its objectives.

May I take this opportunity to thank you for your personal greetings. I wish for you and the people of Brazil the very best of health and success.

Sincerely,

DWIGHT D. EISENHOWER

NOTE: President Kubitschek's message follows:

I wish to congratulate you, Mr. President, on the establishment of the National Advisory Committee for Inter-American Affairs, with the timely purpose of considering current and future problems arising out of the relationship between the United States and Latin America. The fact that you have entrusted the Secretary of State himself with the chairmanship of the new body, as well as your selection of distinguished personalities to integrate it, clearly denote the purpose of carrying out a wise and constructive policy for the maintenance of peace and for a better understanding among the nations of our Continent.

Following our exchange of letters in 1958, and in line with pronouncements by eminent statesmen in Latin America, a movement of continental solidarity was launched which became known as Operation Pan America. The idea behind this movement won the unanimous approval of the twenty one Republics and it has already been the motive for three Inter-American meetings where certain concrete measures, though still insufficient in scope, have been agreed upon. Operation Pan America has a common objective that is both generous and deeply realistic.

Its first practical step will be the joint preparation of an assessment of the needs and of the economic problems of Latin America, in order that concrete measures be undertaken to fight the underdevelopment that plagues so many regions of this New World. I am sure, Mr. President, that a close consideration of the proposals presented within the framework of Operation Pan America by all the participant States will be of the highest value for the work of the newly formed Commission. The problems of development and those of the preservation of the democratic freedoms are inseparably welded together.

In the fervent hope of a thorough continental understanding, I pray God for your personal happiness and for the security and ever increasing greatness of the noble American people.

JUSCELINO KUBITSCHEK

The President authorized the Secretary of State to establish the Committee on November 14, 1959. A White House release of that date, announcing the President's action, states that the Secretary had named as members Ambassador Walter J. Donnelly, Dr. Milton S. Eisenhower, G. Kenneth Holland, O. A. Knight, Charles A. Meyer, and Dr. Dana G. Munro. A report by Dr. Eisenhower following his 1958 tour of Latin American countries, released January 4, 1959, had recommended the establishment of such a committee.

On December 3 the White House announced that the President had met with the members on that day on the occasion of the Committee's inaugural meeting. The release states that the President told the committee members that their meeting was a reflection of the deep interest among the people of the United States in the affairs of the American Republics, and that his meeting with them on the eve of his departure to several countries of the Old World reflected his own interest in the New World and his faith in the future of the inter-American system.

288 ¶ The President's News Conference of *December* 2, 1959.

THE PRESIDENT. Good morning.

There is one short statement I have to make.

For some time, we have been in the process of negotiating a new treaty, revised treaty with Japan; and, it is a matter to which we attach the greatest interest. Mr. Kishi, who is one of the men that the Government as well as I personally admire very much, is coming to visit this country probably in January, and any questions remaining at that moment of course would be taken up then.

So, while there have been some questions presented to me about this matter, until the thing is completed I will not be making any statements about it. However, Mr. Hagerty will have a little statement for you that really relates what I have just said, but in slightly more amplified form.

Q. Merriman Smith, United Press International: Mr. President, in connection with your forthcoming trip, I would like to ask a slightly legalistic question.

Under law, you have the sole authority for the final determination of using nuclear or thermonuclear weapons in event of an emergency. Now, you will be quite some distance from the country during this trip. Have you made any arrangements or are such arrangements feasible where you leave such authority with someone in this country, or would you have to execute such a decision if it became necessary, overseas?

THE PRESIDENT. No, there is no arrangement that puts the President's authority in anybody else. Such decisions that I have to make, though, are of such a character and are kept in such terminology they can be executed from any position and by a simple message that could be delivered instantaneously.

Q. Ray L. Scherer, NBC News: Could you tell us, sir, if you sense any particular feeling, particular sense of mission as you embark on this rather large tour?

THE PRESIDENT. Well, I've been thinking and talking about this so long that I may be repeating myself.

I think that we can conclude, from all of the reports that come to us from abroad, that there is a great deal of doubt remaining in the minds of many people, and including our friends, allies and other friends, as to America's real sincerity in pursuit of peace. We have tried to emphasize this point in every possible way, through diplomatic contacts, through speeches of the Secretary of State, myself, and others, and still it doesn't seem to come through.

Now, I have relatively few months left, and I decided to make an effort that no President ever was called on before to make. I do feel a compulsion to visit a number of countries, and through them hoping to reach many others, and tell them exactly what I believe the United States is trying to do: that our basic aspiration is to search out methods by which peace in the world can be assured with justice for everybody.

I want to prove that we are not aggressive, that we seek nobody else's territories or possessions; we do not seek to violate anybody else's rights. We are simply trying to be a good partner in this business of searching for peace—which means, in the long run, searching also methods in which we, the independent nations together cooperating, can find a better life for all of us; and that means politically and materially.

This is what I'm trying to do, and such prestige and standing as I have on the earth, I want to use it. As long as my other duties do not prevent me from doing so, I'm going to work on this in every possible way I can.

Q. William McGaffin, Chicago Daily News: Mr. President, could you tell us whether you have received the Sigma Delta Chi Freedom of Information Reports; and if so, what was your reaction to them, sir?

THE PRESIDENT. You will have to describe them. There are too many reports for me to remember them by title.

Q. Mr. McGaffin: Well, sir, the reason I asked is that Mr. V. M. Newton, Jr., the chairman of the committee that prepared the reports, says that he sent them to you twice, but he feels that you have not personally seen them, or you would not continue in the belief that you have repeatedly expressed about secrecy in Government during your administration.

THE PRESIDENT. Well, I think I'll have to see the report and give you an answer, because I simply can't answer on something that I can't recall the contents of.

Q. Charles W. Roberts, Newsweek: Sir, last July the committee studying foreign aid under General Draper made a recommendation to you that the United States should assist those countries with which it is cooperating in economic aid programs, on request, in the formulation of their plans designed to deal with problems of rapid population growth. This was generally interpreted as a recommendation that this Government should distribute birth control information on request. I wondered what your reaction to that report was, sir.

THE PRESIDENT. I cannot imagine anything more emphatically a subject that is not a proper political or governmental activity or function or responsibility.

This thing has for very great denominations a religious meaning, definite religious tenet in their own doctrine. I have no quarrel with them; as a matter of fact this being largely the Catholic Church, they are one of the groups that I admire and respect. But this has nothing to do with governmental contact with other governments. We do not intend to interfere with the internal affairs of any other government, and if they want to do something about what is admittedly a very difficult question, almost an explosive question, that is their business. If they want to go to someone for help, they will go unquestionably to professional groups, not to governments. This Government has no, and will not as long as I am here have a positive political doctrine in its program that has to do with this problem of birth control. That's not our business.

Q. Laurence H. Burd, Chicago Tribune: Mr. President, as you are about to undertake this trip, can you tell us how you feel as to health; and second, do you or your doctors or your family have any qualms about the heavy physical exertion that this strenuous trip will require of you?

THE PRESIDENT. I think it's only natural that any man's family begins to think that he is probably here and there taking on a load that he shouldn't; but I think so far as my doctors are concerned—3 days ago I had again my regular monthly examination—they say I'm capable of doing it. And I think that I am as fit as I possibly could be at my time of life to do this thing.

Of course, it demands real resistance to fatigue; but I think I'm capable of carrying it on, and also without losing the last vestiges of what I once thought was a good disposition. [*Laughter*]

Q. Mrs. May Craig, Portland (Maine) Press Herald: With increasing agricultural surpluses, increasing food prices to the housewife, decreasing returns to farmers, do you have any new farm solution in mind?

THE PRESIDENT. I can't say, Mrs. Craig, that I've got a new solution. I believe that for 7 years we've been trying to work on something that's better than we've had, but we have had very little success in finding a formula acceptable to the Congress, that would have been passed by the Congress, to bring about these better conditions.

Actually, our agriculture has become so completely dependent on what Government does, what political action is, that already I think it is too far or too definitely under governmental control. It's too much of a dependent.

There have been a number of ideas brought to me; I've got them now under study by the Agriculture Department. I will have an agricultural program which I hope will do something to free agriculture from its complete dependency, or almost complete dependency upon Government, and make it more prosperous.

Q. Charles H. Mohr, Time Magazine: Mr. President, this is a moment in history in which we have to maintain a large strategic capability in manned aircraft, and at the same time paying for the increasingly expensive development of missile capability, and also an antimissile defense capability.

I wonder if you could discuss and explain to us how, in such a moment in history, the defense budget does not need to rise but can stay relatively stable over a period of 2 or 3 years?

THE PRESIDENT. I think that the first thing is this, since you are going from one defense system, largely, to another, particularly in this matter of deterrent: there is an old saying—what is it—"Be not the first by which the new is tried, nor yet the last to lay the old aside." Now, that's what we're doing.

But if you want to have a really expensive thing, stop everything now that we've been doing and then just put a tremendous hysterical urge about the business of getting something new. Now you will really have, to my mind, a bad answer and an expensive answer.

As we are finding that our Atlas is operational, and is operational, and it comes into this picture, it is only natural that there is shown less concern and less cost in the matter of developing newer and better and bigger airplanes, faster, higher-flying, and so on.

Now, we do not quit that entirely. As you know, the B–58, on a moderate program, is to be completed; and there is an R and D program going on, on one that's even bigger. So we do not feel ourselves within just a matter of 2 or 3 or 4 years completely dependent upon the missile, until we've got these missiles perfected to the point where we think that the deterrent itself needs nothing else.

Q. Mr. Mohr: Would that protection include hardening their bases?

THE PRESIDENT. Well, on that, that's a technical question that no one knows really the right answer yet. I think this: there will be certain types of them that will require, oh, I mean will be much better off if you harden the bases; and I think that it will not be as expensive as we once thought. But there will be other types that still will be in what you might call unhardened bases.

Q. Sarah McClendon, El Paso Times: Sir, I wonder if you think this is a proper matter for you to give your attention to.

Your Attorney General is reportedly presently investigating an affair whereby the Midwestern Gas Transmission Company is going to make about $16 million profit at the expense of the Midwestern consumers for bringing gas in from Canada.

Now, my colleague Joe Huttlinger has discovered whereby the Federal Power Commission had set the rates for this, then they were visited by Mr. Thomas Corcoran, a Democratic Party figure and attorney, who persuaded them to increase these rates.

Now, your Attorney General is looking into this and I wonder if you will discuss this with him and see if you think this is a proper matter for the whole Government to get——

THE PRESIDENT [*addressing Mr. Hagerty*]. Will you remind me to do that? [*Laughter*]

Q. J. F. Ter Horst, Detroit News: Sir, while you are gone on your trip, a lot of us will be left wondering what is going to happen in the steel dispute. We know that it has been an annoying and a plaguing problem to you, and we are wondering, sir, if you have in mind any kind of solution by law or by regulation that might bring two parties together when they cannot seem to do so voluntarily?

THE PRESIDENT. Well, you didn't describe the problem quite correctly. You said it's of course annoying and plaguing to me.

This is vital to America.

Now, my interest in this is not employers and, per se, not employees except as all of them are part of America. I have tried to use every bit of influence I have had officially or personally, in this matter to get these people together. I am going again to insist publicly that they do it. I just know this: if we can't get anywhere on this thing, then finally the Government just cannot sit idly on its hands.

But, I do believe that the day that we abandon honest free collective bargaining, it is going to be a sad day for the United States.

So, it looks to me that unless they get together on a kind of settlement that is equitable to each other and absolutely in the public interest, we are going to lose—something.

Q. Raymond P. Brandt, St. Louis Post-Dispatch: Will the foreign military assistance appropriation be included in the defense budget, and if so, has that been discussed with the congressional appropriation leaders?

THE PRESIDENT. The military section I think is; I think there has been an agreement to do it—for them to defend it next year I think. I have forgotten the details, Mr. Brandt, but I know it has been under study. I think the following year it's to go into the military responsibility, but I can't be sure.

Q. Mr. Brandt: That would be in '62, sir.

THE PRESIDENT. That would be '62 for the defense of this thing. Now, I would have to have looked up what our final agreement on that was because it has been one of these questions that's bandied back and forth for years. So I would think that you could get that directly either from ICA or Defense.

Q. Earl H. Voss, Washington Star: Mr. President, I have a question about nuclear tests.

I wonder if you could tell us how you think the negotiations are going in Geneva, in the light of the information last Saturday from Radio Moscow that the Russians have been creating artificial earthquakes under a lake in Siberia, and under a river there, which they picked up 250 miles away with seismic instruments.

THE PRESIDENT. Well, of course, we've got the scientists working in Geneva, and that kind of information is among the things, among the factors that they are working on. So I couldn't say a great deal about this particular incident or particular report.

We do attach not only great importance to it, but we are more hopeful about some constructive result out of these negotiations than we were a few months back when it looked like they were going to be completely abandoned.

Q. James B. Reston, New York Times: Mr. President, before you go away, sir, I wonder if you could tell us what the outlook is for the new budget, and for the resources coming in—how much has it been hit by the steel strike, for example?

THE PRESIDENT. Well, there is no question that the revenues coming in for this year of '60 are going to be reduced; and this, of course, as Mr. Stans pointed out down at Augusta in a statement, puts the achievement of the balanced budget for 1960 in a very precarious position.

I can only say this: I have had many conferences with all executive divisions and departments, trying to find ways that we can save money in '60 to make up this deficit and try still to achieve that balanced budget. It would have a tremendous effect on the economy, as I see it, and certainly upon all our friends abroad.

So, projecting that same kind of thinking into '61, I think we should strive not only for a balanced budget in '61, but that we must get some small surplus to start paying on this deficit.

Ladies and gentlemen, I want to tell you something. I think the last year that the United States spent less than $9 billion, or spent just about $9 billion for its entire expenses, was 1940. That is less than we are now paying for interest. And it seems to me that this ought to have a very significant meaning for all our people, everybody, everybody in this room that's a taxpayer, thinking about their dollars or their final pension or their final OASI payments. They are the things that are threatened, if we are not more fiscally responsible. I think we are trying to do many things that are not completely necessary; and we should kind of put them off on the shelf until we have got our fiscal system in order, and our financial system.

So for people abroad who are depending on us as the world banker, for ourselves who are hoping to keep a stable dollar, we ought to take this lesson to heart and do something about it.

Q. John M. Hightower, Associated Press: Mr. President, as you travel in these countries on your trip, and meet the leaders of the countries, do you expect to discuss with them a number of specific issues in which they are interested?

What I have in mind particularly is the problem which Mr. Nehru is having with the Chinese Communists on the border.

THE PRESIDENT. Of course I shall be glad to discuss such problems; with respect of this particular one, I don't think the issue, as far as I know, is the exact spots in which this McMahon Line is located. I don't think anyone has ever known exactly. As a matter of fact there is one road and one border of India that was, I believe, in existence 2 years before anybody except its builders knew anything about it. It's a very remote and wild region.

What is important and what is the issue is this: are nations going to settle their differences by negotiation, honest meeting, honest negotiation with each other, or are they going to move in with force and take that course in the settlement of these disputes?

Now, that is the real issue, and on that I am very much on the side of the people that say we must do it by negotiation.

So, when I go through all of these countries, there will be a number of problems. After all, there have been difficulties as we know between Pakistan and India. There are two countries in which we have great interest. All right. There has been a good beginning made through the World Bank in getting the waters of the Indus and other rivers properly stored up, divided. If this leads to the settlement of their outstanding things, this will be a wonderful thing because it will be done not with force, not with threat of force, by negotiation.

This applies to almost every other country in the world.

Q. E. W. Kenworthy, New York Times: Mr. President, a number of leading universities and colleges have decided not to participate in the Federal Student Loan Program because of the loyalty oath required. I wonder if you would give us your views on the loyalty oath and whether you would favor a revision of the law to make this unnecessary.

THE PRESIDENT. Well, the law, of course, was passed by Congress; and while I didn't particularly like the one part of it, why, I, of course, had to put it in the position where it could be executed.

So far as I'm concerned, and I have stated this ever since the question was posed to me, I personally am ready each morning to take an oath that I am not a Communist and that I am loyal to the United States. I think, however, that when we begin to single out any group of citizens and say, "This is a matter of legal compulsion," I can see why they are resentful.

To my mind, anybody who is taking an oath as a citizen, when he becomes naturalized or any other time he is required to take an oath as a public servant, when he says that he is going to defend the United States and its Constitution against all enemies, foreign and domestic, for me that ought to settle the question.

I rather deplore that universities have found it necessary to find, for the moment, a narrow dividing line and therefore keep a number of citizens out of taking advantage of the loan provisions that the Federal Government set up; but for my part, I should think that the loyalty oath, the basic citizenship oath, is sufficient.

Q. Thomas N. Schroth, Congressional Quarterly: Mr. President, do you plan to submit any additional civil rights proposals next year? Specifically I have two in mind: the provision for Federal voting registrars, as proposed in the September 8th report of your Civil Rights Commission; and the so-called part III provision, which would empower the Attorney General to file civil suit in all civil rights cases.

THE PRESIDENT. I have not yet had my final conferences with the Attorney General and the other people interested, but I do say that I would like to see all the parts of the bill that I submitted last year considered, and if possible, enacted this year.

Q. Marianne Means, Hearst Newspapers: Mr. President, in the interest of Latin American relations, is it possible that the United States will let Panama's flag fly beside the United States flag in the Canal Zone?

THE PRESIDENT. This is one of the points that's been talked about for many years, since for 50 years the United States has recognized the titular sovereignty of Panama. There have been numbers of problems over the years that have come about because, first, of what the Panamanians felt were injustices to them in the original treaties; and secondly, by the interpretations of treaties as revised in later years.

These last problems of the differences were under study for the last few months, and we had already agreed with the Panamanians for methods of taking another look at them and trying to see whether we couldn't meet their requirements in this matter. So there has been a very conciliatory attitude toward governments, as far as I have known, and the one question of the flag has never been specifically placed before me, no decision has ever been made about it; but I do in some form or other believe we should have visual evidence that Panama does have titular sovereignty over the region.

Merriman Smith, United Press International: Thank you, Mr. President.

NOTE: President Eisenhower's one hundred and seventy-sixth news conference was held in the Executive Office Building from 10:32 to 11:02 o'clock on Wednesday morning, December 2, 1959. In attendance: 261.

289 ¶ Statement by the President Concerning Treaty Negotiations Between the United States and Japan. *December* 2, 1959

DURING the past months, we have been negotiating a new treaty and other security arrangements with Japan. We attach the greatest importance to this new treaty with Japan which is being negotiated between equals for the mutual benefit and enlightened self-interest of both countries and is therefore in keeping with the new era in our relations with Japan enunciated following my talks with Prime Minister Kishi here in Washington in June 1957. The timing of this new treaty with Japan is particularly opportune since I feel it is most essential at the present juncture in international affairs for the free world to maintain its unity and strength.

Since the negotiations are still in progress, I would prefer not to comment on the details of the new arrangements or the final plans for signing the treaty. However, I understand that Prime Minister Kishi is considering coming to Washington for the signing of the new treaty. If he decides to come, I will welcome the opportunity to talk with him again since he is one of the free world's staunchest leaders and heads a country whose friendship we value most highly.

290 ⁋ Radio and Television Address to the American People Before Leaving on Good Will Trip to Europe, Asia, and Africa. *December* 3, 1959

[Delivered from the President's Office at 7:15 p.m.]

Good Evening Fellow Americans:

I leave, in just a few minutes, on a 3-week journey halfway around the world. During this Mission of Peace and Good Will I hope to promote a better understanding of America and to learn more of our friends abroad.

In every country I hope to make widely known America's deepest desire—a world in which all nations may prosper in freedom, justice, and peace, unmolested and unafraid.

I shall try to convey to everyone our earnestness in striving to reduce the tensions dividing mankind—an effort first requiring, as indeed Mr. Khrushchev agrees, the beginning of mutual disarmament. Of course, I shall stress that the first requirement for mutual disarmament is mutual verification.

Then I hope to make this truth clear—that, on all this earth, not anywhere does our Nation seek territory, selfish gain or unfair advantage for itself. I hope all can understand that beyond her shores, as at home, America aspires only to promote human happiness, justly achieved.

We in America know that for many decades our Nation has practiced and proclaimed these convictions and purposes. But this is not enough. For years doubts about us have been skillfully nurtured in foreign lands by those who oppose America's ideals.

Our country has been unjustly described as one pursuing only materialistic goals; as building a culture whose hallmarks are gadgets and shallow pleasures; as prizing wealth above ideals, machines above spirit, leisure above learning, and war above peace.

Actually, as our declaration proclaims, the core of our Nation is belief in a Creator who has endowed all men with inalienable rights, including life, liberty, and the pursuit of happiness. In that belief is our country's true hallmark—a faith that permeates every aspect of our political, social, and family life. This truth, too, I hope to emphasize abroad.

Of course, as all the world knows, at times, and in some respects, we have fallen short of the high ideals held up for us by our Founding Fathers. But one of the glories of America is that she never ceases her striving toward the shining goal.

And in this striving we know we still can learn much from other cultures. From the ideals and achievements of others we can gain new inspiration. We do not forget that, in the eyes of millions in older lands, our America is still young—in some respects, is still on trial.

So I earnestly make this suggestion, as I start this journey tonight—that you, and those close to you, join with me in a renewed dedication to our moral and spiritual convictions, and in that light re-examine our own record, including our shortcomings. May this examination inspire each of us so to think and so to act, as to hasten our progress toward the goals our fathers established, which have made America an instrument for good. In this rededication we shall replenish the true source of America's strength—her faith; and, flowing from it, her love of liberty, her devotion to justice.

So believing, we look on our Nation's great wealth as more than a hard earned resource to be used only for our own material good. We believe that it should also serve the common good, abroad as well as at home. This is not sheer altruism. If we can truly cooperate with other nations, especially our friends of the free world, we can first defeat the evils of hunger, privation, and disease that throughout the ages have plagued mankind. Thus we can develop a healthier, more prosperous world, and in the process develop greater prosperity for ourselves. Even more than this, we can help reduce the world tensions that are the powder kegs of disaster.

This is why, for more than a decade, America has engaged in cooperative programs with other nations—programs that, in many ways, concern the areas that I set forth to visit tonight.   Our part of this effort is our own Mutual Security Program.   Abroad, it is supplemented and its effects many times multiplied by programs of all the countries associated with us in this work.

Thus we provide a peaceful barrier, erected by freedom, to the continuous probings of predatory force.   Our mutual undertakings support those who strive to forestall aggression, subversion, and penetration.   It helps steady the struggling economies of free nations new and old.   It helps build strength and hope, preventing collapse and despair.   In a world sorely troubled by an atheistic imperialism, it is a strong instrument of hope and of encouragement to others who are eager, with us, to do their part in sustaining the human spirit and human progress.

So we see that our Nation's security, economic health, and hope for peace demand of all of us a continuing support of these cooperative efforts, initiated a dozen years ago.   Of the amounts we devote to our own security and to peace, none yields a more beneficial return than the dollars we apply to these mutual efforts of the free world.

Here at home we are fortunate in having an economy so richly productive as to sustain a most powerful defense without impairment of human values.   Without this military strength our efforts to provide a shield for freedom and to preserve and strengthen peace would be futile. We are determined that in quality and power this force shall forever be kept adequate for our security needs until the conference table can replace the battlefield as the arbiter of world affairs.

This kind of defense is costly and burdensome, as indeed are many other essential Federal programs.   For example, the annual interest alone, on our Federal debt, is now more than nine billion dollars a year—a sum in dollars equal to the entire Federal budget of 1940.   We must, then, for our security and our prosperity, keep our economy vigorous and expanding.   We can keep it so, but only if we meet wisely and responsibly the economic problems that confront us.   To mention a few, there are inflation, public spending, taxation, production costs and foreign trade, agriculture, and labor-management relations.

Of these problems, one cries out for immediate solution.   I refer to the labor-management dispute that is still unresolved in the steel industry.

This, I am sure, is clear to us all: the success of all our efforts to build and sustain the peace depends not only upon our spiritual and military strength, but also upon the health of our economy. Among sovereign nations progress toward a just peace can be achieved only through international cooperation. Likewise, economic strength, in this Nation of free citizens, requires cooperation among us all. We cannot— any of us—indulge our own desires, our own demands, our own emotions, to the extent of working hardship throughout the country.

"Responsible citizenship" in a free country means what it says. It means conducting one's self responsibly, in the interest of others as well as self. America will not—indeed, it cannot—tolerate for long the crippling of the entire economy as the result of labor-management disputes in any one basic industry or any group of industries.

Among our free people there is no one man, no one group, no one industry, no one interest, that measures, in importance, to America.

So, my friends, the choice is up to free American employers and American employees. Voluntarily, in the spirit of free collective bargaining, they will act responsibly; or else, in due course their countrymen will see to it that they do act responsibly. It is up to labor and management, in these disputes, to adjust responsibly and equitably their differences. The Nation is determined to preserve free enterprise, including free collective bargaining. If we are to do this, labor and management alike must see to it, in every dispute and settlement, that the public interest is as carefully protected as the interests of stockholders and of employees. The public will not stand for less.

Tonight, despite months of effort, labor and management in the steel industry are still in disagreement. As I leave tonight, America still faces the possibility of a renewed steel crisis, beginning a few weeks hence.

Day after day, throughout the economy, uncertainty, indecision and hesitation are growing as a result of this continuing controversy. Now, negotiations have just been resumed. The exact methods the parties agree upon to advance these negotiations are of relatively little importance to the American people. The leaders of both segments must realize that the achievement of a voluntary settlement, fair to all, is critically important to the entire Nation. Indeed, it is so important that I am instructing the Director of the Mediation and Conciliation Service to do all that he can to keep the parties negotiating on an around-the-clock basis.

America needs a settlement now.

During these next 3 weeks, while I am talking of peace and of mutual cooperation with our friends abroad, the subject of America's spiritual and economic strength is bound to come up often and importantly. What great news it would be if, during the course of this journey, I should receive word of a settlement of this steel controversy that is fair to the workers, fair to management, and above all, fair to the American people.

One last thought. We have heard much of the phrase, "Peace and friendship." This phrase, in expressing the aspirations of America, is not complete. We should say instead, "Peace and friendship, in freedom." This, I think, is America's real message to the world.

Now, my friends, I set forth as your agent to extend once again to millions of people across the seas assurance of America's sincere friendship. I know you wish me well. And, I wish you well in making your influence felt, individually and collectively, in solving, properly, our pressing problems here at home. For let us remember: these two efforts, the one abroad and the one at home, actually are one and inseparable. Working cooperatively together, here at home, rather than wasting our effort and substance in bitter economic and political strife, we in America will become ever a stronger force on the side of good in the world.

And, as we, through our cooperative efforts abroad, strengthen human understanding and good will throughout the world, we bring ever closer the day of lasting peace.

May the Almighty inspire us all, in these efforts, to do our best.

Good night, and for 3 weeks, goodbye.

291 ¶ Remarks Upon Arrival at Ciampino Airport, Rome. *December* 4, 1959

Mr. President, Your Excellencies, My Friends:

I am most grateful for the warm welcome you have extended to me, President Gronchi, and I am exceedingly proud that as I start this trip I can stay here in your great city, which for so long has been the very symbol of all Western civilization.

I bring a simple message to you from America. It is this: we want to live in peace and friendship—in freedom.

This is the message that I shall carry to every country that I visit. It is the message that I hope will be heard in every country where communications are allowed freely.

And I am particularly glad to come to this country because of the blood ties that join us. In my country there are more than ten million citizens who claim direct heritage from the Italian civilization—people of your blood.

So our friendship is not only an official one, it is a welcome of people clasping their hands across the sea, as relatives—people of the same kind.

I look forward to the discussions that I shall have with you, Mr. President, with Mr. Segni and Mr. Pella, and the others. I look forward again to seeing your beautiful country, and to renewing my acquaintanceship with the people whom I learned to know during my days in NATO. And I assure you that as partners with you in this NATO organization, we shall always do our part and stand with you in the search for peace with justice and in freedom.

I want to say again that it is a great privilege for me to return the visit that you have made to my country—both your Prime Minister and Foreign Minister have been there—we welcomed them warmly, because of the sentiments existing between us, which I have just tried so feebly to express.

Thank you very much.

NOTE: The President spoke at 12:30 p.m. He was met by President Giovanni Gronchi, Prime Minister Antonio Segni, Foreign Minister Giuseppe Pella, other Italian Government officials, members of the diplomatic corps, and U.S. Ambassador James D. Zellerbach.

292 ¶ Remarks to the Staff of the U.S. Embassy in Rome. *December 5, 1959*

GOOD MORNING—good to see you.

It's almost unpardonable in war for an old soldier to be surprised. I am not only surprised this morning, I was astonished. I was invited here to see the Ambassador at his office. I didn't know I was going to meet so many of you good people.

I do congratulate you about one thing, immediately, and that is the beauty of the building in which you have to work. As I came in I noticed the halls and people in it, and I felt it's the kind of office I would like, if I could get it.

I am, as you know, on a visit to try to interpret America to other peoples a little bit more emphatically, a little bit more accurately than sometimes it is done. We do know that the United States is not always admired, we are sometimes suspicioned; and my task is really to try to make them see that America wants nothing but to live in peace, in a just peace. And while I know that this is the task of all of you people— your Ambassador, and everybody down to the last chore boy in this Embassy—I feel that by making the rather dramatic tour of some thousands of miles, that possibly I can support your efforts, to emphasize them, and by going and making this trip, reinforcing the work that you are doing all the time to make certain that the motives of the United States are understood.

We not only want to live with a just peace, we want to help other peoples to raise their standards, to be as content with their lot as humans can be. That is the chore we have set for ourselves.

I think that each of you feels that he has a real mission in trying to do that job, and certainly I have a very great lift when I get a chance to get out and do this kind of thing myself. Because I believe unless the people of the world have confidence that all the nations want peace, we are not going to live the kind of life that we deserve to live.

And since I have four grandchildren, I am very concerned that they get a chance to live, the same kind of opportunity, the same kind of life, at least a better life than I had.

So, to all of you engaged in that same kind of work, my thanks, my felicitations—and thanks very much for your warm welcome.

Goodbye.

NOTE: The President spoke in Ambassador Zellerbach's office at the chancery of the U.S. Embassy.

293 ¶ Joint Statement Following Discussions With President Gronchi. *December* 5, 1959

THE PRESIDENT of the United States, assisted by Ambassador Murphy, the President of the Italian Republic and the President of the Council of Ministers of the Italian Republic, assisted by Minister of Foreign Affairs Pella, concluded on December 5 a two-day series of meetings which were held both at the Quirinal Palace and the Viminal Palace. The conversations were animated by friendship, respect and understanding. They covered a wide range of international topics in which both Italy and the United States are interested.

The meetings were conducted in the clear knowledge that Italy's increasing contribution to the elaboration of a common Western policy is in the interest of the Western countries.

President Eisenhower and President Gronchi discussed plans for their respective visits to the Soviet Union next year. They agreed that these visits are being undertaken in the hope that they will advance the cause of peace and contribute to the search for solutions to outstanding international problems.

Both parties declared that the North Atlantic Alliance remains the cornerstone of their foreign policies. They found themselves in full agreement with regard to the vital role which the North Atlantic Alliance must continue to play.

They confirmed the firm belief that the way to world peace lies through full application of the principles set forth in the United Nations Charter and expressed the dedication of their two countries to the United Nations.

They exchanged views regarding appropriate ways and means to accelerate the economic growth of the less developed countries of the world with the purpose of increasing the combined economic strength of the free world and the well-being of all peoples. They agreed that increased free world participation in assistance to the less developed areas is necessary and that this participation should be coordinated among the free nations.

The participants expressed their determination to pursue policies aimed at reducing the burden of armaments throughout the world. The two Governments also expressed their determination to do all in their power to insure that the ten nation disarmament group, of which both Italy and the United States are members, will lay the groundwork for an acceptable solution to the problem of disarmament, which can only be achieved within the framework of a specific system of controls, inspections and safeguards.

They reviewed developments related to the European Economic Community. They noted the substantial progress which is being achieved in carrying out the Rome treaty and in increasing political and economic unity among the member states of the Community. They were agreed on the continuing importance of these objectives and the need for the Community to evolve policies in order to promote the collaboration with other similar associations and other countries, and also to contribute to the goal of freer, expanded world trade.

President Segni informed President Eisenhower of the measures being taken by the Italian Government to further liberalize trade with the dollar area. President Eisenhower noted this action with satisfaction.

The two Presidents and the Prime Minister considered efforts which are being made through GATT and other appropriate bodies to remove obstacles to world trade. They agreed that further measures should be taken to eliminate discriminatory trade restrictions.

This series of meetings constituted an important step in the progress toward the realization of the ideals of peace, security, justice and social progress which form the basis of all the policies of the two countries.

NOTE: This joint statement was released in Rome.

294 ¶ Remarks at Ciampino Airport, Rome, Upon Leaving for Turkey. *December 6, 1959*

IT NOW becomes my privilege to say goodbye to the people of Italy and to this beautiful country. Every time I come to Italy I am struck by the very warm friendship that I seem to feel between this people and the people of America. And I assure you that that affection is reciprocated.

I have had good talks with the heads of your government—your President and Prime Minister Segni. I am sure that on the vital issues that are now besetting the world, we are in accord—we see them in the same way. We hope to approach them for solutions in the same way.

As I go on this trip, I feel that a very fine beginning has been made here.

And so, as I express the gratitude of my party and myself to all of you, to the heads of your government, and to all the people that hear me, I express the hope that again I may return.

Finally, I want to say I have just come from a visit with His Holiness the Pope, and I have been inspired by his approval of the effort that the free nations together are making to bring some progress toward peace and friendship in freedom.

Thank you again, and goodbye.

NOTE: Prior to making these remarks the President attended services at St. Paul's Protestant Episcopal Church and visited Pope John XXIII at the Vatican. He then left by helicopter from the grounds of the North American Ecclesiastical College for the airport, where he was met by Premier Antonio Segni, Foreign Minister Giuseppe Pella, Manlio Brosio, Italian Ambassador to the United States, and James D. Zellerbach, U.S. Ambassador to Italy.

295 ¶ Remarks Upon Arrival at Esenboga Airport, Ankara. *December 6, 1959*

Mr. President, Citizens of Turkey:

President Bayar, from my heart I thank you and your people for your welcome for my party and myself.

Almost 8 years have passed since my last visit to Ankara. In those years the bonds of friendship and partnership between the Turkish and American peoples have grown stronger. So I return to the capital of this sister republic, hopeful that my visit here will be fruitful for the good of both nations.

My purpose in returning to Turkey is twofold: first, I have wanted to take advantage of a long-standing invitation to visit this nation once again and see all the developments that have taken place since I was here in the spring of 1952.

Second, in my official capacity as President of the United States, I return the visit which you, President Bayar, so graciously paid America.

This visit will permit me to discuss with the leaders of your government some of the problems that confront free nations today. We shall take also the opportunity to talk about opportunities that present themselves to achieve a world of plenty in which all nations can live—independent and prosperous, at peace with their neighbors. I want you to know that we in America greatly respect and highly regard our staunch friend and ally, Turkey. We know that you will be strong and persistent and dedicated in all efforts for peace and friendship in freedom.

President Bayar, I am delighted to be here once again among my Turkish friends, and I know that I speak for all the members of my party when I respond to your warm words of welcome by saying, somewhat haltingly I fear, but nevertheless sincerely, *"Hoş bulduk. Cok tesekkur ederim"* [We are happy to be here. I thank you very much].

NOTE: The President spoke at 3:15 p.m. He was met by President Bayar, Turkish civilian and military officials, members of the diplomatic corps, and by U.S. Ambassador Fletcher Warren.

296 ❡ Remarks by the President at a Dinner Given in His Honor by President Bayar. *December 6, 1959*

Mr. President, distinguished guests:

On this visit, as on my first more than 7 years ago, the unmatched hospitality of our Turkish allies and friends has been for the members of my party and myself a most heartwarming experience. The leaders and people of Turkey have extended to us a welcome that makes us feel more like friends returning to pleasant and well-remembered scenes rather than like strangers in this land.

For myself, it is in truth a return to a land I cannot forget. In March of 1952, I came here to inspect the troops which Turkey had committed to the common defense of the Atlantic nations. Here through a 3-day visit, along with the encouragement and inspiration I got from your armed forces and your leaders, I absorbed evidence of the beauty, the progress, the growth of Turkey. I developed a real admiration for both your military and civil leaders and for the great people they represented.

As tenacious defenders of your land and independence, you of Turkey have achieved a worldwide reputation. From two experiences with you, I can testify that you deserve an equal prestige as gracious hosts. For all of my party, it is indeed a high honor to be welcomed as partners of your nation.

All Americans who know you have a tremendous respect for your courage and your vision of a Republic dedicated to the good of its people, their freedom and their prosperity. You Turks, by your own efforts and by deliberate decision, resolved a generation ago to build a modern nation, free from aggressive intent on its neighbors, at peace with all nations of good will, but resolved never to be cowed by any threat.

Under the outstanding and farsighted leadership of the founder of Modern Turkey, Kemal Ataturk, you of this country have wrought revolutionary changes. In government, customs, and traditions these changes were breathtaking in scope. They were remarkable for the swiftness of their achievement. They are an inspiration and a guiding light to all newly independent nations, determined on progress, prosperity, and peace.

No nation of today encounters greater obstacles to progress than you faced when you made your great national decision. You had just emerged from the ruin and devastation of the first World War. On every side, you were plagued with problems that seemed beyond solution. But you were rich in your spirit and in the idealism and vitality of your leaders. In them you had a wealth and strength beyond money and machines.

You, the people of Turkey forged steadily ahead on the path to industrial development and social progress. You made your country a modern proving ground that democracy and stout hearts are a people's best instruments for the achievement of greatness.

Much, I know, remains to be achieved. But I am impressed—even amazed—as I return to Turkey to see all around me the results of the past 7 years' progress and the evidences of determination and of dynamic growth.

The United States is proud of your achievements—very proud of our increasingly close friendship and associations. The American people understand your desire for progress and for higher standards of living. They are happy that they can provide some measure of assistance to help you realize the goals you yourselves have established.

I am confident that the United States, with other friends and allies, will continue to help in your economic development and security. And no power on earth, no evil, no threat, can frustrate a people of your spirit.

We of America as you in Turkey are much concerned today with the economic progress and political stability of the world's newly emerging nations. We believe that all free nations should cooperate in a great combined effort to achieve increased levels of free world economic strength. But alongside this purpose and because both of us are also concerned with our security and that of our friends we are joined with others in NATO to insure the safety of all of us. Here, my friends, I might as well have brought in CENTO, but since Turkey and ourselves are both full partners of NATO, and we are merely an associate of CENTO, I confine my remarks to NATO.

NATO is a defensive alliance, solely and simply for our mutual security. We know that we are building defenses only against the possibility of an emergency, an aggression, a catastrophe which will never be of our making. Those who say otherwise speak for their own ulterior motives.

The peoples of Turkey and the United States seek peace. But the peace we are striving to achieve, as free, God-fearing nations, must be a just and enduring peace based upon individual freedom and human dignity. These values, the Koran and the Bible teach us, are fundamental to man's life on earth. We will not deviate from our goal nor compromise our principles.

We will continue in our search for peace and in our efforts to reach mutually enforceable agreements with the leaders of the world Communist movement.

With steadfast adherence to our principles, and with faith in Almighty God, we will do our best to achieve the goal we are seeking.

To all our Turkish friends, I express again on behalf of the American people and the members of my party my deep appreciation and sincere thanks for your exceptional welcome and hospitality. In closing I should like to say:

Long live Turkish-American friendship.

Long live the Turkish and American Republics.

Long live world peace, justice, and human freedom.

And in this spirit I propose a toast to your distinguished Head of State—President Bayar.

NOTE: The dinner was held at President Bayar's palace.

297 ¶ Joint Statement Following Discussions With President Bayar. *December 7, 1959*

PRESIDENT EISENHOWER visited Turkey on December 6 through December 7, 1959. The sincere rejoicing of the Turkish Nation and the outstanding reception extended to President Eisenhower and to his party during this brief but meaningful visit reaffirmed in the most impressive way the existing strong friendship and close cooperation between the Governments and peoples of Turkey and the United States. The visit demonstrated anew the desire of both countries to continue this fruitful cooperation in their mutual interest as well as in that of the community of free nations to which they both belong.

In the course of this visit talks were held at President Bayar's residence on Sunday evening between the two Presidents with the participation of Prime Minister Menderes and Foreign Minister Zorlu, Under Secretary of State Murphy, Secretary General Esenbel and Ambassador Warren.

During the talks a full and friendly exchange took place on a wide range of problems of common interest.

The alliance and partnership of Turkey and the United States within the defense organization of NATO and active association in CENTO, together with their common participation in the actions of the United Nations for the preservation of peace, influenced the nature and the scope of the talks. Turkish cooperation in the United Nations Command, Korea, was recalled in this connection.

On the vital question of the creation of an atmosphere that would lead to establishment of a true detente in the whole world, the two Presidents agreed that such a detente, in order to be effective, should be based on justice and equality and provided with the essential safeguards. Since it is not possible to divide the many problems at present separating East and West into separate compartments, they recognized that detente like peace had to be considered as an indivisible entity. It was understood that an efficient, controlled system of disarmament is necessary.

In the course of the discussions particular attention was paid to existing areas of tension and danger throughout the world. President Bayar and President Eisenhower jointly expressed strong conviction that at this point in history the future of humanity depended above all on the degree of solidarity in thought and action which the free nations can master in meeting their common problems. They agreed that cooperation and continuing consultation between the two countries both on a bilateral basis and within NATO and CENTO were paramount.

President Bayar expressed his sincere appreciation of the admirable efforts made by President Eisenhower in order to reduce international tensions and both Presidents voiced the hope that these efforts would bear fruit for the benefit of the whole world. Particular attention was paid to the question of subversive activities in the Middle East and the situation was appraised in the light of an eventual atmosphere of detente.

Economic aspects of the Turkish-American relations, as well as the broader problem of the assistance to underdeveloped countries, were considered. President Bayar stressed the importance of securing a sufficient raising of the living standard of the Turkish people in order to enable Turkey to assume adequately the responsibilities which her geographic position imposes upon her. He outlined the economic progress achieved in the last ten years in Turkey and expressed appreciation for the generous assistance given by the American people to Turkey.

President Eisenhower expressed his appreciation of the economic and social goals met by the Turkish Nation. He expressed confidence that the United States will continue to support, in concert with other friends and allies, the economic development and security efforts of Turkey. He expressed his belief that such efforts would be successful.

The two Presidents recognized that improvement in the standard of living of the less developed countries is a necessary ingredient to the achievement of peace and security in the world. They expressed the view that coordinated action is desirable and that any aid extended would prove most effective when providing and receiving countries were united through a dedication to common goals.

The economic collaboration realized after the war constitutes a remarkable example in the field of economic assistance. The hope was expressed as well that European efforts in this field could be directed to the assistance of the less developed areas of the European continent, like Turkey.

The initiative of Turkey to be an associate member of the European Common Market was also examined and the hope was expressed that such association would foster solidarity among these countries.

In concluding their talk the two Presidents reiterated their dedication to the ideals enshrined in the Charter of the United Nations. They expressed their determination to marshal all their efforts to the attainment of a lasting peace embracing full security and justice for all.

NOTE: This joint statement was released in Ankara.

298 ¶ Remarks at Esenboga Airport, Ankara, Upon Leaving for Pakistan. *December 7, 1959*

Mr. President, Prime Minister Menderes, Members of the Government, Citizens of Turkey:

Through you, President Bayar, and your government, I should like to express to the Turkish people my very warm thanks for the extraordinary reception they accorded to my party and me as we went through Ankara yesterday.

I have been deeply touched. I take their demonstration as a symbol of the true affection that exists between the peoples of America and of Turkey.

For the second time I say goodbye to this country—both times realizing that the visit that I have made is far too short.

This country takes hold of my heart. I should like to stay here and mingle with the people a far longer time than my official duties will permit me to do. But I do assure you that I leave with the greatest expression of appreciation and affection.

Our two countries have been friends for a long time. I think that they have been growing stronger and firmer friends, every year, every month, every day. I am confident this will continue to be so.

We stand together on the major issues that divide the world. And I can see no reason whatsoever that we shouldn't be two of the sturdiest partners standing together always for freedom, security, and the pursuit of peace.

Permit me, as I say Godspeed, good luck to you, to again attempt another Turkish expression, this time: *Allah'a ismarladik.* [I commend you to Allah.]

NOTE: The President spoke at 9:45 a.m., following his arrival by helicopter from the Guest House in Ankara. He was accompanied to the airport by President Bayar. The farewell ceremonies were held in the airport building. A 21-gun salute was fired as President Eisenhower filed through lines of members of the diplomatic corps and Turkish government officials, shaking hands with each on his way across the ramp to his aircraft.

299 ⁋ Remarks Upon Arrival at Mauripur Airport, Karachi. *December 7, 1959*

Mr. President:

I am more than grateful for the words of welcome you have just uttered, and I am particularly pleased by the sentiments you expressed about the ambitions of your country, a new country developing itself to be a force for good and for peace in the world.

For myself, may I say that I have just realized a long-felt ambition to come to your country of Pakistan, knowing something of its history and its traditions and to visit your leaders, your people, and your countryside.

This ambition has been all the stronger in recent years since Pakistan has been an ally of ours. We want to work together for peace, for our own mutual security, but from that position of strength and security to work always for what is good, decent, and just. Believing in our God, believing in the convictions that we have inherited from our Forefathers, we will yet have a world in which a just peace will be the lot of men, in which they can realize and use the fruits of their own toil.

I assure you again, Mr. President, that my party and I are looking forward to this visit with the greatest of anticipation, and we know before we leave that we are not going to be disappointed.

Thank you a lot.

NOTE: The President was met by President Ayub, members of President Ayub's cabinet, military officers, members of the diplomatic corps, and U.S. Ambassador William Rountree.

300 ⁋ Letter to Dr. Erwin D. Canham, President of the U.S. Chamber of Commerce, on the Federal Budget. *December 8, 1959*

[Released December 8, 1959. Dated December 2, 1959]

Dear Dr. Canham:

Your letter of November nineteenth arrived in my office only several days after I had received a report from the Director of the Bureau of the

Budget on improvements in budgeting, present and contemplated.   It occurred to me that this report was directly relevant to the questions you have raised, and I am taking the liberty of forwarding a copy of it to you.

Thank you for sending me so useful and constructive a letter on these important matters.

With warm regard,

Sincerely,

DWIGHT D. EISENHOWER

NOTE: Dr. Canham noted in his letter that the National Chamber had been pleased by the emphasis on budget reform in the 1960 Budget Message and hoped that a similar statement would be included in the Budget Message for 1961. He recommended giving the following deficiencies high priority in any action taken: (1) the failure of Congress to review and act upon the spending program as a whole; (2) the failure of Congress to review the principal aspects of Federal budgeting as a whole—revenues, expenditures, and the debt; (3) the use of "backdoor" spending methods which authorize obligations and/or expenditures outside normal budgetary control processes; (4) the inability of the President to exercise the veto power on items in appropriation legislation or other legislation which authorizes expenditures.

Dr. Canham's letter and the President's reply were released in Washington. The report of the Director of the Bureau of the Budget was made public as part of this release.

301   ¶ Remarks to the Staff of the U.S. Embassy and the American Community in Karachi. *December 8, 1959*

Ladies and Gentlemen:

Wherever an American Embassy is established anywhere in the world, that is a bit of America—that is American territory.   Now, in spite of that fact of international law, anybody that is working in an Embassy, attached to it, duties in connection with it, is nevertheless a guest of the country in which he resides.

We hope of course that Americans, by their customs, their practices, the beliefs and convictions they bring with them, can have some little influence on the country itself.   In turn, they have the problem and the duty of learning.

One of the great duties of an Embassy is to keep the American Government informed of the developments, the progress, the thinking, the aspirations and the hopes and the worries and the dangers that a country feels.

Now this puts on us all a responsibility, a great responsibility. If all of us recognize the dangers that now exist in the world, the tensions and the potentialities for destruction that have been brought about and brought to us by science, there is more than ever a great responsibility to bring about this mutual understanding out of which peaceful negotiation and eventually peace with justice can be achieved.

Now I am particularly interested about these young people right here in front of me. The world as we have known it is going to be different from what they are going to know. And even at these very tender ages, they must learn what is happening in the world, what is developing, and how they themselves can be masters of their own fates and make this a better place in which to live.

Every one of these young people here, Cub Scouts and older and younger—you have yourselves a great job to do, to make the children with whom you play or with whom you go to school, to understand that America wants to be friends with them, to learn more about them, what makes them "tick," why do they have customs different from yours—learning what this all means.

Now I don't mean to say this is a study in the school. This is what we learn by absorption. It is what we as older people learn by absorption that sticks better with us than those things that they try to jam into our heads with a ruler back in the little red schoolhouse, or by merely giving you a grade for the examinations that you didn't want to take in the first place.

But by absorbing and living with people, we learn things. And by your politeness to others, readiness to live and learn from them, rather than just to fight and argue because they are different, that is the kind of thing of which peace is made.

We are all filled with prejudices, preconceptions sometimes based upon religion, other times by race or because we say someone is of a different class, or something of that kind. We try to throw them out as we grow older.

Our problem now is that these kids, these youngsters, have fewer of them than we did. So that understanding grows as they grow. And then we will have a better world.

Now, just a personal word. Probably I am almost as passionately American as anyone could possibly be. I think that I get no thrill in the world quite so much as whenever I see a group of Americans, particularly in another country. Like all people in the uniformed services, I have roamed the world. It has always been a very wonderful thing when I can live and be closer with my American friends, than I think normally we did, because we thought we were in a little bit of a strange land. I am sure I did not take advantage of all the opportunities that were mine, to overcome my prejudices and to learn more fully from these other peoples, their conceptions of everything, from their God to their daily work.

These are the things we need to do. And old as I am, I have at least learned this much: that I have to work at it just as hard as anybody else.

Take one of these youngsters, say one of them is 9 years old, add 60 years to the year in which we now are, that would be two thousand and seventeen when this individual will be attaining my fairly venerable years. This world is going at such a rapid state, they need to know more than we did. They must do it. And you as parents can have no more precious and worthwhile duty than to give them the opportunity to live so far as we can on a basis of a moral code that within human capabilities eliminates prejudices and misconceptions, misapprehension and fear.

Now as usual, whenever I start to talk extemporaneously, I haven't the slightest idea what I am going to say. But I want to tell you this: that the thoughts I have just so haltingly attempted to describe are very deep within me, and while they may not be profound, I do hope all of you, from the youngest one here who is having a little trouble keeping her robe wrapped around her properly, to the oldest person in this audience, at least will ponder them.

Thank you a lot for coming out. It's a great honor you have done me to be here.

NOTE: The President spoke at 8:45 a.m. at the residence of William Rountree, U.S. Ambassador to Pakistan.

302   ¶ Remarks at the Citizens' Welcome for President Eisenhower, the Polo Field, Karachi. *December* 8, 1959

Mr. President, the officials of the City of Karachi, Your Excellencies and Ladies and Gentlemen of Pakistan:

It is a high honor indeed and a personal privilege for me to be a part of this great gathering in your city. And this meeting gives to me an opportunity that I have sought every moment since I first arrived at the outskirts of Karachi. I have never received in the world a warmer, more hospitable greeting than was given to me by the throngs in Karachi. For this greeting, ladies and gentlemen, I am profoundly grateful and I assure you my party, those attending me, feel exactly the same way. And indeed I am sure the people of America will understand that you are trying, through me, to say to them that you are their friend.

I have long desired to visit your magnificent country, and at first hand to learn something of this nation. I bring to you the friendly greetings and heartfelt salutations of the people of the United States for the people of Pakistan.

In the deepest values of life, we feel with you a very close kinship. We have always admired the courage and independent spirit of the Pakistan people, and have respected them because of their religious and spiritual devotion.

Our two countries both believe in human dignity and the brotherhood of man under God. And both of us are determined to be strong—spiritually, materially, militarily—not merely to ensure present security but also that we may be in a better position confidently and effectively to search out the paths to world peace with justice.

Our two countries are staunch allies, each to the other. To strengthen this partnership we must lose no opportunity to increase our mutual understanding.

It is certain that the fuller our knowledge of each other, the more effective will be our alliance for peace.

The many educational and cultural exchanges which have taken place between Pakistan and the United States have already helped greatly. I hope they will be continuously expanded. They will bring about a broader understanding of our common ideals, goals, and purposes. From this both nations will benefit.

Another thing is certain: friends such as Pakistan and the United States must cooperate in many fields, not only for their common security but so that their peoples may be enabled to enjoy more fully the advantages and blessings that modern science can open for mankind.

We are now in the nuclear age. No scientific discovery is of itself evil. It becomes evil only when devoted by unworthy men to wicked purposes. The atom can be used either for the benefit or for the destruction of man. Six years ago this very day, in an address before the United Nations General Assembly, I proposed a study and development of a worldwide program for the peaceful use of atomic energy. Since then, much has been learned in nuclear science, about the production of power and its application to medicine, agriculture, metallurgy, and the like. Very much more remains to be learned as to ways this colossal force can best be utilized to serve mankind.

In order that Pakistan may more rapidly develop its peaceful uses of the atom, the United States has given, in our country, specialized training to a number of your scientists, and has provided various types of equipment for research and medical uses here in your country. American consultants have come here to work with your own scientists. Many other nations are likewise cooperating to find ways by which the miraculous inventiveness of man may be consecrated solely to his progress and welfare.

Another certainty is this: by helping each other in many other ways, the free nations can vastly increase their combined productivity and thus provide both a fuller life and better material advantages for all their peoples.

On its part, the United States, in order to help develop this cooperation, has adopted and prosecuted programs of economic and military assistance to those free countries needing them. Your own country is one of those involved. Military assistance is provided to help you build and participate in the collective security of the free world, while your economy is developing and expanding to promote progress in your nation.

I assure you that the United States will continue to review and give sympathetic consideration to this kind of need in Pakistan.

A final certainty is that discoveries of science in the production of military power increasingly demand that some system of progressive and enforceable disarmament be agreed to among the nations. There is no reason to hesitate in this great undertaking. There can be no winner in any future global war. The world, the entire world, must insist that the conference table, rather than force, be used for the settlement of international disputes. Every national leader worthy of the name must participate in this effort.

The American people especially hope that Pakistan and the other nations in South Asia will succeed in their efforts to improve relations among themselves. Thus they will enhance and practice economic cooperation for the more efficient use and benefit of the resources available to them. Cooperation means prosperity for all—in food, in health, in knowledge, in wealth, in every shape and form of national well being.

The United States urges that good will and patience continue to be exercised, and that the governments concerned here persistently strive to reach mutually satisfactory understandings between themselves. The cause of peace and justice will thereby prosper.

I should like to say at this moment that President Ayub has told me of his very great ambitions and purposes in this very line. And he has, I assure you, the plaudits of America in so doing.

Since my arrival here I have become fortified in a personal certainty: it is my fixed conviction that Pakistan-American friendship is a lasting one, built firmly. Through it we shall have a safer, brighter, happier future together.

My conversations with President Ayub and some of his associates are on the basis that we are two nations with many common interests, two nations which share common goals and which cooperate for mutual security.

Our fruitful talks give me a better appreciation of your problems, and of the courageous manner in which you are attacking them. And when I return home, I shall tell my fellow Americans that the Pakistani are a courageous people, an energetic people, a loyal people who love peace, but who put justice and freedom—as do we—before all else.

All of us know that there is more than one kind of courage. Any courageous man will of course fight for the protection of his home, his family, and his rights. But there is also a patient kind of courage, the kind that in spite of disappointment and discouragement enables a man

817

to persist in working tirelessly to improve the lot of himself, his family, and his community. Pakistani leaders are pointing out the work that needs to be done—America believes that Pakistan has also the kind of courage needed to bring these programs of improvement to fulfillment.

And I shall tell my fellow Americans that in Pakistan are leaders, chief among whom is President Ayub, who are dedicated to the welfare of all their citizens, to the furtherance of universal education, and to the creation of a free republic. In building a truly representative government, they and he are demonstrating themselves to be men of vision, of courage, and of decisive action.

May God prosper their noble purpose.

Thank you very much, ladies and gentlemen.

NOTE: The President spoke at 3:35 p.m.

303 ¶ Joint Statement Following Discussions With President Ayub Khan. *December 8, 1959*

ON THE morning of December 8, 1959, the President of Pakistan and the President of the United States, with advisors of both Governments, met to discuss matters of common interest. These discussions continued at lunch and the two Presidents have had other opportunities to exchange views.

Both Presidents warmly welcomed the opportunity afforded by President Eisenhower's visit to have these talks, which were held in an atmosphere of cordiality and frankness characterizing relations between the two allied nations.

They reviewed generally world-wide political questions, and in particular problems of relations between the Free World and the Sino-Soviet bloc. They were in full agreement as to the essentiality of cooperation among members of the family of free nations in the interest of their mutual security.

They discussed relationships among the nations of the area and the urgent desirability of finding solutions to existing disputes. In this way the energies of the peoples and governments may be directed more fully toward constructive programs adding to stability and progress, and a greater degree of cooperation among them may be achieved.

They reaffirmed their satisfaction with the increasingly close cooperation between Pakistan and the United States. Relations between the countries are based upon mutual respect and friendship, resting on the firm determination of both to work together for the achievement of the purposes and principles of the United Nations.

They emphasized anew the importance of CENTO and SEATO in preserving the stability and security of the areas covered by them. They reiterated the determination of the two Governments to continue strongly to support these regional collective security organizations in accordance with Article 51 of the United Nations Charter.

They recognized the heavy financial burden placed upon Pakistan in its efforts to undertake substantial development projects and at the same time to maintain armed forces consonant with its national security. They reviewed various elements of technical, economic and military aid which is extended to Pakistan by the United States as part of the two nations' mutual assistance which contributes to the security of both.

They reiterated their conviction that the Free World's best interests require closer cooperation in order to advance economic growth and development. They reviewed with gratification the progress being made in Pakistan in this connection, and the President of the United States expressed in particular to President Ayub his admiration for the remarkable achievements in Pakistan toward the resettlement of those elements of the population which have been inadequately housed.

The President of Pakistan explained steps taken by his Government during the past year to strengthen the country. He outlined the "basic democracies plan" and progress toward a new constitution. The President of the United States stated that his Government was following Pakistan's venture with genuine interest.

The two Presidents expressed their belief that the visit had led to an even closer understanding between Pakistan and the United States, had strengthened the strong ties already existing between the two countries, and had underlined the need of continued cooperative programs between them.

NOTE: This joint statement was released in Karachi.

304 ¶ Toast to President Ayub Khan at a Dinner Given in His Honor by the President.
December 8, 1959

Ladies and gentlemen:

I am going to propose a toast to the President of Pakistan, but before doing so I want to assure the President and all his associates in government, whose guests my party and I have been for the past 2 days, that we have had not only an interesting and enjoyable time, but we sincerely believe an instructive time. We think we learned something about your country that will be helpful to us.

If we have done that, that is real reason we should have come.

In addition to that, I want to tell you that it has been a most happy experience for us. The hospitality, the cordiality and the warmth of the reception to all of us have meant a very great deal to each of us.

And so, my friends, I propose a toast to the President of Pakistan.

NOTE: The President proposed this toast at the dinner given at the residence of U.S. Ambassador William Rountree in Karachi at 9:40 p.m.

305 ¶ Remarks at Mauripur Airport, Karachi, Upon Leaving for Afghanistan.
December 9, 1959

MR. PRESIDENT, the time has come for my party and me to say goodbye to you and your friendly country. We have found very interesting and constructive our talks with you and your government, and we hope that you have also received some value from them. Our stay has been all too brief. We have just had a sample of your country and should like to come again. Certainly we have seen enough to know that if we could come we could be sure of the kind of courtesy and hospitality that your country is famous for.

Again, I would like to tell you how much we should each like to thank all the citizens of the city and the countryside for the welcome they have given us. We are grateful from our hearts. Good luck to you and your government, particularly in your leadership for a good, better life for all your citizens, as exemplified in the new village you are building which yesterday we found very interesting.　Good luck to the people of Pakistan and all your associates in government as well as yourself.

NOTE: The President, accompanied by President Ayub and Ambassador Roun-　tree, went by helicopter to the Mauripur Airport.

306　¶ Remarks Upon Arrival at Bagram Airport, Kabul.　*December* 9, 1959

Your Majesty, Your Royal Highnesses, Excellencies, Ladies and Gentlemen:

It is with the greatest pleasure that I address you here this morning in Afghanistan.　I want first to convey the warm and friendly greetings of the American people to Afghanistan and its people.　Ever since His Royal Highness Prince Daud visited us in the United States a year ago last June, I have cherished the hope that I could return his call.　It is a sign of the age in which we live that I am able to travel the many miles involved in this journey in the short space of time available to me.

It is a reminder of the fact that all of us live very close together in the 20th century.　True friendship and mutual respect for nations has become not only desirable, it is an absolute necessity.　My one regret is that my visit here must be so brief.　All my life I have heard and read about this great country, with these magnificent mountains, already snow-capped as I see, its austere beauty, its brave and sturdy people, and its indomitable spirit of independence.

It is a great privilege for me now to be in your country to see a little of it for myself, and to meet more of your people, even though for so short a time.

I thank you, for this welcome.

NOTE: The Presidential motorcade left Bagram Airport at approximately 9:15 a.m. for Chilstoon Palace, the King's residence in Kabul.　Riding with the President were His Majesty Mohammad Zahir Shah, King of Afghanistan, M. H. Maiwandwal, Ambassador to the United States, and Henry A. Byroade, U.S. Ambassador to Afghanistan.

307   ¶ Toast of the President at a Luncheon Given in His Honor by King Mohammad Zahir. *December 9, 1959*

Your Majesty, Your Royal Highnesses, Excellencies, Gentlemen:

First of all, Your Majesty, I should like to thank you very sincerely for the graciousness and generosity of your remarks concerning my country and me personally. More than this, I should like to say a word of thanks for the invitation that made it possible for me to come here to meet Your Majesty, members of your government, and these gentlemen.

So, before I propose a toast to Your Majesty and to your people, I should like to express a few thoughts that are on my mind at this moment.

First, I must express my tremendous respect for the Afghan people; for their integrity, courage, and hardiness, well-proven by history and renowned throughout the world. These qualities, more than anything else, ensure the independence of the Afghan nation.

Second I should like to take note of the desire of the Afghan people for peace and harmony among nations. When all are of a like mind, men will be able to dedicate themselves, not to the building of weapons of destruction but to the ennoblement and enrichment of life.

I wish also to express my admiration for the industriousness and enterprise of the Afghan people. They are determined to share in the dynamic achievements of our time; to enjoy the life which modern science and engineering makes possible today.

The peoples of America and Afghanistan share a steadfast determination to protect and defend their independence and heritage. Because we respect your independence as we do our own, we participate with you in mutual security measures.

We Americans are proud of your advances on the path of economic, educational, and social progress. We are happy that we have been able to assist you even in a small way.

Most importantly, we share with the Afghan people a sense of the great spiritual values deriving from our respective religious heritages. We are drawn together in devotion to the abiding values of religion.

From these values, Afghans and Americans derive a full appreciation of the dignity of man. Without this appreciation, we cannot cope with the problems of our time. With it, we shall be able together to advance the cause of freedom and peace among nations, now and in the future.

And so, I propose a toast to the King—may he continue to enjoy good health and well-being and the benign guidance of the Almighty; and to the people of Afghanistan, may they never falter in their steadfast determination to maintain their honor and independence. May they march ever forward in peace, progress, and prosperity.

NOTE: The luncheon was held at Chilstoon Palace.

308 ¶ Joint Statement Following Discussions With King Mohammad Zahir.
December 9, 1959

THE PRESIDENT of the United States, Honorable Dwight D. Eisenhower, has just paid a visit to Afghanistan, where he met with His Majesty Mohammad Zahir, King of Afghanistan, and other members of the royal family and members of the Afghan Government.

President Eisenhower was accompanied by Ambassador Robert Murphy, Major and Mrs. John Eisenhower and members of the Presidential staff.

President Eisenhower conveyed the warm and friendly greetings of the people of the United States to the people of Afghanistan and expressed his deep appreciation for the reception accorded him and his party.

While the President's visit was primarily an expression of goodwill, talks on questions of mutual interest were carried on. These talks were held in an atmosphere of cordiality.

His Majesty, Mohammad Zahir, King of Afghanistan, explained Afghanistan's policy of independence and neutrality.

Both sides agreed to work unstintingly and patiently toward the limitation of international frictions and tensions.

Note was taken of the strides that Afghanistan is making in economic development and social progress. President Eisenhower gave assurances of an American desire to continue to assist Afghanistan in its task of strengthening its economic and social structure.

Both sides also agreed that in the present day it is imperative that international disputes are settled by peaceful means and further concurred in the need for world peace, especially so as to enable the energies of mankind to be channeled into constructive pursuits of development and human fulfillment.

They endorsed unqualifiedly the principles of the United Nations Charter as standards for international behavior.

His Majesty Mohammad Zahir Shah, King of Afghanistan, expressed high hopes for concrete results from the prospective summit meeting of President Eisenhower with other heads of government and from his forthcoming visit to the Soviet Union.

Both sides further expressed hopes that a workable and enforceable basis for disarmament can soon be found.

Both sides agreed that the visit of President Eisenhower to Afghanistan had strengthened the already warm and friendly relations between the two countries.

NOTE: This joint statement was released in Kabul.

309 ¶ Remarks to the American Community in Kabul. *December* 9, 1959

FELLOW AMERICANS, youngsters, I wish I could start at one end, say "Hello," give my greetings to each one of you, and shake hands with you; but it's just impossible. I do want you to know that the Government of the United States expects a lot of you people, every one of you here. Whether you are 3 or 103, you are Mr. and Mrs. Ambassador. You are trying to picture America in another country. But more than that, you are trying to learn more about another country so you can tell us better how we should conduct ourselves to help bring peace to the earth. No one could have a more important job, and I congratulate every one of you, who has this opportunity. I want to say that so far as I can see in every Embassy that I visited every one of you is doing a good job. I thank you both for the American people and for myself.

Good luck to all of you. Goodbye.

NOTE: The President greeted the members of the American community at the   Bagram Airport before his departure for New Delhi.

310 ¶ Remarks Upon Arrival at Palam Airport, New Delhi. *December* 9, 1959

Mr. President, Mr. Prime Minister, Your Excellencies, and Ladies and Gentlemen:

As I set foot on the soil of India I am fulfilling a cherished wish held for many years. And since the day that your Prime Minister came to visit me in Washington, and came with me to my home where we had talks about India, the work that India is trying now to do, I made up my mind that come what may, the Lord willing, I would come back to India while I was still President of the United States.

Your Prime Minister wrote a very great book about discovering India. I was intrigued with the book, but I am here to do what I can do in 4 short days, to do a little bit of personal discovery about India.

But some of the things I know. India won its freedom and its independence through peaceful means. This in itself was a great accomplishment, and one that has challenged the admiration of the entire world.

But more than that, India, determined to live in peace, has devoted her entire efforts, all her treasure, all her talent, all her brains to raising the standards of her own people, to give them a better chance for a better life.

My friends, these efforts are going to succeed if the world can have peace. All of us know it: the only alternative to global war is peace, or the other alternative is too horrible even to mention.

So I think that I can best explain that the deepest purpose that I have in coming here is this: to symbolize if I can, and if I may so presume, the fact that the United States stands with India, with the leaders of the United States standing with the leaders of India, in our common quest for peace. And the Lord permitting, nations and people so inspired will yet be successful to the complete freeing of men from the fears and tensions that have so long plagued humanity.

So let us all pray that even this little step may have some useful purpose in furthering that great hope.

Thank you—thank you particularly for your welcome and coming here. And I am sorry I was late, I couldn't help it.

NOTE: The President was met by President Prasad, Prime Minister Nehru, other Indian Government officials, members of the diplomatic corps, and U.S. Ambassador Ellsworth Bunker.

311 ¶ Address Delivered Before a Joint Session of the Parliament of India.   *December* 10, 1959

Mr. Chairman, Mr. Speaker, Mr. Vice President, Honorable Members of Parliament, and Ladies and Gentlemen:

Mr. Chairman, I must assure you that our audience here will be aware of a great deal of duplication in our two speeches. It does not dismay me, though, to repeat these sentiments, for the simple reason that one of the reasons that I am here is to assure you of the identity of view on the part of the American people to those that have just been so well expressed.

It is with a sense of high distinction that I accepted the invitation to address you. I deem this a great personal honor, and a bright symbol of the genuine friendship between the peoples you and I represent.

I bring to this nation of four hundred million, assurance from my own people that they feel that the welfare of America is bound up with the welfare of India. America shares with India the deep desire to live in freedom, human dignity, and peace with justice.

A new and great opportunity for that sort of life has been opened up to all men by the startling achievements of men of science during recent decades. The issue placed squarely before us today is the purpose for which we use science.

Before us we see long years of what can be a new era; mankind in each year reaping a richer harvest from the fields of earth—gaining a more sure mastery of elemental power for human benefit—sharing an expanding commerce in goods and in knowledge and in wisdom—dwelling together in peace.

But history portrays a world too often tragically divided by misgiving and mistrust and quarrel. Time and again governments have abused the fields of earth by staining them with blood and scarring them with the weapons of war. They have used a scientific mastery over nature to win a dominance over others—even made commerce an instrument of exploitation.

The most heartening, hopeful phenomenon in the world today is that people have experienced a great awakening. They see the evils of the past as crimes against the moral law, injuring the offender as well as the victim. They recognize that only under the rule of moral law can all of us realize our deepest and noblest aspirations.

One blunt question I put to you, and to all—everyone—everywhere who like myself share responsibility assigned to us by our people:

Must we continue to live with prejudices, practices, and policies that will condemn our children and our children's children to live helplessly in the pattern of the past—awaiting possibly a time of war-borne obliteration?

We all fervently pray not. Indeed, there can be no statesmanship in any person of responsibility who does not concur in this world-wide prayer.

Over most of the earth, men and women are determined that the conference table shall replace the propaganda mill; international exchange of knowledge shall succeed the international trade in threats and accusations; and the fertile works of peace shall supplant the frenzied race in armaments of war.

Our hope is that we are moving into a better era. For my part, I shall do all I can, as one human working with other humans, to push toward peace; toward freedom; toward dignity and a worthy future for every man and woman and child in the world.

If we—and especially all those occupying positions of responsibility—give all that is within us to this cause, the generations that follow us will call us blessed. Should we shirk the task or pursue the ways of war—now become ways to annihilation and race suicide—there may be no generations to follow us.

I come here representing a nation that wants not an acre of another people's land; that seeks no control of another people's government; that pursues no program of expansion in commerce or politics or power of any sort at another people's expense. It is a nation ready to cooperate toward achievement of mankind's deep, eternal aspirations for peace and freedom.

And I come here as a friend of India, speaking for one hundred and eighty million friends of India. In fulfilling a desire of many years I pay, in person, America's tribute to the Indian people, to their culture, to their progress, and to their strength among the independent nations.

All humanity is in debt to this land. But we Americans have, with you, a special community of interest.

You and we from our first days have sought, by national policy, the expansion of democracy. You and we, peopled by many strains and races speaking many tongues, worshipping in many ways, have each achieved national strength out of diversity. And you and we never boast that ours is the only way. We are conscious of our weaknesses and our failings. We both seek the improvement and betterment of all our citizens by assuring that the state will serve, not master, its own people or any other people.

Above all, our basic goals are the same.

Ten years ago, your distinguished Prime Minister, when I was his host at Columbia University in New York, said:

"Political subjection, racial inequality, economic misery—these are the evils we have to remove if we would assure peace."

Our Republic, since its founding, has been committed to a relentless, ceaseless fight against those same three evils: political subjection, racial inequality, economic misery.

Not always has America enjoyed instant success in a particular attack on them. By no means has victory been won over them and, indeed, complete victory can never be won so long as human nature is not transformed. But in my country, through almost two hundred years, our most revered leaders have been those who have exhorted us to give of our lives and our fortunes to the vanquishment of these evils. And in this effort for the good of all our people, we shall not tire nor cease.

Ten years have passed since Mr. Nehru spoke his words. The pessimist might say that, not only do the three evils still infest the world—entrenched, and manifold; but that they will never lose their virulence. And the future, he might conclude, will be a repetition of the past; the world stumbling from crisis in one place to crisis in another; given no respite from anxiety and tension; forever fearful that inevitably some aggression will blaze into global war.

Thus might the pessimist speak. And were we to examine only the record of failure and frustration, we all would be compelled to agree with him.

We Americans have known anxiety and suffering and tragedy, even in the decade just past. Tens of thousands of our families paid a heavy price that the United Nations and the rule of law might be sustained in the Republic of Korea. In millions of our homes there has been, in each, the vacant chair of absent men—a son who performing his duty gave some of the years of his youth that successful aggression might not come to pass. The news, from near and distant places, that has reached us in America through these 10 years, has been marked by a long series of harsh alarms.

These alarms invariably had their source in the aggressive intentions of an alien philosophy backed by great military strength. Faced with this fact, we in America have felt it necessary to make clear our own determination to resist aggression through the provision of adequate armed forces. These forces serve us and those of our friends and allies who like us have perceived the danger. But they so serve for defensive purposes only. In producing this strength, we believe we have made a necessary contribution to a stable peace, for the present and for the future as well.

Historically and by instinct the United States has always repudiated and still repudiates the settlement, by force, of international issues and quarrels. Though we will do our best to provide for free world security, we continue to urge the reduction of armaments on the basis of effective reciprocal verification.

And contrasting with some of our disappointments of the past decade, and the negative purposes of security establishments, Americans have participated, also, in triumphant works of world progress, political, technical, and material. We believe these works support the concept of the dignity and freedom of man. These hearten America that the years ahead will be marked by like and greater works. And America watches, with friendly concern, the valiant efforts of other nations for a better life, particularly those who have newly achieved their independence.

Ten years ago India had just achieved independence; wealthy in courage and determination, but beset with problems of a scale and depth and numbers scarcely paralleled in modern history. Not even the most optimistic of onlookers would then have predicted the success you have enjoyed.

Today, India speaks to the other nations of the world with greatness of conviction and is heard with greatness of respect. The near conclusion of her second 5-year program is proof that the difficulty of a problem is only the measure of its challenge to men and women of determined will. India is a triumph that offsets the world's failures of the past decade; a triumph that, as men read our history a century from now, may offset them all.

India has paced and spurred and inspired men on other continents.

Let anyone take a map of the earth and place on it a flag wherever political subjection has ended, racial prejudice has been reduced, economic misery at least partially relieved during the past 10 years. He will find evidence in the cluster of these flags that the 10 years past may well have been the 10 most fruitful years in the age-old fight against the three evils.

Because of these 10 years, today our feet are set on the road leading to a better life for all men.

What blocks us that we do not move forward instantly into an era of plenty and peace?

The answer is obvious: we have not yet solved the problem of fear among the nations. The consequence is that not one government can exploit the resources of its own territory solely for the good of its people.

Governments are burdened with sterile expenditures—preoccupied with the attainment of a defensive military posture that grows less meaningful against today's weapons carriers.

Much of the world is trapped in the same vicious circle. Weakness in arms often invites aggression or subversion, or externally manipulated revolutions. Fear inspired in others by the increasing military strength of one nation spurs them to concentrate still more of their resources on weapons and warlike measures. The arms race becomes more universal. Doubt as to the true purpose of these weapons intensifies tension. Peoples are robbed of opportunity for their own peaceful development. The hunger for a peace of justice and good will inevitably become more intense.

Controlled, universal disarmament is the imperative of our time. The demand for it by the hundreds of millions whose chief concern is the long future of themselves and their children will, I hope, become so universal and so insistent that no man, no government anywhere, can withstand it.

My nation is committed to a ceaseless search for ways through which genuine disarmament can be reached. And my government, even as I said more than 6 years ago, in April of 1953, still—"is ready to ask its people to join with all nations in devoting a substantial percentage of the savings achieved by disarmament to a fund for world aid and reconstruction."

But armaments of themselves do not cause wars—wars are caused by men.

830

And men are influenced by a fixation on the past, the dead past, with all its abuses of power; its misuses of responsibility; all its futile convictions that force can solve any problem.

In the name of humanity, can we not join in a 5-year or a 50-year plan against mistrust and misgiving and fixations on the wrongs of the past? Can we not apply ourselves to the removal or reduction of the causes of tension that exist in the world? All these are the creations of governments, cherished and nourished by governments. The peoples of the world would never feel them if they were given freedom from propaganda and pressure.

Permit me to cite two simple examples from my own experience. As President of the United States, I welcomed into our Union last year a new sovereign State, Hawaii—peopled by all the races of the earth, men and women of that new State having their ancestral homes in Asia and Africa and Europe, the two Americas, the islands of the earth. Those peoples are of every creed and color, yet they live together in neighborly friendliness, in mutual trust, and each can achieve his own good by helping achieve the good of all.

Hawaii cries insistently to a divided world that all our differences of race and origin are less than the grand and indestructible unity of our common brotherhood. The world should take time to listen with attentive ear to Hawaii.

As President of Columbia University, every year we welcomed to its campus, from every continent, from almost every nation that flew a flag— and some tribes and colonies not yet free. In particular there still lives in my memory, because of their eagerness and enthusiasm for learning, the presence of hundreds of young people from India and China and Japan and the other Asian countries that studied among us, detached from any mutual prejudice or any fixation over past wrongs—indeed, these vices are not easily discernible among the young of any people.

These two simple things from my own experience convince me that much of the world's fear, suspicion, prejudice, can be obliterated. Men and women everywhere need only to lift up their eyes to the heights that can be achieved together; and, ignoring what has been, push together for what can be.

Not one wrong of years ago that still rankles; not one problem that confronts us today; not one transitory profit that might be taken from another's weakness, should distract us from the pursuit of a goal that dwarfs every problem and wrong of the past.

We have the strength and the means and the knowledge. May God inspire us to strive for the world-wide will and the wisdom that are now our first needs.

In this great crusade, from the history of your own nation, I know India will ever be a leader.

Thank you very much.

NOTE: The President was introduced by Vice President Sarvepalli Radhakrishnan, Chairman of the upper house. M. A. Ayyanger, Speaker of the lower house, proposed a vote of thanks to President Eisenhower.

312 ¶ Toast of the President at a Dinner Given in His Honor by President Prasad.
December 10, 1959

Mr. President, Mr. Prime Minister, Your Excellencies, Ladies and Gentlemen—ladies and gentlemen that I hope from this day forward I can call my personal friends:

First, Mr. President, may I thank you sincerely for the overgenerosity of the remarks you have made about my country and about me. I assure you that with whatever talents the good Lord may have endowed me, the effort that I shall make for the peace of the world shall never cease.

As you say, I have been in your great country only a little more than 24 hours, but the welcome accorded me, the things I have seen and the places I have gone, the distinguished citizens with whom I have talked, make this short time an unforgettable experience for me.

In the hours I have been here, I have had the privilege of paying my tribute to your late great leader Mahatma Gandhi and feeling the serene beauty of the Memorial erected to him. I have talked with you and your colleagues, leaders in the victorious struggle for political independence and in the present striving for economic well-being. I have visited your Parliament and have spoken with the men and women there who are together working for the common goal of India and America: peace and friendship, in freedom.

Everywhere I recognize a remarkable unity of purpose as the people of India work together to build the sort of country envisaged by her Constitution. Of course, Ambassador Bunker and others who have lived here had already told me about some of these things. I suppose I had grasped the significance of their words as well as one could who had not himself seen and felt what they had felt and seen.

But, in a scant 24 hours, the strength of India's spirit, which seems to me to be compounded of faith, dedication, courage, and love of country, has been borne in upon me in a most remarkable way. It is a spirit which will not be denied—no one who has felt it could fail to be uplifted by it.

And Mr. President, I should say, too, that this idealism that I felt is not merely one of academic theory; it is a practical idealism. All around me I see evidences of India on the march. I hear of fertilizer plants being built, production in your agriculture multiplied. I hear of students being sent abroad so that they may come back to you with new techniques and disciplines—professors and other technicians have been brought in by your government to help in this whole great work.

To my mind this is the kind of idealism that translates itself into the good of people, to give them the opportunity for the fulfillment of their own destiny in the best possible way.

And you, sir, are the head of a great Republic. To its present world position you have contributed much. Distinguished lawyer, devoted fighter for independence, and President of India fashioned out of years of struggle and now advancing in the light of a grand vision, yours is a life upon which a man may look with satisfaction and a feeling of accomplishment.

Ladies and gentlemen, I ask you to raise your glasses and drink with me to the health of the President of India and Mrs. Prasad.

NOTE: The President proposed this toast at a dinner at Rashtrapati Bhavan, President Prasad's residence in New Delhi.

313   ¶ Remarks to the Staff of the U.S. Embassy and the American Community in New Delhi. *December* 11, 1959

Mr. Ambassador and Ladies and Gentlemen:

For the last few days I have been traveling on a jet airplane. I have found that you have to adjust your schedule, even on an airplane, for the simple reason you get everywhere so rapidly that after you have allowed time for a breakfast or a lunch with a little nap, you have found that the work you were supposed to do has gone by the board and you have landed. The Ambassador does a little bit better than that, he takes you back to Italy from here in a matter of seconds. (*Laughter*)

But on this trip I have been talking a lot about America's deep desire for peace, and I know that the peoples of all nations feel exactly as the people of America do. I have traveled in many countries of the world and I have never yet found a people that were belligerent, I know of no men that just long for the battlefield and I know of no women who want to see their men, their sons and their husbands, their sweethearts or their fathers, on the battlefield.

So, as far as the longing and aspirations of peoples are involved, we know we are one.

But governments have a habit of getting into the way of the sentiments and the feelings of people. It's the governments that conduct propaganda, that put out what they call information—and I am not so sure it always is—people that create problems and then at least say they are attempting to solve them.

Now our problem is how do we get across from people to people, so that we can each try to fulfill our own destinies according to the methods of our own choosing?

Now I think this is one of the problems and the jobs that people like yourselves help to perform. Political leaders—sometimes they like to call themselves statesmen—are apt to have to deal in generalizations. But you, each of you, with the understanding you display toward another, whether he be of another race or another religion, or different from you in his ideals, but no matter how much this individual may differ, if you are working together and you can understand him and you become friends, you are doing some of the practical work that statesmen and political politicians are talking about.

The courtesies that you show to a visitor, no matter how meanly he is dressed or what kind of work he does, when you can show the natural, inborn courtesy and hospitality that is expected of one of God's creatures, because he is talking to another one, that is helping.

This of course is a very simple, homely example. In all of the hours of our daily lives, you people have an unusual opportunity to do this. Of course, the example you show here, as you work among yourselves, in itself is helpful. But as you go further afield, in your clubs, in your restaurants, and your places of recreation and places of work—the more that the American Embassy, whether its employees are Americans or Indians, the more that the American Embassy gets a name for being understanding and sympathetic, this is the stuff of which finally peace will be made. It is not going to be made by two or three people sitting in something that is called a summit, and after exchanging a lot of views that rarely agree, and probably are not pertinent to the subject particularly, anyway; you are not going to get peace that way. This is going to be people that do it— people talking to people.

So I say to you that I believe you are not only having the opportunity to do something that for yourselves would be satisfying, in the sense that for your families, for your country, and for your world community, you are really doing something valuable, but it is the kind of thing that the whole world must be doing, if we are going to have the peace that we seek, a peace with justice and of durability.

And when I take a look at the Cub Scouts and children of that age, and I stop to think what will be the year, what will be the year on the calendar, when they are my age—say they are 9 now and add 60 years to that, that is two thousand and nineteen—what is that world going to be then? What are we teaching these little fellows and girls—young Americans and young Indians—how to do these things better than we have done them? Because if we don't do it, by that time, two thousand and nineteen, then indeed this poor old world, I think, will be in a sick state.

But the point is, if we do our work well, they will do theirs better— and we will have the kind of earth that is moving ahead, with a greater measure of happiness for all people, a greater satisfaction in the work we ourselves have done.

So as I say, when I see this kind of crowd, I think of your opportunity to do practical work, where I go around just talking too much sometimes. You don't. You are doing work that is valuable.

The people to people is what will save the world.

Thank you very much—and goodbye and good luck.

NOTE: The President spoke at 8:55 a.m. at the Chancery of the U.S. Embassy.

314   ¶ Remarks Upon Receiving an Honorary
Degree of Doctor of Laws at Delhi University.
December 11, 1959

*Mr. Chancellor, Mr. Vice Chancellor, Mr. Prime Minister, Members
of the Executive and Academic Councils of the University, Friends of
Delhi University, Ladies and Gentlemen:*

Among the honors which are bestowed upon men in public life, few
awards have the dignity and symbolic importance which attach to an
honorary degree granted by a world-renowned university.   Realizing
this fact, with the deepest gratitude and humility, I am proud to accept—
in the name of the American people, Mr. Chancellor—this token of
spiritual brotherhood.

Universities in the modern world have a difficult dual function to
perform.   They must be at the same time strongholds of traditional
wisdom accumulated during the ages and alert outposts of a world
advancing toward the conquest of the unknown.   Within them, the
traditional and the new are continually being molded together to form
the substance of a better life for humans.

We are fortunate in the United States that we have had the opportunity to draw deeply from the wells of ancient enlightenment in other
cultures.   The treasures of Indian philosophical thought and writing have
not been alien to the intellectual development of America.

In the last 20 years, our long-established interest in Indian studies has
increased in scope and in intensity.   And now, American scholars are
seriously concerning themselves with the economic problems, the politics,
and the social structure of your great experiment in democracy.

This scholarly effort reflects the growing conviction in my country that
no nation can or should live by itself, isolated from the life-giving streams
of other cultures.

I have been glad to learn that American studies are being introduced
into the curriculum of this splendid University and in other outstanding
universities in India.

I know, too, that thousands of your young men and women are studying
in American schools, and that hundreds of our professors have come to
India to learn from a country whose rich history goes back thousands of
years.

Through this exchange of thoughtful people, this trading of ideas and of ideals, this patient building of a bridge of mutual understanding, we accelerate our march toward the goal of world peace.

History teaches us two lessons that are pertinent to the role of a university in this march.

The first is: mutual good is ever the product of mutual understanding.

The second is: a world of swift economic transformation and growth must also be a world of law.

As to the first, the need for great mutual understanding among the peoples, what has been done in the exchange of students should be only a beginning. These young people are a vital, dynamic element in the world's resources for the construction of a just and secure peace.

Most of us who have been given responsibility by our people have reached years of maturity. In some cases, prejudices and antagonisms we have acquired are so much a part of ourselves that they are not easy to eradicate. The older we grow the more stubbornly we cling to conceptions, and misconceptions, that have long been with us in response to real or fancied wrongs.

On the other hand, all of us recognize the ease with which young people absorb new ideas, new insight. I urge then that we amplify our thinking about the security and the peace of the world to embrace the role of our young people.

I propose to you that, while governments discuss a meeting of a few at the summit, universities consider a massive interchange of mutual understanding on the grand plateau of youth.

More enduringly than from the deliberations of high councils, I believe mankind will profit when the young men and women of all nations—and in great numbers—study and learn together. In so doing they will concern themselves with the problems, the possibilities, the resources, and the rewards of a common destiny.

Through centuries nations have sent their youth, armed for war, to oppose their neighbors. Let us, in this day, look on our youth, eager for larger and clearer knowledge, as forces for international understanding; and send them, one nation to the other, on missions of peace.

On the second lesson of history:

The time has come for mankind to make the rule of law in international affairs as normal as it is now in domestic affairs. Of course the structure of such law must be patiently built, stone by stone. The cost will be a great deal of hard work, both in and out of government— particularly in the universities of the world.

Plainly one foundation stone of this structure is the International Court of Justice. It is heartening to note that a strong movement is afoot in many parts of the world to increase acceptance of the obligatory jurisdiction of that Court. And I most heartily congratulate India on the leadership and vision she has shown in her new declaration accepting the jurisdiction of that Court.

Another major stone in the structure of international rule of law must be a body of international law adapted to the changing needs of today's world. There are dozens of countries which have attained their independence since the bulk of existing international law was evolved. What is now needed is to infuse into international law the finest traditions of all the great legal systems of the world. And here the universities of the world can be of tremendous help in gathering and sifting and harmonizing them into universal law.

Universities and research centers in my own country are now beginning specific projects aimed at tapping the deepest wellsprings of major legal systems—as well as the most modern developments of law around the globe.

A reliable framework of law, grounded in the general principles recognized by civilized nations, is of crucial importance in all plans for rapid economic development around the earth. Economic progress has always been accompanied by a reliable legal framework. Law is not a concrete pillbox in which the status quo is armed and entrenched. On the contrary, a single rule of law, the sanctity of contract, has been the vehicle for more explosive and extensive economic change in the world than any other single factor.

One final thought on rule of law between nations: we will all have to remind ourselves that under this system of law one will sometimes lose as well as win. But here is another thought: nations can endure and accept an adverse decision, rendered by competent and impartial tribunals.

This is so, I believe, for one good reason: if an international controversy leads to armed conflict, everyone loses; there is no winner. If armed conflict is avoided, therefore, everyone wins. It is better to lose a point now and then in an international tribunal, and gain a world in which everyone lives at peace under a rule of law.

Here then are two purposes which I see as particularly fitting within the mission of the world's universities:

A more massive mobilization of young people in the centers of learning where truth and wisdom are enshrined and ignorance and witless prejudice are corrected. They whose world this soon will be, can thus begin to make it now a more decent place for their living.

Second, an inquiry and a search into the laws of the nations for the grand principles of justice and righteousness and good, common to all peoples; out of them will be constructed a system of law, welcome to all peoples because it will mean for the world a rule of law—an end to the suicidal strife of war.

In pursuing these purposes, the universities—I most firmly believe—will add new glory to their names for they will be giving leadership to the worthiest human enterprise—the pursuit of peace with justice.

I repeat that I am proud to accept this University's degree—on behalf of the American people.

I thank you for the cordiality of your welcome, and I thank you for the honor you have done me here this morning.

Thank you.

NOTE: The President spoke at 10:18 a.m. His opening words "Mr. Chancellor, Mr. Vice Chancellor, Mr. Prime Minister" referred to Dr. Sarvepalli Radhakrishnan, Vice President of India, Dr. V. K. R. V. Rao, and Prime Minister Jawaharlal Nehru.

315 ¶ Remarks at the Opening of the World Agriculture Fair in New Delhi.
December 11, 1959

Mr. President, Mr. Vice President, Mr. Prime Minister, Mr. President of the Farmers Forum, Distinguished Guests, My Good Friends of India, Ladies and Gentlemen:

I was struck by the Prime Minister's confession of his ignorance of protocol. This means that I have found one other item of contact between my good friend, your distinguished Prime Minister, because let me confess, I don't even know what the word means.

I am signally honored by the invitation to join President Prasad at the opening of the World Agriculture Fair—the first such fair as this ever held. And it is entirely right that it be held here in India. For this nation recognizes in agriculture the fundamental occupation of man and the chief assurance of better living for its citizens.

My own country was quick to accept when invited to participate in this historic event. And today I am particularly honored that India's Chief of State will be with me when, in a few minutes, I officially open the United States exhibit at the Fair. Indeed, the occasion of this Fair gave me the very finest reason I could think of to make this the time of the visit to India that I had long determined upon.

At this American exhibit, all visitors can see how we Americans have managed the soil of our land so that our people might live well for themselves; and have enough food left over to help others. Our way is not necessarily the best, even for us, but here we depict in the American exhibit, American agriculture as it is. We do have a natural pride in what we have accomplished by a creative union of human spirit, fertile earth, and inventive science. But, beyond this, we see in modern agriculture a most effective instrument for a better life among all men. Mela USA points up its use for that high purpose.

On the personal side, I visit this Fair with keen interest. As a boy and young man, I grew up in the heart of the American farmland. A long-held ambition during my professional years—not always too well concealed—has been to return to the farm. And I plan to be a farmer—when my present form of occupation comes to a close. So, I have a keen interest in spending a bit of time at this Fair where so many nations present their achievements in methods and techniques and ways of agriculture. I shall see here much that is new to me. Many of these things are probably improvements on what I have seen or done in the past, and I hope I am still not too old to learn.

For a moment, I hope you will indulge me as I suggest some thoughts on how food can help all of us achieve better lives in a world of justice and peace.

Today, we have the scientific capacity to abolish from the world at least this one evil, we can eliminate the hunger that emaciates the bodies of children; that scars the souls of their parents; that stirs the passions of those who toil endlessly and earn only scraps.

Men, right now, possess the knowledge and the resources for a successful worldwide war against hunger—the sort of war that dignifies and exalts human beings. The different exhibits in this whole Fair are clear proof of that statement.

The call to that genuinely noble war is enunciated in the theme of the American exhibit:

"Food—Family—Friendship—Freedom."

Into these four words are compressed the daily needs, the high purposes, the deep feelings, the ageless aspirations that unite Indians and Americans under one banner—the banner of human dignity.

Here are four words that are mightier than arms and bombs; mightier than machines and money; mightier than any empire that ruled the past or threatens the future.

Here are four words that can lift the souls of men to a high plane of mutual effort, sustained effort, the most rewarding effort that can be proposed to mankind.

First, *Food*—food that our bodies may be fit for every task and duty and service; our minds free from the fear of hunger; our eyes undimmed by the tragedies of famine, searching out new horizons; our aspirations not frustrated by failure of crop or catastrophe of weather.

Family—family that in our homes there may be decent living and bright hope; children no longer doomed to misery in peace and sudden death in war; their elders no longer broken by want and sorrow beyond their control to mend or cure.

Friendship—that among all the peoples of earth the darkness of ignorance and fear and distrust will dissolve in the light of knowledge and understanding. The time has come when we must all live together for our mutual betterment or we shall all suffer harsh, possibly the final, penalty.

Freedom—that on all continents and islands of the earth every man and woman of good will and good life may make the proudest of human boasts: "I am free; slave to no tyranny imposed by other men, by the accident of birth, by the whims of circumstance."

The American exhibit at this Fair presents the role we feel agriculture can play in furtherance of a healthy, fruitful, peaceful world where the families of all nations can live in freedom from fear of famine and war.

841

In no wise whatsoever is the American exhibit an attempt to portray our agriculture as superior to any other. Through centuries of living with the soil and streams, the environment and climate of their own lands, people have learned adjustments and adaptations peculiarly suited to their own circumstances.

What we do present here are ways in which American farmers multiplied their productivity; the fertility of their fields; the vigor and the value of their livestock.

In this exhibit visitors will see the techniques, the changes in old methods, the applications of new discoveries that have best served America's particular requirements. Modified to fit your needs and your circumstances, it is our hope that they might be of value to you.

Of course, they cannot work miracles overnight, in any land. But with each harvest, they may help to bring every people using them closer to a dependable self-sufficiency.

Early this year, I set in motion a new program "to explore anew with other surplus-producing nations all practical means of utilizing the various agricultural surpluses of each in the interest of reinforcing peace and the well-being of free peoples throughout the world—in short, using food for peace."

In keeping with this program my Government and the Government of India have been working together. Whatever strengthens India, my people are convinced, strengthens us, a sister-Republic dedicated to peace. This great nation of 400 million people, rich in culture and history, courageous in the resolve to be free and strong, is a mighty influence for an enduring and just peace in the world. And this is true of every nation so courageous, so determined, so inspired as is India.

With them we shall continue to cooperate to achieve a world free from the pangs of hunger, in which families live full and prosperous lives, where friendship among nations replaces fear and suspicion, and where men are free in the pursuit of happiness.

Thank you for the great honor you have done me by inviting me here.

NOTE: Participating in the ceremonies were President Prasad, Vice President Radhakrishnan, Prime Minister Nehru, and the President of the Farmers Forum and Minister of Agriculture, Dr. Panjabrao S. Deshmukh. Following the ceremonies, President Eisenhower and President Prasad proceeded by car to the U.S. exhibit which was officially opened by the President.

316 ¶ Remarks at the Civic Reception, Ram Lila Grounds, New Delhi. *December* 13, 1959

Mr. Mayor, Mr. Prime Minister, Distinguished Guests, Ladies and Gentlemen:

My good friends, your President and Prime Minister told me several days ago that half a million of you would be gathered here today. I could hardly realize then how impressive and moving and inspiring the sight of you would actually be.

I thank you from my heart for the labor you have imposed on yourselves; the miles you have traveled; the hours you have waited in patience. I thank you for all the personal sacrifice and the civic effort that a reception like this requires.

I see in the magnificent spectacle before me a soul-stirring testimonial by half a million of India's people to America, a sister democracy—and to the cause for which both India and America stand;

That cause is: peace and friendship in freedom.

The critical word and the key idea of this cause is: freedom.

We of these two peaceful nations believe there are greater things in the world even than peace. They are the ideals, the hopes, and aspirations of humanity; our loyalty to conscience. They are the integrity of purpose; unswerving devotion to principle; love of truth and decency. People who believe and practice these things are certain to be friends.

Above all, we believe that only in freedom can men enjoy true and full peace; only in freedom can men be genuine and honest friends.

Freedom must come first, we of India and of America believe.

One of the clearest voices of all time, proclaiming the priority and supremacy of freedom, is your own sainted Mahatma Gandhi.

Speaking of freedom for nations, Mahatma Gandhi said: "Freedom is the gift of God—the right of every nation."

And to his words, America replies: so also we believe.

Speaking of freedom for individuals, he said: "Democracy is not a state in which people act like sheep. Under democracy individual liberty of opinion and action is jealously guarded."

And to his words, America answers: so also we hold.

And then speaking of the responsibility that political freedom demands of those who possess it, he said: "Self-government depends entirely upon our own internal strength, upon our ability to fight against the heaviest odds. Indeed, self-government, which does not require continuous striving to attain it and to sustain it, is not worth the name."

And to his words, America can say: so also we teach.

In what I have quoted from Mahatma Ghandi, I know he spoke the convictions of the American people as clearly as he spoke for India.

We, like you, have won freedom and we strive to assure every individual American the fullness of responsible freedoms.

America's right to maintain a respectable establishment for defense—our duty to join in company with like-thinking peoples for mutual self-defense—would, I am sure, be recognized and upheld by the most saintly men.

Being strong and free, confident that we shall remain strong and free, we are prepared to devote ourselves as a nation—our whole energies and our talents—to the cause of peace and friendship.

We believe that freedom ultimately will be won everywhere. The human hunger for freedom is far too deep-seated in human nature to be put off by a contrived definition or a man-made philosophy.

Freedom, as Ghandi said, is the gift of God. And God's gift cannot forever be kept from his children.

But—immediately—we must search out with all free nations more effective and practical ways to strengthen the cause of peace and friendship in freedom; and, so doing, make our negotiations with other people more persuasive.

One reason I came to India is to tell you that America wants to join with all free men in advancing this cause.

Between the first largest democracy on earth, India, and the second largest, America, lie ten thousand miles of land and ocean. But in our fundamental ideas and convictions about democracy we are close neighbors. We ought to be closer.

We who are free—and we who prize our freedom above all other gifts of God and nature—must know each other better; we must trust each other more; we must support each other.

A free India and a free America could not exist if they were isolated from others in the world. A free society of nations can continue to exist only as it meets the rightful demands of people for security, progress, and increasing opportunity for the betterment of themselves and their children.

Such a society, if some of its nations prosper richly and others barely feed their people, cannot survive.

Now when I consider the potential contribution of India to the prosperity of its own people and of the entire free world—say in the next 10 years—my imagination fails me.

Here will be almost a half billion free men and women well embarked on economic expansion. The productivity of your farmers will have increased enormously—I saw clear signs of that on Friday at the World Agriculture Fair. Their standards of living will rise. You will be turning out textiles and metals and manufactured goods to help meet the multiplied demands of a world ever-growing in its economic appetite. You will be building houses and schools and hospitals and places of worship, centers of recreation and culture, on a scale possibly never before dreamed of—even here. And you will be doing this without abandoning your freedom in favor of forced regimentation.

As you prosper, the whole free world will prosper. Americans, Asians, Africans, Europeans will buy goods from India that they must have to meet their own increasing requirements—that they of themselves cannot meet at all or so well. And you will be able to buy more from them. A spiral of prosperity throughout the free world will lift the living standards of all our peoples.

Of course I don't think that India can achieve its full potential without acquisition of more capital than you now possess. The best means for a nation, determined to maintain its independence, are private investment from outside, governmental loans from others, and where necessary, grants from other free and friendly nations.

One thing I assure you, from now on I shall be quick to assert on every possible occasion that India is becoming one of the great investment opportunities of our time—an investment in the strengthening of freedom and in the prosperity of the world.

India, mighty in the number of its people and in their will to build an ever greater Republic, marches—I am confident—to a great destiny.

Goodbye. God bless you.

NOTE: The President's opening words "Mr. Mayor" referred to Trilok Chand Sharma, Mayor of New Delhi. He attended the reception after a visit to Agra with Prime Minister Nehru, where he visited the Taj Mahal and inspected an agricultural training center and a farming village.

317   ¶ Joint Statement Following Discussions
With Prime Minister Nehru.   *December* 14, 1959

AT THE INVITATION of the Government of India, the President
of the United States of America paid a visit to India, lasting from
December 9 to 14.   President Eisenhower received on his arrival in New
Delhi a warm and cordial welcome, marked by popular enthusiasm and
goodwill.   Throughout his stay and wherever he went, these friendly
manifestations of goodwill were repeated by millions of Delhi citizens and
others who had come to Delhi to join in this welcome.   During his
strenuous four-day visit, President Eisenhower fulfilled a number of public
engagements.   He addressed Members of the Indian Parliament, received
an Honorary Doctorate of Laws from the University of Delhi, participated in the inauguration of the World Agriculture Fair, attended a Civic
Reception on behalf of the City of Delhi and visited rural areas near
Agra.

In thus fulfilling a desire of many years, the President was deeply
touched by the warmth of the welcome extended to him by the people
of India, by the generous hospitality of the Government and the excellence of the arrangements made for him.

The President was impressed by the vitality of India's democratic
institutions, of Parliament, press and University, and by India's strength
of spirit combined with practical idealism.   He saw how India, like the
United States, has created national strength out of diversity, neither
country boasting that theirs is the only way.   He confirmed the bond of
shared ideals between India and the United States, their identity of
objectives, and their common quest for just and lasting peace.

President Eisenhower met the President of India, the Prime Minister
and other members of the Government of India.   He and the Prime
Minister had intimate talks in which they reviewed the world situation
and exchanged views on matters of mutual interest.   Among other
things, the President told the Prime Minister that he was happy to report
to him that all the leaders of the countries he had visited during his recent
journey had expressed to him the hope that problems involving one form
or another of conflict of interest or views could be solved by peaceful
methods of conciliation.   He said that this was true in Italy, Turkey,
Pakistan, and Afghanistan.   The President found this heartening and in

harmony with his own thinking. He did not wish in any way to minimize the importance of or the inherent difficulties involved in some of the problems. The spirit he found was good and forward-looking.

The Prime Minister expressed gratification and pleasure at President Eisenhower's visit to India, and thanked him for the warmth and generosity of the sentiments he had expressed. He assured the President of the wholehearted support of India in his unremitting efforts in the cause of world peace. India herself is dedicated to a policy of peace and has been steadfast in her conviction that differences between nations should be resolved peacefully by the method of negotiation and settlement and not by resort to force. She has consistently pursued this policy in relation to problems of this nature affecting her and other countries. The Prime Minister gave President Eisenhower a review of the major aspects of some of these problems and of recent developments in regard to them.

The Prime Minister also referred to the great effort that India was making, through her Five Year Plans, to develop the country, both in regard to agriculture and industry, so as to raise the living standards of the people as rapidly as possible. To this great task, involving the future of 400 million people, India was devoting herself with all her strength and will.

The President and the Prime Minister expressed their deep satisfaction at the friendly and cordial relations existing between their two countries, and their firm belief that their common ideals and objectives and their quest for peace will ensure the maintenance and development of the strong ties of friendship between the two countries.

President Eisenhower's visit to India has afforded the welcome opportunity of a meeting between the Presidents of the two countries, and for the renewal of the friendship between him and the Prime Minister of India. He was happy to meet other members of the Government, as well as men and women, young and old, in city and village, Parliament and University, and to bring to them, personally, assurance of the genuine friendship of the people of the United States for the people of India and their sincere and continuing interest in India's welfare. To the people of India, this visit, which had been long hoped for, has given the opportunity for the demonstration of the sincere friendship, goodwill and sympathy which they feel for the people of the United States.

NOTE: This joint statement was released in New Delhi.

318 ¶ Remarks Recorded for Broadcast to the
Indian People Upon Leaving for Iran.
December 13, 1959

My Friends of India:

I welcome the privilege of speaking, through your radios, to bid you farewell.

I leave India reluctantly. My visit here has been one of the moving experiences of my life. During these 5 days I have met with your distinguished President, with your eminent Prime Minister—with many others of your great leaders.

I have felt the warmth, the friendship of multitudes of you, wherever I have gone. Most importantly, I have sensed the spirit of the new India, heir to a culture ages old, now possessed by a grand vision—advancing decisively, building a great modern democracy on the foundation of an ancient civilization.

India has filled these past 5 days of my life with so much excitement and wonder, that I shall never forget them. Some similarities between our two countries have become clear to me. India and America believe in the dignity of the individual, in each one's right to live his life in his own way. We both believe in equality of opportunity. We both believe in the right of minorities to have their opinions respected and protected. We both believe in the rule of law in world affairs, and in the peaceful settlement of international disputes, be they great or small. These are indeed fundamental bonds between us.

You are a very old civilization, with an ancient tradition and culture. We are a young country. Our tradition is, as traditions go, young also. But in another sense, in the sense of your independent nationhood, you too are young. You are starting as we did 184 years ago on the path of the development of a new nation. Your problems are different—your difficulties are different—the resources with which you have to work are different. But your purpose is the same as ours was—and still is: to develop your country in which every man and woman may have the opportunity, in freedom, to work out for himself in his own way a rich and satisfying life—a country in which as Abraham Lincoln said, government is of the people, by the people, and for the people.

848

I have been deeply impressed by the way in which you are shouldering the immense problem of raising the standards of living of your people, by the energy and skill and imagination which you are applying to this task. Your achievements in 12 years of independence have been remarkable, and promise even more for the future.

I am leaving India with a reinforced conviction that the people of India and the people of the United States are engaged in a common quest for the improvement of the general welfare of their people—and for peace with justice throughout the world.

So, as I leave, I take away the warmest and friendliest feelings for this great nation. I want to thank you again for the welcome which you have extended to me. On behalf of the people of the United States, I want to wish you good fortune and success. Goodbye.

319 ¶ Remarks Upon Arrival at Mehrabad Airport, Tehran. *December* 14, 1959

Your Majesty, Ladies and Gentlemen:

Your Majesty, before I proceed further, may I express my gratitude for the warmth and generosity of the sentiments you have expressed toward my country and toward me personally. I am truly grateful.

This morning, as I set foot on the soil of Iran, I realize a long-held ambition, to see something of this historic land and a courageous people. I have wanted also to return the visit of Your Majesty to my own country, so that here on this spot we may renew our association and friendship.

In my boyhood, ancient Persia, its kings and their adventures, the nation's marvels of building, its religion, made up a fascinating realm of wonder and romance for a high school student who lived on the Plains of Kansas many thousands of miles away, and half a century ago.

Years later, as a soldier, as a University President, and then President of the United States, Iran became for me one of the most important nations of the world. Three times in the past decade I have had long and searching talks with His Majesty the Shahinshah. He concentrates, in his plans and dreams for Iran, the hopes and aspirations of his people. From him I learned more vividly than from books and papers the present greatness of his country's spirit.

I learned, too, its problems, its strengths, its advances, its vital role in the defense of the free world, and the golden future that is assured Iran and its people in a world of peace with justice.

Now I am here—bringing you from the American people their salute to your courage, their congratulations on their achievements, their best wishes for growth in the years ahead, their pledge of friendship for you and your people.

NOTE: The President was met by Shah Mohammad Reza Pahlavi, members of the Iranian Cabinet, leaders of the Parliament, members of the diplomatic corps, and U.S. Ambassador Edward T. Wailes.

320　¶ Address to the Members of the Parliament of Iran.　*December* 14, 1959

Mr. Prime Minister, Mr. President, Mr. Speaker, Members of the Senate, Members of the Majlis:

The honor you do me with this reception in your handsome new Senate building is a clear indication of the high mutual regard which the Iranian and American peoples have for each other.

Personally, I am deeply touched by your welcome.

We know that people, by meeting together, even if for a limited time, can strengthen their mutual understanding. To increase this mutual understanding has been one of the purposes of my trip to Iran; as it has been to the other countries in which I have stopped along the way.

My conversation this morning with His Imperial Majesty, this convocation, my knowledge of the state of relations between our two countries—and indeed, the cordial warmth of the reception that I received upon the streets of your beautiful city—have all been heartening assurances that our two countries stand side by side. This visit reinforces my conviction that we stand together. We see eye to eye when it comes to the fundamentals which govern the relations between men and between nations.

The message I bring from America is this: "We want to work with you for peace and friendship, in freedom." I emphasize freedom— because without it there can be neither true peace nor lasting friendship among peoples.

Consequently, Americans are dedicated to the improvement of the international climate in which we live. Though militarily we in America devote huge sums to make certain of the security of ourselves and to assist our allies, we do not forget that—in the long term—military strength alone will not bring about peace with justice. The spiritual and economic health of the free world must be likewise strengthened.

All of us realize that while we must, at whatever cost, make freedom secure from any aggression, we could still lose freedom should we fail to cooperate in progress toward achieving the basic aspirations of humanity. The world struggle in which we are engaged is many sided. In one aspect it is ideological, political, and military; in others it is both spiritual and economic.

As I well know, you, and the people of Iran, are not standing on the sidelines in this struggle.

Without flinching, you have borne the force of a powerful propaganda assault, at the same time that you have been working at improving the living standards in your nation.

The people of Iran continue to demonstrate that quality of fortitude which has characterized the long annals of your history as a nation. I know I speak for the American people when I say we are proud to count so valiant a nation as our partner.

Your ideals, expressed in the wise and mature literature of your people, are a source of enrichment to the culture of the world.

By true cooperation with your friends—and among these, America considers herself one—we can proceed together toward success in the struggle for peace and prosperity.

Through trust in one another, we can trust in the fruitful outcome of our efforts together to build a brighter future.

This future—the world we will hand on to our children and to our grandchildren—must occupy our thinking and our planning and our working. The broad outline of our goal is, I think, clear to everyone— to achieve a just peace in freedom.

But peace will be without real meaning—it may even be unattainable—until the peoples of the world have finally overcome the natural enemies of humanity—hunger, privation, and disease. The American people have engaged considerable resources in this work. I am proud of the many dedicated American men and women who have gone out into the world with the single hope that they can ease the pain and want of others.

Some of them are at work in Iran, and I have heard that the people of Iran have found these efforts beneficial.

Of course, their work is effective only because the government of Iran has sturdily shouldered its responsibilities for the development of their country. There are reports of significant accomplishments throughout the length and breadth of your land.

America rejoices with you that this is so.

On the long and difficult climb on the road to true peace, the whole world must some day agree that suspicion and hate should be laid aside in the common interest.

Here, I think, is our central problem. I know that you, too, and all men of good will, are devoting thought and energy to the practical and realistic steps to this great objective.

One such step is, of course, an enforceable agreement on disarmament, or, to be more exact, arms reduction. To achieve this, the governments of the world have chosen a primary instrument, the United Nations.

It could seem that, as the realities of the awful alternative to peace become clearer to all, significant progress in the safeguarded reduction of the arms burden can be made. To such a realistic beginning, there is no feasible alternative for the world.

In the meantime, we cannot abandon our mutual effort to build barriers, such as the peaceful barrier of our Central Treaty Organization, against the persistent dangers of aggression and subversion. This organization, CENTO, has no ulterior or concealed purpose; it exists only to provide security.

Such an effort erects a shield of freedom for our honor and for our lives. With such a shield, we preserve the cherished values of our societies.

To be sure, the people of Iran need no reminder of these simple facts. Only yesterday you celebrated the anniversary of the day on which justice triumphed over force in Azerbaijan. The full weight of world public opinion, as represented in the United Nations, supported you in those difficult times. It will always support the rights of any people threatened by external aggression.

Justice—the rule of law—among nations has not yet been effectively established. But in almost every nation in the world there is a great awakening to the need for such a development. Certainly this is true among the free nations. Because there is such an awakening, the act of any government contrary to the rights of mankind is quickly resented and keenly sensed by people everywhere.

This is the wellspring of our hope. This is why we are right to believe as we do—despite centuries of human turmoil and conflict—that true peace can and will one day be realized.

The impulse toward justice, toward the recognition of the worth and dignity of each and every human being, will not be denied. This is the mainspring of the movement toward freedom and peace.

Now, may I offer my heartfelt thanks for the opportunity you have given me to speak to you, and through you, the representatives of the people of Iran, to your entire nation.

You have conferred upon me an honor which I shall always remember.

Thank you very much.

NOTE: The President's opening words "Mr. Prime Minister, Mr. President, Mr. Speaker" referred to Manuchehr Eqbal, Prime Minister of Iran, Mohsed Sadr, President of the Senate, and Reza Hekmat, Speaker of the lower house (Majlis).

321 ¶ Toast by the President at a Luncheon Given in His Honor by Shah Mohammad Reza Pahlavi. *December* 14, 1959

Your Imperial Majesty:

The American people have the greatest respect and admiration for the Iranian people. Your Kings from Cyrus and Darius are known among those famous monarchs who have advanced the cause of humanity. Your scientists have contributed to the foundations on which we have built our industrial society. Your philosophers and poets have enriched the culture of the West.

The fortitude of the Iranian people in the face of invaders and their resoluteness in maintaining their nation through the centuries have won admiration throughout the world.

Therefore, I propose a toast to the Shahinshah—may he continue to give wise leadership to his people. May God prosper him and them in their work of peace.

Your Majesty, your good health.

NOTE: The President proposed this toast at a luncheon at the Marble Palace of the Shah of Iran, following the presentation of gifts to the President in the Crystal Room.

322 ¶ Joint Statement Following Discussions With the Shah of Iran. *December* 14, 1959

PRESIDENT Eisenhower visited Iran on December 14, 1959. The President and his party were welcomed warmly by the Iranian people. The feelings of the Iranian people shown during this significant visit demonstrated again the strength of the ties between the governments and people of Iran and the United States. The visit attested to the confidence of both countries that their cooperation is of benefit both to themselves and to the world.

During the visit talks were held at the Palace of His Imperial Majesty between the two leaders assisted by Prime Minister Eqbal, Foreign Minister Aram, Ambassador Murphy, and Ambassador Wailes. The President addressed a joint session of the Iranian Parliament.

His Imperial Majesty and the President discussed the CENTO alliance and both emphasized the importance of CENTO in preserving stability and security in the area. They reiterated the determination of their Governments to support CENTO and further recognized the usefulness of their bilateral agreement while, of course, continuing to participate in the action of the United Nations for the furtherance of world peace. Both leaders emphasized their adherence to the goals of peace and freedom.

In the course of their talks the world situation was reviewed. Both leaders expressed their belief in the principles of negotiation as a means of finding just and peaceful solutions to problems which arise between nations. It was agreed that disarmament with adequate controls should be sought in the interest of lasting peace. His Imperial Majesty and the President also exchanged views on various problems, especially those relating to the Middle East. The President recognized the significant contribution Iran is making to the stability of this important world area.

His Imperial Majesty outlined the economic and social progress achieved in Iran and expressed appreciation for the help given by the American people. The President congratulated His Imperial Majesty on the service which Iran is rendering the free world and for his vigorous effort to sustain stability and to further economic development. The President noted that such programs undertaken by Iran have the objective of creating a more bountiful life for the Iranian people. President

Eisenhower also expressed interest in the steps His Imperial Majesty is taking to promote social progress. The President said that the United States intends to continue to assist Iran in the mutual interest of both nations.

The President took the opportunity to express the admiration of the people of the United States for the brave stand of the Iranian people and Government in the face of outside pressure.

NOTE: This joint statement was released in Tehran.

323 ¶ Remarks at the Mehrabad Airport, Tehran, Upon Leaving for Greece.
December 14, 1959

Your Majesty, Ladies and Gentlemen:

During my brief hours here in Iran, I have learned much. First of all, I have learned about the hospitality and cordiality of the Iranian people and their leaders. I appreciate and am grateful for every greeting from every citizen that I saw all along the route.

I am particularly grateful to His Majesty for his many courtesies this morning to me and my party.

I should like to say a special word of farewell to the Diplomatic Corps. I should like to greet you again personally, but the hour grows late for my departure, and I must leave. I am sorry, and I want to apologize to this beautiful country and all its citizens because I didn't and couldn't stay longer. I would like to stay as many days as I have hours.

Thank you until we can meet again. Goodbye.

NOTE: Following the luncheon at the Marble Palace, the President left for the airport accompanied by the Shah of Iran.

324 ¶ Remarks Upon Arrival at Hellinikon Airport, Athens. *December* 14, 1959

Your Majesty, Ladies and Gentlemen:

It is a great privilege to be welcomed to this city for the first time in 7 years. I come back to a country that is responsible for much that belongs to Western culture and civilization.

855

When I came here 7 years ago, I found this nation to be one—in its courage, in its hardihood, in its adherence to principle—truly as great as those Greek city states that we learned to love and admire from the days when as little boys we learned our ancient history.

So I assure you again that the welcome from His Majesty, the audience, and the people—individuals here, it means much to me, and I hope as I have my talks with His Majesty, His Majesty's Government, that we will find much that we can exchange between ourselves that will be fruitful for the solution of any problems between us.

Thank you very much.

NOTE: The President spoke at 4:47 p.m. He was met by King Paul, the Crown Prince, Prime Minister Constantine Kara- manlis, Greek officials, U.S. Ambassador Ellis O. Briggs, and members of the U.S. Embassy.

325 ¶ Address to the Members of the Parliament of Greece. *December* 15, 1959

Mr. Speaker, Mr. Prime Minister, Your Beatitude, Excellencies, Ladies and Gentlemen, Honorable Representatives of the Hellenes:

I am greatly honored that I have been invited to speak before this distinguished Parliament.

Greatness and grandeur are all about us; greatness and grandeur of ideas and ideals that were born and first enunciated nearby; of men forever memorable who walked and lived here, of a people whose valor and vitality and wisdom are written large on the human record. Your present Government and its leaders, your distinguished Prime Minister, are producing a record of achievement that makes them worthy successors to their illustrious predecessors.

I represent in this place 180 million men and women who with you of Greece share the golden legacy of culture and civilization bequeathed by your forebears to the Western World. We Americans, with you Greeks, are fellow-heirs to the glory of Greece.

In this city of Athens, more than a score of centuries ago, democracy—in its principles and in its practices—first won the hearts and minds of men. This house of free representative government symbolizes the vigor of modern democracy in its ancient birthplace; demonstrates that the will of men to be free is imperishable.

In our common dedication to the ideals of democracy our two countries—America and Greece—feel a basic kinship. An American can feel as much at home here as in Washington or Abilene, my own village, or Brooklyn—just as Greeks quickly find themselves at home in those three places in America.

To this Parliament, I come with a message of admiration and respect from the American people to the Greek people, and for the light of inspiration that shone out, in our own day, to all the free world from this land and its islands.

You have proved yourselves fearless of defense in your independence; tireless in your attack on the evils of hardship and privation; ready for sacrifice that your children might enjoy a brighter day. And, beset with hardship and difficulty at home, you joined in cooperation with the other countries of the Atlantic Alliance for mutual defense and security. Your Expeditionary Force to Korea, by its valor and heroism, helped sustain the rule of law and the United Nations in that divided nation.

The American people—and I am sure all the free peoples of the world—salute you, valiant and worthy heirs to the Greek traditions.

And now, briefly, permit me to speak on a cause close to my heart; close, I hope, to the hearts of all who believe in the brotherhood, the dignity, the divine origin and destiny of man as a child of God, created in His image.

The cause is: peace and friendship in freedom.

The Greek and American peoples share a common and deep devotion to peace. We share further the conviction that we must sustain the conditions under which the goal of peace may be pursued effectively.

We must be strong militarily, economically—but above all, spiritually. By developing and preserving such strength—by forever repudiating the use of aggressive force—we shall win the sort of peace we want; with friendship in freedom.

I mean peace that is creative, dynamic, fostering a world climate that will relieve men and their governments of the intolerable burden of armaments; liberate them from the haunting fear of global war and universal death.

I mean friendship that is spontaneous and warm, welling up from a deep conviction that all of us are more concerned with the bettering of our circumstances; giving our children wider opportunity and brighter promise—than in destroying each other.

I mean freedom in which, under the rule of law, every human will have the right and a fair chance to live his own life; to choose his own path; to work out his own destiny; that nations will be free from misgivings and mistrust, able to develop their resources for the good of their people.

To this cause of peace and friendship in freedom, Greeks are contributing all their hearts and minds and energies. Joined with the free men of the world they can help mankind at long last to enjoy the fullness of life envisioned by the sages of ancient Greece.

Honorable Members of Parliament, I want to assure you again of the very deep sense of distinction that I feel in the invitation to address you. I feel that here I am with men who, like myself and all other Americans, love peace and freedom and want to work with you for it.

NOTE: The President spoke at 10:12 a.m. His opening words "Mr. Speaker, Mr. Prime Minister, Your Beatitude" referred to Constantine Rodopoulos, Speaker of the unicameral parliament, Constantine Karamanlis, Prime Minister, and Archbishop Theoklitos, Primate of Greece.

326 ¶ Toast by the President at a Luncheon Given in His Honor by King Paul.
December 15, 1959

Your Majesty:

My heartfelt thanks are extended to the people of Greece for the warm welcome they have accorded me. This welcome reflects the friendship between our two peoples—a friendship cemented in war and in our common effort to preserve and to amplify the concept of liberty, a heritage from the ancient Greeks.

Your Majesty has spoken eloquently of the mission of my country. I believe that the essential element in the alliance of people dedicated to freedom, including those sharing the responsibilities of NATO, is that we are equals who respect each other's interest.

Our alliance is based upon single will to maintain human dignity. This alliance of ours is a union of like-minded peoples, each contributing to the limit of their capacity. The devotion of the Greek people to this common ideal is nowhere more amply attested than in the settlement of the Cyprus problem.

I agree with Your Majesty that we in the free world today confront a great challenge.

How we shall meet it depends in large measure upon our determination, patience, and strength in union. In this test, I have no doubt that the heroic Greek people, who for thousands of years have guarded their independence with fierce decisiveness, will stand in the vanguard.

And so I raise my glass to His Majesty, the King, stalwart standard-bearer of the unquenchable spirit of Hellenism, and to the people of Greece, whose steadfast allegiance to right inspires the admiration of the American people. In union, and with the guidance of the Almighty, may we forge ahead to peace, justice, and prosperity for all mankind.

NOTE: The President proposed this toast at a luncheon at the royal palace.

327 ¶ Joint Statement Following Discussions With Prime Minister Karamanlis. *December* 15, 1959

ON THE occasion of his official visit to Greece on the fourteenth and fifteenth of December, the President of the United States Mr. Dwight Eisenhower concluded talks with the Prime Minister of Greece Mr. Constantine Karamanlis. Present at the talks were the American Ambassador, Mr. Ellis O. Briggs, and the Under Secretary of State Mr. Robert Murphy, and on the Greek side the Deputy Prime Minister, Mr. Panayotis Kanellopoulos, and the Acting Minister of Foreign Affairs, Mr. Constantine Tsatsos.

The President expressed his warm appreciation of the hospitality extended by Their Majesties King Paul and Queen Frederika, and of all the Greek people.

The talks covered a wide range of general and specific topics of common interest to both countries.

Both countries affirmed their faith in the principles of the Charter of the United Nations and their staunch support of the objectives of the North Atlantic Treaty Organization which based on the solidarity of its members, aim at the firm establishment of security, and at peace with justice. The relaxation of world tensions was discussed in this spirit.

The Greek Prime Minister expressed his deep appreciation for the great endeavor for peace undertaken by President Eisenhower. Both agreed that the consolidation of world peace must be pursued in such a way as to guarantee the independence of all nations and the freedom of the individual.

Historic instances in which both countries stood side by side in hard struggles were recalled, and in this context the importance of Greece in the common defense effort was recognized.

Opinions were exchanged concerning those parts of the world of particular interest to Greece. Careful account was taken of her special position in the Balkans and the general situation in this area as well as in the Eastern Mediterranean, was examined. It was agreed that the two governments should exchange views on matters of mutual concern involving these areas. The prospective emergence of an independent Cyprus State was hailed with special satisfaction.

The Greek Prime Minister expressed the gratitude of the Greek people for the enduring interest and help being extended by the American people. He also explained to the President the problems the country faces in seeking to raise the standard of living of the Greek people and maintaining the obligations and responsibilities of its position in the defense structure of the Free World.

President Eisenhower, recognizing the special economic and social conditions of Greece, expressed his admiration for the improvement being accomplished by the country and reaffirmed the interest of the American people in the security and economic development of Greece.

Generally it was recognized that improvement in the standard of living in the economically less developed countries constitutes a vital element in the consolidation of international peace.

The conversations were held in an atmosphere of deep sincerity and warm cordiality such as have traditionally characterized the relations of the two countries, and which were so happily confirmed by the visit to Greece of the President of the United States.

NOTE: This joint statement was released in Athens.

The President took leave of Their Majesties at the royal palace. Prime Minister Karamanlis accompanied him to the sta- dium for departure by helicopter for the U.S.S. Des Moines, the flagship of the Sixth Fleet. The President spent 2 days aboard the Des Moines en route to Tunisia.

328 ¶ Remarks Upon Arrival at La Marsa, Tunisia. *December* 17, 1959

Mr. President, Ladies and Gentlemen:

It is indeed a great honor for me to arrive this morning to greet again you, in your person, President Bourguiba, and to greet the people of free Tunisia.

Our country, America, has welcomed warmly this new nation into the family of independent nations. We wish you good luck in all your endeavors. We hope that we, not only working among ourselves—yourselves, ourselves, and the other free nations—may be able to produce peace with justice in this world, but that as we do it, we can find the opportunities and methods by which all people may be able to raise their own standards, to realize more the happiness that God has meant them to have, and in doing so lead our countries to a nobler, better destiny than ever before they have achieved.

So, sir, in the talks I hope to have with you this morning, and that we have planned, I hope that we can talk over some of the ways in which this cooperation between your country and mine may be as close and as fruitful as our common friendship should promise for it.

Thank you very much.

NOTE: The President, accompanied by Robert O. Blake, First Secretary, U.S. Embassy in Tunis, went by helicopter from the U.S.S. Des Moines to the palace of President Bourguiba of Tunisia at La Marsa, near Tunis. He was met by President Bourguiba and Walter N. Walmsley, U.S. Ambassador to Tunisia. The President spoke at 8:06 a.m.

329 ¶ Joint Statement Following Discussions With President Bourguiba. *December* 17, 1959

PRESIDENT EISENHOWER and President Bourguiba accompanied by their advisers met at La Marsa on December 17.

The two Presidents reviewed in general terms the international situation in a spirit of frankness and cordiality. Their discussions centered on the necessity to continue the progress which is now being made towards strengthening of peace and the reduction of the cause of international tension.

In this connection they examined the situation created by the difficulties in Algeria. They agreed that the fact that a solution has not yet been achieved is a cause of grave concern.

They agreed that the achievement of self-determination by African and Asian peoples is one of the most important events of our times. They welcomed the opportunity offered for the evolution of new relationships and the improvement of old ones based on a common attachment to fundamental principles of human rights and dignity.

President Eisenhower and President Bourguiba expressed their conviction that the efforts by nations to consolidate the peace necessitate increased support from the more industrialized nations for countries in the course of developing their economies.

The conversations between the two Presidents revealed a wide area of understanding of the problems raised.

NOTE: This joint statement was released in Tunis.

330 ¶ Remarks at the Airport in Tunis Before Leaving for France. *December 17, 1959*

Mr. President, Ladies and Gentlemen:

This is the first time that I have been able to visit your beautiful country for 16 years. I left here 16 years ago this month, and we were in the midst of a war. We were fighting a war that we thought would bring permanent peace.

We have found that peace does not come just because the guns are stilled. We have to work for peace, we have to work with our hearts, with our substance, with our hands—we have to work all the time to maintain the peace and to make it more secure.

This cannot be done by any one man, by any one nation—we must all work together, each nation feeling the pride in itself, in its self-respect, with its heart and its soul must work with all other nations in friendship and in freedom, and in this way we will finally make the kind of peace that all of us want and in which all mankind, as brothers, can truly prosper.

So, as I see today, over these 16 years, the great transformations that have come about in your country—your independence, your new buildings, everything about your nation that means progress, I hope and trust that that kind of rate of progress will be sustained. And if I can come back within a few years, I will even see greater signs of prosperity and the advances of Tunisia than I have seen since these last 16 years.

Thank you very much for the great welcome that you and your people have given to my party and me. I assure you that we translate it into terms of friendship that your people feel to the American people—as I assure you that they feel friendship for your people.

Thank you again.

NOTE: The President spoke at 11:20 a.m. before leaving by helicopter for the U.S.S. Des Moines off Cape Carthage.

331 ¶ Remarks to the Ship's Company on Board the U.S.S. Des Moines. *December 18, 1959*

IT HAS BEEN a great pleasure for my party and myself to be embarked in Admiral Anderson's fine fleet. We are particularly grateful, of course, to the officers and men of the Des Moines and Essex who have been our hosts for the past 3 days.

Speaking personally, I cannot tell you how much the opportunity to take a good rest has meant to me. More than that, it has been a very enjoyable experience. As always, when I embark in Navy ships, I have been impressed with the good spirit and dedication to duty that I have seen in this force. You have good reason to be proud of yourselves, and the ships in which you serve.

Yesterday I sent Christmas Greetings to all members of the Armed Forces. I know they will understand when I send the men of the Sixth Fleet special wishes for a Merry Christmas and a Happy New Year.

Thank you—and God bless you.

NOTE: The President spoke over the public address system at 8:30 a.m. Vice Adm. George W. Anderson, Jr., was in command of the Sixth Fleet.

332 ¶ Remarks at the Dock Upon Arrival in Toulon. *December 18, 1959*

Monsieur Jacquinot, Your Excellencies, Ladies and Gentlemen:

Again I am privileged to visit this lovely country of France. Again I have the honor of meeting so many of her citizens.

France and America—the United States of America—have been allies over many years, under many different circumstances. France first came to our aid in 1777, when we were struggling so hard for our independence. Since that time there has existed between our peoples, and certainly on our part, a great sense of obligation to the great French nation.

In the vicissitudes and circumstances of international life, not always has everything been clear sailing, but the underlying affection and respect of the two nations each for the other has never lessened. And because of that, we are stronger today—this nation under the leadership of General de Gaulle and our own nation—we are stronger for the pursuit of peace than possibly we have ever been in our history. We are part of a great coalition that is determined, from a position of strength, to pursue peace with every bit of strength, with every bit of wisdom and certainly with every bit of heartfelt emotion that we possibly can. And in my opinion, if all of us can struggle together in the same way that the United States and France have during these past many decades, we shall, one day, win through to success.

Thank you again, sir, for coming as a personal representative of General de Gaulle to greet me as I put my foot again on this lovely soil of this lovely country. Thank you very much.

NOTE: The President spoke at 1:25 p.m. He was greeted by Louis Jacquinot, French Minister of State and personal representative of President de Gaulle, and by Admiral Henri Nomy and Ambassador Herve Alphand. Secretary of State Christian A. Herter joined the President at Toulon and accompanied him by train to Paris, where they were met by President de Gaulle and Amory Houghton, U.S. Ambassador to France. Ambassador Houghton escorted the President to the U.S. Embassy where the President stayed during the Western summit meeting.

333   ¶ Statement by the President on the Death of the Last Surviving Veteran of the War Between the States.   *December* 20, 1959

WITH MILLIONS of Americans throughout our land, I pause in respectful silence to honor the passing of the last surviving veteran of the War Between the States, Walter W. Williams.

The wounds of the deep and bitter dispute which once divided our nation have long since healed, and a united America in a divided world now holds up on a larger canvas the cherished traditions of liberty and justice for all.

With Mr. Williams' passing, the hosts of Blue and Gray who were the chief actors in that great and tragic drama a century ago have all passed from the world stage. No longer are they the Blue and the Gray. All rest together as Americans in honored glory. An era has ended.

NOTE: This statement was released in Washington. In addition, the President issued Proclamation 3329 (24 F.R. 10711) directing that the flag of the United States be flown at half-staff on all Government buildings, grounds, and naval vessels until interment.

334 ¶ Remarks to the Staff of the U.S. Embassy in Paris. *December* 21, 1959

Ladies and Gentlemen:

I was about to say it was almost a unique experience in the last 2 or 3 weeks for me to speak to a body where every member could understand me. But after thinking it over, I am not so sure that that is entirely an advantage, because some of them, at least, couldn't criticise what I say.

It is indeed a great personal pleasure to meet you this morning. I met the Embassy staffs in every country where the time would permit—in India, Pakistan, and every country where there were more than a few hours to spend, and I did so with a very definite purpose in mind.

We all know in a very real sense that any American coming to a foreign country is an ambassador—his wife is an ambassador, his children are. Now I realize there are people here that are not just Embassy personnel. You are from other organizations the United States maintains in our own interest and in the interest of the free world in other countries. But each of you is an ambassador, and the one thing this poor old world needs more than any other single thing is for all of us not merely to get a greater liking for another country—a country in which you may be living—but try to get a deep understanding, a better understanding, of what makes this people "tick," why do they think what they think, why do we see accounts and opinions and judgments in our newspapers and over our televisions that are so different from those we hear in foreign lands.

And indeed, to talk about my own job for just a moment, I think one of the greatest jobs that any political or governmental leader in the United States, including even the military, has is to make the American people understand what the problems of the world are today. If we can do that among ourselves, we can do a much better job between ourselves and other countries.

Every one of us thinks of the future. Some of us think in terms of the future of our children—with me it's grandchildren, and hopefully, some day, great-grandchildren. But they are the future that we are looking at, and this old world has gotten to the point where unless this future is one of cooperation and of peace—peaceful cooperation, a free opportunity for cooperation, then I say your lives, instead of being fruitful in your pursuit of happiness, in your attempt to see the lives of your children and your grandchildren fulfilled, then instead—if we don't get this understanding, develop this peaceful relationship—it will indeed be a dark and dreary one.

Now I happen to be one of those that is a born optimist, and I suppose most soldiers are, because no soldier ever won a battle if he went into it pessimistically. I make no apologies for being optimistic because I still have the faith in humans, in their individual and their collective good sense and readiness, courage, to look facts in the face, that we can solve these problems. And this is between ourselves—Indians or Africans—the French—any place where differences occur. And one way I think we can keep them from becoming more noticeable—sometimes more irritating than anything—is when we don't help to make them worse. The criticisms we have of another people because they are different, in their background, their traditions and their prejudices—all right, let's ignore them and have a good laugh on it, and drink a Coca Cola—oh, I'll get accused of being commercial—(*laughter*)—have a soft drink, and in this way every one of us will be doing a job.

No leader, no matter who he may be, no matter what his record, no matter how youthful or vigorous or how many years he may have to carry on his work—he can't do it by himself. Millions and millions of Americans can combine, though, with millions and even billions of others, and we will make it a good world.

So that's the reason I would just like to say to all of you, good luck and stick with it—and always remember you are Mr. and Mrs. Ambassador.

Goodbye.

NOTE: The President spoke at the chancery of the U.S. Embassy at 10:23 a.m.

335 ¶ Joint Statement Concerning the Economic
Agreements Reached at the Western Summit
Conference. *December* 21, 1959

THE HEADS of State and Government have discussed the important
changes that have taken place in the international economic situation.
Recognizing the great economic progress of Western Europe, they have
agreed that virtually all of the industrialized part of the free world is now
in a position to devote its energies in increased measure to new and
important tasks of cooperative endeavor with the object of:

(a) furthering the development of the less developed countries,
and

(b) pursuing trade policies directed to the sound use of economic
resources and the maintenance of harmonious international relations, thus
contributing to growth and stability in the world economy and to a general
improvement in the standard of living.

In their view these cooperative principles should also govern the discussions on commercial problems arising from the existence of European
economic regional organizations, which are or will be constituted within
the framework of the GATT, such as the European Economic Community
and the European Free Trade Association. Their relations both with
other countries and with each other should be discussed in this spirit.

The Heads of State and Government, recognizing that the method of
furthering these principles requires intensive study, have agreed to call
an informal meeting to be held in Paris in the near future. They suggest
that the members and participants of the Executive Committee of the
OEEC and the Governments whose nationals are members of the Steering
Board for Trade of the OEEC should be represented at this meeting.

It is proposed that an objective of such a group should be to consider
the need for and methods of continuing consultations dealing with the
above-mentioned problems.

NOTE: This joint statement was released in Paris.

336 ¶ Joint Statement Following the Western Summit Conference.   *December* 21, 1959

THE PRESIDENT of the United States of America, the President of the French Republic, the Prime Minister of the United Kingdom and the Chancellor of the Federal Republic of Germany met in Paris and at Rambouillet on the 19th, 20th and 21st of December 1959 and exchanged views on various subjects of common interest.

In the course of these meetings consideration was given to the views expressed by the member governments of the North Atlantic Treaty Organization at the meeting of the Council held in Paris from the 15th to the 17th of December.

Among the subjects discussed were East-West relations, disarmament and problems relating to Germany including Berlin. On the last point the Heads of State and Government reaffirmed the principles set forth in the Four Power communique of December 14th, 1958, and the Declaration of the North Atlantic Council of December 16th, 1958 on Berlin.

The Heads of State and Government agreed on the desirability of a Four Power conference with the Chairman of the Council of Ministers of the Union of Soviet Socialist Republics. The purpose of this conference would be to consider a number of questions of mutual concern. President Eisenhower, General de Gaulle and Mr. Macmillan have sent letters to Mr. Khrushchev proposing such a meeting beginning on the 27th of April in Paris. These letters were delivered in Moscow this morning. The texts are being immediately released.

The Heads of State and Government have agreed on the procedures to be followed in preparation for the proposed meeting and have issued the necessary directives to this end.

The North Atlantic Council will be informed of the results of the present conversations at the Ministerial Meeting which will take place on the 22nd of December, and the Council will be regularly consulted during the course of the preparatory work.

The Heads of State and Government express the hope that the proposed conference will contribute to the strengthening of peace with justice.

NOTE: This joint statement was released in Paris.

337 ¶ Letter to Chairman Khrushchev Proposing a Four-Power Summit Conference in Paris. *December* 21, 1959

Dear Mr. Chairman:

As you are aware I have just met with President de Gaulle and Prime Minister Macmillan. Among the subjects we discussed was the possibility of our having a meeting with you to consider international questions of mutual concern.

We agreed that it would be desirable for the four Heads of State or Government to meet together from time to time in each other's countries to discuss the main problems affecting the attainment of peace and stability in the world. I therefore wish now to express my readiness to meet with you, President de Gaulle and Prime Minister Macmillan at the earliest feasible time. In view of the engagements of all of us, as they are known to me, we had thought that the opening date for the proposed conference could be April 27 and that Paris would be the most appropriate place for the first meeting.

I very much hope that this proposal is acceptable to you.

Sincerely,

DWIGHT D. EISENHOWER

NOTE: This letter was released in Paris. Gaulle and Prime Minister Macmillan.
Similar letters were sent by President de

338 ¶ Remarks Upon Arrival at Torrejon Air Force Base, Madrid. *December* 21, 1959

Generalissimo, Ladies and Gentlemen:

First of all, let me assure you of my satisfaction that at long last I have fulfilled an ambition of mine, almost of a lifetime, to come to Spain, to Madrid, and to see the Spanish people.

More than four and a half centuries ago, your great Admiral, Columbus, sailed on a voyage which changed the course of history. Not long after that, America began its long role on the world scene.

Since then, Spanish men and women have explored and settled; preached and taught; Spanish culture and language have flourished in the New World beyond the dreams of Isabella and Ferdinand.

In my own country, from Florida to California, across the thousands of miles of the United States, the memory of Spanish explorers and builders, soldiers, and missionaries, lives imperishably in the names of rivers and cities—and even States of the United States of America.

My own life, in part, has been spent against the background of history made by Spanish pioneers. I was born in Texas where de Vaca traveled and the comrades of de Soto wandered after his death. I was raised in Kansas which Coronado reached, and I spent some years in the far-off Philippines.

But I do not come here to recall our ties of old and recent times, important though they are.

I come to this nation, one of the ancestors of the Americas, with a message from the American people to the Spanish people, looking for a brighter future in cooperative labor for the noblest of all human causes: peace and friendship in freedom.

On this mission, I say to Spain and the Spaniards: let us work together so that in our own day we may see a long advance toward a world free from aggression, from hunger and disease—free from war and free of the threat of war.

Let us work together so that we may pass on to our children a golden promise that mankind will achieve peace with justice—friendship in freedom.

By this visit I hope to bring to all of you the personal assurance of America's determination to work toward the attainment of that goal, striving always for stronger bonds of understanding and high purpose between Spain and the United States.

Thank you very much indeed.

NOTE: The President spoke at 4:40 p.m. He was met by Chief of State Generalissimo Francisco Franco, officials of the Spanish Government, members of the diplomatic corps, and U.S. Ambassador John Lodge.

339 ¶ Toast by the President at the Dinner Given in His Honor by General Franco.
December 21, 1959

I AM delighted to be here tonight.

Your words of welcome, General Franco, the heartwarming, friendly reception of the Spanish people; the congeniality of this gathering—are all evidence of Spain's traditional hospitality and courtesy.

As you have said, General, the friendship between the Spanish and American peoples has its roots deep in the history of our two nations. In the very beginnings of the Republic of the United States, the help of Spain and the Spanish people was of great importance to us.

Today, this friendship needs only the nourishment of continuing close relations—in understanding, in trust, in joined effort—to enable us constantly to increase our mutual contribution to peace and friendship in freedom.

Neither Spain nor the United States seeks to exploit other peoples. Neither plots an aggression against any neighbor, near or far. Neither is impelled by an atheistic philosophy to degrade human beings into economic tools of the state.

Rather, both Spain and the United States want to live at peace, at honorable peace, with all their neighbors in the world community. Both want to use their resources for the betterment of their people and to help, so far as they can, in the betterment of all humanity. Both want freedom for themselves and for all nations.

And at this season, when both Spain and the United States celebrate the birth of the Savior, both peoples re-dedicate themselves to the message which heralded His coming: Peace on Earth to Men of Good Will. In the spirit of this Christmas season, in the message of two thousand years ago, we seek divine blessing on today's purpose of Peace and Friendship in Freedom.

General Franco, to you and to the people of Spain, to a fruitful friendship linking our countries.

NOTE: The President proposed this toast at a dinner at the Oriente Palace.

340 ¶ Joint Statement Following Discussions with Chief of State Franco.   *December* 22, 1959

THE PRESIDENT of the United States and the Chief of the Spanish State this morning concluded a series of conversations in which they were joined by other officials of both governments. The President reviewed the purposes which had led him to undertake his good-will tour and the results which he hoped would be achieved. He gave the Chief of State a review of his trip including the Western Summit Conference.

The talks, which covered a wide variety of other international matters of interest to both countries, were conducted in an atmosphere of cordiality and understanding. The President and the Chief of State discussed the President's planned visit to the Soviet Union next year and confirmed their views, as expressed in their exchange of letters of last August, that such consultations to improve the climate of relationships would be beneficial, although a firm defense posture should be maintained.

Gratifying progress was noted in the implementation of the economic and defense agreements signed by the United States and Spain on September 26, 1953. These agreements are based on a recognition of the necessity for efforts on the part of both countries to achieve the common goal of world peace and stability.

During these conversations Spain's admission to the Organization for European Economic Cooperation was mentioned with satisfaction and the President expressed his good wishes for the success of the Spanish economic stabilization program.

The conversation served as another indication of the friendly ties between the Spanish and American peoples and strengthened the bonds of cooperation that exist between the two countries.

NOTE: This joint statement was released in Madrid.

341 ¶ Remarks at Torrejon Air Force Base, Madrid, Upon Leaving for Morocco. *December* 22, 1959

Generalissimo, Your Excellencies, and Ladies and Gentlemen:

The only regret that I have about this visit that I have made to this beautiful country is its shortness. I should like to have stayed here as many days as I have hours. But in spite of the shortness of that time, I am going back with very vivid impressions.

While the courtesy and hospitality of the Spanish people has been proverbial and known throughout the world, one must experience it to really feel its true depth and intensity. I should like to be able to send my personal gratitude and thanks to every individual who has come to this air field to bid me welcome yesterday, or goodbye today—to every individual who came along the street to shout "eekay," which I understand is Spanish for my nickname.

It has been a fruitful visit. I have had useful discussions with the Generalissimo and with the members of his government, and I am quite sure that the traditional ties of friendship and the active cooperation which has been progressing between our countries will be stronger because of this visit.

And finally, I should like on behalf of the American people to bring you their wishes, whether you are here as an American on this base or to all the Spanish people wherever my voice can reach. Best wishes for a Merry Christmas and a Happy New Year. And indeed, after some of the expressions I heard along the street yesterday, I feel that I have your permission to take your best wishes to them for the same kind of fine holiday season.

Goodbye—my appreciation to every official, to every individual that I have had the pleasure of seeing—and good luck to all of you. May God keep you. Goodbye.

NOTE: The President and General Franco went by helicopter to the airport following their breakfast discussion at Pardo Palace.

342   ¶ Letter to the Comptroller General of the
United States Concerning His Request for Reports
Evaluating the Mutual Security Program in Iran
and Thailand.   *December* 22, 1959

[Released December 22, 1959. Dated December 15, 1959]

Dear Mr. Campbell:

I am advised that on November 19, 1959, there was delivered to the
Office of the Director of the International Cooperation Administration
your written request for the disclosure of that Agency's Evaluation Reports
on its programs in Iran and Thailand.

As I have stated on other occasions, it is the established policy of the
Executive Branch to provide the Congress and the public with the fullest
possible information consistent with the national interest. This policy
has guided, and will continue to guide, the Executive Branch in carrying
out the Mutual Security Program so that there may be a full understanding of the program and its vital importance to the national security.

At the same time, however, under the historic doctrine of the separation
of powers between the three great branches of our Government, the
Executive has a recognized Constitutional duty and power with respect
to the disclosure of information, documents, and other materials relating
to its operations. The President has throughout our history, in compliance with his duty in this regard, withheld information when he found
that the disclosure of what was sought would be incompatible with the
national interest.

It is essential to effective administration that employees of the Executive Branch be in a position to be fully candid in advising with each other
on official matters, and that the broadest range of individual opinions
and advice be available in the formulation of decisions and policy. It is
similarly essential that those who have the responsibility for making decisions be able to act with the knowledge that a decision or action will be
judged on its merits and not on whether it happened to conform to or
differ from the opinions or advice of subordinates. The disclosure of
conversations, communications or documents embodying or concerning
such opinions and advice can accordingly tend to impair or inhibit essen-

tial reporting and decision-making processes, and such disclosure has therefore been forbidden in the past, as contrary to the national interest, where that was deemed necessary for the protection of orderly and effective operation of the Executive Branch.

The ICA evaluation reports you have requested are internal Executive Branch communications comprising opinion and advice on official matters. They are of a class of reports prepared by small teams of senior officers on the basis of extensive study in the field and in Washington. The purpose of each such report is to examine basic ICA program objectives and program content in a particular country from the standpoint of determining whether the ICA program in that country is effectively carrying out our foreign policy objectives. Such reports contain the candid personal opinions, suggestions and recommendations of the officers who prepare them, and are prepared for submission directly to the Director of the ICA for his information and use. Reports such as the one which you requested have been an important factor in the decision-making process within the agency, and requests for their release have consistently been denied.

Since the disclosure of the reports requested by you would not be compatible with the national interest, I have forbidden that they be furnished pursuant to your request, and hereby so certify in accordance with section 111(d) of the Mutual Security Appropriation Act, 1960.

As you may know, on November 10, 1959, I made a similar certification in response to a request for an Evaluation Report on the ICA program in Viet-Nam. That request had been made by Senator Mansfield, Chairman of the Subcommittee on State Department Organization and Public Affairs, Committee on Foreign Relations.

Although I have forbidden the furnishing of the Evaluation Reports requested by you, I wish to make it clear that this has not been done for the purpose of preventing the disclosure of any facts shown by the reports. Such facts will be made available to you as promptly as possible.

Sincerely,

Dwight D. Eisenhower

NOTE: This letter, addressed to the Honorable Joseph Campbell, Comptroller General of the United States, was released in Washington.

343   ¶ Remarks Upon Arrival at Nouasseur Air Force Base, Casablanca.   *December* 22, 1959

Your Majesty:

It is indeed a very great honor for me to be received here on the ground of this nation, which was the first nation that recognized the independence of the United States one and three quarters centuries ago.

So it is a definite feeling of kinship with this nation that I sense, as I come here to have these few hours with His Majesty and with his people. And my party and I, I assure you, do so with a feeling of honor and privilege.

NOTE: The President spoke at 11:15 a.m. He was met by His Majesty Mohamed V, King of Morocco, the Crown Prince, Prime Minister Moulay Abdallah Ibrahim, the Moroccan Cabinet, members of the diplomatic corps, and U.S. Ambassador Charles W. Yost.

344   ¶ Remarks at the Luncheon Given in Honor of the President by King Mohamed V. *December* 22, 1959

Your Majesty:

My staff and I are grateful for the great honor you have done us in inviting us to your home, to your table. We have, with you, broken bread, we have shared your food. We are proud that in this sister republic, a sister republic of ours, that we have been enabled to see you and talk with you and with your people.

I could not fail to tell you how deeply we have been impressed by the warmth and indeed the stupendous size of the crowds that greeted us as we came along the road.

I am grateful also for your quick recognition of the reasons for the shortness of my visit. I too wish I could remain longer in this beautiful country. Then I could better appreciate the advances your government and your people have made in education, housing, and commerce— and the general well-being of Morocco. I am grateful also that you have given voice to my own conviction that the friendship between our countries has weathered the test of time.

Moroccans and Americans are old friends, between whom any differences which may arise will always be worked out in sympathy and in understanding.

Your Majesty has honored me in linking my name with the cause for which the Second World War was fought. When I last was in Morocco, I shared with others a heavy responsibility: to win the war which the tyranny of Hitler began, to win it, as Your Majesty has aptly said, for freedom and the dignity of nations and of men.

My mission today is different. This time I represent the American people, bringing to Morocco the message of peace and friendship in freedom. We Americans hope that Morocco and all countries will join us in the effort to assure that devastating war shall not again pit human against human and threaten all of civilization—and even human survival. We Americans seek the rule of law among men and among nations. We are ready to join with all people in its attainment. But so long as the forces of aggression are at large, we must remain strong, in arms, in industrial might, in our faith in ourselves and in our God.

Our strength is for the defense of freedom, the freedom of ourselves, our friends, who with us believe that man was created to be free, to be his own master.

Now, Your Majesty, I thank you for myself, for those with me, for all the American people. The warmth of the welcome from you and the Moroccan people is heartwarming evidence of friendship toward America and Americans—a friendship that I assure you we reciprocate fully.

NOTE: The luncheon was held at the King's palace in Casablanca.

345   ¶ Joint Statement Following Discussions With the King of Morocco.   *December* 22, 1959

THE MEETING between the President and His Majesty took place on December 22, 1959, at Casablanca, and lasted from 1500 to 1700, and took place in an atmosphere of cordiality which is characteristic of the relations which arise from the traditional friendship which has never ceased to exist between the United States of America since the proclamation of their independence and their recognition by the Kingdom of Morocco.

In the course of this interview the two Chiefs of State first of all examined the world situation and the problems which arise therefrom.

They rejoice in the relaxation of international tensions and while reaffirming their faith in the great values of the freedom of peoples and the dignity of men, they feel that any initiative of a nature to lead to the consolidation of peace and ensure international cooperation, should be encouraged.

His Majesty drew President Eisenhower's attention to the multiple bonds which unite Morocco to the other Arab countries and make it sensitive to everything which affects them.

His Majesty emphasized the vital importance to Morocco of the end of the war in Algeria, in view of the profound repercussions which this has on the national life of Morocco and its international relations.

The two Chiefs of State noted with great satisfaction the positive character of the political evolution of the Algerian problem, and rejoice in the progress accomplished towards a peaceful solution of this problem through the acceptance by the interested parties of the principle of self-determination and recourse to consultation.

His Majesty the King of Morocco and the President of the United States have welcomed the opportunity provided by the President's brief visit to Morocco to renew their warm personal friendship and, within the time available, review questions of interest to them. Their exchange of views strengthened their already deep confidence in the possibilities of fruitful cooperation between nations such as Morocco and the United States, sharing common goals of peace and justice among men and guided by the same basic principles of national conduct. This was specifically revealed in their discussions of the withdrawal of United States forces from Morocco, and they were greatly encouraged by the progress that has been made since His Majesty's visit to Washington in 1957.

Preliminary preparations for the departure of United States forces from Morocco will begin in the immediate future, and it is agreed between His Majesty the King of Morocco and the President of the United States of America that United States forces will be withdrawn by the end of 1963. In this connection, immediate steps will be taken to release the airfield at Ben Slimane (Boulhaut). This will be achieved not later than March 31, 1960.

NOTE: This joint statement was released in Casablanca.

346 ¶ Remarks at Andrews Air Force Base Upon Returning From the Good Will Tour.
December 22, 1959

Folks:

Thank you very much indeed for coming out on this cold night to welcome my party and me back home. It is certainly good to be here.

Now I must remind you that this morning we had breakfast in Madrid, lunch in Casablanca—and now we are home at an hour which by our getting up time is five or six o'clock in the morning. So you can realize that it is not a time for a very erudite and informing speech.

But I do want to say just one thing: everywhere we went, people sent this back, a message of Merry Christmas and good will to all the people of the United States. And in that message I join myself this evening to all of you, everybody—everywhere.

Good night.

NOTE: The President spoke at approximately 11 p.m.

347 ¶ Radio and Television Remarks on the Good Will Tour Delivered at the Pageant of Peace Ceremonies. *December* 23, 1959

Fellow Americans, at home and overseas: Friends of America; workers for a just peace wherever you may be in the world, whatever your race or flag or tongue or creed:

Once again I have the privilege of lighting the Pageant of Peace Tree on the eve of the Christmas season. This is the season when men and women of all faiths, pausing to listen, gain new heart from the message that filled the heavens over Bethlehem two thousand years ago—

Peace on earth—good will to men.

Every Christmas through the long march of centuries since then, the message has been echoed in the hopes and prayers of humanity.

This Christmas, for me at least those words have clearer meaning, sharper significance, more urgent counsel.

Last night I came home from a trip that carried me to three continents,

Africa and Asia and Europe. I visited eleven countries whose populations total a quarter of all mankind.

I wish that every American—certainly every American recognized by his fellows as a leader in any field, and every leader in the countries of the West—could see and hear what I have seen and what I have heard. The mutual understanding thereby created could in itself do much to dissolve the issues that plague the world.

My trip was not undertaken as a feature of normal diplomatic procedures. It was not my purpose either to seek specific agreements or to urge new treaty relationships. My purpose was to improve the climate in which diplomacy might work more successfully; a diplomacy that seeks, as its basic objective, peace with justice for all men.

In the crowds that welcomed my party and me, I saw at close hand the faces of millions—many, indeed most, were poor, weary, worn by toil; but others were young, energetic, eager; the children, as always, bright and excited.

The clothes of a few were as modern as today's Paris and New York; of others, as ancient as the garb of Abraham, often soiled and tattered, although sometimes colorful and romantic to the American eye.

They were Buddhist and Moslem and Hindu and Christian.

But seeing them massed along country roads and city streets from the Eastern shore of the Atlantic to Karachi and Delhi, three things—it seemed to me—united them into one family.

The first—their friendship for America and Americans.

The second—their fervent hope—too long frustrated—for betterment of themselves and of their children.

And third—their deep-seated hunger for peace in freedom.

Of this last, permit me to speak first. It must come first. The assurance of peace in freedom is the key to betterment of peoples everywhere; and in a just peace friendship between all peoples will flourish.

I assure you that all the people I saw and visited want peace—nothing in human affairs can be more certain than that.

I talked with Kings and Presidents, Prime Ministers and humble men and women in cottages and in mud huts. Their common denominator was their faith that America will help lead the way toward a just peace.

They believe that we look and work toward the day when the use of force to achieve political or commercial objectives will disappear—when each country can freely draw on the culture, wisdom, experience of other countries and adapt to its own needs and aspirations what it deems is best and most suitable.

They understand that we look and work toward the day when there can be open and peaceful partnership—communication—interchange of goods and ideas between all peoples; toward the day when each people will make its maximum contribution toward the progress and prosperity of the world.

Such is the world condition which we and all the peoples I visited hope—and pray—to see.

Our concept of the good life for humanity does not require an inevitable conflict between peoples and systems—in which one must triumph over the other. Nor does it offer merely a bare coexistence as a satisfactory state for mankind.

After all, an uneasy coexistence could be as barren and sterile, joyless and stale a life for human beings as the coexistence of cellmates in a penitentiary or a labor camp.

We believe that history, the record of human living, is a great and broad stream into which should pour the richness and diversity of many cultures; from which emerge ideas and practices, ideals and purposes, valid for all.

We believe each people of the human family—even the least in number and the most primitive—can contribute something to a developing world embracing all peoples, enhancing the good of all peoples.

But we recognize—we must recognize—that in the often fierce and even vicious battle for survival—against weather and disease and poverty— some peoples need help. Denied it, they could well become so desperate as to create a world catastrophe.

Now in the ultimate sense, a nation must achieve for itself, by its heart and by its will, the standard of living and the strength needed to progress toward peace with justice and freedom. But where necessary resources and technological skills are lacking, people must be assisted— or all the world will suffer.

In the past, America has been generous. Our generosity has been greeted with gratitude and friendship. On my trip, many millions cried and shouted their testimony to that fact.

No country I visited is short on the greatest of all resources—people of good heart and stout will. And this is especially true of the young. Almost every country is, however, short on the technical knowledge, the skills, the machines, the techniques—and the money—needed to enable their people fully to exploit the natural resources of their lands.

Of course, money alone cannot bring about this progress.

Yet America's own best interests—our own hopes for peace—require that we continue our financial investment and aid; and persuade all other free nations to join us—to the limit of their ability—in a long-term program, dependable in its terms and in its duration.

But more importantly—in the spirit of the Christmas season, that there may be peace on earth, and good will among men—we must as individuals, as corporations, labor unions, professional societies, as communities, multiply our interest, our concern in these peoples. They are now our warm friends. They will be our stout and strong partners for peace and friendship in freedom—if they are given the right sort of help in the right sort of spirit.

The American Government and our allies provide the defensive strength against aggression that permits men of good will to work together for peace. Such strength is an absolute requirement until controlled and safeguarded disarmament allows its reduction, step by step.

Protected by our defensive strength against violent disruption of our peaceful efforts, we are trying to produce a workable, practical program that will make each succeeding Christmas a little closer in spirit and reality to the message of the first Christmas long ago.

This is not a matter of charity for the poverty-striken nor of easing our own consciences through doles for the distressed. The help we give to our friends is help and strength for the cause of freedom—American freedom—as well as freedom throughout the world.

In giving it, we must be hardheaded but understanding; enlightened in our own interest but sympathetic and generous in the interest of our friends.

Together we should consider all the ways and the forms such help might take. I fervently hope that in this Christmas Season each of you who is listening will give thought to what you can do for another human, identical with you in his divine origin and destiny—however distant in miles or poor in worldly estate.

With that hope, with that prayer, I wish you all happiness and peace in this season, as I light the Nation's Christmas Tree for the Pageant of Peace.

Merry Christmas!

NOTE: The President spoke at 5:12 p.m. just before lighting the National Community Christmas Tree at the Pageant of Peace Ceremonies on the Ellipse.

348 ¶ Statement by the President on the Expiration of the Voluntary Moratorium on Nuclear Weapons Testing. *December* 29, 1959

THE NEGOTIATIONS with respect to the cessation of nuclear testing have now been in progress for fourteen months. While now recessed, they will soon be resumed. No satisfactory agreement is yet in sight. The prospects for such an agreement have been injured by the recent unwillingness on the part of the politically guided Soviet experts to give serious scientific consideration to the effectiveness of seismic techniques for the detection of underground nuclear explosions. Indeed the atmosphere of the talks has been clouded by the intemperate and technically unsupportable Soviet annex to the report of the technical experts. The distinguished American group of scientists who composed the United States delegation will make public from the verbatim records of the conference the facts which will completely refute this Soviet document.

We will resume negotiations in a continuing spirit of seeking to reach a safeguarded agreement. In the meantime, the voluntary moratorium on testing will expire on December 31.

Although we consider ourselves free to resume nuclear weapons testing, we shall not resume nuclear weapons tests without announcing our intention in advance of any resumption. During the period of voluntary suspension of nuclear weapons tests the United States will continue its active program of weapon research, development and laboratory-type experimentation.

NOTE: This statement was released at Augusta, Ga.

349 ¶ Message to Nikita Khrushchev, Chairman of the Council of Ministers, U.S.S.R., Concerning the Date of the Four-Power Summit Conference. *December 29, 1959*

Dear Mr. Chairman:

I note with satisfaction that you have agreed to participate in a Summit meeting of the Four Powers in Paris which Prime Minister Macmillan, President de Gaulle and myself proposed to you. I can well understand the difficulty of arriving at a date commonly acceptable to the four of us.

I have been in touch with Prime Minister Macmillan and President de Gaulle in regard to the alternative dates which you suggest. Unfortunately, due to other engagements, both President de Gaulle and I would not find it possible to meet on April 21. I further understand that Prime Minister Macmillan has prior commitments which run from May 3 until mid-May.

Provided that this is acceptable to you, the best arrangement would seem to be for the meeting of the Four Powers to open in Paris on May 16.

I trust, Mr. Chairman, that this will not present any difficulties to you and that we may agree to meet in Paris on that date.

> Sincerely,
> DWIGHT D. EISENHOWER

NOTE: This message was released at Augusta, Ga.

350 ¶ Letter to Admiral Jerauld Wright on His Release From the Position of Supreme Allied Commander, Atlantic. *December 31, 1959*

[Released December 31, 1959. Dated December 29, 1959]

Dear Jerry:

The North Atlantic Council has approved my request that you be released from the position of Supreme Allied Commander, Atlantic, effective February 29, 1960, in order that you might retire from active duty in the United States Navy on the following day. At the same time, the Council approved my nomination of Admiral Robert L. Dennison to succeed you in this important post.

I would like to take this opportunity to express my personal thanks and that of the American people for the services which you have performed over a period of the last six years. The North Atlantic Treaty Organization represents an endeavor on the part of fifteen free nations, the success of which is vital to the security and well-being of the United States. Thus, the position of Commander of one of the major commands of this organization is one of the greatest responsibility. The leadership and judgment which you have displayed in this capacity have been a source of deep satisfaction to me personally, and I know has won the great admiration not only of the nations of the North Atlantic Treaty Organization but of all the Free World. Your loss will be felt by all.

At the same time, I do, of course, take note of the fact of your forthcoming retirement from the United States Navy. As you leave, you take with you the gratitude of the people of the United States for your many years of outstanding and devoted service and my very best wishes to you and Phyllis for a happy and rewarding retirement.

With warm regard,

Sincerely,

DWIGHT D. EISENHOWER

NOTE: This letter was released at Augusta, Ga.

A White House release of December 23 stated that the North Atlantic Council had expressed to Admiral Wright, in the name of the governments represented on the Council, lasting gratitude for the distinguished service rendered by him as Supreme Allied Commander, Atlantic, a position in which he served from April 12, 1954, through February 29, 1960.

351 ¶ Letter to Admiral Robert L. Dennison on His Designation as Supreme Allied Commander, Atlantic.   *December* 31, 1959

[Released December 31, 1959. Dated December 29, 1959]

Dear Admiral Dennison:

With the approval of the North Atlantic Council, I have designated you Supreme Allied Commander, Atlantic, to be effective on February 29, 1960.

Your responsibilities and authority as the Supreme Allied Commander, Atlantic, are contained in the Terms of Reference issued by the Standing Group of the Military Committee of the North Atlantic Treaty Organization.

The United States Armed Forces assigned to the United States Atlantic Command will continue to remain under your operational command to the extent necessary for the accomplishment of your mission.

You are hereby authorized to use officers and enlisted personnel of the United States Armed Forces and civilian employees of the United States Government on your staff as you consider appropriate in numbers and grades as necessary.

I am sending copies of this letter to the Secretary of State and to the Secretary of Defense for their guidance.

On behalf of the American people, I wish you the very best as you assume this most important post.

With warm regard,

Sincerely,

DWIGHT D. EISENHOWER

NOTE: This letter was released at Augusta, Ga.

Appendix A—White House Press Releases, 1959

NOTE: Includes releases covering matters with which the President was closely concerned, except announcements of Presidential personnel appointments and approvals of legislation with which there was no accompanying statement.

Releases relating to Proclamations and Executive Orders have not been included. These documents are separately listed in Appendix B.

For list of Press and Radio Conferences, see subject index under "News Conferences."

Appendix A

January   Subject

19 Exchange of messages between the President and President Frondizi of Argentina

20 Remarks of welcome to President Frondizi of Argentina at the Washington National Airport

20 Annual message presenting the economic report to the Congress

20 Toasts of the President and the President of Argentina

21 Letter accepting resignation of Harlow H. Curtice, Chairman, President's Committee for Traffic Safety

22 Letter accepting resignation of Howard Pyle, Administrative Assistant to the President

23 Presidential statement upon signing Executive order establishing the Committee on Government Activities Affecting Prices and Costs

26 Message to the Baghdad Pack Ministerial Council in Karachi

26 Letter accepting resignation of David S. Smith, Assistant Secretary of the Air Force

26 Memorandum on the 1959 Red Cross Campaign

27 Letter accepting resignation of Dudley C. Sharp, Assistant Secretary of the Air Force

28 Special message to the Congress on labor-management relations

28 Exchange of messages between the Secretary of State and Ambassador Carrillo Flores of Mexico concerning the President's visit to Mexico

28 Message to the Congress transmitting the 9th semiannual report under Public Law 480 (83d Cong.)

29 Special message to the Congress on agriculture

30 Remarks to the Third National Conference on Exchange of Persons

31 White House announcement regarding the Cabinet Committee on Price Stability for Economic Growth

31 Letter accepting resignation of J. H. Smith, Jr., Director, International Cooperation Administration

February

2 Message to the Congress transmitting the first annual report under the National Aeronautics and Space Act

February   Subject

3 Statement by the Secretary of State following a discussion with the President before leaving for London, Paris, and Bonn

3 Letter accepting resignation of Thomas S. Gates, Jr., Secretary of the Navy

4 Letter accepting resignation of Paul W. McCracken, member, Council of Economic Advisers

5 Special message to the Congress on civil rights

5 Exchange of messages between the President and President Frondizi of Argentina

6 Statement by the Press Secretary concerning Premier Khrushchev's invitation to the President to visit the Soviet Union

9 Letter from the Secretary of State requesting leave of absence during his illness

11 White House announcement of the President's forthcoming visit to Canada to participate in ceremonies marking the opening of the St. Lawrence Seaway

11 Remarks at the 17th annual meeting of the National Rural Electric Cooperative Association

11 Remarks at the National Lincoln Sesquicentennial Dinner

12 Special message to the Congress on increasing the resources of the International Bank for Reconstruction and Development and the International Monetary Fund

12 Remarks on the 25th anniversary of the Export-Import Bank of Washington

13 Letter to Representative Halleck concerning citizens' views of excessive government spending

14 Statement by the President following his visit to Secretary Dulles in Walter Reed Hospital

14 White House announcement of the President's participation in a meeting on the U.S. Savings Bond program

18 Letter accepting resignation of Willard F. Libby, member, Atomic Energy Commission

888

Appendix A

Appendix A

March	Subject
18	Letter to the Director, Bureau of the Budget, concerning the admission of Hawaii
18	Letter to Governor Quinn certifying to the enactment of the Hawaii statehood bill
18	White House announcement of the presentation by the Austrian Ambassador of the Austrian Tenth Anniversary Volume on the European Recovery Program
18	White House announcement of appointment of Dr. Allen Wallis as Executive Vice Chairman of the Cabinet Committee on Price Stability for Economic Growth
18	Letter to Steve Stahl, Chairman, National Taxpayers Conference, on preserving our national economic strength
19	Toasts of the President and President O'Kelly of Ireland at a luncheon for President Eisenhower
20	Statement by the President on the House Appropriations Committee's rejection of the Development Loan Fund
23	Letter accepting resignation of Malcolm Anderson, Assistant Attorney General
23	White House announcement of the forthcoming visit of King Baudouin I of Belgium
24	White House statement on Easter egg rolling on the White House lawn
24	Toasts of the President and King Hussein I of the Hashemite Kingdom of Jordan
25	Statement by the President concerning disclosure of information on fallout
26	Letter accepting resignation of James S. Plaut, Deputy U.S. Commissioner General for the Brussels Universal and International Exhibition
26	White House statement concerning the report on the Argus experiment
31	Message from President O'Kelly of Ireland

April

1	Letter accepting resignation of Walter S. Robertson, Assistant Secretary of State

April	Subject
1	Letter to Meade Alcorn, Chairman of the Republican National Committee, concerning his resignation
2	Remarks at the opening session of the ministerial meeting of the North Atlantic Council
3	White House statement concerning the organization of the Government's radiological health activities
3	Letter accepting resignation of W. A. Dexheimer, Commissioner, Bureau of Reclamation
4	Address at the Gettysburg College Convocation: "The Importance of Understanding"
6	Memorandum for the President from True D. Morse, Acting Secretary of Agriculture, on food shipments to Kentucky
7	Statement by the Press Secretary concerning release of unemployment figures
7	Letter accepting resignation of Robert L. Farrington, General Counsel, Department of Agriculture
7	Statement by the President on the observance of World Health Day
8	Message to President Garcia of the Philippines on Bataan Day
10	Letter to E. R. Quesada on leaving White House staff to become Administrator of the Federal Aviation Agency
10	Letter to the Director, Bureau of the Budget, on interagency cooperation in aviation matters
11	White House release of list of members of the Advisory Committee on the Arts of the National Cultural Center
13	White House statement following discussions between the President and Secretary Dulles at Walter Reed Hospital
13	Remarks at the seventh annual Republican Women's Conference
13	Remarks to the 15th annual Washington Conference of the Advertising Council
14	Remarks at the dedication of the Robert A. Taft Memorial Bell Tower
15	White House statement on the postponement of the visit of President Lopez Mateos of Mexico

April   Subject

16 Letter accepting the resignation of Secretary Dulles

17 Letter accepting resignation of Victor Hansen, Assistant Attorney General

17 Remarks following the announcement of the Vice President's visit to Moscow to open the American National Exhibition

20 Letter to the Chairman, Council of Ministers, U.S.S.R., on the discontinuance of nuclear weapons tests

21 White House statement, letter to Secretary Anderson, and text of proclamation on woolen textile imports

23 Remarks at the swearing in of John Foster Dulles as Special Consultant to the President with Cabinet rank

23 Remarks at the meeting of the Board of Directors of the National Association of Manufacturers

23 Remarks at the 40th anniversary meeting of the International Chamber of Commerce

27 Message to the Congress transmitting the final report of the National Advisory Committee for Aeronautics

27 Veto of bill concerning the loan approval authority of the Administrator, Rural Electrification Administration

27 White House statement on the Soviet position on nuclear test suspension

27 Remarks at annual meeting of the United States Chamber of Commerce

28 Telegram to the Governor of Mississippi concerning assistance by the FBI in Pearl River County

29 Letter to the President of the Senate and to the Speaker of the House of Representatives on the recommendations of the Committee to Study the U.S. Military Assistance Program

30 Letter to Dean Sayre concerning U.S. participation in the World Refugee Year

30 White House statement concerning Secretary Herter's proposals for the organization of the State Department

May

1 Statement by the Press Secretary on the resignation of Mrs. Clare Boothe Luce, Ambassador to Brazil

May   Subject

1 Letter to the President from Mrs. Clare Boothe Luce submitting her resignation as Ambassador to Brazil

1 Remarks upon receiving the 1958 World Peace Award at the AMVETS luncheon

4 Remarks of welcome to Sir Winston Churchill at the Washington National Airport

4 Statement by the Press Secretary on Ambassador Thompson's interview with Premier Khrushchev concerning the transport plane shot down over Soviet Armenia

5 Message to President Echegoyen on the flood disaster in Uruguay

6 Joint communique following meeting of the Food for Peace Conference

6 Statement by Secretary Benson on the Food for Peace Conference

6 Remarks at the dinner in honor of Sir Winston Churchill

7 Statement by the Press Secretary on the Federal Communications Commission's decision in the Lar Daly case

8 Statement by the President on the death of Donald A. Quarles, Deputy Secretary of Defense

11 Special message to the Congress on the establishment of the Inter-American Development Bank

11 Remarks of welcome to His Majesty Baudouin I, King of the Belgians, at the Washington National Airport

11 Toasts of the President and King Baudouin

12 Special message to the Congress transmitting Reorganization Plan 1 of 1959

13 Remarks at the semiannual conference of State civil defense directors

13 Special message to the Congress urging timely action on the Highway Trust Fund, housing, and wheat

13 White House announcement of a garden party for older residents of D.C. institutions to be given by Mrs. Eisenhower

13 Toasts of the President and the King of the Belgians at the Belgian Embassy

14 Remarks at the ground-breaking ceremonies for the Lincoln Center for the Performing Arts, New York City

May   Subject

14 Address "Science: Hand-Maiden of Freedom," New York City

15 Statement by the President upon approving a Joint Resolution on wheat acreage allotments and marketing quotas

16 Remarks to the cadets at the United States Air Force Academy, Colorado Springs, Colo.

16 Statement by the Press Secretary concerning Premier Khrushchev's reply to the President's letter of May 5

16 Letter to Nikita Khrushchev, Chairman, Council of Ministers, U.S.S.R., on the discontinuance of nuclear tests

17 White House release of an explanatory statement on elementary particle physics and a proposed Federal program in support of high energy accelerator physics

18 Letter to Secretary Gates designating him to act as Secretary of Defense

19 Letter to the Governors of New Hampshire, Rhode Island, and Massachusetts on the establishment of a special inter-agency committee on textile problems

19 Letter to Secretary Strauss on the establishment of an inter-agency textile committee

19 Special message to the Congress transmitting a proposed amendment to the agreement with the United Kingdom for cooperation on uses of atomic energy for mutual defense

19 Memorandum concerning proposed amendment to agreement with the United Kingdom for cooperation on uses of atomic energy for mutual defense

19 Special message to the Congress transmitting a proposed agreement with France on uses of atomic energy for mutual defense

19 Memorandum concerning proposed agreement with France for cooperation on uses of atomic energy for mutual defense

20 Letter to John Foster Dulles awarding him the Medal of Freedom, and accompanying citation

May   Subject

20 White House announcement of the forthcoming ceremonies in connection with the opening of the St. Lawrence Seaway

21 White House announcement of the appointment of a citizens advisory committee for the American National Exhibition to be held in Moscow

21 Message to the Congress transmitting a plan for United States participation and exhibition at the Century 21 Exposition

21 Statement by the President for the White House Conference on Refugees

22 Message to the Congress transmitting a report under the Federal Disaster Act

22 Remarks at the dedication ceremonies at the Francis Scott Key Memorial Auditorium, St. John's College, Annapolis, Maryland

24 Statement by the President on the death of John Foster Dulles

24 Statement by the President on the report of the President's Science Advisory Committee, "Education for the Age of Science"

26 Memorandum concerning proposed agreement with Canada for cooperation on uses of atomic energy for mutual defense

26 Special message to the Congress transmitting agreement with Canada for cooperation on uses of atomic energy for mutual defense

26 Memorandum concerning proposed agreement with Germany for cooperation on uses of atomic energy for mutual defense

26 Special message to the Congress transmitting proposed agreements with Germany, the Netherlands, and Turkey for cooperation on uses of atomic energy for mutual defense

28 Statement by the Press Secretary following the President's meeting with the foreign ministers of France, the United Kingdom, and the Soviet Union

28 Statement by the President following a meeting with Paul F. Foster, U.S. representative to the International Atomic Energy Agency

Appendix A

May	Subject
28	Letter accepting resignation of Dr. James R. Killian, Jr., Special Assistant to the President for Science and Technology

June

1 Letter accepting resignation of S. Everett Gleason, Deputy Executive Secretary of the National Security Council

1 White House announcement of the appointment of Marion W. Boggs as Deputy Executive Secretary of the National Security Council

1 Statement by the President concerning the wheat surplus

4 White House announcement of the forthcoming visit of President Sekou Toure of Guinea

4 Remarks to a group of business magazine editors in the Conference Room

5 White House statement on report of Board of Visitors to the U.S. Naval Academy

6 White House announcement of the opening of the Prince Albert Radar Laboratory in Saskatchewan

6 Message via the moon to the Prime Minister and people of Canada upon the opening of the Prince Albert Radar Laboratory

8 Special message to the Congress on the management of the public debt

8 Remarks and address at testimonial dinner honoring Republicans in Congress

9 Remarks at the National Conference on Civil Rights

9 Address at the annual meeting of the American Medical Association, Atlantic City, New Jersey

11 Special message to the Congress submitting an agreement with Greece for cooperation on uses of atomic energy for mutual defense

11 Memorandum concerning proposed agreement with Greece for cooperation on uses of atomic energy for mutual defense

12 Remarks at the graduation exercises of the Foreign Service Institute

June   *Subject*

15 White House statement on report of Board of Visitors to the U.S. Air Force Academy

16 White House statement on report of Board of Visitors to the U.S. Military Academy

16. Remarks at the opening of the National 4-H Club Center

18 Remarks at the "Industry Salute to the Federal Housing Administration" dinner

19 Statement by the President on the rejection of the nomination of Lewis L. Strauss as Secretary of Commerce

19 Message to members of all scientific expeditions in the Antarctic

23 White House announcement of the Capitol East Front Extension cornerstone laying ceremony on July 4

23 Letter to Chairman, Tariff Commission, on rye import quotas

24 Letter to the President of the Senate and to the Speaker of the House of Representatives transmitting report "The Organization and Administration of the Military Assistance Program"

24 Letter to William H. Draper, Jr., regarding the second interim report of the President's Committee to Study the U.S. Military Assistance Program

25 Statement by the President on the financing of the interstate highway system

25 Veto of bill relating to the wheat program

25 Veto of tobacco price support bill

25 Message to the Congress transmitting Third Annual Report on the Trade Agreements Program

26 Remarks at the formal opening of the St. Lawrence Seaway

27 Letter to David J. McDonald, President of the United Steelworkers of America

29 Statement by the President upon signing bill amending the Federal Airport Act

29 Statement by the President upon making public the interim report of the Cabinet Committee on Price Stability for Economic Growth

Appendix A

June	*Subject*	*July*	*Subject*

June   *Subject*

30 Citation accompanying the Distinguished Service Medal presented to General Maxwell D. Taylor

30 Statement by the President upon signing bill relating to veterans' home, farm, and business loans

30 Letter accepting resignation of Secretary of Commerce Strauss

30 White House announcement of the forthcoming visit of Prime Minister Antonio Segni of Italy

July

2 Letter to the Secretary, Western Association of State Highway Officials, on the interstate highway program

2 Letter to Governor Egan concerning the presentation to Alaska of the first 49-star flag

4 Remarks at the cornerstone-laying ceremony for the extension of the United States Capitol

4 Message recorded for broadcast to Americans overseas

7 Veto of bill relating to housing and urban renewal

8 Letter accepting resignation of Malcolm A. MacIntyre, Under Secretary of the Air Force

8 Letter accepting resignation of Robert B. Dechert, General Counsel, Department of Defense

8 Veto of bill for relief of Harry H. Nakamura

9 Memorandum to Federal agencies on the United Givers Fund campaign in the National Capital area

11 Letter to the President of the Senate and to the Speaker of the House of Representatives transmitting report on mass transportation in the Washington region

11 Exchange of messages between the President and President Diem of Viet-Nam on the occasion of his fifth anniversary as national leader

13 Statement by the Press Secretary on the need for further negotiations before the steel strike deadline

14 Memorandum to Federal agencies on the United Fund and Community Chest campaigns

July   *Subject*

14 Statement by the President on the strike in the steel industry

15 Exchange of messages between the President and Frol R. Kozlov, First Deputy Chairman, Council of Ministers, U.S.S.R.

16 Letter to President Meany acknowledging AFL-CIO support of the Government's position on West Berlin

16 Remarks to the American Field Service students at the Interdepartmental Auditorium

17 Statement by the President on the death of Eugene Meyer

20 Statement by the President on the death of Admiral William D. Leahy

22 Statement by the President on the death of Douglas McKay

22 Remarks to members of Future Farmers of America

23 Letter to the President of the Senate and to the Speaker of the House of Representatives transmitting report "Economic Assistance: Programs and Administration"

24 Statement by the President upon approval of bill amending the Mutual Security Act of 1954

24 Statement by the Press Secretary on the House Committee cuts in mutual security appropriations

25 White House announcement of the Vice President's forthcoming visit to Poland

29 White House announcement of the appointment of Charles A. Coolidge to head a study of U.S. disarmament policy

29 Letter to Chairman, Tariff Commission on imports of almonds

30 Message to the Congress transmitting the Tenth Semiannual Report on activities under Public Law 480, 83d Congress

August

1 Statement by the Press Secretary concerning the President's message to the Vice President on his tour of the Soviet Union

Appendix A

895

October   *Subject*

19 Statement by the President following receipt of the report of the Board of Inquiry in the steel strike

19 Letter to the Attorney General directing him to petition for an injunction in the steel strike

20 Letter to the Chairman, Tariff Commission, regarding cheese imports

21 Statement by the President on the proposed transfer of the Army Ballistic Missiles Agency to the National Aeronautics and Space Administration

21 Letter to Chairmen, Senate Finance and House Ways and Means Committees concerning imports of stainless steel flatware

21 Letter accepting the resignation of Rocco C. Siciliano, Special Assistant to the President for Personnel Management

22 Statement by the President on the effect of the steel strike on national welfare and safety

25 White House release concerning statement by the Cabinet Committee on Price Stability for Economic Growth entitled "Managing Our Money, Our Budget, and Our Debt"

26 Toasts of the President and President Toure of the Republic of Guinea

27 Remarks at the 55th annual meeting of the National Association of Postmasters

28 Letter accepting resignation of Lester D. Mallory, Ambassador to Guatemala

28 Joint statement following discussions with the President of Guinea

28 White House statement on Tariff Commission's finding as to dried figs

28 Letter accepting resignation of Robert D. Murphy, Under Secretary of State for Political Affairs

29 Statement by the President on receipt of the fourth annual report on the rural development program

29 White House announcement of the forthcoming visit of President Lleras Camargo of Colombia

29 Report to the President by a special committee on the feasibility of a proposed world's fair

October   *Subject*

31 Statement by the President's personal physician and the Surgeon General, U.S.A., concerning the President's physical examination

November

1 White House announcement of the forthcoming 4-power meeting in Paris

2 Remarks at the economic conference breakfast

2 Exchange of messages with President Lopez Mateos concerning the cyclone disaster in Mexico

2 White House announcement of the forthcoming visit of a 4-member delegation to Poland

3 Remarks at the cornerstone-laying ceremony for the Central Intelligence Agency building, Langley, Va.

4 Letter accepting resignation of Richard B. Lowe, Governor of Guam

4 Statement by the President concerning his forthcoming good will tour to countries in Europe, Asia, and Africa

4 Letter accepting resignation of Wendell B. Barnes, Administrator, Small Business Administration

5 Statement by the Press Secretary concerning the members of the party to accompany the President on his trip

7 Letter accepting resignation of David K. E. Bruce, Ambassador to the Federal Republic of Germany

10 Memorandum "Essential aspects of a sound farm program," approved by the President following a meeting with the Secretary of Agriculture

10 Letter to the Chairman, Tariff Commission, on cotton textile imports

11 Statement by the Press Secretary concerning the President's plans to meet President Bourguiba of Tunisia and visit Spain and Morocco

12 Letter to the Chairman, Senate Foreign Relations Subcommittee, concerning his request for a report evaluating the mutual security program in Viet-Nam

14 White House announcement of the establishment of the National Advisory Committee on Inter-American Affairs

November   Subject

14 Message to Prime Minister Nehru of India on the occasion of his 70th birthday

16 Letter to Secretary Flemming on receiving the report of the Federal Council on Aging

16 Message to President Prasad accepting his invitation to visit India

17 Exchange of messages between the President and the President of Turkey concerning the President's forthcoming visit to Ankara

17 Exchange of messages between the President and the Prime Minister of Turkey concerning the President's forthcoming visit to Ankara

27 Letter accepting resignation of John H. F. Haskell from the personal rank of Minister conferred upon him as Defense Advisor to the U.S. Permanent Representative to NATO

30 Statement by the Press Secretary announcing a broadcast by the President before departing on his good will tour

December

1 Statement by the President concerning the Antarctic Treaty

1 Letter accepting resignation of Neil H. McElroy as Secretary of Defense

1 Citation accompanying the Medal of Freedom presented to Neil H. McElroy

1 Exchange of messages between the President and the President of Brazil on the establishment of the National Advisory Committee for Inter-American Affairs

2 Statement by the President concerning treaty negotiations between the United States and Japan

3 White House statement concerning tariff on bicycles

3 White house announcement of the designation of Frederick M. Eaton as U.S. representative and chairman of the U.S. delegation to the 10-nation disarmament committee scheduled to meet in Geneva early in 1960

3 White House statement following the meeting of the President with the National Advisory Committee on Inter-American Affairs

December   Subject

3 Radio and television address to the American people before leaving on good will trip to Europe, Asia, Africa

4 Remarks upon arrival at Ciampino Airport, Rome

5 Remarks to the staff of the U.S. Embassy in Rome

5 Joint statement following discussions with President Gronchi

6 Remarks at Ciampino Airport, Rome, upon leaving for Turkey

6 Remarks upon arrival at Esenboga Airport, Ankara

6 Remarks by the President at a dinner given in his honor by President Bayar

7 Letter accepting resignation of William H. G. FitzGerald, Deputy Director for Management, International Cooperation Administration

7 Joint statement following discussions with President Bayar

7 Remarks at Esenboga Airport, Ankara, upon leaving for Pakistan

7 Remarks upon arrival at Mauripur Airport, Karachi

8 White House announcement of appointments by the President to the Advisory Commission on Intergovernmental Relations

8 Letter to Dr. Erwin D. Canham, President of the U.S. Chamber of Commerce, on the Federal budget

8 Memorandum from the Director, Bureau of the Budget, submitting report on improvements in budgeting

8 Remarks to the staff of the U.S. Embassy and the American community in Karachi

8 Remarks at the citizens welcome for President Eisenhower, polo field, Karachi

8 Joint statement following discussions with President Ayub Khan

8 Toast to President Ayub Khan at a dinner given in his honor by the President

9 Remarks at Mauripur Airport, Karachi, upon leaving for Afghanistan

9 Remarks upon arrival at Bagram Airport, Kabul

9 Toast of the President at a luncheon given in his honor by King Mohammad Zahir

Appendix A

Appendix B—Presidential Documents Published in the Federal Register, 1959

PROCLAMATIONS

Appendix B

EXECUTIVE ORDERS

Appendix B

Appendix B

PRESIDENTIAL DOCUMENTS OTHER THAN PROCLAMATIONS AND EXECUTIVE ORDERS

Appendix C—Presidential Reports to the Congress, 1959

Subject	Published	Sent to the Congress	Date of White House release
Middle East, Joint Resolution to promote peace	H. Doc. 43	Jan. 7 (H) Jan. 14 (S)	. . . .
Housing and Home Finance Agency		Jan. 7 (H) Jan. 14 (S)	. . . .
Corregidor Bataan Memorial Commission	H. Doc. 52	Jan. 19 (H) Jan. 20 (S)	. . . .
National Science Foundation, 8th Annual	H. Doc. 53	Jan. 17 (S) Jan. 19 (H)	. . . .
International Cultural Exchange and Trade Fair Participation Act of 1956:			
Fourth semiannual report of operations		Jan. 17 (S) Jan. 19 (H)	. . . .
Fifth semiannual report of operations		Apr. 13	. . . .
Sixth semiannual report of operations		Sept. 14 (S) Sept. 15 (H)	. . . .
Economic Report of the President	H. Doc. 28	Jan. 20	Jan. 20
Mutual Security Program	H. Doc. 451 (85th Cong.)	Jan. 28	. . . .
	H. Doc. 231	Oct. 20 (Sec. of Senate)	. . . .
		Oct. 20 (Clerk of House)	. . . .
National Aeronautics and Space Administration:			
First annual report	H. Doc. 71	Feb. 2	Feb. 2
First semiannual report	H. Doc. 187	June 24	. . . .
Public Law 480 (83d Congress):			
Ninth semiannual report	H. Doc. 60	Jan. 29	Jan. 29
Tenth semiannual report	H. Doc. 206	July 30	July 30
Civil Service Commission	H. Doc. 13	Feb. 3	. . . .
Surgeon General of the Public Health	H. Doc. 73	Feb. 3	. . . .
Commodity Credit Corporation		Feb. 3	. . . .
International Atomic Energy Agency:			
First annual report	H. Doc. 85	Feb. 26	. . . .
Second annual report		Aug. 27	Aug. 27
National Advisory Council on International Monetary and Financial Problems—Special Report	H. Doc. 77	Feb. 12	. . . .

Subject	Published	Sent to the Congress	Date of White House release
Inter-American Development Bank with a special report of the National Advisory Council on International Monetary and Financial Problems	H. Doc. 133	May 11	. . . .
Office of Alien Property.	. . . . . .	Mar. 2	. . . .
National Capital Housing Authority	. . . . . .	Mar. 23	. . . .
Railroad Retirement Board	H. Doc. 27	Mar. 23	. . . .
Semiannual Report of the Secretary of the Interior on Mineral Reserves	. . . . . .	Mar. 23	. . . .
	. . . . . .	Sept. 14 (S)	. . . .
		Sept. 15 (H)	. . . .
National Advisory Committee for Aeronautics— Final Report	S. Doc. 6	Apr. 27	. . . .
St. Lawrence Seaway Development Corporation.	H. Doc. 120	Apr. 24 (S)	. . . .
		Apr. 27 (H)	. . . .
Military Assistance Program:			
Interim report.	. . . . . .	Apr. 29	Apr. 29
Second interim report	H. Doc. 186	June 24	June 24
Final report	H. Doc 215, pt. 1 and pt. 2.	Aug. 20	Aug. 20
World Science Pan-Pacific Exposition	. . . . . .	May 21	May 21
Disaster Relief, Federal Assistance	H. Doc. 157	May 22 (S)	May 22
		May 25 (H)	. . . .
Trade Agreements Program	H. Doc. 31	June 25 (S)	June 25
		June 26 (H)	. . . .
U.S. Participation in the UN for the year 1958.	H. Doc. 104	July 20 (H)	July 20
		July 21 (S)	. . . .
Report on Operations of the Uniformed Services Contingency Option Act of 1953—Fourth annual report	. . . . . .	July 22	. . . .
Commission on Fine Arts	. . . . . .	Aug. 5	. . . .
Lend-Lease Operations	H. Doc. 160	Aug. 19	. . . .

Appendix D—Rules Governing This Publication

[Reprinted from the Federal Register, vol. 24, p. 2354, dated March 26, 1959]

TITLE 1—GENERAL PROVISIONS

Chapter I—Administrative Committee of the Federal Register

PART 32—PUBLIC PAPERS OF THE PRESIDENTS OF THE UNITED STATES

PUBLICATION AND FORMAT

Sec.
32.1   Publication required.
32.2   Coverage of prior years.
32.3   Format, indexes, ancillaries.

SCOPE

32.10   Basic criteria.
32.11   Sources.

FREE DISTRIBUTION

32.15   Members of Congress.
32.16   The Supreme Court.
32.17   Executive agencies.

PAID DISTRIBUTION

32.20   Agency requisitions.
32.21   Extra copies.
32.22   Sale to public.

AUTHORITY: §§ 32.1 to 32.22 issued under sec. 6, 49 Stat. 501, as amended; 44 U.S.C. 306.

PUBLICATION AND FORMAT

§ 32.1 *Publication required.* There shall be published forthwith at the end of each calendar year, beginning with the year 1957, a special edition of the FEDERAL REGISTER designated "Public Papers of the Presidents of the United States." Each volume shall cover one calendar year and shall be identified further by the name of the President and the year covered.

§ 32.2 *Coverage of prior years.* After conferring with the National Historical Publications Commission with respect to the need therefor, the Administrative Committee may from time to time authorize the publication of similar volumes covering specified calendar years prior to 1957.

§ 32.3 *Format, indexes, ancillaries.* Each annual volume, divided into books whenever appropriate, shall be separately published in the binding and style deemed by the Administrative Committee to be suitable to the dignity of the office of President of the United States. Each volume shall be appropriately indexed and shall contain appropriate ancillary information respecting significant Presidential documents not published in full text.

SCOPE

§ 32.10 *Basic criteria.* The basic text of the volumes shall consist of oral utterances by the President or of writings subscribed by him. All materials selected for inclusion under these criteria must also be in the public domain by virtue of White House press release or otherwise.

§ 32.11 *Sources.* (a) The basic text of the volumes shall be selected from the official text of: (1) Communications to the Congress, (2) public addresses, (3) transcripts of press conferences, (4) public letters, (5) messages to heads of state, (6) statements released on miscellaneous subjects, and (7) formal executive documents promulgated in accordance with law.

(b) Ancillary text, notes, and tables shall be derived from official sources only.

Appendix D

Free Distribution

§ 32.15 *Members of Congress.* Each Member of Congress shall be entitled to one copy of each annual volume upon application therefor in writing to the Director.

§ 32.16 *The Supreme Court.* The Supreme Court of the United States shall be entitled to twelve copies of the annual volumes.

§ 32.17 *Executive agencies.* The head of each department and the head of each independent agency in the executive branch of the Government shall be entitled to one copy of each annual volume upon application therefor in writing to the Director.

Paid Distribution

§ 32.20 *Agency requisitions.* Each Federal agency shall be entitled to obtain at cost copies of the annual volumes for official use upon the timely submission to the Government Printing Office of a printing and binding requisition (Standard Form No. 1).

§ 32.21 *Extra copies.* All requests for extra copies of the annual volumes shall be addressed to the Superintendent of Documents, Government Printing Office, Washington 25, D.C. Extra copies shall be paid for by the agency or official requesting them.

§ 32.22 *Sale to public.* The annual volumes shall be placed on sale to the public by the Superintendent of Documents at prices determined by him under the general direction of the Administrative Committee.

* * * * *

ADMINISTRATIVE COMMITTEE OF
THE FEDERAL REGISTER,
WAYNE C. GROVER,
Archivist of the United States,
Chairman.

RAYMOND BLATTENBERGER,
The Public Printer,
Member.

WILLIAM O. BURTNER,
Representative of the Attorney
General, Member.

Approved March 20, 1959.
WILLIAM P. ROGERS,
Attorney General.
FRANKLIN FLOETE,
Administrator of General Services.
[F.R. Doc. 59–2517; Filed, Mar. 25, 1959;
8:45 a. m.]

INDEX

[References are to items except as otherwise indicated]

913

Index

[References are to items except as otherwise indicated]

Index

[References are to items except as otherwise indicated]

Aircraft
  Alleged flights over Cuba from United
    States, 271
  Jet planes, 53
  U.S.-U.K. trade discussions, 67
  See also Aviation
Aircraft, military, 6
  Allies, 55
  Attack on Navy patrol plane over Sea
    of Japan, 132
  Bombers, 7, 48, 57
    B–52, 10 (pp. 57, 60)
    B–58, 10 (p. 60), 288
    B–70, 10 (p. 63)
    Withdrawal from France, 154
  Fighters, 7
  Nuclear, 10 (p. 63)
  Research and development, 288
  Transport plane shot down in Soviet
    Armenia, 94 and ftn. (p. 361)
  Turkish border incidents, 29
Airmen, U.S., shot down in Soviet Ar-
    menia, 94 and ftn. (p. 361)
Airport bill, 26, 29
Airports
  Federal aid for construction, 10 (p. 78)
  Federal Airport Act, amendment, 143
  La Guardia, N.Y., plane crash, 26
  Question of location, 26
Airways, budget message, 10 (p. 45)
Alabama
  Montgomery, 31
  Sparkman, Sen. John, 42
Alaska
  Bartlett, Sen. E. L., 3 n.
  Budget message, 10 (pp. 65, 109, 110)
  Control over schools, 21
  Egan, Gov. William A., 150
  Federal communications facilities, sale
    proposed, 10 (p. 65)
  Funds under amended Federal Airport
    Act, 143
  Gruening, Sen. Ernest, 3 n.
  Oil and gas leases, veto, 182
  Rivers, Repr. Ralph J., 3 n.
  Statehood, 174
    Remarks at admission ceremony, 3

Alaska Railroad, 10 (p. 53)
Alba, Duke of, 100
Alcorn, Meade, 21, 75
Alexander I of Russia, 132, 219
Algeria
  De Gaulle program for, 223
  Joint statement with King Mohamed V,
    345
  Joint statement with President Bour-
    guiba on, 329
Allegheny Ludlum Steel Corporation,
    211 n.
Allen, George V. *See* United States In-
    formation Agency, Director (George
    V. Allen)
Almond, Gov. J. Lindsay, Jr., 17
Alphand, Herve, 332 n.
Ambassadorial appointments, 29
Ambassadors, U.S., 130
American Association for the Advancement
    of Science, 107
American Bar Association, 42
  Conference, remarks, 185
American Council on NATO, Inc., 204 n.
American Field Service students, remarks,
    164
American Meat Institute, 161
American Medical Association, address,
    129
American Republics, 6
  Foreign ministers meeting (1958), 98
  See also American States, Organization
    of; Inter-American; Latin Amer-
    ica; *specific countries*
American States, Organization of, 98, 287
  Caribbean situation, 148, 161
  Joint statement with President Lopez
    Mateos on, 38
  News conference remarks on, 94, 148,
    161
  Technical assistance program, U.S. con-
    tributions, 55
Ames, Iowa, visit by Premier Khrushchev,
    186
Amistad Dam, Rio Grande River, joint
    statement on, 257

Index

Index

[References are to items except as otherwise indicated]

Arrowsmith, Marvin L., 17, 21, 29, 36, 42, 48, 53, 67, 89, 94, 102, 123, 132, 148, 154, 161, 167, 186, 191, 223, 243, 267, 271, 277
Art exhibit in Moscow, U.S., 148
Ashby, Jack L., 211 n.
Asia, South Asia, and Southeast Asia, 302
  Assistance, 55, 71
  Industrial revolution, 55
  Joint statement with President Bourguiba on, 329
  Mission of hospital ship proposed, 29
  News conference remarks, 29, 179
  Visit of President Eisenhower. *See* Visit of the President to Europe, Asia, and Africa
  See also specific countries
Association of State Planning and Development Agencies, remarks, 8
Aswan Dam, comment on, 94
Ataturk, Kemal, 296
Athens
  Arrival, remarks, 324
  Joint statement with Prime Minister Karamanlis, 327
  Luncheon given by King Paul, toast, 326
  Parliament, address to, 325
Atl, Dr. (Gerardo Murillo), 256
Atlantic City, N.J., 129
Atlantic Treaty Association, message, 204
Atlas (ICBM). *See* Missiles
Atlas satellite, 10 (p. 57)
Atomic Energy Act, 120
Atomic Energy Agency, International. *See* International Atomic Energy Agency
Atomic Energy Commission, 102
  Budget message, 10 (pp. 55, 66–68)
  Floberg, John F., 18 n.
  General Advisory Committee, 107
  Radioactive fallout research, 68
Atomic Energy Commission, Chairman (John A. McCone), 68, 119, 121, 243
Atomic energy for mutual defense, 55
  U.S. agreements with Canada, France, Greece, U.K., 119 n., 120 n.

Atomic energy—Continued
  U.S. agreements with Germany, Netherlands, Turkey
    Memorandum, 119 and n.
    Message, 120
Atomic energy for peaceful uses, 55, 189, 217 n., 243
  Atoms for peace program, 121
  Budget message, 10 (pp. 44, 55, 67, 68)
  Geneva conference (1958), 10 (p. 67)
  In Pakistan, 302
  President's address at United Nations (1953), 302
  Project Plowshare, 10 (p. 68)
  See also International Atomic Energy Agency; Power projects
Atoms for peace. *See* Atomic energy for peaceful uses
Attorney General, power to inspect election records, proposed, 27
Attorney General (William P. Rogers)
  Letters, 250, 265
  News conference remarks on, 267, 271, 288
  Steel strike injunction, 267
Atwood, Robert, 3 n.
Augusta, Ga., 73 n., 74 n., 76, 78, 80 n., 81 n., 89, 266 n., 267, 268 n., 271, 277, 279 n., 281 n., 282 n., 283 n., 348 n., 349 n., 350 n., 351 n.
Australia, 96 n.
Austria, Vienna, 121
Automation, 67
Automobiles
  Excise tax on, 187
    Transfer to highway trust fund, 104
  Prices, 53
Averoff-Tossizza, Evanghelos, 40
Aviation
  Budget message, 10 (pp. 78, 79)
  Federal Airport Act, amendment, 143
  Progress in, 169
  See also Aircraft; Aircraft, military
Aviation facilities planning, implementation, report, 74

917

Index

[References are to items except as otherwise indicated]

Index

Index

Index

Canada—Continued
  Gas from, 288
  Montreal, 36, 141 n.
  Oil, discussions on, 51
  Ontario, 141 n.
  Ottawa, 141
  Prince Albert Radar Laboratory, Saskatchewan, 125
  St. Lawrence Seaway dedication ceremonies, 141
  Trade with U.S., 141
Candidates for Presidency
  Attitude of President on, 42, 179
  Democratic, comment on, 172
  News conference remarks, 7, 42, 67, 94, 148, 154, 167, 172, 179
  President's role, 7, 148, 167
  Question of religion, 154
Candidates for public office, equal time on radio and TV, 216
Candidates for Vice Presidency, Milton S. Eisenhower, question of, 179
Canham, Erwin D., letter, 300
Cape Canaveral, Fla., 17
Capehart, Sen. Homer E., 42
Capitalism, 21
Capitol, U.S., cornerstone laying ceremony, remarks, 151
Captive nations
  News conference remarks, 167, 172, 186
  Proclamation, 167 and ftn. (p. 536), 172
"Cardiac Club," 67
Carey, James B., letters to members of Congress on labor bill, 186
Carlbach, William D., 8 n.
Cartier, Jacques, 141 n.
Casablanca, Morocco
  Arrival, remarks, 343
  Joint statement with King Mohamed V, 345
  Luncheon honoring President, remarks, 344
Case, Frank, Jr., 204 n.
Cash, Elba H., indemnity claim, disapproval, 236

Casson, Dollier de, 141 n.
Castiella, Fernando Maria, 200
Castle, Lewis G., 141
Castro, Fidel, news conference remarks on, 21, 161, 271
Cater, S. Douglass, Jr., 94
Catholic Church, position on birth control information, 288
Censorship of TV programs, comment on, 267
CENTO. See Central Treaty Organization
Central America. See Latin America
Central Intelligence Agency, cornerstone-laying ceremony, remarks, 276
Central Intelligence Agency, Director (Allen W. Dulles), 82 n., 89, 276
Central Treaty Organization, 243, 251, 296, 320
  Joint statement with President Ayub Khan on, 303
  Joint statement with President Bayar on, 297
  Joint statement with Shah Mohammad Reza Pahlavi on, 322
Ceylon
  Bandaranaike, S. W. R. D., death of, 241
  Goonetilleke, Oliver E., 241
Chamber of Commerce, International, 40th anniversary, remarks, 84
Chamber of Commerce, U.S.
  Annual meeting, remarks, 87
  Improvements in Federal budgeting, letter, 300
Charleston, S.C., 13
Chequers, 196, 198 n.
Chicago, Ill., 7, 36
Chief Justice of the United States (Earl Warren), 8, 21, 255
Children and youth, White House conference on (1960), 10 (p. 104)
Chile, Santiago, 172
China, Communist, 71
  Aggression in India, 94
  Border dispute with India, 288
  Formosa Strait area. See Formosa (Taiwan) Strait situation

Index

Index

[References are to items except as otherwise indicated]

Index

Index

Index

District of Columbia—Continued
  Home rule, 10 (p. 109), 36
  Increase in benefits for retired police-
    men and firemen, disapproval, 239
  March of unemployed, 36
  Mass transportation survey, report, 157
  U.S. Capitol, cornerstone laying cere-
    mony, remarks, 151
  Voting rights, 36
Docking, Gov. George, 258, 259
Dollar, sound, 6, 15, 43, 75, 76, 83, 87,
    124, 127, 188, 212, 274
  News conference remarks, 17, 29, 36,
    48, 288
Dominican Republic, 148
Donnelly, Walter J., 287 n.
Donovan, Robert J., 89, 132, 161, 167,
    173, 223
Doud, Mrs. John Sheldon, 105 n.
Douglas, Sen. Paul H., 36
Draft (Selective Service), 53
Draper, William H., Jr.
  Letter, 137
  News conference remarks on, 53, 89, 288
Draper Committee. *See* President's Com-
    mittee to Study the U.S. Military
    Assistance Program
Drummond, Roscoe, 48, 89, 154, 186
Dudman, Richard, 173
Dulles, Allen W., 82 n., 89, 276
Dulles, John Foster, 123 ftn. (p. 425), 130,
    200 n.
  Death of, statement, 117
  Discussions on possible Khrushchev visit,
    179
  Illness, 89, 102
  Medal of Freedom, citation, 114
  News conference remarks on, 89, 102,
    123, 179
  Official papers in Eisenhower Library,
    258
  Special Consultant to the President, re-
    marks at oath of office ceremony, 82
  See also State, Secretary of (John Foster
    Dulles)
Dulles, Mrs. John Foster, 82 n., 114 n., 117

Dulles International Airport, 117 n.
  Sewage disposal, 197
Dworshak, Sen. Henry, 154

Earthquake in western United States, 224
East-West contacts, 214
  Broadcast with Prime Minister Macmil-
    lan, 196
  Joint statement with Premier Khru-
    shchev, 242
  News conference remarks, 7, 17, 123
East-West relations, joint statement with
    Western leaders, 336
Eaton, William J., 172, 173, 243
Eber Brothers Wine and Liquor Corp., tax
    refund claim, veto, 215
Echegoyen, Martin R., letter, 95
Economic Advisers, Council of. *See*
    Council of Economic Advisers
Economic assistance, 32, 55, 302
  Budget message, 10 (pp. 44, 69, 74)
  Joint statement with General Franco,
    340
  Joint statement with President Bayar,
    297
  News conference remarks, 94, 148, 288
  Report on, 170, 288
  See also, Foreign assistance; Mutual
    security program
Economic conference, remarks, 274
Economic controls. *See* Controls, Gov-
    ernment economic
Economic growth, 6, 15, 43, 76, 84, 87,
    126, 127, 144
  Budget message, 10 (pp. 37, 39)
  Latin America, 98
  News conference remarks, 17, 36
  Soviet Union, 55
    Incentives, 271
  See also Economy, national
Economic Growth, Committee on Price
    Stability for, 6
  News conference remarks on, 17, 36 and
    ftn. (p. 198), 67
  Report, statement, 144
Economic humanism, 21

[References are to items except as otherwise indicated]

Index

Eisenhower Library, Abilene, Kans., 179
  Ground-breaking ceremony, address, 258
El Alamein, Egypt, 96
Election campaign, Presidential (1960)
  News conference remarks, 7, 123, 148, 179
  Role of President, 179
Election campaigns (1952, 1956), 127
Election of union officers, 22
Elections, split tickets, 123
Electrical machinery, U.S.-U.K. trade discussions, 67
Elephant, gift to the President, 214
Elizabeth II, 96, 141, 193, 196, 198 n., 214
El Salvador, Jose Maria Lemus, 50, 52
  Joint statement with, 54
Emory, Alan S., 36, 42
Employment, 15, 76
  Government, 9, 10 (pp. 108, 109), 36
Engineers, Corps of, 194
  Budget message, 10 (pp. 94, 95)
Enterprise system, 6, 76, 84, 133, 244, 290
  News conference remarks, 21, 53
Eqbal, Manuchehr, 251, 320, 322
Equal Job Opportunity under Government
  Contracts, Commission on, proposed, 27
Equal opportunity. See Civil rights; Integration, public schools
Equal pay for equal work, 10 (p. 101)
Erosion control claim, Madeira Beach, Fla., approval, 232
Esenbel, Melih, 297
Essex, U.S.S., 331
Estes, Lourene O., tax refund claim, disapproval, 234
Euratom. See European Atomic Energy Community
Europe, Western
  Assistance to less developed countries, 271, 335
  Economic recovery, 244
  Joint statement with Chancellor Adenauer on, 192
  Need for unity, comment on, 94

Europe, Western—Continued
  News conference remarks, 36, 48, 94, 191
    Political integration, 191
  Withdrawal of U.S. troops, comment on, 36, 48
  See also specific countries
European Atomic Energy Community
  Budget message, 10 (p. 68)
  News conference remarks, 7, 94
European Coal and Steel Community, 7, 94
European Economic Community, 7, 214
  Joint statement with President Bayar, 297
  Joint statement with Western leaders, 335
  News conference remarks, 7, 94
European Economic Cooperation, Organization for, 200
  Joint statement with General Franco, 340
  Joint statement with Western leaders, 335
European Free Trade Association, joint statement with Western leaders on, 335
Evans, Rowland, Jr., 17, 26, 67, 102, 161
Exchange of persons, 223
  Conference on, remarks, 24
  News conference remarks, 223
  See also Cultural exchange; East-West contacts; People-to-people program
Exchange of students, 222
  American Field Service, 164
Exchange of teachers, 222
Excise taxes. See Taxes
Executive orders, 3, 18, 56, 68 n., 97 n., 111, 117 n., 166 n., 184, 250, 253, 265, 273
  List, Appendix B, p. 904
Executive privilege. See Privileged documents and information
Explorer IV, information on Argus project, 67
Export-Import Bank, 6, 98
  Budget message, 10 (pp. 71, 74)

Index

[References are to items except as otherwise indicated]

Index

Federal Reserve System, Chairman of Board of Governors (William McC. Martin, Jr.), 186
Federal-State Action Committee, Joint, 10 (pp. 68, 98)
Federal-State-local governmental responsibilities, 29
  Budget message, 10 (pp. 96, 98)
  Interstate highway system, 227
Federal Trade Commission, TV quiz investigation, 267, 277
Ferdinand, King, 338
Fermi, Enrico, 107
FHA. *See* Federal Housing Administration
Fillmore, Millard, 151
Firemen, Washington, D.C., increase in benefits, disapproval, 239
Fish and wildlife resources, 10 (p. 95)
Fissionable materials, for International Atomic Energy Agency, 189
Flag, U.S., 97 n., 117 n., 166 n., 262 n., 333 n.
  In Panama Canal Zone, 288
  Letter to Gov. William A. Egan, 150
  New design, remarks, 3, 184
Fleming, Robert H., 267, 271
Flemming, Arthur S. *See* Health, Education, and Welfare, Secretary of (Arthur S. Flemming)
Floberg, John F., 18 n.
Floete, Franklin, 18 n.
Flood control
  Amistad Dam, joint statement on, 257
  Budget message, 10 (pp. 45, 94)
Floods, 45
  Uruguay, 95
Florida
  Cape Canaveral, 17
  Illegal flights to Cuba from, 271
  Madeira Beach, 232
  Miami Beach, 185
FNMA. *See* Federal National Mortgage Association
Folliard, Edward T., 21, 29, 42, 48, 53, 67, 148, 173, 179, 186, 191, 223, 243, 267, 271

Fong, Sen. Hiram, 184 n.
Food and Agriculture Organization, 189
Food and Drug Administration, 10 (p. 46)
Food for Peace program, 226
Food stamp plan, 226
Foot, Sir Hugh, 39
Ford, Henry, II, 154
Fordham University, 21, 106
Foreign affairs, 130, 212, 225
  Budget message, 10 (pp. 71-75)
    Table, 10 (p. 72)
  Leadership of the President, comment on, 179
Foreign aid program. *See* Mutual security program
Foreign assistance, 152
  Afghanistan, 308
  Africa, 55, 71, 269 n.
  Asia, South Asia, and Southeast Asia, 55, 71
  Berlin, 55
  "Buy American" requirement, 267, 271
  Cambodia, 55
  China, Republic of, 10 (p. 69), 55
  Developing countries, 55, 186, 214, 296
  Greece, 55
  India, 94
  Iran, 55, 342
  Jordan, 55
  Korea, 10 (p. 69), 55
  Laos, 55, 186
  Latin America, 55, 94
  Lebanon, 55
  Less developed countries, 10 (pp. 71, 72, 74, 75), 55, 87, 186, 189, 191, 196, 223, 244, 248, 258, 267, 269 n., 293, 297, 329
  Libya, 55
  Middle East, 55
  Morocco, 55
  NATO members, 55
  Pakistan, 55, 94, 302, 303
  Philippines, 55
  Spain, 55, 200, 340
  Sudan, 55
  Thailand, 55, 342
  Tunisia, 55

Index

[References are to items except as otherwise indicated]

Index

Griffin, Repr. Robert P., labor bill, 172, 176, 180

Gromyko, Andrei A., 123 ftn. (p. 425), 148, 218, 242

Gronchi, Giovanni, 291, 294
  Joint statement with, 293

Gruening, Sen. Ernest, 3 n.

Guinea, Sekou Toure, 269, 272

Gundersen, Dr. Gunnar, 129

Hagerty, James C., 7, 17, 21, 26, 29, 36, 42, 48, 53, 67, 78, 89, 94, 102, 123, 132, 148, 154, 161, 167, 171 n., 172, 173, 179, 186, 191, 223, 243, 267, 271, 277, 288

Halleck, Repr. Charles A., 148, 151 n.
  Election as House minority leader, statement, 4
  Letter, 34

Hanley, Edward J., 211 n.

Hannah, John A., 128 n.

Hannibal, 124

Harbor workers, safety code, 10 (p. 101)

Hardy, Royce A., 18 n.

Harkness, Richard, 161

Harmon, Lt. Gen. Hubert R., 109

Harriman, W. Averell
  Interview with Premier Khrushchev, 154
  News conference remarks on, 154, 161
  On recognition of East Germany, 161

Harris, Lou, 267

Hassan, Prince Moulay, 343 n.

Hauck, Arthur A., 222

Hawaii
  Election in, comment on, 172
  Fong, Sen. Hiram, 184 n.
  Inouye, Repr. Daniel K., 184 n.
  Long, Sen. Oren E., 184 n.
  Quinn, Gov. William F., 184 n.
  Statehood, 10 (p. 109), 53, 174, 225, 311
    Approval of act, 60
    Ceremony on admission, remarks, 184
    Letter to Gov. Quinn, 61
    Letter to Maurice H. Stans, 62

Hawaii Statehood Commission, 184 n.

Heads of state and governments, joint statements with. *See* Joint statements with heads of state and governments

Heads of state and governments, meetings
  East-West summit, question of, 29, 42, 48, 57, 67, 89, 94, 102, 123, 132, 148, 161, 167, 179, 191, 196, 214, 243, 267, 271, 277
  In United States, comment on, 67, 102
  Joint statement with President de Gaulle, 202
  Joint statement with King Mohammad Zahir, 308
  Joint statement with Western leaders, 336
  Letters to Premier Khrushchev on, 337, 349
  Geneva (1955), 42, 48
  Paris meeting of Western leaders, 332 n., 335, 336, 337
    Comment on, 267, 271, 277

Heads of state and governments, messages to. *See* Messages to heads of state and governments

Heads of state and governments, visits. *See* Visitors, foreign

Health, Education, and Welfare, Department of, 55
  Appropriation, 181
  Assistance to States on desegregation programs, 27
  Budget message, 10 (pp. 86, 99, 101)

Health, Education, and Welfare, Secretary of (Arthur S. Flemming), 68 n.
  Letters, 49, 280
  Study on medical research and training, 10 (p. 102)
  Study of public assistance programs, 10 (p. 103)

Health Organization, World, 188

Health of the President, 29, 243, 267, 288

Health problems, cooperation with Mexico, 257

Health programs, 6, 181
  International, 55

Health research, 10 (pp. 45, 46)

Index

[References are to items except as otherwise indicated]

Healy, Paul F., 267
Hearing aid anecdote, 107
Hébert, Repr. F. Edward, 167
Hekmat, Reza, 320
Helicopter, purchase by Premier Khrushchev, 243
Helium conservation, 10 (p. 96)
Henderson, Loy W., 19, 91
Hendrickson, Waino, 3 n.
Henry, Patrick, 186
Hensley, Stewart, 148, 179, 277
Herling, John 21, 67, 123, 132, 161, 167
Herter, Christian A., 44, 54, 76, 78
    See also State, Secretary of (Christian A. Herter)
Hesburgh, Father Theodore M., 26
Hester, Adin, 169
Heuss, Theodor, 192
    Meeting with, 214
HEW. *See* Health, Education, and Welfare, Department of
Hightower, John M., 29, 179, 288
Highway Administrator, Federal (Bertram D. Tallamy), report, 138
Highway bill, 161, 167, 179
    Approval, 227
Highway commissioners, State, 138
Highway system, interstate, 104, 187, 225
    Federal aid for, 6, 10 (p. 50), 227
    Federal Aid Highway Act, approval, 227
    Financing of, statement, 138
    Letter to Sen. Gore, 252
    Letter to T. D. Sherard, 149
    News conference remarks, 94, 102, 186
    Study by Gen. Bragdon, 227
Highway trust fund, 104, 138, 149, 187, 226 n., 252
    Budget message, 10 (pp. 80, 81)
Highways
    Accidents, 129, 185
    Budget message, 10 (pp. 45, 50, 80, 81)
    Federal Aid Highway Act, approval, 227
Hill, Robert C., 275
Hitler, Adolf, 7, 212, 344

Hoegh, Leo A. *See* Civil and Defense Mobilization, Office of, Director (Leo A. Hoegh)
Hoffa, James R., 123
Hoffman, Paul, 154
Holeman, Frank, 29, 179
Holland, G. Kenneth, 24, 287 n.
Hollister, John B., 154
Hollmer, Anita, 131
Home rule for District of Columbia, 36
Homer, 116, 129
Homer, Arthur B., 211 n.
Hoover, Herbert, President, 77, 100, 102, 141
    Committee on Recent Social Trends, 6
Hoover Commission recommendations
    Budget message, 10 (p. 53)
    Grouping of Government functions, 221
    Line of authority, 86
Hope, Henry Radford, 148 ftn. (p. 490)
Horner, Garnett D., 17, 21, 26, 36, 42, 48, 53, 102, 132, 179, 243, 277
Horner, John V., 7
Hoskins, Harold B., 130
Hospital ship, mercy mission, 29, 167
Hospitals and medical care facilities, 129, 181
    Budget message, 10 (pp. 45, 102, 107)
Houghton, Amory, 203, 332 n.
Hound Dog missile (air-to-ground). *See* Missiles
Hours of work on Federal construction projects, 10 (p. 101)
Housing, 15
    Budget message, 10 (pp. 46, 63, 82–86)
    College, 10 (pp. 82, 86), 26, 94, 153, 208
    Military, 10 (p. 63), 153
    Older persons, 153, 208
    Public, 10 (pp. 46, 84), 153, 208
    Racial discrimination in, 26
    Veterans, 10 (p. 85), 26, 146
Housing bill
    News conference remarks, 26, 29, 94, 102, 179
    Vetoes, 153, 208

938

Index

Housing and Home Finance Agency
  Budget message, 10 (pp. 51, 85)
  Talle, Henry O., 18 n.
Hull, Cordell, 42
Humphrey, George M., 107
Hunting dog anecdote, 107
Hussein I, exchange of toasts, 66
Huttlinger, Joseph B., 288
Hydro-Electric Power Commission of the
  Province of Ontario, 141 n.
Hydroelectric power projects, 10 (p. 95)
Hydrogen bomb
  Delegation of authority re use, 102
  News conference remarks, 102, 132
  See also Nuclear tests; Nuclear weapons

Ibrahim, Moulay Abdallah, 343 n.
ICA. *See* International Cooperation Ad-
  ministration
ICBM (intercontinental ballistic missiles).
  See Missiles
Idaho, Sen. Henry Dworshak, 154
IGY. *See* International Geophysical
  Year
Illinois
  Chicago, 7, 36
  Dirksen, Sen. Everett McK., 127, 151 n.
  Douglas, Sen. Paul H., 36
  Springfield, 31
Immigration laws, 10 (p. 110)
Immigration and Naturalization Commis-
  sioner (Joseph M. Swing), 161
Imports
  Iron ore, 55
  Minerals and rubber, 55
  Oil, 67
    Statement on control, 51
  Textiles, 267
  U.S.-U.K. discussions on, 67
  Wool, 67, 161
Incentives in Soviet economy, 271
Income taxes, 7
India, 282 n.
  Agra, 317
  Ambassador Ellsworth Bunker, 310 n.,
    312, 313
  Assistance, 94

India—Continued
  Ayyangar, M. A., 311 n.
  Border dispute with Communist China,
    288
  Communist aggression in, 94
  Dispute with Pakistan, 288
  Nehru, Jawaharlal, 31, 94, 279, 288,
    310, 311, 312, 314, 315, 316, 318
    Joint statement with, 317
  Prasad, Rajendra, 310, 312, 315, 316,
    317, 318
    Messsage, 281
  Radhakrishnan, Sarvepalli, 311 n., 314
    n., 315 n.
  Visit of President Eisenhower, 277, 281,
    310, 311, 312, 313, 314, 315, 316,
    317, 318
  See also New Delhi
India and United States, 1959, Washing-
  ton conference on, 94
Indian lands, 10 (p. 95)
Indiana
  Capehart, Sen. Homer E., 42
  Halleck, Repr. Charles A., 4, 34, 148,
    151 n.
  Rensselaer, 4 n.
Indiana University, Fine Arts Depart-
  ment, 148 ftn. (p. 490)
Indus River, 288
Industrial revolution, 55
Infant mortality, 129
Inflation, 6, 11, 15, 43, 63, 76, 83, 124,
  129, 144, 177, 188, 208, 244, 274
  Definition of, 102
  News conference remarks, 17, 21, 42,
    102, 148, 161, 186, 223
Information
  Approval of bill on mutual security pro-
    gram disclosures, 171
  Availability of, 172
  Mutual security evaluation reports, 148,
    172
    Iran and Thailand, 342
    Viet-Nam, 278
  Privileged, 36, 148, 161, 277
  Sigma Delta Chi reports, 288

939

Index

Index

[References are to items except as otherwise indicated]

Index

[References are to items except as otherwise indicated]

Index

[References are to items except as otherwise indicated]

Kabul—Continued
  Joint statement with King Zahir, 308
  Remarks to American community, 309
Kaiser Steel Corporation, 211 n., 271
Kanellopoulos, Panayiotis, 327
Kansas, 75, 338
  Abilene, 177, 179, 186, 258, 259
  Docking, Gov. George, 258, 259
Karachi, Pakistan
  Arrival, remarks, 299
  Dinner honoring President Ayub, toast, 304
  Joint statement with President Ayub, 303
  Meeting of Baghdad Pact Ministerial Council, message, 19
  Remarks at polo field, 302
  Remarks at U.S. embassy, 301
  Remarks on departure, 305
Karamanlis, Constantine, 324 n., 325
  Joint statement with, 327
  Message, 40
Kefauver, Sen. Estes, 42
Kemal, Mustafa. See Ataturk, Kemal
Kennedy, Sen. John F., 42
Kent, Carleton, 17, 29, 48, 94, 123, 223, 267, 277
Kentucky
  Cooper, Sen. John Sherman, 29
  Distribution of surplus farm products, 67 and ftn. (p. 297)
  Morton, Sen. Thruston B., 75, 132
Kenworthy, E. W., 123, 172, 186, 223, 243, 271, 288
Key, Francis Scott, 116
Key (Francis Scott) Memorial Auditorium, St. John's College, dedication, 116
Khrushchev, Madame, 214, 217, 219
Khrushchev, Nikita S., 1 n., 271 ftn. (p. 748), 290
  Address before Congress, question of, 186
  Authority in negotiations, 67
  Disarmament proposal at U.N., 223, 243
  East-West summit, letters, 337, 349

Khrushchev, Nikita S.—Continued
  Helicopter, purchase of, 243
  Interview with Ambassador Thompson re U.S. airmen, 94 and ftn. (p. 361)
  Interview with U.S. Governors in Moscow, 154
  Interview with W. Averell Harriman in Moscow, 154
  Invitation to the President, 29 and ftn. (p. 173)
  Letters to, 81, 110, 337, 349
  Meeting with members of Congress, 223
  Moscow address, 26
  News conference remarks on, 21, 26, 29, 36, 42, 48, 53, 67, 94, 102, 123, 132, 154, 161, 167, 172, 173, 179, 186, 267, 271, 277
  Nuclear test suspension, letters, 81, 110
  On Communist doctrine, 243
  On defense spending, 243
  On Soviet vs. U.S. system, 271
  On Vice President Nixon's visit, 167
  Reaction of Americans to, 223, 243
  Visit to United States, 21, 102, 154, 161, 172, 179, 186, 191, 196, 198 n., 200, 202, 203, 214, 217, 218, 219, 223, 242, 248
    Announcement, 173
    Evaluation of talks with, 243
    Exchange of toasts, 219
    Joint statements with, 218, 242
    Remarks of welcome, 217
Killian, James R., Jr., 107, 267
Kimpton, Lawrence A., 36
Kishi, Nobusuke, 288, 289
Kistiakowsky, George B., 132 ftn. (p. 463)
Knebel, Fletcher, 173
Knight, O. A., 287 n.
Knighton, William H., Jr., 21, 29, 123, 179, 186, 267
Knipp, Howard F., tax claim, disapproval, 240
Know Your America Week, 243, 245
Kohler, Foy D., 218
Korea, 89, 94
  Allied prisoners unaccounted for, 89
  Assistance, 10 (p. 69), 55

943

Index

[References are to items except as otherwise indicated]

Index

Index

[References are to items except as otherwise indicated]

Index

ational Advisory Committee for Inter-American Affairs, message to President Kubitschek, 287

ational Advisory Council on International Monetary and Financial Problems, reports, 32, 98

ational Aeronautics and Space Administration, 25
Army Ballistic Missile Agency, proposed transfer to, 266, 267
Budget message, 10 (pp. 58, 76)
Effect of steel strike on programs, 268
News conference remarks, 102, 267, 277

ational Aeronautics and Space Administrator (T. Keith Glennan), 172, 267
Letter, 46

ational Association for the Advancement of Colored People, 167

ational Association of Manufacturers, remarks, 83

ational Association of Postmasters, remarks, 270

ational Capital Planning Commission, report on transportation survey of Washington area, 157

ational Capital Regional Planning Council, report on transportation survey of Washington area, 157

ational Community Christmas Tree and Pageant of Peace, 347

ational Conference on Civil Rights, remarks, 128

ational Cotton Council of America, 267

ational Council of Churches, remarks, 212

ational debt. *See* Debt, national

ational economy. *See* Economy, national

ational 4–H Club Center, dedication, remarks, 131

ational Fund for Medical Education, 238

ational goals, committee on, 6
News conference remarks on, 36, 89, 154, 179, 271
Selection of members, 271

ational groups. *See* Addresses, remarks, or messages to national groups

National Guard Armory, Washington, D.C., 30 n.

National Institutes of Health, 181
Budget message, 10 (p. 101)

National Labor Relations Board
Areas outside jurisdiction, 89
General Counsel, designation by the President, 22

National Lincoln Sesquicentennial Dinner, remarks, 31

National Newspaper Week, statement, 260

National Press Club, golden anniversary celebration, remarks, 7

National product (GNP), 7, 15, 29, 76

National Rural Electric Cooperative Association, remarks, 30

National Rural Letter Carriers Association, remarks, 177

National Science Foundation, 10 (pp. 98, 99)

National Science Foundation, Director (Alan T. Waterman), 267

National security, 6, 11, 51, 57, 63, 71, 83, 87, 225, 276, 278, 290
Budget message, 10 (pp. 55–71)
Table, 10 (p. 56)
Information affecting, 36
News conference remarks, 7, 36, 42, 53, 148, 186
President's authority, 53

National Security Council, 137, 286 n.

National Service Life Insurance, 236
Claim of Mary D'Agostino, 235

National Society of Editors, 271

National Taxpayers Conference, 63

National Wool Growers Association, 161

National Zoological Park, 214 n.

Nationalism, 55

NATO. *See* North Atlantic Treaty Organization

Natural gas, 10 (p. 96)

Natural resources
Budget message, 10 (pp. 92–96)
Table, 10 (p. 93)
Sea resources, joint statement on, 257

Naval petroleum reserves, 10 (p. 66), 17

951

Index

[References are to items except as otherwise indicated]

Index

News conferences—Continued
  October 28 (No. 174), 271
  November 4 (No. 175), 277
  December 2 (No. 176), 288
Newsmen
  Importance of, 179
  White House dinner, 167
Newspaper Week, National, statement, 260
Newspaperboys and girls of America,
  message, 263
Newton, Virgil M., Jr., 288
Nielsen, Aksel, 133 n.
NIH. *See* National Institutes of Health
Nike-Ajax missile (anti-aircraft). *See*
  Missiles
Nike-Hercules missile (anti-aircraft). *See*
  Missiles
Nike-Zeus missile (anti-missile). *See Missiles*
Nixon, Richard M. *See* Vice President
  (Richard M. Nixon)
Nixon, Mrs. Richard M., 210, 214
NLRB. *See* National Labor Relations
  Board
Nobel Prize, 107
Nomy, Adm. Henri, 332 n.
Nonaggression pacts, comment on, 42
Norfolk, Va., education of children of military personnel, 17
Norstad, Gen Lauris, 206
North American Defense Command, 10
  (p. 61)
North American Ecclesiastical College,
  Vatican City, 294 n.
North Atlantic Council, 350, 351
  Declaration on Berlin (1958), 336
  Foreign ministers meeting, remarks, 70
  Joint statement with Western leaders on,
    336
  Paris meeting, 154
  President (Joseph M. A. H. Luns), 70,
    214
    Meeting with President Eisenhower,
      186
North Atlantic Treaty, question re invoking, 42

North Atlantic Treaty Organization, 40,
  41, 57, 100, 214, 291, 296, 326, 350,
  351
Action on Berlin, comment on, 42
Adherence of Spain, question re, 191
Assistance, 55
Atlantic Treaty Association, message,
  204
Attitude of France, 132
Broadcast in London re, 196
Joint statement with Chancellor Adenauer on, 192
Joint statement with President Bayar on,
  297
Joint statement with President de
  Gaulle on, 202
Joint statement with President Gronchi
  on, 293
Joint statement with Prime Minister
  Karamanlis on, 327
Joint statements with Prime Minister
  Segni on, 203, 248
Joint statement with Western leaders on,
  336
Ministerial Council Meeting, 277 ftn.
  (p. 766)
Mobilization of forces, comment on, 48
Modernization of military forces proposed, 90
News conference remarks, 42, 48, 94,
  132, 186, 191
Permanent Council, remarks, 205
Secretary General (Paul-Henri Spaak),
  70, 214
    Meeting with President Eisenhower,
      186, 214
Tenth anniversary, remarks, 70
Use of nuclear weapons, 120
North Attleboro, Mass., 4 n.
North Dakota, Sen. William Langer, 123
North Polar Sea, submarine voyages under,
  6
Northrup, Doyle L., Award for Distinguished Federal Civilian Service, 9 n.
NS *Savannah*, 10 (p. 80)
  News conference remarks, 48
Nuclear-powered aircraft, 10 (p. 63)

Index

Nuclear-powered ships. *See* Ships, nuclear-powered
Nuclear reactors. *See* Reactors
Nuclear tests
  Atmospheric, 81
  Ban or suspension
    Geneva conference. *See* Geneva conferences
    Letters to Premier Khrushchev, 81, 110
    United States, 10 (p. 67), 186, 191 ftn. (p. 615), 277, 348
    White House statement on Khrushchev letter, 110 n.
  Detection, 81, 110
    Underground tests, 81, 132 and ftn. (p. 463), 277, 288, 348
  Fallout. *See* Radioactive fallout
  In Antarctica, 284
  Inspection and control, 243
    Soviet proposal, 110, 348
    U.K. proposal, 48, 89, 102, 110
    U.S. proposal, 81, 89, 110
  News conference remarks, 48, 89, 102, 132, 186, 191, 243, 277, 288
  See also Nuclear weapons
Nuclear war, 55, 57, 70
  Budget message, 10 (p. 67)
  News conference remarks, 53, 167, 223
Nuclear weapons, 71
  Authority to use during President's absence, comment on, 288
  Budget message, 10 (pp. 66, 67)
  News conference remarks, 53, 154, 288
  Presidential power re use of, 154
  Use by NATO, 120
  See also Bombs; Disarmament; Missiles; Nuclear tests
Nunn, Rear Adm. Ira H., 89
Nurses, 129

OAS. *See* Organization of American States
Oberdorfer, Don, 67, 102, 132
O'Boyle, Archbishop Patrick A., 64
O'Brien, Edward W., 172, 179
Occupational diseases, 129

Oder-Neisse line between Germany an Poland, 191
OEEC. *See* Organization for Europea Economic Cooperation
Office buildings, Federal, construction o 10 (p. 108)
Office of Education, 222 n.
Ohio
  Ayers, Repr. William H., 92 n.
  Brown, Repr. Clarence J., 77 n.
Oil
  Alaskan oil leases, veto, 182
  Imports, 67
    Controls, statement, 51
  Naval petroleum reserves, 10 (p. 66), 1
  Overseas supply, 17
O'Kelly, Sean T.
  Exchange of toasts, 59, 64
  Remarks of welcome, 58
O'Kelly, Mrs. Sean T., 58, 59, 64
Old-age and survivors insurance, 10 (p 102, 104, 105)
Older persons
  Federal Council on Aging, 49
    Report, letter, 280
  Financial security, 124, 129
  Housing, 153, 208
  Medical care, 167
  White House Conference on Agin (1961), 10 (p. 104), 49, 280
O'Leary, J. A., 102, 132, 172
Olympic Committee, International, 132
O'Neill, Michael J., 167, 191
Ontario, Canada, 141 n.
Operation Pan America, 287
Organization of American States, 98, 287
  Caribbean situation, 148, 161
  Joint statement with President Lope Mateos on, 38
  News conference remarks, 94, 148, 161
  Technical assistance program, U.S. cor tributions, 55
Organization for European Economic Cc operation, 200
  Joint statement with General Franco or 340

954

Index

OEEC—Continued
Joint statement with Western leaders on, 335

Orphans, admission to U.S. 10 (p. 110)

Orr, Dr. Louis M., 129

Osler, William, 129

Ottawa, Canada, 141

Outdoor Recreation Resources Review Commission, 10 (pp. 95, 96)

Overlord operation, World War II, 7

Overseas Americans, message, 152

Paarlberg, Don, 161

Pageant of Peace, remarks, 347

Pahlavi, Mohammad Reza, 319, 320, 321, 323
Joint statement with, 322

Pakistan
Ambassador William Rountree, 299 n., 301 n., 304 n., 305 n.
Assistance, 55, 94, 302, 303
Atomic energy for peaceful uses, 302
Ayub Khan, Mohammed, 299, 302, 304, 305
Joint statement with, 303
Cultural exchange with United States, 302
Dispute with India, 288
News conference remarks, 94, 277, 288
Visit to, 299, 301, 302, 303, 304, 305
Comment on, 277
See also Karachi

Palmer, H. Bruce, 274

Pan American Union, 98

Panama, 50
Anti-U.S. demonstrations, comment on, 277
U.S.-Panama treaties, 277, 288

Panama Canal
Flag of Panama flown in Canal Zone, comment on, 288
Internationalization or construction of second canal, comment on, 277

Panel on Seismic Improvement, report (Berkner report), 132 and ftn. (p. 463)

Paris, 202 n., 203 n., 204 n.
Capture plans of allies (1944), 7
East-West summit (1960), proposed, 336, 337, 349
Meeting of Prime Ministers of French Community, 214
Meeting of Western leaders, 271 ftn. (p. 748), 277, 335, 336
Meeting with President de Gaulle, 202, 214
NATO Ministerial Council Meeting, 277 ftn. (p. 766)
Remarks on arrival, 199
Remarks on departure, 207
Remarks at Hotel de Ville, 201
Remarks to Permanent Council, NATO, 205
Remarks at SHAPE headquarters, 206
Remarks at U.S. embassy, 334

Park police, U.S., increase in benefits, disapproval, 239

Parker (Mack Charles) case
News conference remarks, 94, 123
Telegram to Gov. Coleman, 88

Parks, national, conservation, 10 (p. 95)

Parliamentary system of government, comment on, 123

Party responsibility for legislation, comment on, 223

Passchendaele, Belgium, 7

Passport control, authority of Secretary of State, 10 (p. 75)

Pasteur, Louis, 107

Pastore, Sen. John O., 113

Patterson, John S., 18 n.

Paul, Willard S., 71

Paul I, 324, 326, 327

Pay
Equal pay for equal work, 10 (p. 101)
Government employees pay, proposed commission on, 10 (pp. 108, 109)
Military personnel, 10 (p. 59)
Postal employees, 10 (pp. 50, 81)
Teachers, 6, 7, 118
See also Wages

Peaceful uses of atomic energy. See Atomic energy for peaceful uses

955

Public enterprises, 10 (pp. 52, 53)

Public health
Budget message, 10 (pp. 101, 102)
Officials, training for assignments abroad, 6
Research and training, 181

Public Health Service, criteria for research projects and training programs, 181

Public housing, 153, 208
Budget message, 10 (pp. 46, 84)

Public lands, 10 (p. 95)

Public morality, comment on, 277

Public opinion, 274

Public works, 11, 225
Appropriation bills, vetoes, 194, 213
As stimulus to economy, 15
Budget message, 10 (p. 45)
Table, 10 (p. 46)

Puerto Rico, 36
Munoz Marin, Gov. Luis, 102
San Juan, 174
Statehood, question of, 102

"Pump-priming" schemes to aid economy, 225

Pyle, James T., 18 n.

Quarles, Donald A., death of, statement, 97, 102

Quarles, Mrs. Donald A., 97

Quemoy, 55, 267

Quesada, Elwood R., 26
Aviation facilities planning, report, 74

Quezon y Molina, Manuel, 36

Quinn, Gov. William F., 184 n.
Letter, 61

Rabat, Morocco, 277

Racketeering, 6, 10 (p. 101), 21, 123, 176, 223

Radar Laboratory, Prince Albert (Canada), official opening, message, 125

Radford, Adm. Arthur W., 89

Radhakrishnan, Sarvepalli, 311 n., 314 n., 315 n.

Radiation Council, Federal, 68 n.

Radio Moscow, 288

Radio and television, equal time for appearances by candidates for public office, 216

Radio and television addresses to the American people. *See* Messages to the American people

Radioactive fallout, 81
Budget message, 10 (p. 88)
Statement, 68
White House release, 68 n.

Radioactive waste disposal, 161

Radioactivity in outer space, 48

Railroad employee benefits, 10 (pp. 104, 105), 123

Rambouillet, 207 n., 336

Rao, V.K.R.V., 314 n.

Rayburn, Repr. Sam. *See* Speaker of the House of Representatives (Sam Rayburn)

REA. *See* Rural Electrification Administration

Reactors, nuclear
Budget message, 10 (pp. 67, 68)
Japan, request to IAEA for uranium, 189

Recession, 225
Decline of, 6
Of 1957–1958, 15, 223, 244
Recovery from, 76

Reclamation, Bureau of, 194
Budget message, 10 (pp. 94, 95)

Reclamation projects, 42
Budget message, 10 (p. 45)

Records, information re. *See* Information

Records, the President's, 179

Records management, 10 (p. 108)

Recreation Resources Review Commission, Outdoor, 10 (pp. 95, 96)

Red Cross, 156, 159, 238
Campaign, 20
Statement, 45

Redstone Arsenal, Ala., 267

Redstone missile (short-range). *See* Missiles

Reece, Repr. B. Carroll, 77 n.

Refugee Year, World, 115

Refugees, 55
White House Conference, 115

Index

Index

[References are to items except as otherwise indicated]

Index

[References are to items except as otherwise indicated]

Index

[References are to items except as otherwise indicated]

[References are to items except as otherwise indicated]

Index

[References are to items except as otherwise indicated]

Index

Index

Index

Visit of the President to Great Britain, France, and Germany, 196
Broadcast, 214
News conference remarks, 173, 179, 186, 191
Remarks on return, 210
Statement, 186
Visit of the President to Mexico, 36, 254
Visit of the President to Soviet Union (1960), 217 n.
Announcement, 173
Joint statement with General Franco on, 340
Joint statement with President Gronchi on, 293
Joint statement with Premier Khrushchev on, 242
Joint statement with King Mohammad Zahir on, 308
News conference remarks, 173, 191, 223, 243, 267
Visitors, foreign
Baudouin I, 99, 100, 105
Churchill, Winston, 93, 94, 96
Educators, 222
Eqbal, Manuchehr, 251
Frondizi, Arturo, 13, 14, 16, 28
Hussein I, 66
Khrushchev, Nikita S., 21, 154, 161, 172, 179, 186, 191, 196, 198 n., 200, 202, 203, 214, 217, 218, 219, 223, 242, 243, 248, 271
Announcement of visit to U.S., 173
Kozlov, Frol R., 132, 148, 154, 161, 162, 167
Lemus, Jose Maria, 50, 52, 54
Lopez Mateos, Adolfo, 243, 254, 255, 256, 257
Macmillan, Harold, 67
Mikoyan, Anastas I., 7, 17, 21, 48
O'Kelly, Sean T., 58, 59, 64
Segni, Antonio, 203, 243, 247, 248
Toure, Sekou, 269, 272
VMI. See Virginia Military Institute
Vocational education, 10 (p. 98)
Vocational rehabilitation, 10 (pp. 46, 104)
Voice of America, 10 (p. 75), 152 n.

Voluntary Home Mortgage Credit Program, continuance proposed, 153
Von Braun, Wernher
Award for Distinguished Federal Civilian Service, 9 n.
News conference remarks on, 267, 277
Von Brentano, Heinrich, 192
Von Fremd, Charles S., 89
Von Herberg, Mary Philomene, 21, 89
Von Neumann, John, 107
Voroshilov, Kliment E., message, 1
Voss, Earl H., 123, 132, 288
Voting rights, 6, 27
District of Columbia, 36
News conference remarks, 7, 17, 36, 167

Wage and price controls, 21, 94, 124
Wage-price spiral, 6
News conference remarks, 67, 123
Wages
Economic report, 15
Minimum, 10 (p. 46), 17, 161
News conference remarks, 17, 42, 67, 123, 161, 172
Rise in, 15, 17, 42, 161
Steel industry, 42, 67, 172
See also Pay
Wagner, Mayor Robert, 106
Wailes, Edward T., 319 n., 322
Wallis, W. Allen, 144 n.
Walmsley, Walter N., 328 n.
Walter Reed Hospital, 35, 48, 114 n., 262
War
Nuclear war, 10 (p. 67), 55, 57, 70, 167, 223
In Europe, 53
Power of Congress to declare, 48, 179
Preventive war, 48
War Between the States, 129, 255, 333
Warning systems for missile and aircraft detection, 6, 57
Budget message, 10 (pp. 57, 60, 61)
News conference remarks, 26
Warren, Earl. See Chief Justice of the United States (Earl Warren)
Warren, Mrs. Earl, 255
Warren, Fletcher, 295 n., 297

[References are to items except as otherwise indicated]

Washington, D.C. *See* District of Columbia

Washington, George, 31, 107, 151

Washington International Center, 222 n.

Waste treatment facilities, 181
Budget message, 10 (pp. 45, 98, 102)

Water conservation, 10 (pp. 91, 92)

Water conversion, research on, 10 (p. 94)

Water pollution, 181
Potomac River, 197

Water resources development, 6, 194
Budget message, 10 (pp. 38, 45, 94, 95)
Indus River, 288

Water transportation, 10 (pp. 79, 80)

Waterman, Alan T., 267

Watkins, Arthur V., 21

Watkins, Franklin C., 148 ftn. (p. 490)

Waugh, Samuel C., 33

Wayne, John, 127

Weapons
Military assistance program, 55
New, 6, 10 (pp. 38, 55), 11, 55, 57, 286
News conference remarks, 154
See also Bombs; Disarmament; Missiles; Nuclear tests; Nuclear weapons

Webb, James E., 89

Webster, Daniel, 151

Weigle, Richard, 116

Welch, Frank, J., 29

Welfare and pension plans and funds, labor unions, disclosure of, 10 (pp. 46, 101)

Wellington, Duke of, 100

West Point. *See* U.S. Military Academy

Western Association of State Highway Officials, 149

Western summit conference. *See* Heads of state and governments, meetings

Wheat
A c r e a g e allotments and marketing quotas, 108, 139
International Wheat Agreement, 10 (p. 91)
News conference remarks, 102, 132, 167, 179
Price supports, 23
Surpluses, 102, 104, 108, 122, 132, 139
Wheat bill, 132
Veto, 139

Wheat—Continued
Wheat growers referendum, 167
Wheat program (1960), statement, 122

Wheeling Steel Corporation, 211 n.

White, Charles M., 211 n.

White, Gordon E., 21, 48, 161

White, William Allen, 258

White House Conference on Aging (1961), 49, 280
Budget message, 10 (p. 104)

White House Conference on Children and Youth (1960), 10 (p. 104)

White House Conference on Refugees, statement, 115

White House Office
Bragdon, Maj. Gen. John S., 42, 227
Draper, William H., Jr. *See* Draper
Goodpaster, Brig. Gen. Andrew J., 145
Gray, Gordon, 76
Killian, James R., Jr., 107, 267
Kistiakowsky, George B., 132 ftn. (p. 463)
Morgan, Gerald D., 115, 161
Paarlberg, Don, 161
Quesada, E. R., 74

White House Police force, increase in benefits, disapproval, 239

White House releases, partial list, Appendix A, p. 887

Whitman, Walt, 59 n.

Whitney Museum of American Art, 148 ftn. (p. 490)

Wildlife resources, 10 (p. 95)

Wilhelm II of Germany, 75

Wilkins, J. Ernest, death of, statement, 12

Wilkins, Roy, 167

Williams, Mrs. Clare, 75

Williams, Walter W., death of, statement, 333

Wilson, Charles E., 21

Wilson, George C., 123

Wilson, Malcolm, 106

Wilson, Richard L., 17, 26, 36, 48, 89, 148, 167, 271

Wilson, Woodrow, 212
On use of veto, 167

Index

974